David M. Goldfader

The Handbook of
Economic and
Financial Measures

The Handbook of
Economic and
Financial Measures

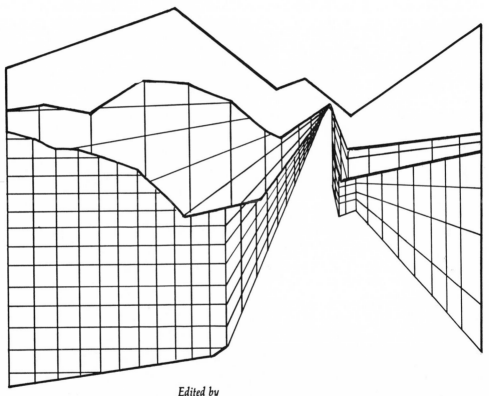

Edited by
Frank J. Fabozzi Walter E. Hanson/ Peat, Marwick,
Mitchell Professor of Business and Finance
Lafayette College
and
Harry I. Greenfield Professor of Economics
Queens College, City University of New York

DOW JONES-IRWIN
Homewood, Illinois 60430

This publication is designed to provide accurate and
authoritative information in regard to the subject matter
covered. It is sold with the understanding that the
publisher is not engaged in rendering legal, accounting, or
other professional service. If legal advice or other expert
assistance is required, the services of a competent
professional person should be sought.

*From a Declaration of Principles jointly adopted by a Committee
of the American Bar Association and a Committee of Publishers.*

ISBN 0-87094-466-5

Library of Congress Catalog Card No. 83–73708

Printed in the United States of America

2 3 4 5 6 7 8 9 0 K 1 0 9 8 7 6

FJF's corner
To Mark Tucciarone

HIG's corner
To my wife

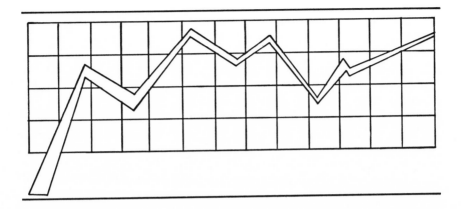

Foreword

Peter L. Bernstein

President
Peter L. Bernstein, Inc.

Way back in 1940 when I started out on my first job as an economist, I worked as a research assistant to one of the vice presidents of the Federal Reserve Bank of New York. While everyone recognizes that the world has changed a lot over the intervening years, one significant but unrecognized difference is in the raw material that an economist has to work with. The economic data that we used then to make critical and complex decisions were pitifully crude and strikingly meager in quantity compared with the oceans of statistics that now wash over us every day of the week.

Although the Federal Reserve Board's index of industrial production was a well-established source for economic activity, GNP data were in their infancy. The National Bureau of Economic Research was doing the basic work and had developed procedures for putting the data together, but the data collection process was extremely primitive in both coverage and composition. Furthermore, the estimates were annual rather than quarterly, and everything was nominal, without adjustments for price changes. The data that were available made their appearance long after the fact—a dramatically different procedure from what we are accustomed to today, when preliminary but detailed estimates appear 21 days after the end of the quarter and flash estimates appear before the quarter is even over.

Money supply? The weekly reporting banks were reporting weekly, just as they do now, but aggregative data appeared only quarterly and received relatively little attention. The focus was on the sources of high-powered money such as member bank borrowing and the burgeoning gold stock rather than on variations in deposits or currency or other sources of liquidity.

An index of consumer confidence, the leading, lagging, and coincident indicator composites, capacity utilization measures, surveys of plant and equipment expenditure plans, and estimates of productivity change simply did not exist. I wonder if anyone even thought about creating them on a regular and systematic basis.

In short, the development of economic information has come a long way during the postwar years, in terms of both coverage and complexity. Indeed, it has come further than most people realize. The consequence is that they use the words that are now part of the popular vocabulary without sufficient attention to the substance that lies behind them. Perhaps the world was safer in the old days, when we had less to work with but at least knew what we were talking about.

The improvement of economic forecasting and interpretation, therefore, lies in the understanding of what these words really mean. What are the limitations of each of the major economic variables in communicating to us what is happening in the economy? What are the difficulties in gathering the data that can have an impact on their accuracy? Is the pressure for early publication of these measures leading to dangerously imprecise preliminary estimates and intolerably large revisions? Are seasonal adjustments and annualizing of short-term changes useful features or a source of distortion? How well do we understand the interrelationships between, say, GNP and industrial production or GNP and unemployment, between M1 and interest rates or interest rates and stock prices, between consumer confidence and residential construction, or between producer prices and consumer prices?

This book is an outstanding and unique effort to address these and many other important questions about the proper uses and inexcusable abuses of economic data. Those of us who study with care what the authors have to tell us will have a significant advantage in interpreting the past, in reporting on the present, and in forecasting the future, over those who use the words but know not whereof they speak.

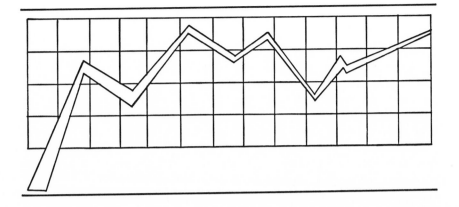

Preface

The origin of this *Handbook* may be traced to the authors' observation that business and financial reporting in the media is becoming more sophisticated, and as a consequence, an information gap is being generated. Measures of economic activity such as gross national product, monetary aggregates, unemployment rates, and the like are reported almost daily, but with the exception of newspapers occasionally printing a box containing short definitions of some of the terms used, clarification is generally lacking. To remedy this deficiency, we selected the measures of economic activity that are most likely to be encountered in business reporting and asked professionals who are intimately familiar with the material to provide relatively in-depth explanations of the background, construction, and uses of these measures. The present *Handbook* is the result of their efforts. For the most part, the level of exposition is neither highly technical nor, on the other hand, oversimplified.

As economic theory develops and as statistical technique becomes more sophisticated, existing indexes will be refined and new ones will be created. This is as it should be. However, the various measures selected have been standard for some time, and we believe that for the near future they will continue to be dominant in the analysis of economic activity.

The contributors to this volume are all professionals from government agencies, academia, or the private sector. Given the natures of the various measures and of the specific backgrounds and perspectives of their respective authors, some inevitable overlapping in treatment has occurred. In the interest of the internal continuity of each piece, we felt that retention rather than excision would be more beneficial.

We wish to thank the contributors individually and collectively for their enthusiastic and knowledgeable participation in this project. We also wish to thank William Costello for his assistance at various stages of this project. It is our hope that the *Handbook* will, in fact, fill the information gap noted above. To the extent that the volume will be a well-thumbed one, our hopes will be realized.

Frank J. Fabozzi
Harry I. Greenfield

CONTRIBUTORS

Peter Asch, Ph.D.   Professor of Economics, *Rutgers University*

Carol S. Carson, Ph.D.   Chief Economist, *Bureau of Economic Analysis, United States Department of Commerce*

Gary Gorton, Ph.D.   Research Economist, *Federal Reserve Bank of Philadelphia*

Elliot S. Grossman, Ph.D.   Associate Professor of Economics, *Lubin Graduate School of Business, Pace University*

Rudolf Hauser, C.F.A.   Vice President, *Oppenheimer Capital Corporation*

Frank J. Jones Ph.D.   Vice President, *Kidder, Peabody & Company, Inc.*

Dolores P. Lynn   Economist, *Federal Home Loan Mortgage Corporation*

Steven R. Malin, Ph.D.   Economist, *The Conference Board, Inc.*

William C. Melton, Ph.D.   Vice President, Senior Economist, *Investors Diversified Services, Inc.*

Edmund A. Mennis, Ph.D., C.F.A.   Consultant to Investment Management

Geoffrey H. Moore, Ph.D.   *Center for International Business Cycle Research, Graduate School of Business, Columbia University*

Philip D. Nathanson, Ph.D.   Vice President and Economist, *Bankers Trust Company*

Janet L. Norwood, Ph.D.   Commissioner, *Bureau of Labor Statistics, United States Department of Labor*

John H. Ortego   *MicroEconometrics*

Joel Popkin, Ph.D.   *Joel Popkin and Company*

Dominick Salvatore, Ph.D.   Professor and Chairman, *Department of Economics, Fordham University*

Joseph Scherer, Ph.D.   Economic Consultant

Marjorie H. Schnader, Ph.D.   Economist, *Brookhaven National Laboratory*

H. O. Stekler, Ph.D.   Professor of Economics, *Industrial College of the Armed Forces, National Defense University*

Kenneth J. Thygerson, Ph.D.   President and Chief Executive Officer, *Federal Home Loan Mortgage Corporation*

Stan West, J.D., M.B.A.   Vice President, *Business Research Division, New York Stock Exchange, Inc.*

Benjamin Wolkowitz, Ph.D.   Vice President, *Citicorp Futures Corporation*

Aubrey H. Zaffuto   Economist, *J. Henry Schroder Bank and Trust Company*

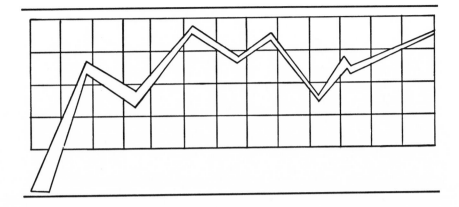

Contents

Activity. International Transactions and Accounting Balances of the United States: *International Transactions of the United States. Accounting Balances.* Disequilibrium in International Transactions: *The Exchange Rate. Disequilibrium under Fixed and Flexible Exchange Rates. Disequilibrium under the Present International Monetary System.* Balance of Payments History of the United States: *The U.S. Balance of Payments over Time. Collapse of the Fixed Exchange Rate System.* The International Investment Position of the United States.

PART THREE   Money Supply and Capital Market Conditions

Construction and Data: *Conduct-Based Measures. Structure Measures. Performance Measures.* An Assessment of Competition Measures: *Data Problems. Conceptual Problems. The Usefulness of Competition Measures.*

PART ONE

Measures of Aggregate Economic Activity

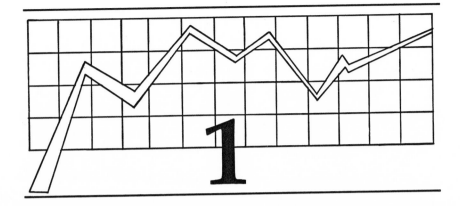

Gross National Product and Related Measures*

Carol S. Carson, Ph.D.
Chief Economist
Bureau of Economic Analysis
U.S. Department of Commerce

The gross national product (GNP), prepared by the Bureau of Economic Analysis (BEA) of the U.S. Department of Commerce, is the most widely used measure of the nation's production. It is the market value of goods and services produced by labor and property supplied by residents of the United States. More specifically, it is the market value of "final" sales of goods and services plus inventory change; purchases by one producing unit from another of intermediate products are not included. In its most familiar form, GNP is the sum of personal consumption expenditures, gross private domestic investment, net exports of goods and services, and government purchases of goods and services. These "product side" components, with estimates for 1982, are on the right side of Exhibit 1.

* The views expressed are the author's own and do not necessarily represent those of the U.S. Department of Commerce. George Jaszi and Robert P. Parker made helpful comments.

EXHIBIT 1   Summary National Income and Product Accounts, 1982

Account 1:   National Income and Product Account ($ billions)

Line		
1	Compensation of employees	1,865.7
2	Wages and salaries	1,568.1
3	Disbursements (2–7)	1,568.1
4	Wage accruals less disbursements (3–12) and (5–4)	0
5	Supplements to wages and salaries	297.6
6	Employer contributions for social insurance (3–20)	140.9
7	Other labor income (2–8)	156.6
8	Proprietors' income with inventory valuation and capital consumption adjustments (2–9)	109.0
9	Rental income of persons with capital consumption adjustment (2–10)	49.9
10	Corporate profits with inventory valuation and capital consumption adjustments	164.8
11	Profits before tax	174.2
12	Profits tax liability (3–17)	59.2
13	Profits after tax	115.1
14	Dividends (2–12)	68.7
15	Undistributed profits (5–6)	46.4
16	Inventory valuation adjustment (5–7)	−8.4
17	Capital consumption adjustment (5–8)	−1.1
18	Net interest (2–15)	261.1
19	*National income*	2,450.4
20	Business transfer payments (2–20)	14.1
21	Indirect business tax and nontax liability (3–18)	258.3
22	Less: Subsidies less current surplus of government enterprises (3–11)	9.5
23	*Charges against net national product*	2,713.3
24	Capital consumption allowances with capital consumption adjustments (5–9)	359.2
25	*Charges against gross national product*	3,072.5
26	Statistical discrepancy (5–12)	.5
	Gross National Product	3,073.0

GNP can also be measured as the costs incurred and the profits earned in the production of GNP. As on the left (income) side of Exhibit 1, these charges against GNP can be thought of in two groups. The first of these—compensation of employees, proprietors' income, rental income of persons, corporate profits, and net interest—are factor charges, so called because they represent income of the factors of production (labor and property). These incomes are recorded in the forms in which they accrue to residents and are measured before deduction of taxes on those incomes. The second group consists of nonfactor charges—that is, charges that must be added to factor charges to arrive at the required total market value of goods and services. These nonfactor charges include business transfer payments, indirect business taxes, the current surplus of government enterprises less subsidies, and capital consump-

Account 1   (*concluded*)

Line		
27	Personal consumption expenditures (2–3)	1,991.9
28	Durable goods	244.5
29	Nondurable goods	761.0
30	Services	986.4
31	Gross private domestic investment (5–1)	414.5
32	Fixed investment	439.1
33	Nonresidential	348.3
34	Structures	141.9
35	Producers' durable equipment	206.4
36	Residential	90.8
37	Change in business inventories	−24.5
38	Net exports of goods and services	17.4
39	Exports (4–1)	347.6
40	Imports (4–3)	330.2
41	Government purchases of goods and services (3–1)	649.2
42	Federal	258.7
43	National defense	179.4
44	Nondefense	79.3
45	State and local	390.5

Gross National Product	3,073.0

Note: Numbers in parentheses indicate accounts and items of counterentry in the accounts. For example, the counterentry for wage and salary disbursements (2–7) is in account 2, line 7.

Source: *Survey of Current Business*, July 1983.

tion allowances. The exhibit's left side also shows the statistical discrepancy. It reflects measurement error, and it is conventionally entered on the left side to secure balance between GNP and the factor and nonfactor charges against GNP.

The exhibit shows, in addition to GNP and charges against GNP, two other production aggregates. The first, national income, is an alternative to GNP in that it reflects, rather than the market value, the factor cost of goods and services produced. In other words, it is the income from the production of goods and services. The second, charges against net national product, is an alternative in that it reflects the value after (that is, net of) depreciation and other allowances for the consumption of fixed capital, rather than the value before deduction of (that is, gross of) such allowances. One further basic distinction can be made in defining the value of production. It is the distinction between domestic measures and national measures. The latter delimit production *by the residence of the supplier* of the labor and property. For example, as mentioned in defining U.S. GNP, it is production that is attributed to labor and property supplied by residents of the United States. The former delimit production *by the location* of the labor and property. National measures exceed domestic measures by the net inflow into a nation of labor and property incomes from abroad. Each of the three national measures has a domestic counterpart: gross domestic product, domestic income, and net domestic product.

The choice of a measure of production from this array depends on the use to which it will be put. For example, national income is often used in studies dealing with the allocation of factors of production to various uses. A market price measure is usually preferred for studies of economic behavior and welfare, because the market price is the basis for choice among alternative products. In most other countries, gross domestic product, rather than GNP, is the primary measure, and thus it is often used in international comparisons.

GNP IN AN ACCOUNTING FRAMEWORK

The usefulness of GNP is derived in part from its being the centerpiece of a set of measures that provides a summary picture of the economic process—that is, the production, distribution, and use of the nation's output. This set of measures is the national income and product accounts (NIPAs). An overview of the NIPAs can be obtained from their summary system. The account in Exhibit 1, which will now be referred to as the national income and product account, is the first of five accounts in this summary system. That account can be viewed as a consolidation of the production accounts of all producing units in the economy. Business units—essentially units that produce goods and services for sale at a price intended to at least cover costs of production—predominate, but production also takes place in units of the other major economic groups (that is, sectors): households, government, and rest-of-the-world.[1]

The national income and product account, in addition to showing total production, provides some information on its distribution and use.

---

[1] For a simplified explanation of GNP by reference to the measurement of the production of a single business unit, see Carol S. Carson and George Jaszi, "The National Income and Product Accounts of the United States: An Overview," *Survey of Current Business*, February 1981, pp. 22–23.

For example, it shows the part of GNP that goes to consumers (in the NIPAs, "persons") and many of the incomes—for example, wages and salaries—that persons receive and use to purchase goods and services. It does not, however, show all the income receipts of persons; nor does it show all the ways persons dispose of their incomes. A similar situation holds for government and foreigners. Finally, information is incomplete for the part of GNP that is saved and invested. The national income and product account shows only the part of GNP that is invested domestically and, among the forms of saving that make investment possible, only business saving.

Accordingly, in the summary system there are accounts for persons, government, and foreigners, to record systematically all the receipts of these sectors and the disposition they make of these receipts; and there is an account for the several forms of domestic saving these sectors generate and the investment their saving makes possible.

The personal income and outlay account, in Exhibit 2, registers income of persons from all sources and its disposition. Persons in the NIPAs consist not only of individuals but also of several kinds of organizations (nonprofit institutions, private noninsured welfare funds, and private trust funds) that are viewed as associations of individuals.

Personal income—the income received by persons from all sources— is sometimes used as a proxy measure of production because it is available for regions of the nation and because the national measure is available monthly. It differs from production because it excludes some incomes that are earned in production but not distributed to persons— for example, social security taxes and undistributed corporate profits— and includes some incomes that do not represent current production— for example, transfer payments. Because (especially in the short run) some of these incomes do not follow the course of total production, the proxy is imperfect. In Exhibit 3, the production incomes that are not distributed to persons are shown as what is subtracted, and the incomes that are not from current production are shown as what is added, in order to derive personal income from national income. Personal income and the measures of its disposition among taxes, outlays, and saving are useful in their own right, especially because persons are the largest among the economic groups whose interaction determines the working of the economy: Persons receive most of the income, account for the single largest share of taxes, give rise to the bulk of the demand for GNP, and contribute substantially to the saving that finances investment.

The government receipts and expenditures account, also in Exhibit 2, can be regarded as a budget statement within the framework of the NIPAs. It covers federal and also state and local agencies (except government enterprises). The foreign transactions account can be regarded as

EXHIBIT 2   Summary National Income and Product Accounts, 1982
Account 2:   Personal Income and Outlay Account ($ billions)

Line		
1	Personal tax and nontax payments (3–16)	402.1
2	Personal outlays	2,051.1
3	Personal consumption expenditures (1–27)	1,991.9
4	Interest paid by consumers to business (2–18)	58.1
5	Personal transfer payments to foreigners (net) (4–5)	1.1
6	Personal saving (5–3)	125.4
	Personal Taxes, Outlays, and Saving	2,578.6

Account 3:   Government Receipts and Expenditures Account ($ billions)

Line		
1	Purchases of goods and services (1–41)	649.2
2	Transfer payments	366.7
3	To persons (2–21)	360.4
4	To foreigners (net) (4–6)	6.3
5	Net interest paid	65.2
6	Interest paid	137.6
7	To persons and business (2–16)	119.4
8	To foreigners (4–7)	18.2
9	Less: Interest received by government (2–17)	72.5
10	Less: Dividends received by government (2–13)	2.3
11	Subsidies less current surplus of government enterprises (1–22)	9.5
12	Less: Wage accruals less disbursements (1–4)	0
13	Surplus or deficit (−), national income and product accounts (5–10)	−115.8
14	Federal	−147.1
15	State and local	31.3
	Government Expenditures and Surplus	972.5

Account 2 (*concluded*)

Line		
7	Wage and salary disbursements (1–3)	1,568.1
8	Other labor income (1–7)	156.6
9	Proprietors' income with inventory valuation and capital consumption adjustments (1–8)	109.0
10	Rental income of persons with capital consumption adjustment (1–9)	49.9
11	Personal dividend income	66.4
12	Dividends (1–14)	68.7
13	Less: Dividends received by government (3–10)	2.3
14	Personal interest income	366.2
15	Net interest (1–18)	261.1
16	Interest paid by government to persons and business (3–7)	119.4
17	Less: Interest received by government (3–9)	72.5
18	Interest paid by consumers to business (2–4)	58.1
19	Transfer payments to persons	374.5
20	From business (1–20)	14.1
21	From government (3–3)	360.4
22	Less: Personal contributions for social insurance (3–21)	112.0
	Personal Income	2,578.6

Account 3 (*concluded*)

Line		
16	Personal tax and nontax payments (2–1)	402.1
17	Corporate profits tax liability (1–12)	59.2
18	Indirect business tax and nontax liability (1–21)	258.3
19	Contributions for social insurance	253.0
20	Employer (1–6)	140.9
21	Personal (2–22)	112.0
	Government Receipts	972.5

EXHIBIT 2   (*continued*)

Account 4:   Foreign Transactions Account ($ billions)

Line		
1	Exports of goods and services (1–39)	347.6
2	Capital grants received by the United States (net) (5–11)	0
	Receipts from Foreigners	347.6

Account 5:   Gross Saving and Investment Account ($ billions)

Line		
1	Gross private domestic investment (1–31)	414.5
2	Net foreign investment (4–8)	−8.3
	Gross Investment	406.2

an embryonic balance of payments statement (see Chapter 10). It covers the transactions of the rest of the world with the United States. The gross saving and investment account cuts across the sectors and shows the saving and investment of all domestic sectors.

This five-account presentation brings out the transactions among sectors. For example, persons pay personal income and other taxes to the government, and government makes transfer payments to persons. Interrelations such as these are indicated by the numbers in parentheses following individual items; these numbers give the account and line where the counterentry occurs, generally in another account. For the first of the examples, in account 2, line 1, the "(3–16)" following "personal tax and nontax payments" indicates that account 3, line 16, shows this item as a receipt of the government sector. Correspondingly, that

Account 4 (*concluded*)

Line		
3	Imports of goods and services (1–40)	330.2
4	Transfer payments to foreigners (net)	7.5
5	From persons (net) (2–5)	1.1
6	From government (net) (3–4)	6.3
7	Interest paid by government to foreigners (3–8)	18.2
8	Net foreign investment (5–2)	−8.3
	Payments to Foreigners	347.6

Account 5 (*concluded*)

Line		
3	Personal saving (2–6)	125.4
4	Wage accruals less disbursements (1–4)	0
5	Undistributed corporate profits with inventory valuation and capital consumption adjustments	37.0
6	Undistributed corporate profits (1–15)	46.4
7	Inventory valuation adjustment (1–16)	−8.4
8	Capital consumption adjustment (1–17)	−1.1
9	Capital consumption allowances with capital consumption adjustment (1–24)	359.2
10	Government surplus or deficit (−), national income and product accounts (3–13)	−115.8
11	Capital grants received by the United States (net) (4–2)	0
12	Statistical discrepancy (1–26)	.5
	Gross Saving and Statistical Discrepancy	406.2

Note: See notes to Exhibit 1.

receipt item will be followed by a "(2–1)," referring back to the payment item.

The summary system is essentially a pedagogical device. The estimates in Exhibits 1 and 2 are only the tip of the iceberg. As will be discussed later, estimates are available not only for years but also for quarters and, in the case of personal income and its disposition, for months. For GNP and its product components, current-dollar measures are separated into measures from which price change has been eliminated—that is, constant-dollar measures—and measures of price change. Finally, most of the items are available in much greater detail. For example, annual estimates of personal consumption expenditures are broken down into about 100 types. Exhibit 4 indicates some of the aspects of the U.S. economy that can be depicted using NIPA estimates.

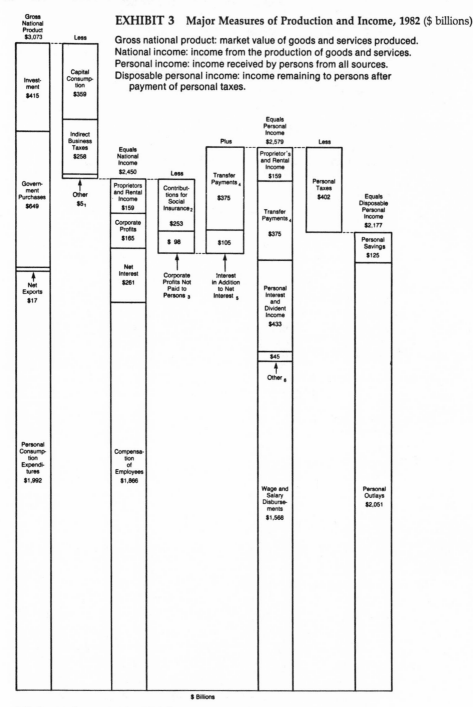

EXHIBIT 3   Major Measures of Production and Income, 1982 ($ billions)

Gross national product: market value of goods and services produced.
National income: income from the production of goods and services.
Personal income: income received by persons from all sources.
Disposable personal income: income remaining to persons after
        payment of personal taxes.

$ Billions

1. Business transfer payments and statistical discrepancy, less subsidies less current surplus of government
   enterprises.
2. Personal and employer contributions, and wage accruals less disbursements.
3. Corporate profits tax liabilities, undistributed corporate profits, and dividends paid to government.
4. Government transfers to persons and business transfer payments.
5. Interest paid by government to persons and business less interest received by government, plus interest paid
   by consumers.
6. Other labor income less personal contributions for social insurance.
Source: July 1983 *Survey of Current Business*, tables 1.7 and 2.1.

EXHIBIT 4   Aspects of U.S. Production, Distribution, and Use of Goods and Services as Depicted in GNP and Related Measures

Economic growth:	Constant-dollar GNP increased at an average annual rate of 3.0 percent from 1929 to 1982, of 3.3 percent from 1948 to 1982, and of 2.6 percent from 1970 to 1982.
	From 1970 to 1982, the average annual rate of growth of U.S. gross domestic product in constant dollars, at 2.6 percent, was in the middle of the range of major industrial countries. Japan, France, and Canada had higher rates (4.7 percent, 3.2 percent, and 3.1 percent); Germany and the United Kingdom had lower rates (2.2 percent and 1.5 percent).
Inflation:	Prices, as measured by the implicit price deflator for GNP, increased at an average annual rate of 3.5 percent from 1929 to 1982, of 4.0 percent from 1948 to 1982, and of 6.9 percent from 1970 to 1982.
Business cycles:	Since 1948, constant-dollar GNP has declined two or more quarters seven times. The largest drop, 4.8 percent, was in 1973–75; the smallest, 0.2 percent, was in 1979. In 1980, a single-quarter decline amounted to 2.5 percent.
Sector and industry shares of GNP:	By sector, 84 percent of GNP originated in business, 11 percent in government, 3 percent in households and institutions, and 2 percent in the rest of the world.
	By industry, the largest shares originated in manufacturing (25 percent), in wholesale and retail trade (17 percent), and in finance, insurance, and real estate (14 percent).
GNP per employee:	Each of the 85 million full-time equivalent employees produced over $36,000 of GNP.
Income distribution:	Employee compensation accounted for by far the largest share of national income—about 76 percent. Net interest accounted for 11 percent, corporate profits for 7 percent, proprietors' income for 4 percent, and rental income of persons for 2 percent.
Use of income:	For each dollar of personal income received, persons used about 79½ cents to purchase goods and services and for other outlays, paid 15½ cents in personal taxes, and saved 5 cents.
Per capita income:	On a per capita basis, disposable personal income was $9,377. By state, Alaska, at $12,680, had the highest per capita income; Mississippi, at $6,690, had the lowest.
	In constant dollars, per capita personal income has doubled since 1948.
Product composition of GNP:	In 1982, as has been typical, personal consumption expenditures accounted for almost two thirds of GNP. Nonresidential investment accounted for 11 percent, residential investment for 3 percent, net exports for 1 percent, and government purchases for 21 percent.
	Purchases of food accounted for 20 percent of personal consumption expenditures, housing for 17 percent, household operation (mainly utilities) for 7 percent, and clothing for 6 percent.
	Fixed investment is volatile. In the last 35 years, fixed nonresidential investment has ranged from a high of 12 percent of GNP to a low of 9 percent, and residential investment has ranged from 7 percent to 3 percent. The net stock of capital resulting from this investment amounted to $5,670 billion.
	Business inventories were drawn down in 1982 to just under $800 billion by year-end. For each $1 of business final sales, business held 30 cents in inventories.

EXHIBIT 4   (concluded)

Over 11 percent of the goods and services produced in the United States were exported. Almost 11 percent of the goods and services sold in the United States were imported.

State and local government purchases have been larger than federal purchases since 1968. About 40 percent of state and local purchases were related to education in 1982. National defense purchases accounted for about 70 percent of federal purchases.

Note: Estimates are for 1982 unless otherwise noted.
Sources: Estimates for 1982 are from the *Survey of Current Business*, July 1983; those for earlier years are from *The National Income and Product Accounts of the United States, 1929–76: Statistical Tables* (Washington, D.C.: Government Printing Office, 1981).

HISTORY

The history of GNP is far shorter than that of national income.[2] Indeed, the idea and statistical implementation of a measure of national income goes at least as far back into economic history as Sir William Petty in 1665. In the United States, several estimates—mainly based on decennial censuses and deriving national income as the sum of incomes by industry—were prepared by individual scholars in the 19th century. During World War I, several estimates were prepared; then, within a few years of its founding in 1919, the National Bureau of Economic Research began publishing the studies that became preeminent in the field.

As a result of a U.S. Senate resolution in 1932, the federal government began the work from which today's estimates are descendants. The resolution was prompted by the fact that, at the depths of the depression, a comprehensive measure of production, even on an annual basis, did not exist for later than 1929. The resulting estimates, published in *National Income, 1929–32*, were prepared at the Department of Commerce under the direction of Simon Kuznets. They showed the origins of national income by industry, and its distribution by type of income payment. Thereafter, beginning in 1935, updates appeared in the *Survey of Current Business*, which has continued to be the journal of record for NIPA estimates. Two major extensions of the estimates, a monthly series (that later evolved into personal income) and a distribution by state, were completed in the late 1930s.

The World War II effort was the immediate impetus to the preparation of estimates as the sum of products. The central question was:

---

[2] Carol S. Carson, "The History and Development of the United States National Income and Product Accounts: The Development of an Analytical Tool," *Review of Income and Wealth*, June 1975, pp. 153–81.

Given the government war effort, how much of total product will be left for civilian consumption? At first, the available estimates of government war expenditures were subtracted from national income. However, because national income is a net measure at factor cost, this procedure was viewed as inappropriate; a measure gross of capital consumption and at market value was needed. Thus, work got underway to derive what was then called gross national expenditures at market prices.

Thereafter, national income, GNP, and some other pieces very quickly jelled into a coherent system of accounts. In July 1947, a basic revision of the estimates of national income and product and of their component series was published. At this time, the estimates were set out as an interrelated and consistent system of national economic accounts. New procedures and source data were introduced as well, and several conceptual changes were made in the aggregates to enhance their usefulness in economic analysis.

The NIPAs have since undergone substantial refinement and elaboration. Estimating techniques were improved, constant-dollar versions of more series were developed and the associated measures of prices were introduced, greater detail is provided in the published estimates, more estimates are provided on a quarterly basis, and the estimates are prepared more quickly.

In addition, beginning in the mid-1950s, the hitherto largely independent segments of economic accounts were to a substantial extent integrated into a system with the NIPAs at its center. These segments can be viewed as elaborations of the five accounts of the summary system:

1.   Input-output accounts are, in essence, disaggregations of the national income and product account along industry lines. They present GNP in terms of both the product and income sides (final demand and value added, respectively, in the input-output table). Both are broken down by industry. However, the distinctive feature of the input-output approach is that it also comprehensively records interindustry transactions in intermediate products.

2.   The regional dimension begun in the 1930s has been further developed. Personal income, from the personal income and outlay account, is estimated for regions, states, and substate areas.

3.   Underlying the government account is substantial detail on receipts and expenditures of federal, state, and local government.

4.   The foreign transactions account is elaborated into balance of payments accounts, and supplemented by information on foreign investment. All of the work just listed is now done within the Bureau of Economic Analysis (BEA).

5.   From the saving and investment account, BEA provides estimates of the stocks of tangible capital by cumulating tangible investment flows. Other work in elaborating this account is done by the Federal

Reserve Board, which prepares the flow-of-funds accounts. These accounts, which can be viewed as providing the direct linkage between the saving and investment account and the associated lending and borrowing, were integrated with the NIPA estimates beginning in 1965.

Finally, there are several areas in which economic accounts are being extended in particular directions. For example, estimates consistent with GNP are available for pollution abatement and control expenditures.

Throughout the period, similar work in setting up and developing systems of economic accounts was going on in other countries. For example, in Great Britain, estimates of national income and expenditures were arranged in a two-sided table in 1941 and used in analysis of economic aspects of the war effort; by 1947, a substantial system of accounts had evolved. After World War II, the economic accounts put in place in several European countries played an important role in the framing of their economic recovery programs.

International consultations began as early as 1944, when U.S., British, and Canadian experts met to compare conceptual and statistical treatments. Shortly thereafter, the League of Nations put in motion efforts that led to the United Nations system of national accounts. This system serves as a guideline for nations in setting up their own accounts and as the vehicle for international reporting. Work is under way to update those guidelines, with the aim of having a revised system in place by 1990.

PUBLICATION OF THE ESTIMATES: FORM, SCHEDULE, AND CONTENT

GNP is prepared for quarters and for years, usually in billions of dollars (Exhibit 5). For quarters, the estimates are usually presented as seasonally adjusted annual rates. The seasonal adjustment is done to remove from the time series the variations—due to events such as weather, holidays, and tax payment dates—that normally occur at about the same time and in about the same magnitude each year. The statistical procedures to do this are based on historical experience; the Census Bureau's X–11 program is widely used. After seasonal adjustment, cyclical and other short-term changes in the economy stand out more clearly. Annual rates are the result of putting values for a quarter or a month at their annual equivalent; that is, they are the value that would be registered if the rate of activity were maintained for a full year. For example, if 2 million cars were sold in a quarter, the annual rate of sales for that quarter would be 8 million. Annual rates make it easier to compare values for time periods of different length—for example, quarters and years

EXHIBIT 5   **Gross National Product, 1956–1982** (seasonally adjusted at annual rates)

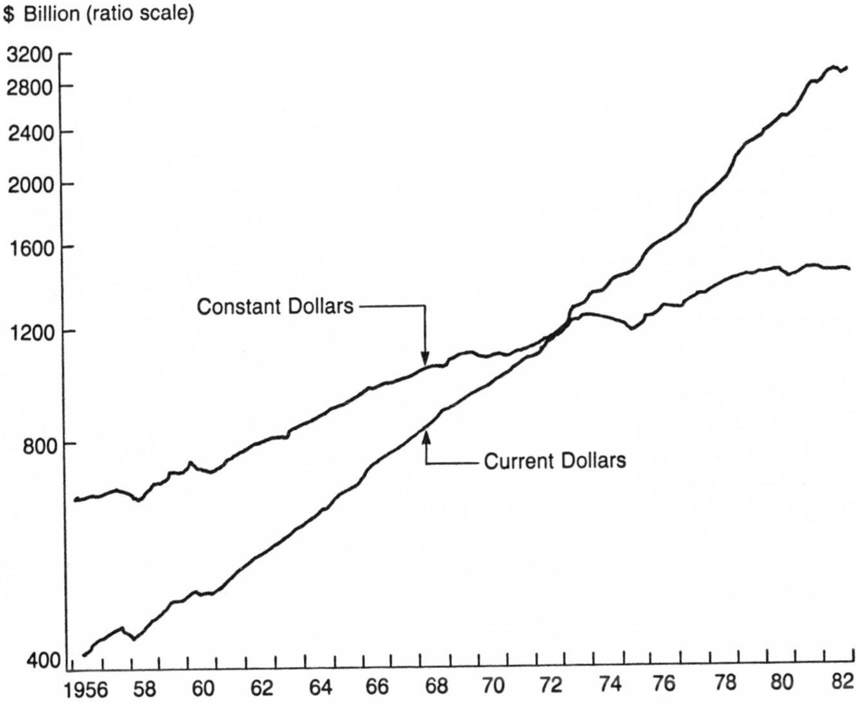

$ Billion (ratio scale)

A preliminary estimate of GNP is released about 15 days after the end of a given quarter.[3] It is based on source data that are incomplete and subject to revision. Revised estimates (known as 45-day and 75-day estimates) for a quarter are released in the two following months; they incorporate the source data that have subsequently become available. In addition, monthly estimates of personal income and its disposition are released.

Ordinarily, the NIPA estimates for the most recent calendar year and usually the two preceding years are revised each year in July, timed to incorporate annual source data. Comprehensive revisions—often called benchmark revisions—are carried out about every five years, timed to incorporate the quinquennial economic censuses. Conceptual, definitional, or classificational changes made to improve the NIPAs as a tool of

---

[3] A "projection," or "flash" estimate, is prepared 15 days before the end of the quarter. As of mid-1983, it is circulated only to high-level policymakers in the federal government and is not released by BEA to the public. Beginning September 1983, the level and change in four summary figures—current-dollar GNP, constant-dollar GNP, the GNP fixed-weighted price index, and the GNP implicit price deflater—were released.

economic analysis are usually introduced at the time of the comprehensive revisions. Such a revision was completed in December 1980. Its major features were the introduction of new source data (including BEA's 1972 input-output tables and summary tabulations of the 1977 economic censuses), methodological improvements in most components, improvements in the treatment of international transactions, and an expansion in the amount of income and product information provided.

The estimates of which GNP is part are published in substantial detail. The full presentation of quarterly estimates in the *Survey of Current Business* consists of about 50 tables. It shows not only GNP in current and constant dollars along with its associated measures of prices, product component detail in current and constant dollars, national and personal income, corporate profits, and other well-known measures but also many others. Among these are auto and truck output, inventory stocks, gross domestic product of corporate business, and merchandise trade by type of product and by end-use category. The estimates as usually presented in the July *Survey*, shown in about 130 tables, provide even more detail. They include several "relationship" tables that show adjustments to source data needed to arrive at NIPA estimates, employ ment estimates consistent with the income and product measures, and industry breakdowns for GNP and several component estimates.

Revisions—conceptual, definitional, and classificational, as well as statistical—to the greatest extent possible have been carried back to early years in order to provide consistent time series. GNP in current and constant dollars is available for years beginning with 1909. Most annual series begin with 1929, and most quarterly series begin with 1946.

SOURCES AND METHODS

This section first provides an overview of the source data and methods used to estimate GNP. Second, it sketches, component by component for both the product and income sides, the sources and methods used in making current-dollar annual estimates usually released in July. Third, it contrasts in general terms the differences between sources and methods used to prepare these estimates and those used to prepare estimates for current quarters. Finally, it describes the sources and methods used to derive constant-dollar estimates.

Overview

With few exceptions, the source data are not collected for the purpose of being transformed into income and product estimates. Aside from this common characteristic, the source data are diverse in terms of collecting agency, primary use, periodicity, statistical techniques, and reliability.

Data collected by federal government agencies—the Census Bureau, Treasury Department, Labor Department, Office of Management and Budget, and Agriculture Department—provide the backbone of the estimates. These data may be classified as administrative and nonadministrative. Administrative data are byproducts of government functions such as welfare and social security programs, tax collection, and regulation. Nonadministrative data include the periodic economic and population censuses and sample surveys, such as those that obtain data on manufacturing activity, corporation finance, and households. The items for which BEA does collect source data used to estimate GNP are related to international activity and include travel expenditures abroad and direct investment. Government data are supplemented by data from trade associations and business, labor organizations, and welfare, educational, and religious groups.

The differences in statistical technique and periodicity of collection are factors in determining how and at what stage in the revision schedule just described a particular data source is used. For benchmarks, use is made of data sources that provide the most complete coverage. Examples are the decennial census of population, the decennial census of housing, the extensive business data collected by the Census Bureau in the quinquennial economic censuses (mainly the censuses of manufactures, wholesale trade, retail trade, service industries, agriculture, and mineral industries), data compiled by the Bureau of Labor Statistics on wages and salaries of employees covered by state unemployment insurance, and data related to business income compiled from tax returns by the Internal Revenue Service and published in its *Statistics of Income* series. The last two sources are available annually and therefore can be used for nonbenchmark as well as benchmark years, although the Internal Revenue Service data are available in complete form only after several years' lag. Annual data sources often are based on samples. Among these are the annual survey of manufactures, the annual retail trade survey, the annual trade survey (for wholesale trade), and the service annual survey. Quarterly and monthly data sources usually are based on samples. These include the monthly surveys of manufacturing, wholesale trade, and retail trade, which are based on smaller samples than their annual counterparts; the *Quarterly Financial Report*, which is prepared by the Census Bureau and provides financial data for manufacturing, mining, and trade corporations; and the monthly surveys of wages and employment by the Bureau of Labor Statistics.

The data pulled together from these diverse sources undergo considerable processing. In part, this involves adjustment of the data to the stipulated definitions of the economic aggregates. An example is the adjustment of corporate profits as reported by business to the NIPA definition. Gaps in information may have to be filled by referring to sources that are themselves incomplete. Conflicting evidence may be received from different sources or for slightly differing periods. BEA stresses the amount of judgment involved in the preparation of the estimates: "The estimating is not a mechanical job. It is not a question of adding up a lot of reported figures. Judgment necessarily enters at every step of the estimating procedure."[4]

Among the estimating procedures are extrapolation and interpolation. They are methods of calculating estimates for one or more periods from estimates for others for which data are more reliable or more abundant. Extrapolation projects estimates from one base period, either forward or backward in time, to other periods. Interpolation fills in estimates between two base periods. Extrapolations and interpolations may use indicator series or trends. Indicators range from samples of the universe being estimated (for example, extrapolating dividend payments on the basis of a sample of large, publicly held corporations) to measures only indirectly related to what is being estimated (for example, extrapolating sales taxes on the basis of retail sales). Because interpolation deals with two base periods, the extent of uncertainty is somewhat less than in extrapolation. The results of both procedures become less reliable the longer the period covered by the calculated estimates.

The commodity-flow procedure provides an example of the complexity of the estimating work. This procedure, developed in its basic form by Simon Kuznets in the 1930s, was a way of obtaining the value of consumer purchases of goods (that is, commodities) or the value of producers' purchases of durable equipment by starting from the value at manufacturers' prices of manufacturing shipments. For consumer purchases, this procedure is preferable to the alternative of utilizing retail sales data, which are detailed by type of store (or by type of department in department stores), and thus do not provide information by commodity group. A generalization of the commodity-flow procedure that takes place within an input-output framework is now followed by BEA for benchmark years. The outline for consumer commodities that follows does not fully indicate the complexity of commodity-flow methods, but it does provide a notion of what is involved in using them.

1. From among the detailed list of products enumerated in the census of manufactures, those destined for consumer use are segregated. This involves, in addition to the straight selection of products destined solely for consumers, an allocation of products whose use is

---

[4] George Jaszi, "The Statistical Foundations of the Gross National Product," *Review of Economics and Statistics*, May 1956, p. 208.

mixed—for example, an estimate of how much flour is used by households directly and how much is used by bakeries.

2. Sales by nonmanufacturing producers of commodities destined for consumer use are taken into account. Among these are the products of agriculture, commercial fisheries, and mining, for which the censuses of agriculture and minerals industries provide information.

3. Transportation charges are added, mainly on the basis of information from the Interstate Commerce Commission.

4. Imports are added, mainly on the basis of Census Bureau data.

5. Producers' sales to consumers need no further processing. For other sales to consumers, wholesale and retail inventory change and wholesale and retail markups, including sales taxes, are taken into account. Information is mainly from Census Bureau surveys and censuses and the Internal Revenue Service.

GNP: Product Side

Personal consumption expenditures are goods and services purchased by individuals (including net purchases of used goods), operating expenses of nonprofit institutions, and the value of food, fuel, clothing, rent of dwellings, and financial services received in kind by individuals.[5]

For benchmark years, the bulk of personal consumption expenditures for goods is estimated, as described earlier, by commodity-flow methods that start with the value of manufacturers' shipments. Between and beyond benchmark years, the estimates are interpolated and extrapolated by Census Bureau data on retail trade (either from the revised *Monthly Retail Trade Report* or, when it becomes available, the *Annual Retail Trade Report*). Of the goods not estimated in this way, motor vehicles (new and used cars, trucks, and recreational vehicles) and gasoline and oil make up the largest part. They are estimated by multiplying quantity purchased by average retail price. For new vehicles, unit sales, information with which to allocate sales among consumer and other purchasers, and average prices are available from trade sources. For gasoline, information on gallons consumed is from the Department of Transportation, information with which to allocate that total is from federal agencies and trade sources, and the average retail price by grade is from the Bureau of Labor Statistics.

Preparation of the services component draws upon several hundred different series. Periodic censuses provide benchmarks for the rental

---

[5] Full definitions of this component and others shown in the exhibits presenting the five-account summary system are in *National Income and Product Accounts of the United States, 1929–76: Statistical Tables* (Washington, D.C.: Government Printing Office, 1981).

value of housing (censuses of population, housing, and agriculture); auto repairs, barbershops, laundries, movie theaters, and similar repair and personal service establishments (census of business); and other components that together account for one half of the dollar value of consumer services. For the rental value of housing, estimates for noncensal years are based on estimates of the housing stock from the Annual Housing Survey when it becomes available and an updated average annual rental. For service establishments, information for noncensal years is available from the Census Bureau's *Service Annual Survey*. Annual reports of government administrative agencies are available for brokerage, financial services, transportation, and private educational outlays. Private organizations provide data on insurance, hospital, telephone, electricity, gas, local transport, and religious and welfare organizations' outlays. Information on physicians, lawyers, and other professional services is obtained from Internal Revenue Service tabulations in *Statistics of Income* and from the *Service Annual Survey*.

Gross private domestic investment consists of fixed capital goods purchased by private business and nonprofit institutions (including net purchases of used goods) and the value of the change in the physical volume of inventories held by private business. All private purchases of residential structures, whether purchased for tenant or owner occupancy, are included.

The principal source for nonresidential structures is the Census Bureau survey of the value of construction put in place. This survey provides the data needed for the nonfarm buildings component. For the other components, several methods are used, depending on the type of information available. Estimates of oil and gas well drilling and exploration are based on data on footage drilled and cost per foot from trade sources and a Census Bureau survey. For utilities, telephone and telegraph, and railroads, companies or trade associations and federal regulatory agencies provide data. Farm construction estimates are based on a Department of Agriculture survey.

Producers' durable equipment is estimated chiefly by commodity-flow methods that start with the value of manufacturers' shipments. Thus, for benchmark years, the major sources are the manufacturing and wholesale trade censuses. For noncensal years, the estimates are based largely on shipments data from the Census Bureau's *Annual Survey of Manufactures*. Estimates for motor vehicles are prepared as described for personal consumption expenditures.

For residential investment, the principal source is similar to that for nonresidential structures. For the nonconstruction components, Census Bureau survey results are used to estimate additions and alterations, and estimates of brokers' commissions on the sales of residences are extrapolations of benchmark levels by a volume measure and a mean price.

Change in business inventories, as noted, is defined as the change in physical volume of inventories valued at average prices of the period. The change in farm inventories is estimated by the Department of Agriculture, using physical quantity data and current prices. For nonfarm inventories, the basic data available are book values. The book values of manufacturing and trade inventories, which make up over 90 percent of the nonfarm total, are derived from Census Bureau censuses or, for noncensal years, sample surveys of wholesalers, retailers, and manufacturers. Annual inventories of all other nonfarm industries are obtained from Internal Revenue Service tabulations of business tax returns.

In general, the change in the book value of inventories does not conform to the NIPA definition, because book values reflect the prices of inventories in the periods in which they were acquired; if prices change, identical physical units in the stock of inventories will generally be valued at different prices. Therefore, adjustments must be made. The adjustments use information on the proportion of inventories reported with different accounting methods (for example, first-in-first-out and last-in-first-out), prices of goods held in inventory, the commodity composition, and the turnover period. The price data are largely from the producer price indexes; the other information comes largely from Census Bureau surveys of manufacturing and trade. The basic steps of the procedure used to derive the NIPA change in business inventories from book values are as follows:

1. Inventory stocks at book value are separated according to the inventory accounting methods that underlie them. This separation is necessary because the mix of acquisition costs differs according to the several accounting methods.
2. Prices that correspond to the costs of different commodities in the stock are selected by reference to turnover periods. In general, the longer the turnover period, the further back in time are the prices that are reflected in these costs.
3. Book-value stocks are divided by indexes based on these prices to convert them into constant-dollar stocks.
4. The differences between the constant-dollar stocks are multiplied by ratios of current prices to constant prices to obtain the NIPA change in business inventories.

Net exports of goods and services are exports less imports of goods and services. The services include factor incomes, measured as compensation of employees, interest, and corporate profits. Exports are part of national production and imports are not; but because imports are included in the other components of GNP (for example, in personal consumption expenditures), they must be deducted in deriving GNP. The net exports component of GNP is related to the balance on goods and services in the international transactions (balance of payments) accounts prepared by BEA.[6]

The estimates of net exports are prepared as part of the balance of payments accounts. The largest components of net exports are merchandise imports and exports, for which data are obtained from import entry forms and shippers' export declarations compiled by the Census Bureau. The Census Bureau data are adjusted for coverage, timing, and valuation. Sources for factor income and other services include reports from the following: U.S. companies on affiliates abroad and U.S. affiliates of foreign companies; federal agencies on their loans, purchases, and sales abroad; companies and federal agencies on transportation; U.S. travelers on their expenditures abroad and foreign travelers on their expenditures in the United States; and agencies or companies handling payments for other services such as income on investments, insurance, royalties, and fees.

Government purchases of goods and services consist of the compensation of government employees and purchases from business and from abroad. They include gross investment, but exclude current outlays, by government enterprises. They include net purchases of used goods and exclude sales and purchases of land and financial assets. Thus, the concept of government purchases is narrower than that of government expenditures, which includes (in addition to purchases) transfer payments, grants-in-aid, net interest paid, and subsidies less the current surplus of government enterprises.

The principal sources for federal expenditures on goods and services are the *Treasury Combined Statement of Receipts, Expenditures, and Balances* and the *Budget of the United States.* From expenditure data in these sources, certain deductions are made—mainly public debt interest, grants-in-aid to state and local governments, transfer payments, subsidies, capital transactions, net expenditures of government enterprises, and foreign currency purchases. Certain additions—mainly capital formation of government enterprises—are also made. The result, after timing adjustments, represents purchases of goods and services.

State and local government purchases of goods and services other than services of employees are derived, mainly from reports made by these governments to the Census Bureau, in a manner analogous to that used in deriving federal purchases. The data are on a fiscal-year, rather

---

[6] A reconciliation of the conceptual and statistical differences is presented in Table 4.5 of the National Income and Product Accounts tables. For more information on the balance of payments, see Chapter 10.

than a calendar-year, basis. For state governments, the calendar-year estimates are prepared as the average of two consecutive fiscal years. For local governments, for which there is a much wider range of ending dates for their fiscal years, the conversion to a calendar-year basis uses information from periodic Census Bureau tabulations of expenditures by ending month of fiscal year. For services of employees (that is, employee compensation), the main source is Bureau of Labor Statistics tabulations of wages and salaries of employees covered by state unemployment insurance.

GNP: Income Side

Compensation of employees is the income accruing to employees as remuneration for their work. It is the sum of wages and salaries and of supplements to wages and salaries. Wages and salaries consist of the monetary remuneration of employees, including the compensation of corporate officers; commissions, tips, and bonuses; and receipts in kind that represent income to the recipients. Supplements to wages and salaries consist of employer contributions for social insurance (such as for federal old-age, survivors, disability, and hospital insurance and for state unemployment insurance) and of other labor income, which includes employer contributions to private pension and welfare funds.

A very large part of the data used to estimate wages and salaries comes from Bureau of Labor Statistics tabulations of wages and salaries of employees covered by state unemployment insurance. For private industries not covered by unemployment insurance, wage information comes from a variety of sources—for example, the Interstate Commerce Commission for railroads and the Department of Agriculture for farms. In only a few instances, such as the estimates of tips as percentages of revenues in applicable industries, are indirect methods employed. For the federal government, information is from the Office of Personnel Management and the *Budget of the United States.*

For supplements to wages and salaries, the information about employer contributions for social insurance comes from the Social Security Administration, other agencies administering social insurance, and Census Bureau surveys of state and local government retirement funds. For other labor income, the information comes largely from trade sources for the insurance industry, Internal Revenue Service tabulations in *Statistics of Income,* and the Health Care Financing Administration.

Proprietors' income with inventory valuation and capital consumption adjustments is the income, including income in kind, of proprietorships and partnerships and of tax-exempt cooperatives. Interest and dividend income received by proprietors and rental income received by persons who are not primarily engaged in the real estate business are excluded; these incomes are included in net interest, dividends, and rental income of persons, respectively. (The inventory valuation adjustment is described under corporate profits, and the capital consumption adjustment is described under capital consumption allowances.)

Nonfarm proprietors' income is estimated, except for the most recent year, from income tax returns tabulated by the Internal Revenue Service. This information is adjusted for understatement of net income on the tax returns and for several conceptual differences between income as reported on tax returns and NIPA income. For the most recent year, extrapolations are prepared by industry. For construction, trade, and services, indicators of activity (such as housing put in place) are used as extrapolators; for most of the remaining nonfarm industries, past trends are used.

Proprietors' income from farming is estimated by the Department of Agriculture on the basis of an extensive reporting system. Basically, the procedure is to obtain an estimate of gross earnings (cash receipts from marketings, inventory change, government payments, other cash income, and nonmoney income) and subtract production expenses to obtain net income.

Rental income of persons with capital consumption adjustment is the income of persons from the rental of real property, except the income of persons primarily engaged in the real estate business; the imputed net rental income of owner-occupants of nonfarm dwellings; and the royalties received by persons from patents, copyrights, and rights to natural resources. (The capital consumption adjustment is described under capital consumption allowances.)

Rental income of persons is estimated as the sum of four components, as follows:

1.   The return from rented nonresidential nonfarm property is estimated largely on the basis of information on rents (paid less received) and on expenses associated with the property (for example, depreciation, taxes, interest, and repairs). The information is from income tax returns as tabulated by the Internal Revenue Service.

2.   Imputed income from owner-occupied nonfarm dwellings is derived by estimating the number of such dwellings, multiplying this estimate by an average annual rent, and then subtracting an estimate of average expenses. The number of dwellings and the average rent are obtained from the census of housing for benchmark years and sample surveys for interpolation and extrapolation; estimates of average expenses are derived from a variety of sources. Income from tenant-occupied nonfarm dwellings is derived using similar sources and methods.

3.   Rent from farm realty is prepared in conjunction with the estimates of farm income.

4. Royalties are largely based on those reported on income tax returns.

Corporate profits with inventory valuation and capital consumption adjustments are the income of corporations organized for profit and of mutual financial institutions that accrues to residents. (The capital consumption adjustment is described under capital consumption allowances.)

The inventory valuation adjustment is the difference between inventories used up when valued at acquisition cost, which is the book valuation used by most businesses, and inventories used up when valued at current replacement cost, which is the valuation used in the NIPAs. (If the sign of the inventory valuation adjustment—which is usually negative—is reversed, this adjustment is recognizable as what is often called "inventory profit.") Because the using up of inventories is an element in the calculation of income of corporations and proprietors, both corporate profits and proprietors' income are shown with an inventory valuation adjustment. The sources and methods used to convert book-value inventories to NIPA inventories were described in the section on gross private domestic investment, where the inventory valuation adjustment appears as the change in business inventories (the GNP component) less the change in book-value inventories.

Corporate profits, except for the two most recent years, are based on tabulations of unaudited corporate income tax returns published by the Internal Revenue Service in *Statistics of Income*. These data are adjusted statistically (including an adjustment for understatement on tax returns) and conceptually. The major conceptual adjustments are to include in profits the depletion allowances on domestic minerals, income of the Federal Reserve and the federally sponsored credit agencies, and the excess of additions to bad debt reserves over losses actually incurred, and to exclude capital gains and losses from sales of property, and dividends from domestic corporations. For the two most recent years, separate extrapolations for about 70 industries are based on the *Quarterly Financial Report*, reports of federal regulatory agencies, and compilations of publicly reported company profits. BEA's surveys of foreign direct investment in the United States and U.S. direct investment abroad provide information on the net inflow of profits from abroad, which is estimated as part of the balance of payments accounts.

Net interest is interest paid by business less interest received by business, plus interest received from abroad less interest paid to abroad. In addition to monetary interest flows, net interest includes flows of interest in kind (imputed interest).

The primary source for the monetary components of the interest paid and received by businesses is *Statistics of Income* from the Internal Revenue Service. For some components in all years and before *Statistics of Income* data are available for others, interest receipts and payments are obtained from data from regulatory agencies (such as the Federal Deposit Insurance Corporation) and from trade sources, or by applying an interest rate to a stock of assets/liabilities. A portion of imputed interest is equal to the value of financial services furnished without explicit payment by commercial banks and other depository institutions. This portion is calculated as the property income earned on investment of deposits less monetary interest paid on deposits (less profits of mutual depositories). The required data are available in the annual reports of the Federal Deposit Insurance Corporation, other regulatory agencies, and the Federal Reserve Board. The remaining portion of imputed interest represents property income earned by life insurance companies and noninsured pension funds (less profits of life insurance companies). The data are obtained mainly from the Internal Revenue Service. Net interest received from abroad is estimated as part of the balance of payments accounts.

Business transfer payments are payments for which the persons paid do not perform current services. They include liability payments for personal injury, corporate gifts to nonprofit institutions, and bad debts incurred by consumers.

The component estimates are based largely on data contained in tax returns tabulated by the Internal Revenue Service. These are supplemented by information from other government and trade sources.

Indirect business tax and nontax liability consists of tax liabilities (except employer contributions for social insurance) that are chargeable to business expense in the calculation of profit-type incomes, and of certain other business liabilities to government agencies—regulatory fees, special assessments, fines and penalties, and rents and royalties—that it is convenient to treat like taxes.

Federal indirect business taxes include liquor and tobacco excise taxes, the windfall profit tax on crude oil production, and customs duties. Estimates are based on collections data from the Internal Revenue Service and other federal agencies. The main state and local taxes are sales taxes and property taxes. Data are largely from the Census Bureau surveys.

Subsidies less current surplus of government enterprises has two parts. Subsidies are grants paid by government to business, including government enterprises at another level of government. The current surplus of government enterprises (for example, the Tennessee Valley Authority and state liquor stores) is their sales receipts less their current outlays.

Subsidies paid by the federal government are compiled from Treasury reports and the *Budget of the United States*. For federal enterprises, the data necessary to derive the current surplus are found either in the profit and loss statements of enterprises organized as corporations or in the financial statements reconstructed from available budgetary data for the others. Information on state enterprises is calculated from summary operating statements compiled by the Census Bureau.

Capital consumption allowances with capital consumption adjustment is the difference between the gross and net measures of production. Capital consumption allowances consist of depreciation charges and accidental damage to fixed business capital. For nonfarm business, depreciation is defined as reported on federal income tax returns; for farms, nonprofit institutions, and owner-occupied houses, depreciation is calculated to conform to NIPA definitions.

The capital consumption adjustment is the tax return–based capital consumption allowances less capital consumption allowances that are designed to provide an economic measure of the using up of capital in production. The adjustment is applied to corporate profits, proprietors' income, and rental income of persons.

The depreciation component of capital consumption allowances, for nonfarm unincorporated enterprises and corporations, is derived from tabulations of income tax returns prepared by the Internal Revenue Service. It is based on the historical acquisition cost of the capital being depreciated and reflects the accounting practices with regard to service lives and depreciation patterns pursued under the Internal Revenue Service regulations. For farms, nonprofit institutions, and owner-occupied houses, the estimates are derived by the perpetual inventory methods used to prepare stocks of capital (see the next paragraph). Estimates of the other component, accidental damage to fixed capital, are based on losses reported to insurance companies and, in cases of weather damage and damage to transport facilities, to government agencies.

The capital consumption adjustment is the sum of two parts: The first is an adjustment that places a historical-cost series for capital used up on a consistent basis with regard to service lives and to a straight-line depreciation pattern, and an adjustment that puts the consistent historical-cost series on a replacement-cost basis. The second part is estimated as the difference between two depreciation measures—one at historical cost and one at replacement cost—derived from a perpetual-inventory calculation. This method starts with investment flows and, by cumulating past investment and deducting the cumulated value of investment that has been discarded, arrives at the gross stock. Depreciation is calculated on the gross stock. The first part is estimated as the difference between two historical-cost measures of depreciation—the one from the perpetual-inventory calculation and the one that is tax return-based.

Sources and Methods for Current Quarterly Estimates

The sources and methods used for the current quarterly estimates—that is, the 15-day, 45-day, and 75-day estimates—differ considerably from those just described for annual estimates. In general, the source data are much less complete and are more subject to revision by the source agency. For example, at the time of the first full presentation of the estimates 15 days after the end of a quarter, the key data available for personal consumption expenditures are the three months of retail sales (of which two months are subject to revision by the source agency); unit sales of new motor vehicles for the three months, one month of information with which to allocate the unit sales among consumers and other purchasers, and two or three months of average list prices (which are subject to modification as information on actual retail prices becomes available), and one or two months of data for services that are about one half of total services.[7] The estimates for most of the remainder of personal consumption expenditures are extrapolations based either on related indicator series or on past trends. For the 45-day and 75-day estimates, the revised retail sales, information on sales and inventories of used cars, and more data on selected services (such as electricity) become available.

As suggested by the release of monthly estimates of personal consumption expenditures, source data for this GNP component are more complete or are more reliable extrapolators than for the others. Among the product components, the change in business inventories and net exports are at the other end of the scale. For the former, book values are limited to those for manufacturing and trade for two months (and data for the second month are subject to revision). For net exports, only merchandise exports and imports (and those only for two months) are available. For both of these components, the difficulty of estimating with only limited data is compounded by their volatility.

Among the income components, source data for wages and salaries are most complete. For almost all private industries, monthly estimates (which are summed to quarterly totals) are prepared by extrapolating annual estimates by the product of employment, hours, and earnings from the Bureau of Labor Statistics monthly survey of establishments. Federal civilian wages and salaries are based on monthly data from the Office of Personnel Management, and other government wages and salaries are based on monthly data on employment and BEA estimates of average earnings. Most other income components are prepared by extrapolating annual estimates either by an indicator series—for example, dividends are extrapolated by reference to dividends paid by a BEA sample of large publicly held corporations—or by past trends. Although

---

[7] BEA makes available a table at the time of the 15-day estimates that shows, by month for a given quarter, the key source data available, whether the data are subject to revision or not, and projections by BEA for data that are not available. The table, "Key Source Data and Projections for National Income and Product Estimates," was described in the *Survey of Current Business*, October 1978.

dividends paid can be estimated monthly for incorporation in personal income, the corporate profits total, which is estimated largely on the basis of industry extrapolations from the *Quarterly Financial Report*, lags one month (and two months for the fourth quarter). Thus, the preliminary estimate for corporate profits and for the income-side total is released 45 days after the close of a quarter (75 days for the fourth quarter).

Constant-Dollar Estimates

Changes in current-dollar GNP reflect changes in both the physical volume of goods and services produced and in their prices. For many purposes, it is essential to have a measure of physical volume alone (and, as a byproduct, a measure of prices).[8] Constant-dollar ("real") estimates are such measures, and they are prepared for GNP and its product components.[9]

To prepare these estimates, each component is valued in principle at its price in a valuation period. Statistically, most constant-dollar estimates are obtained by dividing the most detailed current-dollar components by appropriate price indexes—with 1972, the valuation period as of 1983, equal to 100. Components of the consumer price index and the producer price indexes, prepared by the Bureau of Labor Statistics, are the principal price indexes used.[10] These indexes are used in preparing constant-dollar estimates of components that account for well over three fourths of GNP. Other price information includes the Census Bureau's unit-value indexes for exports and imports and their index for single-family houses, the Federal Highway Administration's indexes for highway construction, BEA's indexes for defense products, and indexes prepared by trade sources. In a few cases, constant-dollar estimates are obtained by extrapolating the current-dollar estimates in 1972 by physical volume measures or by multiplying quantities by 1972 prices.

Several problems are encountered in attempting to match current-dollar components with appropriate price indexes. First, for some im-

---

[8] The major measures of prices associated with GNP and related estimates are implicit price deflators and fixed-weighted price indexes. The former are obtained by dividing a current-dollar estimate by a constant-dollar estimate, and changes in them reflect not only price change but also shifts in the composition of goods and services. The latter use as weights the composition of output in the valuation period, and changes in them reflect only price change.

[9] In general, measures that can be expressed in terms of products can be estimated in constant dollars because price indexes can be associated with them. Also, to serve a practical need, disposable personal income is adjusted for price change even though, strictly speaking, it cannot be expressed in terms of products; the implicit price deflator for personal consumption expenditures is used.

[10] See Chapters 4 and 15.

portant products (mainly some capital goods and some services), price indexes are not available, and indexes of the cost of inputs or other approximations must be substituted. Second, some price indexes are list prices rather than transactions prices. List prices tend to be "sticky" and, when they do change, to do so more abruptly than do transactions prices. Third, some price indexes are not adequately corrected for changes in the quality of the product, that is, they do not represent only price change. Fourth, some indexes are derived from unit values—which are usually computed from mixes of products—rather than from price observations.[11]

In recent years, the quantity and quality of the constant-dollar measures have been substantially improved. Several of the major price indexes have been overhauled and now provide more adequate source data. Also, several new sets of price information have been developed. For example, beginning in the mid-1970s, BEA in cooperation with the Department of Defense developed price indexes at a very detailed level, along with parallel product detail, for defense purchases. Implementation of the standard procedure is especially difficult for defense purchases because defense spending is for unique products that change rapidly and are otherwise difficult to price. As a result of this work, BEA now provides detailed quarterly estimates of constant-dollar defense purchases and of associated price measures. Further, BEA has under way a project to improve the constant-dollar estimates for merchandise exports and imports. A major part of this work is the substitution of price indexes developed by the Bureau of Labor Statistics for the Census Bureau unit-value indexes.

USES

Exhibit 4, referred to earlier, illustrated how GNP and related estimates in the NIPAs can be used to depict different aspects of U.S. production, distribution, and use of goods and services. Another way of describing the uses of these estimates is to refer to the kinds of purposes they serve. In what follows, four purposes are described separately even though they tend to overlap; these purposes are analysis, assessment, forecasts and projections, and policy formulation. This four-way categorization is not the only possible one, but it brings out well the wide range of uses.[12] The importance of the aspects of the economy that can be depicted with

---

[11] See Martin L. Marimont, "Deflating Quarterly GNP," in "Quarterly GNP Estimates Revisited in a Double-Digit Inflationary Economy," BEA Staff Paper No. 25, October 1974.

[12] Two other categorizations of uses are "theoretical" and "applied," and "positive" and "normative." Positive refers to how the economy operates without considering the desirability of the results; normative includes references to the extent to which welfare objectives are obtained.

the NIPAs, together with the wide range of uses they serve, suggest why the development of these estimates has been called one of the major contributions of economists thus far in the 20th century.

Analysis of past economic behavior and relationships as recorded in statistics is generally a first stage in an investigation. Often there is interaction between theory and economic accounts: Theory suggests significant variables and economic accounts provide the data—with detail combined into manageable and useful categories—with which to test and refine theory. The hand-in-hand development of NIPA estimates and macroeconomic theory in the 1930s and 1940s is an example of such interaction. Much of the macroeconomic analysis of the 1980s continues to be done in terms of variables that are part of the NIPAs. For economic growth analysis, for example, the long time series of GNP can be related to factors such as investment and labor force.

Assessment draws upon statistics to help provide a picture of current economic conditions. GNP and related estimates, in combination with employment and financial measures, make up the major part of this picture not only at the national level but also regionally and internationally. For assessment of cyclical developments, for example, the course of the product and income components of GNP provides a solid core.

Forecasts and projections extend estimates of variables and relationships into the future. Estimated future values of accounting aggregates, such as GNP or total wealth, may be their end products. For example, econometric models of the U.S. economy typically are built around NIPA estimates of output, spending, and income, and they integrate employment and financial variables with additional equations. Alternatively, projections may use future values of accounting aggregates as inputs for other types of projections.

Policy formulation, or decision making as it may be called in the private sector, is often the final stage in an investigation. The purpose of policy formulation may be adaptive in the sense that steps are taken to bring a unit into conformity with the projections of the whole; or, as may be the case with government policy formulation, the purpose may be to alter the projected course of events. Business has increasingly used NIPA estimates as background information in making decisions on production, marketing, finance, and capital spending. Government at all levels draws upon the estimates—as evidenced by budget documents that present assumptions about personal income, corporate profits, consumer spending, and other measures. At the federal level, the Council of Economic Advisers, the Treasury, the Office of Management and Budget, the Federal Reserve Board, the Joint Economic Committee, and the Congressional Budget Office all draw heavily upon GNP and related estimates in formulating and evaluating fiscal, monetary, international, and other aspects of economic policy.

RELIABILITY

For measures like GNP, for which statistics such as sampling error are not applicable, it is particularly difficult to draw conclusions about reliability. There are, however, several approaches to the reliability of the GNP estimates that shed some light on the subject.[13]

One approach is to study the sources and methods underlying the estimates. The GNP's estimators have suggested a check list of four factors to be considered in appraising reliability with this approach.

1. Complexity of the reported item. Is the item reported by the economic unit a straightforward, simply defined transaction (often associated with a monetary transaction), or is it one that requires complex calculations or is only vaguely defined?
2. Quality of records kept. Are the records of the reporting unit adequate to provide reliable data or even any data at all?
3. Design of the reporting system. Are the data drawn from a complete enumeration (census) or from a sample, and if from a sample, is it a large one or a small one? Is it a probability sample? Are there possible gaps in the information?
4. Estimating procedure employed. Are the data in nearly the same form as that in which they enter the estimates? If so, potential error may be reduced although this does not suggest that the simpler the procedure the more reliable the estimate; absence of a complex procedure may merely indicate a broad guess.[14]

Two examples suggest how this checklist can be applied. There is little doubt that, on the income side, the wages and salaries component ranks highest in reliability. It is a relatively straightforward item, usually associated with a monetary transaction; both the records kept and the reporting system are high quality, in part reflecting the comprehensive social insurance system to which they are tied; and the adjustments of reported totals are small and statistically well founded. In contrast, the estimates of the change in business inventories present a problem. The item is a complex one; particularly for the noncorporate sector, records are inadequate and the reporting system is not entirely satisfactory. The change in inventories is estimated as a residual between large and volatile stock totals and is thus subject to large percentage errors. The estimating procedure involves complex adjustments, some of which are made on less than secure statistical assumptions.

Another approach to the question of reliability is to view the size of revisions as an indicator of the reliability of the earlier estimates. For

---

[13] The issue of reliability and approaches to appraising it are discussed in Allan H. Young, "Reliability of the Quarterly National Income and Product Accounts of the United States, 1947–71," BEA Staff Paper No. 23, July 1974.

[14] *National Income, 1954* (Washington, D.C.: Government Printing Office, 1954), p. 62.

example, for the 15-day estimates, revisions in the following two months and in July of the following three years can be used to appraise their reliability. Two assumptions underlie this approach: that the second of two estimates being compared is "correct," and that the larger (the smaller) the revision, the less (the more) reliable the first estimate. However, as is suggested by the following case, these assumptions are not completely valid. The case is that of two estimates—say a 15-day and a 45-day estimate—that are based on extrapolation of past trends and for which no new information becomes available to incorporate into the second, so that there is no revision to the first. The second estimate cannot be said to be any more "correct" than the first, and the small revision (in this case, zero) sheds no light on the reliability of the estimate.

Exhibit 6 presents results for estimates of current- and constant-dollar GNP based on this approach. It shows, in percentage points, revisions

EXHIBIT 6	Revisions in Quarter-to-Quarter Percent Change at Annual Rate in GNP (percentage points)		
	Average without Regard	*Range of Revision between Specified Percentiles*	
From 15-Day Estimate to:	*to Sign*	*25 to 75*	*5 to 95*
Current-dollar GNP			
45-day estimate	0.5	−0.1 to +0.6	−0.4 to +1.3
First July estimate	1.0	−0.2 to +1.4	−1.4 to +2.2
Third July estimate	1.4	−0.4 to +1.8	−1.9 to +3.0
Constant-dollar GNP			
45-day estimate	.5	−0.3 to +0.4	−0.8 to +1.1
First July estimate	1.0	−0.5 to +1.1	−1.8 to +2.0
Third July estimate	1.4	−0.8 to +1.5	−2.1 to +3.4

Source: News releases for GNP, BEA.

in the quarter-to-quarter percent change at annual rates for the period 1964–79. Three revisions from the 15-day estimate are shown: to the 45-day estimate, to the first July estimate, and to the third July estimate. For constant-dollar GNP, for example, the average revision (without regard to sign) in the quarter-to-quarter change from the 15-day estimate to the first July estimate was 1.0 percentage point, and 9 times out of 10, the revision was within a range of −1.8 to +2.0 percentage points.[15]

---

[15] The 75-day estimate was introduced in December 1977; it is expected that when there are enough observations to compute the size of revisions between the 45-day and 75-day estimates and between the 75-day estimates and the first July estimates, the revisions will be smaller than those between the 15-day estimate and the 45-day estimate.

For the period since 1979, the last year included in the study on which Exhibit 6 was based, the revisions may turn out to be larger. One possible reason for this to happen is an erosion of the data base by the increasing antipathy of business and others to the burden of reporting their activities and by cuts in budgets of agencies that collect and process the source data. Although this explanation cannot be ruled out, more important as a factor in any increase in the size of revisions is that in recent years the economy has undergone a number of sharp changes due to the rapid runup in energy prices, high and volatile interest rates, and the shifting U.S. position in the international economy, to mention a few. The task of estimating GNP and related measures is much more difficult when the economy is undergoing such rapid change.

ALTERNATIVE MEASURES

In the early 1930s, one of the reasons that work on national income estimates was encouraged was that the available measures of aggregate economic activity were not comprehensive enough to serve some major analytical and policy uses. One of the measures then available was the index of industrial production. It has since been expanded, and remains the only other major measure of U.S. production. The GNP itself is sometimes criticized as lacking comprehensiveness, and proposals have been made for more comprehensive measures—for example, measures with a welfare orientation and measures that would take into account the "underground" economy. The index of industrial production and two measures more comprehensive than GNP are briefly contrasted with GNP in what follows.

Index of Industrial Production

The index of industrial production (IIP), prepared by the Federal Reserve Board, measures the output of manufacturing and mining industries and of gas and electric utilities.[16] The output originating in these industries accounts for only about one third of GNP. Further, for current estimates, the sources that are used in preparing the IIP differ substantially from those used in preparing GNP. About one half of the IIP is based on physical volume measures, and the bulk of the remainder is based on electric power inputs and employee hours (both adjusted for estimated productivity change).

As can be seen in Exhibit 7, real GNP and the IIP show similar cyclical movements although there are differences in turning points and in am-

---

[16] See Chapters 4 and 18.

EXHIBIT 7 Real Gross National Product and the Index of Industrial Production
(percent change from preceding quarter at an annual rate)

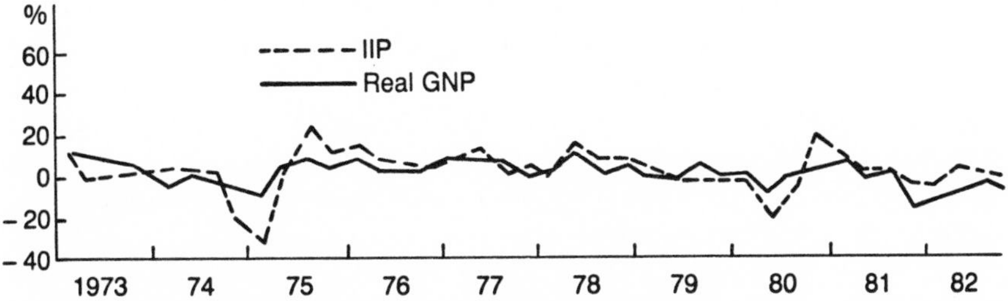

Source: Issues of the *Survey of Current Business* and the *Federal Reserve Bulletin.*

plitude. Fluctuations in the IIP tend to be larger because the IIP measures production in a volatile sector. An adjusted real GNP may be constructed to bring the coverage of the two series closer together. It is defined as GNP goods plus 40 percent of structures less gross farm production and used car margins plus personal consumption expenditures on gas and electric services. Quarter-to-quarter changes in the IIP and in adjusted real GNP are fairly close although the differences are substantial in some quarters.

Comparisons may also be made of some components of the two series—for example, the consumer goods market grouping of the IIP with the goods part of personal consumption expenditures, and the business equipment grouping with producers' durable equipment. Also, components of the annual GNP by industry series can be compared with industry groupings for the IIP. The two source agencies cooperate in comparisons of the two sets of measures with the aim of improving them.

Welfare-Oriented Measures

The production that GNP measures is limited largely to that of goods and services sold on the market. The main nonmarket additions were mentioned in discussing the sources and methods for the income and product components: wages and salaries in kind, the value of services of owner-occupied dwellings, food and fuel produced and consumed on farms, and the value of services furnished without payment by financial intermediaries except life insurance carriers. These imputations amount to less than 10 percent of GNP and are made in order to obtain a better view of total national output and its distribution.

It has been suggested that more nonmarket production—for example, the services of housewives, the services of volunteers, and the services provided by the stock of consumer durables—should be taken into account in order to provide a measure of economic welfare. It is proposed that this be done by adding them to GNP or, in the case of consumer durables, replacing a purchase component with a value-of-services component. On the other hand, it is pointed out that a number of goods and services now included in GNP either subtract from the population's welfare or at least do not add to it. Products whose production or use pollutes the environment and government expenditures for police and fire protection are often mentioned, and it is proposed that GNP be adjusted to exclude them.

In answer to these proposals, others have argued that, even if agreement on the conceptual basis of these changes could be reached and if they could be implemented statistically, it would be undesirable to introduce such vast changes in the GNP. A measure of production, generally defined as at present, now serves and will continue to serve many uses. This argument does not deny that analysis related to welfare-oriented topics should be encouraged. Along these lines, BEA has developed estimates of expenditure on pollution abatement and control that are consistent with GNP, thus providing a tool for analysis (including welfare analysis) consistent with GNP without restructuring it. Further, for several years, BEA did exploratory research on the value of the services provided by consumer durables, the value of household work, and several similar topics. However, BEA does not plan to restructure GNP to make it a measure of welfare.

The Underground Economy

The estimates of GNP have been criticized as being understated because they do not include all the activities that take place in the "underground" (or "hidden," or "informal," or "subterranean"—there are a number of names) economy. Some of the estimates of understatement are quite high—over 25 percent. However, by convention grounded in practicality, GNP does not include illegal activities, such as illegal trade in narcotics and illegal gambling. Accordingly, the term *understatement* is not fully appropriate.

The criticism of GNP thus narrows to the question of the extent to which GNP understates legal activities because it is based on source data that miss amounts of legal, but underground, activities. A BEA review of its sources and methods has shown that, on the income side, a little more than one half of GNP is accounted for by three components that are subject to understatement because their source data are understated. These three—nonfarm proprietors' income, domestic corporate profits, and private wages and salaries—all rely on income tax return tabulations. BEA procedure has long recognized the potential for understatement in the tabulations and has added amounts for unreported tips to private wages and salaries, added to nonfarm proprietors' income, and added to corporate profits mainly on the basis of audit studies and examinations done by the Internal Revenue Service. On the product side, about 40 percent of GNP is potentially subject to shortfall, and BEA has made adjustments.

BEA's review of its sources and methods pointed to a minimum shortfall of legal activities of about 1 percent of GNP in 1979.[17] Since completing the review for 1979, a somewhat larger shortfall due to non-reporting and underreporting on business income tax returns has been identified: On the income side, it is in the range of 3–4 percent. BEA is refining these estimates and plans to explore other topics related to the underground economy.

---

[17] Update of Robert P. Parker, "The Understatement of GNP and Charges against GNP in 1976 due to Legal Source Income Not Reported on Individual Income Tax Returns," Bureau of Economic Analysis, August 1980.

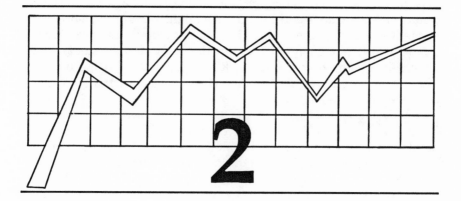

Corporate Profits

Edmund A. Mennis, Ph.D., C.F.A.
Consultant to Investment Management

Prior to a discussion of the various measures of corporate profits, some understanding of the conceptual differences among the different types of profits is necessary. Profit measures have various sources and are used for different purposes. Therefore, conceptual differences should not be surprising, although users of the various measures often are not aware of their existence.

TYPES OF PROFIT MEASURES

Basically, three major types of profits measures may be distinguished: (1) profits as reported for tax purposes, (2) profits as reported in the national income accounts, and (3) profits as reported to shareholders.

Profits Reported for Tax Purposes

Corporate management is required to submit an annual report of its operations to the Internal Revenue Service as a part of filing the corporate income tax return. These reports have a substantial degree of uniformity because they must be prepared in conformance with the Internal Revenue Code. However, complete uniformity is not possible because of the varying treatment permitted under the code for such items as depreciation, depletion, installment sales, and gains and losses on property sales. Treatment of foreign profits and the degree of consolidation used in reporting for related corporations also affect the comparability of the data. As a generalization, intercorporate dividends and capital gains and losses are included, special reserves are excluded, and foreign subsidiary earnings are included only to the extent that dividends are remitted to the parent company.

Profits Reported in the National Income Accounts

Perhaps the most widely quoted profits aggregate is that reported by the Department of Commerce as a part of the national income and product accounts (NIPA). This profits series is not intended to reflect an estimate of profits reported by all the corporations in the country. In the national income accounts, corporate profits represent the remuneration to one factor of production (or factor cost, in national income terminology) in what might be called a closed economic system for the United States. This factor cost of profits is distinguished from the other costs of employee compensation, interest, and rent.

This profits figure is an attempt to measure the distribution to the residents of the nation of the earnings of corporations, which are a portion of the aggregate earnings of labor and property arising from the nation's current production. The basic source of information for this profit series is corporate income tax returns; however, adjustments are made to conform to national income account conventions.[1]

National income profits reflect the income of corporations organized for profit and of mutual financial institutions that accrues to U.S. residents and is measured before profit taxes, before deduction of depletion, after the exclusion of capital gains and losses, and net of dividends received from domestic corporations. Bad-debt expenses are measured by actual losses, not additions to reserves. The profit or loss of bankrupt corporations includes the gain from unsatisfied debt. Profits also include net inflows (from abroad to U.S. corporations and residents) of dividends and reinvested earnings of direct investors' incorporated foreign affiliates and earnings of unincorporated foreign affiliates.

---

[1] A reconciliation of corporate profits, taxes, and dividends in the national income and product accounts with corresponding totals as published by the Internal Revenue Service is published annually in the July *Survey of Current Business*, Table 8.12.

Two other important adjustments are made in this series to reflect current-period accounting rather than historical costs. An inventory valuation adjustment (IVA) is made to adjust the usual change in book value of inventories, as reported by business, to reflect instead the change in physical volume of inventories valued at prices of the current period. The IVA therefore is equal to the excess of the replacement cost of inventories used up over their historical acquisition cost. The second adjustment is a capital consumption adjustment (CCAdj), which converts tax return–based capital consumption allowances to a replacement-cost valuation and to uniform service lives and depreciation formulas. The adjustment is equal to the new measure of capital consumption allowances minus the previous measure based upon historical costs.

Profits Reported to Shareholders

A third conceptual view of profits is that of profits reported to shareholders, which reflect management's evaluation of the company's operations, ordinarily checked by an annual independent audit. In order to receive the auditor's certification without qualification, these financial results have to be prepared in accordance with generally accepted accounting principles, and the Financial Accounting Standards Board has been making substantial progress in recent years to bring greater uniformity to the ways that companies may report their operations. However, considerable latitude is still possible, especially in the areas of consolidation and treatment of depreciation.

As a broad generalization, shareholder reports ordinarily reflect worldwide consolidation of earnings and assets and also depreciation on a straight-line basis. Government profit reports generally reflect domestic operations, with foreign dividends and profits reported separately. In addition, those government profit series that are based upon tax returns reflect the depreciation policies used in the tax returns rather than those used in shareholder reports. Consequently, compilations of shareholder profits may differ considerably from reports based upon either of the other two types of profits.

PROFIT COMPILATIONS

Reports on profits are available in two forms: continuous time series and periodic compilations of individual company reports.

Continuous Time Series of Profits

Several reports of annual or quarterly profits that provide a continuous time series are released by the federal government or by private sources. These series are described briefly in the following sections. However, users should consult the basic source documents for each of these reports in order to obtain more detailed information about their construction.

National Income and Product Account Series. The Department of Commerce, Bureau of Economic Analysis, publishes quarterly estimates of corporate profits on the third Thursday of the second month following the end of each calendar quarter. Annual revisions are published in the July issue of the *Survey of Current Business*. The information provided is as follows:

Corporate profits with IVA and CCAdj.

Corporate profits with IVA.

Profits before tax.

Profits tax liability.

Dividends.

Undistributed profits.

Corporate profits after tax with IVA and CCAdj.

Undistributed profits with IVA and CCAdj.

In addition, on the same publication basis, the department provides a particularly useful breakdown of gross domestic product of corporate business in current dollars, gross domestic product of nonfinancial corporate business in current and constant dollars, and current-dollar cost and profit per unit of constant-dollar gross domestic product of nonfinancial corporate business. These series are useful for analysis of current profits trends, and they are the basis of many economists' forecasts of corporate profits.[2]

Because this terminology may not be too familiar, some clarification may be helpful. Nonfinancial gross corporate product (NFGCP) reflects the contribution of the domestic operations of nonfinancial corporations

---

[2] This information is adapted from Edmund A. Mennis, "Forecasting Corporate Profits" in *Methods and Techniques of Business Forecasting,* ed. William F. Butler, Robert A. Kavesh, and Robert B. Platt (Englewood Cliffs, N.J.: Prentice-Hall, 1974), pp. 517–42. For a fuller explanation and a discussion of the use of this information to prepare forecasts of corporate profits, see Mennis and also Grace E. Wickersham, "The Latest Tools for Profit Analysis" in *C.F.A. Readings in Financial Analysis,* 5th ed. (Homewood, Ill.: Richard D. Irwin, 1981), pp. 87–94.

to gross national product. NFGCP has both a sales or product side and a balancing income or factor cost side. On one hand, it can be viewed as the sales of nonfinancial firms to other businesses, consumers, government, and foreigners, plus inventory change less purchases from other firms, both domestic and foreign. NFGCP also can be defined as the sum of incomes and charges to this gross product. From this viewpoint, it is therefore the sum of: (1) capital consumption allowances, (2) indirect business taxes less subsidies plus business transfer payments, (3) compensation of employees, (4) net interest, and (5) corporate profits before taxes and inventory valuation and capital consumption adjustments.

Capital consumption allowances in national income terminology include depreciation and accidental damage to fixed capital. Indirect business taxes represent primarily sales, excise, and property taxes and the windfall profits taxes of crude oil producers. Business transfer payments include liability payments for personal injury, corporate gifts to nonprofit organizations, and consumer bad debts. Employee compensation includes monetary remuneration plus supplements such as contributions to social insurance, pension, health, welfare, and unemployment funds as well as compensation for injuries.

In addition to the figures for NFGCP and its factor cost components in current dollars, the Department of Commerce also provides data for NFGCP in 1972 prices together with implicit price deflators. The price deflator for NFGCP reflects the current cost per unit of 1972 dollar NFGCP—that is, the costs incurred and the profits earned in producing one 1972 dollar's worth of output in the current period. The current factor costs of capital consumption allowances, indirect business taxes, net interest, employee compensation, and profits also have been related to NFGCP in 1972 dollars, so that we have not only the dollar costs but also the unit labor costs, unit nonlabor costs, and unit profits.

This additional information is especially useful in profits analysis because the movement of costs and profits can be traced in constant-dollar terms. Profits per unit of real NFGCP can be used as a measure of profit margins. However, this measure is not exactly comparable with pretax margins as ordinarily computed by a financial analyst. Pretax margins normally reflect the proportion of pretax dollars to sales dollars. Unit profits represent the percent that current-dollar pretax profits are of current output measured in 1972 prices; unit profits relate to profits per unit of real output rather than current-dollar sales.

Also on a quarterly basis in the *Survey of Current Business*, the department provides a breakdown of corporate profits by major industry groupings as well as national income without capital consumption by industry. The major industry groupings are subdivided into domestic and "rest of the world"; the latter series reflects the net inflow of profits from abroad to U.S. corporations and residents. Domestic industries are divided further into financial and nonfinancial. In the financial sector, data for the Federal Reserve banks are separated from those of other financial industries. Nonfinancial sectors are subdivided into 10 manufacturing segments as well as transportation and public utilities and wholesale and retail trade.

Flow of Funds Data.   Another useful source of information about profits is contained in the flow-of-funds data published by the Board of Governors of the Federal Reserve System. Annual and quarterly data are published about six weeks after the end of the current quarter. Base data are available in annual form from year-end 1945 and in quarterly form from 1952.

The purpose of the flow-of-funds accounts is to provide aggregate measures of transactions needed to identify both the influences of the nonfinancial economy on the financial markets, and the reciprocal influences of developments in financial markets on demand for goods and services, sources and amounts of saving and investment, and the structure of income. This chapter will discuss only that portion of the accounts that reports information on corporate profits.[3] A more complete discussion of flow of funds is provided in Chapter 12.

In the system, profits are based upon NIPA corporate profits. Therefore, data for corporate nonfinancial business are identical to those in the series used in the NIPA tables except that they include farm corporations. Like the NIPA series, this sector covers only domestic activities of corporations and does not represent worldwide financial position or investment or borrowing by U.S. corporations. No breakdown of information beyond the nonfinancial sector is provided.

Information is reported in terms of both flows and outstandings. In the flow information, private domestic nonfinancial business is both a supplier and a user of funds. Internal sources of funds include retained earnings, capital consumption allowances, foreign earnings, and inventory valuation adjustment. Outside sources include new equity and credit market instruments as well as trade credit. Uses of funds represent capital expenditures, including plant and equipment and change in inventories. Sources and uses of funds should balance, but the statistical discrepancy can at times be substantial. In addition to a significant amount of detail on the items described, the flow account tables also provide certain ratios indicating the effective tax rate, the ratio of capital outlays to internal funds, and also the ratio of credit market borrowing to capital expenditures.

---

[3] For a description of the concept and organization of the total system of the flow of funds, see *Introduction to Flow of Funds* (Washington, D.C.: Board of Governors, Federal Reserve System, June 1980). See also chapter 18.

In addition to flows, the account system shows, on an annual and a quarterly basis, outstanding financial assets and liabilities. This information does not provide a complete balance sheet, but it does provide considerable detail on financial assets such as liquid assets (demand deposits, time deposits, government security holdings, and commercial paper), consumer and trade credit, and other miscellaneous financial assets. The liability side includes credit market instruments (both long- and short-term), profit taxes payable, and trade debt. Also included in the reports are ratios of long-term debt to credit market debt, short-term debt to credit market debt, and liquid assets to short-term liabilities.

Quarterly Financial Data of the Bureau of the Census.   Another widely used source of corporate profits information is the *Quarterly Financial Report for Manufacturing, Mining, and Trade Corporations* (QFR), now issued by the Bureau of the Census, U.S. Department of Commerce.[4] Publication is about 75 days after the end of each of the first three calendar quarters and about 95 days after the end of the fourth quarter. The series dates back to 1947, but a change in consolidation rules in 1973 has lessened the comparability between earlier and later periods.

The QFR is useful for several reasons. It provides considerable industry detail, ordinarily by two-digit categories as described in *Enterprise Standard Industrial Classification Manual, 1974*. Classification also is provided by asset size, broadly divided into six asset classes as well as individual industry categories more than and less than $25 million in assets. Balance sheet and income account data are provided in some detail, and balance sheet and operating ratios are given.

The data are prepared on a sampling basis: All corporations with assets of more than $25 million are included, and smaller companies are represented by means of a statistically selected sampling process.

The conventional accounting concept of profits is used in QFR estimates, which means that the figures may differ from those used in reports for income tax purposes. In addition, when the QFR series began in 1947, corporations were instructed to consolidate all of their subsidiaries taxable under the U.S. Internal Revenue Code and fully consolidated in the latest report to shareholders; all other subsidiaries were counted as investments. Beginning in the fourth quarter of 1973, foreign entities (either corporate or noncorporate), foreign branch operations, and domestic corporations primarily engaged in foreign operations were specifically excluded from consolidation. Also excluded from consolida-

---

[4] The Federal Trade Commission had responsibility for the program from 1947 until December 1982, and the responsibility was shared with the Securities and Exchange Commission until 1971.

tion are domestic corporations engaged primarily in banking, finance, or insurance. Nonconsolidated subsidiaries are accounted for either on the cost (dividend income only) or the equity (equity in earnings or losses) method. This change has affected comparability of the pre- and post-1973 data.

Standard & Poor's Profits Data.   Standard & Poor's Corporation in the *Trade and Securities Statistics Manual* publishes annual earnings-per-share data for the S&P industrial, transportation, utility, financial, and composite averages from 1926 to date. For these same series, quarterly earnings are available since 1935. Earnings per share generally are taken as reported by the company.

Standard and Poor's also has a publication, *The Analysts Handbook*, which provides for each industry in the S&P Index of 500 Stocks the following information of the years 1950 to date: sales, operating profit, depreciation, income taxes, earnings, dividends, book value, working capital, and capital expenditures. The continuity of the per share figures is maintained through adjustments made similar to those in the stock price indexes. The companies in each industry correspond to the companies in the S&P stock indexes, so that direct comparisons with stock prices can be made. A monthly supplement to the *Handbook* provides quarterly information on per share sales, earnings, dividends, and prices. In addition, the *Handbook* provides complete income account and balance sheet information for the past six years for each Standard & Poor's industry that is a part of the 400 industrial group.

Other Continuous Time Series.   For a good overview of important profits information, the Department of Commerce in its monthly publication *Business Cycle Developments* charts a number of series on profits. The series and their titles are as follows:

Series 16   Corporate Profits after Taxes in Current Dollars.
Series 18   Corporate Profits after Taxes in 1972 Dollars.
Series 79   Corporate Profits after Taxes with Inventory Valuation and Capital Consumption Adjustments in Current Dollars.
Series 80   Corporate Profits after Taxes with Inventory Valuation and Capital Consumption Adjustments in 1972 Dollars.
Series 22   Ratio of Profits (after Taxes) to Total Corporate Domestic Income.
Series 81   Ratio of Profits (after Taxes) with Inventory Valuation and Capital Consumption Adjustments to Total Corporate Domestic Net Income.
Series 34   Net Cash Flow, Corporate, in Current Dollars.

Series 35 Net Cash Flow, Corporate, in 1972 Dollars.
Series 295 Business Saving—Undistributed Corporate Profits plus Capital Consumption Allowances with Inventory Valuation and Capital Consumption Adjustments.
Series 286 Corporate Profits with Inventory Valuation and Capital Consumption Adjustments.
Series 287 Corporate Profits with Inventory Valuation and Capital Consumption Adjustments as a Percent of National Income.

Compilations of Individual Profit Reports

In addition to the time series reports described in the prior section, a number of reports on corporate profits are available that cover only one time period.

Tax Return Information. The broadest report of corporate profits is published annually by the Internal Revenue Service in the *Statistics of Income—Corporate Income Tax Returns*. This report reflects the annual compilation of the income tax returns of all corporations in the United States and represents a stratified sample of corporate returns selected from the active corporate returns filed for the most recent year.[5] The main disadvantage of the report is that, because of the time necessary to collect the data, the lag in publication is about two years after the reporting year. For example, data for taxable years that ended between July 1980 to June 1981 were not published until mid-1983.

Data are presented for the total of all active corporations and also for corporations with net income, by major divisions and also down to the two-digit level of the enterprise standard industrial classification code. In addition, information is presented by size of corporation. Substantial income and balance sheet accounting detail is provided. Consolidation of returns is permitted where 80 percent of the voting and nonvoting stock is held. Foreign dividends only are included.

Other Individual Compilations. Several business magazines regularly publish one-period compilations of corporate profits data. All of these compilations reflect profits as reported to shareholders, although some adjustments may be made to make the data more comparable from company to company.

Perhaps the most extensive work is done by *Business Week*, a weekly publication of McGraw-Hill, Inc. Annually in March, *Business Week* publishes a compilation of 1,200 companies ranked by sales and divided

---

[5] For 1980, the sample was 85,500 returns selected from 2.8 million filed.

into 39 industry groupings. Information covers the fourth quarter of the previous year as well as the full previous year and includes sales, net income before extraordinary items, the ratio of net income to sales, return on common equity for the previous year, earnings per share, and the price-earnings ratio of the company's stock. About one and one-half months after the close of each calendar quarter, *Business Week* publishes quarterly information for about 900 companies that contains the same detail as the annual data. In addition, when the first quarter data are published, information is added on return on invested capital and 10-year growth rates for common equity and earnings per share.

Business Week also publishes special reports annually for the 200 top banks (published in mid-April), corporate research and development spending for about 775 companies grouped by industry (published in mid-June), balance sheet data and ratios for about 890 companies (published at the end of July), and sales, profits, and earnings data for more than 900 companies in 57 countries (published in mid-July). The data are prepared for *Business Week* by Standard & Poor's Compustat Services, Inc. In addition, in early May, *Business Week* publishes a report prepared by their own staff on inflation-adjusted earnings for more than 500 companies. Finally, in the last issue of *Business Week* each year, 900 large companies are listed alphabetically together with financial analysts' estimates of earnings for the past and the next year as well as other financial data.

Another well-known compilation of profits data is the annual publication by *Fortune* magazine each May of the *Fortune* 500. This report covers the largest 500 U.S. industrial companies ranked by sales, and data are provided for the previous year on sales, assets, net income, stockholders' equity, number of employees, net income as a percent of sales and of stockholders' equity, earnings per share, earnings growth rates, and the total return to investors for the previous year and the previous 10 years. Similar information is published in mid-June on the 500 largest U.S. service companies and in August on the 500 largest industrial companies and the 100 largest commercial banks outside of the United States.

Forbes magazine every May publishes information on *Forbes* 500, which ranks U.S. corporations four ways: by dollar sales, by asset size, by profits, and by market value. In January, Forbes also publishes a list of companies by industry with sales of $450 million or more; included in the tabulation is information on profitability, growth, earnings, and stock market performance.

An interesting source of information on expectations for profits is a weekly publication, *The Icarus Service*, by Zacks Investment Research, Inc., in Chicago and a similar publication by Lynch, Jones, & Ryan in New York called *I/B/E/S*. Both of these publications present the current consensus of brokerage analysts earnings-per-share estimates for the next two years. The information also is combined by industry, and summaries are provided for the Standard & Poor's 500 Stock Index and for the total universe of companies covered. The value of these reports is not only the information about the individual companies but also the ability to track the changing earnings estimates of analysts for the market or for industry groups. Financial analysts' estimates characteristically lag the market, underestimating earnings in cyclical recoveries and overestimating in cyclical declines. Nevertheless, comparisons of industry groups are most useful in identifying the cyclical impact on profits of changes in the economy.

One other source of information for profits data should be mentioned. Standard & Poor's Compustat Services has available computer tapes of detailed financial information for more than 6,000 industrial companies listed on the New York Stock Exchange, the American Stock Exchange, and the over-the-counter market. Data go back 20 years on an annual basis and 10 years on a quarterly basis. On an annual basis, 175 items of accounting information are available, and 70 items on a quarterly basis. Tapes also are available for 250 utility companies, with 400 items of annual data and 80 of quarterly data. Tapes are available for 90 telecommunications companies, with 290 items of annual data and 150 of quarterly data. A business information file also provides data on product lines and segments for 600 companies. The tapes can be purchased and individual computer programs written that can arrange the data in whatever form the user wishes.

COMPARISONS AND CAVEATS

Given the wealth of information available on corporate profits, a wide assortment of analyses could be prepared. Only a few significant comparisons are presented here.

NIPA Profits

Exhibit 1 shows corporate profits after taxes from 1950 to 1982 both in nominal terms and also adjusted for inflation. The data plotted are those reported in NIPA.

As the chart indicates, current-dollar and inflation-adjusted profits moved closely together from 1950 through 1972. Thereafter nominal profits soared until 1979 and then fell sharply. The growth in inflation-adjusted profits was slower from 1972 until 1978, and then these profits were relatively flat. Note that the inflation-adjusted profit figures are not

EXHIBIT 1   NIPA Corporate Profits after Taxes, 1950–1982 (current-dollar versus inflation-adjusted)

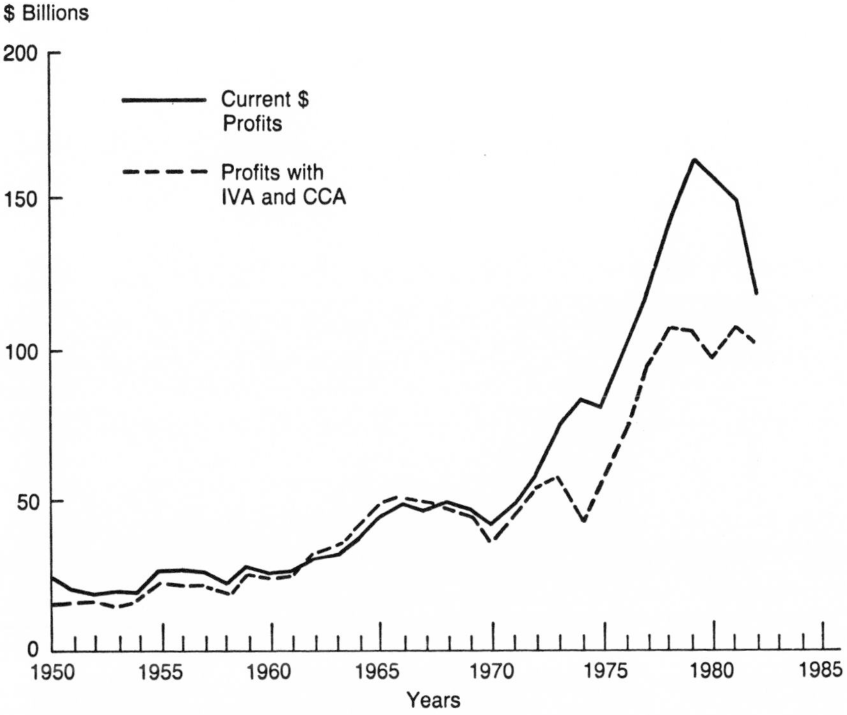

$ Billions

Source: NIPA, U.S. Department of Commerce.

adjusted by some price index but rather reflect current-dollar after-tax profits with the IVA and CCAdj. Consequently, the adjustment reflects the overstatement of inventory values caused by inflation and the adjustment for the runup in replacement costs of capital.

Exhibit 2 reflects the relationship of current-dollar corporate profits after taxes to gross national product from 1950 to 1982. During this period, profits averaged about 5.8 percent of GNP, as shown on the chart, but the impact of the 1981–82 business contraction caused this ratio to fall to its lowest level in the postwar period. However, no particular trend seems discernible, so that the share of profits, although volatile, does not seem to be shrinking over time.

Exhibit 3 charts the differences between the NIPA concepts of profits (before taxes and after adjustment for IVA and CCAdj) and corporate profits after taxes as reported in the NIPA. The series are plotted on a

EXHIBIT 2   NIPA Corporate Profits after Taxes, 1950–1982 (as a percent of gross national product)

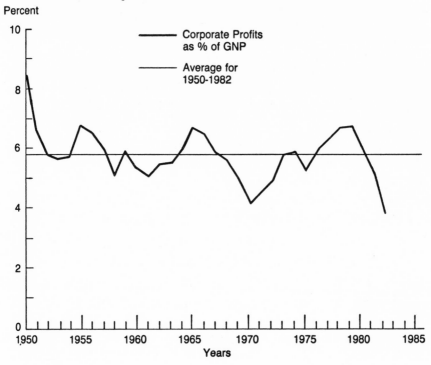

Source: NIPA, U.S. Department of Commerce.

semilogarithmic chart, so that percent changes can be compared directly. The movement of the two series is similar except for the 1950–53 period, when after-tax profits were reduced because of the excess profits tax during the Korean War, and for the period beginning in 1973, when aftertax profits were inflated due to inventory profits and understatement of depreciation.

NIPA versus Shareholder Profits

An interesting question is how various profit series compare, given the conceptual differences between them. Exhibit 4 plots a comparison of nonfinancial corporate profits after taxes as presented in NIPA with shareholder after-tax profits as reflected in the dollars of after-tax profits of the S&P 500 Stock Price Index as taken from the Compustat tapes. These data also are plotted on a semilogarithmic grid.

Nonfinancial profits are used because financial profits in the NIPA are

EXHIBIT 3   NIPA Corporate Profits, 1950–1982 (national income concept versus after-tax profits)

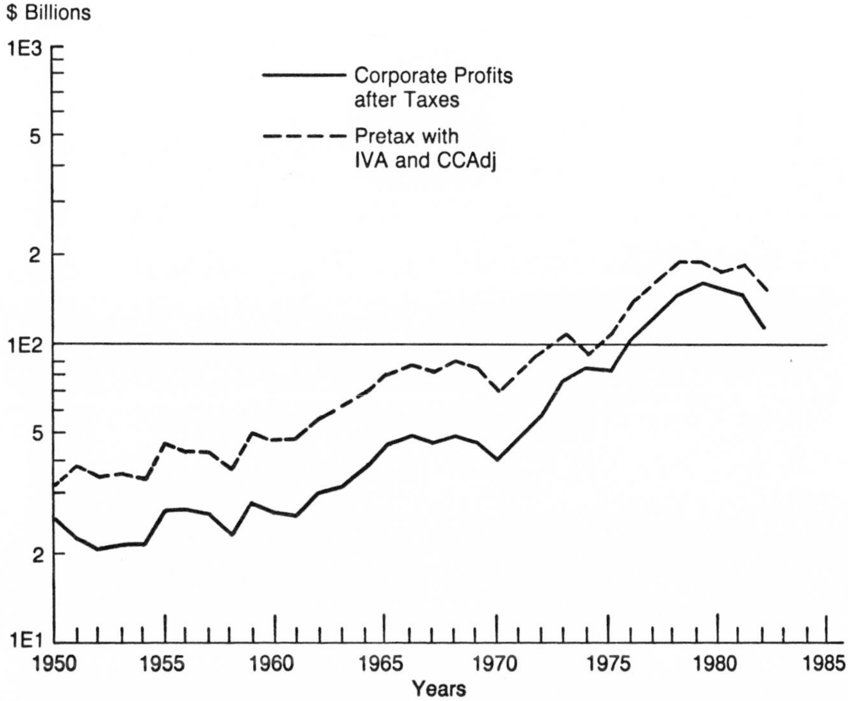

$ Billions

Source: NIPA, U.S. Department of Commerce.

distorted by inclusion of profits of the Federal Reserve banks, which account for almost 30 percent of pretax profits but only about 2 to 4 percent of aftertax profits. The other components of the two financial profit composites also are quite different.[6]

As the chart indicates, the two series are similar although the 1966–69 decline in NIPA profits was more than that of S&P profits, the growth of NIPA profits was greater from 1970 to 1979, and more recently the S&P series has increased faster. The differences are probably due to the accounting differences between the two series and also because the S&P series is heavily weighted by large, successful corporations.

---

[6] Federal Reserve profits are included in the NIPA series because the Federal Reserve banks are owned by the member banks in the commercial banking system. The difference between pretax and aftertax percentages is caused by the fact that, after paying a nominal dividend to the owner banks, the balance of Federal Reserve profits is paid to the U.S. Treasury, and the payment is considered an income tax payment in NIPA.

EXHIBIT 4 NIPA versus S&P 500 Nonfinancial Corporate Profits, 1963–1981

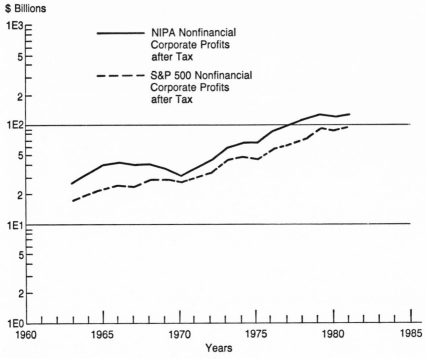

Source: NIPA, U.S. Department of Commerce, and S&P Compustat Tapes.

Tax Rates

Another interesting comparison is the difference between the implicit tax rates (corporate income taxes as a percent of pretax profits) as shown in the nonfinancial corporate profits data as reported by NIPA and as reported to shareholders. This information clearly indicates the effect of the conceptual differences between the two series. As shown in Exhibit 5, the implicit tax rates of the two series were not much different between 1963 and 1972. However, the chart suggests that U.S. corporations' tax rate computed on the NIPA series has been decreasing since 1970, while shareholders would have the impression that tax rates went up from 1970 to 1975 and have only recently returned to the pre-1973 level. The difference is accounted for primarily by the petroleum industry, beginning in 1973 when the overseas earnings of the oil companies surged due to the rapid increase in the price of oil, causing taxes paid to

EXHIBIT 5   NIPA versus S&P 500 Nonfinancial Implicit Tax Rate, 1963–1981

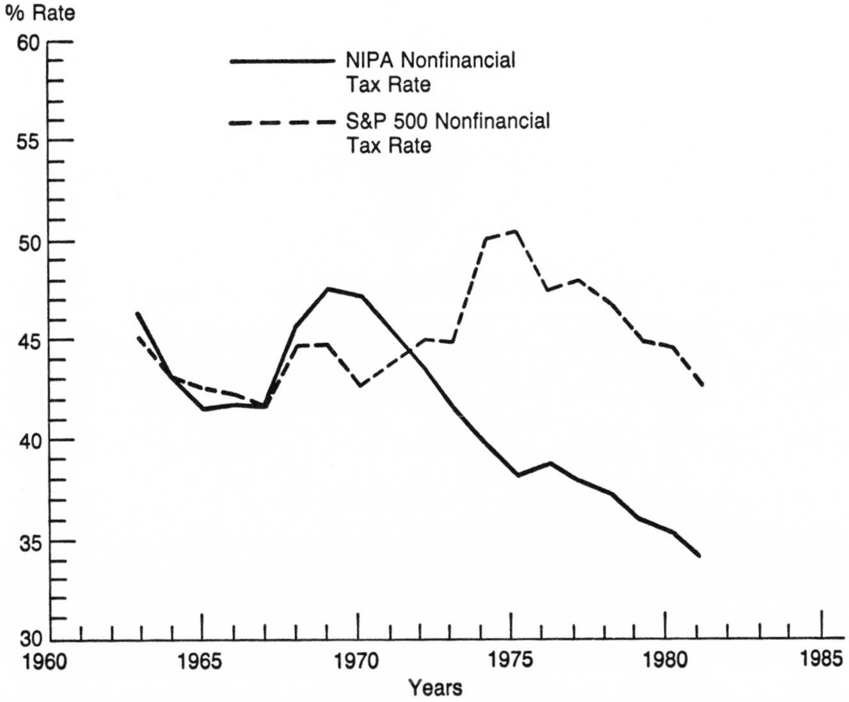

% Rate

Source: NIPA, U.S. Department of Commerce, and S&P Compustat Tapes.

foreign countries to increase. As a result, on U.S. income tax returns, which are not consolidated on a worldwide basis, tax credits claimed for foreign taxes paid increased substantially.

Caveats

Profits information has many users: economists, financial analysts, shareholders, government officials. The primary message of this chapter is not so much a description of where profits information can be found, but rather a warning to users of any aggregate of profits to consider the source, the basis on which the profits were reported for individual companies, and the rules that were followed when the profits were aggregated. The various measures are sufficiently different so that care should be taken not to move from one to another in the belief that they all measure the same thing.

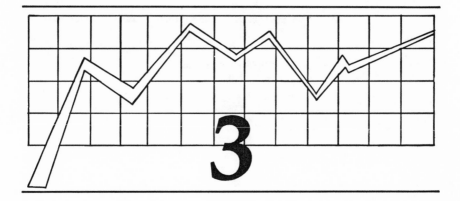

Capital Spending

Aubrey H. Zaffuto
Economist
J. Henry Schroder Bank and Trust Company

INTRODUCTION

Capital spending refers to investment in structures and equipment by businesses operating in the United States. Capital spending's share of total constant-dollar gross national product averaged just under 10 percent for the period 1950–82. This share is only about ⅙ of that contributed by consumer spending, but it has ranged from two to four times larger than housing's share of real GNP. However, the relatively modest segment that capital spending claims out of total GNP belies its actual importance to the health of the economy. Expenditure on new plant and equipment lays the base for productivity growth, which is the prime determinant of the economy's ability to expand.

Capital spending is a cyclical sector and therefore plays an important role in the fluctuations in aggregate economic activity. The cyclicality of capital spending is largely related to uncertainties or changes in both the cost of capital and the expected return on the capital investment. The cost of capital is particularly variable because of interest rate fluctuations and changes in tax laws. The expected returns associated with a capital

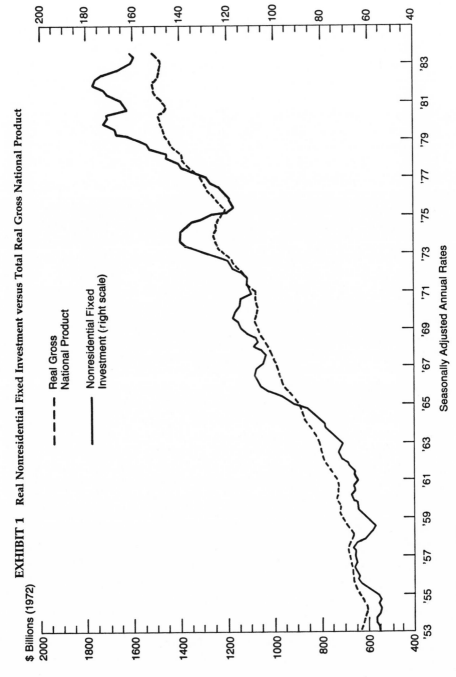

EXHIBIT 1 Real Nonresidential Fixed Investment versus Total Real Gross National Product

Real Gross
National Product

Nonresidential Fixed
Investment (right scale)

$ Billions (1972)

Seasonally Adjusted Annual Rates

Source: U.S. Department of Commerce.

project are usually analyzed in light of a combined macroeconomic, industry, and company outlook. Therefore, the business cycle itself is a further source of cyclicality for capital spending.

Exhibit 1 illustrates the trends in constant-dollar capital spending (measured by nonresidential fixed investment) and compares them to total real GNP. During the period illustrated, capital spending expanded at an average compound annual rate of 3.8 percent, outpacing GNP which grew at an average 3.2 percent. There were six major cycles during the 30-year period, and the healthiest periods for capital expenditure were 1960–66 and 1975–79. In each of these instances, the tax code was amended to include new investment incentives in the early stages of the cycle.

In the 1979–82 period, economic growth came to a virtual standstill, and capital spending plateaued at a cyclical peak. Capital spending finally began to decline significantly in early 1982, and this drop continued for the entire year. Economic recovery from the 1981–82 recession commenced in the fourth quarter of 1982, and capital spending stabilized in early 1983 and began to recover in the second quarter of the year. Given the severity of the recession, the contraction in capital spending in 1982 was mild. Significantly accelerated depreciation schedules offered by the Reagan administration for both equipment and structures provided powerful props for investment at a time when extraordinarily high interest rates and depressed economic activity could well have led to a much deeper contraction.

Nonresidential fixed investment, which is illustrated in Exhibit 1, is the capital spending component in the U.S. national income and product accounts (GNP). The information used to construct this measure comes from *producers* of capital goods. The other type of capital spending indicator, best represented by the Commerce Department's plant and equipment spending survey, is a measure of demand for capital goods from the *user's* perspective. This chapter will discuss many indicators of capital spending, some of which are compiled from production data and others of which are put together using information gathered from the users of capital goods. More attention will be paid to the two aforementioned indicators because they are the most comprehensive measures of capital spending which exist.

PRINCIPAL CAPITAL SPENDING INDICATORS

Nonresidential Fixed Investment

The nonresidential fixed investment component of GNP is broken down into two major categories labeled "producers' durable equipment" and "structures." The indicator has been compiled since 1929 on an annual basis and since 1946 on a quarterly basis. The U.S. Department of Commerce's Bureau of Economic Analysis is the entity responsible for producing this series. The bureau relies heavily on a myriad of primary data sources to derive its estimates for the components of fixed investment. The nonresidential fixed investment component of GNP is seasonally adjusted and is available both in current- and constant-dollar (1972) form.

The structures category records construction activity on a value-put-in-place basis. In constant dollars, it has averaged 3.2 percent compound annual growth in the past 30 years. In compiling this series, the Bureau of Economic Analysis relies heavily on Census Bureau reports of construction activity as well as on other reports which are listed in Exhibit 2. The dollar amount of the structures category represents the value of work underway in the quarter in question regardless of when the work commenced, and value refers to the cost of materials, labor, equipment, rent, depreciation, architectural and engineering fees, and contractors' profits. Land costs are not included, nor are maintenance and repair costs. The major subcomponents of the structures category are commercial, industrial, religious, educational, hospital and other institutional, public utilities, farm, and petroleum and mining.

Producers' durable equipment (PDE) is a larger category of fixed investment than is structures. In constant dollars, it has grown at a 4.1 percent average compound annual rate in the past 30 years. The Bureau of Economic Analysis derives its estimates for the various subcomponents of PDE from a wide variety of primary sources, the most important of which are listed in Exhibit 3. The fastest-growing components of PDE in the late 1970s and early 1980s have been the high technology and productivity-oriented areas of office and store machinery, service-sector machinery, communications equipment, and instruments and photographic equipment. Other components of PDE are much more cyclical in nature.

Before further discussion of nonresidential fixed investment and its components, it is useful to first review the particulars of another comprehensive indicator of capital expenditure so that comparisons can be made between the two.

Commerce Department Plant and Equipment Expenditure Survey

The Commerce Department's plant and equipment expenditure survey measures spending on new plant and equipment by U.S. nonfarm business. The published data are derived directly from a quarterly sur-

EXHIBIT 2 Summary of Source Data Used in Estimating Current Dollar Structure Expenditures*

Nonresidential Structures	*Benchmark Revision*	*Annual Revision*	*15-Day Estimate*	*45-Day Estimate*	*75-Day Estimate*
Nonresidential buildings, excluding farm	Bureau of the Census new construction put in place	Same as benchmark	2-mo. census survey, BEA estimate for third month	3-mo. census survey	Same
Public utilities					
Railroads	Census Bureau estimates based on Interstate Commerce Commission data	Same as benchmark	2-mo. census projection using BEA and ICC data, BEA estimate for third month	3-mo. census projection	Same
Telephone and telegraph	Census compilation of AT&T and Western Union reports, BEA adjustment from AT&T data	Same as benchmark	2-mo. census data, BEA estimate for third month	3-mo. census data	Same
Electric light and power	Census compilation of Federal Energy Regulatory Commission (FERC) and BEA data, BEA adjustment from FERC data	Same as benchmark	2-mo. census projection using BEA plant and equipment survey data, BEA estimate for third month	3-mo. census projection	Same
Gas	Census compilation of FERC and American Gas Association data	Same as benchmark	2-mo. census projection using BEA plant and equipment survey data, BEA estimate for third month	3-mo. census projection	Same
Petroleum pipeline	Census Bureau estimates based on ICC data	Same as benchmark	2-mo. census projection, BEA estimate for third month	3-mo. census projection	Same

Farm	Department of Agriculture survey of farm expenditures	USDA estimates	Census projection of USDA annual estimate	Same	Same
Mining exploration, shafts, and wells					
Petroleum and natural gas	Input-output studies based on census of minerals data	American Petroleum Institute (API), Census Bureau oil & gas survey, Independent Petroleum Assoc. of America, and Mid-Continent Oil & Gas Assoc. *Joint Association Survey of the U.S. Oil & Gas Producing Industry.*	Drilling footage—2-mo. data on drilling footage of well completed from API. Cost per foot—annual cost projected by BEA index, 2-mo. PPI's BEA trend estimates	3-mo. data	Same
Mining	Census of minerals	BEA plant and equipment survey	BEA extrapolation of annual estimate	Same	Same
Brokers' commission on sale of structures	BEA input-output table	Benchmark extrapolated in nonresidential buildings excluding farm and mobile homes	2-mo. census survey data of nonresidential buildings value put in place, BEA estimate for third month	3-mo. census data	Same
Net purchases of used structures	Census of state and local gov't. finances, GSA excess of surplus real property—disposal by sale	Same as benchmark	Quarters of current year are held constant	Same	Same

* Final three columns refer to number of days following end of quarter that estimate is released.

Note concerning BEA estimates for detailed groups: The nonresidential fixed investment estimates for detailed groups are not published quarterly by the Bureau of Economic Analysis (BEA). The data are made available to users only upon request with the understanding that individual group estimates may contain considerable error. While such errors tend to offset each other when aggregated to the higher levels shown in the published tables, the more detailed estimates are subject to large revisions. BEA strongly recommends that the detailed figures be used with caution.

EXHIBIT 3   Summary of Source Data Used in Estimating Current Dollar Producers' Durable Equipment Expenditures*

Producers' Durable Equipment	Benchmark Revision	Annual Revision	15-Day Estimate	45-Day Estimate	75-Day Estimate
Tractors	Commodity—flow estimate based on manufacturers' shipment, inventories, and foreign trade data	Census M35S[1]	Census M35S for first and second month, BEA estimate for third month	Census M35S, three months	Same
Trucks, buses, and truck trailers	Registration and use data	Motor Vehicle Mfg, Assoc. unit sales of trucks and buses, plus census M37L[2]	Motor Vehicle Mfg, Assoc. unit sales; two months	Same, with BEA trend estimate for third month.	Same
Autos	Registration and use data	MVMA unit domestic sales of new and used cars, Ward's unit sales of imported cars.	Same	Same	Same
Aircraft	Commodity—flow estimate based on manufacturers' shipment, inventories, and foreign trade data	Census M37G[3]	Census M37G for first and second month, BEA estimate for third month	Census M376, three months	Same
Scrap	Commodity—flow estimate based on manufacturers' shipment, inventories, and foreign trade data	GSA, ICC, and Bureau of Mines data	Extrapolated by 1972 commodity flow less autos, reflated by PDE deflator	Same	Same
All other[5]	Commodity—flow estimate based on manufacturers' shipment, inventories, and foreign trade data	Census M-3[4]	Census M-3 shipments, merchandise exports and imports, two months. BEA estimate for third month	Census M-3, three months	Same

* Final three columns refer to number of days following end of quarter that estimate is released.
[1] Current Industrial Reports, Series M35S, "Tractors, Except Garden Tractors" (Bureau of the Census).
[2] Current Industrial Reports, Series M37L, "Truck Trailers" (Bureau of the Census).
[3] Current Industrial Reports, Series M37G, "Complete Aircraft and Aircraft Engines" (Bureau of the Census).
[4] Current Industrial Reports, Series M3, "Manufacturers' Shipments, Inventories, and Orders Survey" (Bureau of the Census).
[5] All other: Household Furniture; Other Furniture; Fabricated Metals; Steam Engines; Internal Combustion Engines; Construction Tractors; Agricultural Machines; Construction Machines; Mining & Oilfield Machines; Metalworking Machines; Special Industrial Machines; General Industrial Machines; Office & Store Machines; Service Industry Machines; Communication Equipment; Electrical Transmission & Distribution; Household Appliances; Miscellaneous Electrical; Ships & Boats; Railroad Equipment; Instruments Science & Engineering; Photographic Equipment; Miscellaneous.

vey conducted by the Commerce Department. The survey measures both current capital spending activity as well as anticipated spending levels. The series dates back to 1947 and is now under the auspices of the Bureau of Economic Analysis. The survey is seasonally adjusted, is available both in current and constant dollars, contains considerable industry detail, and is also broken down by spending on equipment and structures. A quarterly summary of the carry-over of investment projects for manufacturers and utilities is also available.

The survey is taken once a quarter in February, May, August, and November, and it asks companies to report their actual and planned capital spending budgets. The current survey sample includes 15,000 companies, and respondents account for 53 percent of total nonfarm business plant and equipment expenditure in the United States. Expenditure covered by the survey includes that which is generally charged to fixed accounts and which is depreciated or amortized by the company (certain oil drilling which is expensed does not show up in the survey results).

The methodology used to estimate total plant and equipment spending from the survey results is threefold. The first step includes benchmark surveys which encompass all nonfarm business. These surveys were taken in 1948, 1958, 1963, 1967, and 1972. The second step is interpolation between benchmark years in order to arrive at interim results. The third step is extrapolation past the final benchmark period (1972).

The quarterly survey results of future spending plans are subject to a systematic bias due to factors other than economic or operational conditions. The Commerce Department adjusts for these biases at an industry level and in total. Totals unadjusted for this bias are noted in a footnote in the survey.

A study undertaken by the Federal Reserve Bank of New York in 1977–78 and recently updated by the author of this chapter indicates that the survey results which are unadjusted for systematic bias are actually a more accurate predicter of actual capital spending than are the adjusted results.[1] Unfortunately, these unadjusted series are reported only for manufacturing and nonmanufacturing concerns, with no industry breakdown provided. Additionally, these data are reported for annual values, with quarterly data provided only in adjusted form.

Since the plant and equipment survey and nonresidential fixed investment are the most comprehensive measures of capital spending and are derived in distinctly different ways, it is useful to compare their

---

[1] Karen Bradley and Avril Euba, "How Accurate Are Capital Spending Surveys?" Federal Reserve Bank of New York *Quarterly Review*, Winter 1977–78, pp. 10–15.

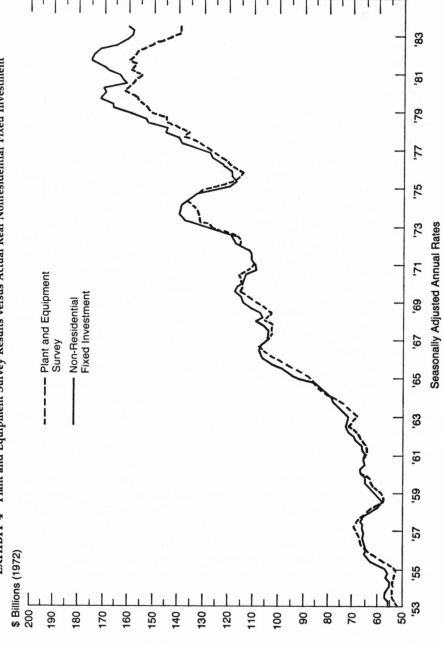

EXHIBIT 4 Plant and Equipment Survey Results versus Actual Real Nonresidential Fixed Investment

$ Billions (1972)

- - - - Plant and Equipment Survey

——— Non-Residential Fixed Investment

Seasonally Adjusted Annual Rates

Source: U.S. Department of Commerce.

results over a period of time. Exhibit 4 demonstrates the behavior of these two series in constant dollars from 1953 to 1982.

The measures tracked together fairly closely until 1974–75; then the indicators began to deviate, with capital spending measured by the survey lagging behind the GNP measure. Definitional differences explain part of the gap as oil drilling equipment, farm spending, and other items are included in fixed investment but are for the most part excluded from the plant and equipment survey. However, even after adjusting for these definitional differences, there still exists a puzzling divergence between the two indicators which widens significantly in 1982 and 1983. The Bureau of Economic Analysis has to date been unable to account for this dichotomy.

THE SUPPORTING CAST: ADDITIONAL INDICATORS OF CAPITAL SPENDING

There are many other measures looked at by analysts trying to gauge the outlook for capital spending. Aside from a private study taken by McGraw-Hill which complements the more comprehensive Commerce Department survey, most of these reflect activity levels of specific capital spending components, and most represent the primary-source information which is used as the building block for the construction of the nonresidential fixed investment components of GNP. Examples of these sources include the monthly values of nonresidential construction put in place and shipments of nondefense capital goods. Other measures are used to indicate pressures building which point to a change in investment needs. The capacity utilization estimates published by the Federal Reserve Board are a good example of this type of indicator.

A summary follows of selected additional indicators of capital spending.

McGraw-Hill Plant and Equipment Survey

This privately compiled survey of capital spending plans started in 1947 and currently surveys the capital spending intentions of every public corporation in the United States. However, only about 450 responses are received by McGraw-Hill, therefore providing them with a significantly smaller sample that that used in the Commerce Department's survey. McGraw-Hill takes its survey twice a year in the autumn and spring, with a supporting survey taken each March. Respondents are asked for their capital spending plans for the next one, two, and sometimes three years, compared to Commerce's survey which focuses on estimates for only one year in the future. These estimates are available in current dollars, and the companies surveyed are grouped by industry according to their major source of business.

The McGraw-Hill survey adds a further dimension to understanding the capital investment environment by gathering data on operating rates, sales expectations, inflation expectations, and whether the intended investment is largely expansion or modernization related. Other supporting surveys are taken on pollution control expenditures, research and development spending, and overseas capital spending.

The Conference Board Quarterly Survey of Manufacturing Capital Investment

For many companies, appropriation of funds is an early stage in the investment process. The Conference Board, a private nonprofit business organization, takes a quarterly survey measuring the capital appropriations of the nation's 1,000 largest manufacturing concerns. The survey also tabulates cancellations of appropriations as well as actual spending in the quarter. The survey officially began in 1956–57, but the Conference Board has data extending back to 1953. Also available is the backlog of appropriations, which has been derived from the survey results after being benchmarked in 1972.

The data are grouped in 17 industry groups and constitute an extremely valuable leading indicator of capital spending trends in the volatile manufacturing sector of the economy. An average of 470 of the 1,000 firms queried actually respond to the survey, and these companies represent 70 percent of the assets of the entire sample. The survey results are seasonally adjusted and are available in both current and constant dollars.

The appropriations series has proven to be a good leading indicator of shifts in manufacturing-capital outlays. In the six capital spending cycles since 1953, the constant-dollar appropriations series signaled an impending downturn in constant-dollar spending by an average four- to five-quarter lead time. Appropriations led spending by an average of about two quarters when signaling an upturn. The Conference Board also publishes a quarterly appropriations series for gas and electric utilities.

Private Nonresidential Construction Put in Place

This series is a component of the Bureau of the Census monthly report on the value of all construction put in place in the United States. It is a key source of primary data for the nonresidential construction component of GNP. The data are available in both current and constant (1977) dollars and is seasonally adjusted. The series is based on contract awards in 37 eastern states and the District of Columbia (which are reported by F. W. Dodge division of McGraw-Hill) and on permit data and surveys of activity in the remaining western states.

Aside from commercial and industrial projects, this series also includes nonresidential farm construction, utility construction, and building on petroleum, gas, and railroad projects. The series measures only the value of work performed during the period being measured, regardless of when the work was initiated. Some of the monthly estimates are based on samples and may differ from statistics gathered by a complete census.

F. W. Dodge Construction Potentials

The F. W. Dodge division of McGraw-Hill has been collecting monthly reports on potential construction activity since 1919. The intent of the service is to provide building contractors with information on potential sources of business. The construction potentials report is a byproduct of that effort in that it takes over as a source of information once the contract is actually issued. The report classifies projects by type. In the nonresidential sector, they include commercial, manufacturing, educational, hospital and other health related, public amusement and recreation, utility, and other nonbuilding projects.

The projects are valued both in current-dollar and in square-footage terms (except for utility construction, which is only reported on a dollar basis). Dodge provides seasonal adjustment factors so that users of the data can seasonally adjust it if they desire. However, it would facilitate use of the data if they were reported by Dodge in seasonally adjusted terms. Contract data are highly volatile on a month-to-month basis, but they usually do provide some degree of lead time in determining shifts in capital expenditure patterns.

Nondefense Capital Goods Shipments and Orders

Shipments and orders of nondefense capital goods are reported as a component of the Census Bureau's monthly report on manufacturer's shipments, inventories, and orders. Nondefense capital goods shipments have been calculated since 1968 and are a key source used in the compilation of many components of the producers' durable equipment series in nonresidential fixed investment.

Nondefense capital goods shipments are designed to measure current activity levels of domestic manufacturers of capital equipment excluding that shipped to the U.S. Department of Defense. Manufacturers are classified into industries based on their primary product specialization. Industries covered by the series include machinery, except electrical (excluding farm machinery and equipment and machine shops); electrical machinery (excluding household appliances, ratio and TV, and electronic components); railroad equipment; and the nondefense portions of equipment, aircraft, aircraft parts, and ordinance.

Information used in compiling this data is collected through the use of a monthly survey distributed to companies with 2,500 or more employees. Responses are voluntary; and because the surveys are distributed at the operating level, larger companies are probably surveyed more than once. The monthly data are revised using annual surveys which cover about 55 percent of the value of shipments. Further revision occurs after a census of manufacturers which covers around 350,000 companies. These data are available in both seasonally adjusted and unadjusted form, and they are not deflated.

The nondefense capital goods orders series is constructed similarly to the shipments data. The orders data are more volatile than shipments, but nevertheless provide a reliable leading indicator of the equipment component of capital spending.

U.S. capital equipment manufacturers have had a large export market in post-World War II history. In the early 1980s, however, the world recession combined with a strong dollar, and the debt-related problems of the developing world curbed this export demand. Exhibit 5 illustrates that although domestic capital spending has held up reasonably well during this period, U.S. producers of capital equipment have nonetheless had a difficult time. Evidence of this difficulty is the large gap which developed between the GNP-based measure of equipment expenditure and the order and shipment rates of U.S. producers.

Industry Estimate of Machine Tool New Orders, Cancellations, Shipments, and Backlog

New machine tool orders and associated data are estimated monthly by the National Machine Tool Builders' Association (NMTBA). Machine tools are used to cut and form metal; therefore, orders for these tools are considered a leading indicator of spending on heavy equipment.

Information for these series is collected by the NMTBA surveying companies belonging to the trade association. Machine tool manufacturers who participate in the survey account for more than two thirds of total U.S. machine tool shipments. These figures, which are gathered

EXHIBIT 5 Real Nondefense Capital Goods Orders and Shipments versus Real Purchases of Machines and Equipment

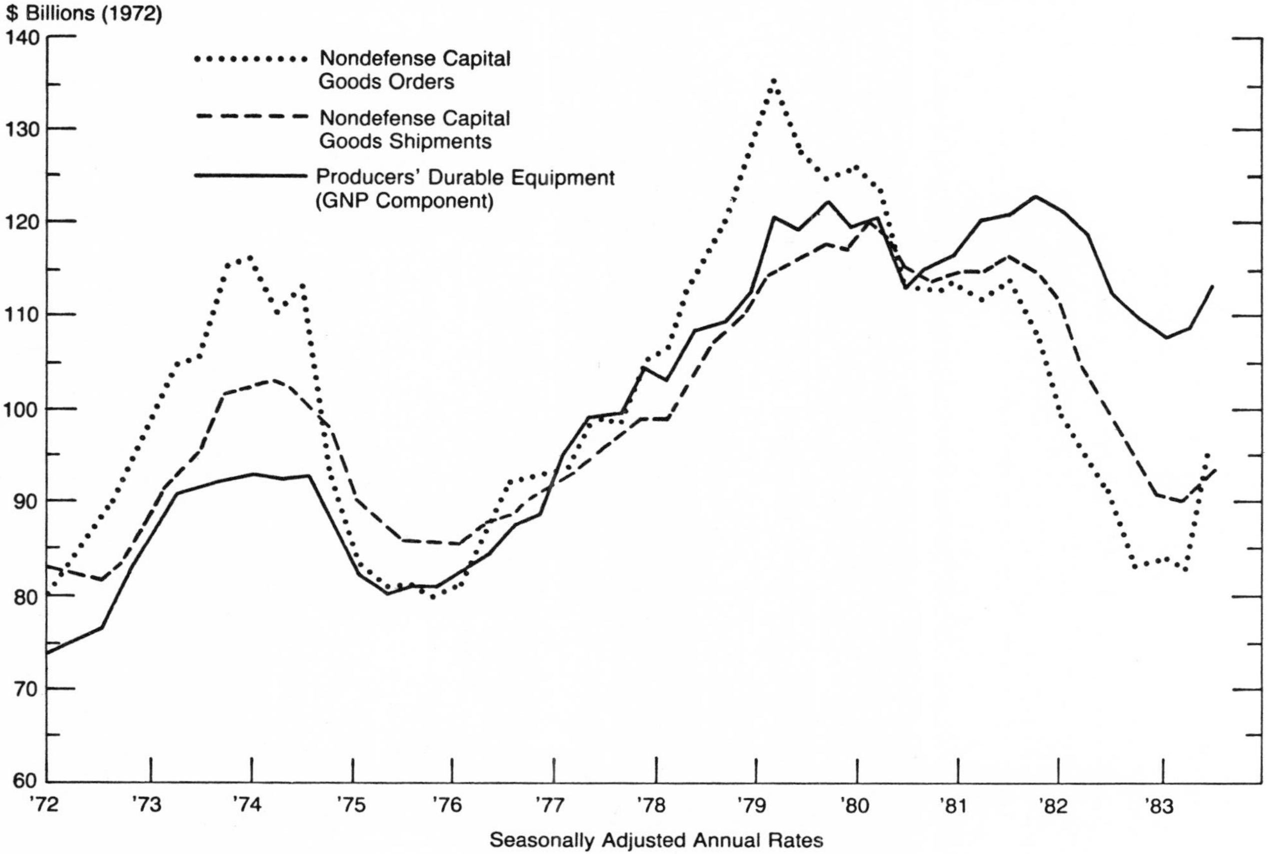

$ Billions (1972)

········· Nondefense Capital
          Goods Orders

— — — Nondefense Capital
          Goods Shipments

———— Producers' Durable Equipment
          (GNP Component)

Seasonally Adjusted Annual Rates

Source: U.S. Department of Commerce.

monthly, are then expanded to an estimate of the industry total by the NMTBA's statistical department. This expansion is designed so that the monthly estimates are compatible with comprehensive data published much later in the Census Bureau's Current Industrial Report, "Metalworking Machinery" (MQ–35W). The NMTBA's estimates are usually published three to four weeks after the end of the month reported. The data are in current dollars and are not seasonally adjusted.

Hughes Tool Company Active Rotary Rig Count

Oil and gas drilling is a sector of capital spending which is included in the petroleum and mining component of the structures category of nonresidential fixed investment. The Hughes Tool Company has been keeping track of active rotary drilling rigs in the United States for over 40 years. Most of the weekly data are collected by Hughes Tool division field representatives in the course of performing their other duties.

Generally, rig count data are useful for spotting trends in drilling expenditure. In conjunction with using rig count data, drilling activity should be analyzed according to type of drilling (deep versus shallow). Additionally, drilling activity is highly seasonal, with lowest activity occurring generally in the first quarter of the year and higher levels of activity late in the year. The Hughes Tool Company rig count is not seasonally adjusted, so care must be taken in analyzing week-to-week or monthly changes in the series.

Capital Stock

The nation's capital stock refers to the value of capital equipment and structures in place in the United States. Capital stock levels are derived by the Bureau of Economic Analysis, utilizing published GNP data. The derivation is of a perpetual-inventory type, in which the previous year's gross capital stock is adjusted by adding new investment (measured on a nonresidential fixed investment basis) and subtracting retirements of plant and equipment.

The data are available back to 1929 and are valued in both current and constant dollars. The data are also broken down into subcomponents detailing the makeup of the structures and equipment groups. Data are also grouped by major industry groups. The series are available on both a gross and a net basis. The net stock data are clear of depreciation, which is calculated using the straight-line method over 85 percent of an item's service life.

All of the capital stock data can be used to assist in analyzing shifts in capital formation. A most useful ratio is depicted in Exhibit 6. The chart illustrates the capital output ratio, which is simply constant-dollar gross capital stock divided by constant-dollar GNP. (The ratio can also be

EXHIBIT 6   U.S. Real Capital Output Ratio (real gross capital stock/real GNP)

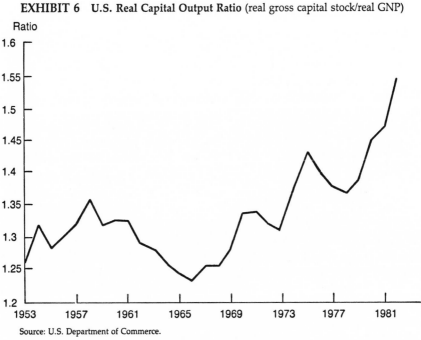

Source: U.S. Department of Commerce.

calculated on a net basis, and the trends are similar.) As demonstrated, the United States has improved its capital output ratio in a secular manner since the mid-1960s, with each peak being higher than the previous one. This increase in the capital stock relative to output can be explained by business's reaction to rising labor and energy costs, as well as by the rapid advent of new technology. The investment in new capital goods to increase labor and energy productivity has caused capital stock to increase more rapidly than GNP.

Index of Business Equipment Production

In its monthly report on the output of the nation's factories, mines, and utilities, the Federal Reserve Board publishes a component on the production of business equipment. The business equipment grouping is broken down into the two major components of industrial equipment and commercial, transit, and farm equipment. Each component consists of a further breakdown into three subcomponents. The indexes are seasonally adjusted and are based on average 1967 production equaling 100.0 percent. Data are available from 1947 for the group as a whole and from 1954 for the subcomponents.

The business equipment grouping in the industrial production release is the most difficult for the Federal Reserve to calculate. Most of the items being produced take considerably longer than one month to build; therefore, actual output data are very difficult to define. Consequently, the major sources used in calculating these indexes comes from employment data collected by the Bureau of Labor Statistics and from electricity-generation data collected by regional Federal Reserve banks.

The bulk of the production data are estimated using labor-hour data collected at the establishment level and reported in the monthly employment release distributed by the Bureau of Labor Statistics. These data must be analyzed in light of secular and cyclical productivity trends, so changes in business equipment production are not necessarily directly proportional to changes in labor-hours in the industries under study.

Most of the remaining production data are estimated using detailed reports of electricity usage which are collected by the regional Federal Reserve banks. The surveys used to collect this data cover about 80 percent of all electricity produced for industrial use in the United States.

As a consequence of the difficulty involved in arriving at their estimates for the production of business equipment, the Federal Reserve acknowledges that these figures are based on little "hard" data. Therefore, they are best used in conjunction with other capital equipment data when analyzing trends in this sector of the economy.

Indexes of Capacity Utilization[2]

The Federal Reserve also publishes monthly estimates of capacity utilization of the nation's factories, mines, and utilities. Capacity utilization refers to the percent of available capacity actually being utilized for production. The manufacturing data are broken down by industry and are available from 1948. The utility and mining components are available from 1967. The data are seasonally adjusted, and the ratio is constructed using 1967 as the base year for output and capacity.

Capacity utilization is constructed as a ratio of output to capacity. The output data come from the Federal Reserve's industrial production re-

---

[2] See Chapter 4 for a detailed discussion of capacity utilization measures.

port. Capacity data are estimated in an eclectic manner by the Federal Reserve. In general, the Federal Reserve relies on McGraw-Hill data as well as data provided by industry trade groups to estimate capacity values. These values are then smoothed using capital stock data and sophisticated statistical techniques. Monthly values are arrived at by extrapolating the capacity data forward. Revisions occur at periodic intervals, and the data between revision points are interpolated and revised.

Capacity utilization data are used to determine when pressure is building for either increases or decreases in capital spending. Typically, 80–82 percent capacity utilization is considered the point where capital spending begins to turn up. However, this relationship varies considerably depending on the industry in question, and factors other than capacity utilization obviously enter a firm's capital spending decision. Therefore, capacity utilization data, while important to use in projecting changes in capital spending, should always be supplemented by analysis of other indicators as well.

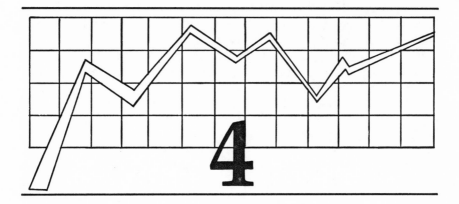

Capacity Utilization

Marjorie H. Schnader, Ph.D.

Economist
Brookhaven National Laboratory

INTRODUCTION

Measures of capacity utilization are measures of actual production levels relative to maximum possible production levels. For the economy as a whole, economists subtract actual output from potential output and call that difference the "GNP gap." The conventional capacity utilization measure for industry—applied primarily to manufacturing, mining, and utilities—is actual output divided by production capacity and expressed as a percent.

Measures of capacity utilization in U.S. industry based on production data and capacity indexes have been developed by the Board of Governors of the Federal Reserve System and by Wharton Econometric Forecasting Associates, Inc. In addition, the McGraw-Hill Publications Company, the Bureau of the Census (U.S. Department of Commerce), the Bureau of Economic Analysis (also U.S. Department of Commerce), and Rinfret Associates, Inc., each conduct periodic surveys of capacity utilization in American business.

Capacity utilization rates are widely used in business conditions analysis and forecasting to explain changes in capital spending, prices, and productivity. Low utilization rates discourage capital spending. Rising operating rates may be harbingers both of rising expenditures for new plant and equipment and of rapidly rising output prices. Capacity utilization rates are used in econometric forecasting models. "The original Wharton index of industrial capacity utilization was developed in the early 60s as a relatively simple means to measure capacity pressure in the cyclically sensitive investment and price equations of an early variant of the Wharton econometric model."[1]

In studies of the relationship between capacity utilization rates and other economic variables, analysts often attempt to estimate "equilibrium" rates of utilization. An equilibrium rate of capacity utilization is a rate at which there is no pressure for change in the rate of change of another variable, usually productivity or prices. A recent study of the relationship between capacity utilization and labor productivity found the equilibrium utilization rate to be approximately 82 percent for the Federal Reserve series on total manufacturing and roughly 88 percent for the Wharton series.[2] Earlier studies estimated the equilibrium rate of capacity utilization for stable price change as approximately 82 percent.[3] In general, business economists expect to find capital spending pressures and an increase in the rate of change of output prices when the Federal Reserve total manufacturing series approaches 82–83 percent. This "threshold" number, however, should be used with great care. Some researchers have questioned the effectiveness of aggregate manufacturing capacity utilization measures to explain changes in investment, prices, and productivity, especially since the rise in energy prices in the early 1970s.[4]

Measures of capacity utilization are regarded as business cycle indicators. Both the Federal Reserve index of capacity utilization in manufacturing and the Federal Reserve series for materials are classified as leading indicators at business cycle peaks, and roughly coincident indicators at troughs (see Chapters 7 and 8). It should be noted that within the set of 110 economic time series classified as cyclical indicators, the capacity

---

[1] F. Gerard Adams and Robert Summers, "The Wharton Indexes of Capacity Utilization: A Ten-Year Perspective," *Proceedings of the American Statistical Association, Business and Economic Statistics Section*, 1973, p. 67.

[2] Michael Ellis, "Supply-Side Linkage of Capacity Utilization and Labor Productivity: U.S. Manufacturing, 1954–1980," *Business Economics*, May 1983, pp. 62–69.

[3] Ibid., p. 63.

[4] Ernst R. Berndt and Catherine J. Morrison, "Capacity Utilization Measures: Underlying Economic Theory and an Alternative Approach." *American Economic Review*, May 1981, pp. 48–52.

utilization series rank in the lowest group with respect to statistical adequacy.[5]

There is no doubt that extreme utilization rates, especially low ones, are very dramatic and that accurate utilization rates would be very valuable analytical tools. However, capacity utilization is difficult to measure; even the goal is elusive. While the measurement of output is relatively straightforward, capacity is a moving target for many industries and products.

An historical overview of the six alternative measures of capacity utilization is contained in the next section. This is followed by a description of the standard measure of industrial output—the Federal Reserve index of industrial production—and a discussion of concepts of capacity and difficulties in construction of capacity indexes. Separate sections are then devoted to each of the six capacity utilization series. Included in each of these sections is information on history of the measure, method of construction, industries covered, availability of the series, and timeliness. Time series on capacity utilization for total manufacturing are compared to each other with respect to average level and cyclical variability. This information is summarized in the final section.

HISTORICAL OVERVIEW

The earliest measures of capacity utilization in U.S. industry were available from data on output and capacity collected and maintained by industry and trade associations for capital-intensive, continuous process industries—steel, cement, paper, petroleum refining, and others. In 1954, the McGraw-Hill Publications Company, pioneering in the collection of survey data on industrial operating rates, started collecting data from companies representing all of the major manufacturing industries. In 1965, mining and utility companies were added to the McGraw-Hill survey.

The Federal Reserve Board and Wharton Econometric Forecasting Associates, Inc. began their reports on capacity utilization in industry in the 1960s. Both use the Federal Reserve Board's industrial production indexes as estimates of actual output; their methodologies differ in the calculation of the denominator of the ratio—capacity. Wharton uses a "trend through peaks" method which assumes that previous peaks in the industrial production indexes represent capacity output. The Federal

---

[5] Statistical adequacy consists of "a number of attributes such as the quality of the reporting system, coverage of process and time unit, availability of estimates of sampling and reporting errors, frequency of revisions, length of series, and comparability over time." Victor Zarnowitz, "On Functions, Quality, and Timeliness of Economic Information," Reprint No. 250, National Bureau of Economic Research, February 1982.

Reserve has developed an eclectic method for estimating capacity which uses industrial production data, capacity utilization survey data, capital stock estimates, information on net investment, and physical capacity estimates from business and trade associations and government agencies. The Wharton measure is available for all of the market and industry categories covered by the industrial production index. The Federal Reserve publishes manufacturing, mining, utilities, and materials series.

In 1965, the Bureau of Economic Analysis (BEA) began collecting operating rates from manufacturing companies in its quarterly survey of capital expenditures. The BEA data is organized both by industry and by asset size. The Bureau of the Census began its extensive survey of operating rates of manufacturing establishments in the early 1970s. Census data are available at very detailed industry levels. Rinfret Associates' quarterly surveys of operating rates of both manufacturing and non-manufacturing companies started in 1974.

INDEXES OF INDUSTRIAL PRODUCTION

The Federal Reserve Board's indexes of industrial production are the standard reference measures of the actual physical output of U.S. factories, mines, and electric and gas utilities. This output is expressed as a percentage of production in a base-year period, currently 1967. Component series of the indexes of industrial production are either based on physical product data or estimated with the use of data on production-worker hours and electric power consumed. As of the 1976 revision, there were 235 individual series organized into industry groups and major markets (see Exhibit 1). Monthly, quarterly, and annual data are published for each industry and market category. The components of each index are weighted according to their relative proportion of value added in 1967.

Monthly data releases from the Federal Reserve, available approximately midmonth, report preliminary estimates for the previous month; these are revised in later months. Annual revisions reflect new seasonal factors and more complete data, largely data from the Bureau of the Census annual surveys of manufacturers and censuses of manufacturers and mineral industries. The last major revision of the Federal Reserve indexes of industrial production was the 1976 one. Another major revision is currently underway.[6]

---

[6] The latest major reference on these series, published by the Board of Governors of the Federal Reserve System, is *Industrial Production, 1976 Revision*. Unfortunately, this is out of print as of this writing. Another useful reference is *Indexes of Production*, vol. IV of the 1972 Census of Manufactures and Mineral Industries, U.S. Department of Commerce, Bureau of the Census, December 1977. Also helpful: "Revision of Industrial Production Index," *Federal Reserve Bulletin*, August 1979, pp. 603–5.

EXHIBIT 1   Federal Reserve Industrial Production Index Groupings: Wharton Econometric Forecasting Associates, Inc. Capacity Utilization Series

	Grouping	*1967 Proportion*		Grouping	*1967 Proportion*
Major market:					
1	Total Index	100.00	29	Building and mining	1.44
2.	Products	60.71	30	Manufacturing	3.85
3	Final products	47.82	31	Power	1.47
4	Consumer goods	27.68	32	Commercial transit, farm	5.86
5	Equipment	20.14	33	Commercial	3.26
6	Intermediate products	12.89	34	Transit	1.93
7	Materials	39.29	35	Farm	.67
	Consumer goods		36	Defense and space	7.51
8	Durable consumer goods	7.89		*Intermediate products*	
9	Automotive products	2.83	37	Construction supplies	6.42
10	Autos and utility		38	Business supplies	6.47
	vehicles	2.03	39	Commercial energy	
11	Autos	1.90		products	1.14
12	Auto parts and allied			*Materials*	
	goods	.80	40	Durable goods materials	20.35
13	Home goods	5.06	41	Durable consumer parts	4.58
14	Appliances, A/C, and TV	1.40	42	Equipment parts	5.44
15	Appliances and TV	1.33	43	Durable materials	10.34
16	Carpeting and furniture	1.07	44	Basic metal materials	5.57
17	Miscellaneous home		45	Nondurable goods materials	10.47
	goods	2.59	46	Textile, paper, and	
18	Nondurable consumer goods	19.79		chemical materials	7.62
19	Clothing	4.29	47	Textile materials	1.85
20	Consumer staples	15.50	48	Paper materials	1.62
21	Consumer foods and		49	Chemical materials	4.15
	tobacco	8.33	50	Containers, nondurable	1.70
22	Nonfood staples	7.17	51	Nondurable materials	
23	Consumer chemical			n.e.c.	1.14
	products	2.63	52	Energy materials	8.48
24	Consumer paper		53	Primary energy	4.65
	products	1.92	54	Converted fuel materials	3.82
25	Consumer energy			*Supplementary groups*	
	products	2.62	55	Home goods and clothing	9.35
26	Residential utilities	1.45	56	Energy, total	12.23
	Equipment		57	Products	3.76
27	Business	12.63	58	Materials	8.48
28	Industrial	6.77			

Note: Published groupings include some series and subtotals not shown separately. For description and historical data, **see** *Industrial Production—1976 Revision* Washington, D.C.: Board for Governors of the Federal Reserve System, December 1977).
Source: *Federal Reserve Bulletin*, December 1982, A48 and A49.

EXHIBIT 1 *(concluded)*

Grouping	SIC Code	1967 Proportion
Major industry:		
1 Mining and utilities		12.05
2 Mining		6.36
3 Utilities		5.69
4 Electric		3.88
5 Manufacturing		87.95
6 Nondurable		35.97
7 Durable		51.98
Mining		
8 Metal	10	.51
9 Coal	11.12	.69
10 Oil and gas extraction	13	4.40
11 Stone and earth minerals	14	.75
Nondurable manufactures		
12 Foods	20	8.75
13 Tobacco products	21	.67
14 Textile mill products	22	2.68
15 Apparel products	23	3.31
16 Paper and products	26	3.21
17 Printing and publishing	27	4.72
18 Chemicals and products	28	7.74
19 Petroleum products	29	1.79
20 Rubber and plastic products	30	2.24
21 Leather and products	31	.86
Durable manufactures		
22 Ordnance, private and government	19.91	3.64
23 Lumber and products	24	1.64
24 Furniture and fixtures	25	1.37
25 Clay, glass, stone products	32	2.74
26 Primary metals	33	6.57
27 Iron and steel	331.2	4.21
28 Fabricated metal products	34	5.93
29 Nonelectrical machinery	35	9.15
30 Electrical machinery	36	8.05
31 Transportation equipment	37	9.27
32 Motor vehicles and parts	371	4.50
33 Aerospace and miscellaneous transportation equipment	372–9	4.77
34 Instruments	38	2.11
35 Miscellaneous manufactures	39	1.51

CONCEPTS AND MEASURES OF CAPACITY

In contrast to the unambiguous goal of the industrial production index, there is no definitive concept of capacity. When capacity is considered relative to capital alone, the empirical measure is "rated capacity," an engineering (technological) assessment of maximum annual plant output with allowance for normal downtime for maintenance and repair. This engineering measure is conventionally reported for establishments in the continuous process industries (for example, petroleum refineries or electric power plants). However, in other industries and for most analytical and forecasting purposes, economic capacity is the relevant concept. The use of an engineering measure of capacity implies that output is constrained by the physical capacity of the plant to produce rather than by labor, materials, or other constraints. The various economic measures of capacity consider the output of all resources combined.

Economic capacity is a planned level of maximum production which will fulfill goals such as the maximization of profits or minimization of average or marginal cost. Clearly economic capacity can be a moving target in many industries and for many products. Changes in relative labor and materials costs, overtime costs, and product mix are some of the considerations which may affect capacity production levels. There is also the problem of how to classify abandoned plant and equipment which might be used under different price or demand conditions. It is difficult to measure changes in capacity *utilization* if capacity changes in the short run. It is also hard to estimate industrial capacity, because planned maximum output may include a great deal of idle "engineering" capacity for many reasons: (1) Optimum production levels which will maximize profit, minimize average or marginal cost, or protect market share may command physical facilities with planned excess engineering capacity due to economies of scale. (2) Desire to fulfill seasonal or other periodic demands, or need to meet irregular peak demands, leads to planned maximum annual output which is less than engineering capacity. (3) Periodic or irregular patterns in the supply of required materials can lead to planned excess physical plant capacity. (4) High labor costs relative to capital costs, or social and/or institutional constraints on use of labor around the clock, lead to the planned use of capital for less than technological capacity.[7]

The notion of practical capacity is the concept which underlies all of the surveys of utilization rates. Practical capacity is defined by the Census Bureau as the greatest level of output "this establishment could

---

[7] An excellent reference on intended idle capital is Gordon C. Winston, "The Theory of Capital Utilization and Idleness," *Journal of Economic Literature*, December 1974, pp. 1301–20.

reasonably expect to attain using a realistic employee work schedule and the machinery and equipment in place during the time periods covered by this survey."[8] In its questionnaire, the bureau instructs respondents to assume a normal product mix; shifts and hours of plant operation which are reasonably attainable within the community; only the use of machinery and equipment in place and ready to operate; sufficiently available labor, materials, and utilities to operate capital in place; and normal downtime for maintenance & repairs. The Census Bureau also specifically requests respondents not to consider overtime pay, added costs for materials, or other cost increases as limitations in the determination of capacity. Although other survey questionnaires are not as explicit in their definitions of capacity, it is generally assumed that most respondents to these surveys do use the concept of practical capacity.

Even though capacity is defined similarly in surveys of industrial operating rates, the capacity levels implied in survey data may differ from one survey to another for statistical reasons, such as differences in coverage or aggregation methods. For example, data on industrial capacity will be affected by the type of economic unit which is being measured. A single establishment (e.g., a factory, refinery, or warehouse) will have one estimate of its potential production level; a company consisting of many individual establishments and taking into account intracompany bottlenecks will estimate its maximum output at less than the sum of the maximum output levels of individual units. In the aggregate, actual output will be the same, but capacity will be greater for establishment data. Therefore, operating rates based on establishment data will be lower than those based on company data. This phenomenon is evident in comparing Bureau of the Census survey data (based on a sample of establishments) with the other capacity utilization survey data (based on samples of companies); the Census survey operating rates are distinctly lower than the others.

That the capacity estimates which underlie survey data on utilization rates may not be the definitive measures we are looking for becomes particularly evident when capacity indexes are calculated by dividing industrial production indexes by survey measures of capacity utilization.[9] Time series of capacity indexes derived in this way tend to have short-term cyclical movements. These cyclical movements cannot be ex-

---

[8] Bureau of the Census, Instructions and Definitions, Form MQ–Cl(1), *1982 Survey of Plant Capacity Utilization* (Washington D.C.: U.S. Government Printing Office).

[9]
$$\text{Capacity utilization} = \frac{\text{Output}}{\text{Capacity}}$$

therefore,

$$\text{Capacity} = \frac{\text{Output}}{\text{Capacity utilization}}$$

plained by time series of capital stock changes, net investment, or survey data on capacity expansion. On the other hand, the capital stock and investment data are, by themselves, insufficient data from which to derive capacity estimates. The development of capital stock series for manufacturing industries has its own statistical problems. More important, the relationship between the growth in capital stock and changes in capacity is not always consistent by any means. "In the case of steel, for example, estimates indicate a more rapid growth of both capital stock and investment during the 1960s than during the 1950s. Yet capacity expanded by nearly 50 percent between 1950 and 1960 and by less than 5 percent in the subsequent decade."[10]

It is thought that a time series of industrial capacity ought to move in a relatively smooth, trend-like fashion over time. The Federal Reserve Board has designed a capacity index based upon this premise which it publishes along with the board's industrial production indexes and capacity utilization series. These capacity series take into account the level and longer-term trends in capacity implied by the survey data on operating rates; the short-term movements are smoothed out to reflect the less cyclical movements in capital stock and investment expenditure data. This index is available monthly. The other available measure of capacity, the Wharton capacity indexes, is a trend line based upon peaks in an industrial production index. The Wharton capacity index is a measure of attainable output, a different concept from that defined empirically by the Federal Reserve.

SOURCES OF CAPACITY UTILIZATION MEASURES
Board of Governors of the Federal Reserve System

The Federal Reserve Board publishes capacity utilization rates for manufacturing, mining, utilities, and the production of industrial materials. The manufacturing series first become available in the 1960s; historical data begins with 1948. The industrial materials series, which covers the entire materials group in the Federal Reserve industrial production index, was introduced with a major revision of the utilization series in 1976. This series is an expansion of the previously available major-materials index which covered less than one quarter of the materials section of the industrial production index. Historical data on the materials index is available back to 1967. Mining and utilities were introduced in July 1983 together with a new, total industry aggregate which covers manufacturing, mining and utilities. Data for the total industry

---

[10] Barry Bosworth, "Capacity Creation in Basic-Materials Industries," *Brookings Papers on Economic Activity* 2 (Washington, D.C.: Brookings Institution, 1976), pp. 311.

series and for the mining and utility industries are available for the years 1967–82 in a supplement to the Federal Reserve statistical release on capacity utilization, dated July 18, 1983.

Manufacturing Series. The Federal Reserve manufacturing utilization series include separate time series for total U.S. manufacturing, advanced processing and primary processing industries, durable and nondurable manufacturing, and each of 16 major manufacturing industries (see Exhibit 2). Federal Reserve manufacturing operating rates are the ratio of a seasonally adjusted industrial production index to an estimate of capacity. The indexes of industrial production are monthly, available about 15 days after the end of the month. The capacity series are developed from industrial production data, McGraw-Hill and Bureau of Economic Analysis (BEA) survey data, capital stock and capital expenditure data from various groups within the Department of Commerce, and physical capacity estimates from business and trade associations and government agencies.

Capacity Measures for Manufacturing Industries. The July 1983 major revision of the Federal Reserve capacity utilization series covered the period 1967–82. In this revision, the Federal Reserve introduced a revised methodology for construction of the manufacturing capacity indexes.

In the new methodology, three distinct time series of capacity estimates were developed for each industry. One set of estimates was obtained by dividing annual (December) McGraw-Hill survey operating rates into the appropriate industrial production indexes. The resultant capacity estimates were then regressed on trend variables and variables that permitted breaks in trend. These equations provided time series of capacity which were smoother than the original data points. Using the same technique, but this time with BEA survey operating rates, a second set of capacity estimates was made for each industry. The third set of estimates was provided by regressing capacity points derived from the McGraw-Hill capacity survey (which is independent of the McGraw-Hill annual operating rate survey) on trend variables and variables allowing breaks in trend.

These three sets of capacity estimates were not formally combined. Rather, the final capacity series for each industry was the result of industry-by-industry evaluation of all regression results in the context of other information. Consideration was given to the statistical quality of each set of regression estimates; other information which was considered in the final determination included capital stock data from the Department of Commerce and other sources, capacity data from various business and trade organizations and government agencies, Federal Reserve tabulations of plant closings reported by the media, and Federal Reserve data

EXHIBIT 2   Federal Reserve and McGraw-Hill Industry Categories

	Federal Reserve Board*		McGraw-Hill Publications Company Department of Economics†
	Series	1967 Proportion of Total Industrial Production[1]	Industry
A.	Total industry	100.00	Iron and steel
	Manufacturing	87.95	Nonferrous metals
	Primary processing[2]	30.59	Electrical machinery
	Advanced processing[3]	57.36	Machinery
	Durable manufacturing	51.98	Autos, trucks and parts
	Stone, clay, and glass products	2.74	Aerospace
	Iron and steel, subtotal	4.21	Other transportation
	Nonferrous metals, subtotal	2.36	equipment[6]
	Fabricated metal products	5.93	Fabricated metals
	Nonelectrical machinery	9.15	Instruments
	Electrical machinery	8.05	Stone, clay and glass
	Motor vehicles and parts	4.50	Other durables
	Autos	1.90	Total durables
	Aerospace and miscellaneous	4.77	Chemicals
	transportation equipment		Paper and pulp
	Instruments	2.11	Rubber
	Nondurable manufacturing	35.97	Petroleum
	Foods	8.75	Food and Beverages
	Textile mill products	8.75	Textiles
	Paper and products	3.21	Other nondurables
	Petroleum products	7.74	Total nondurables
	Rubber and plastics products	1.79	All manufacturing
	Mining	2.24	Mining
	Utilities	6.36	Electric utilities
	Electric utilities	5.69	Gas utilities
B.	Industrial materials[4]	3.88	All industry
	Durable goods materials	39.29	
	Metal materials[5]	20.35	
	Raw steel	6.39	
	Aluminum	0.72	
	Nondurable goods materials	0.27	
	Textile, paper, and chemical	10.47	
	Paper materials	7.62	
	Chemical materials	1.62	
	Energy materials	8.48	

[1] The proportions are based on value added. Total industrial production covers mining, gas and electric utilities, and manufacturing. The industries shown under durable and nondurable manufacturing do not include all industries in these categories.

[2] Primary processing, which incorporates many of the same manufacturing industries that are represented in materials, includes textile mill products; industrial chemicals; petroleum products; rubber and plastics products; lumber and products; stone, clay, and glass products; primary metals; and fabricated metal products.

[3] Advanced processing includes foods; tobacco products; apparel products; printing and publishing; chemical products such as drugs and toiletries; leather and products; ordnance; furniture and fixtures; machinery; transportation equipment; instruments; and miscellaneous manufactures.

[4] A detailed list of components of the materials grouping is found in Industrial Production—1976 Revision, pp. S–8 to S–10.

[5] Grouping includes basic metal materials, consumer durable steel, and equipment steel.

[6] As of 1979, other transportation equipment is included in other durables.

* Source: Federal Reserve statistical release, "Capacity Utilization: Manufacturing, Mining, Utilities, and Industrial Materials," July 18, 1983, p. 4.

† Source: McGraw-Hill Historical Capital Expenditures and Related Data, Table IX.

on industrial production. "For some industries, historically reliable data on capacity provided by industry associations or government agencies were major determinants of the final estimates of capacity."[11]

The major change of the July 1983 revisions was the revision downward of estimates of capacity growth for the period since 1973, with the major downward thrust occurring since 1979. As a consequence, utilization rates were revised upward. For example, for the period 1973–79, the annual rate of change in capacity growth rates for total manufacturing was revised from 3.2 percent to 3.1 percent; for 1979–82, the revision was from 3.0 percent to 2.4 percent. Thus, the utilization rate for all manufacturing for March 1979 was raised from 87.2 percent to 87.5 percent; for December 1982, the manufacturing operating rate was raised to 68.9 percent from the previously estimated 67.5 percent.[12]

Materials Series. The Federal Reserve capacity utilization series for industrial materials are developed in a less formal manner. For the July 1983 revision, "all 96 series on industrial materials were reevaluated using essentially the same methodology as in the past."[13]

For many key materials, particularly those produced in a continuous production process (such as iron and steel), actual physical output and physical capacity data are available and are used for first estimates of utilization rates. Where physical capacity data are unavailable, the ratio of output to survey utilization rate affords a first approximation of capacity. A third alternative is the use of past peaks and trends in the corresponding industrial production index to provide estimates of capacity levels and movements. The first approximation of a materials capacity series is then refined using other evidence as available—for example, investment expenditure series. The final capacity estimates are divided into the appropriate, seasonally adjusted production indexes for calculation of utilization rates.

Utilities and Mining Series. The general description of methodology for the materials series also applies for utilities and mining. Sixty percent of the electric utility industry and 85 percent of the mining industry had long been included in the industrial materials group. For the electric

---

[11] In the July 1983 revision of the Federal Reserve capacity series, "data on real growth in the capital stock played a less important role in the estimation procedure than it had in the past." Department of Commerce revised data on capital stock had indicated substantial growth in real capital stock over the past decade, while evidence from surveys and data on capacity provided by business and trade associations indicated a slowdown in capacity growth. The relationship between growth in capital stock and growth in capacity had changed since the late 1960s.

Ronald F. Rost, "New Federal Reserve Measures of Capacity and Capacity Utilization," *Federal Reserve Bulletin*, July 1983, p. 520.

[12] Ibid., Table 2, p. 517.

[13] Ibid., p. 519.

utilities, Edison Electric Institute is the basic data source. Edison Electric's estimates of engineering capacity are scaled down to estimates of sustainable capacity by eliminating generating capability planned as reserve against outages, peak demands, and necessary repair and maintenance. Gas utility capacity data are inferred from McGraw-Hill survey data on operating rates. Capacity estimates for the 15 percent of the mining industry which had not previously been covered are inferred mainly from previous peaks in the appropriate industrial production indexes.

EXHIBIT 3   **Capacity Utilization, Total Manufacturing* 1958:2–1982:4** (quarterly data, seasonally adjusted)

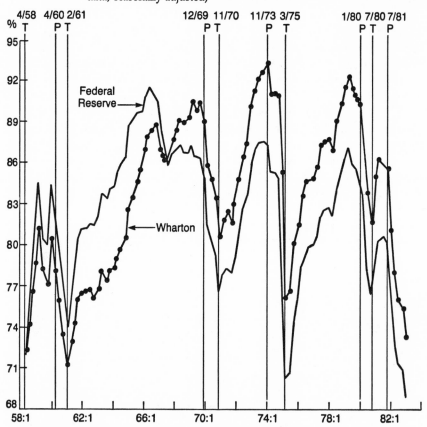

* Correlation coefficient: 0.67.

   Source: Federal Reserve data for 1967–82 from statistical release, "Capacity Utilization," July 18, 1983; earlier data from *Federal Reserve Measures of Capacity and Capacity Utilization,* Board of Governors of the Federal Reserve System, February 1978. Wharton data, received from Wharton Econometric Forecasting Associates, updated on October 16, 1983. Business cycles dates from *Business Conditions Digest,* Bureau of Economic Analysis, U.S. Department of Commerce, January 1983, p. 103.

Aggregation. Aggregate utilization rates are derived by dividing an aggregate production index by an aggregate capacity index. The capacity series are combined with value-added weights, using the same techniques and weights used for aggregating the production indexes.

Comparison with Other Series. Federal Reserve quarterly operating rates for total manufacturing for 1958 through 1982 are shown in Exhibit 3 together with the Wharton quarterly series. One obvious difference between these two sets of data is that the Wharton operating rates have been higher than the Federal Reserve series since the middle of 1967. In Exhibit 4, the Federal Reserve quarterly manufacturing series is compared with the Wharton series with respect to average level and variability. Also in Exhibit 4, statistics are shown for fourth-quarter data only, in order to facilitate comparison with the McGraw-Hill December series. In Exhibit 5, a similar comparison is made for end-of-the-year time series for all six capacity utilization measures for 1974 through 1981. For the later period, the Federal Reserve series falls into middle ground with respect to average level and cyclical amplitude and most closely resembles the McGraw-Hill December rates. (The Federal Reserve fourth-quarter rates form a somewhat smoother time series than the Reserve's December rates, which is to be expected; but both have tracked the McGraw-Hill series closely for the past decades.)

In the 1974–81 period, the two series which are "outliers" are the Census fourth-quarter rates, which have the lowest average level and the least volatility, and the Rinfret January rates, with the greatest volatility. A Federal Reserve time series of total manufacturing operating rates for the months corresponding to the Rinfret survey data is shown in Exhibit 6 along with the Rinfret series. Summary statistics describing

EXHIBIT 4   Summary Statistics: Capacity Utilization—Total Manufacturing

	1958–1982		1954–1982		
	FRB *(quarterly)*	*Wharton* *(quarterly)*	*FRB* *(4th quarter)*	*McGraw-Hill* *(December)*	*Wharton* *(4th quarter)*
Mean	82.3	83.6	82.2	82.5	83.8
High	91.6 (1966:2)	93.1 (1973:4)	90.6 (1966)	92 (1955)	93.1 (1973)
Low	69 (1982:4)	71.2 (1961:1)	69 (1982)	69.1 (1982)	73.1 (1960)
High-low / Mean	27%	26%	26%	28%	24%
Standard deviation	5.0	5.8	5.0	5.3	5.8

Data sources: Federal Reserve data for 1967–82 from statistical release, "Capacity Utilization," July 18, 1983; earlier data from *Federal Reserve Measures of Capacity and Capacity Utilization,* Board of Governors of the Federal Reserve System, February 1978. Wharton data, received from Wharton Econometric Forecasting Associates, updated on October 16, 1983. McGraw-Hill data from Economics Department Information Products, McGraw-Hill Publications Company.

EXHIBIT 5   Summary Statistics: Capacity Utilization—Total Manufacturing, 1974–1981*

	FRB (4th quarter)	McGraw-Hill (December)	Wharton (4th quarter)	BEA (December)	Census (4th quarter)	Rinfret (January)†
Mean	80.7	80.2	86	79.4	69.8	81.6
High (all 1978)	86.6	87	91.8	84	74‡	90
Low (all 1981)	75.9	73.9	81.2	72	66	67
High-low / Mean	13.2%	16.3%	12.3%	15.1%	11.5%	28.1%
Standard deviation	3.9	4.9	3.8	3.6	3.2	6.8

* 1982 was not included because the 1982 Census survey data was not available at this writing.
† December 1974; January 1976 to 1982.
‡ Also 1979.
Data sources: Federal Reserve data for 1967–82 from statistical release, "Capacity Utilization," July 18, 1983; earlier data from *Federal Reserve Measures of Capacity and Capacity Utilization*, Board of Governors of the Federal Reserve System, February 1978. Wharton data, received from Wharton Econometric Forecasting Associates, updated on October 16, 1983. McGraw-Hill data from Economics Department Information Products, McGraw-Hill Publications Company. BEA data received from the Bureau of Economic Analysis, U.S. Department of Commerce. Census data comes from "Survey of Plant Capacity, 1981," Current Industrial Reports, Bureau of the Census, U.S. Department of Commerce, Table 1B, Practical Capacity Utilization Rates, p. 9. Rinfret data by permission of Rinfret Associates, Inc., New York.

---

average level and volatility for these two series are presented in Exhibit 7.

Summary and Notes.   The philosophy behind the Federal Reserve operating rates is that changes in industrial capacity occur in a reasonably smooth fashion, and short-term movements in operating rates ought to reflect changes in output rather than "lost" or "found" capacity. Federal Reserve operating rates tend to have short-term movements closely akin to movements in the industrial production indexes. Revised total manufacturing rates tend to track the McGraw-Hill survey rates. The average level of manufacturing rates falls somewhere in the middle of the pack, in recent years, for the end-of-the-year series compared here.

The latest discussion of Federal Reserve methodology can be found in "New Federal Reserve Measures of Capacity and Capacity Utilization," *Federal Reserve Bulletin*, July 1983. This article partially supersedes *Federal Reserve Measures of Capacity and Capacity Utilization*, Board of Governors of the Federal Reserve System, February 1978. Another very useful publication of the Board of Governors is *Measures of Capacity Utilization: Problems and Tasks*, July 1979. Included in the latter is a paper by Raddock in which he compares alternative measures of capacity utilization for individual manufacturing industries.

Monthly capacity utilization rates are available midmonth for the previous month. They are published along with the Federal Reserve companion series of output and capacity.

EXHIBIT 6   Capacity Utilization—Total Manufacturing* 1974–1983 (monthly data for four months of each year)†

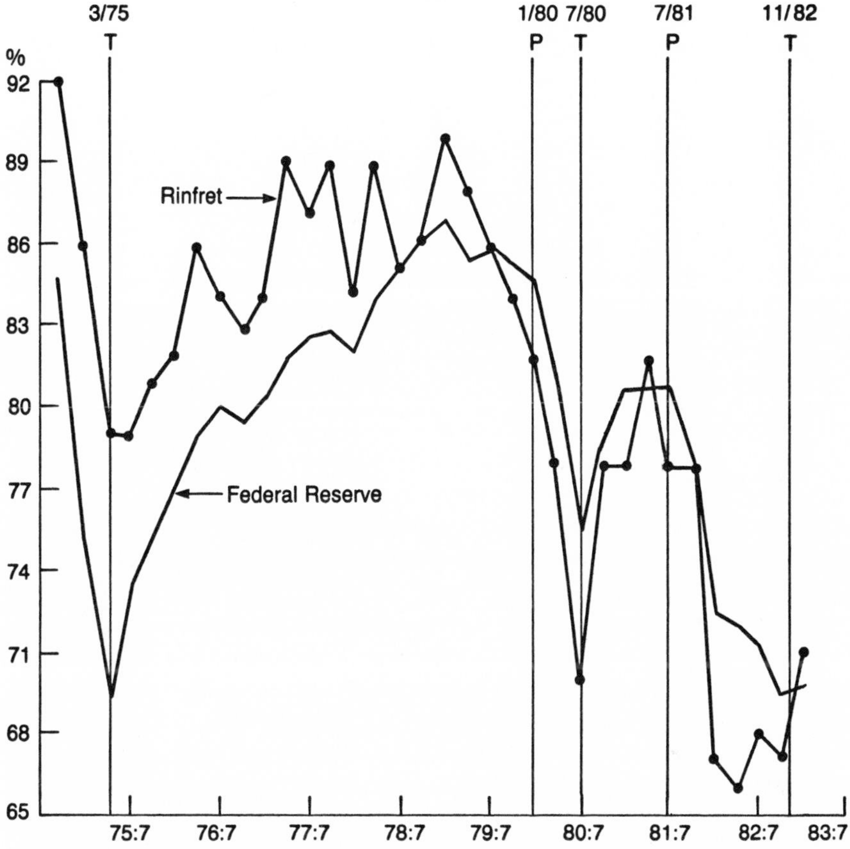

* Correlation Coefficient: 0.79.

† September and December 1974; March, July, and October 1975; January, April, July, and October for 1976 through 1982; January 1983. These are the available survey dates for the Rinfret capacity utilization survey.

Data sources: Federal Reserve statistical release "Capacity Utilization," July 18, 1983; Rinfret series used by permission of Rinfret Associates, Inc., New York City; business cycle dates from *Business Conditions Digest*, January 1983.

Wharton Econometric Forecasting Associates, Inc.

Wharton Econometric Forecasting Associates, Inc. (Wharton EFA) maintains a quarterly and annual index of capacity utilization for each of the component series of the Federal Reserve total index of industrial production. Accordingly, there are industrial capacity utilization rates organized by major market group: consumer goods, business and defense equipment, intermediate products, materials and supplementary

EXHIBIT 7 Summary Statistics: Capacity Utilization, Total Manufacturing 1974–1983*

	FRB	Rinfret
Mean	79.3	81
High	86.9 (1979:1)	92 (1974:9)
Low	69 (1975:3)	66 (1982:4)
$\frac{\text{High-low}}{\text{Mean}}$	23%	32%
Standard deviation	5.3	7.2

* September and December 1974; March, July, and October 1975; January, April, July, and October for 1976–82; January 1983.
Source: Based on data received spring 1983 from Federal Reserve Board and Rinfret Associates, New York City.

groups; from the same component data come operating rate series for manufacturing, mining, and utilities (see Exhibit 1).

Prior to 1980, Wharton EFA was a nonprofit corporation owned by the University of Pennsylvania. As of this writing, Wharton EFA is owned by Compagnie Internationale de Services Informatique, a Paris computer company. The Wharton capacity utilization series are proprietary and available by subscription only. At various times in the past, the index for total manufacturing has been available routinely in publications of the government or nonprofit industry groups.

In basic technique and conceptual foundation, the Wharton indexes of capacity utilization have changed very little since they were first introduced in the early 1960s. The Wharton series are based upon the Federal Reserve indexes of industrial production. The industrial production component series are used directly as estimates of output. The uniqueness of the Wharton indexes is in the trend-through-peaks method used to calculate capacity.

Trend-through-Peaks. The idea behind the trend-through-peaks method is that capacity is a "general notion of attainable output under other than extraordinary working conditions . . . and . . . peak observed performance is a realistic measure of attainable output. . . ."[14] Previous peaks in each of the component series of industrial production are estimates of capacity output at that time. These estimates are validated by reference to a variety of other data, especially engineering-type data. Linear interpolation between historic peaks provides a measure of

---

[14] Adams and Summers, "The Wharton Indexes," p. 67.

capacity output between peaks. The most difficult part of the trend-through-peaks method is extrapolation from past peaks to the estimate of contemporaneous capacity.

Aggregation. Industries are combined into groups, and operating rates for the broader categories are the weighted arithmetic mean of the individual utilization rates. The weights are the proportion of total national income each industry contributes at full employment.

Comparison with Other Series. A comparison of Wharton fourth-quarter operating rates for total manufacturing with the similarly or closely dated time series of the other manufacturing capacity utilization measures indicates that the Wharton series has the highest average level of any of the measures. For the 1954–82 period, the average level of the Wharton series was 83.8 percent compared to 82.5 and 82.2 for McGraw-Hill and the Federal Reserve, respectively (Exhibit 4). For 1974 through 1981, the Wharton fourth-quarter series had an average level of 86.0 percent, almost 4½ percentage points above the second-highest series, the Rinfret time series for January (Exhibit 5).

Exhibit 3 shows the Wharton quarterly manufacturing utilization series plotted against the Federal Reserve quarterly data. The Wharton series was lower than the Federal Reserve series before 1967, but has been higher since then.

Comments. The Wharton indexes of capacity utilization have a number of advantages. They are relatively easy to calculate and, since they are based on the Federal Reserve indexes of industrial production, can cover all of the industries for which this output data are available. They are available on a timely basis and are not difficult to interpret.

The limitation of the Wharton method is that the indexes must be revised often as new data becomes available. Substantial revisions may be necessary in estimates of current capacity levels.

A final and important note is that the basic component series of the Wharton indexes do reach 100 percent at peaks because of the way that they are constructed. This is not true of any of the other measures of capacity utilization. The utilization rate for a group of the component series, however, does not generally reach 100 percent since the component series are usually not at their peaks at exactly the same time. The aggregates may come close to 100 percent, however. For example, in the first quarter of 1980, nondurable consumer goods registered 96.9 percent of capacity, energy materials 99 percent, and total materials 95.8 percent.

McGraw-Hill Publications Company

The McGraw-Hill Publications Company has been collecting data on capacity utilization in industry for the past three decades. The information is collected as part of its annual survey of business's plans for new plants and equipment, a survey of American business firms covering roughly half of all capital spending each year. Respondents use their own definitions of capacity. It is assumed that these definitions correspond to maximum practical capacity.

Annual Survey. End-of-the-year (December) operating rates are collected in a spring survey and are available generally by the end of May. The series have been available since 1954 for total manufacturing and for major manufacturing industries. Mining companies and electric and gas utilities were added in 1965. Between 1957 and 1965, manufacturing rates were also available for September of each year, but on an intermittent basis. The list of available series appears in Exhibit 2. There are occasional gaps in the McGraw-Hill survey data, but by and large, each series is continuous.

Aggregation. Employment weights are used for combining companies into industries. Industries are combined into durable, nondurable, and total manufacturing, using the same 1967 value-added weights used for the industrial production indexes.

Monthly Series. McGraw-Hill also estimates monthly operating rates based upon December benchmark figures and annual survey information on planned capacity expansion. Assuming that capacity additions occur evenly throughout the year, expected percent change in capacity is combined with percent change in industrial production each month to calculate a percent change in operating rate. This change in operating rates is used to roll forward the most recently available December survey data. In May of each year, when data for the previous December becomes available, estimates of monthly operating rates for the previous year are revised.

Comparisons. As discussed in a previous section, the Federal Reserve relies heavily on the McGraw-Hill survey data for its estimates of capacity. The McGraw-Hill series for total manufacturing is tracked closely by the Federal Reserve's total manufacturing time series for December. This is evident in the correlation statistics shown in Exhibit 8 and the graph in Exhibit 9, which shows December operating rates for McGraw-Hill, the Federal Reserve, and BEA for the period 1965–82. For 1965–82, the volatility of the McGraw-Hill series is close to that of the Federal Reserve series (a standard deviation of 5.7 versus 6.0 for the Federal Reserve

EXHIBIT 8 Correlation Coefficients—Total
Manufacturing
1954–1982*

		McGraw-Hill (December)
	Wharton (fourth quarter)	0.59
FRB (fourth quarter)	0.71	0.94

1965–1982†
(December only)

		McGraw-Hill
	BEA	0.92
FRB	0.94	0.98

* Based on data referred to in Exhibit 4.
† Based on data shown in Exhibit 9.

data) and greater than the BEA series (which has a standard deviation of 4.8).

Comments. The McGraw-Hill survey data provide the longest-running series of survey data on capacity utilization and also provide valuable companion series on capital expenditures and capacity expansion. The series have been widely used for academic and business research, particularly in the study of investment expenditures. The five-month publications time lag is a limitation of the annual series. The estimated monthly series are more timely; data for the previous month for all industries is available by the 25th day of the current month. Annual and monthly operating rates are available from McGraw-Hill by subscription. The monthly series for all manufacturing is published routinely in *Business Week*, a McGraw-Hill publication.

Bureau of Economic Analysis (Department of Commerce)

As part of its continuing program of quarterly capital spending surveys, the Bureau of Economic Analysis (BEA) has been collecting capacity utilization data from manufacturing companies since the end of 1965. Of the three company-based surveys (McGraw-Hill, BEA, and Rinfret), this one is largest, covering over 2,400 firms and accounting for 75 per-

EXHIBIT 9   Capacity Utilization Rates 1965–1982*

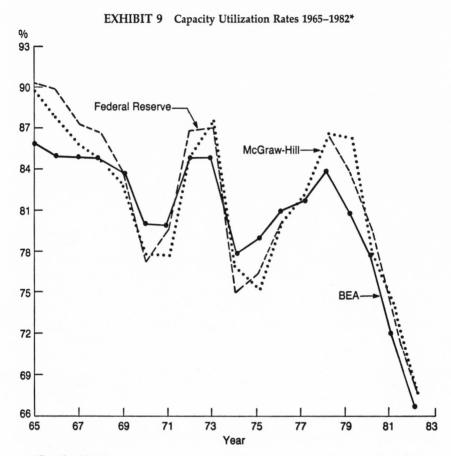

* December data only.
  Data source: Federal Reserve data for 1967–82 from statistical release, "Capacity Utilization," July 18, 1983; earlier data from *Federal Reserve Measures of Capacity and Capacity Utilization*, Board of Governors of the Federal Reserve System, February 1978. McGraw-Hill data from Economics Department Information Products, McGraw-Hill Publications Company. BEA data received form the Bureau of Economic Analysis, U.S. Department of Commerce.

cent of gross depreciable assets in 1969. Each quarter, the companies are asked to report on actual operating rates and preferred rates for the last month of that quarter (March, June, September, or December). Capacity is not specifically defined, but respondents are instructed to follow the company's usual operating practices with respect to the use of productive facilities, overtime, work shifts, holidays, and so forth. The respondents appear to be using a measure of maximum practical capacity in answering the questions. The data have been available quarterly since December 1967 and were collected semiannually for the two previous years.

BEA estimates of manufacturing operating rates are available two and a half months after the end of each quarter (e.g., December survey data are available approximately mid-March). The series are available both seasonally adjusted and unadjusted.

Aggregation. BEA company data are assigned to major industry groups, appropriate major manufacturing divisions—durable, nondurable, primary processed and advanced processed goods—and also to one of three asset-size classes (Exhibit 10). The organization by asset size is unique, weights used for aggregation are company capacity output. The BEA combines information from several sources to estimate these weights.

Comparison. The BEA operating rate series are the longest-running quarterly survey data. They are similar to the McGraw-Hill and Rinfret series in that the data are company-based, and the concept of capacity (determined by respondents) is assumed to be maximum practical capacity. On the other hand, McGraw-Hill uses employment weights for aggregation to the industry level which would tend to lend more weight to the labor-intensive companies within a given industry.

Shown in Exhibit 9 is a comparison of a time series of BEA December operating rates for total manufacturing with the McGraw-Hill series and a time series of December Federal Reserve rates. The BEA series exhibits the least extreme movements over the business cycle, thus indicating cyclical movements in implied capacity of greater amplitude than would be exhibited by other survey-based time series.

Comments. The BEA survey-based manufacturing utilization series are useful because their coverage is extensive and because the series are available quarterly and have been available over a long enough time period so that their characteristics can be properly evaluated. The availability of companion series on capital expenditures are a definite advantage. Although they are not as timely as the Federal Reserve estimates, they are also not subject to the extensive revisions of the production-based series. The lesser degree of cyclical amplitude should be kept in mind in using the data. Another important note: published annual capacity utilization rates are averages of the four end-of-the-quarter series.

The standard reference on the BEA series is "The Utilization of Manufacturing Capacity, 1965–1973," *Survey of Current Business*, July 1974.

Bureau of the Census

The Bureau of the Census annual survey of fourth-quarter capacity utilization rates, available since the early 1970s, is a comprehensive survey of approximately 8,500 individual manufacturing establishments. An establishment is an economic unit, generally at a single physical location. Examples of manufacturing establishments are factories, mills, and refineries. Thus the sample unit is different from that of the other capacity utilization surveys, all of which sample entire companies rather than single establishments.

The Census survey requests information on both actual operating rates, defined as percentage of practical capacity, and preferred operating rates. The instructions include specific discussion of what is meant by practical capacity. Information on preferred rates is used for the calculation of actual operating rates as a percent of preferred, and this calculation is also routinely published.

Census fourth-quarter operating rates are reported for all manufacturing, durable and nondurable manufacturers, primary and advanced processing industries, and the major (two-digit SIC) manufacturing industries. Census data are also available at the three- and four-digit SIC levels. A selected list of industry groups appears in Exhibit 10. In addition, manufacturing capacity utilization rates are available for selected standard metropolitan statistical areas and by employment size of the establishment (five categories). These utilization series are weighted by value added. The Census survey collects information on reasons for operating at less than 100 percent of practical capacity and reports these reasons by priority assigned to each one by each industry. Information is elicited on time required to expand practical capacity and length of time capacity output could be maintained. In addition to the questions on operating rates, specific information is requested on dollar value of production and the major components of production levels (e.g., number of shifts, production workers, overtime hours, etc.). Respondents are asked to answer these questions for actual, preferred, and practical levels of operation. Thus, the Census survey collects a unique mine of raw data in this area.

Comparisons. In comparison with other capacity utilization series, Census operating rates expressed as a percent of practical capacity are significantly lower and are less variable. The average level for all manufacturing for 1974 through 1981 was 69.8 percent—much lower than the other comparable series—and its peak in 1978 was only 74 percent (Exhibit 5). The high-to-low amplitude was 11.5 percent of the mean, smaller than the cyclical amplitude of other survey data and smaller than either of the other two fourth-quarter series, the Wharton or the Federal Reserve series. Census survey data based on output as a percent of practical capacity and as a percent of preferred capacity are shown in comparison to fourth-quarter Federal Reserve data in Exhibit 11. The level of the Census operating rate series defined as percent of preferred capacity is higher than the "practical capacity" series but still lower than other measures. Census estimates are probably lower in large part because of the differences in sampling unit. "Utilization rates in the company-based surveys may be higher because large, multiestablishment firms with integrated operations probably view total company capacity as less than the sum of the capacity of their separate establishments because of intracompany bottlenecks which do not affect the capacity of individual plants."[15] If the estimates of capacity are lower for companies than for establishments, then actual output as a percent of capacity for companies will be higher than actual output as a percent of capacity when the data are collected from manufacturing establishments.

Comments. Further details on methodology, detailed survey results for 1981 and 1980, and operating rates for selected industries for 1974–81, are available in *Survey of Plant Capacity, 1981,* Bureau of the Census, October 1982. At the time of this writing, 1982 survey results were not yet available. In addition, earlier data have been retabulated, but the revised figures were also unavailable at this time.

Finally, the 1982 survey instruction form and questionnaire is somewhat different from the previous forms. In particular, specific reference is made to the reporting of idle plants. Respondents are asked to complete the questionnaire in its entirety even if the plant was temporarily idle during the entire period. Since this instruction was not included prior to the 1982 survey, it is possible that many idle plants were not being reported at all. This could have caused some of the lack of volatility which is evident in the Census data.

Rinfret Associates

Rinfret Associates, Inc., has been conducting a quarterly capacity utilization survey of manufacturing and nonmanufacturing companies since 1974. Information is collected for the months of January, April, July, and October. In the latest 1983 survey, questionnaires were sent to 700 companies which account for 40 percent of total fixed corporate assets in the United States. Responses were received from 51 percent of the companies surveyed. The concept of capacity which underlies responses is assumed to be comparable to the concept of practical capacity used by respondents in other capacity utilization surveys. Assignment of companies to specific industries is done in accordance with the assignments designated for each company in the BEA survey of capital

---

[15] Bureau of the Census, Current Industrial Report, Series MQ–Cl(81)–1 *Survey of Plant Capacity, 1981* (Washington, D.C.: U.S. Government Printing Office, 1982), p. 2.

EXHIBIT 10 Capacity Utilization Series—Classification Systems

Bureau of Economic Analysis *U.S. Department of Commerce*	*Rinfret Associates*	*Bureau of the Census* *(Selected Industry Groups)*
Industry and asset size		*Industry group and SIC code*

All manufacturing	All industries	United States
Asset size:	Manufacturing	Nondurable (20–23, 26–31)
$100.0 million and over	Durables	Food and kindred products (20)
$10.0 to $99.9 million	Nondurables	Meat products (201)
Under $10.0 million	Nonmanufacturing	Tobacco manufacturers (21)
		Textile mill products (22)
Durable goods[1]	Durables manufacturing	Apparel and other textile products (23)
Asset size:	Primary metals	Paper and allied products (26)
$100.0 million and over	Iron and steel	Printing and publishing (27)
$10.0 to $99.9 million	Nonferrous	Chemicals and allied products (28)
Under $10.0 million	Electrical machinery	Petroleum and coal products (29)
	Nonelectrical machinery	Petroleum refining (291)
Primary metals	Transportation equipment	Rubber and plastics products, n.c.c. (30)
Electrical machinery	Motor vehicles	Miscellaneous plastics products (307)
Machinery, except electrical	Aerospace	Leather and leather products (31)
Transportation equipment[2]	Stone, clay, and glass	
Motor vehicles		Durable (24, 25, 32–39)
Aircraft	Nondurables manufacturing	Lumber and wood products (24)
Stone, clay, and glass	Food and beverages	Sawmills and planning mills (242)
	Textiles	Furniture and fixtures (25)
Nondurable goods[3]	Paper	Household furniture (251)
Asset size:	Chemicals	Stone, clay, and glass products (32)
$100.0 million and over	Petroleum	

$10.0 to $99.9 million
Under $10.0 million
Food including beverage
Textiles
Paper
Chemicals
Petroleum
Rubber
Primary processed goods[4]
Advanced processed goods[5]

Rubber
Nonmanufacturing
Mining
Railroads
Air transportation
Other transportation
Public utilities
  Electric
  Gas
Commercial and other[6]

Primary metal industries (33)
  Blast furnaces, steel works, and rolling and finishing mills (331)
  Iron and steel foundaries (332)
Fabricated metal products (34)
  Fabricated structural metal products (344)
  Metal forgings and stampings (346)
Machinery, except electrical (35)
  Construction, mining, and materials handling machinery and equipment (353)
Metal working machinery and equipment (354)
General industrial machinery and equipment (356)
Electrical equipment and supplies (36)
  Electrical industrial apparatus (362)
  Communication equipment (366)
Transportation equipment (37)
  Motor vehicles and motor vehicle equipment (371)
  Aircraft and parts (372)
Instruments and related products (38)
Miscellaneous manufacturing industries (39)

[1] Also includes lumber, furniture, fabricated metals, instruments, and miscellaneous.
[2] Also includes other transportation equipment
[3] Also includes tobacco, apparel, printing-publishing, and leather.
[4] Consists of lumber; stone, clay, and glass; primary metals; fabricated metals; textiles; paper; chemicals (at ½ weight); petroleum; and rubber.
[5] Consists of furniture, electrical machinery, machinery except electrical, motor vehicles, aircraft, other transportation equipment, instruments, food including beverage, tobacco, apparel, printing-publishing, chemicals (at ½ weight), leather, and miscellaneous.
[6] Aggregates include industries not shown separately.
Source: U.S. Department of Commerce News, BEA 82-13, March 17, 1983; reproduced by permission of Rinfret Associates, Inc., New York City; Bureau of the Census, *Survey of Plant Capacity 1981*, Tables 1A, 1B.

EXHIBIT 11   Fourth-Quarter Capacity Utilization Rates 1974–1981

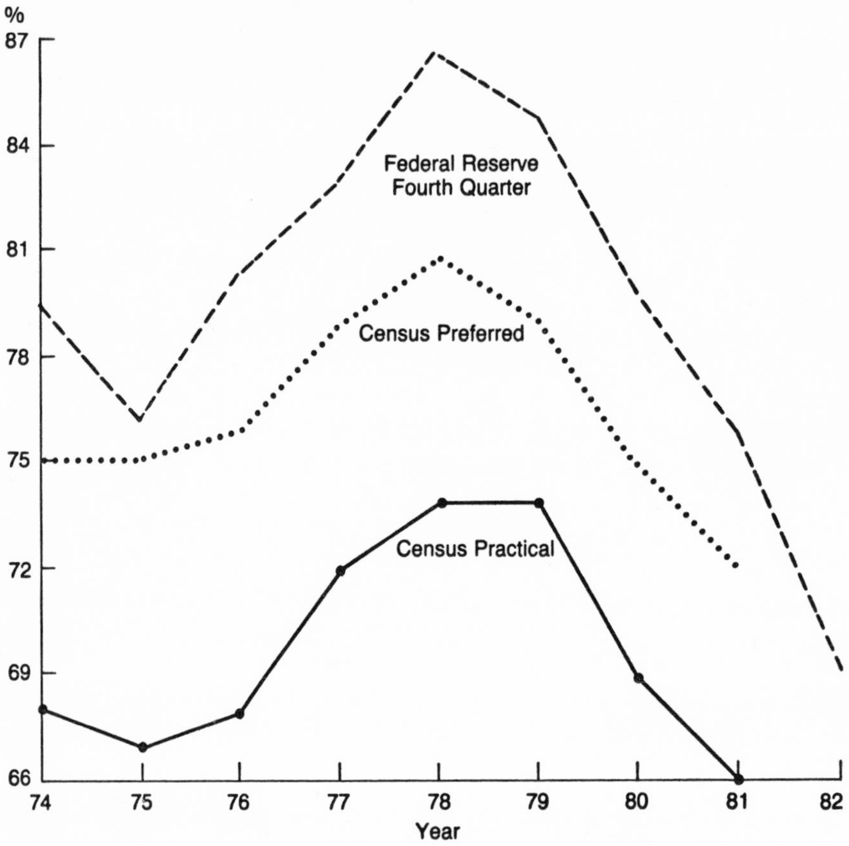

Data sources: Federal Reserve statistical release, "Capacity Utilization," July 18, 1983; Bureau of the Census, *Survey of Plant Capacity 1981*, pp. 8–9.

expenditures which covers all industries. Industries reported in addition to manufacturing are mining, transportation, and public utilities (Exhibit 10). A utilization series for the commercial sector was available until 1979, then discontinued.

Comparisons.   In Exhibit 5, the average level and volatility of a series of Rinfret January survey rates is compared with coterminous series of the other five sources of capacity utilization measures. Both measures of amplitude—high minus low divided by the mean, and the standard deviation—indicate that the Rinfret series is significantly more volatile than any of the others. In Exhibits 6 and 7, the Rinfret series for total manufacturing, from its inception in 1974 through January 1983, is compared to a Federal Reserve series based on the same months of each year. There, too, the greater volatility is evident. This variability is an interesting phenomenon because it implies a capacity index whose short-term movements may be more "accurate" than the short-term movements typical of the capacity indexes implied by the other survey-based capacity utilization measures. The greater the cyclical variability reflected in a utilization series, the less cyclical variability expected in the implied capacity index.

Availability and Timeliness. Rinfret Associates sends out its first request for information at the end of each quarter, e.g., at the end of January. Companies are asked for their actual operating rates for the recently completed quarter and for a forecast of rates for the coincident quarter. A follow-up is sent two weeks later, and companies are expected to respond within three weeks of this second request. As soon as the responses come in (which should be about five weeks after the end of the quarter), results are tabulated and available within a few days. Results are available to subscribers and companies which participate in the survey.

SUMMARY

There are six well-known measures of capacity utilization in U.S. industry: four survey-based measures and two production-based (see Exhibit 12). Each of the production-based measures uses the Federal Reserve

EXHIBIT 12	Summary Information					
	FRB	*Wharton*	*McGraw*	*BEA*	*Census*	*Rinfret*
Primary information base						
Industrial production index	•	•				
Survey of companies	•		•	•		•
Survey of establishments					•	
Industry categories						
Manufacturing	•	•	•	•	•	•
Materials	•	•				
Mining and utilities	•	•	•			•
Other		•				•
Periodicity						
Annual	•	•				
Quarterly	•	•				
Monthly	•		•			
Four times/year				•		•
Fourth quarter					•	
December			•			

indexes of industrial production as measures of output and develops explicit capacity indexes in order to estimate the utilization rates. Accordingly, each of the production-based measures, the Federal Reserve series and the Wharton series, have associated with them a capacity index which is available either publicly or by subscription. The survey-based measures are based on questionnaires which ask businesses to report their operating rates for particular months or quarters of the year. An implied capacity index may be derived from each survey-based utilization series by dividing operating rates into estimates of output expressed as an index. The industrial production indexes are used for this purpose.

The two production-based series of operating rates are different in concept and construction. The Wharton series uses previous peaks in the industrial production indexes as estimates of capacity output, thereby defining capacity as a realistically obtainable level of maximum output. In consequence, the Wharton operating rates can equal 100 percent, and this does happen at the more detailed industry level. The Federal Reserve series is constructed using capacity indexes which reflect the level and long-term trend movements implied by dividing an industrial production index by a survey measure of operating rates. This construction was developed as a practical solution to a difficult problem. For some industries, data on capacity provided by industry associations or government agencies play a major role in the development of final estimates.

Most respondents to the various capacity utilization surveys assume "capacity" to mean some version of the concept of practical maximum output. The Census Bureau explicitly defines practical capacity as maximum output assuming a realistic work pattern but without consideration of supply shortages (other than capital) or additional costs from expanding operations. Significant differences among the survey-based series would appear to stem primarily from differences in coverage: nature of sample unit and extent of coverage.

Each of these operating rate series is different from the others for either conceptual or statistical reasons, or both. There is no "target," or benchmark utilization series, against which the measures can be evaluated for accuracy as, for example, population estimates can be evaluated against census counts or output estimates against actual data. Nevertheless, a great deal of effort has gone into the development of these measures, and they are succinct descriptions of the general economic condition of U.S. industry at any given time. The most important point to remember is that the numerical value of any of the series at a point in time is meaningful only in the context of past history of the series—i.e., the level of past highs and lows, the history of cyclical amplitude, and the relationship to the business cycle in general. Each series must be evaluated separately to determine its usefulness for a particular purpose. Some simple and obvious considerations such as industry detail, accessibility, and timeliness may be very important to the user.

REFERENCES

Adams, F. Gerard, and Robert Summers. "The Wharton Indexes of Capacity Utilization: A Ten-Year Perspective." *Proceedings of the American Statistical Association, Business and Economic Statistics Section,* 1973, pp. 67–72.

Armitage, Kenneth, and Joan D. Hasley. "Revision of Industrial Production Index." *Federal Reserve Bulletin,* August 1979, pp. 603–5.

Berndt, Ernst R., and Catherine J. Morrison. "Capacity Utilization Measures: Underlying Economic Theory and an Alternative Approach." *American Economic Review,* May, 1981, pp. 48–52.

Betaucourt, Roger R., and Christopher K. Clague. *Capital Utilization: A Theoretical and Empirical Analysis.* Cambridge, Eng.: Cambridge University Press, 1981.

Board of Governors of the Federal Reserve System. *Federal Reserve Measures of Capacity and Capacity Utilization.* Washington, D.C.: February 1978.

Board of Governors of the Federal Reserve System. *Industrial Production, 1976 Revision.* Washington, D.C.: December 1977.

Bosworth, Barry. "Capacity Creation in Basic-Materials Industries." *Brookings Papers on Economic Activity,* vol. 2 (Washington, D.C.: Brookings Institution, 1976), pp. 297–341.

Bureau of the Census. Census of Manufacturers, 1972. Volume IV, *Indexes of Production.* Washington, D.C.: U.S. Government Printing Office, 1972.

Bureau of the Census. Current Industrial Reports, Series *MQ–Cl(81)–1 Survey of Plant Capacity, 1981.* Washington, D.C.: U.S. Government Printing Office, October 1982.

Christiano, Lawrence J. "A Survey of Measures of Capacity Utilization." *International Monetary Fund Staff Papers,* 1981, pp. 144–99.

Cremeans, John E. "Capacity Utilization Rates—What Do They Really Mean?" *Business Economics,* May 1978, pp. 41–46.

de Leeuw, Frank. "The Concept of Capacity." *Journal of the American Statistical Association,* September 1962, pp. 826–40.

de Leeuw, Frank; Lawrence R. Forest, Jr.; Richard D. Raddock; and Zoltan E. Kenessey. *Measurement of Capacity Utilization: Problems and Tasks.* Washington, D.C.: Board of Governors of the Federal Reserve System, July 1979.

Ellis, Michael. "Supply-Side Linkage of Capacity Utilization and Labor Productivity: U.S. Manufacturing, 1954–1980." *Business Economics,* May 1983, pp. 62–69.

Hertzberg, Marie P.; Alfred I. Jacobs; and Jon E. Trearathan. "The Utilization of Manufacturing Capacity, 1965–1973." *Survey of Current Business*, July 1974, pp. 47–57.

Raddock, Richard. "Revision of Capacity Utilization Rates." *Federal Reserve Bulletin*, August 1979, pp. 606–7.

Rost, Ronald F. "New Federal Reserve Measures of Capacity and Capa city Utilization." *Federal Reserve Bulletin*, July 1983, pp. 515–21.

Winston, Gordon C. "Capacity: An Integrated Micro and Macro Analysis." *American Economic Review*, February 1977, pp. 418–22.

Winston, Gordon C. "The Theory of Capital Utilization and Idleness." *Journal of Economic Literature*, December 1974, pp. 1301–20.

Zarnowitz, Victor. "On Functions, Quality, and Timeliness of Economic Information." Reprint No. 250, National Bureau of Economic Research, February 1982.

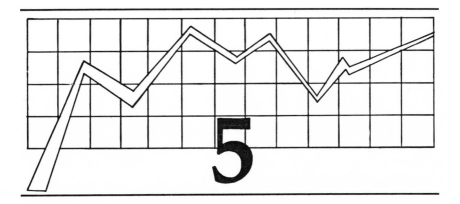

Construction Activity

Kenneth J. Thygerson, Ph.D.
President and Chief Executive Officer
Federal Home Loan Mortgage Corporation

Dolores P. Lynn
Economist
Federal Home Loan Mortgage Corporation

The primary source of comprehensive statistics on residential construction activity in the United States is the federal government. Based on continuous surveys of small geographical areas throughout the nation, the Bureau of the Census of the U.S. Department of Commerce publishes current measurements of the quantity of new housing production at several stages of planning and execution. It also publishes qualitative data on new housing and estimates of the monetary and real value created over time by residential construction activities.

The Census Bureau's data on new housing activity are published in *Construction Reports*, a group of nine publication series, eight of which relate exclusively to residential construction. The specific statistical indicators contained in these series appear in set formats and are updated at regular monthly, quarterly, or annual intervals according to the frequency of the data. The statistics used to measure physical construction activity are number of housing units rather than number of structures. New housing that is authorized, started, or completed in a given period, for example, is expressed in number of housing units.

The government's monetary measure of construction activity is largely based on builder estimates of the cost of construction projects, as stated in applications for local building permits. These permit-value data, adjusted to compensate for systematic understatement, are distributed over the life of construction projects in order to estimate the value of residential construction put in place during specific time periods. The "value in place" estimates then enter the gross national product (GNP) accounts as the major component of fixed residential investment. Here, alongside comparable statistics for other productive sectors of the economy, these data allow the residential construction sector to be evaluated in terms of size, relative performance, and contribution to overall economic growth.

With their extremely broad scope, the federal government's construction series are capable of serving a wide range of needs. Builders, suppliers of construction materials, real estate brokers, and lenders of construction and permanent mortgage funds, for example, are likely to find the data of practical benefit, particularly where geographical details are supplied. At the same time, policymakers and others concerned with the macroeconomy and/or the housing sector may find the overall measures of residential construction activity ideal for their purposes.

In this chapter, we will examine closely the eight *Construction Reports* series related to new residential construction. The ninth series, dealing with housing units authorized for demolition, will not be discussed. Our main interest will be in the sources, methodology, usefulness, and (where appropriate) shortcomings of the statistics. The series are as follows:

C–40 on housing units authorized by building permits.

C–20 on housing starts.

C–22 on housing completions.

C–21 on new residential activity in selected standard metropolitan statistical areas (SMSAs).

C–25 on new one-family homes sold and for sale.

C–27 on prices of new one-family houses.

C–50 on expenditures for residential alterations and repairs.

C–30 on the value of new construction put in place.

Because the statistics share a common definitional framework, however, we will first describe the Census Bureau's concept of a housing unit, its guidelines for classifying housing units by type of structure, and the geographical content of regions and smaller areas for which data may be reported.

Housing Units

The Census Bureau defines a housing unit as a single room or group of rooms intended for occupancy as separate living quarters by a family, by a group of unrelated persons living together, or by a person living alone. Separate living quarters are those in which occupants do not live and eat with any other persons in the structure. Also, they must have direct access from the outside of the building or through a common hall, and they must have complete kitchen facilities for the exclusive use of the occupant(s).

Certain types of shelter units are not considered by the Census Bureau to be new housing units. One type is nonhousekeeping units, such as those found in group living quarters (e.g., dormitories) and in transient accommodations (hotels). Another is housing units created by conversions of, or additions and alterations to, existing buildings. A third type is mobile homes, which are portable dwellings designed to be towed on their own chassis and without need of a permanent foundation. Because mobile homes are dwellings and additions to the housing stock, however, the Census Bureau provides separate data on mobile home activity in the *Construction Reports*. Elsewhere in Commerce Department statistics, expenditures on mobile homes and additions and alterations are treated as residential investment.

Unit Size of Residential Structures

In the *Construction Reports*, total housing units are broken down by the size of structures in which they are located. Structure size, or type, is determined by the number of housing units contained in the building. In some of the published data tables, there are four structure types— one-unit, two-unit, three-to-four-unit, and five-or-more-unit buildings. In other tables where the two-unit and three-to-four-unit categories are combined, the breakdown is into three structure types.

The one-unit structure category includes fully detached single-family houses and also semidetached houses, rowhouses, and townhouses with qualifying structural characteristics. To be classified as one-unit structures, attached houses must be separated from the adjacent structure by a ground-to-roof party wall. In addition, they must not share heating systems or interstructural facilities such as water/power supply or sewage disposal.

All other housing units, including those built on top of one another, are categorized by the total number of units in the structure. Apartments are defined as buildings with five or more units. Since ownership is not a criterion for classification, condominium units may be classified either as one-unit structures or as units in larger buildings, depending upon their structural characteristics.

Geographical Subdivisions

The basic geographical subdivisions used in *Construction Reports* are Census regions and standard metropolitan statistical areas. There are four Census regions containing the 50 states—Northeast, North Central, South, and West. These regions are broken down into nine Census divisions. The state composition of the Census regions and divisions and the relative amounts of residential construction activity occurring in these areas are shown in the table below.

States Composing Census Regions and Divisions

Region	Division	State
Northeast	New England	Maine
		New Hampshire
		Vermont
		Massachusetts
		Rhode Island
		Connecticut
	Middle Atlantic	New York
		New Jersey
		Pennsylvania
North Central	East North Central	Ohio
		Indiana
		Illinois
		Michigan
		Wisconsin
	West North Central	Minnesota
		Iowa
		Missouri
		North Dakota
		South Dakota
		Nebraska
		Kansas
South	South Atlantic	Delaware
		Maryland
		District of Columbia
		Virginia
		West Virginia
		North Carolina
		South Carolina
		Georgia
		Florida
	East South Central	Kentucky
		Tennessee
		Alabama
		Mississippi

Region	Division	State
	West South Central	Arkansas
		Louisiana
		Oklahoma
		Texas
West	Mountain	Montana
		Idaho
		Wyoming
		Colorado
		New Mexico
		Arizona
		Utah
		Nevada
	Pacific	Washington
		Oregon
		California
		Alaska
		Hawaii

An SMSA is a metropolitan area containing a large population nucleus and adjacent communities with a high degree of economic and social integration with the nucleus. The specific criteria for defining and establishing SMSAs were modified in 1980 by the Office of Management and Budget. Under the revised standards, an SMSA must include at least one city with a population of 50,000 or more or an urbanized area of at least 50,000 inhabitants and a total SMSA population of at least 100,000. In 1981, 36 new metropolitan areas were designated as SMSAs, bringing the total number of SMSAs to 323.

The amount of geographical detail in the construction activity data varies extremely. Most of the published data contain totals for the four Census regions and for combined areas inside and outside SMSAs. In the case of housing units authorized by building permits, however, monthly data are given for individual states grouped into Census divisions and regions, for 131 SMSAs and for approximately 4,700 counties or smaller places requiring building permits. Annual data are given for all SMSAs and all permit-issuing places that have been identified by the Census Bureau.

HOUSING UNITS AUTHORIZED BY BUILDING PERMITS AND PUBLIC CONTRACTS (C–40)

The housing permits series, as it is commonly called, is an indicator of the amount of housing activity that can occur in the future as a result of new construction authorizations currently granted to builders. In the case of privately owned construction, authorizations are in the form of building permits issued by local governmental bodies. Publicly owned construction is counted as newly authorized when public housing agencies (PHAs) notify developers to proceed with projects under programs of the U.S. Department of Housing and Urban Development (HUD) or when other federal agencies award construction contracts.

Sources of Data

The data on publicly owned housing are for all buildings owned by the federal, state, and local governments at the time of construction. These data are reported to the Census Bureau each month by HUD and other federal agencies. The HUD statistics cover conventional programs for low-income public housing and Native American public housing as well as Section 8 projects that are publicly owned during the construction period. They do not include "turnkey" public housing projects, which are privately owned during construction and sold to local PHAs upon completion. Data reported by the other federal agencies cover construction contracts awarded for new military housing, caretaker quarters on federal lands, and housing for federal officials.

In all, authorizations for new public housing account for only a minor share of the Census Bureau's housing permits series. During the five-year period of 1978–82, total new housing units reported by the federal agencies represented less than 1 percent of all newly authorized housing units.

Information on privately owned housing authorized is obtained by the Census Bureau through a monthly mail survey of local building permit officials. Currently, the data universe consists of approximately 16,000 places in the United States that were identified in 1978 as having local building permit systems. Earlier, the universe contained 14,000 places from 1972 to 1977, 13,000 places from 1968 to 1971, 12,000 places from 1963 to 1967, and 10,000 places from 1959 to 1962. Beginning in 1985, the published permits data will be for 17,000 permit places.

The Census Bureau's program of continuously identifying new permit-issuing places has been necessitated by population and household growth and the spread of housing activity beyond the limits of established urban and suburban areas. The periodic enlargement of the data universe, at roughly five-year intervals, reflects both conversions of new areas and the adoption of building permit systems by active jurisdictions previously without them. The permit coverage of new housing activity, or the ratio of housing starts in permit areas to total housing starts, has risen from 83 percent in 1963 to 89 percent in 1982.

Permit-issuing jurisdictions may be counties, municipalities, townships, or towns. Below the county level, the statistics reported by the Census Bureau normally reflect permit activity within the bounds of the jurisdiction indicated. For counties, the data usually apply to all unincorporated territory or to the areas not covered by municipal permit systems. Some townships subject only part of their areas to building permit requirements. Some municipalities have permit authority beyond their boundaries, and in these cases, the data for the additional areas are included in the municipal figures. A few permit-issuing municipalities and townships also come under the permit jurisdiction of the county. In these cases, the permit data are reported once under the county.

Data Publication

The most detailed statistics on housing permits are published in the C–40 *Construction Reports,* issued monthly and annually by the Census Bureau. The monthly data presented in the monthly reports contain preliminary estimates for the 16,000-place universe based on a 3,700-place sample survey, and revised estimates based on the full sample survey of 8,000 places. The annual reports present calendar-year totals obtained from surveys of all 16,000 permit-issuing places. Imputed data are included for places either not responding to the survey or responding inadequately.

Both the monthly and annual publications contain data on the dollar value of construction authorized by permits as well as on the number of housing units. The valuation data come from individual building permit applications, where the estimated cost of construction is recorded along with the number of structures and housing units. Because these cost estimates exclude some items—site development and heating and electrical installations, for example—the permit valuation data understate the value of the finished construction.

The monthly C–40 reports contain five statistical tables on new housing authorized in permit-issuing places. The first table of summary data has two sections. The first section gives monthly data, at seasonally adjusted annual rates, on privately owned housing units, with breakdowns into Census regions and three structure types. For the U.S. total, in addition, a four-month moving average of seasonally adjusted annual rates is given.

The second section presents annual, year-to-date, and unadjusted monthly data on total, public, and private housing authorizations in terms of both housing units and permit valuation. The national private-activity data are broken into four types of structures, location with respect to SMSAs, and Census regions. The SMSA breakdown includes totals for inside SMSAs, inside central cities of SMSAs, and outside SMSAs.

The second table in the monthly C–40 reports presents data for the latest month on total, public, and private housing authorized in individual states grouped into Census divisions and regions. Totals for the regions and divisions are shown. The data include both housing units and permit valuation, except that valuation statistics are not available for public contract awards. Private activity is shown by three structure types. Also, there is a count of the number of privately owned structures containing five or more housing units.

The third table gives data for the latest month on 131 selected SMSAs for which statistics are available from the 8,000-place sample. The data presented are the same as in the preceding table, except that there are four structure types rather than three. The 131 SMSAs are listed alphabetically by title; they are not grouped by states or regions. Under each individual SMSA heading, subtotals are given for the central city or cities and for combined areas outside the central city. Table totals for all 131 SMSAs are shown, including separate totals for all areas inside and outside central cities of these SMSAs.

The fourth table gives data for the latest month for approximately 4,700 individual permit-issuing places. These places are listed alphabetically under the counties in which they are located, as are the counties under states. Private permit activity is measured here in terms of housing units, but not dollar value. The statistics given are current-year-to-date and current-month totals of housing units authorized. In addition, for the current month, permit authorizations for single-family housing are shown.

The fifth table reports on publicly owned housing units authorized in the latest month, by government agency and by type of HUD program. The data are for the particular cities in which new projects were authorized during the period, and only those cities (and states in which they are located) are listed each month.

The annual C–40 tables are basically the same as the monthly ones in format and content, with a few exceptions. The monthly data given in the annual U.S. summary tables are not seasonally adjusted. The annual table of state data contains a breakdown of private activity by four structure types rather than three. The SMSA table gives data for all currently defined SMSAs in the nation rather than a selection. Finally, the fourth data table lists individually all known permit-issuing places in the nation, including those identified by the Census Bureau since the 16,000-place universe was adopted in 1978.

Limitations of the Data

The housing permits data are essentially information about proposed or planned construction rather than about actual construction in progress or completed. They are, however, a useful indicator of near-term trends in construction activity at the national level. Continuing sample surveys show that, nationally, only 2 percent of the housing units authorized by permits are never constructed. They also indicate that construction normally follows close on the heels of permit issuance, with a major proportion of units getting started in the month of authorization and most of the remainder within the following three months.

On the negative side, the permits series reflects only that housing activity occurring in places with building permit systems. As noted before, about 11 percent of new housing units on which construction started in 1982 were outside of permit-issuing places. The permit series, moreover, tends to underestimate activity in permit-issuing places, because an estimated 2 percent of new housing units in these areas are started without the required permits. All of the underestimation occurs in the single-family sector, where more than 3 percent of starts in permit areas are not permit authorized. To the extent that these limitations apply consistently over an extended time period, they do not seriously impair the usefulness of the national data.

The flaws in the permit statistics are much more apparent at the regional and local levels, and care must be taken in using the data to make interarea comparisons or to analyze trends in specific areas over time. Boundaries of permit-issuing places change, and so do definitions of SMSAs. Moreover, there is a wide variation in the use of building permit systems among geographic areas.

In 1982, permit places accounted for 100 percent of new residential construction (based on housing units started) in the Census Bureau's West region, 94 percent in the Northeast, 86 percent in the South, and 79 percent in the North Central region. The coverage of total residential construction by permit systems fluctuates from year to year in all regions. Since the mid-1960s, permit coverage has tended to decline somewhat in the North Central region and to climb sharply in the South. In the West, nearly all residential construction has been permit-authorized at least since the early 1960s. In the Northeast, where permit coverage has been extensive but not complete, there has been a moderate trend of increase.

HOUSING STARTS (C–20)

The housing starts series provides a count of the number of new housing units on which construction has begun each month. For publicly owned housing units, construction is assumed to have begun in the month of the contract award. The start of construction of privately owned units is when excavation begins for the footings or foundation. All units in a multifamily building are defined as started when excavation for that building has begun.

Sources and Methodology

The statistics on private housing starts are compiled in a multistage process that involves different sets of procedures for permit-authorized and other housing activity. The estimates of starts in permit-issuing places flow directly from the building permits survey, which identifies potential new construction activity and cases for continuing observation. The estimates of starts in areas where permits are not required result from direct contacts initiated by the Census Bureau within a sample of land areas.

Housing starts in permit places are estimated by applying housing start rates to numbers of housing units authorized by building permits. A start rate is a ratio of units started to total units for which there are permits. To estimate start rates, the Census Bureau conducts an independent monthly survey of a sample of permits within 137 land areas (counties or groups of counties) included in the permit survey. From each of approximately 850 permit places in these land areas, a sample of building permits is selected. For each permit selected, the owner or builder is asked to report the month and year in which the unit covered by permit was started. For each unit not started in the month of permit authorization, follow-up inquiries are made in successive months until the unit is started or the permit is reported as expired, revoked, canceled, or abandoned.

From these sample data, the Census Bureau each month calculates sets of 14 different start rates for use in estimating the number of housing units started from permits of the survey month and of each preceding month. The multiple start rates take account of differences in activity patterns due to differences in structure type and geographical location. Eight of these start rates are for one-family houses, including a metropolitan area and a nonmetropolitan area rate for each of the four Census regions. Four additional start rates—one for each region—are for large apartment buildings. The remaining two start rates include one each for two-unit structures and three-to-four-unit structures.

After these start rates are applied to the appropriate estimates of housing units authorized by permits and after starts for each month of authorization are calculated, the results are aggregated to structural totals within the four Census regions. To complete the estimate of starts in permit areas during the latest month, the Census Bureau makes two further adjustments. It raises the total number of single-family starts by 3.3 percent to take care of units started without the required permits. It also makes upward adjustments for late reports. This estimation procedure occurs first on the basis of preliminary permits data from the 3,700-place survey and later on the basis of revised permits data from the full 8,000-place sample.

The estimate of housing starts in areas without building permit systems comes from Census Bureau contacts within the same 137 places sampled to determine rates at which starts from permits are occurring. Of these 137 places, 100 contain nonpermit areas in which the Census Bureau obtains, through interviews with persons assumed to be knowledgeable about local housing activity, a sample of housing units started in the latest month. This information is verified through field visits or interviews with owners or builders of the projects identified. In addition, to assure the accuracy of the sample, Census employees canvass a subsample of 170 small land areas for information about housing starts that may not have been reported by other sources.

Data Publication

Housing starts data are published monthly in the C–20 *Construction Reports*. Seven basic tables devoted to measures of the volume of new housing activity appear every month.

The first of the regular monthly tables contains statistics on total, publicly owned, and privately owned housing starts, with private starts for the United States broken down by four structure types, by location inside or outside SMSAs, and by Census region. The data are shown annually for approximately two decades and monthly for at least three years. The monthly statistics are actual unadjusted totals.

The second table provides annual and monthly data on private housing starts in permit-issuing places. The monthly statistics are presented both unadjusted and at seasonally adjusted annual rates. Breakdowns of the U.S. data are by Census region and by four structure types.

The third C–20 table provides adjusted monthly data—by structure type and Census region—only on private housing starts. For each month, the table contains a seasonally adjusted annual rate and a four-month moving average of seasonally adjusted annual rates centered on the third month.

The fourth table gives annual and monthly U.S. data—by structure type, by Census region, and by location with respect to SMSAs—on private housing units authorized by permits. The annual statistics cover past periods when the data universe contained fewer than 16,000 permit-issuing places. At points where the universe was expanded, permit totals for both the old and the new universe are shown for at least one overlapping year. The monthly section of the table includes seasonally adjusted annual rate data and unadjusted year-to-date totals for the current and previous years.

The fifth table provides a count of the number of housing units authorized but not yet started as of the end of each month or year shown.

These data measure the backlog of all construction projects approved at any past time up to the report date and for which permits are still alive. In each reporting period, the data in this series are increased by new permit authorizations and decreased by housing starts and by permit cancellations, expirations, revocations, and abandonments. For the United States and each of the four Census regions, data are provided for all structures and for three structure types.

The sixth C–20 table shows, separately and in combination, the number of mobile homes shipped by manufacturers and the number of privately owned single-family structures started in the United States during monthly and annual periods. The monthly data are given in actual unadjusted totals and at seasonally adjusted annual rates.

The seventh table expands on the information contained in the first table by providing structural breakdowns of private housing starts for geographical subdivisions. Thus, the starts totals for areas inside and outside SMSAs and for each Census region are broken into two structural categories—single-family and five-or-more units. The data are annual totals and unadjusted quarterly totals.

Limitations of the Data

The housing starts series is a more direct and complete measurement of new construction activity than the permits series. It reflects decisions to actually put projects into construction, and it includes additional information about housing activity in areas without building permit systems. The housing starts data are also useful because they facilitate calculations of the backlog of new construction or the number of unstarted housing units for which permit authorizations are still valid.

The usefulness of current monthly statistics on housing starts in analyzing residential construction trends, however, is diminished by the somewhat erratic nature of the monthly data. In some periods, three or four months of data may be needed before a basic trend can be identified. To a large extent, the irregular pattern of the monthly series on private housing starts reflects the speculative component of the one-family segment of the construction market. Roughly two thirds of total private starts are one-family houses; of this, nearly two thirds consist of construction initiated by builders at their own risk for inventory and sale. The amount of inventory a builder is willing to carry varies with the anticipated demand for homes and with the current and projected cost of construction financing. Upward and downward adjustments in desired inventory levels tend to destabilize activity in the built-for-sale market. Because of the market's particular sensitivity to interest rates, moreover, and the ability of interest rates to move quickly in the short run, irregular fluctuations in the monthly data may be all the more pronounced.

Certain issues of the monthly C–20 *Construction Reports* present data that are compiled and published quarterly or annually only. These statistics focus primarily on the qualitative aspects of residential construction activity. These series are discussed below.

C–20 Data on Qualitative Aspects of Construction Activity

Private Housing Units Started, by Purpose of Construction (C–20). Four times a year, in the February, May, August, and November issues of C–20, the Census Bureau publishes unadjusted quarterly data on private housing starts in the United States by purpose of construction at the time of start. These data are a product of the housing starts sample survey.

The purpose-of-construction breakdowns are provided for two types of structures—one-unit houses and buildings of two or more units. Single-family starts are distributed among three categories—for sale, for owner occupancy, and for rent. The rental category has recently accounted for less than 2 percent of the total. Dwellings slated for owner occupancy are shown in two subcategories—contractor built and owner built. In either case, the land on which they are built is owned by the party intending to occupy them. Houses built for sale by builders include those for which sales contracts have already been written at the time of start. Housing units started in structures of two or more units are divided into two categories—for sale and for rent.

In March of each year, the C–20 reports contain a supplementary table on new private housing units by intended use at the time of start. The data are less frequent—annual versus quarterly—but more detailed. Breakdowns are provided for three structure types, with the two-or-more-unit category broken into two-to-four-unit structures and apartment buildings. For all structure types, housing units intended for sale as condominiums are shown separately. The data are annual totals for the latest and preceding calendar years for the United States and for each of the four Census regions.

Private Housing Units Started, by Design (C–20). In another supplementary table in the March C–20, annual data on private housing starts in the United States and the four Census regions are broken down by design characteristics. One-unit starts are divided into detached houses and townhouses. Units in large buildings of five or more units are broken into townhouse apartments and conventional apartments. Design information on structures of two- to four-units is not available, but this structural category contains a relatively small share—8 percent—of new private housing starts.

Selected Characteristics of Housing Units in Privately Owned Buildings with Five Units or More (C–20). In two quarterly tables appearing regularly in the February, May, August, and November C–20 issues, the Census Bureau publishes descriptive information on new private multifamily construction started in annual and quarterly periods. In the first table, the number of buildings with five or more units started in the United States is distributed two ways—by number of units per building and by number of floors per building. There are five structural categories into which apartment buildings are divided: 5–9 units, 10–19 units, 20–29 units, 30–49 units, and 50 or more units. There are only two height categories—one to three floors and four or more floors.

The second table of characteristics contains breakdowns of housing units started in multifamily buildings—by number of floors per building, units per building, structure size, number of bedrooms per unit, and number of bathrooms per unit. In addition, the table provides data on the median and average square feet per unit for all new multifamily units started. Bedroom categories include efficiency apartment, and one, two, and three or more bedrooms. Bathroom categories include one, one and a half, and two or more.

Total Time from Start of Construction to Completion of Private Residential Buildings (C–20). From the survey of construction, which produces the data on new housing units started, the Census Bureau is able to determine the length of time needed to complete private residential buildings of different types and sizes. As noted before, the beginning of excavation for the building is considered by the Census Bureau to be the time of start of a housing unit. Completion time is defined differently, however, for one-family and multifamily structures. A one-family house is classified as completed either when all finish flooring (or carpeting) is installed or when it becomes occupied. All the units in a multifamily structure are considered as completed when at least 50 percent of the units are occupied or available for occupancy.

The construction time for a building can be accurately calculated as the number of days from start to completion. Since the survey of construction is designed for monthly data collection, however, a day count is not possible. The Census Bureau, therefore, has developed a system of measuring construction time that overcomes this difficulty. Under this system, a building that is reported as started and finished in the same month is assumed to have taken a full month to construct. One completed in the month after start took one and one-half months; in the second month after start, two and one-half months; in the third and fourth months after start, three and four months, and so on.

The Census Bureau's statistics on time to completion for private residential buildings are annual data published once a year in three supplementary tables in either the April or May issue of the C–20 *Construction Reports*. The first two tables present about a decade of annual data on completion time, in average number of months, for new residential construction. The first table, covering one-family houses, shows construction time by Census region and by construction purpose. The listed purposes are: built for sale, where the house and lot are to be included in the sales transactions; contractor built, where the house is built on the owner's land under the supervision of a single general contractor; and owner built, where the owner supervises the house-building on his own land.

The second table, dealing with multifamily construction, provides separate data on two-to-four-unit buildings and on structures with five or more units. In addition, for large apartment buildings, construction times are given for five structure sizes ranging from 5–9 units up to 50 or more units. The third table gives the percentage distribution of buildings completed during the latest survey year, by number of months from start. Separate data are given for one-unit, two-to-four-unit, and five-or-more-unit buildings and for the five size groups of apartment buildings. In using the data on completion times for multifamily structures, it should be borne in mind that a completed building may have up to 50 percent of its units still uncompleted. By a different definition, calculated construction times would most likely be longer.

Survey of New Mobile Home Placements (C–20). Although the mobile home does not conform to the Census Bureau's definition of a housing unit, it is recognized to be an addition to the nation's housing stock and a form of residential investment. As we have noted, the C–20 monthly report on new housing units started includes data regularly on mobile home shipments to dealers by manufacturers. These published data are not compiled by the Census Bureau. For the period from November 1977 forward, they are compiled by the National Conference of States on Building Codes and Standards (NCSBCS) from reports submitted by manufacturers of mobile homes. The prior data were obtained from the Manufactured Housing Institute (MHI), which now publishes the NCSBCS data.

Through a sample survey sponsored by HUD, however, the Census Bureau does collect data on mobile home placements for residential use. Beginning with 1980, the monthly survey has involved a sample of new mobile homes shipped. The dealer to whom the sampled unit was shipped is contacted by telephone and questioned about the status of the unit. The process is repeated each month until the unit is reported placed. From 1974 through 1979, the methodology for collecting information was different in that the survey sample was constructed of dealers in selected geographic areas across the nation rather than of mobile home units.

The information obtained through the survey is published by the Census Bureau in the C–20 reports as a supplement four times a year, although not necessarily at regular intervals. Each of the three tables contained in the supplement provides quarterly and annual statistics on total, single-wide, and double-wide mobile home placements for the United States and for each of the four Census regions. The three sets of data are the number of mobile homes placed during each period, average sales price per unit placed, and number of new mobile homes on dealer lots at the end of each period.

HOUSING COMPLETIONS (C–22)

Statistics on new housing units completed and under construction are compiled monthly by the Census Bureau and published in the monthly C–22 *Construction Reports*. The data are a product of the housing starts survey, and the compilation procedure is basically the same for completions and housing under construction as it is for starts.

Once a housing unit is reported to be started in the housing starts survey, it continues to be surveyed in successive months until it is found to be completed. For permit areas, these monthly sample data are used to calculate, by structure type, ratios of the number of housing units under construction and completed to the number of units authorized by permit, in the same manner as housing start rates for a sample of permits are calculated. Separate ratios are calculated for units authorized by permit in the current month and in each preceding month. These ratios are then applied to total housing units authorized in corresponding months, in order to obtain estimates for the current month of total housing units under construction and completed in permit-issuing places. The calculated results for one-unit structures are then adjusted upward by 3.3 percent to account for houses built without permits in places where permits are required.

The C–22 reports contain three data tables that are nearly identical in format for housing completed and for housing under construction. The statistics in these tables refer to total activity during each period in the case of completions and to the number of units at the end of each period in the case of housing under construction. One of these three tables contains annual and unadjusted monthly data on private housing units—by four structure types, by location inside and outside SMSAs, and by Census region. All data are shown for total private housing and for private housing in permit-issuing places. A second table gives seasonally adjusted data on private housing units by two structure types. The third table provides annual and unadjusted quarterly breakdowns by structure type for geographical areas. These areas are Census regions and combined places inside and outside SMSAs.

The C–22 release also contains a monthly table of four-month moving averages of seasonally adjusted annual rates of housing completions centered on the third month. These data are for all private structures and for two structure types.

Finally, the C–22 reports contain a table of monthly seasonal factors used to adjust both private housing completions and housing under construction. Projected as well as historical seasonal factors are provided for each of three structure types.

NEW RESIDENTIAL CONSTRUCTION IN SELECTED SMSAs (C–21)

Under contract from HUD, the Census Bureau publishes statistics on housing activity for 20 SMSAs individually. These SMSAs cover land areas in 16 states and the District of Columbia. The four Census regions and six of the nine Census divisions are represented on this list of SMSAs. The divisions not represented are New England, West North Central, and East South Central. Data for calendar quarters and annual periods are published in the C–21 *Construction Reports* four times a year at irregular intervals.

The individual SMSA tables in this report cover total and one-family housing units in permit-issuing places. The five statistical series contained in each table include housing unit: authorized by permits, authorized but not started, started, under construction, and completed. The data are obtained from the building permits and housing starts surveys, which were designed to provide reliable national and regional estimates. The 20 SMSAs chosen for this report are ones for which the sample coverage is considered to produce reliable estimates for total housing units and one-family houses. All permit-issuing jurisdictions in these SMSAs are in the monthly survey of new permit activity, and there are no large land areas within the SMSAs where building permits are not required.

One potential limitation on the usefulness of the SMSA construction statistics is the fact that one sample survey on which they are based has not been revised to reflect changes in SMSA definitions since 1970. Currently, however, the bias in the data from this factor is considered to be small.

NEW ONE-FAMILY HOUSES SOLD AND FOR SALE (C–25)

The Census Bureau, under contract with HUD, compiles data on the number of new one-family houses sold during the month and for sale at the end of each month. These data are published monthly in the C–25 *Construction Reports* along with related statistics on builders' inventories and the average and median prices of new homes sold.

The statistics in this data series are obtained from the housing sales survey, whose monthly sample includes all new one-family houses in permit and nonpermit areas that are shown by the housing starts survey to be either sold or for sale. In the sales survey, monthly interviews are conducted with the builder or owner of each new house until the house is reported sold or withdrawn from the sales market. The survey covers only those one-family houses that are built for sale with lot included in the transaction. It excludes contractor-built and owner-built houses which are constructed on the owner's land and assumed to be for land-owner's use.

The C–25 reports contain six tables. The first presents annual and monthly data for the United States on the number of houses sold during the period and for sale at the end of the period and on the number of months' supply of unsold houses on the market at the current sales rate. All of these data are given in unadjusted form and on a seasonally adjusted basis. The second table contains annual and monthly data on houses sold and for sale by Census region. Seasonally adjusted data are also given for houses sold. The third table contains breakdowns, for annual and monthly periods, by stage of construction of houses sold and for sale. In the Census Bureau data, there are three possible stages of construction for new one-family houses on the sales market—completed, under construction, and not yet started. The houses not started which appear in these statistics are ones for which builders have already obtained permits.

The fourth table shows the number and percent distribution of homes sold across the United States by six price groups ranging from under $50,000 to $120,000 and over. It also provides data on the U.S. median and average sales prices for each annual and monthly period. The fifth table contains data on median and average sales prices of new homes sold in the United States and in each Census region during calendar quarters. The sales price of a new home reported in this survey is that agreed on by buyer and seller, and reported by the seller, at the time a contract is signed. It does not reflect any subsequent adjustments, and it does not include extras or options paid for in cash by the purchaser.

The sixth table is concerned with the median length of time, in months, that houses are on the sales market. This measure is calculated separately for all houses sold during the month and for houses still for sale at the end of the month. In both cases, time on the market is measured from the month of the housing start, and data are given both unadjusted and seasonally adjusted. In the case of houses still for sale at the end of the month, time on the market is also measured from the month of completion. These numbers are not seasonally adjusted.

In addition to the six regular monthly tables, the C–25 series has four tables of quarterly data on new house sales and prices. These appear in the March, June, September, and December issues. The first of these tables contains data on the number and percent of new houses sold during annual and quarterly periods by 10 sales price categories ranging from under $40,000 to $150,000 and over. Another table presents similar statistics for each of the four Census regions. The regional data are distributed among four price groups, from under $50,000 to $100,000 and over.

A third quarterly table shows, for annual as well as quarterly periods, the number and percent of new homes financed by each of the five alternative methods. The financing methods are FHA-insured loans, VA-guaranteed loans, conventional mortgages, Farmers Home Administration loans, and cash. The fourth quarterly C–25 table provides, by each type of financing, both median and average sales prices of new homes sold.

In each January issue of C–25, the Census Bureau publishes an appendix table containing the monthly seasonal indexes used to adjust various new home sales series. For most of the series, projected as well as historical seasonal factors are provided. In the case of new homes sold, however, the projected seasonal factors are given only for the Census regions. The U.S. seasonal index for homes sold cannot be projected, since it is an implicit index derived as the ratio of unadjusted houses sold to the sum of seasonally adjusted houses sold in the four regions.

The data series for which past and projected monthly and seasonal factors are published are: new houses for sale, the ratio of houses for sale to houses sold, and median months on the sales market for houses sold and for houses for sale. The seasonal indexes for the two time-on-the-market series apply to data calculated from the month of housing start, not completion.

Data Limitations

Several features of the C–25 data on house sales and prices may tend to reduce the accuracy and reliability of the data.

In the data collection process, a relatively large imputation factor is used in the first estimate of houses sold. One reason is to cover late reports for new houses sold prior to the issuance of a building permit in permit places and prior to start in nonpermit areas. Another is for late reports on houses sold subsequent to authorization or start, usually the result of failure to contact respondents. Although the published data reflecting imputations are subsequently revised as actual reports come in, the preliminary data should probably be interpreted with caution.

The basic concept of a house sale used for the C–25 reports is one that might, under certain mortgage market conditions, produce misleading information on sales and prices. The Census Bureau counts a house as sold when a contract is signed or a deposit made. Subsequently, however, there are no follow-up interviews to determine whether, in fact, the sale was closed. The possibility that the aggregate price measures reflect new house sales that did not occur, or occurred at other-than-reported prices, makes the accuracy of the data subject to question. In addition, even in the majority of the cases where reported sales occur, final selling prices could differ from initial contract prices because of changes made to new homes by builders prior to closing.

PRICE INDEX OF NEW ONE-FAMILY HOMES
SOLD (C–27)

Four times a year, in March, June, September, and December, the Census Bureau publishes the C–27 *Construction Reports*, a series devoted exclusively to price information on new one-family houses sold. The C–27 reports feature one house price-indicator that is not among those included in the C–25 series on new homes sold and for sale. This indicator is the quarterly price index of new one-family houses sold, which is intended to measure changes over time in the sales price of new homes of consistently the same quality. The price index provides a basis for calculating the rate of house price change that is due to inflation and other nonquality factors. In addition, the rate of change in the price index, when compared to the rate of change in average sales price of homes actually sold for the same period, reveals the direction and the extent of the shift in homebuyer preferences toward higher- or lower-quality homes.

Like the new home price data contained in the C–25 reports, the price index of new one-family homes sold is a product of the housing sales survey. The price index, however, is unique in that its calculation draws on detailed information on the physical characteristics of new homes sold, which has been obtained since the beginning of the survey in 1963. The end product is a 1977-based index of the sales price of new houses that are, with respect to 10 characteristics, the same as the houses sold in the United States in 1977. The 10 characteristics used to calculate the average sales price of "kinds of houses sold in 1977" are floor area, number of stories, number of bathrooms, air conditioning, type of parking facility, type of foundation, geographic division within region, metropolitan area location, presence of fireplace, and size of lot. Prior to 1974, eight characteristics, not including fireplace and lot size, were used. A multiple regression procedure involving these 10 basic characteristics is used to show what the average price on this kind of house would have been in time periods other than 1977. Index numbers are then calculated from these estimated average prices.

Since the 10 characteristics account for approximately two thirds of the variation in selling prices of new one-family houses, changes in the average price of "kinds of houses sold" reflect relatively little quality difference from one period to the next as compared to changes in average actual transactions prices. Both price series, however, reflect a variety of other influences on house price movements. These include supply factors such as wage rates, materials costs, and productivity and demand factors such as demographic changes and the cost and availability of mortgage funds to homebuyers.

The C–27 reports present the house price data in two regular quarterly tables and in one annual table appearing in the fourth-quarter issue published in March. The first quarterly table contains the price index for the same kinds of houses as those sold in 1977. The data are given for the period from 1963 to the most current quarter or year. The U.S. data are annual and quarterly. The data for the Census regions are annual only.

The second quarterly table contains average sales prices, in dollars, of kinds of new one-family houses sold, and of new houses actually sold, for annual and quarterly periods. These data are for the United States. The same data are given for Census regions, annually back to 1963, in the annual table appearing in the fourth-quarter C–27 issues.

RESIDENTIAL ALTERATIONS AND REPAIRS (C–50)

The Census Bureau compiles quarterly estimates of expenditures made by property owners (but not by renters) for maintenance and repairs of residential properties and for construction improvements to these properties. For this purpose, residential properties are defined as all those having at least half of the enclosed space devoted to nontransient residential use. Publicly and privately owned structures are covered in the data. Both farm and nonfarm properties and properties that are either occupied or vacant are included. Each ownership unit for which expenditures are reported consists of the land, all residential structures on the land, and any facilities attached to the land.

The data tabulated in this series refer to expenditures on the main dwelling or another structure incidental to the use of the main dwelling. Expenditures on the grounds—other than for gardening—are also included. Generally, the payments must be for work done under contract or by hired labor, for materials purchased by owners, and for the cost of tool and equipment rental. Excluded are the cost of purchased tools, the value of labor in do-it-yourself jobs, and financing costs arising out of installment borrowing by property owners.

The types of expenditures covered in the C–50 reports differ basically. Maintenance and repair expenditures are current costs for property upkeep rather than additional investment in a property. Expenditures on construction improvements are usually considered as capital investment in property. These fall into two main categories—additions and alterations to properties, and major replacements of such items as furnace, roof, plumbing, and electrical wiring. In preparing the estimate of residential investment for the GNP accounts, the Commerce Department includes expenditures on additions and alterations, but not those for major replacements. The distinction between the two is that replacements, however costly, do not create anything new.

The Census Bureau obtains the data presented in the C–50 reports through two sample surveys in 103 areas (counties or groups of counties) throughout the nation. In one survey, owners living in their own one-to-four-unit residential properties are interviewed personally. In 1982, approximately 4,900 owner-occupied housing units were sampled; of these, about 98 percent were interviewed. In the second survey, the nonresidential owners of one-to-four-unit properties and all owners of larger structures are sent mail questionnaires. Approximately 94 percent of these nonresident owners provide information in each quarter.

The C–50 *Construction Reports* are issued quarterly and annually. The quarterly edition contains five data tables. The first table provides statistics by individual categories on total expenditures for residential alterations and repairs. These include maintenance and repairs, total construction improvements, additions and alterations, and major replacements. Additions and alterations are divided into three subcategories—additions to residential structures, alterations to residential structures, and additions and alterations to property outside of residential structures. The latter would include, for example, spending for the construction of swimming pools, detached garages, and greenhouses. These quarterly and annual data are given for all residential properties, one-unit owner-occupied properties, one-to-four-unit owner-occupied properties, and one-to-four-unit properties not owner-occupied plus all properties with five or more units.

The second table provides up to 10 years of quarterly data on expenditures for upkeep and improvement on all residential properties. The spending categories differ from those in the first table in that all additions and alterations are combined under one heading. All expenditure statistics are at seasonally adjusted annual rates. In addition, for each spending category and each year shown, the seasonal indexes used to adjust the raw data are given.

The third table shows the total of all expenditures of $25 or more on one-unit owner-occupied housing and gives a breakdown of the total between payments to contractor or hired labor and payments for building materials purchased by the owner. The data are annual and quarterly.

The fourth table contains data for one-to-four-unit owner-occupied properties on average expenditures per property and for average and median expenditures per property with expenditures. Also given are distributions of total expenditures and of total properties by categories of expenditure size. These data are provided quarterly for the current and preceding three years.

The fifth table presents quarterly data on total expenditures for additions and alterations to all residential properties, at seasonally adjusted annual rates and deflated by the Census Bureau's price index of new one-family homes of the kind sold in 1977 (from the C–27 *Construction Reports*).

The annual issues of the C–50 reports present basically the same type of data as the quarterly reports, but with added detail. Annual spending figures are further broken down by type of job (e.g., plumbing, roofing, painting), Census region, year structure was built, and year the owner making the expenditure moved into the structure.

Data Limitations

The sampling errors of some estimates in the C–50 data series are too great to allow comparisons involving these items to be meaningful. The data on additions to residential structures have a particularly high error, and the statistics for other types of construction improvements also tend to be unreliable on a quarterly basis. Quarterly estimates of payments to contractors by owners of one-family houses may also be wide of the mark. In cases such as these, it is recommended that the figures be regarded as orders of magnitude rather than absolute measurements and that quarterly changes be viewed with caution.

VALUE OF NEW CONSTRUCTION PUT IN PLACE (C–30)

The value of new construction put in place is a dollar measurement of the value of construction installed or erected at a site during a given period. For each project, it includes the cost of materials and labor, a proportionate share of the cost of construction equipment rental, the project owner's overhead costs, the contractor's profit, architectural and engineering fees, interest and taxes paid during construction, and miscellaneous costs charged to the project owner. The value-in-place concept does not include land value or the cost of land acquisition. It also does not include maintenance or repairs on existing structures or the replacement of major equipment items.

The Census Bureau calculates monthly estimates of the total value put in place as the sum of the value put in place on all projects under way during the month, regardless of when work on each individual project was started or when payments were made to contractors. The data, published monthly in the C–30 *Construction Reports*, cover all new residential and nonresidential construction in the United States, including projects owned privately and those owned by federal, state, or local governments. In this chapter, we are concerned only with the residential portion of the C–30 data.

The bulk of the value created by private residential construction activ ity stems from the production of new housing units, and most of the remainder arises out of additions and alterations to existing buildings. A minor portion reflects the construction of nonhousekeeping residential buildings, such as hotels and dormitories.

Published estimates of value in place for these categories are obtained in different ways. The data on nonhousekeeping residential buildings are derived from the same survey that is used to estimate the value of private nonresidential buildings put in place. The data on additions and alterations are estimates of expenditures made by property owners, based on the Census Bureau's quarterly survey and reported in the quarterly C–50 *Construction Reports*. The monthly value-in-place estimates for additions and alterations are interpolations from actual quarterly data or, until actual data become available, extrapolations from a linear regression of seasonally adjusted estimates. For new housing units, the monthly value-in-place data are estimates derived by distributing the total cost of individual projects over months according to past construction progress patterns.

The value of new housing units put in place reflects separate estimating procedures for one-unit housing and two-or-more-unit buildings. The data on one-unit houses are derived from the building permits survey and the housing starts survey. The estimated construction cost is obtained by multiplying the number of units started by the average cost per unit. For permit-issuing areas, the average cost per unit is the average permit value, as reported in approved permit applications, increased by 17.6 percent. Of this adjustment, 13.9 percent is made to compensate for permit undervaluation and the remaining 3.7 percent is to cover architectural and engineering fees. For nonpermit areas, the average cost per unit is derived as 95 percent of the average value for permit-covered units.

The combined cost of single houses in permit and nonpermit areas is converted into monthly value-in-place estimates using data on construction progress patterns. According to these data, about 75 percent of one-unit houses are completed in the fourth month of construction and 85 percent in the fifth month. Progress is the fastest for buildings started in June and July and the slowest for those started in October and November.

The value-in-place estimates for buildings of two or more units are measured directly from monthly progress reports of a sample of new residential construction projects selected from housing units reported in the housing starts survey. Once a project is selected, monthly construction progress reports are requested from the owner until it is completed. About 2,500 projects are in the sample each month, including both newly selected projects and carry-over projects from previous months.

The monthly value-in-place estimates of private residential construction in current dollars are converted to a 1977 constant-dollar series on the basis of two indexes. One of these is the Census Bureau's quarterly price index of new one-family houses sold, which measures changes in the sales price of homes which are the same with respect to 10 characteristics as homes sold in 1977. For the purpose of value-in-place estimates, this price index is adjusted to exclude the value of the lot. Information on lot value has been provided since 1969 by the Census Bureau's housing sales survey. The second deflator used for residential value-in-place estimates is the monthly index of national construction cost for buildings, compiled by the Engineering News–Record with a 1913 base and converted to a 1977 base by the Census Bureau. This index has three materials components—steel, cement, and lumber—and one labor component—a 20-city average cost for skilled labor.

The Role of Residential Activity in Total Construction Value Put in Place

As mentioned earlier, the value-in-place statistics published monthly in C–30 *Construction Reports* cover all private and public construction in the United States, both residential and nonresidential. During the five years 1978–82, the nonresidential portion accounted for 60 percent of total construction value put in place and the residential portion for 40 percent. Nonresidential construction includes such projects as commercial and industrial buildings, public utilities, and highways and sewers. The residential portion includes all new private housing units, additions and alterations to existing properties, and nonhousekeeping residential buildings as well as publicly owned residential construction activity.

During the five years ended 1982, the public sector accounted for less than 2 percent of residential value put in place. Of the public activity, state and local government-owned projects accounted for 90 percent.

Data Publications

The monthly C–30 reports consist of 10 standard tables of U.S. monthly or annual data. These contain detailed breakdowns of private and public construction by type. In addition, public construction data are given for separate ownership categories—federal, and state and local. All data are presented in both current dollars and 1977 dollars, and monthly data are shown in unadjusted form and at seasonally adjusted annual rates. Value-in-place estimates for the Census regions and divisions are published on an annual basis only, and then only for state and local government construction.

Residential Investment in the GNP Accounts

The Census Bureau's estimates of construction value put in place are the basic source of the estimates of fixed investment in residential structures contained in the nation's GNP accounts. The GNP data are prepared by the Bureau of Economic Analysis (BEA) of the U.S. Department of Commerce, using the Census Bureau data and other sources.

The GNP data on investment in residential structures differ somewhat from the Census Bureau's residential value-in-place total, reflecting differences in coverage and in estimation procedures. With respect to coverage, the GNP data exclude hotels and recreational-type buildings from the residential category, instead counting them as nonresidential investment. The data, however, include other nonhousekeeping residences such as dormitories and nursing homes. The GNP estimates of residential investment also incorporate certain expenditures that are not in the value-in-place estimates. These are the value of mobile home sales, brokers' commissions on the sale of new and existing structures, net purchases of used government-owned structures by the private sector, and investment in producers' durable equipment needed for construction.

MOVEMENTS IN SELECTED CONSTRUCTION INDICATORS

In this section, we present exhibits depicting movements in the major indicators of residential construction activity, since the early 1970s in the case of data plotted quarterly and earlier for annual series. So that they will cover a period containing more than one business cycle, monthly time series are plotted on a quarterly basis. The exhibits will demonstrate both the response of the residential construction markets to economic and financial change over the business cycle and changes in the characteristics of new construction.

Exhibit 1:   Quarterly Rates of Change in GNP and Private Fixed Residential Investment

The data plotted in this exhibit are quarterly percentage growth rates, compounded annually, in GNP and private fixed residential investment. The rates are calculated from dollar GNP and residential investment data deflated to remove the effects of price change on the series. Thus, the exhibit illustrates changes in real activity in the economy and in residential investment activity.

Even on a quarterly basis, Exhibit 1 shows residential investment to be erratic and extremely volatile relative to the behavior of overall activity in the economy. Nevertheless, there is a clear-cut cyclical pattern in

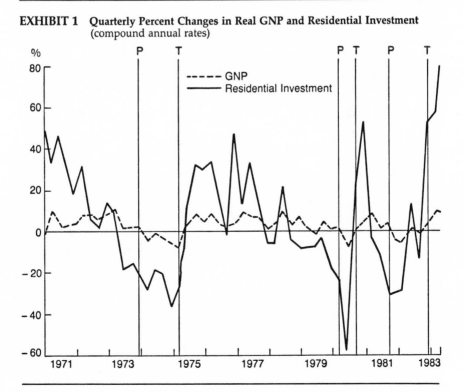

EXHIBIT 1   Quarterly Percent Changes in Real GNP and Residential Investment (compound annual rates)

residential spending, with rapid positive growth early in business expansions giving way to sharp declines later. The vertical lines in the exhibit mark off the major cyclical phases of economic activity—expansions from trough to peak and contractions from peak to trough. As can be seen, residential investment begins to weaken well before business cycle peaks and to start rising while the economy is still in recession. In all three recessions shown, 1973–75, 1980, and 1981–82, the residential sector helped to lead the economy out of recession.

Exhibit 2:   *Private Fixed Residential Investment and Market Rate on Three-Month U.S. Treasury Bills*

Residential investment expenditures, deflated by cost indexes to reflect real activity, are here plotted against a short-term money market rate—that on three-month U.S. Treasury bills. From the exhibit, it is evident that the cyclical pattern of residential spending is the inverse of the cyclical pattern of interest rates. Also, it is apparent that the unusually sharp rise of interest rates beginning around the mid-1970s and the

EXHIBIT 2   Residential Investment and Market Rate on Three-Month Treasury Bills

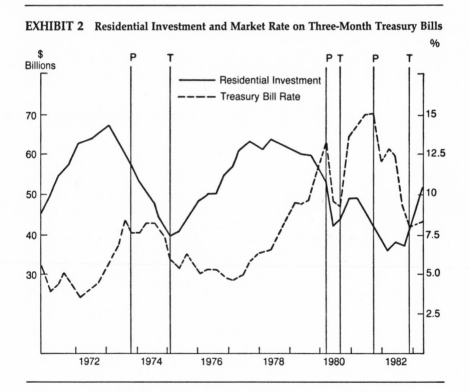

unprecedentedly high rate levels prevailing since then have been accompanied by depressed real residential investment.

Higher interest rates have worked to restrain housing activity through their effects on the availability and cost of mortgage financing. Prior to 1978, interest rates payable on savings accounts in thrift institutions were held by government regulation to rigid and often unrealistically low ceilings. When market rates of interest rose above these ceilings, savers withdrew funds from savings accounts to invest directly in money market instruments. As a result of this "disintermediation" process, thrift institutions—the main providers of home mortgage credit—experienced shortages of funds leading to a curtailment of lending.

In 1978, the regulatory authorities allowed thrifts and banks to issue a new savings instrument—the money market certificate (MMC)—with issuing rates tied to the weekly auction rate on six-month U.S. Treasury bills. Subsequently, under the guidance of the Depository Institutions Deregulation Committee (DIDC) set up by the Congress for the purpose, deregulation has proceeded to the point where there are virtually no restrictions on rates or terms of savings accounts. While thrift institutions can now obtain any desired-volume funds during high-rate periods, residential market activity is still depressed at these times by mortgage lending rates that are unacceptable or unaffordable for consumers.

Exhibit 3: Value of Residential Construction Put in Place in Current and Constant Dollars

Trends in nominal and real expenditures on new private residential construction, as defined in the Census C–30 value-in-place reports, are illustrated in Exhibit 3. While the concept of residential spending is somewhat narrower here than in the GNP accounts, the cyclical pattern is identical to that in the GNP data. As seen, the weakening trend of real residential construction after the mid-1970s occurred as the current-dollar value of construction put in place rose to new peaks. These divergent trends reflect a sharp acceleration in construction cost inflation.

Exhibit 4: Comparative Rates of Change in Residential Construction Costs and Consumer Prices

The rates of inflation shown in this exhibit are year-over-year percent changes in quarterly indexes of construction cost and consumer prices. The construction cost index is implicit in the published C–40 data on residential construction value put in place. It is calculated as the current-dollar value of residential construction put in place divided by the value in 1977 dollars.

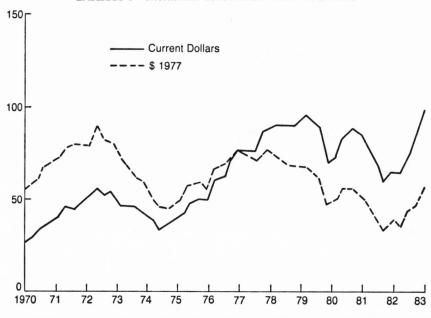

EXHIBIT 3 Residential Construction Value Put in Place

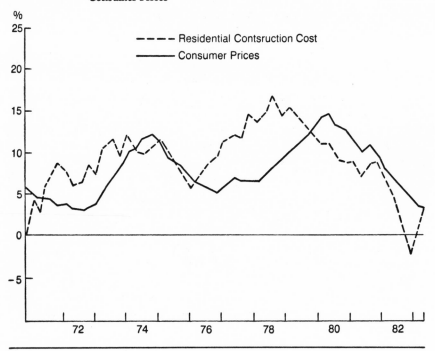

EXHIBIT 4 Comparative Rates of Change in Residential Construction Cost and Consumer Prices

Residential construction costs respond very quickly to changes in the demand for housing. As Exhibit 4 shows, construction cost inflation starts to accelerate early in business expansions, reflecting the lead role of housing activity in the economy.

While the inflation of construction costs exceeded overall price inflation during most of the 1970s, it entered a long, steep slide in 1979 which kept it beneath the consumer inflation rate until mid-1983. The pronounced weakening of construction costs in the late 1970s and early 1980s reflected a sharp reduction in housing demand induced by historically high mortgage interest rates and the earlier steep rise in residential building costs.

Exhibit 5:   Real Spending for Additions and Alterations and Increase in Prices of Existing One-Family Homes

Real spending by property owners on additions and alterations to existing homes was sustained at relatively high levels in the 1970s and

EXHIBIT 5   Real Spending for Additions and Alterations and Increase in Selling Price of Existing Homes

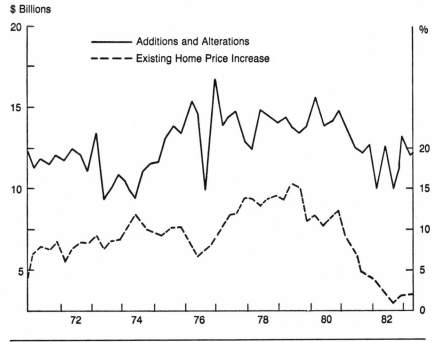

early 1980s, contrary to the trend of weakening in total residential investment. As seen in the exhibit, spending on additions and alterations did not show a decline of any significance until 1982. The strong pattern of such spending is consistent with the acute inflation of new home selling prices that persisted at rates of over 10 percent through mid-1980. In that environment, remodeling or expanding a home already owned was, for many, an affordable alternative to purchasing a new home. Although new home prices stopped rising in 1982 and actually fell in the final quarter, the decline in spending on additions and alterations has so far been moderate. With mortgage interest rates remaining in the 13 percent area, home remodeling will continue to be of interest to property owners with low-rate mortgages.

Exhibit 6:   Percent of Private Housing Starts Occurring in Permit-Issuing Places

The exhibit contains regional data, for annual periods beginning with 1963, on the percent of new residential construction occurring in places identified by the Census Bureau as having building permit systems. During this time span, the number of permit places included in the

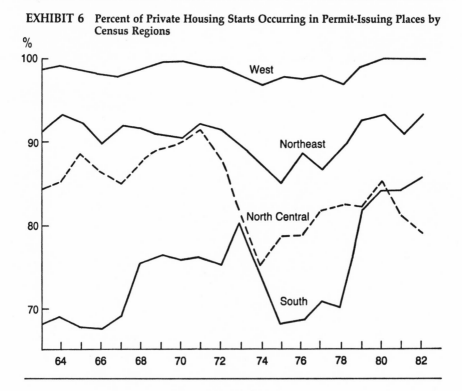

EXHIBIT 6   Percent of Private Housing Starts Occurring in Permit-Issuing Places by Census Regions

building permits universe rose from 12,000 in 1963 to 16,000 in 1982, and the coverage of construction activity by the building permits data series, nationally, rose from 83 percent to 89 percent.

Exhibit 6 is intended to demonstrate that there is a fairly significant variation in the use of building permit systems among Census regions and that, therefore, the value of the housing permits series as an indicator of future construction may be greater in some regions than in others. Also, the exhibit shows that the national trend of increase in permit coverage of construction reflects increases in all regions but the North Central and a particularly sharp improvement in the South.

Exhibit 7:   *Private New Housing Units Authorized by Permits and Rate of Change in Nonfarm Payroll Employment*

Trends in housing permit activity reflect the sensitivity of housing demand to economic change, particularly as it affects the consumer.

EXHIBIT 7   Private New Housing Authorized by Permits and Rate of Change in Nonagricultural Payroll Employment

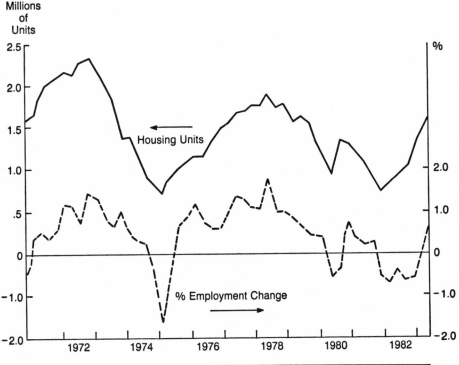

This shows clearly in Exhibit 7, where private housing units authorized by permits are plotted against percentage changes in nonfarm payroll employment. During the 1970s and early 1980s, permit activity responded quickly to change in the employment situation, with major turning points in employment growth and permit issuance corresponding almost exactly.

Exhibit 8:   New Single-Family Housing Units Authorized by Permits, and Rate on Fixed-Rate Conventional Mortgages to Homebuyers

From this exhibit, it is evident that even relatively small changes in the mortgage interest rate to homebuyers have direct short-run effects on permit activity in the single-family housing market. It is also apparent, however, that over time this market can adapt itself to higher levels of interest rates. For example, during the period from 1977 to 1980 when the mortgage lending rate accelerated upward from about 9 percent to

EXHIBIT 8   New Single-Family Housing Units Authorized by Permits, and Rate on Fixed-Rate Conventional Mortgages to Homebuyers

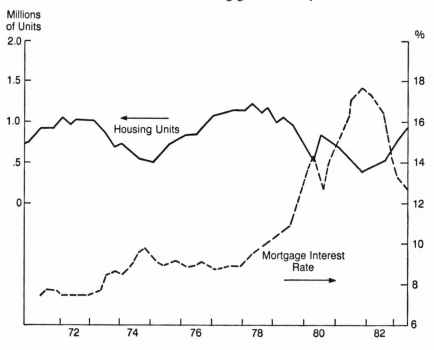

an unprecedented 14 percent, single-family permit activity remained above its cyclical low of early 1975. At mid-1983, new permits for single homes were being issued at a relatively high annual rate of one million units with the mortgage lending rate at more than 13 percent. The mortgage interest rate plotted in the chart is the rate charged by savings and loan associations for 80 percent loan-to-value, 30-year conventional fixed-rate loans.

Exhibit 9:   Private Housing Starts

This exhibit illustrates trends in all private new residential construction activity over recent business cycles, and it also provides an indication of the comparative size and behavior of the single-family and multifamily markets. As the exhibit suggests, one-family construction has accounted for about two thirds of total private housing starts, on average, since 1969. Of the remainder of housing activity, four fifths has been in apartment buildings—large multifamily structures of five or more units.

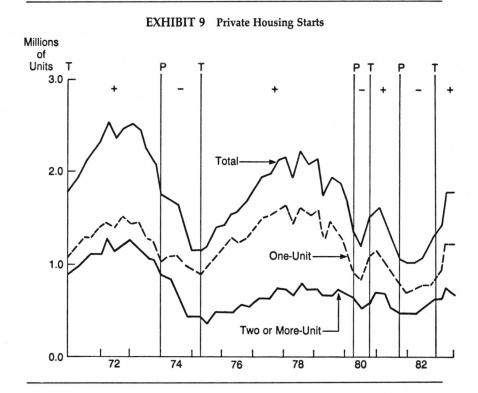

EXHIBIT 9   Private Housing Starts

Cyclical patterns of activity in the single- and multifamily housing markets tend to be basically similar, as seen in Exhibit 9. Both types of construction activity peak out and begin declining several quarters in advance of the business cycle peak, and both tend to revive while the economy is in recession. During the recession of 1973–75 and the ensuing expansion lasting through early 1980, however, the multifamily pattern diverged sharply. Starts in two-or-more-unit buildings fell precipitously during the recession and barely recovered in the expansion, never regaining the high levels prior to the recession.

Exhibit 10: *Multifamily Housing Starts and the Rental Vacancy Rate*

This exhibit throws into sharper focus the prolonged recession in multifamily construction activity occurring after 1972. As seen, the precipitous drop in multifamily activity during 1973–75 followed a sharp surge in such activity in 1971–72 to unprecedented levels of 900,000 to 1 million units per year. As also illustrated in the exhibit, the early 1970s

EXHIBIT 10   Multifamily Housing Starts and the Rental Vacancy Rate

boom in multifamily construction caused a concurrent rise in the rental vacancy rate, indicating that the market was considerably overbuilt. Subsequently, the flat recovery of multifamily activity contrasted with the relatively dynamic revival of single-family desire for homeowner-ship during this period of inflation and rapid escalation of house prices.

Exhibit 11:   Private Starts of One-Family Homes and Builder's Supply of Unsold Inventories

The fundamental forces determining trends in single-family house .starts are housing needs, construction costs, mortgage interest rates, and the building industry's capacity to produce. The timing of these starts, however, is also influenced by the inventory situation in the new home market. As seen in Exhibit 11, changes in single-family starts on a quarterly basis move inversely to changes in the builders' inventory burden. This burden is measured as the median number of months'

EXHIBIT 11   Private Starts of One-Family Homes and Builders' Supply of Unsold Inventories

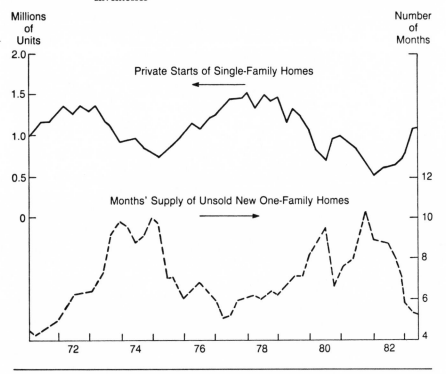

supply of unsold homes on the market at the current selling rate, and it is reported in the C–25 Census reports.

CONCLUSION

In this chapter, we have described the basic data available from the federal government on residential construction activity, as well as the form and content of the printed reports in which they are published. It should be noted that these construction activity data may be obtained by other means. The Bureau of the Census makes available on microfiche, within two months after they are issued in print, all publications that provide final data from censuses and surveys. Census will also prepare for a particular customer, at cost, special tabulations from their data files according to mutually agreed-upon specifications. These tabulations can be furnished on tape or as a computer printout. In addition, in tape or printout, the Census Bureau will also provide unpublished data on building permits for residential (and nonresidential) construction. Specifically, monthly data may be obtained for 10,500 individual permit places of the current 16,000-place universe, or more than twice as many places as are covered each month in the printed reports.

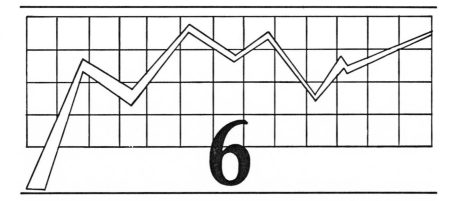

Unemployment and Associated Measures*

Janet L. Norwood, Ph.D.
Commissioner
Bureau of Labor Statistics
U.S. Department of Labor

The unemployment rate is as well known to the public today as the world series and super bowl scores. It is no wonder. The popular notion is that the unemployment rate has become a barometer of the success or failure of government policies to improve the state of the economy. But we must look far beyond the unemployment rate itself for these judgments. Unemployment statistics represent people—people seeking a first job, people changing jobs, and people losing jobs. The jobless figures and related data released by the Bureau of Labor Statistics on the first Friday of every month provide a comprehensive set of data which make up what might be called a management information system of social and economic data for monitoring the U.S. economy. Although employment and unemployment figures have been used by economic analysts and policymakers for over 40 years, the data are not always well understood.

---

* The author wishes to express thanks for the contributions of Robert W. Bednarzik and Harvey R. Hamel of the Bureau of Labor Statistics staff.

BACKGROUND

Our modern systems of surveying households to measure unemployment began in 1940 with the Works Progress Administration (WPA). Prior to that time, some attempts had been made to determine the number of "gainful workers" through decennial censuses of population. These estimates, however, were not based upon statistical samples, and the definitions used were often vague and limited in scope.[1] Attempts at clarification of concepts occurred in 1935 in a census for the state of Michigan and in a 1937 WPA enumerative check census using probability sampling techniques. These were followed by WPA experimental surveys in local labor markets and finally by the WPA monthly sample survey of unemployment in 1940.

Responsibility for the monthly survey was transferred to the Census Bureau in 1942. The survey was renamed the monthly report on the labor force, and in the mid-1940s, Census introduced a revised survey questionnaire and new approaches to sample selection, data coverage, and survey size.

Changes in survey techniques and concepts were introduced through most of the 1940s. In 1947, the survey assumed its present name, the Current Population Survey (CPS); and concepts and techniques were further standardized. Thus, the year 1948 really marks the start of the modern era of labor force statistics.[2] Official data are available for comparison as far back as 1948, although users need to take account of the effect of changes introduced since that time.[3]

Overall responsibility for concepts, analysis, and publication of labor force data was shifted from the Census Bureau to the Bureau of Labor Statistics (BLS) in 1959. Since that time, BLS has contracted with Census to carry out survey operations. The BLS is the program agency responsible for concept, content, and analysis. It carries out the seasonal adjustment of the estimates, analyzes and publishes the data, and maintains the historical files. Initial publication takes place in "The Employment Situation" news release, which typically is issued by the BLS on the first Friday of the month following the reference month. Data in much greater detail appear later in the BLS monthly labor force data compen-

---

[1] Among other things, no fixed reference period was established, retirees were included, new workers were excluded, and employment status was not clearly differentiated from unemployment status.

[2] Labor force series back to 1900 have been constructed retrospectively. See Stanley Lebergott, *Manpower in Economic Growth: The American Record since 1800* (New York: McGraw-Hill, 1964).

[3] For a detailed account of the history of the CPS sample design, see *The Current Population Survey: Design and Methodology*, Technical Paper No. 40, Bureau of the Census, U.S. Department of Commerce, January 1978; or Bureau of Labor Statistics, *Concepts and Methods Used in Labor Force Statistics Derived from the Current Population Survey*, Report 463, October 1976.

dium, *Employment and Earnings*. Much of the analysis appears in special articles in the BLS journal, the *Monthly Labor Review*.

The official definition of unemployment has gone through several stages of development. Several independent reviews of the entire data system have been conducted over the years, and many of the recommendations that were made have been implemented. In 1957, for example, two groups previously classified as employed were added to the unemployment count—persons on temporary layoff who expected to return to work within 30 days and persons, except students, waiting to start new jobs within 30 days.[4]

The unemployment definition was changed again in 1967 to implement recommendations of a presidentially appointed committee chaired by Professor Robert A. Gordon of the University of California and usually referred to as the Gordon Committee.[5] The job search time period required for classification as unemployed was extended to the four weeks prior to the survey. In addition, those classified as unemployed had to be currently available for work. An important implication of the 1967 changes was that those not working who *volunteered* that they had not sought work in the immediate past either because of illness or because no jobs were available were excluded from the unemployment totals. Although not a specific recommendation of the Gordon Committee, 14–15-year-olds were dropped from the labor force counts in the 1967 revisions.[6]

Whenever unemployment rises, the system for compiling the figures is subjected to intensive examination, and considerable controversy arises at times. In response to the heightened interest in the concepts and methodology used to arrive at the measure during the 1970s, another presidential commission was established in 1978—the National Commission on Employment and Unemployment Statistics (NCEUS), chaired by Professor Sar Levitan of George Washington University.[7] After deliberating for 18 months, the NCEUS found the national employment and unemployment statistics fundamentally sound and left the basic labor force definitions almost completely intact.[8] One impor-

---

[4] These changes were recommended in the "Interim Report of the Review of Concepts Subcommittee to the Committee on Labor Supply, Employment, and Unemployment Statistics." Employment and Unemployment Statistics, Joint Economic Committee, 84th Congress, 1st Session, November 7–8, 1955, p. 7.

[5] President's Committee to Appraise Employment and Unemployment Statistics, *Measuring Employment and Unemployment* (Washington, D.C.: Government Printing Office, 1962). Also see Robert L. Stein, "New Definitions for Employment and Unemployment," *Employment and Earnings and Monthly Report on the Labor Force*, February 1967, pp. 1–25.

[6] Ibid.

[7] John E. Bregger, "Establishment of a New Employment Statistics Review Commission," *Monthly Labor Review*, March 1977, pp. 14–20.

[8] National Commission on Employment and Unemployment Statistics, *Counting the Labor Force* (Washington, D.C.: Government Printing Office, 1979).

tant recommendation was for publication of an overall national unemployment rate including resident members of the Armed Forces in the labor force and the employed. The Bureau of Labor Statistics began publication of the new series in January 1983.[9] Consistency over time was maintained by providing the new series back to 1950. All civilian-based data series have also continued to be retained.

MEASUREMENT

Current Population Survey (CPS)

The official unemployment figures continue to be derived from the CPS—a scientifically designed monthly sample survey of some 60,000 households across the nation. The sample is designed to reflect urban and rural areas, different types of industrial and farming areas, and the major geographic divisions of the country in the same proportion as they occur in the nation as a whole.[10]

In order to reduce the burden on respondents, a household is interviewed for four consecutive months, omitted from the interviewing for the following eight months, and then interviewed for four more months before being dropped from the sample for good. Personal visits are combined with telephone collection in order to develop data of high quality within operational cost constraints.

The data collected in the survey refer to the week containing the 12th day of the month, the "survey reference week." Trained interviewers contact a responsible person in each sample household to obtain, through a carefully structured questionnaire, data on each household member 16 years old and over. Each person is classified as employed, unemployed, or out of the labor force, as a result of their responses to the survey questions. The results are then adjusted to independent population estimates, taking into account the age, sex, race, and urban-rural distribution of the population.

Employment and Unemployment Defined

The following basic definitions are used to classify survey respondents as employed or unemployed. To be counted as *employed*, a person must have worked for 1 hour or more for pay or profit during the

---

[9] Ibid., pp. 49–51. Also see John E. Bregger, "Labor Force Data from the CPS to Undergo Revision in January 1983," *Monthly Labor Review*, November 1982, pp. 3–6.

[10] For a more detailed discussion, see *The Current Population Survey: Design and Methodology*.

reference week or, if an unpaid family worker, for at least 15 hours without pay in a family farm or business. Also included as employed are those temporarily absent from a job for such reasons as illness, vacation, or industrial dispute, whether or not they were paid for the time off.

Persons are classified as *unemployed* if they did not work during the survey week, were available for work, and searched for a job sometime during the preceding four weeks. Workers on layoff (and thus expecting recall to their jobs) and persons waiting to start a new job within 30 days are classified as unemployed, even if they have not engaged in any job-seeking activity.[11]

The sum of the employed and the unemployed constitutes the *civilian labor force*. Persons not in the labor force combined with those in the civilian labor force constitute the civilian noninstitutional population 16 years old and over. The inclusion of the resident Armed Forces—based on figures obtained from the Department of Defense—yields total labor force and total noninstitutional population figures. The unemployment rate is obtained by dividing the number unemployed by the number in the labor force.

In order to permit analysis of economic change from one month to the next, the data are seasonally adjusted. Over the course of a year, the size of the nation's labor force and the levels of employment and unemployment regularly exhibit sharp movements due to such recurring seasonal events as changes in the weather, major holidays, harvests, and the opening and closing of schools. Because these events usually follow a regular pattern each year, their influence needs to be removed before economic trends can be fully assessed. The Bureau of Labor Statistics publishes the data both on a seasonally adjusted and on a nonadjusted basis to accomodate users with different purposes.[12]

VARIETY OF MEASURES AVAILABLE

It can be seen in Exhibit 1 that the nation has entered each recession with a higher unemployment rate than that which prevailed at the beginning of the preceding recession. Thus, because the 1981–82 recession started with the highest unemployment rate for any business cycle peak, the increase registered during the recession caused the jobless rate to be higher than that in any previous post–World War II recession. Numerous factors—including the entrance into the labor force of large numbers of women, minorities, and young workers, as well as other social and

---

[11] U.S. Department of Labor, Bureau of Labor Statistics, *How the Government Measures Unemployment*, Report 505 (Washington, D.C.: Government Printing Office, 1976).

[12] U.S. Department of Labor, Bureau of Labor Statistics, *A Guide to Seasonal Adjustment of Labor Force Data*, Bulletin 2114 (Washington, D.C.: Government Printing Office, 1982).

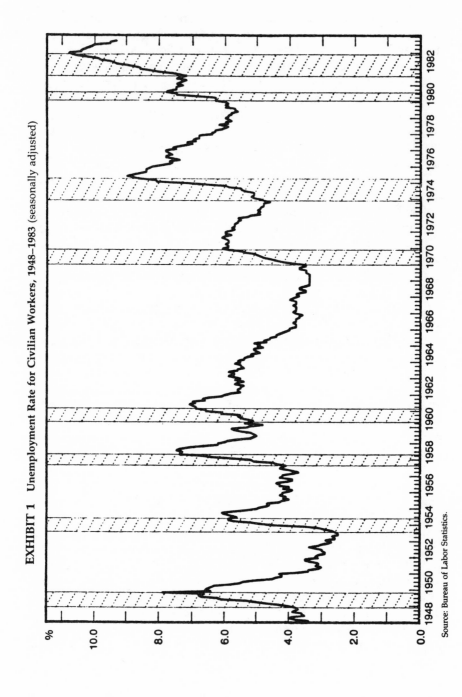

EXHIBIT 1 Unemployment Rate for Civilian Workers, 1948–1983 (seasonally adjusted)

Source: Bureau of Labor Statistics.

economic policy changes—have been suggested as partly responsible for this trend.[13]

To meet the multiple needs of data users, the Bureau of Labor Statistics publishes a wide variety of unemployment rates and indicators. One useful disaggregation of the data for analytical purposes is by the major age-sex groups—teenagers, adult men, and adult women. Exhibit 2 illustrates that, as would be expected, the incidence of joblessness is higher among young workers than among older ones. Teenagers have less experience than older workers, frequently combine school with periods of work, and change their employment status more frequently than older workers do. Over the postwar period, the jobless rate for teenagers averaged about twice the rate for adults. The rate for adult women is generally higher than that for men in good times as well as bad, although this relationship was reversed during most of the 1981–82 recession and into 1983. This reversal in pattern occurred because the recession was focused sharply in the goods-producing sector, especially durable goods manufacturing, where males represent a large proportion of the work force.

Data provided each month on the labor market experience of the minority population show that the nation's black workers have had an increasingly difficult time in the labor market, especially since the mid–1970s. The unemployment rates for black workers have for some time been more than twice the rates for whites, and the proportion of black adult males and teenagers who are employed (employment-population ratio) has been considerably lower than for whites.

The employment-population ratio, derived by dividing total employment by the noninstitutional population age 16 years and over, provides an indicator of the economy's ability to generate jobs for a changing population.[14] The unemployment rate may vary because of special developments that affect the extent of labor force growth. The employment-population ratio, on the other hand, is a relatively stable time series because its base is not affected by the continuity of job search activities and consequently by the shift of workers into and out of the labor force (see Exhibit 3).

Groups Identified with the Unemployed.   Data on the number of persons involuntarily working less than full time and the number of workers discouraged over job prospects, two groups often included in a broader context of overall underutilization of human resources, are also published on a regular basis. (See Exhibit 4.)

---

[13] For more on this topic, see series of articles in the *Monthly Labor Review*, March 1979, pp. 13–53.

[14] Carol Boyd Leon, "The Employment-Population Ratio: Its Value in Labor Force Analysis," *Monthly Labor Review*, February 1981, pp. 36–45.

EXHIBIT 2   Unemployment Rates by Major Age-Sex group, 1948–1983 (seasonally adjusted)

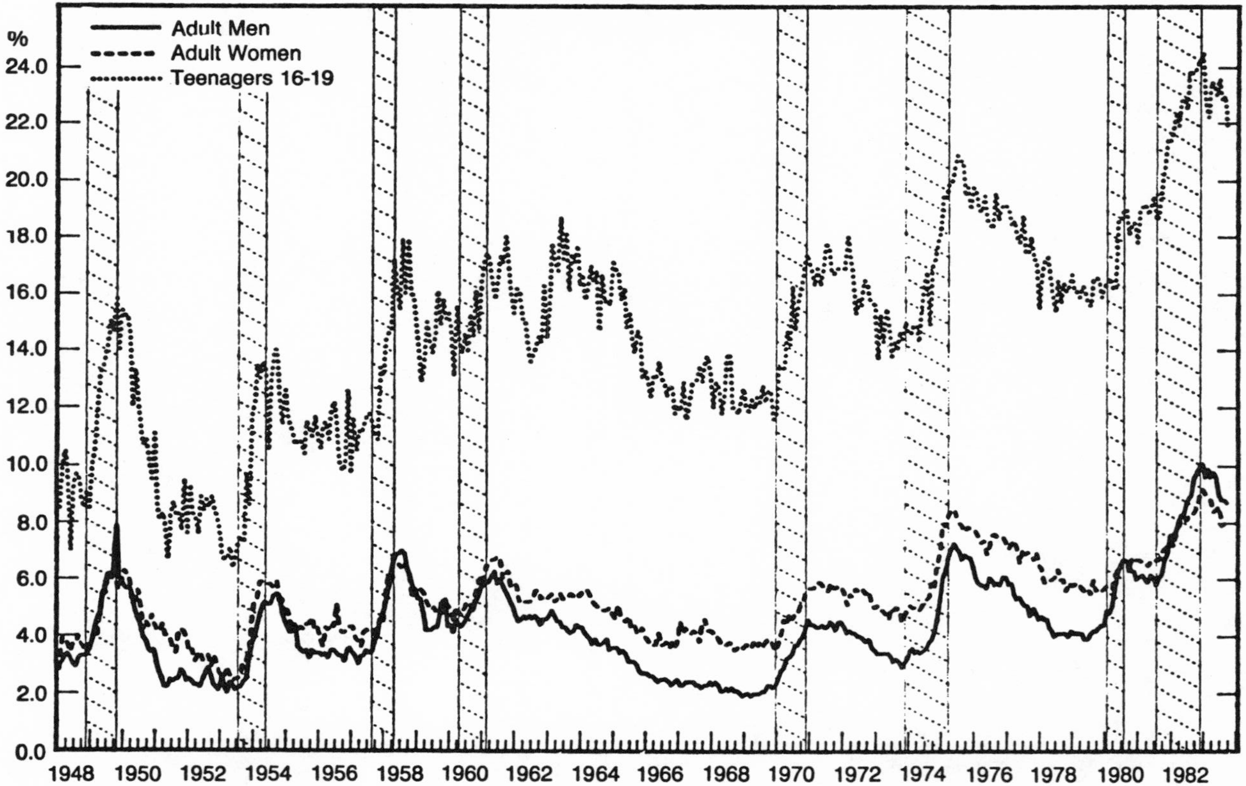

Adult Men
Adult Women
Teenagers 16-19

%
24.0
22.0
20.0
18.0
16.0
14.0
12.0
10.0
8.0
6.0
4.0
2.0
0.0

1948 1950 1952 1954 1956 1958 1960 1962 1964 1966 1968 1970 1972 1974 1976 1978 1980 1982

Source: Bureau of Labor Statistics.

EXHIBIT 3 Unemployment Rate and Employment-Population Ratio of all Civilian Workers, 1948–1983
(seasonally adjusted)

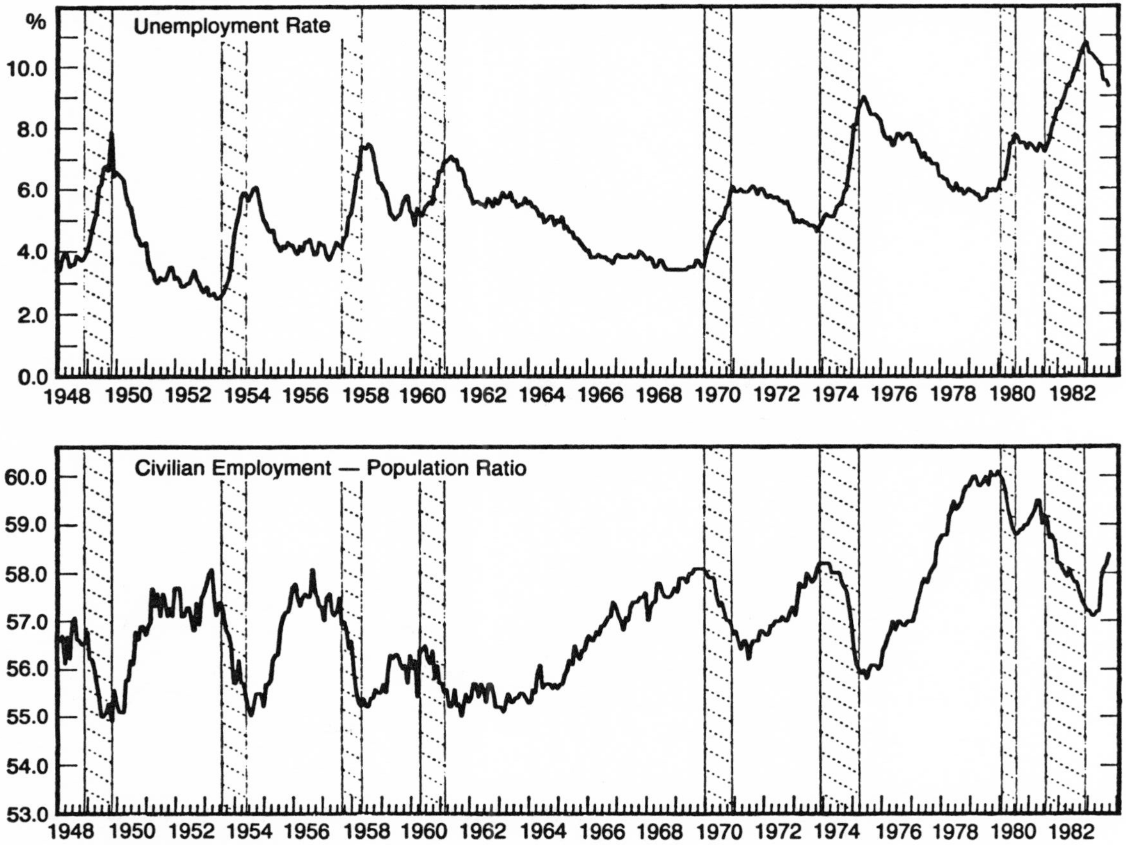

Source: Bureau of Labor Statistics.

EXHIBIT 4 The Number of Persons Unemployed, Employed Part Time for Economic Reasons, and Discouraged Workers, 1970–1983 (seasonally adjusted)

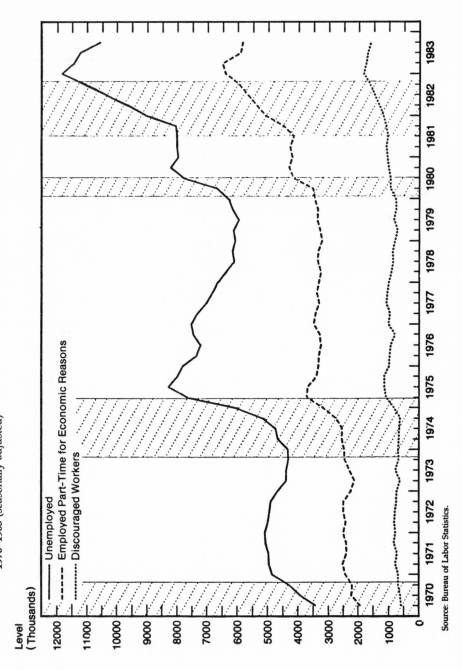

Source: Bureau of Labor Statistics.

Employed persons actually at work are divided into those on full-time schedules (35 hours or more a week) and those working part time (1–34 hours a week). Persons working less than 35 hours are asked their reasons for their short hours. Those who wish to work full time but are involuntarily on shortened workweeks—either because their hours were reduced or because a part-time job was all they could find—are classified as working *part time for economic reasons*. These data have been collected monthly beginning in May 1955.

Discouraged workers are persons who want to work but feel their search for a job would be in vain. Discouragement over job prospects is a state of mind which is sometimes difficult to measure with precision. Those classified as discouraged workers in the CPS are those who say they (*a*) are not working, (*b*) currently want a job, but (*c*) are not engaged in any job search because they believe that one cannot be found. Those who searched in the past but gave up or who believe that no jobs are available are classified as discouraged because of "job market factors." Those discouraged because they believe they lack the necessary skills, have handicaps, or believe they are too old or too young to be considered for employment are classified as discouraged because of "personal factors."

Data on labor force discouragement, available since 1967, are collected from only a part of the CPS sample, accumulated into quarterly averages, and published once each calendar quarter. The National Commission on Employment and Unemployment Statistics recommended that prior job search must have taken place sometime within the prior six months for a person to be counted as discouraged. This recommendation, accepted in reports to the Congress by Secretaries of Labor Ray Marshall and Raymond Donovan, is being tested by BLS and the Census Bureau.[15]

The NCEUS report supported continuation of the current BLS practice of counting discouraged workers as outside of the labor force. Although persons involuntarily working part time or classified in the survey as discouraged are excluded from the official measures of unemployment, the Bureau of Labor Statistics also publishes an unem-

---

[15] The NCEUS argued that the present measure is too arbitrary and subjective and that more objective criteria, such as job search and availability for work, should be the basis for the classification of discouraged workers. The current procedure for identifying availability for work is based upon certain reasons—school attendance, home responsibilities, and illness—which are assumed to indicate unavailability for work, even if the respondent cites additional reasons of discouragement. In the questionnaire items being tested, availability for work is asked directly. However, it will be several years, at best, before any new definition can be introduced. In a related recommendation, the NCEUS agreed that discouraged workers should continue to be classified as not in the labor force. See National Commission, *Counting the Labor Force*, pp. 44–48.

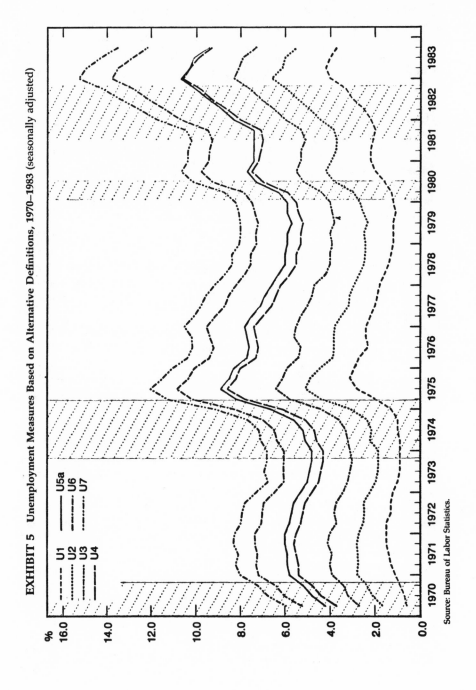

EXHIBIT 5 Unemployment Measures Based on Alternative Definitions, 1970–1983 (seasonally adjusted)

Source: Bureau of Labor Statistics.

ployment measure which includes both of these categories with the unemployed. Designated as "U–7," it is one of seven alternative measures of unemployment regularly published by the BLS in recognition of the fact that no single measure of unemployment can satisfy the diverse needs of all users. The definitions for these alternatives are provided below, and their trends during the past few decades are presented in Exhibit 5. It should be noted that these alternative rates differ from the official rates in level but not in trend.

U–1   Persons unemployed 15 weeks or longer as a percent of the civilian labor force.

U–2   Job losers as a percent of the civilian labor force.

U–3   Unemployed persons 25 years of age and over as a percent of the civilian labor force 25 years and over.

U–4   Unemployed full-time job seekers as a percent of the full-time civilian labor force.

U–5a Total unemployed as a percent of the labor force, including the resident Armed Forces.

U–5b Total unemployed as a percent of the civilian labor force.

U–6   Total full-time job seekers plus half part-time job seekers plus half total on part time for economic reasons, as a percent of the civilian labor force less half of the part-time labor force.

U–7   Total full-time job seekers plus half part-time job seekers plus half total on part time for economic reasons plus discouraged workers, as a percent of the civilian labor force plus discouraged workers less half of the part-time labor force.

These alternative measures represent a broad range of possibilities— several being more restrictive and several being less restrictive than the official measures. For instance, U–1 includes in the numerator only those unemployed 15 weeks or longer, while U–2 counts only job losers as unemployed and thus excludes all entrants and reentrants to the labor force as well as all those who voluntarily left their last job. The broadest of the series, U–7, which has consistently been several points higher than the official rates (U–5a and U–5b), includes involuntary part-time workers as "partially" unemployed and discouraged workers as fully unemployed.

RELATED STATISTICS AND DATA SOURCES

There are other labor force measures from the CPS and other sources of data which users of unemployment statistics need to be aware of.

Work Experience Data

The CPS work experience survey, conducted in March of each year as a supplement to the basic CPS, covers the labor market status of the civilian noninstitutional population during the previous calendar year. Because many persons enter and leave the labor force during the course of a year, the total number of persons with some unemployment during the year, as determined through the work experience questions, is much greater than the average for the year based on the total unemployed in each month. For example, in 1982, the total number of persons who had some unemployment during the year, at 26.5 million, was 2.5 times greater than the average monthly figure. The March data provide insights into the experience over the entire year, whereas the monthly survey serves to provide us with a snapshot of conditions at a particular point in time—the week containing the 12th of the month. The March data are published in BLS news releases, *Monthly Labor Review* articles, and special reports, as are data and analyses based on other supplements to the CPS. The work experience data also form the basis for BLS analysis of linkages of the employment experience of individuals over a full year with earnings and family income status.

Subnational Unemployment Data

The CPS also yields a set of unemployment statistics for states and areas—the local area unemployment statistics (LAUS) program. CPS monthly labor force and unemployment data in 10 large states (New York, California, Illinois, Ohio, New Jersey, Pennsylvania, Michigan, Texas, Massachusetts, and Florida) and two metropolitan areas (Los Angeles–Long Beach and New York City) are published and used directly from the national survey. Monthly estimates for the remaining 40 states and the District of Columbia are prepared using a combination of CPS data, data from the BLS survey of nonagricultural establishments, and unemployment insurance statistics. When they become available, annual average labor force data from the CPS are used as benchmarks in these states. Below the state level, monthly employment and unemployment estimates are prepared for all standard metropolitan statistical areas (SMSAs), counties, and cities of 50,000 or more. The LAUS data are developed by individual state employment security agencies in accordance with stipulated BLS procedures which ensure consistency and adherence to CPS concepts.[16] These data are published in the Bureau's

---

[16] For additional detail, see "Measurement of Unemployment in States and Local Areas," Chapter 4 in *BLS Handbook of Methods*, Bulletin 2134–1 (Washington, D.C.: 1982).

monthly news release, "State and Metropolitan Area Employment and Unemployment," as well as in *Employment and Earnings*. Monthly data for the 10 states from the CPS are published in "The Employment Situation" news release.

These LAUS estimates are indicators of local economic conditions and are used by state and local governments for planning and budgetary purposes and as an indication of the need for local employment and training services and programs. Local area unemployment estimates are also used to determine the eligibility of an area for benefits in various federal assistance programs. For example, they are used as a basis for eligibility and allocation of funds under the Job Training Partnership Act, labor surplus area determinations, and several other federal assistance programs.

Establishment Data

Another data source relevant to an understanding of the labor market is the Current Employment Statistics (CES) program, often referred to as the "establishment survey." The CES program is a BLS survey conducted in cooperation with state employment security agencies. Data are collected each month on payroll employment, hours, and earnings from a sample of almost 200,000 nonagricultural establishments. The sample is large, covering about 40 percent of total employment. From these data, a large amount of industry and geographic detail are prepared and published each month. The employment series include data for all employees, women workers, and production or nonsupervisory workers; and the survey also provides data on average weekly hours, average weekly overtime hours, and average hourly and weekly earnings for production or nonsupervisory workers. It is one of the oldest Bureau surveys, with some statistics dating back to 1919.

The monthly sample-based data are updated, or "benchmarked," periodically to a comprehensive count of employment compiled principally from quarterly reports of establishments covered under state unemployment insurance laws. Monthly sample data issued between benchmarks are subject to revision.

The establishment series of nonagricultural employment differs from the CPS in concept as well as the survey technique.[17] Movements in the two series often diverge from month to month; over the long run, however, the two surveys show very similar trends.

The establishment series are widely used by business, labor, academic, and other researchers as economic indicators in marketing stud-

---

[17] John Stinson, "Comparison of Nonagricultural Employment Estimates from Two Surveys," *Employment and Earnings*, March 1983.

ies, in economic research and planning, and in regional analysis. And they are one of the major components used by state employment security agencies in the development of the subnational unemployment rates.

The data are published monthly in "The Employment Situation" news release and in *Employment and Earnings*, as well as in the annual publications *Supplement to Employment and Earnings, United States* and *Supplement to Employment and Earnings, States and Areas*, which present updated and revised historical series following each benchmark revision.

Insured Unemployment Data

Another set of labor force statistics generated from state administrative operations are data from each state's unemployment insurance (UI) system. These are primarily the weekly counts of initial and continued UI claimants. UI claims data are compiled from the administrative records of local claims offices throughout the country and published in *Unemployment Insurance Claims* by the Employment and Training Administration (ETA) of the Department of Labor. For the nation as a whole, an insured unemployment rate is published which relates seasonally adjusted continued claims for a week to covered employment in the first four of the last six calendar quarters.

Not all persons who are reported as unemployed in the CPS are included in the UI statistics, and vice versa. Although each state law differs in its requirements, all states require some minimum of time worked before a worker is qualified to receive benefits.[18] Thus, jobless persons entering the labor force for the first time or reentering the labor force after a period of absence typically do not qualify for benefits and are thus excluded from the UI figures although they are included in the total unemployment count from the CPS. Also excluded are the very long-term unemployed, since most states allow for a maximum of 26 weeks of regular benefits. In addition, some persons disqualified from receiving UI benefits may be counted as unemployed in the CPS. For example, jobless workers who have voluntarily left their jobs but remained in the labor force to seek other jobs are excluded from the UI counts, except under certain circumstances. These worker groups are, however, included in the definition of unemployment used in the CPS. It is also the case that not all persons receiving UI benefits would be classified as unemployed in the CPS. Persons working for a low level of

---

[18] Saul J. Blaustein, "Insured Unemployment Data," in *Data Collection, Processing, and Presentation: National and Local* (Washington, D.C.: Government Printing Office, 1979).

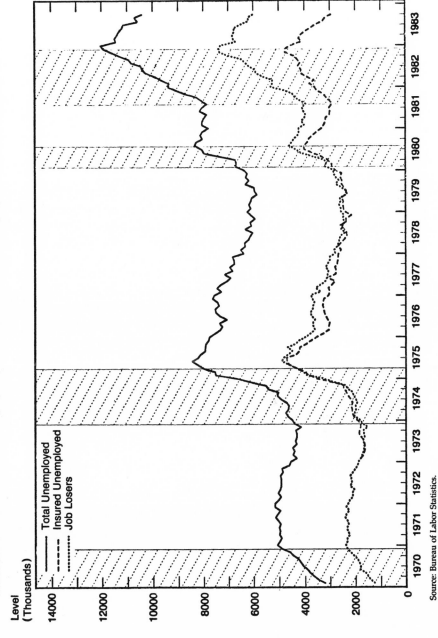

EXHIBIT 6 The Number of Unemployed, Job Losers, and Insured Unemployed, 1970–1983 (seasonally adjusted)

Source: Bureau of Labor Statistics.

earnings would be classified as employed in the CPS and could also be receiving UI benefits.

The CPS figures on job losers—unemployed workers on layoff who expect to be called back to their jobs, and those who have permanently lost their job—are closer in concept to the UI figures. The UI series and the CPS series on job losers usually track well together over time. During the 1980 and 1981–82 recessions, however, these series diverged, as the UI series declined relative to the job-loser series. Although the reasons for this divergence cannot be fully explained, some of it stemmed from changes in the programs of extended duration benefits and revisions in state UI laws and practices.[19] (See Exhibit 6.)

RELIABILITY OF THE DATA

The accuracy of estimates of unemployment and other CPS data based on a sample survey is, in theory, measured by the difference between the value of the survey estimate itself (for example, the estimate based on a particular month's sample) and the "true" value that would be obtained from a complete and perfect census. The goal is to design and implement a survey in which this difference, or total error, is minimized. Sample surveys and the estimates they produce are subject to two sources of survey error which users of the data should be aware of for a more complete understanding of the figures. These are: (1) sampling error, that is, survey error arising from the fact that the estimates are based on information from a sample of the population rather than from a complete count; and (2) nonsampling error, that is, errors or bias in the conduct of field collection, in the process of data compilation, or in the concept or definition of the phenomenon to be measured.

Sampling Error

Estimates from a sample survey may differ from those that would be obtained from a complete survey of the entire universe. The differences—referred to as sampling variance or standard error—can be calculated directly from the sample survey data. The size of the variance is dependent on the size of the sample and of the universe or total population of the group, the sample design, and the characteristic being measured. The variance for the unemployment rate for blacks, for example, is considerably higher than that for whites because the black population

---

[19] See Gary Burtless, "Why is Insured Unemployment so Low?" *Brookings Paper on Economic Activity*, vol. I (Washington, D.C.: Brookings Institution, 1983).

makes up a much smaller percentage of the total population. Estimates of the standard errors, as well as illustrations of their use, are published regularly in considerable demographic detail in *Employment and Earnings* and are available from the BLS upon request.

Nonsampling Error

It is much more difficult to quantify the effect of nonsampling error. Sources of nonsampling error can be attributed to such factors as nonresponse; differences in interviewer handling of questions; incorrect responses; errors made in recording, coding, or processing the data; and failure to represent all sample households and all persons within sample households (undercoverage). Although these nonsampling errors are difficult to measure, considerable effort is expended in preventing the occurrence of errors, identifying those that do occur, and quantifying their effect.[20] A regular reinterview program is conducted to check the accuracy of the original interview, and interviewer training is carried out on a continuing basis. Also, the effects of some components of nonsampling error can be examined by tabulating the data separately for each of the eight rotation groups used in the sample, since the levels of the estimates vary by rotation group. Over time, for example, it has been shown that persons in the initial interview and those who come back into the survey after a period of eight months absence show a higher incidence of labor force participation.

CPS sample results are weighted by independent estimates of the population by age, sex, and race, derived initially from the decennial census of population. In intercensal years, these population estimates are adjusted for births, deaths, immigration, and other administrative data in order to keep them up to date. In addition, procedures have been developed to provide for proper coverage of new households or dwelling units.

Some nonsampling error can result from incorrect concepts as well as from differences between what the survey questions are *intended* to measure and what the survey respondent *perceives* as that intent. Thus, the measurement of social and economic phenomena, which are complex and can at times be subjective, is more difficult than simple counts of the population. Some error can result from the survey procedures chosen, although considerable care is taken to ensure complete coverage. This kind of error can be important if the group not fully covered has labor

---

[20] See Camilla A. Brooks and Barbara A. Bailar, *An Error Profile: Employment as Measured by the Current Population Survey,* Statistical Policy Working Paper (U.S. Department of Commerce, Office of Federal Statistical Policy and Standards, September 1978).

market experience which differs very much from the total who are represented.

The impact of nonsampling error is important in evaluating estimates of labor market behavior and may, in fact, differ among subsamples by age, sex, and race. Publication of a more complete set of sources of nonsampling errors and additional research on the nature of these errors was one of the recommendations made by the NCEUS,[21] and work is currently underway to address some of these issues.

In some cases, where work concepts and practices may shift over time, the BLS may request the Census Bureau to add a new labor force measure as the need develops. However, no change in questionnaire or definition is actually implemented into the ongoing survey until it has been fully tested and tried out under survey conditions. These issues are constantly under review; currently, new questions are being tested and reviewed relating to persons on layoff, discouraged workers, and the school enrollment status of teenagers and young adults, as well as several other questionnaire changes. Periodic examinations of the entire survey process are also conducted by outside presidential commissions, such as the Gordon Committee and the Levitan Commission, in order to assure that the labor force survey is kept on track.

CRITICISMS OF THE UNEMPLOYMENT MEASURE

Over the years, some have argued that the unemployment concept and definition should be revised. Some argue for a more limited coverage, while others believe the concept is already too narrow and would like to see it broadened. Some look at the unemployment rate as a measure of available labor supply; others expect it to provide information on economic hardship and social distress; and still others see the unemployment rate as a measure of overall economic performance.[22]

In general, critics on the overstatement side contend that the unemployment figures include some persons who do not really need jobs. They argue that persons are counted frequently as unemployed when their major activity during the reference period is something else, such as keeping house or going to school. For example, full-time students are included in the unemployment count when they are seeking part-time

---

[21] National Commission, *Counting the Labor Force*, p. 132.

[22] See Julius Shiskin, *Unemployment: Measurement Problems and Recent Trends*, Report 445 (Washington, D.C.: U.S. Department of Labor, Bureau of Labor Statistics, 1975, pp. 9–10). Also see Janet L. Norwood, *Some Social Aspects of Unemployment*, Report 469 (Washington, D.C.: U.S. Department of Labor, Bureau of Labor Statistics, 1976); Bregger, "Establishment of a New Employment Statistics"; and E. E. Liebhafsky, John E. Gnuschke, and William L. McKee, "Value Judgments Inherent in Criticisms of CPS Measurement of Unemployment," *Social Science Quarterly*, September 1980, pp. 237–52.

jobs (and as employed when working part time). Some overstatement critics would limit the unemployment counts to "breadwinners" (defined broadly as persons supporting themselves and others) who have lost their jobs or to persons who have been unemployed for only a short period of time. They would thereby exclude from the unemployed most seekers of part-time jobs, wives or husbands who are not a primary source of family support, youth, job leavers, and persons coming into the labor force—new entrants and reentrants.

Another popular contention of those arguing that the unemployed counts are overstated is that the definition of job search is too loose. They believe that some job seekers are not really serious in their efforts to find work.

In contrast to the overstatement group are those who believe that certain groups presently excluded from the unemployed count should be included. They argue that present concepts are too narrowly conceived. They point out that some persons who may have worked only a few hours in a week, and therefore have been counted as employed, may indeed want full-time work and may need the earnings of a full-time job. Still others would broaden the unemployment concept by relaxing the job search criterion so as to include "discouraged workers." They argue that exclusion of those not looking for work because they believe no jobs are available seriously underestimates the unemployment rate.

Finally, it is argued by some critics that the unemployment concept captures only the "tip of the iceberg" in regard to labor market problems, because it does not address low earnings. This thinking has spawned a host of "subemployment" measures to account simultaneously for inadequate hours worked and inadequate earnings. Following a NCEUS recommendation, the BLS began regular annual publication of a report linking unemployment and low income. In January 1982, the first such report was published, and this has been followed by two subsequent reports.[23] Recently, the Job Training Partnership Act of 1982 mandated the issuance of annual reports relating labor force status to earnings and income.[24]

The unemployment rate, by itself, was never intended to be the only measure of importance in measuring changes in the labor market and the overall economy. The unemployment rate is a summary measure. We must look at the more detailed data to assess the extent of labor market–related economic hardship and the extent of unutilized labor

---

[23] Data for 1979 are published in *Linking Employment Problems to Economic Status*, Bulletin 2123 (Washington, D.C.: U.S. Department of Labor, Bureau of Labor Statistics, 1982). Information for 1980 is available through the National Technical Information Service, no. PB83115345. Information for 1981 was published in BLS Bulletin 2169.

[24] See P. L. 97–300, Job Training Partnership Act of 1982.

supply. Obviously, any simple categorization of working-age persons as employed, unemployed, or not in the labor force cannot reflect the extensive movements which actually occur in the labor market.

In spite of these difficulties, we can expect unemployment statistics to continue to play a crucial role in the assessment of the performance of the nation's economy and to shed some light on economic and social distress. Unemployment rates will also continue to serve as an allocator of federal aid to states and local communities. And, as the trend toward closer interaction between government policy and statistics continues, we can anticipate that unemployment and related measures will more than ever before provide input to policy formulation, a tradition which began with the very inception of the concepts more than 40 years ago.

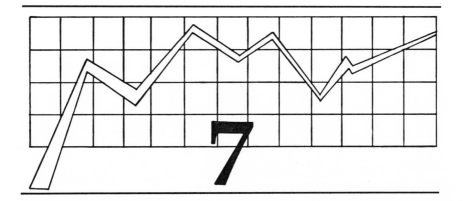

Measures of Recession and Expansion

Geoffrey H. Moore, Ph.D.

Center for International Business Cycle Research
Graduate School of Business
Columbia University

BUSINESS CYCLE PEAK AND TROUGH DATES

Basic to the measurement of recessions and expansions are the dates when they begin and end. For many years the National Bureau of Economic Research, a private organization with headquarters in Cambridge, Massachusetts, has established such dates for the United States. They are used in the Department of Commerce's monthly publication on business cycle indicators, *Business Conditions Digest*, and are widely accepted as authoritative. A complete listing, covering 35 business cycles from 1834 to 1982, is contained in Exhibit 1.

The dates are based upon a definition of business cycles that was first formulated in the 1920s and revised in the 1940s. It reads as follows:

> Business cycles are a type of fluctuation found in the aggregate economic activity of nations that organize their work mainly in business enterprises: a cycle consists of expansions occurring at about the same time in many economic activities, followed by similarly general recessions, contractions, and revivals which merge into the expansion phase of the next cycle; the sequence of changes is recurrent but not periodic; in duration, business

EXHIBIT 1 Business Cycle Peak and Trough Dates: United States, 1834–1982

Dates of Peaks and Troughs*						Duration in Months		Cycle	
By Months		By Quarters		By Calendar Years		Contraction (peak to trough)	Expansion (trough to peak)	Trough to Trough	Peak to Peak
Trough	Peak	Trough	Peak	Trough	Peak				
				1834	1836	24†	24†	48†	36†
				1838	1839	48†	12†	60†	72†
				1843	1845	12†	24†	36†	24†
				1846	1847	12†	12†	24†	72†
				1848	1853	24†	60†	84†	36†
Dec. 1854	June 1857	4Q 1854	2Q 1857	1855	1856	18	30	48	40
Dec. 1858	Oct. 1860	4Q 1858	3Q 1860	1858	1860	8	22	30	54
June 1861	Apr. 1865	3Q 1861	1Q 1865	1861	1864	32	46	78	50
Dec. 1867	June 1869	1Q 1868	2Q 1869	1867	1869	18	18	36	52
Dec. 1870	Oct. 1873	4Q 1870	3Q 1873	1870	1873	65	34	99	101
Mar. 1879	Mar. 1882	1Q 1879	1Q 1882	1878	1882	38	36	74	60
May 1885	Mar. 1887	2Q 1885	2Q 1887	1885	1887	13	22	35	40
Apr. 1888	July 1890	1Q 1888	3Q 1890	1888	1890	10	27	37	30
May 1891	Jan. 1893	2Q 1891	1Q 1893	1891	1892	17	20	36	35
June 1894	Dec. 1895	2Q 1894	4Q 1895	1894	1895	18	18	36	42
June 1897	June 1899	2Q 1897	3Q 1899	1896	1899	18	24	42	39
Dec. 1900	Sep. 1902	4Q 1900	4Q 1902	1900	1903	18	21		

Trough	Peak	Trough	Peak	Trough	Peak	Contraction	Expansion	Trough-to-Trough	Peak-to-Peak
Aug. 1904	May 1907	3Q 1904	2Q 1907	1904	1907	23	33	44	56
June 1908	Jan. 1910	2Q 1908	1Q 1910	1908	1910	13	19	46	32
Jan. 1912	Jan. 1913	4Q 1911	1Q 1913	1911	1913	24	12	43	36
Dec. 1914	Aug. 1918	4Q 1914	3Q 1918	1914	1918	23	44	35	67
Mar. 1919	Jan. 1920	1Q 1919	1Q 1920	1919	1920	7	10	51	17
July 1921	May 1923	3Q 1921	2Q 1923	1921	1923	18	22	28	40
July 1924	Oct. 1926	3Q 1924	3Q 1926	1924	1926	14	27	36	41
Nov. 1927	Aug. 1929	4Q 1927	3Q 1929	1927	1929	13	21	40	34
Mar. 1933	May 1937	1Q 1933	2Q 1937	1932	1937	43	50	64	93
June 1938	Feb. 1945	2Q 1938	1Q 1945	1938	1944	13	80	63	93
Oct. 1945	Nov. 1948	4Q 1945	4Q 1948	1946	1948	8	37	88	45
Oct. 1949	July 1953	4Q 1949	2Q 1953	1949	1953	11	45	48	56
May 1954	Aug. 1957	2Q 1954	3Q 1957	1954	1957	10	39	55	49
Apr. 1958	Apr. 1960	2Q 1958	2Q 1960	1958	1960	8	24	47	32
Feb. 1961	Dec. 1969	1Q 1961	4Q 1969	1961	1969	10	106	34	116
Nov. 1970	Nov. 1973	4Q 1970	4Q 1973	1970	1973	11	36	117	47
Mar. 1975	Jan. 1980	1Q 1975	1Q 1980	1975	1979	16	58	52	74
July 1980	July 1981	3Q 1980	3Q 1981	1980	1981	6	12	64	18
Nov. 1982		4Q 1982		1982		16		28	

Averages (35 cycles, 1834–1982)

						19	32	51	51

* The quarterly and annual dates are based upon data summed or averaged by quarter or by year. Quarterly peaks and troughs are placed in the same quarter as the monthly date if the latter is the midmonth of the quarter. Otherwise, it is placed either in the same quarter or the adjacent quarter. Annual dates may or may not be in the same year as the monthly dates, depending on the behavior of the annual totals or averages.

† Based upon calendar year dates.

Source: National Bureau of Economic Research.

EXHIBIT 2   Growth Cycle Peak and Trough Dates: Thirteen Countries, 1948–1980*

Peak or Trough	United States	Australia	Belgium	Canada	France	Italy	Japan	South Korea
P	7/48							
T	10/49							
P	3/51	8/51		4/51				
T	7/52	9/52		12/51				
P	3/53			3/53			12/53	
T	8/54			10/54			6/55	
P	2/57	8/55		11/56	8/57	10/56	5/57	
T	4/58	1/58		8/58	8/59	7/59	1/59	
P	2/60	9/60		10/59				
T	2/61	9/61		3/61				
P	5/62			3/62	2/64	9/63	1/62	
T	10/64			5/63	6/65	3/65	1/63	
P							7/64	
T							2/66	
P	6/66	4/65	10/64	3/66	6/66			
T	10/67	1/68	7/68	2/68	5/68			8/66
P	3/69	12/70	9/70	2/69	11/69	8/69	6/70	1/69
T	11/70	1/72	7/71	12/70	11/71	9/72	1/72	3/72
P	3/73	2/74	7/74	2/74	5/74	4/74	11/73	2/74
T	3/75	5/75	10/75	10/75	6/75	5/75	3/75	6/75
P		11/76		5/76		12/76		7/76
T		12/77		7/77		10/77		
P	12/78		6/79	9/79	8/79	2/80	2/80	
T				6/80				

* The chronologies begin at different dates because appropriate data are not available earlier. The absence of a recent date does not necessarily mean that one has not occurred.

† The four-, six-, and seven-country chronologies are based on composite indexes of output, income, employment, and trade, weighted by each country's GNP in 1970, expressed in U.S. dollars. The four countries are the United Kingdom, West Germany, France, and Italy. The six countries include these four plus Canada and Japan, and the seven countries include the United States as well.

Source: For the United States, National Bureau of Economic Research; for other countries, Center for International Business Cycle Research.

cycles vary from more than 1 year to 10 or 12 years; they are not divisible into shorter cycles of similar character with amplitudes approximating their own.[1]

In using this definition to determine peak and trough dates, the National Bureau assembles a number of monthly and quarterly series representing different aspects of aggregate economic activity. They include measures of output, such as gross national product from real terms and industrial production, employment and unemployment, total personal income in real terms, and total sales of business enterprises in real terms. The series are adjusted to eliminate seasonal variations but otherwise are not smoothed. The choice of peak or trough date depends upon

[1] Arthur F. Burns, and Wesley C. Mitchell, *Measuring Business Cycles* (New York: National Bureau of Economic Research, 1946), p. 3.

EXHIBIT 2 (concluded)

Netherlands	Sweden	Switzerland	United Kingdom	West Germany	Four Countries†	Six Countries†	Seven Countries†
		2/50					
7/50		3/51	3/51	2/51			
6/52		2/53	8/52				
				2/54			
10/56		6/57	12/55	10/55	5/57	2/57	2/57
5/58		9/58	11/58	4/59	2/59	2/59	5/58
							2/60
							2/61
3/61		4/64	3/61	2/61	3/61	3/61	2/62
2/63			2/63	2/63	2/63	2/63	2/63
						7/64	
11/65	2/65		2/66	5/65	3/66		3/66
8/67	7/67	5/68	8/67	8/67	5/68	5/68	10/67
11/70	7/70	5/70	6/69	5/70	5/70	6/70	8/69
8/72	7/72	1/71	2/72	12/71	2/72	2/72	8/71
8/74	6/74	4/74	6/73	8/73	7/74	11/73	11/73
7/75		8/75	8/75	5/75	8/75	9/75	5/75
9/76							
11/77	7/78						
12/79			6/79	2/80	11/70	2/80	9/79

a reading of the consensus among this collection of measures, since they do not ordinarily reach their highs and lows at the same time. Since most of the individual series are subject to revision from time to time, the consensus has a degree of stability that the use of a single series to fix the dates would not have. Nevertheless, the dates are reviewed occasionally and sometimes revised.

GROWTH CYCLE PEAK AND TROUGH DATES

An alternative type of business cycle chronology, known as the growth cycle, has come into use in recent years. It is used especially for international comparisons and for analyzing the relations between the business cycle and inflation. The growth cycle represents a fluctuation in economic activity around the long-run growth trend of the economy. In order to establish peak and trough dates, therefore, long-run trends are fitted to the data. The figures are then expressed as deviations from the trend. Peak and trough dates, selected from these deviation series, mark the points when aggregate economic activity was farthest above (peak) or farthest below (trough) its long-run trend path.

Growth cycle chronologies for the United States and 12 other countries, prepared by the Center for International Business Cycle Research, are shown in Exhibit 2. The intervals from peak to trough represent periods of slow growth or recession. The intervals from trough to peak represent periods of rapid growth—i.e., in excess of the long-run trend. The number of growth cycles usually exceeds the number of business cycles during a given period, because slowdowns sometimes occur during long business cycle expansions. Also, growth cycle peaks usually occur some months before business cycle peaks, because activity usually slows down before a business cycle peak is reached.

MEASURES OF THE DURATION, DEPTH, AND DIFFUSION OF RECESSIONS

A recession's severity depends upon how long it lasts, how deep it gets, and how widely it is felt among different industries or sectors of the economy. These dimensions are interrelated, but do not all yield the same verdict. The variations among them from one recession to another during the past 60 years are demonstrated in Exhibit 3.

Here the Great Depression of 1929–1933 stands out as the longest, deepest, and most pervasive decline of any in the record. The 1920–21 and 1937–38 episodes belong in second rank, as major depressions. A third group, which can be called severe recessions, includes six periods: 1923–24, 1948–49, 1953–54, 1957–58, 1973–75, and 1981–82. Finally, there are five mild recessions: 1926–27, 1945, 1960–61, 1969–70, and 1980. Although these groupings are arbitrary, averages for each group (as shown in Exhibit 4) provide a rough guide to the range of experience with recession in the United States since 1920.

MEASURES OF THE DURATION, VIGOR, AND SCOPE OF EXPANSIONS

The variation among business cycle expansions is as wide as, if not wider than, among recessions. In the United States, expansions have been as short as 10 months and as long as 8 years (Exhibits 1 and 5). The longer expansions have often been interrupted by slowdowns, or

		Jan. 1920 July 1921	May 1923 July 1924	Oct. 1926 Nov. 1927	Aug. 1929 Mar. 1933	May 1937 June 1938	Feb. 1945 Oct. 1945
	EXHIBIT 3 Measures of Duration, Depth, and Diffusion of Recessions						

EXHIBIT 3 Measures of Duration, Depth, and Diffusion of Recessions

Business Cycle Peak: *Business Cycle Trough:*	Jan. 1920 July 1921	May 1923 July 1924	Oct. 1926 Nov. 1927	Aug. 1929 Mar. 1933	May 1937 June 1938	Feb. 1945 Oct. 1945
Duration (months)						
Business cycle (Exhibit 1)	18	14	13	43	13	8
GNP, current dollars	n.a.[a]	6	12	42	9	6
GNP, constant dollars	n.a.	3	3	36	6	n.a.
Industrial production	14	14	8	36	12	27
Nonfarm employment	n.a.	n.a.	n.a.	43	11	22
Depth (percent)[b]						
GNP, current dollars	n.a.	−4.9	−3.0	−49.6	−16.2	−11.9
GNP, constant dollars	n.a.	−4.1	−2.0	−32.6	−13.2	n.a.
Industrial production	−32.4	−17.9	−7.0	−53.4	−32.4	−38.3
Nonfarm employment	n.a.	n.a.	n.a.	−31.6	−10.8	−10.1
Unemployment rate						
Maximum	11.9[c]	5.5[c]	4.4[c]	24.9[c]	20.0	4.3
Increase	+10.3[c]	+2.6[c]	+2.4[c]	+21.7[c]	+9.0	+3.4
Diffusion (percent)						
Nonfarm industries, maximum percentage with declining employment	97	95	71	100	97	n.a.
Date when maximum was reached[d]	Sept. 1920	April 1924	Nov. 1927	June 1933	Dec. 1937	

EXHIBIT 3 (concluded)

Business Cycle Peak: Business Cycle Trough:	Nov. 1948 Oct. 1949	July 1953 May 1954	Aug. 1957 Apr. 1958	Apr. 1960 Feb. 1961	Dec. 1969 Nov. 1970	Nov. 1973 Mar. 1975	Jan. 1980 July 1980	July 1981 Nov. 1982
Duration (months)								
Business cycle (Exhibit 1)	11	10	8	10	11	16	6	16
GNP, current dollars	12	12	6	3	[e]	[e]	[e]	3
GNP, constant dollars	6	12	6	9	6	15	3	6
Industrial production	15	9	13	13	13	9	16	16
Nonfarm employment	13	14	14	10	8	6	4	17
Depth (percent)[b]								
GNP, current dollars	-3.4	-1.9	-2.8	-0.6	[e]	[e]	[e]	-0.4
GNP, constant dollars	-1.5	-3.2	-3.3	-1.2	-1.0	-4.9	-2.3	-3.0
Industrial production	-10.1	-9.4	-13.5	-8.6	-6.8	-15.3	-8.5	-12.3
Nonfarm employment	-5.2	-3.5	-4.3	-2.2	-1.5	-2.9	-1.4	-3.1
Unemployment rate								
Maximum	7.8	5.9	7.3	6.9	5.9	8.8	7.7	10.7
Increase	+4.5	+3.4	+3.7	+2.0	+2.6	+4.3	+2.2	+3.6
Diffusion (percent)								
Nonfarm industries, maximum percentage with declining employment	90	87	88	80	80	88	77	79
Date when maximum was reached[d]	Feb. 1949	Mar. 1954	Sept. 1957	Oct. 1960	May 1970	Jan. 1975	Apr. 1980	Aug. 1982

[a] n.a. = Not available.

[b] Percentage change from the peak month or quarter in the series to the trough month or quarter, over the intervals shown. For the unemployment rate, the maximum figure is the highest for any month during the contraction; the increases are from the lowest month to the highest, in percentage points.

[c] The maximum figures are annual averages for 1921, 1924, 1928, and 1933 (monthly data not available). Increases, in percentage points, are for 1919–21, 1923–24, 1926–28, and 1929–33.

[d] Since 1948, based on changes in employment over six-month spans, centered on the fourth month of the span, in 30 nonagricultural industries, 1948–59; 172 industries, 1960–71; 186 industries, 1972–80. Prior to 1948, based on cyclical changes in employment in 41 industries.

[e] No decline.

Source: U.S. Department of Commerce, U.S. Department of Labor, Board of Governors of the Federal Reserve System, National Bureau of Economic Research. For a fuller version of this table, see Solomon Fabricant, "The Recession of 1969–1970," in The Business Cycle Today, ed. V. Zarnowitz, (New York: National Bureau of Economic Research, 1972), pp. 100–10.

EXHIBIT 4　A Capsule History of Recessions and Depressions, 1920–1982

How Deep? (percent)

	How Long? (months)	Real GNP	Industrial production	Nonfarm employment	Unemployment Rate		How Wide? (percent of industries with employment decline)
					High	Increase	
1. The Great Depression (1933)	43	−33	−53	−32	25	+22	100
2. Two major depressions (1921, 1938)	16	−13	−32	−11	16	+10	97
3. Six sharp recessions (1924, 1949, 1954, 1958, 1975, 1982)	12	−3	−13	−4	8	+4	88
4. Five mild recessions (1927, 1945, 1961, 1970, 1980)	10	−2	−8	−2	6	+3	77

Explanation of exhibit: The first column is the period from the peak of the business cycle to the trough, as determined by the National Bureau of Economic Research. The next three columns show the percentage declines in output or employment from its high month or quarter to its low. For unemployment, the highest monthly figure reached is shown (column 5) as well as the increase from the low to the high (column 6). The last column is the percentage of industries that experienced a decline in employment over a six-month interval. The figure shown is the highest percentage reached during the depression or recession. All the entries on lines 2, 3, and 4 are averages covering the respective depressions or recessions. For individual recessions see Exhibit 3.
　Source: Center for International Business Cycle Research.

EXHIBIT 5   Measures of the Duration, Vigor, and Diffusion of Expansions

Business Cycle Trough: Business Cycle Peak:	Oct. 1949 July 1953	May 1954 Aug. 1957	Apr. 1958 Apr. 1960	Feb. 1961 Dec. 1969	Nov. 1970 Nov. 1973	Mar. 1975 Jan. 1980	July 1980 July 1981	Average Seven Expansions
Duration (months)								
Business cycle	45	39	24	106	36	58	12	46
GNP, current dollars	42	39	30	*	*	*	*	n.a.
GNP, constant dollars	48	39	24	105	45	60	15	48
Industrial production	45	35	21	104	43	48	12	44
Nonfarm employment	44	31	23	109	47	59	12	46
Increase (percent)†								
GNP, current dollars	43.8	24.0	16.3	*	*	*	*	n.a.
GNP, constant dollars	28.1	13.2	11.3	49.2	17.1	24.3	4.4	21.1
Industrial production	50.1	23.7	26.0	78.9	25.9	37.4	9.6	35.9
Nonfarm employment	17.7	9.1	7.5	33.7	11.9	19.1	1.9	14.4
Unemployment rate								
Minimum	2.5	3.6	4.9	3.3	4.5	5.5	7.1	4.5
Decrease	−5.3	−2.3	−2.4	−3.6	−1.4	−3.3	−0.6	−2.7
Rate of increase (percent per year)								
GNP, current dollars	10.9	6.9	6.2	*	*	*	*	n.a.
GNP, constant dollars	6.4	3.9	5.5	4.7	4.3	4.4	3.5	4.7
Industrial production	11.4	7.6	14.1	6.9	6.6	8.3	9.6	9.2
Nonfarm employment	4.5	3.4	3.8	3.2	2.9	3.6	1.9	3.3
Diffusion (percent)								
Nonfarm industries, maximum percentage with rising employment	100	95	92	91	86	85	73	89
Date when maximum was reached‡	July 1950	May 1955	Jan. 1959	Dec. 1965	Mar. 1972	Feb. 1977	Oct. 1980	

* No cycle.
† Percentage change from trough month or quarter in the series to the peak month or quarter, over the intervals shown. For the unemployment rate, the minimum figure is the lowest for any month during the expansion, and the decreases are from the highest month to the lowest, in percentage points.
‡ Based on changes in employment over six-month spans, centered on the fourth month of the span, in 30 nonagricultural industries, 1948–59; 172 industries, 1960–71; 186 industries, 1972–80.
Source: U.S. Department of Commerce, U.S. Department of Labor, Board of Governors of the Federal Reserve System, National Bureau of Economic Research.

growth recessions, as noted above. Nevertheless, the overall rate of gain per year has not been closely associated with the length of upswings. Hence, long expansions have usually achieved bigger total increases in activity, putting the economy on a much higher level. Another rule is that expansions that have become large in magnitude have also been wide in scope, embracing more industries and sectors of the economy than mild or moderate expansions.

The character of expansions is governed in some degree by the nature of the preceding recession. The pace of expansion (rate of gain) is likely to be greater, at least for the first year or so, the deeper the preceding recession. This is especially true for the goods-producing sector of the economy—i.e., manufacturing—where sharp recessions deplete inventories that are built up rapidly during the ensuing expansion. Despite the more rapid advance in recoveries from sharp recessions, it takes longer, as a rule, for output to regain its previous peak level after a sharp recession than after a mild one. Most expansions, however, go well beyond the preceding peak level before succumbing to the next recession.

MEASURES OF RECESSION AND RECOVERIES IN PROGRESS

Although business cycles are far from uniform, they do have many repetitive features. This makes it possible to make useful judgements about what is likely to happen next by comparing a current recession or recovery, while it is in progress, with its predecessors when they were at the same stage. These comparisons have been called recession-recovery patterns. Some recent examples are shown in Exhibit 6.

The Exhibit is designed to answer such questions as whether production in the first 10 months, say, after a recession began exceeded its decline during the first 10 months of previous recessions. When the following month's data become available, the comparison can be updated. At the same time, one can see what happened in subsequent months during past recessions, using this as a guide as to what is likely to happen next. Similar patterns can be constructed for recovery periods. By applying the technique to a range of variables that influence one another and affect the course of the business cycle, one can obtain a perception of the nature of cyclical movements and their future course.

Exhibit 6 shows how this type of measurement worked during the recession of 1981–82 and the subsequent recovery. The two series shown are the index of industrial production compiled by the Federal Reserve Board[2] and the index of leading economic indicators compiled

---

[2] See Chapter 4.

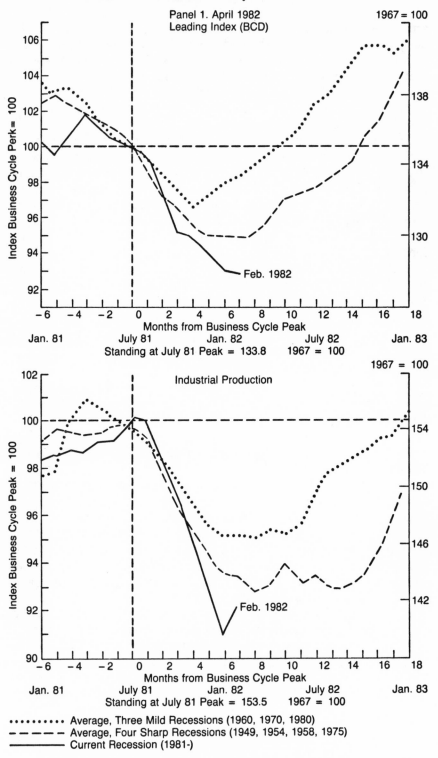

EXHIBIT 6   Recession-Recovery Patterns, 1981–1983

Panel 1. April 1982
Leading Index (BCD)

1967 = 100

Index Business Cycle Perk = 100

Feb. 1982

Months from Business Cycle Peak

Jan. 81   July 81   Jan. 82   July 82   Jan. 83
Standing at July 81 Peak = 133.8   1967 = 100

1967 = 100

Industrial Production

Index Business Cycle Peak = 100

Feb. 1982

Months from Business Cycle Peak

Jan. 81   July 81   Jan. 82   July 82   Jan. 83
Standing at July 81 Peak = 153.5   1967 = 100

• • • • • • • • •   Average, Three Mild Recessions (1960, 1970, 1980)
– – – – – –   Average, Four Sharp Recessions (1949, 1954, 1958, 1975)
———————   Current Recession (1981-)

EXHIBIT 6 (*continued*)

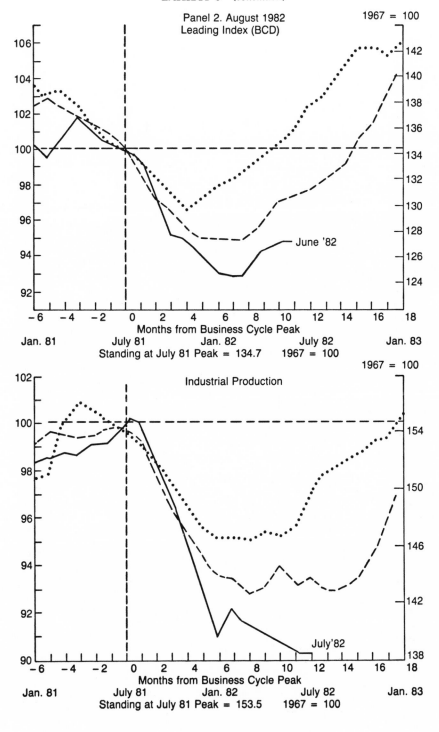

Panel 2. August 1982
Leading Index (BCD)
1967 = 100

June '82

Months from Business Cycle Peak

Jan. 81   July 81   Jan. 82   July 82   Jan. 83
Standing at July 81 Peak = 134.7   1967 = 100

1967 = 100

Industrial Production

July'82

Months from Business Cycle Peak

Jan. 81   July 81   Jan. 82   July 82   Jan. 83
Standing at July 81 Peak = 153.5   1967 = 100

EXHIBIT 6 *(continued)*

Panel 3. December 1982

Leading Index (BCD)

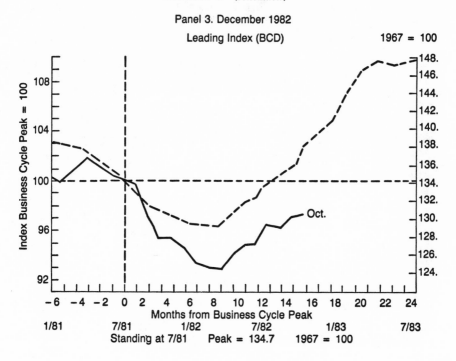

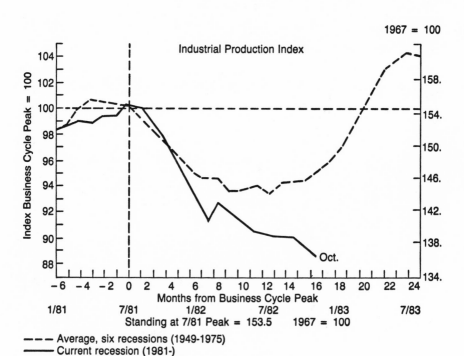

--- Average, six recessions (1949-1975)
— Current recession (1981-)

EXHIBIT 6 (*continued*)

Panel 4. April 1983

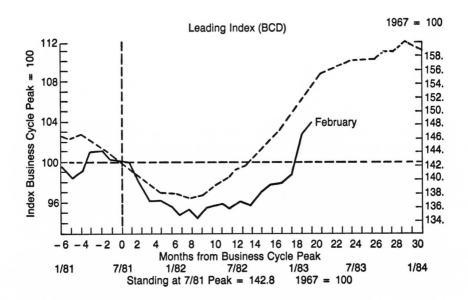

Leading Index (BCD)   1967 = 100

Standing at 7/81 Peak = 142.8   1967 = 100

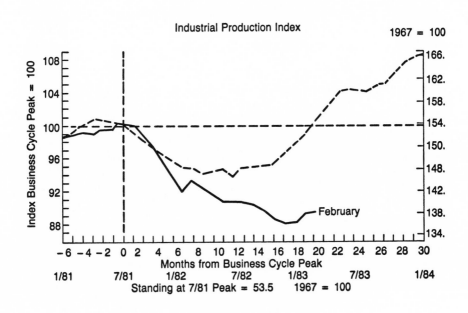

Industrial Production Index   1967 = 100

Standing at 7/81 Peak = 53.5   1967 = 100

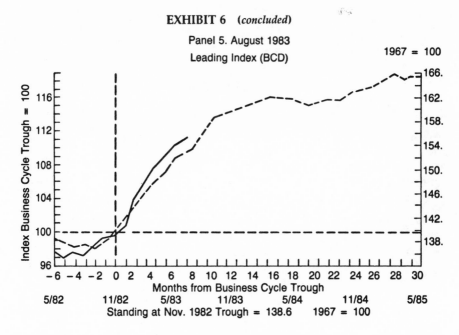

EXHIBIT 6 (*concluded*)

Panel 5. August 1983

Leading Index (BCD)

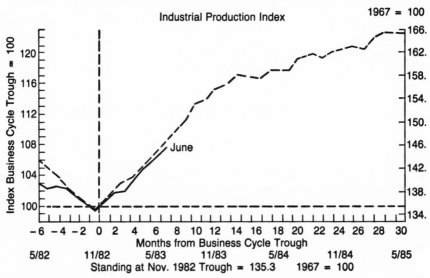

Industrial Production Index

----- = Average, six expansions (1949-1980)
——— = Current recovery (1982-)

Source: *Recession-Recovery Watch*, Center for International Business Cycle Research.

by the Department of Commerce.[3] The first panel (published in April 1982) depicts the movement of these indexes starting in January 1981, six months before the recession began, through February 1982, seven months after it began. Shown also are the average patterns of these indexes during the four sharp recessions of 1949, 1954, 1958, and 1975, and the three mild recessions of 1961, 1970, and 1980. Both indexes had declined further in 1981–82 than either of these averages. Apparent are the earlier downturns and upturns in the leading index than in the production index in past cycles.

In the next panel, published in August 1982, an upturn had appeared in the leading index but not in the production index. By December, four months later, the upturn in the leading index had been extended, but there was still no sign of it in production. Here and in subsequent panels, only one average is shown, covering both mild and severe recessions.

The April 1983 panel revealed a vigorous upswing in the leading index, carrying it well above its level when the recession began and paralleling its action in previous recoveries. As for industrial production, a small improvement had occurred in the figures for January and February. Four months after that, in August 1983, the recovery was well under way, and the method of constructing the charts had been changed. The business cycle trough of November 1982 was now lined up with previous business cycle troughs, so that the current expansion could be compared directly with previous expansions. The leading index was rising more vigorously than it had in the average previous expansion, while the production index was duplicating its previous performance. Both indexes show that the historical pattern is for slower growth after an initial period of rapid growth and that this has happened first in the leading index.

---

[3] See Chapter 8.

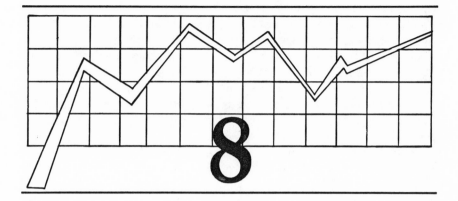

Leading, Lagging, and Coincident Indicators

Gary Gorton, Ph.D.
Research Economist
Federal Reserve Bank of Philadelphia

Business cycles are irregularly recurring alternations of prosperity and recession.[1] Measuring, detecting, and appraising these movements of aggregate economic activity are notoriously difficult tasks. Forecasting business cycles is the toughest task. Since the 1930s, indexes of leading, lagging, and coincident indicators have been widely used as an inexpensive and practical method for guiding the economic decisions of a wide variety of market participants, as well as policymakers, who must act in the context of the rhythm of the macroeconomy. Indeed, announcements of the index of leading indicators are widely reported in the popular press and on TV.

The popularity of the approach is no doubt partly related to the fact that since 1961 the U.S. Department of Commerce, in its *Business Conditions Digest*, has been publishing monthly values of indexes of leading, lagging, and coincident indicators (as well as a large number of other series). But beyond the fact that the information is fairly cheap to obtain,

---

[1] This chapter is partly drawn from the author's article "Forecasting with the Index of Leading Indicators," Federal Reserve Bank of Philadelphia *Business Review*, November–December 1982, pp. 15–27.

lies the simplicity of the approach.[2] Unlike econometric modeling, the index approach does not require assumptions about what causes peoples' economic behavior. Instead, the index approach relies on atheoretically detecting historic patterns among economic variables which can, when combined in an index, be used to appraise the overall behavior of the economy. A change in the direction of an index immediately allows an assessment about the macroeconomy. In the case of the index of leading indicators, for example, if the index changes direction today, the direction of economic activity should go the same way tomorrow.

The simplicity of the approach is more apparent than real. Interpreting the meaning of the indexes is a tricky business. In fact, it is not clear conceptually how their behavior ought to be interpreted. Consequently, users of the indexes should be aware of how the indexes are constructed and be sensitive to the problems involved in inferring conclusions from their behavior. On balance, however, the indexes have some particular strengths which, when used carefully, make them powerful tools.

CONSTRUCTION OF THE INDEXES

Remarkably, the basic approach used to construct the indexes of leading, lagging, and coincident indicators was originated in the 1930s and has changed little since then.[3] During the sharp recession of 1937–38, Henry Morgenthau, Jr., the Secretary of the Treasury, asked the National Bureau of Economic Research to devise a system of indicators that would signal when the recession was nearing its end.[4] The National Bureau, under the leadership of Wesley C. Mitchell and Arthur F. Burns, had assembled and analyzed hundreds of economic time series. Burns and Mitchell selected a number of series which seemed to have been good predictors of past business upturns. The Treasury published the list in May 1938.

The National Bureau Business Cycle Chronology

The approach originated by Burns and Mitchell begins by using statistical techniques to separate the cyclical component from other move-

---

[2] A domestic subscription to the *Business Conditions Digest* costs $55.00. It is available from the Superintendent of Documents, U.S. Government Printing Office, Washington, D.C. 20402.

[3] Actually there was an earlier system of indicators published by the Harvard Economic Service called the Harvard ABC curves. These indicators were discontinued when they failed to predict the Great Depression.

[4] The National Bureau of Economic Research is a private, not-for-profit, research group.

ments (such as seasonal and trend-related changes) in a particular economic time series.[5] Then the cyclical component of each series is plotted against calendar time and the movements of the series are inspected for common turning points. Historical plots of the series will show that there are dates around which many of the series move downwards and other dates around which many of the series move upwards. The dates of these clusters of turning points are called reference dates, and the collection of reference dates is called the business cycle chronology.[6] This chronology shows the peaks and troughs, when booms turn into recessions and recessions turn into upswings.

The cyclical components of different series do not all move in the same way, but inferences about historical business cycle patterns can be made by identifying clusters of turning points. If the turning points of many different series are bunched closely together, then the procedure will not likely go astray, though the method of visually examining the plots of the series in search of turning points is somewhat arbitrary.

Given the business cycle chronology, various economic series can be classified with respect to the reference dates. The cyclical components of some series almost always have peaks just *before* the reference peaks, and troughs just *before* the reference troughs. Such series are called *leading indicators.* Series which have peaks and troughs just *after* the corresponding reference peaks and troughs are *lagging indicators. Coincident indicators* have peaks and troughs roughly corresponding to those of the business cycle chronology. Finally, some series have no cyclical component and are *unclassified.*[7]

The classification of series by lining up peaks and troughs with reference to the business cycle chronology does not rely on economic theory (or on statistical theory). In many cases, the relation between a series and the cycle is easy to explain. Some series (such as housing starts, contracts for construction, and new orders for machinery and equipment) represent decisions made early in a lengthy investment process. For example, changes in actual production lag behind new orders because the orders must first be filled, and how soon they are filled depends on the volume of unfilled orders and on the state of inventories. Thus, unfilled orders and order backlogs are leading indicators of production activity. The behavior of some coincident and lagging series can also be explained, but for most series, the relations are not so clearcut. Rather than analyze very complicated economic relations, the National

---

[5] See Arthur F. Burns and Wesley C. Mitchell, *Measuring Business Cycles* (New York: National Bureau of Economic Research, 1946).

[6] The business cycle chronology is published in the January issue of the *Business Conditions Digest.*

[7] The *Business Conditions Digest* reports on and has classified over a hundred series.

Bureau procedure classifies series without assuming a theory of the business cycle.

Choosing Series and Choosing Weights

The Bureau of Economic Analysis, a division of the Commerce Department, constantly refines and revises the classification of a large number of economic time series, measuring their leads and lags against the common standard of the business cycle chronology. The BEA also constructs the leading, lagging, or coincident series. Then the series must be appropriately weighted in importance and added together.

Candidate series for the leading, lagging, and coincident indexes are evaluated by the BEA according to six criteria: (1) economic significance, (2) statistical adequacy, (3) timing at turning points, (4) conformity to historical business cycles, (5) smoothness, and (6) currency or availability of data. Candidate series are "scored"—that is, points are given to each series for each criterion and then totaled. Since diversified coverage

EXHIBIT 1   Component Series and Weights for the Indexes

BEA Series Number	Series	Weight
	Leading index	
1	Average workweek, production workers, manufacturing	1.014
5	Average weekly initial claims, state unemployment insurance	1.041
8	New orders for consumer goods and materials in 1972 dollars	.973
32	Vendor performance, companies receiving slower deliveries	1.081
12	New business formation	.973
20	Contracts and orders for plant and equipment in 1972 dollars	.946
29	New building permits, private housing units	1.054
36	Change in inventories on hand and on order, 1972 dollars	.986
99	Change in sensitive materials prices	.892
19	Stock prices, 500 common stocks	1.149
106	Money supply (M2) in 1972 dollars	.932
111	Change in credit outstanding—business and consumer borrowing	.959
	Coincident index	
41	Employees on nonagricultural payrolls	1.064
51	Personal income less transfer payments in 1972 dollars	1.003
47	Industrial production, total	1.028
57	Manufacturing and trade sales in 1972 dollars	.905
	Lagging index	
91	Average duration of unemployment	1.098
77	Ratio, constant-dollar inventories to sales, manufacturing, and trade	.894
62	Labor cost per unit of output, manufacturing	.868
109	Average prime rate charged by banks	1.123
101	Commercial and industrial loans outstanding in 1972 dollars	1.009
95	Ratio, consumer installment credit to personal income	1.009

Source: *Business Conditions Digest*, February 1983, p. 108.

of economic activity is also desirable, the series chosen are not necessarily those with the highest scores. Exhibit 1 lists the component series of the three indexes. The weights used to add the series together are the evaluation scores.[8]

EVALUATING THE PERFORMANCE OF THE INDEXES

Inspection of the behavior of the three indexes in Exhibit 2 suggests that the methods used to construct the indexes are successful. In Exhibit 2, the shaded areas are recessions. The Federal Reserve Board index of industrial production is also plotted in Exhibit 2 as a measure of aggregate economic activity. Determining the accuracy of the indexes, however, requires closer examination.

The performance of the three indexes as indicators of aggregate economic activity can be evaluated in two ways. One way is to examine the movements of the indexes in relation to business cycle turning points. The other is to examine the behavior of the indexes at all points of the cycle. Evaluation of the performance of the indexes requires a measure of economic activity as a standard of comparison. A frequently used measure of economic activity is the Federal Reserve Board index of industrial production.[9] This measure will be employed when the second evaluation method is used. With the first evaluation method, the National Bureau business cycle chronology is used as the standard of comparison.

The Turning-Point Approach

The first method of evaluation accepts the National Bureau's emphasis on turning points. Problems immediately arise in deciding when an index is indicating a turning point. The usual approach is to decide that an upturn (downturn) in economic activity has occurred if the index has been above (below) its previous high (low) for a specified number of months. The problem is to decide how many months should be looked at before deciding that an upturn or downturn is indicated.

---

[8] For a complete description of the criteria used to select series and the scoring procedure, see Victor Zarnowitz and Charlotte Boschan, "Cyclical Indicators: An Evaluation and New Leading Indexes," in *Handbook of Cyclical Indicators* (Washington, D.C.: Bureau of Economic Analysis, U.S. Department of Commerce, May 1977).

[9] The gross national product would be a natural measure to use as a standard of comparison, but it is available only on a quarterly basis while the indicator indexes come out monthly.

EXHIBIT 2 Recent Behavior of the Indexes

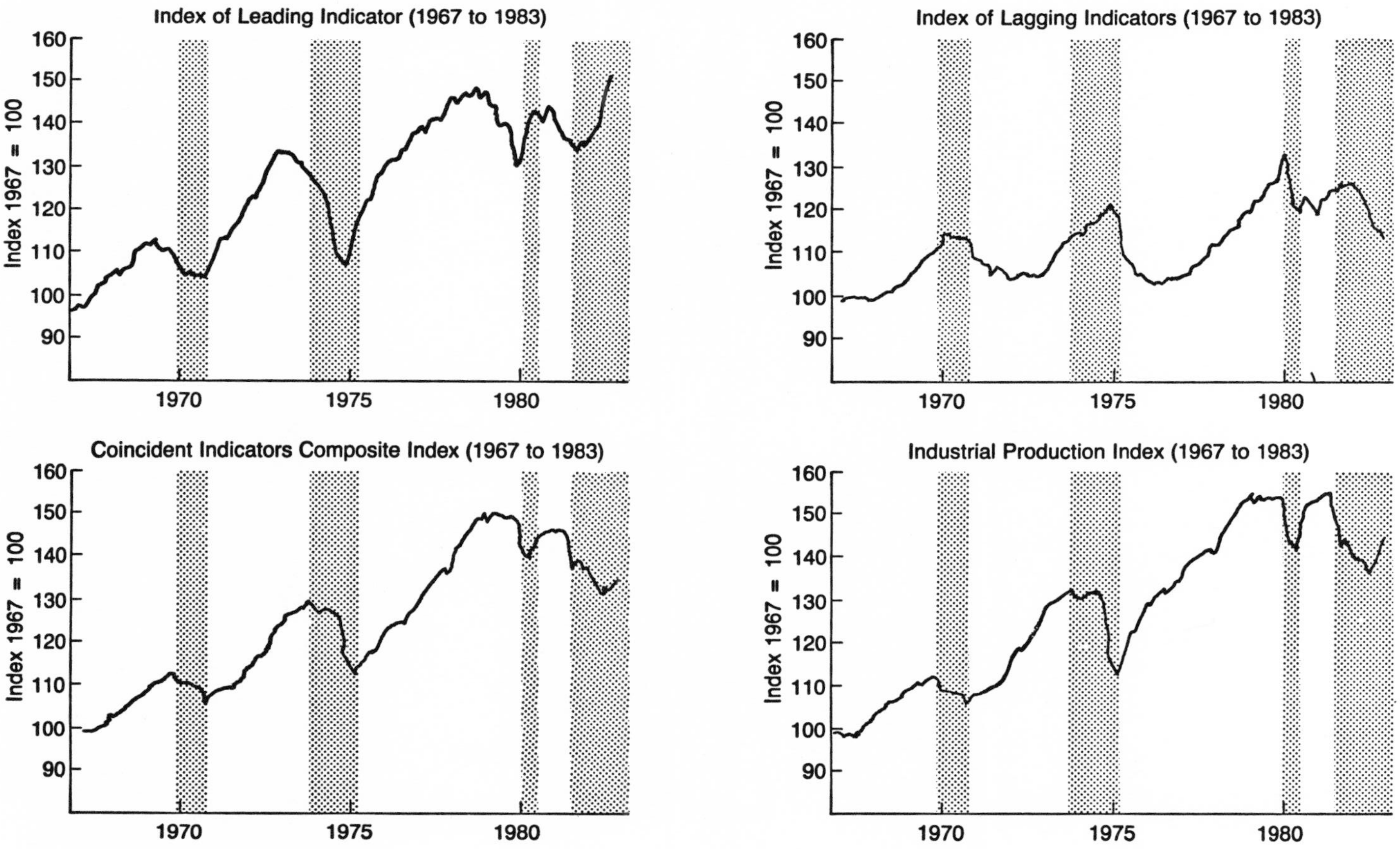
Index of Leading Indicator (1967 to 1983)
Index of Lagging Indicators (1967 to 1983)
Coincident Indicators Composite Index (1967 to 1983)
Industrial Production Index (1967 to 1983)
Index 1967 = 100
160
150
140
130
120
110
100
90
1970
1975
1980

Since movements in the indexes are partly random, many upward or downward movements are reversed if we wait long enough. Suppose, for example, that the index of leading indicators declines for two months in a row. If we adopt a two-month rule, we would conclude that the index is predicting a downturn in economic activity. It could well be the case, though, that in the next month the index will rise to a level above that of three months ago. Then, under a three-months rule, it would *not* predict a downturn. There is an inherent arbitrariness to the number-of-months approach. It is not obvious how many months an index must move in the same direction before a turning point in economic activity is indicated. Moreover, different rules for determining turning points in the three indexes result in different conclusions.

Using the one-month rule, the three indexes successfully indicate all the turning points in the National Bureau chronology during the period 1950–82 (see Exhibit 3). The indexes under the one-month rule are also successful in terms of timing. On average, the index of leading indicators does have turning points which lead the National Bureau's turning points. The index of coincident indicators and the index of industrial production have turning points at roughly the same time as the National Bureau's turning points.[10] Finally, the index of lagging indicators' turning points do lag.

Exhibit 3 seems to present persuasive evidence of the abilities of the indexes to indicate turning points in the desired manner. The indexes, however, produce a number of false signals over the same period: one-month changes appear in the indexes which do not correspond to any turning point in the National Bureau chronology. Under the one-month rule, over the period 1950–82, the index of leading indicators predicted 50 peaks and 50 troughs *which did not happen* (see Exhibit 4).[11] The number of false signals given by the other two indexes is similar in magnitude.

Exhibit 4 shows that as the number of months used to make a decision is increased, the number of false turns indicated declines, but so does the number of true turns indicated. In addition, as the number of months used to make a decision is increased, the timing properties of the indexes are lost. Under a four- or five-month rule, the average lead

---

[10] The index of industrial production is included because it will be used as the standard of comparison when the second evaluation method is used.

[11] Similar studies of the index of leading indicators have also found this problem. See H. O. Stekler and Martin Schepsman, "Forecasting with an Index of Leading Series," *Journal of the American Statistical Association,* June 1973, pp. 291–96. Also see Saul H. Hymans, "On the Use of Leading Indicators to Predict Cyclical Turning Points," *Brookings Papers on Economic Activity,* vol. 2 (Washington, D.C.: Brookings Institution, 1973), pp. 339–84.

EXHIBIT 3 Behavior of the Indexes, One-Month Rule, 1950–1982

NBER Troughs	Turn in ILI*	Lead Months	Turn in ICI†	Months Difference	Turn in IIP‡	Months Difference	Turn in LII§	Lag Months
May 1954	Dec. 1953	5	(Jul. 1953)	—	May 1954	0	Feb. 1955	9
Apr. 1958	Mar. 1958	1	May 1958	1	May 1958	1	Sep. 1958	5
Feb. 1961	Jan. 1961	1	Mar. 1961	1	Jan. 1961	1	Sep. 1961	7
Nov. 1970	Sep. 1970	2	Dec. 1970	1	Dec. 1970	1	May 1971	6
Mar. 1975	Mar. 1975	0	Apr. 1975	1	Apr. 1975	1	Oct. 1975	7
Jul. 1980	Jun. 1980	1	Aug. 1980	1	Aug. 1980	1	Nov. 1980	4
Average		1.66		1		1		6.3
NBER Peaks								
Jul. 1953	Apr. 1953	3	Jun. 1953	1	Jun. 1953	1	Jan. 1954	6
Aug. 1957	Jul. 1957	1	Mar. 1957	5	Jan. 1957	7	Oct. 1957	2
Apr. 1960	Jan. 1960	3	Feb. 1960	2	Feb. 1960	2	Jul. 1960	3
Dec. 1969	Oct. 1969	2	Nov. 1969	1	Nov. 1969	1	Apr. 1970	4
Nov. 1973	Jun. 1973	5	Dec. 1973	1	Dec. 1973	1	Feb. 1974	3
Jan. 1980	Jun. 1979	7	Feb. 1980	1	Feb. 1980	1	May 1980	4
Jul. 1981	May 1981	2	Aug. 1981	1	Aug. 1981	1	Nov. 1981	4
Average		3.28		1.7		2.0		3.7

* ILI = Index of leading indicators.
† ICI = Index of coincident indicators.
‡ IIP = Index of industrial production.
§ LII = Index of lagging indicators.
Source: Calculated by author.

EXHIBIT 4   True and False Turns of the Indices, 1950–1982

Index of leading indicators

	Peaks			Troughs		
Months Rule	Average Lead	True Turns Predicted	False Turns Predicted	Average Lead	True Turns Predicted	False Turns Predicted
1	3.28	7	50	1.66	6	50
2	2.1	7	20	.33	6	33
3	1.1	7	11	−.66	6	19
4	−1.6	6	2	−3.1	6	14
5	−2.3	3	2	−4.1	6	13

Index of coincident indicators

	Peaks			Troughs		
Months Rule	Average Difference	True Turns Indicated	False Turns Indicated	Average Difference	True Turns Indicated	False Turns Indicated
1	1.7	7	41	1.0	5	42
2	3.1	7	9	2.0	5	29
3	4.0	7	4	3.4	5	17
4	5.2	6	4	4.4	5	12
5	5.0	5	2	5.0	4	11

Index of lagging indicators

	Peaks			Troughs		
Months Rule	Average Difference	True Turns Indicated	False Turns Indicated	Average Difference	True Turns Indicated	False Turns Indicated
1	3.7	7	46	6.3	6	44
2	5.1	7	15	8.6	5	27
3	9.1	7	5	15.5	2	21
4	11.1	7	2	16.5	2	13
5	12.1	7	2	17.5	2	9

Source: Calculated by author.

time of the index of leading indicators is negative which means that this index is "predicting" turning points which have already happened. The index of coincident indicators shows lagging behavior under a four- or five-month rule. Under these rules, the index of lagging indicators is indicating turns a year or more after they have happened!

Considering these difficulties, choosing the best months rule is a very difficult task. There is a trade-off between the accuracy of the indexes and their timing behavior. But whichever months rule is chosen, if the indexes could be used as indicators of economic activity at all points in time, and not just around turning points, then the difficulties of choosing a months rule could be eliminated.

The Whole-Cycle Approach

The historic lead-lag behavior of the indexes with respect to economic activity over *all* points in the cycle, rather than just near turning points, can be investigated using a type of time series analysis called spectral analysis.[12] The length of time it takes for a complete business cycle, up–down–up, is called its period. The National Bureau has found that business cycles average about three years from peak to peak, for a period of 36 months. Roughly speaking, spectral analysis decomposes an individual series into a number of other series, each of which is a periodic series with a specific amplitude. The periodic series, or waves, into which the original series is decomposed sum to the original series. Spectral analysis provides a measure, the "power," of how much of the movement in the original series is due to each of the component periodic series.

Applying spectral analysis to two series, called cross-spectral analysis, yields two important measures for each periodicity. The first is a measure of the correlation, or strength of association, between cycles of the same periodicity. This measure, the squared coherence, is analogous to the coefficient-of-determination (R^2) statistic in regression analysis. The more closely a periodic component of one series is related to the like component of the other series, the closer is the squared coherence to unity. Calculating the squared coherence for the whole range of periodicities yields a profile, called the cross-spectrum, of the degree of association between two series.

The second important measure derived from cross-spectral analysis is the phase displacement. The phase displacement is the number of time units, here months, separating the peaks (or troughs) of a periodic component of one series from the like component of the other series. Calculating the phase displacement for the whole range of periodicities yields a profile of the leads and lags between the two series.

Exhibit 5 presents the squared coherences and phase displacements for each of the indicator indexes and the index of industrial production. For business cycle periodicities, 20–40 months, all three indexes have high squared coherences and the appropriate phase lead or lag behavior. At periodicities lower than 12 months, however, the squared coherences for the leading and lagging indexes decline dramatically. Also, the timing behavior of these two indexes degenerates at these lower periodicities. The index of leading indicators becomes coincident and the index of lagging indicators lags by only about a month.

---

[12] Some useful references on spectral analysis are Gwilym M. Jenkins and Donald G. Watts, *Spectral Analysis and Its Applications* (San Francisco: Holden Day, 1968); and George S. Fishman, *Spectral Methods in Econometrics* (Cambridge, Mass. Harvard University Press, 1969).

EXHIBIT 5 Behavior of the Indexes over the Whole Cycle

	ILI* and IIP†		ICI‡ and IIP		LII† and IIP	
Periodicity (months)	Squared Coherence	Phase Lead (+) or Lag (−)‖	Squared Coherence	Phase Lead (+) or Lag (−)‖	Squared Coherence	Phase Lead (+) or Lag (−)‖
66	.86	7.2	.97	−1.0	.77	−12.7
40	.92	4.2	.96	−.5	.81	−9.4
30	.96	3.5	.97	−.2	.87	−8.1
25	.92	2.9	.96	−.4	.90	−6.9
20	.79	2.1	.96	−.5	.85	−6.8
12	.52	1.8	.75	−.1	.13	−3.9
8	.61	1.0	.88	−.1	.14	−2.3
6	.25	.8	.69	.0	.58	−2.1
4	.23	−1.2	.75	.0	.46	−2.0
3	.28	.1	.57	−.1	.05	−1.2
2.5	.42	−.3	.66	−.1	.31	−1.2
2.4	.18	.1	.66	.1	.14	−.8
2.3	.15	−.5	.33	−.1	.11	1.1
2.0	.21	.1	.10	−.1	.43	1.0

* ILI = Index of leading indicators.
† IIP = Index of industrial production.
‡ ICI = Index of coincident indicators.
§ LII = Index of lagging indicators.
‖ Phase leads and lags are measured in months.
Source: Calculated by author.

The lead length of the index of leading indicators is highly variable depending on which periodic component dominates the movements of the index. Moreover, if movements in the index are heavily influenced by movements of low-periodicity components, then false signals can arise because of the low squared coherences at these periodicities. The index of lagging indicators also exhibits these types of problems. Since the index of coincident indicators has only four component series, one of which is the index of industrial production, it is not surprising that the movements of these two series are so closely related.

When the indexes are evaluated using the whole-cycle approach, many of the same conclusions reached in the turning-point analysis reappear. False signals can be given, and the timing behavior is not consistent. It is clear, however, that the indexes do contain valuable information. At business cycle periodicities, the indexes are basically reliable indicators.

PROBLEMS WITH THE INDEXES

False signals and variable lead-lag behavior appear whether the three indexes are evaluated by the turning-point approach or by the whole-cycle approach. Perhaps these problems are, at least partially, the result of the methods used to construct the indexes. Construction of the indexes involves choosing the component series and then deciding how to weight each of them in importance in adding them together. Both of these steps, as currently carried out, involve the largely subjective "scoring procedure" and do not rely on statistical theory. Choosing the component series for each index relies on the notion of a turning point, a concept deriving more from intuition than from statistical theory.

The National Bureau's notion of a turning point rests on the idea that the underlying structure of economic activity, which the indexes are designed to detect, undergoes an important or special change at certain points in time, the turning points. In particular, the idea presupposes that the underlying structure of the economy during upturns is different than during downturns. There is little theoretical or empirical evidence to support this conception of the business cycle.[13] Moreover, there is little statistical theory which can guide the construction of indexes to detect such movements in economic activity.

The National Bureau approach, however, does seem to fit naturally into the well-developed statistical theory of time series.[14] Instead of predicting or detecting turning points, this theory is the whole-cycle approach which seeks to detect the mean or trend of economic activity. Like the National Bureau approach, time series models tend not to rely on economic theory. Instead, time series methods seek to detect significant patterns of relations between economic variables by analyzing the variables with purely statistical models. Some of these methods have been applied to the index of leading indicators, yielding results suggesting where the problems with the National Bureau's procedure lie.

Choosing Series

Using time series methods, the component series of the index of leading indicators can be tested to see if they contain information which is really useful for predicting movements in the index of industrial production. Forecasts about future industrial production can be made using only past and current values of the index of industrial production alone. If forecasts of industrial production using the leading indicators of the index of leading indicators are more accurate than forecasts using only

---

[13] Some work on the theory of turning points has been done. See William E. Weckes, "Predicting the Turning Points of a Time Series," *Journal of Business* 52, no. 1 (1979), pp. 35–49; also Salih N. Neftci, "Optimal Prediction of Cyclical Downturns," *Journal of Economic Dynamics and Control* 4, (1982), pp. 225–41.

[14] See Thomas J. Sargent and Christopher A. Sims, "Business Cycle Modeling without Pretending to Have Too Much A Priori Economic Theory," in *New Methods in Business Cycle Research* (Minneapolis: Federal Reserve Bank of Minneapolis, October 1977).

the current and past values of the index of industrial production, then the component leading series contain valuable information. Such tests are called "Granger-causality" tests.[15]

Testing for Granger-causality in the leading series in this way makes rigorous the concept of a "leading series." The National Bureau's only criterion for leading indicators is that the peaks and troughs of these series consistently lead those of the business cycle chronology as determined by a visual inspection of the plots of the data. But a leading series chosen in this way does *not* necessarily help predict the index of industrial production any better than using only current and past values of the index of industrial production.[16] In other words, from the standpoint of predicting future values of industrial production and not turning points per se, there may be no additional information in a leading indicator.

Testing the information content of 11 of the 12 component series of the index of leading indicators reveals that 6 of the component series are not helpful predictors when the data are seasonally adjusted. When nonseasonally adjusted data are used, only one component series is not helpful.[17] These results suggest that it would be better not to seasonally adjust the data, contrary to the Commerce Department's current procedure. Also, other series which are not presently used as components of the index of leading indicators have yet to be tested to see if they could improve the forecasting power of this index.

Choosing Weights

In a statistical sense, the weights for the component series of each index were not chosen in the best way—that is, they were not estimated from the data, but rather were computed according to the "scoring procedure." The scoring procedure is largely subjective because there is simply no other way to combine the component series without a statistical theory of turning-point prediction. In fact, the indexes are almost unweighted, since all the weights are near unity (see Exhibit 1). From the standpoint of detecting the trend in economic activity at all points in time, ignoring turning points, the weights can be statistically estimated.

[15] See C. W. J. Granger, "Investigating Causal Relations by Econometric Models and Cross-Spectral Methods," *Econometrica* 37, no. 3 (1969); and Christopher A. Sims, "Money, Income, and Causality," *American Economic Review* 62, no. 4 (1972).

[16] Thomas Sargent gives some theoretical examples of this in his book *Macroeconomic Theory* (New York: Academic Press, 1979), pp. 247–48.

[17] These tests were conducted on an earlier version of the index of leading indicators. The results are from Salih N. Neftci, "Lead-Lag Relations, Exogeneity, and Prediction of Economic Time Series," *Econometrica* (January 1979), pp. 101–13.

Perhaps the indexes could be improved if the weights of the component series were chosen in this way.

When the weights for the index of leading indicators are statistically estimated, they do not resemble the Commerce Department weights. Indeed, some of the statistically estimated weights turn out to be negative. Moreover, one researcher found that estimating the weights over different sample periods indicated that the relations were not stable between the component series of the index of leading indicators and the underlying business cycle pattern, since different weights for the index were chosen for each sample. This finding suggests that over time the relations change between the individual series used to construct this index and the underlying pattern of economic activity.[18]

When the weights are estimated over one sample period and the index of leading indicators so constructed is employed to forecast over another sample period, the results are poor compared to the Commerce Department's weights.[19] Even though the weights chosen by the Commerce Department do not seem to be the best in a statistical sense, no obviously superior set of weights has yet been found.

SUMMARY

The main problem with the indexes is that they are based on the ambiguous concept of a turning point. Consequently, there is little statistical theory justifying the classification of series into leading, lagging, and coincident indicators. Also, there is no theory suggesting how the best indexes should be constructed to detect turning points. Consideration of the construction of the indexes from the standpoint of the whole-cycle approach, for which there is a theory, reveals some problems and puzzles but not necessarily answers and solutions. Only more research can resolve the issues about constructing indexes.

The practical forecaster is left with the difficulty of interpreting the behavior of the indexes. If the turning-point approach is correct, then it is not clear that any significance can be attached to the magnitude of an index's movement, but only to the direction. If the whole-cycle approach is correct, then significance can be attached to the magnitude of the movement of an index, but months rules to detect turning points make no sense. No theory implies that one index can do both. Which-

---

[18] These results were reported by Alan J. Auerbach, "The Index of Leading Indicators: Measurement Without Theory, Twenty-Five Years Later" (Cambridge, Mass.), National Bureau of Economic Research, Working Paper No. 761.

[19] Ibid.

ever view is adopted, the indexes contain some valuable information even though they also give false signals.

It would be easy to conclude that difficulties with the indexes are so serious that the indexes should be discarded. But other methods of forecasting and measuring aggregate economic activity also have problems. The indexes have proven useful, and the general approach seems fruitful. Progress in the spirit of the National Bureau's approach is being made toward improved indexes.[20]

---

[20] See Robert B. Litterman, "A Use of Index Models in Macroeconomic Forecasting," Federal Reserve Bank of Minneapolis, Staff Report 78 (March 1982). Also see Stephen Beveridge and Charles R. Nelson, "A New Approach to Decomposition of Economic Time Series with Attention to Measurement of the Business Cycle," *Journal of Monetary Economics* 7, (1981) pp. 151–74.

PART TWO

Government Deficit and Trade Balance

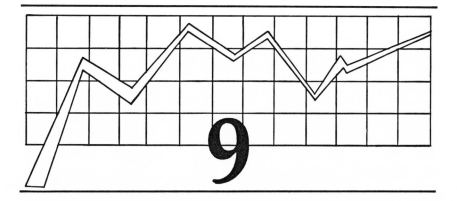

Government Deficits and the Budget

Joseph Scherer, Ph.D.
Economic Consultant
Georgetown, Maine

In mid-1984, the consensus forecasts for the federal government budget projected future annual deficits in the neighborhood of $200 billion. The size of these deficits is unprecedented. Even more serious, however, was the expectation that, for the first time, the federal deficit would not be reduced appreciably (if not actually eliminated) in a recovery period, the usual case following a recession. In fact, there was widespread concern that the deficit might become larger despite the expansion of economic activity. To label this unhappy set of economic circumstances, a new phrase was coined—*the structural deficit.* While the federal budget has long been one of the prime variables in any assessment of the economic outlook, it moved to center stage in the 80s and carried with it a heightened concern—more strongly, fears—that Federal Reserve monetary policy might become increasingly tight again in an attempt to offset the huge budget deficit and that interest rates, both nominal and real, would climb to new peaks.

Federal government taxes and spending, of course, affect the economy in many diverse ways, depending on the specifics of each tax and spending program. In turn, the budget and its resultant surplus or deficit as a total aggregative package affects the overall functioning of the economy. Financial and business analysts, therefore, must constantly rework their analyses to determine whether the changing picture of the budget will promote or hinder business activity with particular emphasis on how the budget will affect the level of inflation, the level of interest rates, and how much of the available new savings (investment funds) will be siphoned off to finance the unfolding deficit.

There are no simple one-sentence answers to these questions; much depends on surrounding circumstances. Consequently, it is helpful to see how we have arrived at the present condition. It is also helpful to understand the different analytical ways the budget is viewed and the way a new budget comes into being. In the process of building this background, the meaning of some seemingly identical terms, which are quite different in meaning and interpretation, must be clearly differentiated. A sample list of these terms include *unified budget, current services budget, high-employment budget, federal sector in the national income accounts, budget resolution, structural deficit, budget deficit,* and *total deficit.* All these terms refer to interrelated but quite different aspects of the federal budget and their relationships to other financial and economic variables. Each provides some analytical help in assessing budget performance and impact. The uses and limitations of these and other terms must be explored both to arrive at a balanced assessment of a given budget with its likely impact on current and future business activity.

BUDGET TRENDS

The bulk of any new budget, on both the revenue and the spending sides, is determined by past legislation. New legislation in any one year, whether reducing or eliminating some outlays and taxes or expanding existing programs and introducing new ones, is only the tip of the total budget iceberg. While changes have only a relatively small impact in the year of introduction, they can have a very large impact in future years. Social security and medicare are prime examples of programs introduced years ago that have expanded greatly on both the outlays and tax sides. More recently, the expansion of defense spending by the Reagan administration, the 1983 social security legislation, and the multiyear tax cut passed in 1981 (although relatively small in the first year) will have substantial impacts in future years. A look at trends since the end of World War II is useful in placing the current budget picture in perspective.

Summary Budget Trends

Since World War II, federal government revenue and spending have traced a generally similar upward path, although the revenue side of the budget tends to move somewhat more erratically. As is well known, spending typically has exceeded revenues so that only in eight years has there been a budget surplus and none since fiscal 1969. For many years, the deficits were under $5 billion and, until the 70s, rarely over $10 billion (see Exhibit 1). Thereafter, the deficits began ranging toward the record deficits of $47–55 billion associated with the World War II years. Unfortunately, the upward deficit trend continued into the 80s to establish a new peak of $195 billion in fiscal 1983, with the prospect that annual deficits would continue to run in the neighborhood of $200 billion, and possibly higher, through the rest of the 80's.

In dollar terms, federal spending exploded from $55 billion in fiscal 1946 to more than $796 billion in fiscal 1983. It must be noted, however, that the economy as a whole, as measured by the gross national product (GNP), has also expanded sharply over the same time span. Since government spending has grown at a more rapid pace, it has risen as a percentage of GNP from about 14 percent to 25 percent in fiscal 1983. Exhibit 2 provides annual data for the period since 1965 for GNP, budget receipts, outlays, surplus or deficit, and federal debt, as well as each item as a percentage of GNP. All the budget items have increased far faster in dollar magnitudes than they have as a percentage of GNP. Except in years when the deficit is quite large, both receipts and outlays generally are about the same percentage of GNP and show an upward trend from around 18 percent in 1965 to 20 percent in 1979. The combination of recession and tax cuts in the period since then is reflected in receipts falling to 19 percent of GNP while spending climbed to 25 percent by 1983.

Trends in Receipts

The long-run trend of tax receipts since 1946 has been upward for all of the broad categories, but there have been shifts in the relative importance among the tax categories. Individual income taxes rose from $16 billion in 1946 to $289 billion in 1983 and constitute the backbone of the government's revenue stream, contributing in the neighborhood of 45 percent of total revenue over much of the period (see Exhibit 3). This position has been maintained even though there were some sizable tax cuts during the period. On the other hand, corporate profits taxes, even though they increased from $12 billion to $37 billion from 1946 to 1983, produced a declining share of total revenue, dropping from 31 percent of total revenue to 6 percent. Social security taxes have replaced corporate profits taxes as the second largest component of receipts, rising from $3 billion to $209 billion—in percentage terms, going from less than 8 percent to almost 35 percent. In 1982, the two major forms of taxation, individual income taxes and social insurance taxes, accounted for 83 percent of the total tax take. Estate and gift taxes, custom duties, excise taxes, and other miscellaneous taxes are small in percentage terms

EXHIBIT 1   Federal Budget, 1946–1983

A. Outlays and Receipts

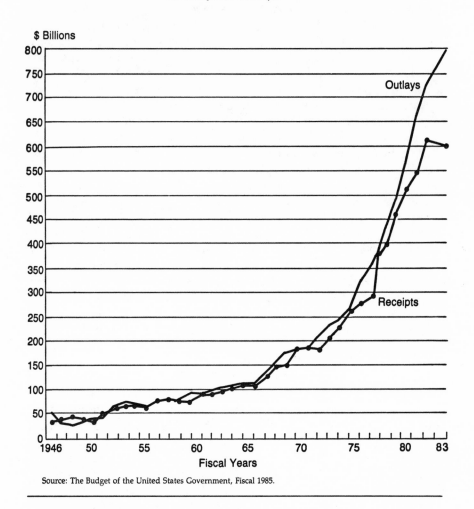

Source: The Budget of the United States Government, Fiscal 1985.

but together contributed $66 billion in 1983, $29 billion more than the corporate profits tax.

Trends in Spending

On the spending side, it is convenient to use the broad categories of the federal government expenditures in the national income accounts

EXHIBIT 1   (*concluded*)

B. Surpluses and Deficits

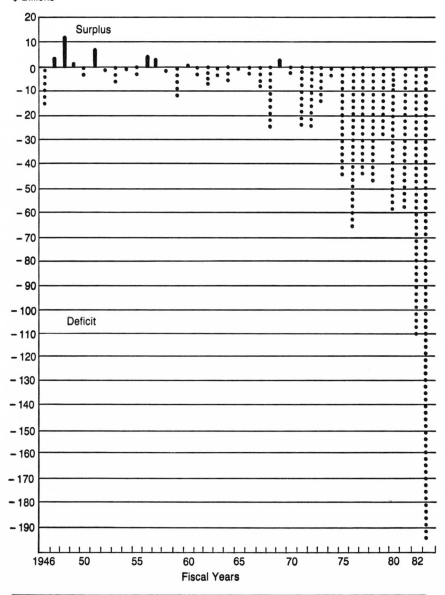

EXHIBIT 2   Federal Finances and the Gross National Product, 1965–1983 ($ billions)

					Outlays		
						Off-Budget Federal Entities	
		Budget Receipts					
Fiscal Year	Gross National Product	Amount	Percent of GNP	Amount	Percent of GNP	Amount	Percent of GNP	Amount
1965	659.5	116.8	17.7	118.4	18.0			118.4
1966	724.1	130.9	18.1	134.7	18.6			134.7
1967	777.3	148.9	19.2	157.6	20.2			157.6
1968	831.3	153.0	18.4	178.1	21.4			178.1
1969	910.6	189.6	20.5	183.6	20.2			183.6
1970	968.8	192.8	19.9	195.7	20.2			195.7
1971	1,031.5	187.1	18.1	210.2	20.4			210.2
1972	1,128.8	207.3	18.4	230.7	20.4			230.7
1973	1,252.0	230.8	18.4	245.6	19.6	.1	†	245.7
1974	1,379.4	263.2	19.1	267.9	19.4	1.4	.1	269.4
1975	1,479.9	279.1	18.9	324.2	21.9	8.1	.6	332.3
1976	1,640.1	298.1	18.2	364.5	22.2	7.3	.4	371.8
1977	1,862.8	355.6	19.1	400.5	21.5	8.7	.5	409.2
1978	2,091.3	399.6	19.1	448.4	21.4	10.4	.5	458.7
1979	2,357.7	463.3	19.7	491.0	20.8	12.5	.5	503.5
1980	2,575.8	517.1	20.1	576.7	22.4	14.2	.6	590.9
1981	2,882.0	559.3	20.8	657.2	22.8	21.0	.7	678.2
1982	3,057.3	617.8	20.2	728.4	23.8	17.3	.6	745.7
1983	3,228.8	600.6	18.6	796.0	24.7	12.4	.4	808.3

* The off-budget deficits are equal to the off-budget outlays but with the opposite sign.
† 0.05% or less.
Source: The Budget of the United States Government, fiscal 1985.

(NIA), since the multiple spending divisions used in the unified budget are reclassified in the NIA into only five major groups. In Exhibit 4, the dollar level and the percentage each category is of the total are shown for selected years.

Total spending for any given year in the NIA differs slightly from the spending total in the unified budget because the accounting system used is different in the two accounts; but over a long period, the small differences in the totals are not important. Total spending on an NIA basis has risen sharply from $40 billion in 1946 to $816 billion in 1983. The category "purchases of goods and services" represents the amount of current output in the economy that has been absorbed by the government. It rose from about $20 billion in 1946 to $275 billion in 1983. As a percentage of total spending, the purchases component declined from 50 percent in 1946 to 34 percent by 1983. Within the purchases component, the defense segment represented 43 percent of total spending in 1946 and was 23 percent of total spending in 1982.

EXHIBIT 2 (*concluded*)

Total	Budget		Total (including off-budget)*		Total		Held by the Public	
Percent of GNP	*Amount*	*Percent of GNP*	*Amount*	*Percent of GNP*	*Amount*	*Percent of GNP*	*Amount*	*Percent of GNP*
17.9	−1.6	.2	−1.6	.2	323.2	49.0	361.6	39.6
18.6	−3.8	.5	−3.8	.5	329.5	45.5	264.7	36.5
20.3	−8.7	1.1	−8.7	1.1	341.3	43.9	267.5	34.5
21.4	−25.2	3.0	−25.2	3.0	369.8	44.5	290.6	34.8
20.2	3.2	.4	3.2	.4	367.1	40.3	279.5	30.7
20.2	−2.8	.3	−2.8	.3	382.6	39.5	284.9	29.4
20.4	−23.0	2.2	−23.0	2.2	409.5	39.7	304.3	29.5
20.4	−23.4	2.1	−23.4	2.1	437.3	38.7	323.8	28.7
19.6	−14.8	1.2	−14.9	1.2	468.4	37.4	343.0	27.4
19.5	−4.7	.3	−6.1	.4	486.2	35.3	346.1	25.1
22.5	−45.2	3.1	−53.2	3.6	544.1	36.8	396.9	26.8
22.7	−66.4	4.0	−73.7	4.5	631.9	38.5	480.3	29.3
22.0	−44.9	2.4	−53.6	2.9	709.1	38.1	551.8	29.6
21.9	−48.8	2.3	−59.2	2.8	780.4	37.3	610.9	29.2
21.4	−27.7	1.2	−40.2	1.7	833.8	35.4	644.6	27.3
23.0	−59.6	2.3	−73.8	2.9	914.3	35.5	715.1	27.8
23.6	−57.9	2.0	−78.9	2.8	1,003.9	34.8	794.4	27.6
24.6	−110.7	3.6	−127.9	4.2	1,147.0	37.5	929.4	30.4
25.0	195.4	6.1	−207.8	6.4	1,381.9	42.8	1,141.8	35.4

Surplus or Deficit (−) spans the Total, Budget, and Total (including off-budget) columns. *Federal Debt, End of Year* spans the Total and Held by the Public columns.

EXHIBIT 3   **Federal Budget Receipts: Distribution by Source**

	Fiscal 1946*		Fiscal 1976*		Fiscal 1983*	
Individual income taxes	41.0%	$16.1	43.9%	$131.6	48.1%	$288.9
Corporation income taxes	31.1	12.2	13.8	41.4	6.2	37.0
Social insurance taxes and contributions	7.8	3.1	30.9	92.7	34.8	209.0
Excise taxes	16.9	6.6	5.7	17.0	5.9	35.3
Estate and gift taxes	1.7	0.7	1.7	5.2	1.0	6.1
Customs duties	0.9	0.4	1.4	4.1	1.4	8.7
Miscellaneous receipts	0.5	0.2	2.7	8.0	2.6	15.6
Total receipts†	100.0%	$39.3	100.0%	$300.0	100.0%	$600.6

* Amounts given for each fiscal year in percent of total receipts and $ billions.
† Details may not add to totals because of rounding.
Source: The Budget of the United States Government.

EXHIBIT 4   Federal Spending in the National Income Accounts

$ Billions

Account	Fiscal 1946*		Fiscal 1976*		Fiscal 1983	
Purchases of goods and services	50%	$20	34%	$125	34%	$275
(Defense purchases)	(43)	(17)	(23)	(84)	(24)	(197)
Transfer payments	33	13	42	157	42	345
Grants-in-aid to state and local governments	2	1	16	58	11	86
Net interest paid	10	4	7	25	11	91
Subsidies less current surplus of government enterprises	5	2	2	6	2	20
Total*	100%	$40	100%	$371	100%	$816

* Amounts given for each fiscal year in percent of total spending and $ billions.
† Details may not add to totals because of rounding.
Source: The Budget of the United States Government.

Transfer payments rose from $13 billion in 1946 to $345 billion in 1983 and, as a percentage of total spending, rose from 33 percent to 42 percent from 1946 to 1983—thereby moving up from second place to first. The transfer-payments category represents the so-called entitlement programs for which individuals meeting the standards for eligibility automatically draw benefits. The major components in the transfer-payments category in 1983 are shown in Exhibit 5.

For the remaining 25 percent of spending, two categories—grants-in-aid and interest—were each 11 percent of the total in 1983. The grants-

EXHIBIT 5   Major Components in the Transfer-Payments Category, 1983

	$ Billions	Percent of Total
1. Social security (old age and survivors and disability insurance)	160	47
2. Medicare	56	17
3. Unemployment benefits	30	9
4. Civil service retirement	22	6
5. Military retirement	16	5
6. Veterans benefits	17	5
7. Railroad retirement	6	2
8. Other transfers	33	10
Total*	339	100

* Details may not add to totals because of rounding.
Foreign transfer payments ($6 billion) omitted from this table.

in-aid programs, which provide funds to state and local governments for activities thought to be administered best below the federal level, have grown rapidly since 1946. Some of these activities (such as highway building) are long established, while others are relatively new (such as medicaid). By contrast, the percentage of the total comprised by interest payments is little changed since 1946, but will begin to rise as outsized deficits continue, with additional pressures if interest rates remain high.

THE BUDGET PROCESS[1]

Until the passage of the Congressional Budget and Impoundment Control Act on July 12, 1974, the budget process in the Congress was fragmented; indeed, there was virtually no satisfactory congressional control over total federal spending. In addition, the Congress had no committees charged with consolidating the various pieces of budget legislation into a meaningful whole as they entered the legislative hopper. Nor did it have a staff that could have provided it with such an overview. The new budget control act established a budget committee in the House and in the Senate to coordinate budget policy. It also established a Congressional Budget Office (CBO) to provide information and analysis comparable to that which the OMB provides the executive branch.

The 1974 budget act sets up a timetable for the congressional budget process which is summarized in Exhibit 6. In addition to setting new requirements, the act integrates previously existing executive and congressional schedules. Under the new procedures, the president still submits his budget at approximately the same time in January as in the past; the present schedule specifies it be done by the 15th day after the Congress convenes. The actual budget process, of course, begins well before the president submits his budget, for that document represents the culmination of budget making within the executive branch. A new part of the whole budget process is the requirement laid down by the Congress that the president submit to it a "current services budget" much earlier—by November 10.

The Current Services Budget

The current services budget is meant to provide a benchmark or baseline against which any changes later proposed by the president or by the

---

[1] This section has been adapted from material in the author's article, "New Directions for the Federal Budget," Federal Reserve Bank of New York *Quarterly Review*, Spring 1977. For a discussion of budget concepts used prior to the unified budget, see Joseph Scherer, "A Primer on Federal Budgets," Federal Reserve Bank of New York *Monthly Review*, April 1965.

EXHIBIT 6   Timetable For Budget Action

On or Before:	Action to be Completed
November 10	President submits current services budget
Fifteen days after Congress convenes	President submits official budget
March 15	Committees and joint committees submit reports to budget committees in House and Senate
April 1	Congressional Budget Office submits report to budget committees
April 15	Budget committees report first concurrent resolution on the budget to their respective houses
May 15	Legislative committees report bills and resolutions authorizing new budget authority
May 15	Congress completes action on first concurrent resolution on the budget
Seventh day after Labor Day	Congress completes action on bills and resolutions providing new budget authority and new spending authority
September 15	Congress completes action on second required concurrent resolution on the budget
September 25	If necessary, Congress completes action on reconciliation bill or resolution, or both, implementing second required concurrent resolution
October 1	New fiscal year begins

Congress can be measured. A current services budget is one that estimates federal tax and spending programs on the assumption that they are continued without any change in policies. These estimates are presented for the current fiscal year and also for the fiscal year ahead. This budget must also take into account the effects of expected changes in economic activity or of other trends. Examples of such changes are higher or lower levels of unemployment or inflation, variation in the number of social insurance beneficiaries, or variation in the number of recipients under programs that are mandated by existing legislation (such as those for veterans).

The Standard Appropriation Process

The standard procedure has been and continues to be that each new activity of the federal government—or the expansion of an old activity—must be authorized by a bill which has been passed by both houses of the Congress and has been signed by the president. Such bills are considered first by the appropriate legislative committee (in both the House of Representatives and the Senate) responsible for the subject the bill addresses. If necessary, the bill includes an *authorization* to appropriate up to a specified amount of money for the program. If the committees approve, the bill is brought to a vote before the full membership of each branch of the Congress. If the bills passed by the two houses differ in any respect, these differences must be resolved by a conference committee composed of members of the two houses. If there is an acceptable resolution, then identical bills are resubmitted for passage in each house and transmitted to the president for signature.

Actual authority to spend funds typically involves a further step—the passage of the *appropriation* bill, again by both houses of the Congress. (The stated amount on the appropriation bill may be no more, but may be less than, the amount in the authorization bill.) The appropriation bill must also be signed by the president. An appropriation specifically permits a federal agency to order goods and services and to draw funds from the Treasury to pay for these goods and services as well as to meet payrolls up to some stated amount. Other spending may take the form of transfers of funds to state and local governments, to individuals, or to governments abroad and international agencies. Spending in any single fiscal year is always made up of a combination of spending from some appropriations carried over from previous years as well as from appropriations newly legislated.

AN ANALYTICAL FRAMEWORK FOR BUDGET ANALYSIS

With the background of how the budget comes into being each year and knowing the broad contours of the budget picture in the postwar period, an analytical framework can be put into place for evaluating the massive deficits looming over the next several years. A number of elements which interact with each other and influence other economic and financial variables will be described. It will be noted, however, that these variables, in turn, have repercussions which affect the budget picture, so that there is a mutual interaction making it difficult to isolate causal relationships. As different variables change—particularly when the magnitudes and direction of change differ from what had been expected—it is necessary to go back to the drawing board to rework the analysis.

The Current Services Budget

The current services budget, as noted previously, provides estimates for all items of receipts and outlays on the assumption that there have been no policy changes. The same approach is also called a "baseline projection." For example, spending for social security in the budget next year would take into account all those who currently draw benefits plus the number expected to be added in the next budget year less those expected to die; under current law, any expected increase in the cost of living adjustment would then be factored in. Similarly, on the receipts side, individual income taxes would be estimated on the basis of the projected level of economic activity, with particular importance placed on the level of expected personal income. Thus, the current services budget for fiscal 1985 indicates how much total receipts, total spending, and the resultant deficit would be in the absence of any new legislation. It serves as a guide to compare a no-change budget (i.e., the current services budget) with one containing changes proposed by the president or by others.

In estimating the current services budget for future years, a critical element is the economic assumptions underlying the estimates for each succeeding year. The estimate of the future level of GNP, rate of inflation, unemployment rate, and interest rates—to name a few—will greatly affect both the receipts and spending sides of the budget. For example, a change of one percentage point in the Treasury bill rate might make a difference of some $4–5 billion in annual interest costs.

Using the current services budget for comparing a no-change budget with various proposed budgets, an analyst must determine whether the economic assumptions are reasonable and, if they are not, what a reasonable set of assumptions might do to the estimates. The adoption of the current-services-budget device, as described in the section on the budget process, together with the requirement that the proposed budget be projected for future years, was a significant improvement in budgetary techniques and can be credited with calling attention to the outlook for $200 billion deficits for the mid-80s despite an economic recovery and moderate growth in the economy.

Role of the High-Employment Budget

The high-employment budget is an estimate of the budget on the assumption that the economy is operating at high-employment levels of economic activity. In the past, a budget surplus was viewed as restrictive fiscal policy, a budget deficit was considered stimulative fiscal policy, and a balanced budget was seen as neutral in its impact on the economy. The budget and the economy, however are not independent of each other but are interrelated. Thus, a very restrictive budget which at high employment would generate a large surplus might cause the economy to fall into a recession, and that budget would consequently show an actual end-of-year deficit. Since the actual budget outcome was a deficit, it would be viewed as stimulative with the simplistic rule cited above, when in fact it was so restrictive that it caused a severe slowdown in the economy. To correct for the impact of the economy on the budget outcome, the analytical device was developed of estimating budgets by using a standard level of economic activity—the high-employment level of activity.

The high-employment calculation simply provides a standard yardstick to compare the economic role of different budget structures; it does not follow that a balanced budget at high employment is the desired goal at a particular time. The desired budget policy is one that will impart the appropriate impulse to the economy, moving it from the existing level of economic activity to the level of activity desired in the future, near-term and long-term.

Role of the Structural Deficit

The term *structural deficit* is relatively new; it refers to a budget deficit that will occur even if the economy is functioning at high-employment levels—a time when a budget is often presumed to be in balance. A cyclical deficit, by contrast, is a deficit that takes place because the economy is functioning at less than high-employment levels or below its full potential. In other words, there is a deficit because there is a recession-induced shortfall in receipts and a recession-induced increase in spending because of higher unemployment benefit payments and other recession-related spending increases. Thus, a given deficit might be decomposed into two segments—a portion that arises from cyclical elements and a portion that arises from structural elements, as is expected to be the case through much of the 80s. This can be done by calculating a budget at actual expected levels of economic activity (i.e., a current services budget) and comparing it to the equivalent high-employment budget.

If a sizable structural deficit exists at high-employment levels, it means that the budget (fiscal policy) is stimulative at a time when much, if not all, of this stimulis is not needed or desired. In the absence of an appropriate offsetting monetary policy, the budget would generate inflationary pressures. To eliminate a structural deficit requires raising taxes or cutting spending, or some combination of the two. Whatever policy changes are made, the impact is not likely to be felt uniformly among various income groups, industries, and geographic areas. Much of the existing structural deficit (1984 and on) can be traced to the large increase in defense spending and the multiyear tax cut whose final stage was effective in 1983; some of the structural deficit is imbedded in the entitlement programs and the failure to weed out waste and inefficiency.

One segment of the structural deficit, however, is generally not discussed when the deficit problem is under examination—the deficit of the off-budget agencies. The off-budget federal entities are federal agencies or programs that have been excluded from the unified budget under the legislation passed when these agencies were set up or when they were removed from the budget at a later time. In fiscal 1983, the off-budget entities added an additional $12 billion to the $195 billion unified budget deficit to give a total deficit of $208 billion (see Exhibit 2). As will be noted in the next section, the off-budget deficit adds to the total amount of borrowing that the Treasury must do.

Role of the Federal Debt

The federal government debt at the end of fiscal 1983 was $1.4 trillion. The major factor, by far, responsible for the change in the debt from one year to the next is the deficit (budget and off-budget) that must be financed by the Treasury. But for any given year-to-year change, the amount of borrowing is not exactly equal to the deficit. The amount of borrowing will also depend on such matters as how large a balance the Treasury had when the previous year ended and how much has been gained from seigniorage in minting new coins. For the 80s, the deficit with its resultant drain on the nation's capital markets has become a critical variable in the business and financial outlook because it will absorb a much more sizable portion of the new savings (investment funds) of each year, so that some private borrowers will be unable to borrow and those who do will pay higher interest rates than would have been the case.

A somewhat neglected aspect of the government debt picture is the role played by the Federal Reserve System's monetary policy. Federal Reserve open market operations are the major tool used for implementing its policy objectives. Open market operations are carried out by buying or selling *outstanding* issues of U.S. government securities. If the Fed should embark on a tighter monetary policy over the next several years and sell government securities out of its portfolio to tighten the reserve positions of the banks, it means that the private sector must not only absorb all the new securities issued by the Treasury to finance the huge deficit, but the public must also buy the already outstanding issues sold by the Fed. Thus, savings available to the private sector are further reduced from the amount that would have been the case if only the deficit had to be financed, therefore adding further restraint to the primary impact of open market sales by the Fed. Moreover, even if the Fed does not, on balance, actually reduce its portfolio of government securities but merely refrains from buying more, it means that a growing economy must get along without any growth in the money supply, so that interest rates are still being subjected to some upward pressure.

The General Approach

The various elements in the analytical framework and other background material are pulled together here to suggest the probable direction of the budget and its interaction with the economy. As noted previously, the dominant theme for the mid-80s is the outsized federal budget deficit. It is almost impossible to find anyone who does not view with alarm the current and prospective deficits, no matter what the political or economic persuasion of the viewer.

What does the analyst who is not an expert in budgetary matters do to keep himself informed about developments? To begin, there are the experts (official and nonofficial) who provide a good deal of information and analysis, which is generally reported in the newspapers and business press. On the official side, the administration releases the bulk of its budgetary material through the Office of Management and Budget (OMB). An independent assessment for the Congress is provided by the Congressional Budget Office (CBO). Then, there are the knowledgeable commentators, particularly those associated with financial organizations, who write regular newsletters which are quoted in the press. Another set of knowledgeable commentators are those associated with independent research organizations such as the Brookings Institution, the American Enterprise Institute, and the Conference Board.

If one does not wish to rely completely on some outside "expert," however, there is the need to have a set of tools to evaluate the evidence and opinion available in such profusion. For self-guidance, the material developed earlier comes in handy.

First, it is necessary to know what the actuals have been for the previous fiscal year. Then, you should know what is expected for the current fiscal year, which starts in October and runs through the following September. By the middle of the fiscal year, particularly after the April figures are in, official estimates and unofficial estimates are likely to be in the ball park in years when things seem to be reasonably "normal." Moving forward, you begin focusing on the future, most particularly on the next fiscal year, which is engaging the attention of the president and the Congress. On the basis of the schedule summarized in Exhibit 6, by late August or certainly by late September, the necessary legislation for the next fiscal year should be in place. Unfortunately, this has not been the case in recent years, when major legislation (including some important appropriations bills) still had not been passed.

As long as major pieces of legislation are still pending, the size of the new budget remains uncertain so that it is necessary to put together a package of possible or probable alternatives. Under these circumstances, an outside analyst probably depends on the detailed analyses available in the releases of the OMB and CBO for making up his own combination.

In examining the projections for any budget in the so-called out-years, it is important to know what the economic assumptions are for each year, for reasons discussed earlier. Whether the projected budget deficit is reasonable is closely linked to the reasonableness of the economic assumptions. Moreover, as long as the federal sector continues to have a number of agencies off-budget, the unified budget deficit is not sufficient; it is necessary to add the off-budget deficit to it, and that will add some $15–20 billion.

While the annual totals in the federal sector in the NIAs are similar to those in the unified budget, the quarterly data reported for the federal sector in those accounts do not provide any clue to the demands that the Treasury will put on the credit markets, because the NIA data are seasonally adjusted annual rates. The actual seasonally unadjusted pattern of spending by the government from one month to the next is fairly even; but tax receipts are very erratic during the year, so that certain months are always deficit months and a few others (particularly April and June) are almost always surplus months, even in years when the annual deficit is quite large.

THE OUTLOOK

If there are no changes in the tax structure and in spending programs, the current-service-budget estimates by all experts (regardless of political or economic persuasion) show budgets running in triple-digit billions of dollars on the deficit side through the mid-80s even if the economy should continue to expand. Moreover, even if the economy were to reach the high employment level, the deficits probably would run in the range of $150–200 billion. In light of these potential outsized deficits over the next several years, the need for legislation to generate more revenue and/or restrain the growth of spending is gaining broad support among quite diverse political groups.

To finance these large deficits, the Treasury is expected to preempt a larger portion of the annual savings stream (investment funds) than it had in the past and thereby crowd out some private borrowers who otherwise would have obtained funds. Greater demand for available savings puts upward pressure on interest rates, raising the cost of capital to the private sector as well as substantially raising the interest costs of the government, not only for its new borrowing but also for refinancing the large volume of existing debt that matures every year. In addition, the U.S. interest rates higher than in other countries attract foreign funds to the United States. While the inflow of foreign funds helps provide more loanable funds here than would otherwise be the case, it also pushes up the exchange rate of the dollar relative to other currencies. The high exchange rate for the dollar in turn makes foreign goods cheaper, thereby increasing imports while raising the price of American goods sold abroad. Thus, American products become less competitive, so that the balance of trade and the balance of payments problems are made more difficult.

With the large deficits generating inflationary pressures, the Federal Reserve finds itself on the horns of a dilemma. If it follows a monetary policy that is typical for a growing economy—that is, taking those steps that increase the money supply to facilitate the growth—the monetary policy combined with the stimulative fiscal policy would tend to add further upward pressure on interest rates by fostering greater fears about the potential upticks in inflationary pressures down the road. If it takes steps to offset the stimulative fiscal policy, credit availability is curtailed so that interest rates again might reach new peaks (similar to the situation that existed in the early 80s).

The major role in coping with this difficult situation therefore falls into the fiscal area to construct budget changes that point toward steady and substantial declines in the deficit over the next several years. These economic requirements must then be resolved by new legislation on tax changes and spending changes that are politically acceptable. There is little question that additional revenue must be raised, but there are no easy answers on how policy should be implemented. Similarly, hard decisions must be made in the spending area. It remains for the electoral process to reveal how and where that ball will bounce.

SOURCES OF DATA

Budget of the U.S. Government with supporting documents is presented to the Congress by the president, usually in the last week in January (see Exhibit 6). It contains annual data, actuals for some previous years, reestimates of the current year, estimates for new fiscal year, and current services budgets.

Congressional Budget Office reports to the Senate and House committees on the budget. Coverage similar to *Budget* and its supporting documents.

Federal Reserve Bulletin—monthly. Summary data on budget and debt.

Survey of Current Business—monthly. NIA federal sector data, quarterly.

U.S. Treasury: *Monthly Statement of the Public Debt.* Summary totals and details on all outstanding issues.

U.S. Treasury: *Monthly Statement of Receipts and Outlays.* Summary totals and major breakdowns by agency and function.

U.S. Treasury: *Treasury Bulletin*—quarterly since 1982, previously monthly. Budget and debt data, less detailed than in *Monthly Statements*, plus data not elsewhere published.

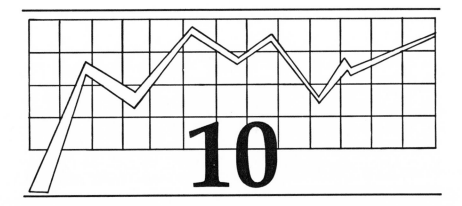

The Balance of Payments

Dominick Salvatore, Ph.D.
Professor and Chairman
Department of Economics
Fordham University

The purpose of this chapter is to examine the meaning and measurement of the balance of payments in general, and the balance of payments of the United States in particular. We begin with the definition of the balance of payments and the purpose of such a measure. Then we introduce some balance of payments accounting principles. The third section examines the relationship between a nation's balance of payments and the level of the nation's gross national product (GNP). We then present and analyze the international transactions of the United States for the year 1982. Subsequently, the meaning of a disequilibrium in international transactions and in the balance of payments is examined. This is followed by a brief balance of payments history of the United States. Finally, the related international investment position of the United States is presented. The Appendix presents the complete, unabridged statement of the international transactions of the United States for the years 1981 and 1982.

DEFINITION AND PURPOSE OF THE BALANCE
OF PAYMENTS

The balance of payments is a statement which summarizes all of the international transactions of the residents of a nation with the residents of all other nations during the course of a year. Some nations, including the United States, also keep the balance of payments on a quarterly basis. The information contained in the balance of payments is indispensible for the nation's monetary authorities in formulating monetary, fiscal, and commercial policies. It is also invaluable for banks, firms, and individuals who are either directly or indirectly involved in international trade and finance.

Some clarifications and elaborations are in order with regard to the above definition of the balance of payments. First of all, the balance of payments summarizes into a few major categories the literally millions of international transactions taking place each year, rather than presenting each transaction individually. Thus, all merchandise trade is subdivided and grouped into a few large categories such as foods, fuels, and capital goods. Because of the difficulty in tracking down gross international capital flows, only the balance of each type of international capital flow is recorded. There are then some transactions recorded in the balance of payments in which the residents of other nations are not directly involved. An example occurs when a bank purchases the currency of another nation from the nation's central bank.

What then is an international transaction, and who is a resident? An international transaction refers to the exchange of a good, service, or asset (for which payment is usually required) between the residents of one nation and the residents of other nations. However, gifts and certain other transfer payments are also included into the nation's balance of payments even though no payments are made. As for residency, tourists, temporary migrants, diplomats, and military personnel abroad are the residents of the nation of which they are citizens. Similarly, a corporation is the resident of the nation in which it is incorporated, but its foreign branches and subsidiaries are not. International institutions such as the United Nations, the International Monetary Fund, and the World Bank are not the residents of the nation in which they are located (by their very nature, they are the residents of no nation).

BALANCE OF PAYMENTS
ACCOUNTING PRINCIPLES

We now introduce some essential balance of payments accounting principles. We begin by defining debits and credits, and then examine and give examples of double-entry bookkeeping.

Debits and Credits

International transactions are classified as debits or credits. *Credit transactions* (entered with a positive sign) are defined as those transactions that lead to the receipt of payments *from* foreigners. *Debit transactions* (entered with a negative sign) are those that lead to payments *to* foreigners.

The export of goods and services, unilateral transfers (gifts) received from foreigners, and capital inflows are entered as credits (+) in the nation's balance of payments because they lead to the receipt of payments from foreigners. On the other hand, the import of goods and services, unilateral transfers or gifts made to foreigners, and capital outflows are debits (−) because they lead to payments made to foreigners.

Capital inflows can take the form of either an increase of foreign assets in the nation or a reduction in the nation's assets abroad. For example, the purchase of a U.S. stock by a foreign resident is an increase of foreign assets in the United States and a credit of the United States because it leads to a payment from foreigners. The sale of a foreign stock by a U.S. resident is a reduction in U.S. assets abroad. This is also a credit of the United States because it leads to the receipt of a payment from foreigners. Thus, both the purchase of a U.S. stock by a foreign resident and the sale of a foreign stock by a U.S. resident lead to the receipt of a payment from foreigners, and so they are both entered as credits (+) in the U.S. balance of payments.

On the other hand, *capital outflows* can take either the form of an increase in the nation's assets abroad or a reduction in foreign assets in the nation. Both lead to a payment to foreigners. For example, the purchase of a German Treasury bill by a U.S. resident increases U.S. assets abroad, and it is a U.S. debit because it leads to a payment to foreigners. Similarly, the sale by a French firm of a U.S. subsidiary reduces foreign assets in the United States, and it also leads to a payment to foreigners. Both the purchase of a foreign treasury bill and the foreign sale of a U.S. firm are capital outflows of the United States and are entered as debits (−) in the U.S. balance of payments.

These definitions—of capital inflows into the United States as increases in foreign assets in United States or reductions in U.S. assets abroad, and of capital outflows from the United States as increases in U.S. assets abroad or reduction in foreign assets in the United States—can be confusing and are somewhat unfortunate. However, this is the terminology actually used in all U.S. government publications and cannot be avoided.

To summarize, the export of goods and services, the receipt of unilateral transfers, and capital inflows are credits (+) because they all lead to the receipt of payments from foreigners. On the other hand, the import of goods and services, unilateral transfers to foreigners, and capital out-flows are debits (−) because they lead to payments to foreigners.

Double-Entry Bookkeeping

Each transaction is recorded twice in the nation's balance of pay-ments—once as a credit and again as a debit of an equal amount. This accounting procedure is known as *double-entry bookkeeping.* It is used because a transaction usually has two sides to it. When we sell some-thing, we record the sale as a credit (because it leads to a payment from foreigners), and the actual payment from foreigners is then recorded as an equal debit. On the other hand, when we buy something, we record the purchase as a debit (because it leads to a payment to foreigners), and the actual payment we make to foreigners is then entered as a credit of an equal amount. We can clarify the double-entry bookkeeping proce-dure with few examples.

As a first example, suppose that a U.S. firm exports $1,000 of mer-chandise and agrees to be paid in three months. The United States credits merchandise exports for $1,000 since this leads to a payment from foreigners. The foreigner's promise to pay is instead entered as a U.S. short-term capital outflow (a debit) because, by accepting to be paid in three months, the U.S. exporter has acquired a claim on the foreign importer. This is an increase in U.S. assets abroad and a debit. The entire transaction is entered as follows in the U.S. balance of payments:

	Debit (−)	Credit (+)
Short-Term Capital Outflow	1,000	
Merchandise Exports		1,000

As another example, suppose that a U.S. tourist in Paris spends $400 on hotels, meals, sightseeing trips, and so on. The U.S. tourist is pur-chasing travel services from French people, requiring a payment to them. The only difference between this and an import of a good or service from France is that the service that the American tourist pur-chases is consumed in France rather than in the U.S. Thus, the United States debits services for $400. The payment itself is then recorded as a short-term credit of $400 in the U.S. balance of payments. It is an in-crease in foreign claims on the United States, since French people can subsequently use the $400 to purchase U.S. goods and services equal to that amount. This is equivalent to an increase in foreign assets in the United States and is recorded as a short-term capital inflow (a credit or +) in the U.S. balance of payments. The entire transaction is entered as follows:

	Debit (−)	Credit (+)
Services Purchased from Foreigners	400	
Short-Term Capital Inflow...........................		400

As a third example, assume that the U.S. government ships $100 worth of grains to India as part of its foreign aid program. The United States debits unilateral transfers for $100 and credits exports (even though it does not actually receive a payment for the grains). The transaction is entered in the U.S. balance of payments as follows:

	Debit (−)	Credit (+)
Unilateral Transfers Made............................	100	
Merchandise Exports................................		100

As a fourth transaction, suppose a foreign resident purchases a U.S. stock for $600 and pays for it by drawing down his or her bank balances in the United States by $600. The purchase by the foreigner of a U.S. stock increases foreign assets in the United States and is recorded as a long-term capital inflow or credit of $600 in the U.S. balance of payments. The reduction in foreign bank balances in the United States is a decrease in foreign assets in the United States (a short-term capital outflow) and is recorded as a short-term debit in the U.S. balance of payments. Note that both sides of this transaction are financial. The entire transaction is recorded as follows in the U.S. balance of payments:

	Debit (−)	Credit (+)
Short-Term Capital Outflow	600	
Long-Term Capital Inflow		600

Finally, suppose that a U.S. resident purchases $200 of U.K. Treasury bills and pays $200 into the foreigner's bank account in the United States. The purchase of the U.K. Treasury bills increases U.S. assets abroad by $200. This is a capital outflow from the United States and is recorded as a short-term capital debit of $200 in the U.S. balance of payments. On the other hand, the payment by the U.S. resident increases foreign bank balances in the United States by $200. This is a capital inflow of the United States and is recorded as a short-term capital credit in the U.S. balance of payments. Note that both entries are now short-term capital flows:

	Debit (−)	Credit (+)
Short-Term Capital Outflow (the purchase of U.K. Treasury bills by the U.S. resident)	200	
Short-Term Capital Inflow (the increase in foreign bank balances in the United States)		200

If the above five transactions were all the international transactions of the United States during the year, the U.S. balance of payments would be as follows:

	Debit (−)	Credit (+)
Services..	400	
Unilateral Transfers	100	
Short-Term Capital, Net..............................	1,200	
Merchandise		1,100
Long-Term Capital...............................		600
Total	1,700	1,700

The net merchandise credit balance of $1,100 was obtained by adding the $1,000 exports and the $100 worth of grains shipped as part of the U.S. foreign aid program. The net short-term capital debit balance of $1,200 resulted from adding the five short-term capital entries (−$1,000, $400, −$600, −$200, $200) examined separately earlier. Total debits equal total credits because of double-entry bookkeeping.

THE BALANCE OF PAYMENTS AND THE LEVEL OF ECONOMIC ACTIVITY

The balance of payments is related to the level of economic activity, or gross national product, of the nation. Imported goods and services generate employment in the foreign nation where the goods are produced, rather than in the nation consuming the imported goods. On the other hand, the production of goods and services for export generates employment in the exporting nation. On balance, the level of economic activity or GNP in a nation is stimulated by an export surplus (the value of exports minus the value of imports) and reduced by an import surplus.

A nation facing a recession or excessive unemployment might be tempted to restrict imports in order to stimulate domestic economic activity. However, as the nation's imports are the exports of other nations, other nations are likely to retaliate. The net result would then be a shrinking of international trade and a loss, in all nations concerned, of the grains from specialization in production and trade. A nation could balance an import surplus with an inflow of capital from abroad and should attempt to cure a recession with other policies (such as expansionary fiscal and monetary policies) rather than with trade restrictions.

The actual value of imports of a nation during a particular year is directly related to the level of economic activity, or GNP, of the nation in that year. With an increase in economic activity, a nation demands more goods, services, and resources; and part of this increase in demand spills into imports. For example, a $100 million increase in GNP results in a $13 million increase in U.S. imports, and this has been rising over time as the United States became more dependent on foreign mineral resources (such as petroleum imports). On the other hand, the level of a nation's exports depends on the level of economic activity in the rest of the world. Thus, expansion of economic activity in a nation tends to increase its import surplus or reduce its export surplus.

INTERNATIONAL TRANSACTIONS AND ACCOUNTING BALANCES OF THE UNITED STATES

We are now ready to examine the international transactions of the United States and several accounting balances of international transactions.

International Transactions of the United States

Exhibit 1 presents a summary of the International transactions of the United States for the year 1982 (the last year for which complete data were available as this book went to press). The complete unabridged statement of U.S. international transactions for 1981 and 1982 is presented as Exhibit 5 in the Appendix. In Exhibit 1, credits are entered with a positive sign and debits with a negative sign.

Exhibit 1 shows that the United States exported (+)$348.3 billion goods and services in 1982. Merchandise exports of (+)$211.2 billion included aircrafts, computers, machinery, chemicals, agricultural products, and so on. Service exports of (+)$137.1 billion included travel and transportation services provided to foreigners, fees and royalties received from foreigners, and interest and dividends earned on U.S. foreign investments. Note that while capital outflows from the United States are recorded as capital debits, the earnings received from abroad for the *services* of U.S. foreign investments are recorded as credits under services.

On the other hand, the United States imported goods and services for an amount equal to (−)$351.5 billions in 1982. Merchandise imports of (−)$247.6 billion included automobiles, petroleum, television sets, shoes, textiles, and many other products. Imports of services of (−)$103.9 billion included the travel and transportation services purchased by U.S. citizens from other nations, fees and royalties paid to foreigners, and the interest and dividends paid for the services of foreign investments in the United States.

EXHIBIT 1   Summary of U.S. International Transactions for 1982
                 ($ billions)

Exports of goods and services	$ 348.3
Merchandise	211.2
Services	137.1
Imports of goods and services	−351.5
Merchandise	−247.6
Services	−103.9
Unilateral transfers, net	−8.0
U.S. government grants	−5.4
U.S. government pensions and other transfers	−1.5
Private remittances and other transfers	−1.1
U.S. assets abroad, net [increase/capital outflow (−)]	−118.0
U.S. official reserve assets, net	−5.0
U.S. government assets, other than official reserve assets, net	−5.7
U.S. private assets, net	−107.3
Direct investment abroad	+3.0
Foreign securities	−8.0
Nonbank claims	7.0
Bank claims	−109.3
Foreign assets in the U.S., net [increase/capital inflow (+)]	87.9
Foreign official assets in the U.S., net	3.2
Other foreign assets in the U.S., net	84.7
Direct investment in the U.S.	10.4
U.S. Treasury and other U.S. securities	13.1
Nonbank liabilities	−3.1
Bank liabilities	64.3
Statistical discrepancy	41.3
Accounting balances	
Balance on current account	−11.2
Balance on capital account	−28.3
Balance of payments	1.8
Balance on official reserve account	−1.8

Source: Compiled from Exhibit 5 in the Appendix.

The United States made *net* unilateral transfers to foreigners of (−) $8.0 billion during 1982. This included (−)$5.4 billion of grants to foreign nations for economic and military aid, (−)$1.5 in U.S. government pensions and other transfers to foreign nations, and (−)$1.1 billion of private remittances and other transfers. Private remittances and other transfers refer to emigrant remittances to relatives abroad and to other private gifts. The net debit balance on all these items resulted from U.S. government and private transfers abroad exceeding foreign transfers to the United States.

The stock of U.S. assets abroad increased (a capital outflow of the United States and a debit) by the net amount of (−)$118.0 billion during 1982. This included a net increase of (−)$5.0 billion in the stock of U.S.

official reserve assets, a net increase of (−)$5.7 billion in the stock of U.S. government assets other than official reserve assets, and the net increase in the stock of U.S. *private* assets abroad of (−)$107.3 billion.

The official reserve assets of the United States include the gold holdings of U.S. monetary authorities, special drawing rights, the U.S. reserve position in the International Monetary Fund (IMF), and the official holdings of foreign currencies by U.S. monetary authorities (see lines 39–42 in Exhibit 5). Special drawing rights (SDRs, or "paper gold") are international reserves created by IMF and distributed to member nations according to their importance in international trade. The reserve position in the IMF refers to gold paid in by the nation upon joining the IMF and which the nation can borrow automatically from the IMF in case of need. Member nations can borrow further amounts subject to the conditions imposed by the IMF.

The increase in U.S. private assets abroad of (−)$107.3 included the decline in U.S. foreign direct investments abroad of (+)$3.0 billion, the increase in U.S. holdings of foreign securities of (−)$8.0 billion, the decline in U.S. nonbank claims of (+)$7.0 billion, and the increase of (−)$109.3 billion in U.S. bank claims against foreigners.

The stock of foreign assets in the United States increased (a capital inflow of the United States and a credit) by (+)$87.9 billion in 1982. This included the net increase of foreign official assets in the United States of (+)$3.2 billion and the net increase in other foreign assets in the United States by (+)$84.7 billion. The latter was made up by the net increase in foreign direct investments in the United States of (+)$10.4 billion, the net increase in foreign holdings of U.S. Treasury and other U.S. securities of (+)$13.1 billion, the net decline in U.S. nonbank liabilities of (−)$3.1 billion, and the increase in U.S. bank liabilities of (+)$64.3 billion.

There was no allocation of special drawing rights (SDRs) during 1982.

The overall total credits of the United States during 1982 were thus equal to (+)$436.2 billion [(+)$348.3 billion of exports of goods and services, plus (+)$87.9 billion of the net increase in foreign assets in the United States]. On the other hand, the overall total debits of the United States during 1982 were equal to (−)$477.5 billion [the net debit balance of (−)$351.5 billion of imports of goods and services, plus the (−)$8.0 net unilateral transfers of the United States plus the (−)$118.0 net increase in U.S. assets abroad].

With the overall debit total of (−)$477.5 and the overall credit total of (+)$436.2 billion, the need arose for a net credit entry called *statistical discrepancy* for (+)$41.3 billion in order to make the overall debits equal to the overall credits, as required by double-entry bookkeeping. The statistical discrepancy arises from recording mistakes or unreported items, especially unreported capital outflows.

Accounting Balances

We now examine the accounting balances appearing at the bottom of Exhibit 1. The first is the balance on *current account* which shows a net debit balance of (−)$11.2 billion for the United States in 1982. This was obtained by subtracting the value of the imports of goods and services of (−)$351.5 and the net unilateral balance of (−)$8.0 billion from the exports of (+)$348.3 billion for the U.S. in 1982.

The second balance at the bottom of Exhibit 1 gives the balance on capital account for the United States in 1982. The *capital account* of the United States measures the change in U.S. assets abroad and foreign assets in the United States, *other than official reserve assets*. The increase in U.S. assets abroad other than official reserve assets is (−)$113.0 billion, obtained by adding the (−)$5.7 billion increase in U.S. government nonreserve assets to the (−)$107.3 increase in U.S. private assets abroad during 1982. On the other hand, the increase in foreign nonreserve assets in the United States is (+)$84.7 billion. Thus, the balance in the U.S. capital account in 1982 is equal to (−)$28.3 billion (−$113.0 + $84.7). Official reserve assets are excluded from the measure of the capital account because they reflect government policy and intervention rather than market forces.

Adding together the balance on current account of −$11.2 billion, the balance on capital account of −$28.3 billion, and the statistical discrepancy of +$41.3 billion, we get the *balance of payments* of +$1.8 billion for the United States for the year 1982. The net credit balance of $1.8 billion means that the United States had a *surplus* of that amount in its balance of payments in 1982. It resulted from foreigners spending $1.8 billion more in the United States than the United States spent abroad.

The last balance in Exhibit 1 gives the balance on official reserve account. This shows a net debit balance of (−)$1.8 billion. It was obtained by adding the −$5.0 billion increase in U.S. official reserve assets to the $3.2 billion increase in foreign official assets in the United States. The balance in the official reserve account is equal in magnitude and opposite in sign to the balance on U.S. payments for 1982. This is the way by which the U.S. balance of payments surplus was settled—that is, by a net increase in U.S. official reserve assets (a debit) of (−)$1.8 billion. (Actually, the U.S. balance of payments surplus for 1982 was $2.3 billion because $0.5 billion was deducted from the net increase in official foreign assets in the United States of $3.2 billion. See Exhibit 5, line 81).

Had total debits exceeded total credits in the current and capital accounts and for the statistical discrepancy when taken together, the net debit balance would have indicated a deficit of that amount in the U.S. balance of payments. There would then have been a net credit balance of equal magnitude in the official reserve account in order to settle the deficit in the U.S. balance of payments. As will be seen later, the United States had a deficit in its balance of payments in every year since 1970, except in 1979 and 1982.

The items in the current and capital accounts (as well as the statistical discrepancy) are sometimes called *autonomous items* because they take place for business or profit motives (except for unilateral transfers) and are independent of balance of payments considerations. On the other hand, transactions in official reserve assets are called *accommodating items* because they result from, and are needed to, balance international payments and receipts.

DISEQUILIBRIUM IN
INTERNATIONAL TRANSACTIONS

We now discuss the concept and the measurement of disequilibrium in international transactions and payments under fixed and flexible exchange rate systems.

The Exchange Rate

The definition and measure, given in the previous section, of the deficit or surplus in a nation's balance of payments is strictly applicable only under a fixed exchange rate system and not under the type of flexible exchange rate system in operation today. In order to understand this, we must first examine the meaning of the exchange rate, of a depreciation or appreciation of a nation's currency, of a fixed exchange rate system, and of a flexible exchange rate system. This will be accomplished with the aid of Exhibit 2.

For simplicity we assume that there are only two nations, the United States and the United Kingdom, and only two currencies, the U.S. dollar ($) and the British pound sterling (£). The *exchange rate* of the dollar is then defined as the price of one pound in terms of dollars. That is, the exchange rate (R) of the dollar is the number of dollars required to purchase one pound, or $/£. This is measured along the vertical axis of Exhibit 2. For example, R = 1.60 means that $1.60 is required to purchase £1.

An increase of R (a movement upward along the vertical axis of the figure in Exhibit 2) is referred to as a *depreciation* of the dollar, since more dollars would be required to purchase £1. For example, an increase in the exchange rate from R = 1.60 to R = 1.80 means that 20 cents more would be required to purchase £1. On the other hand, a decrease in the

EXHIBIT 2   The U.S. Foreign Exchange Market for Pounds (£)

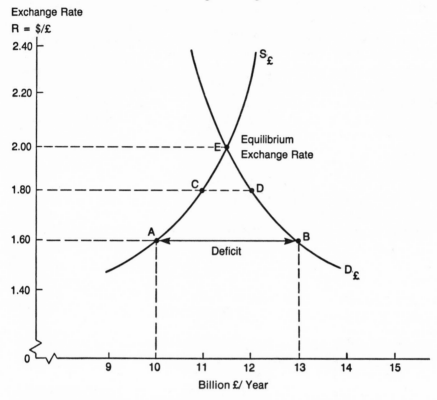

dollar price of the pound refers to an *appreciation* of the dollar, since fewer dollars would then be required to purchase £1. For example, a decline in the exchange rate from R = 1.60 to R = 1.50 means that 10 cents less would be required to purchase £1.

The horizontal axis of the figure in Exhibit 2 measures the quantity of pounds per year. $D_£$ is then the U.S. demand curve for pounds. It arises in the process of U.S. residents purchasing goods and services from and investing in the U.K. When the exchange rate of the dollar falls, British goods and investments become cheaper and more attractive to Americans. For example, a record costing £3 in the U.K. costs $5.40 to U.S. residents if R = 1.80, but only $4.80 at R = 1.60. Therefore, $D_£$ is usually negatively sloped, indicating that at lower exchange rates Americans demand a greater quantity of pounds (just as a greater quantity of any commodity is demanded when the price of the commodity falls).

On the other hand, the U.S. supply of pounds ($S_£$) arises in the process of Americans exporting goods and services to the U.K. and receiving British investments. An increase in the exchange rate of the dollar makes American goods and investments cheaper to English residents. For example, a $14.40 American calculator costs £9 at R = 1.60, but only £8 at R = 1.80. As a result, at higher exchange rates of the dollar, British residents purchase more goods and services and invest more in the United States. That is, they usually supply greater quantities of pounds to the United States so that the U.S. $S_£$ curve is positively sloped (just as the supply of any commodity).

Disequilibrium under Fixed and Flexible Exchange Rates

We are now ready to examine how a deficit or surplus in a nation's balance of payments arises under a fixed exchange rate system. Under this system (which was in operation up to 1973), the exchange rate is not allowed to vary. Any excess in the quantity demanded over the quantity supplied of the foreign currency at the prevailing (fixed) exchange rate represents the deficit in the nation's balance of payments. This must be covered (settled) by a loss of an equal amount of international reserves by the nation. For example, at the exchange rate of R = 1.60, £13 billion are demanded by the United States, but only £10 billion are supplied (see Exhibit 2). The excess demand of £3 billion (AB = $4.8 billion at R = 1.60) represents the deficit in the U.S. balance of payments for the year. The United States would then have to draw down its official pound reserves by £3 billion ($4.8 billion) to cover the deficit.

Had the exchange rate been allowed to find its own equilibrium level, the exchange rate would have risen (i.e., the dollar would have depreciated) to R = 2.00. At R = 2.00, the quantity demanded of pounds of £11.5 is equal to the quantity supplied of pounds, so that the U.S. balance of payments would be in equilibrium. Then R = 2.00 would be the *equilibrium exchange rate*. It is only because the exchange rate is not allowed to fluctuate freely to find its own equilibrium level that a balance of payments deficit or surplus arises under a fixed exchange rate system. This is no different than if the price of any good is fixed below in its equilibrium level: a shortage (deficit) of the good would arise.

On the other hand, a balance of payments surplus arises when the exchange rate is above the equilibrium level, because the quantity supplied of the foreign currency would then exceed the quantity demanded of it (see Exhibit 2). Under a freely flexible exchange rate system, the exchange rate would then fall (i.e., the nation's currency would appreciate) until the surplus is eliminated. Only if the exchange rate were fixed above its equilibrium level would the balance of payments surplus persist. The surplus nation would then continue to accumulate international reserves.

If a balance of payments disequilibrium (deficit or surplus) is automatically corrected under a freely flexible exchange rate system, the logical question then is why monetary authorities would ever want a system of fixed exchange rates. One reason is that under a freely flexible exchange rate system, exchange rates can vary frequently and erratically over time. This discourages international trade and investments, as traders and investors face ever changing prices (in terms of their own currency) for traded goods and foreign investments. On the other hand, in a rapidly changing world, an exchange rate originally fixed at the equilibrium level will soon be out of equilibrium, leading to balance of payments deficits or surpluses which must be settled.

If a balance of payments deficit is not quickly corrected, the deficit nation may soon run out of official reserves. On the other hand, a surplus nation is usually unwilling to continue to accumulate international reserves after it feels it has an adequate amount. Thus, both balance of payments deficits and surpluses require adjustment. In our discussion, we concentrate on balance of payments deficits rather than on surpluses because the need to correct a deficit is more compelling and immediate (the nation would simply run out of international reserves). Furthermore, the United States has had balance of payments deficits over most of the last decade.

Disequilibrium under the Present International Monetary System

While exchange rates are allowed to vary under the present system, they are not *freely* flexible—monetary authorities usually intervene in foreign exchange markets, allegedly to prevent erratic fluctuations in exchange rates, while allowing some exchange rate adjustment to take place. For example, the United States may not want to allow the exchange rate of the dollar to rise (i.e., the dollar to depreciate) all the way to the equilibrium rate of R = 2.00 in Exhibit 2. U.S. monetary authorities may feel that this large depreciation would make U.S. imports (especially of needed raw materials) too expensive. If the United States allowed the dollar to depreciate only from R = 1.60 to R = 1.80, the U.S. balance of payments deficit would be cut from £3 billion (AB in Exhibit 2) to £1 billion (CF = $1.8 billion). This system is called a *managed float*, or *dirty float*, and it is the system in actual operation today.

Since under a *freely flexible* exchange rate system, a balance of payments disequilibrium (deficit or surplus) would be automatically and entirely eliminated by the exchange rate moving to its equilibrium level, a balance of payments disequilibrium would only be temporary and not of much consequence. Even under the present managed floating system, the excess demand for foreign exchange only measures the degree of official intervention in the foreign exchange markets and not the actual disequilibrium itself, since part of the disequilibrium is eliminated by the allowed change in the exchange rate. Only under a fixed exchange rate system would the excess demand of foreign exchange measure the true deficit in the nation's balance of payments, and the excess supply measure the true surplus.

Because of the type of exchange rate system in operation today, U.S. monetary authorities refuse to measure explicitly the size of the excess demand or the excess supply of foreign exchange of the nation (see the memoranda items at the bottom of Exhibit 5). What we have called the balance of payments in Exhibit 1 thus represents simply the amount of official intervention in the market for foreign exchange (to keep the dollar from appreciating further as required to eliminate the U.S. balance of payments surplus in 1982).

However, most other nations, the International Monetary Fund, and newspapers and other media keep on discussing the "deficit" or "surplus" in the nation's balance of payments and so we are compelled to do so too. This is fine as long as it is kept clearly in mind that a deficit or surplus today refers only to the amount of official intervention to stabilize exchange rates. The true deficit or surplus would be larger without the adjustment occurring through the allowed fluctuation in exchange rates.

BALANCE OF PAYMENTS HISTORY OF THE UNITED STATES

We can now briefly examine the postwar balance of payments history of the United States and the events that led to the collapse in 1971 of the fixed exchange rate system set up at the end of World War II and to the establishment of the present managed floating exchange rate system.

The U.S. Balance of Payments over Time

From 1945 to 1949, the United States had huge balance of payments surpluses as most nations, ravaged by the war, had little to sell to the United States while wanting to purchase many U.S. goods and services. This was the time of the so-called dollar shortage. The United States used part of its balance of payments surpluses to finance the Marshall Plan, aimed at helping reconstruction in war-torn nations in Europe.

With reconstruction more or less complete by 1950 in Europe and Japan, the U.S. balance of payments turned in deficits. These deficits were rather small (averaging about $1.5 billion per year) until 1957, and the United States did not view them unfavorably because they allowed European nations and Japan to rebuild their international reserves.

Starting in 1958 and continuing until 1969, U.S. balance of payments deficits more than doubled in size because of (1) sharply increased U.S. direct investments to Europe (a capital outflow and debit for the United States), (2) a higher inflation rate in the United States than in most other developed nations of the world (which further eroded the competitiveness of U.S. products on world markets), and later (3) because of the cost of the Vietnam war. These large U.S. deficits were an important contributing factor to the collapse of the fixed exchange rate system in 1971 and to the establishment in 1973 of the present managed floating exchange rate system (discussed in the next section).

Exhibit 3 summarizes the U.S. balance of payments from 1970 to 1982. The last column shows that the United States had a deficit in its balance

EXHIBIT 3   Summary of U.S. International Transactions, 1970–1982 ($ billions)

Year	Exports of Goods and Services	Imports of Goods and Services	Balance of Merchandise Trade	Balance on Goods and Services	Balance on Current Account	Balance of Payments
1970	66	−60	3	6	2	−9
1971	69	−66	−2	2	−1	−29
1972	77	−79	−6	−2	−6	−10
1973	110	−99	1	11	7	−5
1974	146	−137	−5	9	2	−9
1975	156	−133	9	23	18	−5
1976	172	−162	−9	9	4	−10
1977	184	−194	−31	−9	−14	−35
1978	221	−230	−34	−9	−14	−32
1979	289	−282	−27	7	1	+15
1980	345	−334	−25	11	4	−7
1981	373	−362	−28	11	4	0
1982	350	−350	−36	0	−8	−2

Source: U.S. Department of Commerce, Bureau of Economic Analysis, *Survey of Current Business* (Washington, D.C.: U.S. Government Printing Office, June 1983), pp. 38–39.

of payments in every year except 1979 and 1982. Note that the difference between the balance on current account and the balance on goods and services gives the balance on unilateral transfers (not shown), and the difference between the balance of payments deficit or surplus and the balance on current account gives the sum of the balance in the capital account and the statistical discrepancy.

Several important things must be kept in mind in interpreting balance of payments data. First, as pointed out earlier, balance of payments deficits and surpluses measure only the amount of official intervention in foreign exchange markets rather than the true deficit or surplus, under the exchange rate system in operation since 1973. Second, too much attention is usually placed on the trade balance. The reason may be that this is the first of the balance of payments data to become available. Third, it is dangerous to extrapolate yearly figures from quarterly data. Fourth, the items in the balance of payments are closely interdependent. Thus, the attempt by a nation to reduce a balance of payments deficit by restricting capital outflows (a debit) will also diminish the future stream of earnings from foreign investments (a credit). Similarly, a reduction in foreign aid will usually reduce the exports of the donor nation, especially if foreign aid is tied to be spent in the donor nation (as most foreign aid is today).

Collapse of the Fixed Exchange Rate System

Under the fixed exchange rate system established after World War II, nations were committed to keeping exchange rates fixed, except in case of fundamental disequilibrium. This was defined as a large and persistent actual or potential deficit of a continuing nature. In fact, nations were very reluctant to change exchange rates (devalue or revalue), even when in fundamental disequilibrium, for fear of triggering off wild currency speculation. For example, if a holder of French francs felt that the franc was about to be devalued (reduced in value in relation to another currency, say the German mark), he or she would sell francs to purchase marks (a capital outflow and a debit of France) before the expected devaluation. This would result in great instability in international finance and in the money supply of the nation. However, with fixed exchange rates, deficit and surplus nations were generally unable to quickly and smoothly correct a balance of payments disequilibria.

The United States, for its part, was in a unique position. The dollar was used, together with gold, as an international reserve or currency. Thus, the United States could use dollars to cover its balance of payments deficits. Other nations were willing to accept dollars to cover U.S. deficits because they could then use these dollars to pay for goods and services from the United States and from other nations. The dollar was as good as gold, since the United States stood ready to exchange any foreign-held dollar or gold at $35 per ounce. However, starting around the mid-60s, the amount of dollars held by foreign official monetary authorities began to exceed the official gold reserves of the United

States. In addition, there was an even greater amount of foreign, privately held dollars, which also represented a claim on U.S. gold reserves.

As U.S. balance of payments deficits continued and increased in size over the years, the feeling became widespread that the United States would have to devalue the dollar. This led to a mass conversion of foreign-held dollars into other, more secure currencies (such as the German mark and the Swiss franc), thereby leading to even larger U.S. balance of payments deficits. In the face of a huge balance of payments deficit in 1970 and an even greater one in 1971, the United States was forced to devalue the dollar and cut the link between the dollar and gold. This brought the end of the Bretton Woods system, as the postwar monetary arrangements had come to be known.

The period from mid–1971 to March 1973 was a period of very unsettled conditions in international trade and finance, as various attempts to reestablish a fixed exchange rate system failed. Finally, exchange rates were allowed to fluctuate (with some government intervention in foreign exchange markets), and the current exchange rate system came into existence. Thus, the immediate cause of the collapse of the fixed exchange rate system was the huge U.S. balance of payments deficit in 1971. The fundamental cause was the lack of an effective mechanism for adjusting balance of payments disequilibria. While the present exchange rate system was to some extent forced on the world, it has served the world community reasonably well since its inception. To be sure, exchange rates have sometimes fluctuated very widely. But international trade and investments did not suffer much, as hedging was available to cover foreign exchange risks.

THE INTERNATIONAL INVESTMENT POSITION OF THE UNITED STATES

While a nation's balance of payments measures the international *flow* of goods, services, and capital over a one-year period of time, *the international investment position* of a nation measures the total amount and the distribution of a nation's assets abroad and foreign assets in the nation at the end of each year. Thus, the balance of payments is a flow concept just like the income statement, while the international investment position (sometimes called the balance of international indebtedness) is a stock concept just like the balance sheet.

The international investment position of a nation is useful, among other things, to project the nation's future flows of income or earnings from foreign investments. The international investment position of the nation in a particular year can theoretically be obtained by adding the capital flows between the nation and the rest of the world to the previous year's international investment position of the nation. In reality, this is seldom if ever true, because of unrecorded changes in the domestic currency value of past foreign direct investments, resulting from domestic inflation and from fluctuations in exchange rates over the year.

Exhibit 4 presents the international investment position of the United States at the end of 1970, 1980, 1981, and 1982. Exhibit 4 shows that the

EXHIBIT 4 International Investment Position of the United States at Year-End, Selected Years ($ billions)	1970	1980	1981	1982
Net U.S. international investment position	59	121	156	169
U.S. assets abroad	166	607	717	834
Official reserve assets	15	27	30	34
Gold	11	11	11	11
SDRs	1	3	4	5
Reserve position in the IMF	2	3	5	8
Foreign currencies	1	10	10	10
Other government assets	32	64	68	74
Private assets	118	516	618	726
Direct investments	78	215	226	221
Foreign securities	20	62	63	75
Bank claims	13	204	293	402
Other	7	35	36	27
Foreign assets in the U.S.	107	486	561	665
Official assets	26	176	181	189
Private assets	81	310	380	476
Direct investments	13	68	90	102
Other	67	242	290	374

Source: *Survey of Current Business*, August 1981, p. 56, and August 1983, p. 44.

net international investment position of the United States increased from $59 billion at the end of 1970 to $169 billion at the end of 1982. Over this period, U.S. assets abroad more than quintupled, rising from $166 billion at the end of 1970 to $834 billion at the end of 1982. The amount of foreign assets in the United States rose even more sharply (increasing more than six times) from $107 billion to $665 billion. A very sharp increase in the stock of foreign capital remained even after excluding the effect of inflation (which, over this period, was very high the world over).

Looking at the subcategories of U.S. assets abroad, we find that U.S. official reserve assets and other U.S. government assets abroad more than doubled over the 1970–82 period, while U.S. private assets abroad increased more than six times. In 1982, U.S. private assets abroad were almost seven times larger than U.S. government assets abroad. More than five sixths of U.S. private assets abroad in 1982 were accounted for

EXHIBIT 5 The International Transactions of the United States ($ millions)

Line		1981	1982
1	Exports of goods and services	374,621	348,324
2	Merchandise, adjusted, excluding military	237,019	211,217
3	Transfers under U.S. military agency sale contracts	9,727	12,097
4	Travel	12,163	11,293
5	Passenger fares	2,991	2,979
6	Other transportation	12,593	12,437
7	Fees and royalties from affiliated foreigners	5,813	5,572
8	Fees and royalties from unaffiliated foreigners	1,480	1,567
9	Other private services	6,167	6,576
10	U.S. government miscellaneous services	426	440
	Receipts of income on U.S. assets abroad		
11	Direct investment	32,446	22,888
12	Interest, dividends, and earnings of unincorporated affiliates	18,963	17,565
13	Reinvested earnings of incorporated affiliates	13,483	5,323
14	Other private receipts	50,113	57,127
15	U.S. government receipts	3,684	4,131
16	Transfers of goods and services under U.S. military grant programs, net	680	644
17	Imports of goods and services	−363,098	−351,502
18	Merchandise, adjusted, excluding military	−265,086	−247,606
19	Direct defense expenditures	−11,082	−11,918
20	Travel	−11,479	−12,394
21	Passenger fares	−4,487	−4,772
22	Other transportation	−12,379	−11,638
23	Fees and royalties to affiliated foreigners	−413	−42
24	Fees and royalties to unaffiliated foreigners	−298	−295
25	Private payments for other services	−3,183	−3,700
26	U.S. government payments for miscellaneous services	−1,932	−2,296
	Payments of income on foreign assets in the U.S.		
27	Direct investment	−7,454	−4,844
28	Interest, dividends, and earnings of unincorporated affiliates	−3,694	−5,008
29	Reinvested earnings of incorporated affiliates	−3,761	164

30	Other private payments	−28,553	−33,769
31	U.S. government payments	−16,753	−18,229
32	U.S. military grants of goods and services, net	−680	−644
33	Unilateral transfers (excluding military grants of goods and services), net	−6,931	−8,034
34	U.S. government grants (excluding military grants of goods and services)	−4,549	−5,413
35	U.S. government pensions and other transfers	−1,464	−1,493
36	Private remittances and other transfers	−918	−1,128
37	U.S. assets abroad, net [increase/capital outflow (−)]	−110,601	−118,045
38	U.S. official reserve assets, net	−5,175	−4,965
39	Gold	—	—
40	Special drawing rights	−1,824	−1,371
41	Reserve position in the International Monetary Fund	−2,491	−2,552
42	Foreign currencies	−861	−1,041
43	U.S. government assets, other than official reserve assets, net	−5,078	−5,732
44	U.S. loans and other long-term assets	−9,717	−10,117
45	Repayments on U.S. loans	4,419	4,334
46	U.S. foreign currency holdings and U.S. short-term assets, net	220	51
47	U.S. private assets, net	−100,348	−107,348
48	Direct investment	−9,680	3,008
49	Equity and intercompany accounts	3,803	8,331
50	Reinvested earnings of incorporated affiliates	−13,483	−5,323
51	Foreign securities	−5,636	−7,986
52, 53	U.S. claims on unaffiliated foreigners, reported by U.S. nonbanking concerns — Long-term / Short-term	−1,181	6,976
54, 55	U.S. claims reported by U.S. banks, not included elsewhere — Long-term / Short-term	−83,851	−109,346
56	Foreign assets in the U.S., net [increase/capital inflow (+)]	80,678	86,866
57	Foreign official assets in the U.S., net	5,430	3,172
58	U.S. government securities	6,272	5,089
59	U.S. Treasury securities	4,983	5,759
60	Other	1,289	−670
61	Other U.S. government liabilities	−28	504

EXHIBIT 5 (*concluded*)

Line		1981	1982	Line
62	U.S. liabilities reported by U.S. banks, not included elsewhere	−3,479	−2,054	62
63	Other foreign official assets	2,665	−367	63
64	Other foreign assets in the U.S., net	75,248	84,694	64
65	Direct investment	21,998	10,390	65
66	Equity and intercompany accounts	18,238	10,554	66
67	Reinvested earnings of incorporated affiliates	3,761	−164	67
68	U.S. Treasury securities	2,982	7,004	68
69	U.S. securities other than U.S. Treasury securities	7,171	6,141	69
	U.S. liabilities to unaffiliated foreigners reported by U.S. nonbanking concerns			
70	Long-term	942	−3,104	{70
71	Short-term			71
	U.S. liabilities reported by U.S. banks, not included elsewhere			
72	Long-term	42,154	64,263	{72
73	Short-term			73
74	Allocations of special drawing rights	1,093	—	74
75	Statistical discrepancy (sum of above items with sign reversed)	24,238	41,390	75
	Memoranda			
76	Balance on merchandise trade (lines 2 and 18)	−28,067	−36,389	76
77	Balance on goods and services (lines 1 and 17)	11,523	−3,177	77
78	Balance on goods, services, and remittances (lines 77, 35, and 36)	9,141	−5,799	78
79	Balance on current account (lines 77 and 33)	4,592	−11,211	79
	Transactions in U.S. official reserve assets and in foreign official assets in the U.S.			
80	Increase (−) in U.S. official reserve assets, net (line 38)	−5,175	−4,965	80
81	Increase (+) in foreign official assets in the United States (line 57 less line 61)	5,458	2,668	81

Note: Credits +; debits −.

Source: *Survey of Current Business*, June 1983, pp. 38–39.

by U.S. private bank claims on foreigners (i.e., bank deposits of U.S. residents in banks abroad) and by U.S. direct investments abroad. On the other hand, foreign official assets in the United States were about two fifths of foreign private assets in the United States at the end of 1982. Note also that U.S. direct investments abroad were more than double the amount of foreign direct investments in the United States at the end of 1982, but the latter grew almost three times as fast as the former over the 1970–82 period.

With a large and increasing net U.S. international investment position, the United States did not have a solvency problem in 1982 (nor at any times in the postwar period). Indeed, U.S. foreign lending and investments contributed net earnings of about $41 billion to the U.S. balance of payments (see Exhibit 5) in 1982 ($80 billion in gross earnings received minus $39 billion in gross payments made on foreign investments and lending to the United States). On the other hand, the United States does seem to have a liquidity problem, since U.S. official reserve assets were only $34 billion while foreign official assets in the United States (mostly in the form of dollars or very liquid claims on the United States) were $189 billion at the end of 1982. However, this is based on valuing U.S. gold reserves at the old official gold price, which was about 10 times less than the market price of gold (over $400 per ounce) in 1982.[1]

---

[1] For a more detailed discussion of the topics covered in this chapter, see D. Salvatore, *International Economics* (New York: Macmillan, 1983), chapters 14 and 20; and D. Salvatore, *International Economics: Theory and Problems*, 2d ed. (New York: McGraw-Hill, 1984), chapters 8 and 12 (English, Spanish, French, and Portuguese editions).

PART THREE

Money Supply and Capital Market Conditions

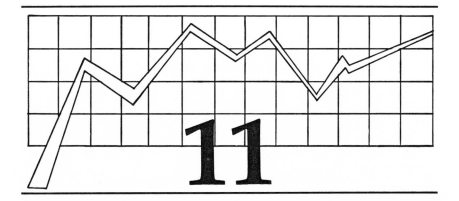

Monetary Aggregates

Steven R. Malin, Ph.D.
Economist
The Conference Board, Inc.

On October 6, 1979, the Federal Reserve—the central bank in the United States—adopted a new operating procedure designed to strengthen control over money supply growth rates. With inflation rates in double digits and the federal budget structurally out of balance, members of Congress and foreign central bankers looked to the Federal Reserve for the only anti-inflation policy with clout. However, the first 40 months of monetary policy under the Fed's new money-growth targeting procedures were highlighted by excessive volatility in money and financial markets and dramatic shifts in policy.[1] In the interim, domestic inflation rates were reduced sharply, but the world economy suffered its deepest recession since World War II. In the second half of 1982, monetary policy

---

[1] For a detailed description and chart of Federal Reserve operating procedures, see Michael E. Levy and Steven R. Malin, "Monetary Policy in Transition: Sorting Out the Confusion," in *Economic Policy Issues*, no. 1 (The Conference Board, 1981), pp. 7–9. An assessment of the Fed's first 40 months under the money-growth target operating procedure is provided in Steven R. Malin and Michael E. Levy, "Changing Designs in Monetary Policy: Toward a New Pragmatism?" in *Economic Policy Issues*, no. 1 (The Conference Board, 1983), pp. 1–15.

turned decidedly stimulative once again, interest rates collapsed, and by January 1983 a robust economic recovery had begun. Economic performance once again proved that money matters.

Ironically, the intensified worldwide focus on U.S. monetary policy coincided with the apparent breakdown of long-established relationships between measures of the money supply and macroeconomic performance. Most economists—including some within the Federal Reserve—attribute this breakdown to the whirlwind pace of financial innovation and changes in financial regulations that blur the distinctions between narrowly and broadly defined money supply aggregates. Since 1970, changes in the financial environment have forced the Federal Reserve to revise the composition of the various monetary aggregates. With each new round of revisions, macroeconomic relationships involving the monetary aggregates become more attenuated and less predictable. For the Fed, the execution of monetary policy becomes increasingly complicated and its results less assured.

DEVELOPING MONETARY AGGREGATES: A TRANSACTIONS APPROACH

Since 1960, economists, associating economic instability with fluctuations in the money supply, have looked to the Federal Reserve for detailed money supply figures. In 1970, 10 years after the Fed published statistics for "the" money supply for the first time, the central bank began to adopt short-run growth targets for the monetary aggregate. This move was hailed by money watchers as the most significant development in domestic monetary policy in a decade. In 1975 under Concurrent Resolution 133 and again in 1978 under the Humphrey-Hawkins Act, the Fed was *required* to establish and report to Congress annual money growth targets consistent with the achievement of full employment and price stability. Private economic analysts came to focus on such announcements; for a decade, comparing each Thursday's new money statistics with corresponding target levels became the (ritualistic) highlight of the week in financial markets. (From 1980–1983, weekly money supply reports were released every Friday afternoon; beginning in February 1984, the Fed began to report money supply data on Thursday once again.)

For some time before 1978, the Federal Reserve targeted monetary aggregates; but by targeting the growth of monetary aggregates as a matter of law, Congress established a yardstick for measuring the Fed's performance and a formal criterion by which the Fed could govern its own operations. The Humphrey-Hawkins Act made the Federal Reserve responsible to the Congress for the financial variables over which it has a reasonable degree of influence. Thus, the chairman of the Federal Reserve Board is required to report to the Congress twice a year (in February and again in July) on the objectives and performance of monetary policy and to state long-term targets for growth of various money and credit aggregates. However, definition of money and credit aggregates, and the importance assigned to them in monetary policy, remain entirely at the discretion of the Fed.

Since 1970, Federal Reserve policy implementation as well as substantial economic research have focused on the "transactions approach" to the definition of monetary aggregates. According to that approach, assets that perform as media of exchange represent generalized purchasing power that reduces the cost of exchanging goods and services; this attribute distinguishes media of exchange from other assets which serve primarily as stores of value. Among many monetary economists (including some within the Fed), aggregate transactions balances have long been believed to have a reliable and predictable relationship to total spending and—under some conditions—to inflation. Since the essential feature of money is assumed to reside in its general acceptability as a means of payment, the influence of money on the economy is widely believed to operate through its influence on aggregate demand.

The Original Money Supply Definitions

The original money supply measure introduced by the Fed in 1960, called M–1 (defined as the public's holdings of currency, coins, and demand deposits at commercial banks), included all of the assets generally used as means of payment—that is, to facilitate transactions—and excluded all assets that typically serve as stores of value. Thus, none of the media of exchange included in M–1 earned a positive interest income. In fact, outright prohibition of interest on demand deposits from 1933 through 1976 made demand deposits and currency close substitutes for each other, made the narrowly defined money supply aggregate a conceptually pure measure of transactions balances, and created disincentives to maintaining large checking account balances.[2]

In 1971, the Fed began to publish additional monetary statistics, designated M–2 and M–3, intended to take account of the nontransactions

---

[2] A discussion of some of the legal and institutional foundations of the original money supply aggregates is found in Stephen H. Axilrod, "Monetary Policy, Money Supply, and the Federal Reserve's Operating Procedures," *Federal Reserve Bulletin*, January 1982, pp. 13–24. The rationale behind the transactions approach to defining monetary aggregates is explained in Bryon Higgins and Jon Faust, "NOWS and Super-NOWS: Implications for Defining and Measuring Money," Federal Reserve Bank of Kansas City *Economic Review*, January 1983, pp. 3–18.

functions of money. Generally, these broader monetary aggregates grouped together various financial assets according to their relative liquidity and the type of financial institution where they are held—commercial banks or thrift institutions (savings banks, savings and loan associations, mutual savings banks, and credit unions). In defining the M–2 aggregate—which included M–1 plus commercial bank time and savings deposits other than large negotiable certificates of deposit (CDs) issued by large money-center banks—the Fed acknowledged that various savings instruments provide potential purchasing power even though they usually have to be converted first into cash or demand deposits before they could be used for transactions. The aggregate M–3 expanded the coverage of M–2 to include accounts not only at commercial banks, but also at mutual savings banks and savings and loan associations. In 1975, when the Fed increased the number of published monetary aggregates to five, M–3 was redefined to also include credit union shares.

The two additional money stock measures, M–4 and M–5, introduced in 1975 were defined by adding large negotiable CDs to M–2 and M–3, respectively. Thus, M–4 represented a comprehensive measure of currency, coins, and *all* deposits at *commercial banks;* M–5 covered currency, coins, and *all* deposits at *commercial banks and thrift institutions.*

Economic Relationships Begin to Break Down

It is somewhat ironic that the proliferation of money supply measures, and the increasing focus on their growth targets, coincided with the apparent breakdown in the close association between fluctuations in money supply, incomes, and prices. Beginning in the mid–1970s, exceptionally high short-term interest rates and opportunity costs of holding noninterest-earning demand deposits encouraged businesses and individuals to reevaluate their cash needs. Money managers accelerated the transfer of funds held for transactions and precautionary purposes from demand deposits into short-term liquid interest-earning assets—for example, savings accounts, Treasury bills, and commercial paper. Thus, inflation models that related changes in the GNP deflator (the broadest measure of inflation) to present and past growth rates in the narrowly defined M–1 money supply, performed quite well in the 1960s and early 1970s, but *under*estimated inflation in 1974 and 1975.[3] After the middle of 1974, standard money-demand equations consistently *over*estimated the

---

[3] A detailed econometric assessment of the short-run relationship between growth in money supply and the rate of inflation is provided in Peter I. Berman, *Inflation and the Money Supply in the United States: 1956–1977* (Lexington, Mass.: Lexington Books, 1978).

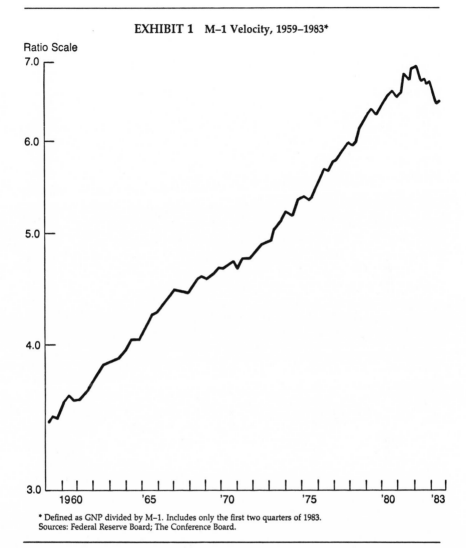

EXHIBIT 1   M–1 Velocity, 1959–1983*

Ratio Scale

* Defined as GNP divided by M–1. Includes only the first two quarters of 1983.
Sources: Federal Reserve Board; The Conference Board.

amount of money people wanted to hold.[4] In 1975 and 1976, GNP grew significantly faster, relative to the narrowly defined M–1 money supply, than its trend rate of increase over many previous years. In effect, each

---

[4] An analysis by econometric means of the overestimation of money demand is provided in two classic articles by Stephen Goldfeld, "The Demand for Money Revisited," *Brookings Papers on Economic Activity* 3 (Washington, D.C.: Brookings Institution, 1973); and "The Case of the Missing Money," *Brookings Papers on Economic Activity* 3 (Washington, D.C.: Brookings Institution, 1976).

dollar of M–1 money supply was supporting a larger volume of transactions than previously: the "velocity of money" had increased (see Exhibit 1).

Many econometricians viewed these findings not as valid indications of fundamental changes in economic relationships but as statistical artifacts or the result of poor economic analysis—a kind of econometric malpractice. Thus, the poor performance of money/inflation models in 1974–75 has been attributed to omitted variables (especially measures of private wealth and long-term bond yields) as well as those that would capture the effects of the 1974 oil price explosion, agricultural shortages, the lifting of wage and price controls, and other "shocks" to the economy. Standard money-demand equations allegedly mistracked after 1974, either because of econometric misspecification (changes in money demand both depend on and cause changes in GNP) or because a stable money/income relationship cannot be found econometrically. Some economists attribute the breakdown of money-demand equations in the mid–1970s to the unwillingness of borrowers to hold large compensating balances during the 1974 period of weak loan demand and to the restructuring of corporate debt into short-term issues.[5] Regardless of the proximate causes, economists grew increasingly uncertain of the relationships between money and economic performance; achievement of Federal Reserve policy goals set in terms of money supply growth targets became less assured.

A WHIRLWIND OF FINANCIAL INNOVATIONS: NEW "MONEY SUBSTITUTES" AND CASH MANAGEMENT PRACTICES

It is not coincidental that uncertainties about the relationship between monetary expansion and economic performance became acute from the early 1970s through the end of that decade, a time of great regulatory and institutional changes in the banking and financial markets. For more than four decades, preoccupation with preserving the viability of individual banks had dominated regulatory philosophy. Thus, some bank regulations—particularly the prohibition of interest payments on demand deposits and limitations on interest payments for savings deposits—were designed explicitly to discourage competition among financial institutions. However, high market interest rates, as well as evolving foreign and nonbank competition for money market funds,

---

[5] For a summary of explanations of the breakdown of money-demand equations, see John Wenninger, Lawrence Radecki and Elizabeth Hammond, "Recent Instability in the Demand for Money," Federal Reserve Bank of New York *Quarterly Review*, Summer 1981, pp. 1–9.

forced major changes in bank regulatory philosophy and a revamping of the banking and financial markets.

Beginning around 1970, major regulatory and institutional changes led to the development of new transactions-oriented accounts, to increased liquidity of savings accounts, to new liquid deposits and nondeposit alternatives, and to changes in liquidity and maturity of time accounts.[6] New money substitutes permitted individuals and businesses to hold funds in relatively liquid forms that earn positive interest yields not available on conventional demand deposits or cash balances. These developments encouraged competition, but began to blur the distinctions between deposits at commercial banks, thrift institutions, and other financial institutions. Changes in bank holding-company laws, liberalization of regulations governing thrift institutions, and a more competitive international banking environment reinforced the move to more intensive competition and more daring innovations.

The various new transactions-oriented financial instruments that developed during the 1970s were not counted in the narrowly defined money supply (M–1). This made M–1 a less comprehensive measure of transactions balances than when it was originally conceived. Among the new liquid deposit alternatives were several "checkable" accounts, including negotiable orders of withdrawal (NOW) in New England and New York State, credit union share drafts, and demand deposits at savings and loan associations. After the mid-1970s, the new checkable accounts became important substitutes for traditional demand deposits at commercial banks. Between 1974 and 1979, the volume of these accounts increased from $0.8 billion (0.1 percent of M–1) to $13.9 billion (3.9 percent of M–1).

Money market mutual funds (MMMFs)—another form of checkable account—also expanded rapidly during the second half of the 1970s. (Deposits in MMMFs earn market rates of return and may be withdrawn by negotiable order—typically in $500 minimum amounts—at designated banks, by wire transfer, or by mail.) After their introduction in 1973, shares in MMMFs expanded to $3.0 billion in the second quarter of 1975 and redoubled to $5.8 billion in 1978. In 1979, money market mutual funds grew spectacularly, smashing the $40 billion level by the year's end.

A variety of other developments at commercial banks and thrift institutions increased the liquidity of savings accounts. Prearranged automatic fund transfer systems (ATS) from savings to checking accounts created a highly liquid savings device that feeds funds directly into an individual's bill-paying system. During the 1960s, thrift institutions re-

---

[6] A chronicle of regulatory changes and financial innovations of the 1960s and 1970s is found in Anne Marie Laporte, "Proposed Redefinition of the Money Stock Measures," Federal Reserve Bank of Chicago *Economic Perspectives*, March/April 1979, pp. 7–13.

ceived legal authorization to transfer funds from savings accounts to checking accounts by telephone; beginning in April 1975, this facility was extended to commercial banks as well. In September 1975, federally chartered savings and loan associations were authorized to make prearranged payments to a third party from savings accounts.

Nondeposit alternatives to traditional demand deposit accounts also became increasingly important to commercial banks and nonfinancial corporations. One such arrangement—overnight security repurchase agreements (RPs or repos)—permits firms to earn a return, often a single day's interest, in the short-term market on funds not immediately needed for transactions. In the first half of the 1970s, the volume of RPs quadrupled, from $1.8 billion to $7.7 billion; by the end of the decade, RP volume exceeded $21 billion. Since corporations obtain RPs with less expense—i.e., at lower transactions costs—than many other assets of comparable yields, their use in cash management strategies reduces the volume of demand deposits and cash held, regardless of interest rates. For depository institutions, RPs provided an attractive new outlet through which to market short-term investment opportunities to businesses, the market segment that maintains the largest transactions balances. (Shifting of funds from demand deposits with relatively high reserve requirements to RPs and CDs with relatively lower reserve requirements defrayed some of the higher interest expense incurred by banks.)

Improved Cash Management Practices

Intensified use of RPs and other financial arrangements was a rational response by businesses and individuals to the general increase in interest rates in 1973–74 and 1978–79. During both of those periods, short-term rates broke through their previous record levels by wide margins. The interest rate on 90-day Treasury bills, for example, climbed to 9 percent in 1974 and to 12 percent in 1979. These record-high rates sensitized virtually everybody to the advantages of economizing on their holdings of cash and noninterest-bearing demand deposits.

Business managers intensified their use of a variety of cash management techniques that improve information about near-term cash flows and minimize their cash balances.[7] One technique, known as control disbursement, widely used by businesses involves keeping a zero- or fixed-dollar balance checking account. Under this arrangement, the

---

[7] For a summary of cash management procedures designed to minimize holdings of ..oninterest-earning accounts, see Marvin Goodfriend, James Parthemos and Bruce Summers, "Recent Financial Innovations: Causes, Consequences for the Payments System, and Implications for Monetary Control," Federal Reserve Bank of Richmond *Economic Review*, March/April 1980, pp. 14–27.

bank notifies the firm whenever it receives checks written against the firm's account; the firm then transfers to the bank, usually by wire transfer, just enough funds to cover the checks. In this way, the firm avoids holding excess balances in a noninterest-bearing account. Control disbursement is often practiced through banks at remote locations, because their checks take several extra days to clear. This practice allows the firm to earn additional interest for as long as possible.

From an empirical standpoint, two factors make it difficult to evaluate the impact of increasingly sophisticated cash management procedures on historical relationships between money supply aggregates and economic performance:

1. Historical experience with cash management is limited.
2. Incentives for cash management are closely tied to changes in regulations, interest rates, technology, and competition.

The timing, frequency, and magnitude of these changes are difficult to isolate and predict; and to the extent that cash management is predictable, funds shift back and forth among accounts included in the narrowly and broadly defined monetary aggregates. Fluctuations in interest-bearing components of the aggregates may themselves be difficult to predict if they are held—at least in part—for portfolio purposes rather than for transactions.

REVISED MONETARY AGGREGATES FOR THE 1980s

On February 7, 1980, the Federal Reserve took a much needed step to facilitate the evaluation of monetary policy: it issued a revised set of monetary definitions that take into account the many financial developments and regulatory changes of the 1960s and 1970s.[8] The Fed had long recognized that movements in money supply, especially the narrowly defined M-1 money supply, were increasingly difficult to predict with conventional money-demand equations and other economic measures. Faced with uncertainty about macroeconomic relationships involving money (particularly M-1), achievement of policy goals set in terms of money supply growth targets became less assured. Consequently, a redefinition of the monetary aggregates was needed.[9]

---

[8] See Thomas D. Simpson, "The Redefined Monetary Aggregates," *Federal Reserve Bulletin*, February 1980, pp. 97–114.

[9] A concise discussion of the motives for redefinition of the money supply aggregates is found in Steven R. Malin, "Money Watching," *Across the Board*, September 1980, pp. 57–64. Also see Anne Marie L. Gonczy, "Monetary Aggregates Redefined," Federal Reserve Bank of Chicago *Economic Perspectives*, March/April 1980, pp. 11–18; and Neil G. Berkman,

In general, the revised money supply definitions adopted in 1980 regroup the new and more conventional forms of money into two broad divisions: funds used to conduct transactions and funds held for a longer period of time (as a store of wealth).[10] Five new aggregates were defined, consisting first of those assets that correspond to the narrowest definition of medium of exchange and extending to ever broader measures of money and near-money (see Exhibit 2). On the whole, each successively broader measure incorporates assets less liquid than those in the aggregates preceding it. Assets that serve similar functions—and presumably are close substitutes in the eyes of the public—are grouped together irrespective of the financial institution at which they are held. By contrast, the Fed's original formulation of the aggregates was along institutional lines, a satisfactory approach before the whirlwind of regulatory, legislative, and technological changes that blur the distinctions between the various kinds of financial institutions.

The narrowest money supply aggregate, dubbed M–1A, was defined exactly like the original M–1 except that it excluded demand deposits held by foreign commercial banks and official institutions (a small change that amounted to $10.2 billion in 1979). In January 1982, the Fed eliminated M–1A from the dictionary of monetary aggregates when its growth pattern became grossly unreliable as an indicator of economic performance or the relative ease of monetary policy.

The most comprehensive measure of transactions money, labeled M–1B, added to M–1A the various forms of deposits that behave like checking accounts—such as NOW accounts (limited to New England and New York State), ATS, credit union share drafts, and demand deposits at thrift institutions. Although their composite volume probably overstated their net addition to transactions balances per se—some portion probably reflected hard-core savings deposits—the inclusion of these checkable accounts in a narrowly defined monetary aggregate

---

"Some Comments on the New Monetary Aggregates," Federal Reserve Bank of Boston *New England Economic Review*, March/April 1980, pp. 45–63. For a discussion of monetary aggregates that includes revisions incorporated through 1982, see Daniel J. Larkins, "The Monetary Aggregates: An Introduction to Definitional Issues," *Survey of Current Business*, January 1983, pp. 34–46.

[10] The revised monetary aggregates announced in 1980 were not the only formulations considered by the Fed. A proposed set of redefined aggregates had been presented by the staff of the Board of Governors in the January 1979 *Federal Reserve Bulletin*. The definitions proposed at that time grouped together those assets most alike in terms of their liquidity, regardless of whether they are deposited at commercial banks or thrift institutions. For example, all deposits subject to withdrawal by check or negotiable order, whether located at commercial banks or thrift institutions, would be counted in the narrowly defined money supply. The proposed definitions did not include highly liquid *nondeposit* assets such as MMMFs and RPs, principally for lack of up-to-date data. By leaving out these assets, the proposed definitions failed to achieve the predictability sought by the Fed. Further redefinition was needed.

EXHIBIT 2   Two Measures of Money, 1959–1982

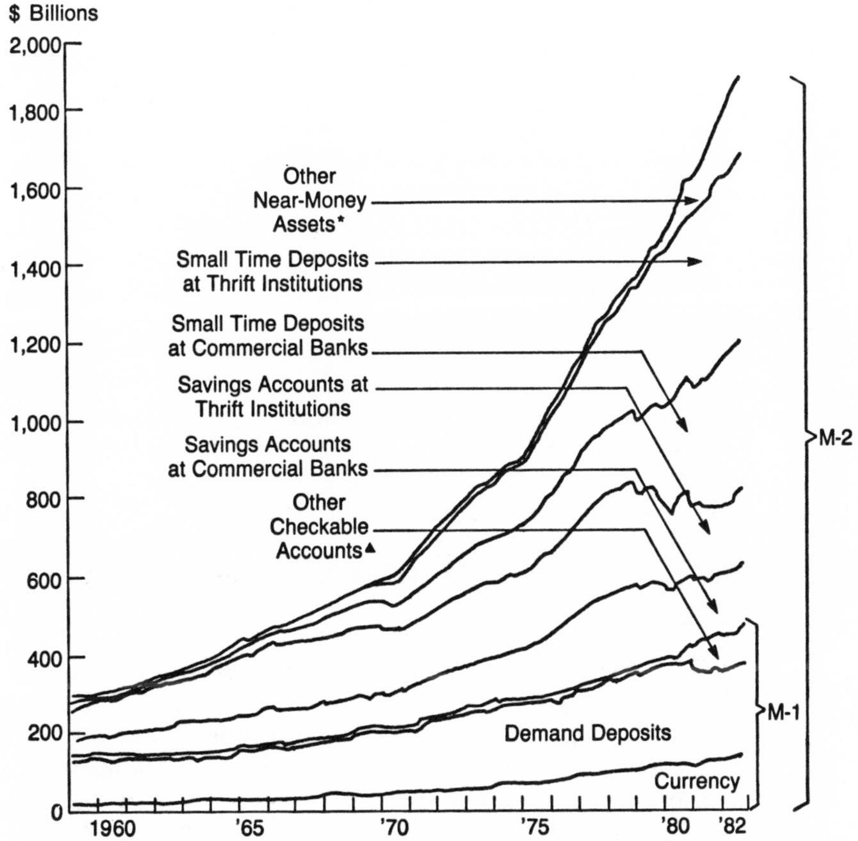

$ Billions

* Includes money market mutual fund shares, overnight repurchase agreements and overnight Eurodollar deposits at Caribbean branches of U.S. banks.
† Includes demand deposits at thrift institutions, negotiable orders of withdrawal, automatic fund transfers, credit union share drafts, and traveler's checks.
Sources: Federal Reserve Board; The Conference Board.

filled in a major omission from the original M–1 measure of transactions money.

Redefined M–2 covered M–1B plus a variety of relatively liquid savings instruments never before included in official monetary definitions—overnight RPs at commercial banks, overnight Eurodollars held by U.S. residents other than at Caribbean branches of member banks, and MMMF shares. Revised M–2 also included passbook savings accounts and all small (less than $100,000) time deposits, about 60 percent of which had maturities longer than six months in 1979 and imposed substantial penalties for early withdrawal. Such relatively illiquid deposits were included here because they are widely used as substitutes for savings accounts, especially during periods of rising interest rates.

The revised M–3 was closer in concept and magnitude to the original M–5 (coins, currency, plus all deposits at banks and thrift institutions) than to the original M–3 or M–4. Under the 1980 revisions, M–3 was redefined by adding to the revised M–2 all large time deposits and longer-term RPs. Defined in this way, the revised M–3 included all of the assets in the old M–5 plus long-term RPs and the new nondeposit assets included in the two narrower measures of money.

Finally, a new broad measure of easily marketable financial assets, known as L, was added to the lexicon of monetary definitions. Aggregate L included the revised M–3 plus a variety of funds never included before in any monetary aggregate—e.g., Treasury bills and other liquid Treasury securities, U.S. savings bonds, term Eurodollars held by U.S. residents other than banks, commercial paper, and bankers' acceptances. Because of its broad inclusiveness, L was not expected to be influenced by shifts of funds from one financial asset to another; it was expected to remain stable even during periods of financial change. However, it is not clear what, if any, policy implications the Fed hoped to derive from changes in the level of such a broadly defined measure.

Money-Demand Shortfalls Remain Unexplained

The Fed approached the task of redefinition with full awareness that the composition of the aggregates would require periodic adjustments as the financial and regulatory environments continued to change. For the time being, however, the revised monetary data promised to be more stable than the original measures in their relation to particular economic variables. Thus, for example, various money/inflation models performed significantly better in 1976–79 with the new M–1B measure of transactions balances than with either the original M–1 or the new M–1A measures.[11]

Yet inclusion of the redefined monetary measures in standard money-demand equations still did not adequately explain the shortfall in demand for money since the second half of the 1970s. Unusually slow growth in demand for the original M–1 had been attributed to the introduction of ATS and NOW accounts; and the shift of funds into these accounts seemed to be manifest in the higher velocity of M–1B—which included these accounts—relative to the original M–1. However, econometric estimates by the Federal Reserve Board's staff indicated that ATS

---

[11] See Levy and Malin, "Monetary Policy," p. 14.

and NOW accounts explained no more than about one fourth of the estimated shortfall in M–1 growth. This result led the Federal Reserve to conclude that "much of the weakness in the demand deposit component of the original M–1 is attributable to other source."[12]

Inclusion of RPs and MMMFs in the broader M–2 aggregate was expected to explain the remainder of the money-demand shortfall. Monetary economists widely believed that the record-high interest rates of 1974 and 1979 induced widespread shifts out of demand deposits into short-term earning assets. Indeed, much of the weakness in demand deposits relative to GNP had been in the holdings of nonfinancial corporations, the principal users of repos. However, a study by Federal Reserve Board economists indicated that the addition of RPs to M–1B barely improved the predictability of the money supply aggregate from 1974 through 1978 and *increased* forecast errors thereafter. The addition of MMMFs, on the other hand, caused the prediction errors to *increase* between the second quarter of 1974 and the third quarter of 1977, although they *decreased* sharply thereafter. Based on its own evidence, the Fed cautiously concluded that "the demand deposit puzzle is not resolved by arguing that demand deposit growth suffered at the expense of RPs and the like."[13] For money watchers, fresh doubts were cast on the permanence of the revised aggregates as tools of monetary policy.

Nationwide Expansion of NOW Accounts

Barely seven weeks after the Fed announced the revised money supply aggregates, Congress passed new legislation that provided fresh impetus to reexamination of the relationship between conventional transactions balances and new financial assets. On March 31, 1980, Congress approved the Depository Institutions Deregulation and Monetary Control Act of 1980 (P. L. 96–211), the most comprehensive banking legislation since the passage of the Federal Reserve Act in 1913. The legislation was designed to enhance the Fed's ability to implement monetary policy, apply operating requirements more uniformly to all depository institutions, allow small savers a market rate of return, remove impediments to competition between depository institutions and other financial institutions, and increase the availability of financial services to the public. The act also authorized nationwide introduction of NOW accounts by all depository institutions beginning in January 1981 and

---

[12] David J. Bennett, Flint Brayton, Eileen Mauskopf, Edward K. Offenbacher and Richard D. Porter, *Econometric Properties of the Redefined Monetary Aggregates* (Federal Reserve Board, Division of Research and Statistics, February 1980), p. 18.

[13] Ibid., p. 27.

stipulated that interest rate ceilings on all time and savings deposits be phased out by 1986.

Yet instead of facilitating the monitoring and execution of monetary policy, the act made the Fed's task more complicated. In the first two months of 1981, the "other checkable deposits" component of M–1B—which included NOW accounts—roughly doubled (to $52 billion); by the end of 1981, "other checkable deposits" increased by $50 billion while ordinary demand deposits decreased by $31 billion. These shifts were not entirely unexpected. Shifts into NOW accounts from sources such as savings deposits included in M–2 were expected to bloat M–1B; inflows of funds from existing checking accounts already counted in M–1B were expected to have no net impact on M–1B. To the extent that some fraction of the funds shifted into NOW accounts represented non-transactions balances, the reliability of relationships became even less assured between the narrowly defined monetary aggregate, real economic activity, and inflation.

In order to prevent shifts of nontransactions balances into M–1B from adversely affecting the measurement of these relationships, the Fed adjusted actual M–1B figures and monitored a "shift-adjusted" M–1B.[14] The shift-adjusted measure excluded nontransactions balances estimated by the Fed to have been deposited mostly between January 1981 and April 1981, after which the difference between the actual and shift-adjusted measures of M–1B remained relatively constant at roughly $11 billion. By the end of 1981, the Fed concluded that the one-time increase in M–1B attributable to NOW accounts had run its course; thus, as of January 1982, M–1A was dropped from the list of money supply aggregates, and M–1B was renamed M–1.

Nonetheless, the "other checkable deposits" component of the new M–1 continued to grow strongly well into 1982. This component surged by 28.1 percent in the third quarter of 1981, by 33.9 percent in the fourth quarter of 1981, and by an additional 44.8 percent in the first quarter of 1982 (at annual rates)—despite a consistently tight Federal Reserve monetary policy and cyclical declines in conventional demand deposits. For all of 1982, "other checkables" increased by over 33 percent, while demand deposits were relatively flat (see Exhibit 3).

Money watchers offered a variety of explanations for the continued growth of the "other-checkable-deposits component." The most widely held of these explanations attributes its rapid growth to precautionary savings associated with the weak and uncertain state of the economy.

---

[14] For an excellent brief discussion of the behavioral characteristics of M–1B and its shift-adjusted counterpart, see Higgins and Faust, "NOWs and Super-NOWs," pp. 3–18. A technical discussion is provided in Thomas D. Simpson, John R. Williams and others, "Recent Revisions in the Money Stock: Benchmark, Seasonal Adjustment, and Calculation of Shift-Adjusted M1–B," *Federal Reserve Bulletin*, July 1981, pp. 539–42.

EXHIBIT 3   Liquid Deposits and Nondeposit Balances, 1977–1983
($ millions)

		Demand Deposits	Other Checkable Deposits	Overnight Repurchase Agreements	Money Market Mutual Funds
1977	I	$226.3	$ 2.9	$10.0	$ 2.4
	II	230.4	3.2	11.5	2.3
	III	233.4	3.6	12.4	2.3
	IV	241.8	4.0	13.3	2.4
1978	I	240.4	4.4	13.7	2.9
	II	246.6	4.8	14.0	3.5
	III	251.2	5.1	14.6	4.5
	IV	257.5	6.8	16.8	5.8
1979	I	249.4	11.0	18.8	9.4
	II	255.0	14.0	21.5	14.8
	III	259.6	16.1	22.1	22.0
	IV	265.2	16.7	19.6	30.6
1980	I	261.3	18.0	17.5	43.8
	II	256.4	19.5	17.3	52.0
	III	264.3	23.2	22.8	60.9
	IV	273.7	26.6	23.3	61.7
1981	I	245.2	51.2	24.3	74.8
	II	240.1	65.8	26.3	98.7
	III	235.9	70.0	27.7	121.5
	IV	239.7	75.3	27.3	144.1
1982	I	234.2	82.6	31.3	156.8
	II	232.1	87.4	32.3	165.6
	III	231.4	90.3	33.8	180.1
	IV	242.0	100.9	38.1	187.0
1983	I	237.7	110.6	40.7	160.1
	II	240.9	119.8	45.0	142.5

Source: Federal Reserve Board.

Accordingly, NOW accounts are assumed to differ fundamentally from demand deposits and currency in that their explicit yield removes the incentive to hold only the minimum balance necessary to meet transactions needs. Thus, depositors with NOW accounts are presumed to store precautionary balances that would have formerly been placed in a higher-yielding liquid asset.[15] (Growth of 6.1 percent in balances held in passbook savings accounts in the 12 months ending November 1982 similarly indicates a general shift toward liquidity by savers.) To the extent that this explanation is valid, funds "saved" in NOW accounts continued a process that blurred the distinctiveness of M–1 as a measure of transactions balances. Among money watchers, doubts intensified

---

[15] Early in 1983, the Federal Reserve repeatedly cited the bulge in precautionary balances as a major cause of the rapid acceleration of M–1 growth rates during the second half of 1982. See, for example, "Monetary Policy Report to Congress, February 16, 1983," *Federal Reserve Bulletin*, March 1983, pp. 132–35.

about the reliability of the revised money supply aggregates as indicators of economic performance or the Fed's policy stance.

MMMFs Spawn New Liquid Savings Instruments

Despite the critical role of NOW accounts in blurring the distinction between transactions and nontransactions balances, many financial experts point to the rapid expansion of MMMFs as the single most critical financial development of the 1970s and early 1980s. According to the Investment Company Institute, the assets of MMMFs increased from $0.1 billion in 1973 to a peak of $172.4 billion in 1982. Yet despite their checkwriting facility, money market mutual funds typically have modest rates of share redemption compared with the turnover of conventional demand deposits. Between 1975 and 1979, relatively high minimum check sizes (often $500 or more), as well as other implicit and explicit costs associated with writing checks against fund balances, limited the number of drafts, on average, to about four per account per year. Thus, in their first decade of existence, MMMFs competed predominantly with savings accounts and other "stores of value" rather than with transactions balances of the M–1 type.

The ascendancy of MMMFs forced major adjustments in the menu of financial instruments offered by depository institutions. In order to maintain their competitiveness, banks and thrifts introduced an array of financial instruments that bear money market rates of interest. By 1982, about two thirds of the non-M–1 component of M–2 bore market rates of return, compared to only about 5 percent in 1978. Six-month CDs, the most popular of the new accounts, attracted the bulk of funds deposited in the new accounts. Effective October 1, 1981, banks were authorized to offer all-saver certificates with 12 month maturities and limited tax exemption of interest earnings. Beginning in May 1982, banks gained authorization to offer negotiable and nonnegotiable certificates of deposit with unrestricted yields and maturities of 3½ years or more. By summer of 1982, depository institutions introduced 90–day CDs with yields tied to the Treasury bill rate, as well as CDs with maturities from 7 to 31 days with yields tied to Treasury securities.[16]

Proliferation and growth of new liquid savings accounts in 1981 and 1982 further complicated interpretation of the economic significance of fluctuations in the monetary aggregates. During periods of sharply changing interest rates, relative growth rates of the narrowly and

---

[16] As early as 1961, large commercial banks had begun to offer negotiable certificates of deposits (CDs) in order to compete for money market funds. By the mid-1960s, both large and small banks—which had previously shown relatively little interest in consumer-type savings deposits—had moved into the CD market.

broadly defined monetary aggregates reflect changes in accrued interest earnings as well as deliberate adjustments in the level of deposits held by depositors. For example, unprecedented high interest rates during 1981 contributed to sharp increases in MMMF assets and to the growth of M–2 in excess of its target growth limit; over the same period, growth in M–1 was modest.[17] Moreover, relatively high yields offered by MMMFs from 1978 through 1982 forced banks to raise the yield on short-term CDs and to offer deposit incentives. Net outflows of funds from thrift institutions virtually dried up funds normally available for mortgage financing. With declines in average balances in conventional checking accounts, banks experienced the loss of their cheapest source of reserves.

Money Market Deposit Accounts and Super-NOWs: Liquid Savings Accounts or Savings Accounts With Checking?

Despite the growth of new financial instruments offered by banks and thrifts, the relatively high yields and other features of MMMFs contributed to disintermediation from banks and thrifts. In order to increase the competitiveness of depository institutions against purveyors of MMMFs, Congress authorized depository institutions to offer money market deposit accounts (MMDAs) free of interest restrictions, beginning on December 14, 1982. The Garn–St. Germain Depository Institutions Act of 1982 required the account to be "directly equivalent to and competitive with money market mutual funds."[18] Moreover, the act specified that MMDAs have no minimum maturity and that they allow up to three checks or automatic transfers to a third party per month. Because of their comparability to MMMFs, the Fed included MMDA balances in M–2.[19]

The Garn–St. Germain Act also cleared the way for the Depository Institutions Deregulation Committee to issue rules governing a so-called super-NOW account to be offered after January 4, 1983. Super-NOW accounts offer unlimited checking or third-party transfers and, unlike

---

[17] More than 90 percent of the increase in M–2 during 1982 was attributable to interest earned on money market mutual fund balances.

[18] U.S. Congress, Garn–St. Germain Depository Institutions Act of 1982, 97th Congress, 2d session, September 8, 1982.

[19] An excellent discussion of the characteristics and expected economic behavior of money market deposit accounts and super-NOWs is found in John A. Tatom, "Money Market Deposit Accounts, Super-NOWs and Monetary Policy," Federal Reserve Bank of St. Louis *Review*, March 1983, pp. 5–16. For the Fed's own expectations about the characteristics of MMDAs and super-NOWs, see Frederick T. Furlong, "New Deposit Instruments," *Federal Reserve Bulletin*, May 1983, pp. 319–21.

conventional NOW accounts, an unrestricted interest rate. Both super-NOWs and MMDAs require initial and minimum average balances of at least $2,500. The primary difference between the two accounts is the transaction orientation of super-NOWs provided by their unlimited checkwriting privileges and, accordingly, their lower reserve requirements. Super-NOWs are included in M–1 (see Exhibit 4).

EXHIBIT 4   Official Definitions of Money Supply and Credit Aggregates*

M–1 is defined as the sum of the currency held by the public plus demand deposits; other checkable deposits, including negotiable order of withdrawal (NOW and super-NOW) accounts, automatic transfer service (ATS) accounts, and credit union share draft accounts; and traveler's checks.

M–2 is defined as the sum of M–1 plus savings and small-denomination time deposits, money market deposit accounts, shares in money market mutual funds (other than those restricted to institutional investors), overnight repurchase agreements, and Eurodollar deposits held by U.S. residents other than banks at Caribbean branches of Federal Reserve member banks.

M–3 is M–2, plus large time deposits, large-denomination term repurchase agreements, and shares in money market mutual funds restricted to institutional investors.

Total Domestic Nonfinancial Sector Debt is outstanding debt of domestic governmental units (federal, state, and local), households, and nonfinancial businesses.

* As of July 1983.
Source: Federal Reserve Board.

Depository institutions marketed the new accounts heavily, and the depositors reacted swiftly and positively. Flows of funds into MMDAs averaged more than $35 billion per week in the first six weeks that the accounts were offered. By late March 1983, the weekly inflows had subsided to about $5 billion per week, but were well ahead of expectations. By mid-April 1983, MMDA balances totaled more than $340 billion; in comparison, it took nearly two full years for the popular six-month money market certificate (MMC) to reach that level. According to survey results and econometric estimates, most MMDA balances came from other deposit accounts, particularly savings and small-denomination time accounts. Indeed, between November 1982 and March 1983, savings deposits at all institutions fell a record $48 billion; over the same period, assets in MMMFs declined by $37 billion (although part of the decline resulted from a sharp drop in short-term interest rates). Most of the transfers to MMDAs from small-denomination time deposits came from relatively short-term certificates with market-related yields, particularly six-month money market certificates. Despite measures by some depository institutions to limit the size of balances in MMDAs earning high introductory rates of return, some depositors shifted funds from large CDs into the new accounts.

The extraordinary growth of MMDAs overshadowed the otherwise strong introduction of super-NOWs. Between January and mid-April 1983, balances in super-NOWs rose to over $29 billion, about one fourth of the total other-checkable-accounts component of M–1. With interest rates on super-NOWs generally below the yields on MMMFs, MMDAs, and other short-term investments, the bulk of funds entering super-NOW accounts came mostly from other transactions-oriented accounts; funds attracted from nontransactions accounts most likely came from savings and small time deposits, rather than from nondeposit sources (such as MMMFs). Thus, on balance, the volume of transactions deposits included in M–1 probably did not increase significantly as a result of the introduction of super-NOW accounts. Nevertheless, as funds in super-NOWs promised to become a larger share of household transactions balances and as cash managers became less sensitive to the opportunity cost of holding transactions balances, the behavior of M–1 relative to other economic variables threatened to deviate even more widely from past historical experience.

The Recasting Must Continue

For money watchers within the Federal Reserve, continued breakdown of long-established relationships between the official money supply measures and other economic variables complicates the development and the conduct of monetary policy. This does not mean that the establishment of monetary growth targets, for example, is a half-deaf attempt to "fine tune" economic performance. (There are those, including some prominent monetarists, who argue that the Fed should not vary the growth in the money supply in response to short-run changes in other economic conditions.) Other developments—like those in the credit markets, in foreign exchange markets, and in prices—also play important roles in monetary policy. It is against the background of analysis and projection of these fundamental developments that the Federal Open Market Committee (FOMC) establishes quarterly and annual targets for several monetary and credit aggregates.

While instability complicates policy, it does not completely frustrate it. Establishment of monetary policy in 1983, for example, required an accurate interpretation of unusually high growth rates of M–1 relative to GNP (i.e., unusually sharp declines in M–1 velocity) during late 1981 and 1982. A serious policy dilemma was posed for the Fed by double-digit declines in M–1 velocity during three of the quarters of 1982 and large increases in nontransactions balances parked in M–1-type accounts. With the economy deep in recession, persistently strong demand for liquidity seemed to necessitate a policy of continued monetary ease in order to fuel the expansion of private credit needed to support a strong economic recovery. If, however, the unusual behavior of M–1 velocity reflected primarily a cyclical slowdown in GNP—rather than a permanent shift in liquidity preferences—the Fed's policy options for 1983 would be more limited. A sharp increase in velocity during 1983 could quickly revive inflation once economic recovery got under way (particularly if large federal budget deficits persist)—unless new restraint was applied. Prematurely rising interest rates (whether triggered by the revival of inflationary expectations or by a shift to greater monetary restraint) would then endanger the sustainability of the recovery.[20]

Faced with a difficult policy dilemma and faulty tools of policy, the Fed continued a policy of monetary accommodation through spring 1983, followed by gradual tightening during early summer. In its semiannual report to the Congress on February 16, 1983, the FOMC stated that the goal of monetary policy was "to provide enough liquidity to facilitate an early upturn in economic activity while maintaining the monetary discipline needed to sustain the progress toward lower rates of inflation—a crucial element in satisfactory economic performance over the longer run."[21] Financial market participants ratified the Fed's policy with a strong favorable response in both the stock and bond markets. Yet the FOMC conceded that the rapid pace of financial innovations complicated the setting of money supply growth targets and made achievement of the broader macroeconomic goals more difficult. The FOMC report concluded that "an unusual degree of judgment would be necessary in interpreting the growth of money and credit in coming months."[22]

The need to exercise caution in the interpretation of money supply fluctuations does not render the monetary aggregates unimportant. Money supply definitions are only *basic tools* designed to assist the mechanics of monetary policy and its evaluation, which is always a tricky art. The economy does not adjust immediately, swiftly, and mechanically to monetary policy actions. Its adjustments are delayed, slow, and complicated. Under such conditions, sophisticated and crude empirical evidence alike may be misleading; all money watchers, not just those within the Federal Reserve System, must be vigilant and flexible. At times, the focus of monetary policy must shift from M–1 to M–2 and back to M–1 again as the composition of the aggregates changes and the messages they convey about the economy conflict. At other times,

---

[20] Implications of the Fed's 1983 policy dilemma are discussed in Malin and Levy, "Changing Designs," pp. 14–15. Also see Daniel L. Thornton, "The FOMC in 1982: Deemphasizing M–1," Federal Reserve Bank of St. Louis *Review*, June/July 1983, pp. 26–35.

[21] See "Monetary Policy Report to the Congress," *Federal Reserve Bulletin*, March 1983, p. 132.

[22] Ibid., p. 136.

money watchers will abandon their favorite monetary aggregate and focus their attention on some credit aggregate. (In fact, beginning in 1983, the Fed replaced the L monetary aggregate with a measure of total nonfinancial sector debt.)[23]

Critics of the monetary aggregates decry their occasional unpredictability. (Indeed, predictability of outcomes is the hallmark of science.) Yet those who voice those proclivities forget that economic uncertainty is always heightened in a period of rapid structural change. No statistical procedure or survey technique, no matter how well conceived, can identify with precision the impact of such change on the monetary aggregates. In the words of Paul Volcker, "No single concept or definition of money or credit can reasonably be expected always to provide reliable signals about economic performance or about the course of monetary policy. . . . Definitions of monetary aggregates can be, and have been, adapted to significant institutional changes, although all definitions of money necessarily involve, at the margin, a degree of arbitrariness."[24] As long as the money market continues to adjust to regulatory changes and financial innovations, the money supply definitions must continue to be recast.

---

[23] For an excellent discussion of the Fed's changing emphasis on M–1 and M–2, see Donald E. Maude, "The 'New' Monetary Policy Environment," *Economic Policy Issues* no. 1 (The Conference Board, 1983), pp. 11–13.

[24] See "Monetary Policy Report to the Congress, July 20, 1983," Federal Reserve Board processed, p. 17.

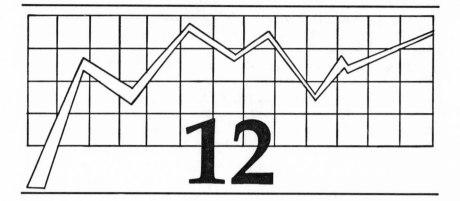

Flow of Funds

Rudolf Hauser, C.F.A.
Vice President
Oppenheimer Capital Corporation

INTRODUCTION: BRIEF DEFINITIONS AND WHERE TO OBTAIN THE NUMBERS

In a narrow sense, flow of funds is a series of tables which trace financial transactions from current savings to ultimate investment in physical assets, revealing the uses and sources of funds of all major sectors in the economy, including financial intermediaries. In a broader sense, which is the sense in which it is used in this chapter, reference to flow of funds also includes the balance sheets (outstandings) of these major sectors and use of statistics on particular flows and amounts outstanding to analyze such issues as interest rates, security prices, and the economic outlook for certain sectors. If one wants to know how a particular sector, such as mutual savings banks, obtains and invests its funds or which sectors absorb net issuance of particular types of financial instruments, the flow of fund tables are a convenient place to find out.

The most comprehensive tables on flows and amounts outstanding are published by the Flow of Funds Section of the Board of Governors of the Federal Reserve System under the able direction of Stephen P. Taylor. Quarterly flow tables are available as Release Z.1 (780), *Flow of Funds Accounts*. Tables on outstandings have been completely or partially published annually.[1] Summary tables also appear in the *Federal Reserve Bulletin* and the 2.7 release. The detailed tables show both actual and quarterly data and seasonally adjusted flows at annual rates.

Annual historical data and forecasts for the year ahead are also regularly made available to their clients by various organizations, two of the most prominent being Bankers Trust Company *(Credit and Capital Markets)* and Salomon Brothers *(Prospects for the Credit Markets In . . .)*, both of which contain descriptive text in addition to their tables. In terms of historical analysis, the most prominent are probably the numerous studies by Raymond Goldsmith, writing for the National Bureau of Economic Research in the 1950s and 1960s.

There is a need for this information in a complex system such as ours in order to understand how the economy functions. With so much individual savings not directly invested in physical assets, so much investment dependent on funds from sources other than owner-managers, and so much borrowing being done to finance current consumption and government spending, the institutions and processes that channel the flow of savings (in excess of what the savers themselves can invest in physical assets) into final uses are a factor in the determination of the long-run real growth potential of our economy, the cyclical pattern of the economy, the relative health and prosperity of various sectors in the economy, and relative and absolute levels of various interest rates and security prices. A full understanding of this process requires knowledge of the nature of the instruments and institutions in the market, including legal and other restraints, institutional custom, and the purposes for, and investment needs of, the various institutions. This has to be related to real activity in the economy, inflation rates and relative price changes, exchange rates, tax laws, monetary policy, and innumerable political, fiscal, and social factors.

We shall first examine the accounting basics that are necessary to understand the flow of funds accounts and then examine what is contained in the flow of funds tables. Thereafter, we describe the relation of the flow of funds to other economic statistics and their potential uses and discuss the accuracy of the numbers, their use in understanding

---

[1] As of summer 1983, these tables were available without charge from the Publication Services, Mail Stop 138, Board of Governors of the Federal Reserve System, Washington, D.C. 20551. Annual historical data is published every few years. The *Flow of Funds Accounts 1949–1978*, which is available for a charge, was the most recent as of mid-1983. The Flow of Funds Section, Division of Research and Statistics, will upon request make available *Balance Sheets For the U.S. Economy*, which in addition to containing financial assets and liabilities also includes current-cost values of physical assets for major sectors. Within reason, they will also make available quarterly historical data on both flows and outstandings for particular sectors or instruments.

interest rates and security price trends, and what improvements would be desirable in the statistics.

FLOW OF FUNDS ACCOUNTS AND SOME ACCOUNTING BASICS—STOCKS VERSUS FLOWS

It is evident from experience that people without accounting back-grounds sometimes find flow of funds concepts confusing, so a review of some accounting is in order. The first concept of importance is that the two sides of the balance sheet are equal and that debits must always equal credits. The left (or debit) side of the traditional balance sheet consists of assets, and the right (or credit) side of the balance sheet consists of claims against those assets—that is, liabilities and equity (residual ownership interest).[2] In the Fed's flow of funds accounts these are referred to as the uses and sources sides, respectively.

If any transactions take place, this identity is maintained; debits must equal credits, uses must equal sources. Debit entries consist of increases in assets, decreases in liabilities, and decreases in equity (such as expenses or dividends); credit entries consist of decreases in assets, increases in liabilities, and increases in equity (such as revenues or sale of stock). For example, if a corporation issues bonds, debit cash and credit bonds. If it purchases raw materials on credit, debit raw materials and credit accounts payable. When the account is paid, debit accounts payable and credit cash.

The balance sheet measures all assets held and liabilities and equity at one point in time. These are also referred to as stocks or outstandings. Flows measure those transactions that change one balance sheet to another at a later point in time. They consist of income flows—that, is transactions which affect net income, mainly revenues and expenses (also reported in income statements)—and of capital flows such as sale and purchase of assets, raising new debt, selling stock, or paying dividends. These flows can be shown as gross or net: If $10 million of debt is paid off and $100 million of debt is raised, it can be shown in that detail (gross) or as a net increase of $90 million in debt outstanding. The Fed's flow of funds uses the net approach although some of the private flow of funds tables show both gross and net issuance of certain securities.

Flows include some nonmarket noncash transactions which are imputed, the most important of which is depreciation. Not shown in flows are changes in market value of outstandings, which are necessary to trace the change from one balance sheet date to another because, unlike

---

[2] If not shown in traditional left-right sequence, assets are shown before (on top of) liabilities and equity.

the conventional accounting balance sheets which value assets at historical cost, the flow of funds values many assets and equity at current cost values. For a fixed-asset category such as machinery, the balance sheet value at the termination of the flow period is equal to the starting value of such, plus new purchases of machinery (net of any sales to another entity or sector), less depreciation, plus (less) the increase (decrease) in market value of the machinery. This detail is shown in the stock-flow reconciliation tables in the Balance Sheets for the U.S. Economy.

The balance sheet represents all transactions since the beginning of time that have not been extinguished. For example, some unredeemed debt might have been issued 25 years ago or some railroad bridge built 50 years ago. Flows, in contrast, represent only those transactions that have taken place during the period in question, typically a quarter or a year. One frequent analytical error is to concentrate only on the need for the flows to balance—that is, the need to sell the new net issuance of an instrument. In reality, the stocks must also balance; and aside from certain legal restrictions (such as letter stock) or other illiquidity considerations, the true potential supply consists not only of the net flows or issuance of the instrument in a particular period but of the net issuance plus the entire amount thereof outstanding at the beginning of the period.

The equilibrium price must be such that old owners plus new owners in the aggregate desire to hold the entire outstanding supply. During periods of little fundamental change, one can perhaps concentrate more on the net issuance; but during periods of great changes in economic, social, and legal factors, major price changes may be necessary to balance the outstandings even when such price changes would not appear warranted by the net flows alone. That movement to restore equilibrium may only require relatively few transactions at changing prices, because all stocks are basically valued by current transaction prices. Those prices are determined at the margin. That is, the price is the one at which the least anxious buyer is willing to part with his money *and* is able to accommodate the least anxious seller who is willing to part with his security or whatever for money, all more reluctant potential buyers or sellers not being able to transact. The potential willingness to buy or sell at the current price or some specified price is referred to as ex ante; and as the price changes to accommodate the imbalance between potential buyers and sellers at the ex ante price, the actual outcome is referred to as ex post. There is no way to measure ex ante quantities; the flow of funds represents only ex post results.

Every transaction between sectors results in at least four rather than just two accounting entries. For example, if a corporation sells a bond to a pension fund, the gain in cash and increase in liabilities of corporations would not only equal one another but also equal the decrease in cash and increase in bond holdings of pension funds.

The final concept, which is more an economic than it is an accounting concept, is the difference between current transactions (that is, current production and consumption) and noncurrent (most capital) transactions. In essence, current transactions in an economic sense, and as used in the national income and flow of funds accounts, refer to those transactions related to the production and sale of goods and services, with costs measured at prices prevailing at the time of sale, to distribution of the income on capital to the ultimate recipients (that is, the payment of interest and dividends), and to current consumption. Hence profits are exclusive of inventory profits and depreciation is measured at replacement cost values in order to calculate profits on a current cost basis. (Depreciation is also measured using constant asset lives rather than at lives in use for tax purposes at the time.) This differs from conventional accounting income statements which include realized income from price appreciation such as inventory profits, underdepreciation of assets, and certain writedowns of asset values. Because the emphasis is on gross investment, depreciation (or capital consumption as it is referred to in the economic accounts) is added back to net savings to obtain gross savings, or current surplus, that is available for capital expenditures and net financial investment.[3] The emphasis of the flow of funds accounts naturally is on capital expenditures and financial flows. Although the major current account items for major sectors are summarized, only the current surplus amount is shown for other sectors.

WHAT THE FEDERAL RESERVE FLOW OF FUNDS TABLES COVER—SECTORS AND INSTRUMENTS

Federal Reserve flow of funds accounts consist of summary accounts and detailed accounts by sectors and by financial transaction categories (instruments). Those detailed accounts, as of 1983, are shown in Exhibit 1. In addition to 25 detailed accounts by sector, there are summary tables for nonfinancial business—total; commercial banking; private nonbank financial institutions—total; and savings institutions combined. There is also a table on amount and composition of individuals' savings, which combines the accounts on households, farm business, and noncorporate business and reconciles savings on this basis with personal savings in the national income accounts. In addition to the 28 detailed tables by transaction category, there is a summary table for mortgages, and the miscellaneous financial claims table provides subsector detail on six ar-

---

[3] Strictly speaking, capital consumption allowances include the destruction of items in addition to depreciation.

EXHIBIT 1   Federal Reserve Flow-of-Funds Detailed Accounts

By Sector	*By Transaction Category*
Households, personal trusts, and nonprofit organizations	Gold and official foreign exchange holdings
Farm business	Treasury currency and SDR certificates
Nonfarm noncorporate business	Insurance and pension fund reserves
Nonfinancial corporate business, excluding farms	Net interbank claims
	Currency and checkable deposits
State and local governments—general funds	Small time and savings deposits
	Money market mutual fund shares
Foreign sector	Large time deposits
U.S. government	Federal funds and security repurchase agreements
Federally sponsored credit agencies and mortgage pools	U.S. deposits in foreign countries
Monetary authority	U.S. government securities
U.S. chartered commercial banks	State and local government obligations
Domestic affiliates of commercial banks	Corporate and foreign bonds
Foreign banking offices in U.S.	Corporate equities
Banks in U.S. possessions	Home mortgages
Savings and loan associations	Multifamily residential mortgages
Mutual savings banks	Commercial mortgages
Credit unions	Farm mortgages
Life insurance companies	Consumer credit
Private pension funds	Bank loans not elsewhere classified
State and local government employee retirement funds	Open market paper
	Other loans
Other insurance companies	Security credit
Finance companies	Trade credit
Real estate investment trusts	Profit taxes payable
Open-end investment companies (mutual funds)	Proprietor's equity in noncorporate business
Money market mutual funds	Miscellaneous financial claims
Security brokers and dealers	

---

eas. There are also tables on sector discrepancies and transaction discrepancies. Quarterly tables show annual data for about the past 10 years and quarterly data for the past six quarters.

The summary tables are shown for both borrowing (Exhibit 2) and lending. Note in Exhibit 2 the table on net credit market borrowing by nonfinancial sectors. This table is important because it shows borrowing by the ultimate users of funds, those who will buy goods and services for tangible investment or for consumption. A sizable amount of funds is raised by financial intermediaries, one of whose main purposes it is to channel fund flows from savers to ultimate borrowers. Although their raising of funds inflates the volume of financial activity and has an important impact on what parts of the economy will prosper, it does not directly increase the pressure on the available claims on goods and services offered by savers.

The economists in the Flow of Funds Section at the Federal Reserve do not themselves obtain and tabulate raw data to construct the flow of

EXHIBIT 2 Summary of Net Funds Raised in Credit and Equity Markets (seasonally adjusted annual rates, $ billions)

		1978	1979	1980	1981	1982	1981 IV	1982 I	1982 II	1982 III	1982 IV	1983 I
1	Total net borrowing by domestic nonfinancial sectors	368.6	388.8	355.0	391.1	412.7	372.7	348.0	383.7	463.6	455.5	457.4
	Net credit market borrowing by nonfinancial sectors											
2	U.S. government	53.7	37.4	79.2	87.4	161.3	123.0	99.7	100.6	215.5	229.2	189.1
3	Treasury issues	55.1	38.8	79.8	87.8	162.1	123.4	102.2	100.8	215.8	229.7	189.0
4	Agency issues + mortgages	-1.4	-1.4	-.6	-.5	-.9	-.4	-2.5	-.2	-.3	-.5	.1
5	Private domestic nonfinancial sectors	314.9	351.5	275.8	303.7	251.5	249.7	248.3	283.1	248.1	226.3	268.3
6	Debt capital instruments	198.7	216.0	204.1	175.0	168.4	150.0	154.8	159.5	150.8	208.6	222.2
7	Tax-exempt obligations	28.4	29.8	35.9	32.9	59.5	35.0	39.1	66.3	50.1	82.6	62.0
8	Corporate bonds	20.1	22.5	33.2	23.9	25.5	26.4	14.5	12.3	33.6	41.9	25.7
9	Mortgages	150.2	163.7	135.1	118.3	83.3	88.6	101.2	80.9	67.1	84.1	134.5
10	Home mortgages	112.1	120.1	96.7	78.6	58.8	51.6	68.2	49.1	57.7	60.3	105.4
11	Multifamily resid.	9.2	7.8	8.8	4.6	1.3	4.2	5.7	2.8	-3.4	.2	6.8
12	Commercial	21.7	23.9	20.2	25.3	18.0	22.6	20.1	25.5	8.3	18.3	23.4
13	Farm	7.2	11.8	9.3	9.8	5.2	10.2	7.3	3.6	4.6	5.2	-1.1
14	Other debt instruments	116.2	135.5	71.7	128.8	83.0	99.6	93.5	123.6	97.3	17.7	46.1
15	Consumer credit	48.8	45.4	4.9	25.3	14.4	8.3	5.5	23.4	6.0	22.8	28.1
16	Bank loans n.e.c.	37.1	49.2	35.4	51.1	57.4	43.2	67.5	87.2	61.9	13.1	18.1
17	Open market paper	5.2	11.1	6.6	19.2	-2.8	22.3	12.2	-3.4	-1.8	-18.1	-16.8
18	Other	25.1	29.7	24.9	33.1	14.0	25.9	8.3	16.4	31.2	-.1	16.7
19	By borrowing sector:	314.9	351.5	275.8	303.7	251.5	249.7	248.3	283.1	248.1	226.3	268.3
20	State + local governments	19.1	20.2	27.3	22.3	45.8	24.3	26.4	55.8	33.4	67.5	52.4
21	Households	169.3	176.5	117.5	120.4	88.5	71.7	82.1	94.0	80.8	97.3	125.5
22	Nonfinancial business	126.4	154.8	131.0	161.0	117.2	153.7	139.8	133.3	134.0	61.6	90.5
23	Farm	14.6	21.4	14.4	16.4	9.0	9.6	5.5	11.3	12.8	6.5	-.7
24	Nonfarm noncorporate	32.4	34.4	33.8	40.5	24.7	38.5	28.1	36.8	12.2	21.6	26.0
25	Corporate	79.4	99.0	82.8	104.1	83.5	105.5	106.2	85.1	109.0	33.5	65.2

#												
26	Fgn. net borrowing in U.S.	2.7	18.2	8.3	18.4	16.5	20.8	15.3	27.3	27.2	20.2	33.8
27	Bonds	4.2	8.9	12.5	1.4	3.0	11.3	6.4	5.5	.8	3.9	4.2
28	Bank loans n.e.c.	7.5	-9.5	-14.6	4.8	-5.6	-3.8	-6.2	3.7	11.5	2.3	19.1
29	Open market paper	-16.8	17.4	.5	8.5	16.4	10.1	10.7	13.9	10.1	11.2	6.6
30	U.S. government loans	7.9	1.4	9.9	3.7	2.8	3.2	4.4	4.3	4.7	2.9	3.9
31	Total domestic plus foreign	460.1	473.7	471.8	402.1	364.5	393.5	428.0	418.4	382.2	409.1	402.3

Net credit market borrowing by financial sectors

#												
1	Total net borrowing by financial sectors	69.5	45.1	43.2	118.4	68.6	27.6	68.8	80.7	61.3	80.7	75.0
2	U.S. government-related	60.7	62.3	69.5	73.2	45.3	30.1	62.6	45.1	43.6	47.3	36.7
3	Sponsored credit ag. sec.	-12.2	-9.0	18.4	33.8	9.1	13.5	13.1	30.1	24.4	24.3	23.1
4	Mortgage pool securities	72.9	71.3	51.1	39.5	36.2	16.6	49.5	15.0	19.2	23.1	13.6
5	Loans from U.S. government	—	—	—	—	—	—	—	—	—	—	—
6	Private financial sectors	8.8	-17.1	-26.4	45.2	23.2	-2.5	6.2	35.6	17.7	33.4	38.3
7	Corporate bonds	12.4	7.4	8.3	-4.5	-2.1	4.1	2.3	-.8	7.1	7.8	7.5
8	Mortgages	.1	.1	3.2	.8	2.9	-3.2	1.8	-2.9	-.9	-1.2	.9
9	Bank loans n.e.c.	5.3	-.9	1.9	-1.9	13.8	-.5	3.2	2.2	-.4	-.4	2.8
10	Open market paper	4.6	-15.7	-23.6	37.2	-5.3	-4.0	-1.8	20.9	4.8	18.0	14.6
11	Fed. Home Loan Bank loans	-13.7	-8.1	-16.2	13.5	14.0	1.2	.8	16.2	7.1	9.2	12.5
12	Total, by sector	69.5	45.1	43.2	118.4	68.6	27.6	68.8	80.7	61.3	80.7	75.0
13	Sponsored credit agencies	-12.2	-9.0	18.4	33.8	9.1	13.5	13.1	30.1	24.4	24.3	23.1
14	Mortgage pools	72.9	71.3	51.1	39.5	36.2	16.6	49.5	15.0	19.2	23.1	13.6
15	Private financial sectors	8.8	-17.1	-26.4	45.2	23.2	-2.5	6.2	35.6	17.7	33.4	38.3
16	Commercial banks	1.1	2.0	1.4	1.0	.4	1.0	1.2	.4	.5	1.6	1.3
17	Bank affiliates	5.6	4.0	-15.7	12.7	6.6	4.5	1.9	8.3	6.9	6.5	7.2
18	Savings and loan assos.	-6.3	-15.1	-24.7	12.4	20.8	-7.4	-1.7	13.1	6.6	11.4	14.3
19	Finance companies	9.0	-7.4	13.2	19.6	-4.2	.1	5.3	14.1	6.3	16.6	18.1
20	Reits	.1	.1	.1	.1	.1	-.1	.2	.2	-2.2	-1.3	-1.4

Total net credit market borrowing, all sectors, by type

#												
1	Total net borrowing	529.6	518.8	515.0	520.5	433.1	421.1	496.9	499.1	443.5	489.7	477.4
2	U.S. government securities	249.8	291.6	285.2	174.0	145.1	153.2	224.0	132.6	122.9	84.8	90.5
3	State + local obligations	62.0	82.6	50.1	66.3	39.1	35.0	59.5	32.9	35.9	29.8	28.4
4	Corporate + foreign bonds	42.3	58.2	54.4	9.1	15.3	41.8	34.2	28.5	41.1	34.2	31.8
5	Mortgages	134.5	84.1	70.1	81.6	104.0	85.3	85.0	115.2	134.0	162.4	151.0

EXHIBIT 2 (concluded)

						1981	1982				1983
	1978	1979	1980	1981	1982	IV	I	II	III	IV	I
6 Consumer credit	48.8	45.4	4.9	25.3	14.4	8.3	5.5	23.4	6.0	22.8	28.1
7 Bank loans n.e.c.	59.0	51.0	46.5	57.0	54.4	38.8	75.7	90.1	49.3	2.7	30.9
8 Open market paper	26.4	40.3	21.6	54.0	6.1	28.4	23.3	42.4	-24.8	-16.4	-28.9
9 Other loans	41.5	41.8	36.6	53.7	19.2	30.2	25.1	33.6	24.9	-6.8	10.9
10 Memo: U.S. govt. cash balance	3.8	.6	-3.8	*	7.3	-3.9	22.0	-29.2	46.2	-9.9	9.9
Totals net of changes in U.S. govt. cash balances:											
11 Net borrowing by dom. nonfin.	364.8	388.2	358.8	391.1	405.5	376.6	326.0	413.0	417.4	465.5	447.5
12 By U.S. government	49.9	36.8	83.0	87.4	154.0	126.9	77.7	129.9	169.3	239.1	179.1
External corporate equity funds raised in U.S. markets											
1 Total net share issues	1.9	-3.8	22.1	-2.9	34.5	-13.1	16.7	30.2	28.7	62.5	85.9
2 Mutual funds	-.1	.1	5.0	7.7	19.6	8.7	16.5	12.4	27.1	22.4	44.3
3 All other	1.9	-3.9	17.1	-10.6	14.9	-21.7	.2	17.8	1.6	40.1	41.6
4 Nonfinancial corporations	-.1	-7.8	12.9	-11.5	11.4	-23.0	-1.1	15.1	-1.1	32.6	35.3
5 Financial corporations	2.5	3.2	2.1	.9	2.2	1.2	2.1	2.3	2.2	2.3	2.2
6 Foreign shares purchased in U.S.	-.5	.8	2.1	*	1.3	.1	-.9	.4	.4	5.3	4.0

Note: I/83 based on incomplete information.

Source: Board of Governors of the Federal Reserve System, *Flow of Funds Accounts, First Quarter 1983*, May 23, 1983.

funds accounts; rather they rely on data compiled by government departments and agencies, trade associations, other sectors of the Federal Reserve, and private organizations. At times, ownership data are only partial, and households are assumed to be the residual owners or provider of funds. At other times, data are complete, but are not altogether consistent, giving rise to an explicit discrepancy item, which is buried in the household category when that is obtained as a residual item. Some of this discrepancy comes about because of timing differences. For example, a business will send a check in the mail and reduce its accounts payable and cash accordingly, but the seller of the merchandise will still show unpaid accounts receivable on that date. Discrepancies in net interbank claims will arise for similar reasons because of checks in transit. More about some major discrepancy items later on.

An excellent summary of the Fed's tabulations is found in the booklet *Introduction to Flow of Funds*, published and sold by the Board of Governors, which covers much of the same areas and also lists the key sources of data. The main data sources and most recent data available are also listed in the front of the quarterly flow of funds tables. Not all data are available for the most recent quarter covered, nor is everything available even for all prior quarters; to the extent it is not, the staff of the Flow of Funds Section guesses at the missing items as best it can. The users should be careful to separate such guesses from actual or more carefully estimated data. Too often one sees careless references to these recent guesses that treat them as reality.

It should be realized that the flow of funds data cannot be any more accurate than the various original sources, which vary considerably in quality. Such data are not always broken down in the detail or exact classifications necessary to make them comparable with flow of funds classifications, and then it becomes necessary to make some estimates consistent with the underlying data. As new benchmark data, new data sources, information and methods become available, data revisions are often made that go back many years. Although the present format of the flow of funds has been basically unchanged for quite some years, it is necessary to make changes to conform to the emergence of new instruments and financial sectors, such as mortgage pool securities and money market mutual funds.

SOME USES OF THE FLOW OF FUNDS STATISTICS IN ECONOMIC ANALYSIS, AND WHERE THOSE TABLES FIT IN WITH OTHER ECONOMIC STATISTICS

There are numerous types of summary economic statistics which ideally should interrelate and be comparable to one another. One of the most important and familiar is the system of national income accounts, which details the production and income of the nation. The balance of payment statistics present detailed information on international flows of both goods and services relevant to the national income accounts and on financial flows relevant to the flow of funds accounts. There are also series on industrial production, input-output relationships, prices, employment, productivity, demographics, and so forth.

Yet it is not enough to know how income is obtained, how production is paid for, how relative prices change, etc., to understand how the economy functions. It is also necessary to know how claims on current production of goods and services in excess of those desired by individuals or organizations for consumption and for their own nonfinancial investment are made available to those who would bid for the use of those claims. Although net credit market borrowing by nonfinancial sectors was only equal to 12.9 percent of gross national product in 1982 (a not insignificant number in itself), the importance of these transferred claims on real resources is far more important to specific activities, particularly how much money will be available for increases in the housing stock and for net productive investment in the economy.

The latter—along with such inputs as investment in human capital (education, training), technology (research and development), managerial techniques, and the production mix—will determine labor productivity and real growth potential. Net residential mortgage extensions were equal to 63.7 percent of residential construction in 1982, and net financial borrowings (net of financial investment) of nonfinancial corporations were equal on average to 101.4 percent of their net investment in plant and equipment in the five years through 1982.[4] The flow of funds provides important information on these flows and also on the current financial position of the various sectors, which, along with the flows, is critical for understanding the cyclical behavior of those economic activities most dependent on outside financing.

Housing is so dependent on borrowed funds that a forecaster needs to know what sources of financing are available and what the cost of those funds will be. Given the specialized nature of mortgage financing, that means having a knowledge of the balance sheet positions and cash flows of those institutional investors who will make mortgage loans. Forecasting cash flow requires forecasts of whether interest rates will be so high as to encourage disintermediation because the average return on outstanding assets and/or legal regulations prevent the thrift industry from offering competitive rates. It requires an analysis of whether the equity and liquidity positions of those institutions will allow them to

---

[4] This figure is, perhaps, somewhat misleading because of the large statistical discrepancy for this sector, causing sources of funds to exceed known uses.

undertake long-term fixed-rate loans as more of their sources of funds become short-term and interest sensitive in nature. It requires a knowledge of innovations such as variable-rate mortgages and pooled mortgage securities which widen the source of funds for mortgages beyond those traditionally available in the past.

Some of the necessary information in this regard is available from the Federal Reserve's flow of funds data. A fuller analysis requires examination of more detailed data of both the flow and outstanding variety provided by the original data sources such as the Federal Home Loan Bank Board and National Association of Mutual Savings Banks. As with all economic analysis, it requires a knowledge of all related background information and the changes therein that cannot be known just from the numbers, although the numbers can often alert one to changes. For example, an examination of the trends in the amount of gross mortgage financing relative to housing construction in the late 1970s would have alerted one to the realization of capital gains on homes through refinancing associated with the increased turnover of existing homes and issuance of second mortgages.

What the aggregate flow of funds and other macroeconomic statistics do miss are certain details on the microlevel that can be important for economic analysis. For the housing forecast, for example, it would be useful to know what saturation levels of home ownership were among those groups of the population whose income and financial position would enable them to qualify for mortgage financing and whether the apparent potential demand based on demographics and housing trends is not real because it is concentrated in the parts of the population that do not qualify for such financing. Pioneering work by those such as William Fitzgerald on spending patterns and finances by age-income cohorts may fill in this data gap eventually. In addition, the potential of certain thrift institutions for bankruptcy, if realized, might make all other thrifts more cautious in making long-term loans, influence their funds flows, and influence monetary policy. Nonetheless, too much data can also make analysis difficult, and aggregation of the flow of funds data is a very valuable analytical tool.

The capital spending outlook will be influenced by the strength of the corporate balance sheet, internally generated funds, and the state of financial markets, along with other factors less evident from a flow of funds analysis and forecast. The impact of government deficits is likewise a macroeconomic question the analysis of which can be enhanced by a reference to the flow of funds. This is also the case in the longer-term analysis of how much money is available for investment in productive assets and why more is not available.

In the analysis of corporate profitability in nominal and real terms, corporate growth and productivity, the various series interrelate in useful ways. The Bureau of Labor Statistics has productivity data that are consistent with data on the income statement of the nonfinancial corporate sector in the national income accounts. The flow of funds numbers are also comparable aside from the fact that farm corporations are excluded from this group in that series. In addition to the financial activities of corporations and the financial part of the balance sheets made available, the annual balance sheet data on current costs and historical costs of tangible assets, including land, are most useful, as these data are less conveniently available from other sources.

Indeed, so useful are the flow of funds for economic analysis that the entire textual part of the May 1982 issue of the *Survey of Current Business* was devoted to a proposal by Richard and Nancy Ruggles for the creation of integrated economic accounts, one of the key features of which would be an integration of some of the flow of funds accounts into the national income accounts.

SOME DIFFERENCES BETWEEN THE FLOW OF FUNDS ACCOUNTS AND THE NATIONAL INCOME ACCOUNTS, AND MAJOR DISCREPANCIES

As desirable as it would be and despite the effort made to make the economic statistics consistent with one another, there are still some significant comparability problems that the user should be aware of. The differences in classification are in some respects the easiest to deal with. The major classification difference is that the flow of funds includes investment in durable goods as part of noncurrent expenditures, whereas the national income accounts treat it as a consumption item.[5]

The other major difference in household savings is that government life insurance and retirement funds reserves (other than social security) are attributed to households, whereas in the national income accounts they are treated as part of the savings of the federal and state and local governments. The flow of funds treatment is consistent with the way nongovernment pension fund reserves are treated in both sets of economic statistics. Minor classification differences relate both to the inclusion of capital gains dividends paid by mutual funds as part of the

---

[5] One of the terms that can be confusing to noneconomists is *savings*. It can refer to either the stock or flow of savings, depending on the context in which it is used. More confusing is that under the definition used for the Milton Friedman permanent-income hypothesis, consumption includes only the capital consumption allowances for durables and treats as savings net investment in durables, which tends to fall in recessions, whereas financial savings tend to rise during the recessions. The Ruggles-proposed integrated economic accounts would also include government net investment in tangibles such as savings, which the flow of funds does not do.

individual savings (and correspondingly as a reduction of savings by the financial sector) and to the treatment of wages on a disbursement rather than an accrual basis.

On the investment side, household investment in owner-occupied housing, including condominiums (along with related capital consumption allowances and mortgage debt), is logically attributed directly to the household sector rather than to an imaginary noncorporate business enterprise sector as in the national income accounts. (However, the imputed rental income on owner-occupied housing of the national income accounts is still included in personal income, consumption, and savings.) Purchases of mineral rights are included as investment by nonfinancial corporations and as a sale of capital assets by the federal government.

One major problem in the balance of payments accounts is the large size of the statistical discrepancy (that is, nonreported transactions), equal to a net inflow of $38.5 billion in 1982. Some of this may be due to unreported service exports, but most is probably related to unreported financial investment in the United States by foreigners. In the national income accounts, this discrepancy is treated as part of net foreign investment, whereas the flow of funds accounts (with their need to allocate such amounts by instruments) only considers reported capital transactions as part of net foreign investment. One small difference is the inclusion of allocations of special drawing rights (SDRs) as part of savings in the national income accounts but not in the flow of funds accounts.[6]

This brings us to the other major statistical discrepancies in the flow of funds accounts. The difference in 1982 between personal savings using national income account definitions as reported in the flow of funds data and as reported in the national income accounts was $96.7 billion, an amount that would increase national income account personal savings by 77.1 percent. This amount has been growing in recent years; it was minimal back in 1974. Part of this may be a direct result of the foreign discrepancy. Because many household purchases of financial assets are calculated as residuals, some of the unreported foreign purchases may be attributed to households by mistake. Discrepancies were even larger before it was realized that much commercial construction was being financed by limited partnerships rather than corporations and that a substantial amount of mortgage borrowing formerly attributed to nonfinancial corporations is properly that of individuals, inclusive of their unincorporated business activity.

---

[6] Most of the discussion of the differences between the flow of funds and the national income accounts is based on *Introduction to Flow of Funds* (Board of Governors of the Federal Reserve System, June 1980), p. 27–31.

It is tempting to explain away part of the remaining discrepancy by reference to the underground economy, but a more careful consideration reveals this is not a very plausible explanation. By its very nature, an underground transaction implies an unrecorded current account transaction. The difference between known income and known consumption is treated as savings. Any recorded purchases by those producing in the underground economy are deducted from their known income, producing dissavings if they have no known income. Unless the item produced was an investment item such as a house, the underground activity will produce unrecorded income and consumption in equal measure, leaving the total reported national income account's savings unchanged. The known savings may in fact be saved by individuals other than those assumed, but the underground economy is not an explanation for the national income accounts/flow of funds accounts savings discrepancy on personal savings.

The final major discrepancy is that between the known need for external financing by nonfinancial corporations and their net financial flows, which indicated $57.7 billion of funds raised in 1982 in excess of their known need for funds. Transactions in existing land and plant and equipment between sectors are not included and may account for a small portion of this discrepancy. It is difficult to believe that profits would be overstated by corporations anxious to keep tax payments low. These discrepancies clearly indicate the need for improvements in our reporting systems. Most of these discrepancies are offsetting, so that the net discrepancy overall is actually much more modest—for example, $3.9 billion in 1982—and attributable to the type of problems referred to earlier in the section on what the flow of funds cover.

FLOW OF FUNDS DATA AND THE FORECASTING OF INTEREST RATES AND STOCK PRICES

Probably the greatest interest in the flow of funds is as a method for forecasting interest rates and stock prices. The usual approach to interest rates forecasting by this method is to forecast the ex post flow of funds for the year ahead and how much of the demand for funds will have to be met by direct security purchases by individual investors, on the assumption that higher interest rates will be needed to encourage such investments. A quick glance at the annual data on Moody's Aaa corporate bond yields and net investment in credit market instruments by households (either in dollar terms or as a percent of total domestic plus foreign net borrowing by nonfinancial sectors) raises some question about this simple assumption, even aside from the ability to correctly forecast these ex post numbers. As one would expect, there are a good number of years in which the relationship appears to hold, but there are significant exceptions. For example, there was a sharp increase in the average bond rate in 1980 despite a decline in the aforementioned ratio from 22.1 percent in 1979 to 16.0 percent in 1980.

This should not really be surprising because there are many factors that influence interest rates through their impact on shifting the supply and demand curves for funds of the various sectors that are more important than the levels of specific fund flows, such as inflation expectations and liquidity conditions. (The latter is related to flow of funds analysis but different from the simple type of relationship referred to above.) One would expect an emphasis on household direct investment in credit market instruments to work better when economic, monetary, and inflation conditions are more stable than when they were experiencing significant changes.

This might be more obvious if one looked theoretically at how to go about making a flow of funds projection. One would start with an interest rate assumption, the assumed economic outlook, and known institutional framework and ask what demand for or supply of funds would exist in every sector under those ex ante assumptions. As noted in the section on accounting, all outstanding holdings must be considered potential supply. If inflation accelerates, for example, many holders of bonds might prefer to sell them and buy tangible assets or short-term securities at the previously existing interest rate level. Because the bonds will not just disappear, some interest rate level must be found at which all outstanding plus new net issuance thereof will be held willingly by someone. The first estimates completed, one would change the interest rate assumption in the direction necessary to balance the difference between the ex ante supply and demands for funds, make the necessary adjustments to the economic assumptions so that they will be consistent, and again ask what level of funds will be demanded and supplied by each sector under the changed assumptions. This process should be repeated until a balance is determined. Surely one would have to count on many offsetting errors to obtain a correct interest rate forecast or one for individual direct investment in credit market instruments, etc.

An examination of the Bankers Trust forecasts from 1970 on and a reading of Sally Ronk's dissertation focusing on the Bankers Trust forecasts from 1953 to 1963 reveals that a major source of flow of funds forecast errors is the forecast of the business cycle used and that a correct forecast of the business cycle is in itself very useful in forecasting interest rate trends.[7] In essence, the main value of a first run through flow of funds forecast is that it adds one more dimension to an interest rate

---

[7] Sally Stuart Ronk, *The Sources and Uses of Funds Approach to Analysis of Interest Rate Developments* (Ann Arbor, Mich.: University Microfilms, reproduction of 1965 Ph.D. dissertation at the Graduate School of Business Administration, New York University). This dissertation also provides much useful information on the history of the early development of the flow of funds.

forecast, making sure one does not miss some important imbalances likely in the flows at assumed interest levels. It should be a supplement to other methods rather than the sole method of forecasting rates.

We made a brief reference to liquidity pressures before, by which we mean a greater desire to hold liquid assets because of a disequilibrium in money supply relative to greater demand therefor. This is much more of a problem in the 1980s than in the 1950s because the leverage in many businesses and financial institutions has become so much greater that the impact of tightening liquidity is also greater than at the time when borrowers did not have to worry as much about not being able to roll over maturing obligations, and so forth. An analysis of interest coverage in a period of economic contraction and the need for gross borrowing in such a period can be very useful in gauging the impact of a given change in monetary policy. Monetary policy is an exogenous factor, but flow of funds analysis can be very useful in understanding the environment in which it operates.

In addition to an overall level of interest rates, flow of funds analysis can perhaps be of greater use in forecasting trends in specific relative interest rates. For example, the outlook in municipal securities is importantly influenced by the demand therefor by property-liability insurance companies and commercial banks. In turn, the demand by these two financial instruments is influenced by their need for tax-exempt income at the time and, in the case of banks, by the strength of loan demand. Because prices are set at the margin, the exhaustion of usual sources of demand might force large price changes to entice the marginal buyers who may demand a much higher relative return that the usual class of buyers who may have limited investment alternatives or have special advantages of investing in the particular security that other buyers do not have. At times, such forecasts will be off because the market will innovate—such as the expansion of the mortgage market via the issuance of mortgage-backed securities to participants who required more liquidity than mortgages provide. Nonetheless, for such analysis, the flow of funds approach can be most useful.

For this type of analysis, as for the use of the flow of funds approach in predicting stock prices, it is often enough (given the accuracy of the data and inherent imprecision in the approach) to have a rough feel for the ex ante demands of participant sectors, without making a precise numerical forecast. Among other reasons for not attempting a precise forecast of the numbers to obtain a residual demand in forecasting the direction of stock prices is that the household sector is hardly a residual in the usual sense in that households own more stock than institutions do in total. For another, as noted before, it is the ex ante, not ex post, demand that matters in determining pressures on security prices, and those numbers cannot be measured or verified.

Rather, one examines anticipated action by the various sectors in light of the assumed overall economic and financial environment, what is happening to each sector, and valuation levels. To do this, one ideally desires to have numbers on cash flow, balance sheet breakdowns of asset holdings at current prices, the levels of cash and liquid cash equivalents, recent transactions in securities, and any other information that may be relevant to a specific sector, such as historical cost values if legal limits on holdings are determined by such values.

Sectors should be grouped so that they are relatively homogeneous in the main factors influencing their portfolio activity. For example, life insurance company general accounts are limited in the amount of equity securities they can hold by law and by the fact that they guarantee investment performance but only have modest surplus and/or equity positions to cover poor performance. In their separate accounts, in contrast, the investment risk is borne by the owner of the account, not the life insurance company, and there is no legal limit on stockholdings. For a proper analysis, these two sectors should be separated—which they are not in the flow of funds accounts—so that one must look at the original source data from the American Council of Life Insurance.

One must be aware of the traditional behavior patterns, legal restraints, specific circumstances, and operational developments. For example, life insurance companies used to commit much of their expected cash flows to long-term fixed-income investment in advance, are obligated to make policy loans at low fixed-interest rates, hold many illiquid investments, and can carry fixed-income securities at amortized costs but must value common stocks at market values. Given this, one knew that when rising interest rates caught them unawares in 1978–79, life insurance companies might be forced to sell, which they did, some common stocks because they were liquid and the sale would not cause additional reported losses. Unlike life insurance companies, which have a mandatory securities valuation reserve to rely on to cushion declines in equity prices, property-liability insurance companies must also value common stock at market, but have no such reserves. Although they have much larger equity positions than life companies, one could foresee that, given declining premium-to-surplus ratios because of operating losses and declining stock prices in 1974, they would probably sell stock to prevent further erosion in their surplus positions lest they be forced significantly to reduce their insurance activities. With such analysis, it was possible to correctly predict that they would become sellers of common stock.

Sometimes, such an analysis by sectors offers clear-cut indications of security price trends. Often it only provides crucial information about the environment, an idea of what's going to happen if certain other developments fall into place. In none of this can the flow of funds approach be used in a vacuum, but rather as a useful adjunct to other factors determining price trends.

At times when the economy was more stable than from 1973 to 1982, there was an approximate pattern one could expect with regard to the stock market and the flow of funds. If we start our cycle analysis when the economy was well into a recession, one would expect monetary policy to be easing, thereby improving the liquidity situation, or at least anticipated to be easing soon to combat the recession. Common stock offerings and leading indicators thereof, the backlog of issues in registration, would be greatly reduced because of declining stock prices and less need for external financing as inventories were liquidated and capital spending cut back. Mutual fund cash positions would be relatively high; margin debt levels would be down. Other institutional investors, after they became more prominent and had their initial moves into stocks behind them, would also have been expected to have cut back on their net stock purchases and to have increased cash positions. In essence, all that was needed was something to spark the psychology in order to put the potential demand to work.

Then, as the market advanced, cash positions would be reduced to buy securities, and common stock offerings would increase as would the level of margin debt. Eventually, as the economy developed imbalances and monetary policy became more restrictive, the market would be ready for its descending phase. Corporations needing funds would continue to issue new stock. Mutual fund sales would drop as investors needed their cash for other activities and/or wanted to avoid additional stock price declines. Institutional investors would cut back on stock purchases or even sell to increase cash positions. In time, the cycle will be ready to repeat itself.

Naturally this is a simplified pattern with many variations in practice. Developments that do not return every cycle such as those described for insurance companies above, are part of the evaluation. Precise timing is not always possible. For example, in 1972, pension funds and insurance companies had become extremely aggressive in stock investing relative to past behavior. Mutual funds were continuing to experience net redemptions. Margin debt positions had been built up considerably. Yet private pension funds might continue to sell bonds in order to buy stocks somewhat longer, just as life insurance companies could continue to maintain net stock purchases relative to cash flow in excess of their legal maximum holding ratio because their holding levels at cost were still significantly below those legal limits. But one knew that, when the psychology turned, the stage had been set for a major bear market because such extreme trends were not sustainable and were likely to be reversed, which is exactly what happened in early 1973.

Subsequent years were more difficult ones because of the considerable changes in the fundamental factors that influence usual demand patterns. One knew that institutions, having been hurt severely in the 1973–74 bear market, would want much larger cash positions, which earned not insignificant returns in most of the 1970s. Knowing the environment gave one a sense of parameters of possible behavior, but the old behavior benchmarks were being changed, making forecasts of actual behavior more difficult and stock price forecasting even more dependent on non-flow of funds variables than usual.

This discussion could continue, but the brief glimpses should give readers an idea as to how the flow of funds data can be used for such forecasts. Remember that in all forecasts of interest rates or stock prices, it is necessary to consider the entire picture and not just specific facets. Note that the Fed's flow of funds tables are not nearly as useful as the original source data, which are both more timely and provide much more detail (such as foreign buying by country and margin debt positions by equity status) that can be very useful in analysis.

NEEDS FOR IMPROVEMENTS IN, AND SUGGESTIONS FOR EXPANSION OF, THE FLOW OF FUNDS AND OUTSTANDING SERIES

The above observations, along with the discussion of discrepancies, raise some questions of what might be done to improve the Federal Reserve flow of funds tables. One urgent need is for more accurate statistics. In general, where statistics are required by law to be provided to the government on a periodic basis and enough resources are devoted to tabulating those statistics and checking the incoming reports, they are often reasonably accurate, although financial innovations often present problems until those innovations are recognized, understood, and accounted for. Hence, numbers on the banking system, thrift institutions, and the federal government should be satisfactory though still with problems. For example, Commerce, in compiling U.S. government data for the national income accounts, does so using figures that the Fed cannot totally reconcile to the Treasury's unified budget. In other areas, statistics may be required; but too much slips by unreported, particularly in the area of international transactions. Even when data is provided, it is not always in the desired detail needed for flow of funds accounts.

The main problem areas include private net security issuance, private noninsured pension funds, and nonfinancial corporations. The SEC has discontinued its series on net change in stocks and corporate bonds outstanding. There are figures on gross public offerings but not on retirements, sales to employees, conversions of debt to stock, and sales under dividend reinvestment plans. Despite all the data required by the SEC, these series were always deficient; but with the absence of any SEC data, the Flow of Funds Section can only make an educated guess based on remaining data on gross offerings and public announcements on mergers, etc.

The SEC data on private noninsured pension funds were based on voluntary survey data, which were shown to understate reality considerably by the benchmark tabulation of the ERISA-required 5500 form reports for 1977. Because of general budgetary pressures and the effort that would have been needed to improve the SEC quarterly survey, the SEC discontinued that series and a related one on property-liability insurance companies, leaving insufficient data on the pension funds. As of mid-1983, the possibility of obtaining survey data from some of the pension fund performance evaluation services was being explored. Data on other sectors is available but often deficient. For example, the data on state and local government retirement systems only provide information on book value of assets, not on the actual transactions, and are not even internally consistent with data on receipts and disbursements.[8]

The above are all problems for agencies other than the Flow of Funds Section, which only compiles the data. There are other changes that could be made using existing data that would make the flow of funds more useful. For now, users should be aware of these deficiencies and, where possible, turn to the original data sources if these would improve their analysis. Separate categories could be made for instruments that are quite different in nature from others they are now included with. Common stock could be shown separately from preferred stock and limited partnership tax shelters, all of which are now combined. Ownership of mortgage pool securities could be shown separately from agency securities. Analysis of thrift institutions and banks would be aided if time deposits were broken out more by type, as they are in the more detailed original source statistics. It might also help to break out the issuance of corporate bonds by feature—convertible, floating rate, fixed interest, etc.—and all bond issuance by more maturity classifications than just short-term (for under one year) and everything else. To the extent available, gross issuance and retirements might be disclosed in addition to the net issuance figure. These changes would help those trying to forecast stock prices, relative interest rates, bank and thrift investment activities, and the outlook for mortgage finance. One problem with introducing changes of this type in the flow of funds statistics is that the data are not available for all sectors, so that the unity of the

---

[8] For more detailed information on what is available and the problem with the data, see Rudolf Hauser, *Measuring the Flow Funds in Equities-Problems and Needs* (New York: Oppenheimer & Co., November 5, 1982).

current system would be lost. However, this should not prevent such information being presented as supplementary data for those sectors for which it is available.

The Fed should also publish separate tables for farm corporations so that economists trying to combine the Fed statistics on nonfinancial corporations with those of the Labor Department and the national income accounts can do so on a comparable basis. Some economists have also felt that more detailed breakdowns of nonfinancial corporations by major industry groups could be helpful because "the major industry groups differ in behavior and in their reactions to financial forces," although this could really only be done for sources of funds by type of instrument and uses of funds because adequate ownership data on the instruments on that detailed level would be very difficult to obtain.[9]

Other useful data changes that are more difficult to implement include changes to make the series more consistent with inflation. One problem is that fixed-income securities are valued at book value rather than current market values in the balance sheet presentations, whereas market values are used for equity and physical assets. The market and book values would be expected to become much more divergent because of inflation-induced increases in interest rates. The market value figures should ideally be used because that is what is relevant for portfolio theory, and the historical-cost values should be shown in footnote information as is now the case for tangible assets of nonfinancial corporations. Inflation implications on interest expense and debt issuance should at least be shown in footnote information.

One problem in both the national income and flow of funds accounts is that interest expense is incorrectly deducted to obtain operating income of equity owners. Only the real interest costs should be considered an operating cost, although this may be quite difficult to do in practice because there is perhaps no satisfactory way to estimate the inflation premium on debt at the time of its issuance.[10] The nominal interest rate contains an inflation premium designed to account for the failure to index principal to inflation that should be earned from the appreciation of asset values. The result of the present treatment of interest is that operating earnings to equity owners are understated. Individual interest income and resultant savings are overstated but equally offset by understatement of corporate and government savings.

One important use for the flow of funds statistics as part of an analysis of economic growth is to trace how savings are utilized and funds

[9] David Meiselman and Eli Shapiro, *The Measurement of Corporate Sources and Uses of Funds* (New York: National Bureau of Economic Research, 1964), p. 1.

[10] For further explanation, see Rudolf Hauser, *How Profitability Should be Measured in an Inflationary Environment and How FAS33 Compares with the Theoretical Ideal* (New York: Oppenheimer & Co., August 4, 1980).

obtained for productive and nonproductive investment. Those wishing to examine the issue of productivity might find it useful if constant-dollar values of tangible assets were included along with the current-cost and historical-cost information in the balance sheets of the U.S. economy, although such information is available elsewhere. A case can be made for including information on other investment activity that could help future productivity. Then, a summary of all noncurrent transactions could be found in one set of statistics, even if some are classified as current in the national income accounts. This would ideally include government-financed infrastructure and investment in human capital and in research and development, along with related capital consumption and revaluation accounts. This is possible now for infrastructure but much more difficult for the latter two categories.

Those who now only view the role of the accounts as being related to financial flows might disagree, but a broader point of view might consider these accounts an ideal place to consolidate all such information, should a plausible set of estimates become possible. With all these reforms along with others in other economic series implemented, Commerce national income accounts, Labor Department employment/productivity series, and Federal Reserve flow of funds data (along with supplemental detailed information on balance of payments, industrial production, input/output, and pricing information) could become even better integrated keystones for understanding economic activity.

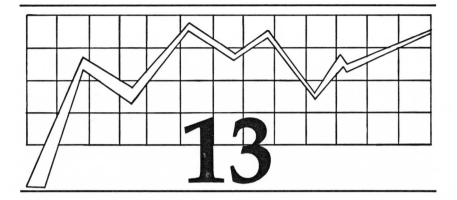

Interest Rates

Frank J. Jones, Ph.D.
Vice President
Kidder, Peabody & Company, Inc.

Benjamin Wolkowitz, Ph.D.
Vice President
Citicorp Futures Corporation

Interest rates on securities issued by the U.S. Department of the Treasury are commonly accepted as being reflective of the general level of interest rates in the U.S. economy. This is because there are more Treasury securities outstanding than any other securities in the world, the Treasury issues securities of every maturity spectrum on a regular basis, and Treasury securities have virtually no credit risk. At any given point in time, however, there are factors that cause differences among interest rates for different Treasury securities and among non-Treasury securities.

In this chapter, we present an overview of the determination of the general level of interest rates, and we explain why there are differences in interest rates among securities at various stages of the business cycle. In the last section of this chapter, we discuss interest rate forecasting.

THE GENERAL LEVEL OF INTEREST RATES

In a broad sense, the economy can be conceived of as being composed of two sectors—the real sector and the financial sector. The real sector is involved with the production of goods and services with physical resources—labor and capital. Important examples of components of the real sector include automobile production, steel production, and housing construction. The financial sector is concerned with the transfer of funds from lenders to borrowers. Important examples of components of the financial sector include commercial banks, insurance companies, and securities dealers.

In the financial sector, equilibrium is attained when the demand for borrowed funds equals the supply of loanable funds. The catalyst for achieving equality between the aggregate supply of funds and the aggregate demand for funds in the financial system is the interest rate. The financial sector is not, however, one uniform, homogeneous market. Rather, the financial sector is composed of a number of financial institutions and markets that, although distinct, are interrelated. Each of these specific components of the financial sector is specialized, attracting funds from specific types of savers and making funds available to specific types of borrowers.

There is, however, some substitution in which savers and/or borrowers who usually borrow or lend in one part of the financial sector may switch to a different part because of a change in relative interest rates. For example, in the recent high-rate environment, small savers that had typically deposited their funds in thrift institutions have responded to relative interest rates and shifted to money market funds.

Interest rates bring the supply and demand for funds into equality in each part of the financial system and operate in the same way to bring the total or aggregate supply and demand for funds in the financial system into equality.

Interest rates are not constant, rather they vary over time. The determination of the general level and variability of interest rates is explainable by several different theories or frameworks. The three major theories—liquidity preference, loanable funds, and inflation and the real rate of interest—are described below. In addition to a general conceptual explanation of the theories, a discussion of how these theories can be used in practice is provided. The focus in this section is on the general level of interest rates, not on any particular interest rate.

Liquidity Preference

Liquidity preference is synonymous with "demand for money." And, as is the case with the demand for other financial assets and liabilities, the demand for money is dependent on the level of interest rates.

The relationship between the demand for money and interest rates can be explained in two ways. The first relies on a Keynesian construction called the speculative demand for money. In this approach, it is assumed that the investor has as investment alternatives either holding cash, which has a zero return and no risk, or holding a bond that has two forms of return, a coupon return and a potential capital gain or loss. If the capital loss on bonds is large enough to exceed the coupon return, the total return on bonds will be negative, and holding money, even at a zero return, would be preferable.

Since the prices of, and interest rates on, fixed income securities move inversely, bonds incur a capital loss when interest rates rise and a capital gain when interest rates fall. When interest rates are low, there will typically be an expectation that they will rise—thus resulting in a capital loss on bonds. In anticipation of such a capital loss, holding cash is preferable. Conversely, if interest rates are presently high, they will typically be expected to decline—so that a capital gain on bonds is anticipated, and holding bonds is preferable.

Interest rates affect the relative demand for money and bonds, as illustrated by a downward-sloping demand curve shown in Exhibit 1. The demand for money increases as the current interest rate decreases, because the lower the present interest rate is, the more it is expected to rise—thus, the greater the expected capital loss is, and the more inves-

EXHIBIT 1   The Supply and Demand of Money

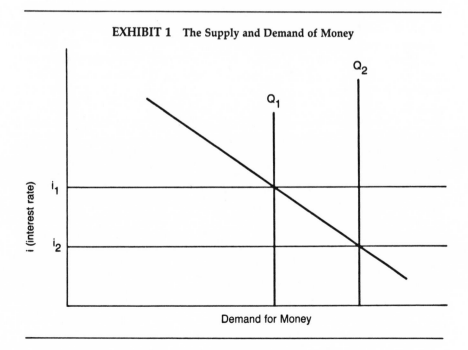

tors are inclined to hold money. With respect to Exhibit 1, as the interest rate rises from i_2 to i_1, the quantity of money demanded decreases from Q_2 to Q_1.

A second way to explain the relationship between interest rates and the demand for money is to conceive of the interest rate as the foregone return for holding money instead of an interest-bearing asset. Consequently, the higher the rate of interest, the greater is the return foregone by holding money and the less money is held. In other words (according to Exhibit 1), as interest rates rise, the cost of holding money rather than an interest-earning asset rises. Consequently, as interest rates rise, a smaller amount of money is held.

According to either explanation, the liquidity preference theory of interest rates explains the level of the interest rate in terms of the supply and demand for money. Thus, if the Fed increases (decreases) the supply of money and there is no change in the demand relationship, the interest rate will decrease (increase). Again referring to Exhibit 1, increasing the supply of money from Q_1 to Q_2 while leaving the demand relationship unchanged results in a lower equilibrium interest rate. In general, an increase in the supply or a decrease in the demand for money will cause interest rates to decline, whereas a decrease in supply or an increase in demand will cause interest rates to rise.

The liquidity preference theory of interest rate determination can be used for determining both short-term and long-term changes in interest rates.

A partial, short-term analysis of interest rate determination is based solely on tracking and analyzing short-term movements in the money supply.[1] Since the Fed has the primary responsibility for determining the money supply, there has developed a school of interest rate analysts commonly known as Fedwatchers who continually monitor and interpret the Fed's activities to infer the Fed's intentions regarding future activities that will affect the money supply and, consequently, interest rates.[2] The weekly money supply statistics announced by the Fed on Friday afternoons and widely disseminated by the financial press are carefully examined for indications of changes in Fed policy that could affect interest rates. Exhibit 2 provides a weekly table of Federal Reserve money supply statistics. An additional discussion of how the Fed's money supply data are interpreted is provided below.

In addition to their market money supply data being watched and interpreted, the Fed's open market operations and their effect on the federal funds rate are continuously monitored. As an example, a discus-

---

[1] The money supply is discussed in Chapter 11.

[2] Fedwatching is the subject of Chapter 20.

EXHIBIT 2   Weekly Federal Reserve Money Supply Statistics—Wednesday, July 28, 1982 ($ millions)

Federal Reserve

Wednesday, July 28, 1982 All data in millions of dollars	Latest Week	Previous Week	Year Ago
Monetary Aggregates Daily averages			
M-1 (One-Week Lag) *	$450,800	R $451,600	$428,500
Adj. Monetary Base (Fed. Res. Board) *	172,713	R172,686	n.a.
Adj. Monetary Base (St. Louis Fed) *ᐟ	178,100	178,600	n.a.
Reserve Position, All Member Banks Daily averages			
Required Reserves	40,056	40,359	40,884
Total Reserves Held, Including Vault Cash	40,327	R 40,665	41,285
Excess (Deficit) Reserves	271	R 306	401
Less: Non-seasonal, Non-extended Borrowing at Federal Reserve Banks	336	323	1,720
Equals: Free (Net Borrowed) Reserves	(65)	R (17)	(1,319)
Reserve Position, Eight Major New York Banks Daily averages			
Excess (Deficit) Reserves	0	64	n.a.
Borrowings at Federal Reserve	57	39	n.a.
Net Federal Funds Purchases	10,269	R11,238	n.a.
Basic Reserve Surplus (Deficit)	(10,326)	R(11,213)	n.a.
Federal Reserve Credit Outstanding Daily averages			
Gov'ts. and Agencies Held Outright	141,220	142,215	130,298
Gov'ts. and Agencies Under Repurchase	0	1,252	1,389
Float	1,708	R 2,011	3,094
Other Assets	9,057	8,916	10,261
Other Factors Affecting Reserves Daily averages			
Gold Stock	11,149	11,149	11,154
Special Drawing Rights	4,018	3,875	3,068
Currency in Circulation	147,103	147,899	137,732
Treasury Deposits	3,358	3,181	3,063
International			
Gov't. Securities Held for Foreign Central Banks and Int'l. Fin. Institutions	95,851	96,479	n.a.
Ten New York Banks, Balance Sheet Items Wednesday, July 21			
Total Loans, Adjusted	113,491	115,301	n.a.
United States Treasury Securities	6,062	5,834	n.a.
Tax-Exempt Securities	11,376	11,725	n.a.
Demand Deposits, Adjusted	24,959	25,764	n.a.
Total Time and Savings Deposits Excluding Large† C.D.'s	34,941	34,807	n.a.
Large Negotiable Certificates of Deposit	35,329	34,846	n.a.
Total Loans, Credit Demand Wednesday, July 21			
Business Loans, All Large Banks	210,426	212,092	181,014
All Other Commercial, Industrial Loans**	206,508	207,769	176,844
Business Loans, New York Banks**	59,467	60,779	n.a.
Business Loans, Chicago Banks**	n.a.	24,022	19.599
Commercial Paper	182,877	181,285	n.a.

R Revised.   * Seasonally adjusted.   † Over $100,000.   ** Excluding acceptances.
n.a. Not available.

Source: The *New York Times.*

sion which appeared in *The Wall Street Journal*, January 20, 1982, included the following comment:

> Some specialists said the recent rise in the funds rate reflected an apparently tougher stance adopted by the Fed late last month in supplying reserves to the banking system. And many contend the recent surge in the money supply will force the Fed to get even tougher.

A longer-term application of the liquidity preference theory is based on the relationship between the money supply and the level of gross national product (GNP). This relationship is formally expressed M × V = P × Y (called the quantity theory of money), where V is velocity of money, P is the price level, and Y is real gross national product. The product of P and Y, P × Y, is nominal GNP, referred to simply as GNP.

According to this theory, if the level of the money supply over some future time period is less (greater) than the actual amount needed to support the expected level of GNP, then the level of interest rates is likely to rise (fall). It is due to this relationship that economic forecasters go through the complex exercise of predicting GNP, the money supply, and their interrelationship in order to provide forecasts of interest rates.

Predicting GNP and money supply relationships is usually conducted in the context of large econometric models of the U.S. economy. These multiequation models attempt to capture the complex interactions in the economy that result in the determination of interest rates, GNP, and money supply. The results of such models are frequently the basis for long-range financial planning by corporations and others.

Loanable Funds

The loanable funds theory of interest rate determination is based on the reasoning related to the supply and demand for loanable funds noted earlier. This theory of interest rate determination depends on the supply of funds available for lending by savers and on the demand for such loanable funds by borrowers. As the return to lending rises (as interest rates rise), the supply of loanable funds increases. Conversely, when interest rates decline, the return to lenders declines and so does the supply of such funds. Since interest rates represent a cost to borrowers, the opposite relationship applies to borrowers: As interest rates rise, borrowers' demand for funds decreases; as interest rates decline, borrowers' demand for funds increases.

The loanable funds theory of interest rate determination applies to aggregate borrowing and lending in the economy. If, at a given interest rate, intended aggregate borrowing is greater than intended aggregate lending, then interest rates will rise. Then the actual measured levels of borrowing and lending at the higher level of interest rates will be equal. If intended aggregate borrowing is less than intended aggregate lending, interest rates will decline until the actual measured levels of borrowing and lending will be equal at the lower level of interest rates.

To apply the loanable funds theory, aggregate borrowing and lending are typically divided into their components, or sectors (as illustrated in Exhibit 3).[3] Even though some borrowers and lenders can shift among types and maturities of sources and uses of funds and some cannot, a structure or taxonomy such as shown in Exhibit 3 can be used in either case for determining aggregate borrowing and lending. This structure is useful for summarizing actual, measured aggregate borrowing and lending for past years, as done for 1976–81 in the exhibit; as indicated above, borrowing and lending must be equal.

The structure is also useful for forecasting interest rates. For this purpose, an estimate is developed of the expected or intended levels of borrowing and lending, over a period of time, of each type shown in Exhibit 3. Then the sum of all types of borrowing (aggregate borrowing) is compared with the sum of all types of lending (aggregate lending). If the former is greater than the latter, interest rates are forecast to increase. And due to the increase in interest rates, actual borrowing would be less than expected borrowing and actual lending would be greater than expected lending. Then, ex post, actual measured borrowing and lending would be equal. For example, the data in Exhibit 3 provide estimates of the actual measured sources and uses of funds in 1982 after interest rates changed to their equilibrium levels.

Often, instead of developing as complete a taxonomy of borrowing and lending as described above, analysts focus only on the major types of borrowing and lending, such as federal government borrowing, business borrowing, and mortgage borrowing. Then, by forecasting increases or decreases in these types of borrowing, the analysts assess whether there will be upward or downward pressures on the interest rate.

A popularization of the application of the loanable funds theory on a sectoral basis is referred to as "crowding out." Large federal deficits require the U.S. Department of the Treasury to increase the amount of debt it has outstanding; and the issue of Treasury debt is alleged to compete with private-sector borrowing, assuming a fixed supply of available credit. Thus, an increase in the demand for funds by the Treasury causes interest rates to increase and forces out the private-sector

---

[3] Flow of funds is explained in Chapter 12.

EXHIBIT 3   Summary of Supply and Demand for Credit ($ billions)

1. Summary of Supply and Demand for Credit ($ Billions)

	Annual Net Increases in Amounts Outstanding							Amt Out 31Dec81e	Table Refer
	1976	1977	1978	1979	1980	1981e	1982p		
Net Demand									
Privately Held Mortgages	70.5	108.0	116.0	105.0	70.9	72.2	71.7	1,230.3	2
Corporate & Foreign Bonds	39.1	39.1	31.8	36.1	37.9	27.4	28.8	536.9	3
Subtotal Long-Term Private	109.6	147.1	147.8	141.1	108.8	99.6	100.5	1,767.2	
Short-Term Business Borrowing	14.1	49.0	76.0	91.4	55.0	127.1	142.1	742.7	8
Short-Term Other Borrowing	40.7	50.7	65.5	52.8	20.7	47.0	59.7	555.9	8
Subtotal Short-Term Private	54.8	99.7	141.5	144.2	75.7	174.1	201.8	1,298.6	
Privately Held Federal Debt	73.0	74.5	81.7	77.4	118.0	113.5	135.4	1,003.6	6
Tax-Exempt Notes and Bonds	17.6	28.9	32.5	27.7	33.0	31.0	30.7	397.5	4
Subtotal Government Debt	90.6	103.4	114.2	105.1	151.0	144.5	166.1	1,401.1	
Total Net Demand for Credit	**255.0**	**350.2**	**403.5**	**390.4**	**335.5**	**418.2**	**468.4**	**4,466.9**	▼
Net Supply[1]									
Thrift Institutions	70.5	82.0	73.5	55.9	57.9	-39.7	41.1	832.8	9
Insurance, Pensions, Endowments	49.0	68.1	73.2	63.6	75.4	70.8	76.7	808.8	9
Investment Companies	2.9	7.0	6.4	25.5	22.5	69.4	64.0	149.9	9
Other Nonbank Finance	12.9	13.4	18.9	26.4	16.6	33.3	41.4	240.4	9
Subtotal Nonbank Finance	135.3	170.6	172.0	171.3	172.3	213.2	223.1	2,031.8	9
Commercial Banks[2]	60.8	84.1	105.9	103.9	83.3	115.0	126.8	1,289.9	10
Business Corporations	9.0	-2.3	-0.9	8.3	3.7	6.8	7.7	98.9	11
State & Local Government	4.0	13.3	11.1	9.5	7.3	11.0	8.2	87.1	11
Foreign[3]	19.6	47.2	58.8	8.9	37.9	17.9	16.0	296.1	11
Subtotal	228.7	312.9	346.9	301.9	304.5	363.9	381.8	3,803.8	
Residual (mostly household direct)	26.3	37.3	56.6	88.5	31.0	54.3	86.6	663.1	12
Total Net Supply of Credit	**255.0**	**350.2**	**403.5**	**390.4**	**335.5**	**418.2**	**468.4**	**4,466.9**	▲
Percentage Growth in Outstandings									
Total Credit	11.0	13.6	13.8	11.7	9.0	10.3	10.5		
Government	13.1	13.2	12.9	10.5	13.7	11.5	11.9		
Household	11.5	14.7	14.7	11.1	5.8	7.2	7.4		
Corporate	8.1	12.4	13.5	14.1	9.0	13.7	13.4		
Long-Term	10.3	12.9	11.7	9.8	7.5	6.4	6.1		
Short-Term	11.9	14.5	16.2	13.9	10.6	14.3	14.6		
Held by Nonbank Finance	13.6	15.1	13.2	11.6	10.5	11.7	11.0		
Commercial Banks	8.3	10.5	12.0	10.5	7.6	9.8	9.8		
Foreign	18.5	37.6	34.1	3.8	15.8	6.4	5.4		
Household Direct	7.1	9.4	13.1	18.1	5.4	8.9	13.1		

[1] Excludes funds for equities, cash and miscellaneous demands not tabulated above.
[2] Domestically chartered banks and their domestic affiliates.
[3] Includes U.S. branches of foreign banks.

Note: Figures in tables may not add to totals due to rounding.

Source: "1982 Prospects for Financial Markets," Salomon Brothers, January 4, 1982, p. 20.

issues. An example of the crowding-out application of the loanable funds theory appeared in *The Wall Street Journal* in 1981:

> Many dealers said they continue to be concerned about the size of the Treasury's financing needs. Traders also expressed nervousness over recent increases in short-term interest rates. But many said they remain confident that bond prices will rebound early next year, mainly because they anticipate further evidence of erosion in the economy.

And another example appeared the same year in a *New York Times* story:

> Unusually heavy year-end government borrowings continued to weigh on the money market last week, raising short-term rates a point on average and reducing prices of longer-term coupon securities as much as two points, or $20 for each $1,000 of face value.

Thus the crowding-out concept derives from the loanable funds theory but focuses only on Treasury borrowing. Most applications of loanable funds use an intermediate approach between a complete taxonomy of sources and uses of funds and only a single use of funds; they consider a few major uses of funds and perhaps changes in the aggregate supply of funds.

Inflation and the Real Rate of Interest

Interest rates represent a rate of return for lenders and a cost to borrowers. To be a meaningful representation of cost or return, however, interest rates should be related to the rate of change of prices. The significance of this relationship can be considered by the following example. Consider a saver who has placed $5,000 in a money market fund earning a return of 12 percent per year. At the end of a year, the saver has $5,600, a 12 percent increase in purchasing power. If, however, the price level had increased by 10 percent per year, then the net increase in purchasing power of the savings would be only 2 percent.

The 12 percent return on the savings is referred to as the nominal rate of interest, since it measures the percent increase in the nominal number of dollars earned or paid over a period of time. The measure of change in purchasing power of 2 percent is referred to as the real rate of interest since it measures the real change in purchasing power. The difference between these two rates is the rate of inflation. Thus the real rate of interest equals the nominal rate of interest minus the rate of inflation.

From the lender's perspective, the real rate of interest represents the increase in real purchasing power resulting from foregone consumption—savings. From the borrower's perspective, the real rate of interest represents the real cost of borrowing. The inflation component of the nominal rate of interest the borrower pays on the borrowed funds represents a deterioration of the principal of the loan (often described as paying back in cheap dollars), not a real cost of borrowed funds. A business should, as a rule, continue to borrow and invest until the real rate of return on investments equals the real rate of interest paid on borrowing.

Thus, there are two major determinants of the real rate of interest. The first is the return on investment—the return to capital. If a business can improve its efficiency of operations and earn a higher rate of return from investment, it will be inclined to pay a higher real rate of return on borrowed funds. The other influence is the preference of consumers. The more consumers want to consume currently rather than forego consumption, the higher the real rate of return will have to be to induce them to alter their plans and save.

Then the real rate of interest and the rate of inflation jointly determine the nominal rate of interest. The effect of the rate of inflation on the nominal rate of interest is to cause the nominal rate to change so that the real rate is unaffected by the rate of inflation. Lenders, unless subject to a "dollar illusion," are concerned with the return of the real purchasing power on their savings rather than the nominal return. Such concern causes consumers to negotiate for nominal rates that keep their real rate of return at least constant. Thus, to the extent their savings are sensitive to the real rate of interest, an increase in inflation without a corresponding increase in the real rate of interest will cause a decrease in savings. Consequently, there is upward pressure on the nominal rate of interest during periods of inflation, which prevents the real rate of interest from decreasing below its original level. To prevent savings from decreasing requires an increase in the nominal rate equal to the increase in the rate of inflation.

Inflation has a somewhat similar effect on the willingness of borrowers to pay a higher nominal rate of interest for funds. Inflation affects the return on investment by affecting the prices of goods and services produced. An investment earning a given amount net of the interest on borrowings will earn a higher nominal amount after inflation because the value of the goods and services produced by the investment have been inflated. If the interest payments on the borrowings do not increase as well, then the real rate of return on investment will also increase. Under such circumstances, borrowers presumably will continue to increase their demand for funds until the nominal cost of borrowing has increased such that the real cost is at its preinflation level.

Over time, however, the real rate of interest may change for two reasons. First, the real rate of interest, since it is the real return on capital, may decrease during recessions because of a substantial amount of unused capital and a low return to the used capital. Similarly, it may increase during periods of economic growth because all capital is productively employed.

The second reason for changes in the real rate relates to *unexpected* changes in the rate of inflation. The nominal interest rate on a security at any time should reflect the *expected* average rate of inflation over the maturity of the security. If the financial markets *expect* a higher rate of inflation in the future, nominal interest rates should increase to reflect these expectations. However, if inflation changes unexpectedly, the initial nominal rate of interest will not correctly reflect the change, and the actual real rate of interest over the period will be different from the normal level of the real rate in the opposite direction of the unexpected change in the rate of inflation.

Consider the following example. Between times T_0 and T_1, the nominal rate of interest is 8 percent, the rate of inflation is 5 percent, and the real rate of interest is 3 percent. Assume these are the normal levels.

Assume that at T_1 the rate of inflation *unexpectedly* increases to 6 percent. Since the change is unexpected, the nominal rate does not change; thus, the real rate of interest decreases to 2 percent. Assume that by T_2 the financial markets recognize the change in the rate of inflation, and the nominal rate of interest increases to 9 percent, restoring the real rate of interest to 3 percent.

At T_3, the rate of inflation *unexpectedly* decreases to its original level of 5 percent. Because the change is unexpected, the nominal rate remains at 9 percent, so the real rate increases to 4 percent. By T_4, the financial market recognizes the change in the rate of inflation, the nominal rate of interest decreases to 8 percent, and the real rate of interest decreases to its original normal level of 3 percent. Thus, although expected changes in the rate of inflation should have no effect on the real rate of interest, unexpected changes in inflation will cause the real rate of interest to change in the opposite direction.

Typically, interest rates are referred to in nominal terms. Similarly, interest rate determination models relate to the nominal rate of interest. As discussed above, the nominal rate of interest and the rate of inflation are directly related. Since the nominal rate of interest is by definition equal to the real rate of interest plus the rate of inflation, the rate of inflation is a major component of the level of the nominal rates of interest. In fact, given the levels of inflation and interest rates that have been observed during the last decade, changes in the nominal rate of interest have been due in greater measure to changes in inflation than to changes in the real rate of interest.

Exhibit 4 provides a plot of the real rate of interest from 1965 until recently. Calculations of the real rate of interest can be made from different measures of the rate of inflation and different interest rates, although in concept the measure of the inflation rate used should be the expected inflation rate over the maturity of the security whose interest rate is used. The interest rate can be either a short-term or a long-term interest rate. Very often, the inflation rate used is based on an average over several previous periods or a projection of the trend of the past inflation rate into the future. The real rate of interest in the plot in Exhibit 4 equals the 91-day Treasury bill interest rate minus the contemporaneous quarterly change in the consumer price index (CPI). Alternatively, the real rate plotted could have been the long-term Treasury bond rate minus an expected long-term rate of inflation.

Exhibit 4 shows that there has been considerable variation in the real rate of interest (the difference between the interest rate and the inflation rate) since 1981. These changes in the real rate have been due both to changes in the strength of the economy and to errors in inflationary expectations.[4] Although the correlation is less than perfect, the real rate of interest tends to be low during recessions and high during periods of economic strength. Recently, the real rate of interest has been at historic highs.

To summarize, in models of the determination of the nominal rate of interest, the factors that affect the rate of inflation and the real rate of interest should be considered separately. Since there has been even greater volatility in the rate of inflation than in the real rate of interest, an accurate determination of the rate of inflation is an important part of an accurate determination of the nominal rate of interest.

Synthesis

The three different theories or rationales of the level of interest rates that were described in this section are not exclusive, but rather are compatible and complementary ways of considering interest rate determination. The liquidity preference theory, which considers the supply and demand for money, and the loanable funds theory, which considers the supply of and demand for loanable funds, are equivalent ways of considering interest rate determination. A model that included both money and loanable funds would show that these two theories would determine the same interest rate. The impact of the theory of inflation

---

[4] Some observers claim that the real rate of interest has been high recently because the real rate contains a risk premium to account for the increased volatility of interest rates since October 1979, when the Fed announced that it would devote more attention to controlling the money supply and less to controlling the interest rate.

EXHIBIT 4   The Real Rate of Interest

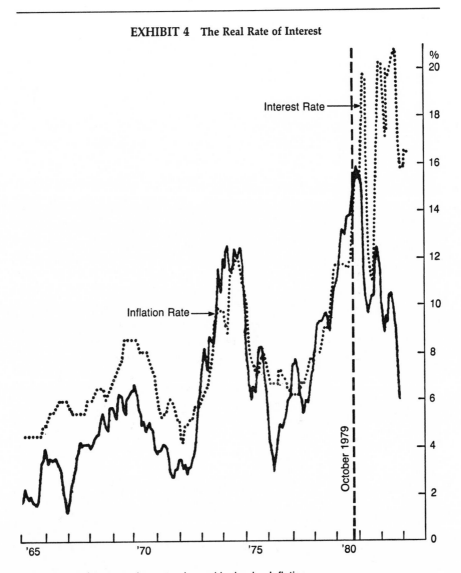

Interest rate: Average prime rate charged by banks. Inflation
rate: Consumer price movement, six-month spens (annual rate).

* Average prime rate charged by banks.
† Consumer price movement, six-month spans (annual rate).
Source: U.S. Department of Commerce.

and the real rate of interest on the level of interest rates is complementary to the other two explanations by introducing the effect of inflation to either. Thus, the three theories described in this section should be viewed as a unified approach to interest rate determination.

Tone of the Market

The factors discussed above that affect interest rates—the supply and demand for money, the supply and demand for funds, and the inflation rate—are objective in nature. These fundamental factors undoubtedly determine the level of interest rates after some lag. But there is another type of influence on interest rates that responds very quickly—within hours or even minutes, and at times includes subjective as well as objective factors. This type of influence is called the tone of the market.

The tone of the market determines the very short-run direction and volatility of interest rates and is due to actions by professionals in the interest rate markets, mainly dealers in government securities, corporate bonds, and municipal bonds and also large institutional investors in these securities. The professionals continually monitor the nation's and the world's economic, political, and social condition and quickly assess their likely impacts on interest rates. In particular, they watch for changes in the condition of the nation's economic goals, inflation, unemployment, economic growth, and balance of payments and watch for changes in economic policies, monetary policy, and fiscal policy. Even more specifically, they monitor the volume of new issues of Treasury, corporate, and municipal debt that will be brought to the market in the next few days and weeks as well as Fed open market operations and monetary policy.

By monitoring and quickly assessing the likely impact of these factors on interest rates, the professionals are able to rapidly alter their portfolio strategies in view of new information. If dealers and portfolio managers expect interest rates to increase, they reduce the size of their portfolios to avoid losses, thus lowering the demand for securities and increasing interest rates. In response to the same expectations, they may reduce their holdings of long-term securities but increase their holdings of short-term securities, thus increasing long-term rates relative to short-term rates, a normal phenomenon during times of rising interest rates. Through these portfolio activities, the expectation that interest rates will rise actually causes interest rates to rise, at least for a short period of time. The opposite will occur if interest rates are expected to decrease.

At times, professionals may respond not only to recent information but to expectations or anticipations of future information. Operating on the basis of future information is more subjective than operating after the release of new information. And at times, the psychology of the market may be counter to the fundamental factors: Professionals may expect future information that will reverse interest rate trends based on recently available data.

The tone of the market, whether determined by objective (fundamental) or subjective (psychological) factors, affects interest rates very quickly. And activities by professionals that set the tone of the market by quickly translating new information or expectations of future information into present interest rate changes add to the efficiency of the financial markets.

The following quote from *The Wall Street Journal* indicates the nature and importance of the tone of the market:

> Bond prices swung widely as speculators stepped up their involvement in the credit markets.
>
> The Treasury recently offered 8⅜ percent bonds of 2008, for example opened at 99²²⁄₃₂ bid, 99²⁴⁄₃₂ asked, traded as high as 100 bid, 100⁴⁄₃₂ asked only to finish the session at their opening levels.
>
> The earlier firming came as dealers purchased inventory for possible markups in any subsequent resumption of the strong price rally of the past two weeks.

THE STRUCTURES OF INTEREST RATES

It is often asked what determines or affects "the" interest rate—as if there were a single interest rate. However, from the financial markets, it is obvious that there is not one but several interest rates. And although these interest rates may generally move in the same direction at the same time, the amounts of their movements and, at times, even the direction of their movements may differ substantially. Thus the spreads, or differences, between interest rates vary. These observations are illustrated by Exhibit 5.

This section discusses the factors that tend to make interest rates differ among themselves. These factors are often the basis for the "structures" of interest rates. There are three different structures of interest rates—even if securities are identical in every other respect, their interest rates may differ because of maturity, credit risk, and taxability.

Maturity Structure (Term Structure) of Interest Rates

Let us first consider the relationship between a security's interest rate and its term to maturity. This relationship is usually referred to as the maturity structure or term structure of interest rates. A common analyti-

EXHIBIT 5 Plot of Interest Rates (monthly averages of daily figures)

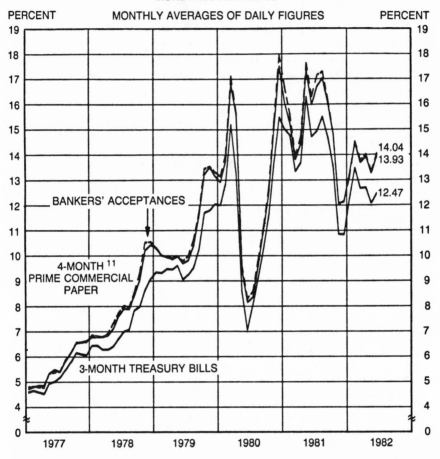

MONEY MARKET RATES

PERCENT   MONTHLY AVERAGES OF DAILY FIGURES   PERCENT

DATA PRIOR TO NOVEMBER 1,1979 ARE 4.6 MONTH COMMERCIAL PAPER RATES.
LATEST DATA PLOTTED: JUNE
PREPARED BY FEDERAL RESERVE BANK OF ST. LOUIS

Source: "Monetary Trends," *Federal Reserve Bank of St. Louis.*

cal construct in this context is the yield curve (or term structure curve),
which is a curve illustrating the relationship between the interest rate
and the maturity of securities that are identical in every way other than
maturity. Exhibit 6 shows three yield curves that have been observed at
various dates.

EXHIBIT 5   (*concluded*)

LONG—TERM INTEREST RATES

MONTHLY AVERAGES OF DAILY FIGURES

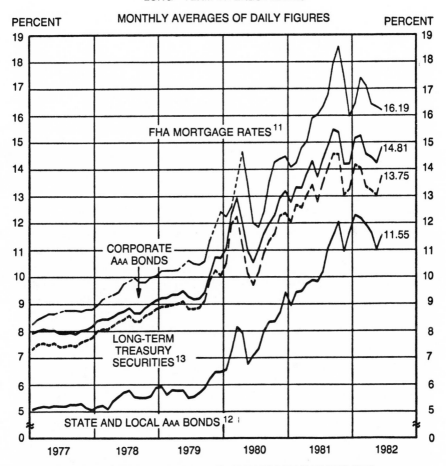

PERCENT

PERCENT

FHA MORTGAGE RATES [11]

16.19

14.81

13.75

CORPORATE
Aaa BONDS

11.55

LONG-TERM
TREASURY
SECURITIES [13]

STATE AND LOCAL Aaa BONDS [12]

1977   1978   1979   1980   1981   1982

11 FHA 30-YEAR MORTGAGES. DASHED LINES INDICATE DATA NOT AVAILABLE.

12 MONTHLY AVERAGES OF THURSDAY FIGURES.

13 AVERAGE OF YIELDS ON COUPON ISSUES DUE OR CALLABLE IN TEN YEARS OR MORE,
EXCLUDING ISSUES WITH FEDERAL ESTATE TAX PRIVILEGES. YIELDS ARE COMPUTED
BY THIS BANK.

LATEST DATA PLOTTED: JUNE
PREPARED BY FEDERAL RESERVE BANK OF ST. LOUIS

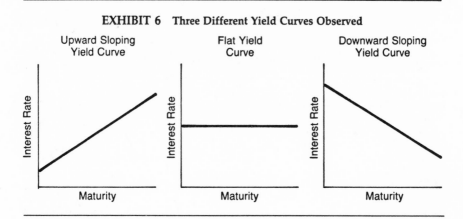

EXHIBIT 6   Three Different Yield Curves Observed

There are three distinct explanations of the relationship between the maturities of securities and their interest rates (i.e., shape of the yield curve)—liquidity hypothesis, expectations hypothesis, and segmentation hypothesis.[5]

The liquidity hypothesis predicts an upward-sloping yield for all economic environments. However, the liquidity hypothesis is not intended to be a complete explanation of the term structure of interest rates. Rather, it is intended to supplement the expectations hypothesis. The combined effects of the liquidity hypothesis and the expectations hypothesis are shown in Exhibit 7.

The expectations hypothesis produces a horizontal (flat) yield curve when interest rates are normal, an upward-sloping yield curve when interest rates are low, and a downward-sloping yield curve when interest rates are high. Supplementing the expectations hypothesis with the liquidity hypothesis, which always predicts an upward-sloping yield curve, provides an upward bias to a yield curve based only on the expectations hypothesis. Indeed, upward sloping yield curves historically have been the most frequently observed; and for this reason, upward-sloping yield curves are frequently referred to as normal yield curves. During recessionary periods, when interest rates are low and are expected to increase, the yield curve has a steep upward slope. When the economy is strong, credit is tight, and interest rates are high; however, downward-sloping yield curves are observed. Both observations

---

[5] For a more detailed treatment of these three theories, see Frank J. Jones and Benjamin Wolkowitz, "The Determinants of Interest Rates on Fixed Income Securities," Chapter 5, and Richard W. McEnally, "The Term Structure of Interest Rates" Chapter 46, in *The Handbook of Fixed Income Securities* ed. Frank J. Fabozzi and Irving M. Pollack (Homewood, Ill.: Dow Jones-Irwin, 1983).

EXHIBIT 7 Expectations Hypothesis plus Liquidity Hypothesis

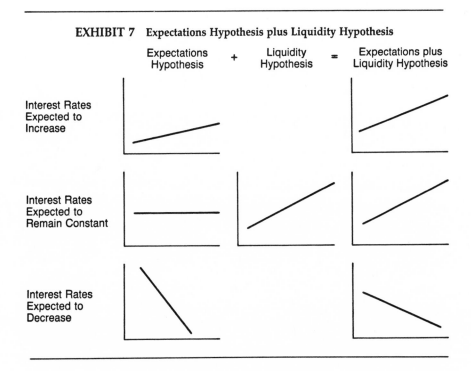

are consistent with the expectations hypothesis. Most observers of debt markets tend to support the expectations hypothesis complemented by the liquidity hypothesis as the dominant explanation for the observed relationship between interest rates and maturity.

The combined expectations hypothesis/liquidity hypothesis description of the maturity structure of interest rates can be applied to the actual behavior of the financial markets. The conclusions that can be drawn from a combination of the expectations hypothesis and the liquidity hypothesis are: When the level of interest rates is normal, the yield curve will have a slight upward slope—the long-term rates will be slightly greater than short-term rates. When the general level of interest rates is low, the term structure will have a steeper upward slope. Finally, when the level of interest rates is high, the term structure will have a downward slope. Pragmatically, the segmentation hypothesis adds nothing that either contradicts or supports this observation.

Empirical observations support conclusions derived from the expectations and the liquidity hypotheses. Exhibits 8, 9, and 10 show yield curves on different dates with various slopes. Note that the general level of interest rates is higher for the downward-sloping yield curve.

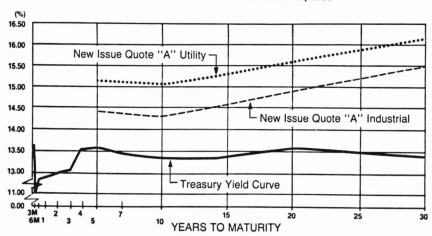

EXHIBIT 8 Yield Curve—November 12, 1981

Source: Paine, Webber Fixed Income Research.

EXHIBIT 9 Yield Curve—September 3, 1981

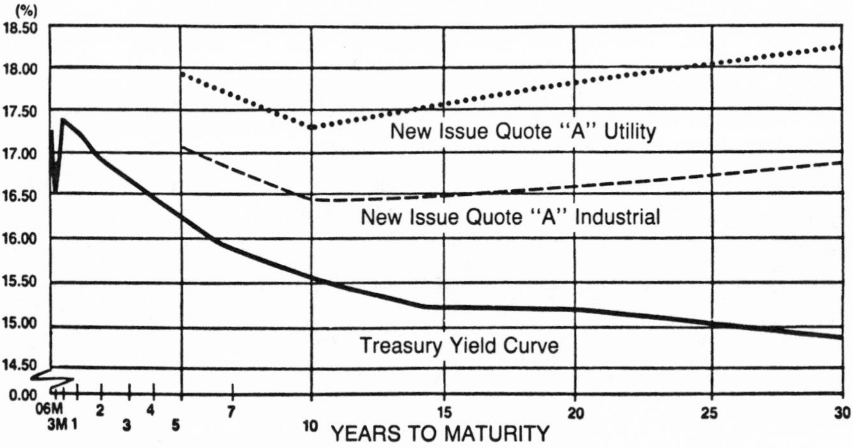

(%)

18.50
18.00
17.50
17.00
16.50
16.00
15.50
15.00
14.50
0.00

New Issue Quote "A" Utility

New Issue Quote "A" Industrial

Treasury Yield Curve

06M 2   4   7   15   20   25   30
3M 1   3   5   10 YEARS TO MATURITY

Source: Paine, Webber Fixed Income Research.

EXHIBIT 10   Yield Curve—August 5, 1982

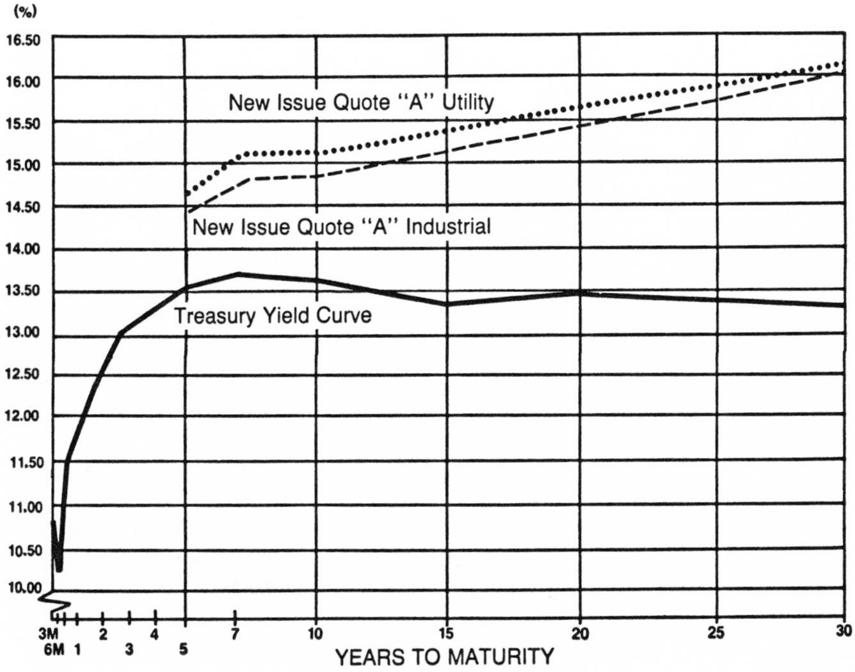

Source: Paine, Webber Fixed Income Research.

Exhibit 11 shows a plot of the spread of the long-term Treasury bond rate minus the 91-day Treasury bill rate over recent interest rate cycles. Note that the spread tends to be large and positive at low levels of interest rates and negative at high levels of interest rates. These results are consistent with the conclusions of the combined expectation hypothesis and the liquidity hypothesis.

Credit Risk

The two major characteristics of a security are return and risk. In turn, there are two major types of risk: market risk and credit risk. Market risk refers to the volatility of the price of a security due to changes in the general level of interest rates. The market risk of a security is thus determined primarily by its maturity, since the longer the maturity, the greater the price change of the security for a given magnitude of interest rate change in the opposite direction. Thus the term structure of interest

EXHIBIT 11   30-Year Treasury Bond minus 91-Day Treasury Bill Yield Spread

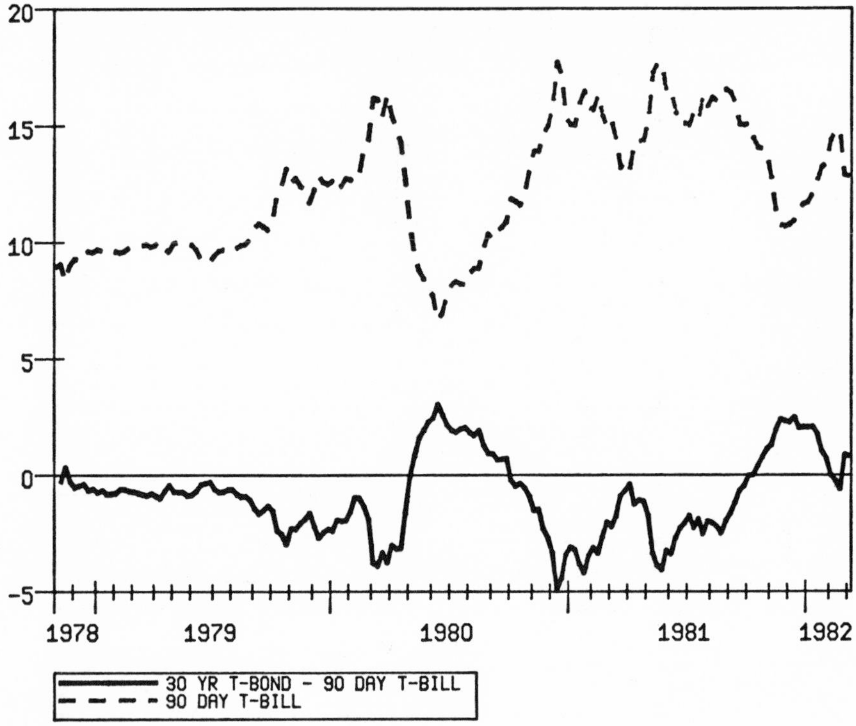

rates relates to the market risk of a security. This section considers the other type of risk, credit risk.

The credit risk of a security is a measure of the likelihood that the issuer of the security, the borrower, will be unable to pay the interest or principal on the security when due. Credit risk is thus a measure of the creditworthiness of the issuer of the security. Federal securities—that is, issues of the U.S. Department of the Treasury—have the lowest credit risk. Federal agencies are perceived to have the next lowest credit risk because they are backed by the federal government. Corporate securities are rated lower than federal agencies with respect to credit risk. The relative credit risks of long-term corporate securities are rated by two private financial corporations—Moody's and Standard & Poor's. Exhibit 12 describes their rating categories.

Although the creditworthiness of different issuers of bonds affects the bonds' credit risk, even different bonds of the same issuer can have different credit risk depending on the characteristic of the specific bond.

EXHIBIT 12   Corporate Bond Rating Categories*

Standard & Poor's Rating Categories†	Description
AAA (Aaa)	Bonds rated AAA have the highest rating assigned by Standard & Poor's to a debt obligation. Capacity to pay interest and repay principal is extremely strong.
AA (Aa)	Bonds rated AA have a very strong capacity to pay interest and repay principal and differ from the highest-rated issues only in small degree.
A (A)	Bonds rated A have a strong capacity to pay interest and repay principal, although they are somewhat more susceptible to the adverse effects of changes in circumstances and economic conditions than bonds in higher-rated categories.
BBB (Baa)	Bonds rated BBB are regarded as having an adequate capacity to pay interest and repay principal. Whereas they normally exhibit adequate protection parameters, adverse economic conditions or changing circumstances are more likely to lead to a weakened capacity to pay interest and repay principal for bonds in this category than for bonds in higher-rated categories.
BB (Ba) B (B) CCC (CCa) CC (Ca)	Bonds rated BB, B, CCC, and CC are regarded, on balance, as predominantly speculative with respect to capacity to pay interest and repay principal in accordance with the terms of the obligation. BB indicates the lowest degree of speculation and CC the highest degree of speculation. While such bonds will likely have some quality and protective characteristics, these are outweighed by large uncertainties or major risk exposures to adverse conditions.
C	The rating C is reserved for income bonds on which no interest is being paid.
D	Bonds rated D are in default, and payment of interest and/or repayment of principal is in arrears.
Plus (+) or Minus (−):	The ratings from AA to B may be modified by the addition of a plus or minus sign to show relative standing within the major rating categories.

* These Standard & Poor's corporate bond rating categories also apply to municipal bonds.
† The ratings in parentheses refer to the corresponding ratings of Moody's Investors Service, Inc.
Source: Standard & Poor's Corporation.

For example, a debenture (an unsecured bond) may have a higher credit risk than a bond that is collateralized by real or financial assets or a sinking-fund bond of the same issuer.

Interest rates are higher for securities with greater credit risk, since investors have to be compensated for the additional risk. Consequently, the interest rate on a Treasury security is less than that on a AAA corporate security, which is in turn less than that on an A corporate security, all with the same maturity. Exhibit 13 shows the spread between 30-year Treasury bonds and 30-year AAA corporate bonds and

EXHIBIT 13   30-Year AAA Corporate Bond minus 30-Year Treasury Bond Yield Spread and 30-Year A Corporate Bond minus 30-Year AAA Corporate Bond Yield Spread

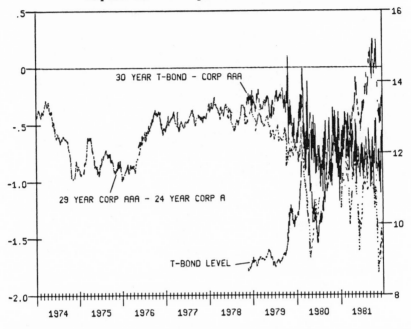

the spread between 30-year corporate AAA bonds and 30-year A corporate bonds against the level of the 30-year Treasury bond interest rate. Note that these spreads tend to widen when interest rates are high and to narrow when interest rates are low. This is consistent with a "flight to quality," an increased preference by investors for low credit risk instruments when interest rates are high and investors perceive high credit risk borrowers as vulnerable. Exhibit 14 shows the interest rates by credit rating at a specific time.

EXHIBIT 14   Bond Interest Rates by Credit Rating

	Industrials	Treasuries	Utilities
Baa	17.25%		18.70%
A	16.25		17.75
Aa	15.55		17.50
Aaa	15.15		—
Bell System debentures			17.00
30-year Treasuries		14.40%	

Source: *Bondweek*, February 8, 1983, p. 9.

EXHIBIT 15   90-Day Commercial Paper minus 90-Day Treasury Bill Yield Spread

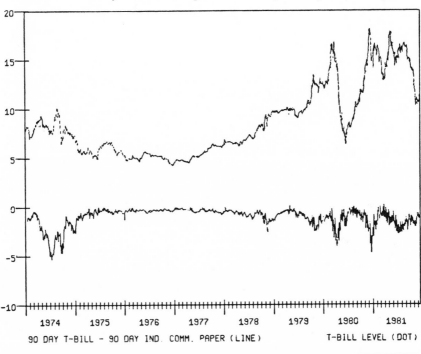

90 DAY T-BILL - 90 DAY IND. COMM. PAPER (LINE)   T-BILL LEVEL (DOT)

Exhibit 15 shows a plot of the spread between 90-day Treasury bills and 90-day industrial commercial paper against the Treasury bill interest rate level. The money market spread similarly shows a widening when interest rates are high and a narrowing when interest rates are low— that is, a flight to quality at high interest rates.

The credit risk structure of interest rates explains variations in the interest rates on various securities of the same maturity due to differences in the credit risk of the issuers and issues. In addition, the size of the spreads between securities with high credit risk and low credit risk varies with the level of interest rates.

Taxability Structure

There are three aspects of taxability that cause interest rates on different securities to differ at a specific time.

Tax-Exempt Municipals.   The coupon payments on Treasury and corporate bonds are subject to the federal personal income tax. Consequently, the aftertax yield on Treasury and corporate bonds is less than the coupon yield, by an amount determined by the bondholder's tax bracket. It is not legal, however, for the federal government to tax the coupon payment on state and local securities.[6] Since municipal securities are tax exempt, their aftertax yield is the same as their pretax yield. Because investors are concerned with aftertax rather than pretax yields, municipal securities can be issued with lower coupons than the coupons on similar Treasury or corporate securities. For example, to an investor in the 50 percent tax bracket, a 6 percent municipal security selling at par has the same aftertax yield as a 12 percent Treasury or corporate security.

Thus, municipal bond interest rates differ from the interest rates on Treasury and corporate bonds because of the difference in taxability. Exhibit 16 shows the spread in the yields between a 30-year Treasury bond and a 30-year AAA municipal security. Notice that the yield spread is always positive—that is, the yield on Treasury bonds is higher than the yield on municipal bonds.

The magnitude of the spread changes over the interest rate cycle for two reasons. First, municipal bonds have a higher credit risk than Treasury bonds, and the phenomenon related to the flight to quality discussed in the last section is applicable. Here the flight to quality is from municipals to Treasuries when interest rates are high. In this case, however, since the rate on Treasury bonds is higher than the rate on municipal bonds, the flight to Treasury bonds during times of high interest rates tends to narrow the spread.

In addition, the spread between Treasury and municipal bond yields changes over the interest rate cycle for reasons of taxability. The spread is the absolute difference between the Treasury and the municipal bond interest rates. However, the tax rate as it is applied to the coupon on Treasury securities has a relative or proportional effect. Thus, for example, to an investor in the 50 percent tax bracket, a 4 percent municipal security has the same aftertax yield as an 8 percent Treasury security, for a spread of 4 percent. However, a 6 percent municipal security has the same aftertax yield as a 12 percent Treasury security, for a spread of 6 percent. Similarly, an 8 percent municipal security has the same aftertax yield as a 16 percent Treasury security, for a spread of 8 percent. Thus, because of the proportional nature of the federal personal income tax, the absolute spread between Treasury and municipal bonds varies over the interest rate cycle, being larger when interest rates are high and smaller when interest rates are low.

---

[6] Neither can state and local governments tax the coupon payments of federal securities. But this exemption is not as important as the federal exemption on state and local government securities, because the income tax rates of state and local government are lower than federal income tax rates.

EXHIBIT 16   30-Year Treasury Bond minus 30-Year Municipal Bond Yield Spread

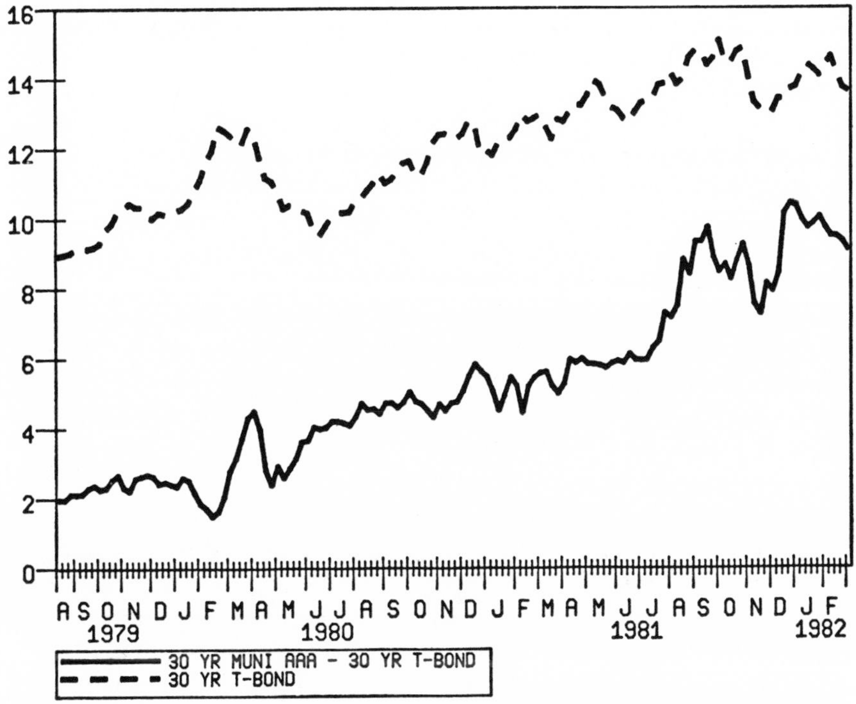

Overall, due to the flight to quality, the spread between Treasury and municipal bonds narrows when interest rates are high; and due to the proportional nature of the income tax, the spread widens when interest rates are high. Thus, the two effects are countervailing. Based on the Treasury bond/municipal bond interest rate spread shown in Exhibit 16, the latter effect of interest rates on the spread dominates the former effect.

The spread between municipal and Treasury bonds may also vary structurally due to changes in tax legislation that affect the level of the personal income tax and the attractiveness of other tax shelters that compete with municipal securities as tax-reducing investments.

Level of Coupons.   A second aspect of taxability also causes interest rates among different securities, even of the same issuer and maturity, to differ. This aspect is the magnitude of the coupon of the security. Although coupon payments on Treasury and corporate bonds are taxed at the personal income tax rate, capital gains are taxed at the capital gains tax rate. If a bond is held for more than one year, the long-term capital gains tax rate, which is 40 percent of the personal income tax rate, will apply. Consequently, the aftertax value of 1 percent of pretax coupon return is less to an investor than the aftertax value of 1 percent of pretax capital gains.

The yield-to-maturity of a bond, as it is commonly calculated, includes both the coupon return and the return due to capital gain or loss (the difference between the current market price and the par value of the bond) on an annual basis as if the security were held to maturity. If, for example, a 30-year security with an $80 coupon is selling for $1,000, its 8 percent yield-to-maturity is entirely due to the coupon return. If another 30-year security with a $60 coupon is initially selling for $773.77 for an 8 percent yield-to-maturity, its yield-to-maturity consists of a 7.75 percent coupon return, and the remainder is due to the capital gain over the 30-year life. Since this low-coupon "discount security" (a security selling for less than its maturity value of $1,000) has a portion of its return due

EXHIBIT 17   11¾ Percent Treasury Bond minus 7⅝ Percent Treasury Bond Yield Spread

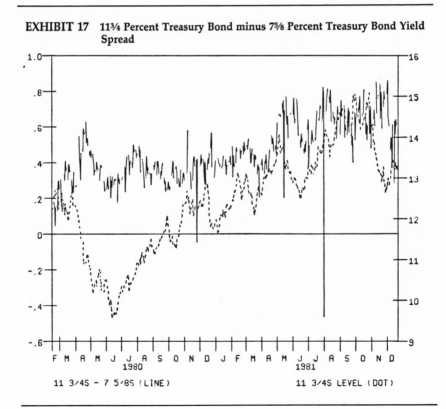

11 3/4S − 7 5/8S (LINE)   11 3/4S LEVEL (DOT)

to capital gains, which is taxed at a lower rate, the aftertax return on the low-coupon discount bond is greater than that of the high-coupon bond selling at "par" (its maturity value of $1,000). Therefore, the price of the discount bond will be bid up; and thus, the yield-to-maturity at its new actual trading price will be somewhat less than the 8 percent yield on the par bond. The lower yield on the discount bond will compensate for its more favorable tax treatment.

Thus low-coupon discount bonds normally sell at a yield somewhat lower than high-coupon bonds selling at par or at a premium (at a price greater than its maturity value) or even at a smaller discount because of this tax advantage. Exhibit 17 shows the yield spread between high-coupon, 11¾ percent, and low-coupon, 7⅝ percent, Treasury securities over the past two years. Notice that the yield spread, almost without exception, is positive (the yield on the high-coupon bond is greater than the yield on the low-coupon bond).

Exhibit 18 illustrates that although the pretax yield of the highest coupon Treasury bonds shown is highest, the aftertax yield of these

EXHIBIT 18   Before-Tax and Aftertax Yields on U.S. Treasury Bonds—December 4, 1981

Coupon	Pretax Yield-To-Maturity	Aftertax Yield	Issue Date	Maturity Date
7⅝%	12.12†	7.11	2/15/77	2/15/07/02
7⅞	12.14	7.08	11/15/77	11/15/07/02
8¼	12.45	7.23*	5/15/75	5/15/05/00
8⅜	12.37	7.15	8/15/78	8/15/08/03
8¾	12.45	7.14	11/15/78	11/15/08/03
9⅛	12.51	7.11	5/15/79	5/15/09/04
10	12.59	7.01	5/15/80	5/15/10/05
10⅜	12.66	6.99	11/15/79	11/15/09/04
11¾	12.79	6.84	2/15/80	2/15/10/05
12¾	12.77	6.65†	11/17/80	11/15/10/05
13⅞	12.85*	6.68	5/15/81	5/15/11/06
14	12.85*	6.68	11/16/81	11/15/11/06

* Highest.
† Lowest.
Note: Due to their tax advantages, the (pretax) yields on these bonds is lower than on other Treasury bonds without the estate-tax eligibility provision.
Source: "Government Securities Quotations," Continental Bank, Chicago.

bonds is not. Due to taxability alone, the yields on all these bonds would be equal if they were identical in every way other than coupon. However, they also have different maturities and different times since issuance.

Flower Bonds. Several Treasury bonds issued during the 1950s and early 1960s exhibit another type of taxability. These bonds, known as flower bonds, are acceptable at par in payment of federal estate taxes when owned by the decedent at death. These bonds were issued with low coupons. On January 1, 1977, the capital gain realized at the holder's death was made taxable, thus reducing the tax advantage of flower bonds to some extent.

BOND YIELD INDEXES

To gauge the general level of interest, several organizations construct bond yield indexes, where yield is measured by the issue's yield-to-maturity. Some of the more popular bond yield indexes are listed in Exhibit 19. One of the problems with bond yield indexes is that, unlike their counterpart in the common stock area,[7] it is difficult to find accurate and consistent information on bond prices at a point in time. This is because bonds are traded in the over-the-counter market, and trading on a given issue may not be frequent.

FORECASTING INTEREST RATES

Loans and deposits that have variable interest rates will typically have those rates pegged to a particular government security or an index of such securities. Thus, the periodic resetting of the rate will depend on the behavior of a predetermined benchmark rate. Adjustable-rate mortgages as well as commercial loan arrangements typically reprice in this fashion. Variable-rate corporate debt issues as well as variable-rate CDs will also reprice periodically, with rates fixed in relationship to some market rate. Because of the proliferation of such instruments, the general level of concern over interest rate behavior has been heightened.

The primary question for anyone affected by the pattern of interest rates is how will they behave in the future. Decisions affected by interest rates depend not only on the current level of rates but on their likely future levels. Thus, as the constituency concerned with interest rates has grown (whether because of new variable rate instruments or because of the continuing growth of the public and corporate debt), the concern over interest rate forecasting has intensified.

Forecasting, at its best, is a combination of analytical techniques, experience, and sound judgment. A perhaps trite but nevertheless accurate way of describing forecasting is to recognize that it is an art as much

---

[7] Stock market indexes are discussed in the next chapter.

EXHIBIT 19   List of Popular Bond Yield Indexes

U.S. government indexes
  Standard & Poor's long-term government bond yield average
  Standard & Poor's intermediate-term government bond yield average
  Standard & Poor's short-term government bond yield average

Corporate Indexes
  Barron's best-grade bonds
  Barron's intermediate-grade bonds
  Dow Jones 20 bonds average
  Dow Jones 10 industrial bonds average
  Dow Jones 10 public utility bond average
  Moody's Aaa industrial bond average
  Moody's Aa industrial bond average
  Moody's Baa industrial bond average
  Moody's Industrial average
  Moody's Aaa public utility average
  Moody's Aa public utility average
  Moody's A public utility average
  Moody's Baa public utility average
  Moody's public utility average
  Moody's Aa railroad bond average
  Moody's A railroad bond average
  Moody's Baa railroad bond average
  Moody's railroad bond average
  Moody's Aaa corporate composite
  Moody's Aa corporate composite
  Moody's A corporate composite
  Moody's Baa corporate Composite
  Moody's corporate average composite
  Standard & Poor's corporate composite bond yield average—AAA
  Standard & Poor's corporate composite bond yield average—AA
  Standard & Poor's corporate composite bond yield average—A
  Standard & Poor's corporate composite bond yield average—BBB
  Standard & Poor's industrial bond yield average—AAA
  Standard & Poor's industrial bond yield average—AA
  Standard & Poor's industrial bond yield average—A
  Standard & Poor's industrial bond yield average—BBB

Municipal Indexes
  Dow Jones municipal bond yield index
  Bond Buyer revenue bond index
  Bond Buyer 20-bond index
  Bond Buyer 11-bond index
  Standard & Poor's municipal bond average yield

---

as, if not more than, a science. Certainly, there are scientifically grounded techniques, mostly statistical, which are useful in analyzing trends and relationships in an effort to uncover the future pattern of interest rates. Interpreting these patterns is where the judgmental or artistic aspect of forecasting enters.

Interest rate forecasting is generally divided into two categories, short-term and long-term forecasting. The difference between these two types of forecasting, besides the obvious difference in the time period being focused on, is the relative importance of the various factors influencing interest rates.

Short-term interest rate forecasting is for the most part equivalent to Fedwatching.[8] The relationship between weekly movements in the money supply and the Federal Reserve's publicized targets is viewed as an important indicator of likely changes in Federal Reserve policy. The securities markets do indeed respond to changes in the money supply numbers; therefore, being able to forecast the weekly money supply figures accurately is tantamount to forecasting a major influence on short-term rates. These weekly transient money supply numbers are of most importance to money managers and securities dealers whose decisions are dependent on short-term changes in interest rates.

Long-term interest rate forecasting is also a function of Federal Reserve actions and policies. In addition, such forecasts also require analysis of the overall behavior of the economy with emphasis on long-term economic trends. For example, budget deficits may not have an impact on interest rates in the near term and therefore can be relegated to a position of lesser importance in short-term forecasts. When forecasting the future behavior of interest rates, budget deficits are likely to take on a more significant role. In general, longer-term forecasting requires a broader and more comprehensive view of the economy than short-term forecasts. This activity frequently incorporates the use of large-scale models that attempt to explain the interrelationships of the real and financial sectors of the economy in an effort to predict interest rates.

The actual job of preparing forecasts has generally been the responsibility of economists assisted by statisticians, and economists with particular expertise in statistics known as econometricians. This forecasting activity is, for the most part, either conducted by security dealers or by corporations that provide economic analyses including interest rate forecasts. Securities dealers typically provide interest rate forecasts as a service to their clients. The information is disseminated through publications which are often sent to prospective as well as actual clients and through direct contact with the dealers' staffs. In a few cases, interest rate forecasters employed by dealers have received almost celebrity status, and their pronouncements on interest rates receive widespread attention.

The other major source of interest rate forecasts is advisory services without dealer connections. These forecasts are generally available via subscription and can be obtained in hard copy or, in several cases, through quote services such as Telerate or Reuters. Several of these services also offer tailored consultations to their clients.

---

[8] See Chapter 20.

Information on interest rate forecasts is, of course, rated by its accuracy. Assessing the accuracy of forecasts is a straightforward activity that will quickly indicate that no one has a monopoly on predicting the future. Although certain forecasters have a better record than others, no one is infallible.

Forecasts, even if they are not perfect, should be consulted regularly by anyone involved in decision making influenced by interest rates. The activity of routinely consulting forecasts will enhance one's understanding of the dynamics of interest rate determination. This will provide a better understanding of interest rate behavior and enable one to intelligently sift through forecasts to reach a personal prediction of future interest rate behavior.

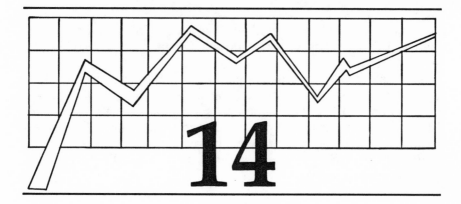

Stock Market Indicators

Stan West, J.D., M.B.A.
Vice President, Business Research Division
New York Stock Exchange, Inc.

For decades, the stock market has fascinated observers—whether they be professional security analysts, academic researchers, investors and traders, newspaper financial editors, or just ordinary laymen. Ironically, too, "reading" the market may be easier than in most other fields of endeavor because of the enormous flow of statistical information about the stock market. Being familiar with the various kinds of data about the market is no guarantee of investment success, but knowledge of the major statistical indicators can certainly facilitate an understanding of what one reads in the newspapers, hears on the radio, or sees on television about that intriguing subject: the stock market.

This chapter is not designed to cover statistical measurements that may be guides to investment decisions—e.g., dividend yields, price/earnings ratios, analyses of corporate balance sheets, or income statements. Nor will it examine so-called technical approaches such as relative strength measures or moving averages of stock prices. Instead, it takes a macroview of the subject, focusing on overall aggregate indicators of stock market conditions.

STOCK PRICE INDEXES

The most commonly used stock market measure is the index or average which reflects the price movements of a group of stocks or an entire market of stocks. The index or average is simply an effort to express in a single number the price movements of a larger number of items. While every index of stock prices, no matter how compiled, can be criticized as not truly describing the portfolio of any one individual or institution, several indexes do reflect the composite portfolio of *all* individual and institutional investors in the particular marketplace being measured.

No index or average of stock prices, however, remains for very long near the actual average dollar-and-cents price per share traded in the particular marketplace. Over a period of time, stock splits tend to hold down the actual average price, while market appreciation pulls up the index of all stock prices.

Although many stock price indexes and averages have been devised over the years, only a few have attained widespread use. These are available at least daily, some hourly or half-hourly, and some (through the miracle of computerization) even minute-to-minute. Many of the major indexes are supplemented by whole families of indexes. Composite indexes of a market may be subdivided into large-sector components covering industrial, transportation, utility, or finance companies. Some families of indexes may be further broken down into smaller, less frequently published industry categories such as air freight, air transport, railroads, truckers—under transportation; electric power, natural gas distributors, natural gas pipelines, telephone—under utilities. The principles of construction are compatible with the aggregate types of indexes, so they will not be discussed in detail.

Dow Jones

Probably the most widely quoted and popularly used measure of the stock market is the Dow Jones Industrial Average (Exhibit 1). Unfortunately, it is the least valid measure of the market. It survives because of its long history (extending back nearly 100 years), the body of investment theory built around it, and its support in the financial press. While over the long run it tends to move in the same direction as broader measures, on a day-to-day basis, the Dow industrials often move counter to the trend of the market. Indeed, technical market analysts attach significance to longer-term divergences between the Dow and broader measures.

The Dow industrials consist of 30 highly capitalized issues, largely from heavy industry, listed on the New York Stock Exchange (NYSE).

EXHIBIT 1 Dow Jones Industrial Average

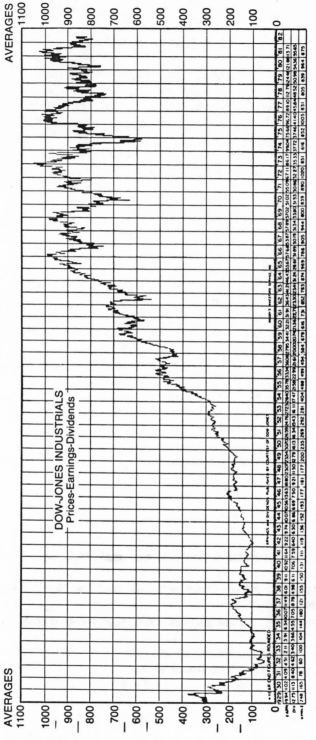

Source: Moody's Investors Service, *Industrial Manual* 1.

They accounted for less than 23 percent of the market value of the entire NYSE common stock list as of the end of 1982. (Dow Jones also publishes transportation, utility, and composite averages.) The industrials are computed by simply adding the per share prices of the 30 components and then dividing the total price by a number called the divisor. In its early years, the Dow was a true arithmetic mean—an average that was created by summing the prices of the component issues and dividing by the number of issues. As a result of stock splits, stock dividends, and issue substitutions, the divisor as of December 31, 1982, was 1.359 rather than 30.

A stock split or large stock dividend necessitates an adjustment in the average to eliminate the effect of the split on the average price. Consequently, the divisor is changed to produce the same average before and after the split. Other capitalization changes, rights offerings, or substitutions of one stock for another require similar adjustments. The end result, the Dow Jones Industrial Average, is carried on virtually every financial page and every financial broadcast or telecast in the country—and many overseas.

Standard & Poor's

The next major set of indexes to make an appearance on the stock market scene emanated from Standard & Poor's Corporation (Exhibit 2). The composite, industrial, transportation, and utility indexes are available on a daily basis back to 1928, although their composition has been broadened from the 90 issues included until 1957; the composite now encompasses 500 common stocks (including some not traded on the NYSE). Their recent value was equivalent to approximately three fourths of the value of the common stocks on the NYSE.

The S&P indexes are market value weighted. The market value of each of the component issues is aggregated and divided by a base value figure; the result is multiplied by 10, since the base period was 1941–43 = 10. No adjustments are needed for splits, inasmuch as a split does not alter the market value of the stock. Changes in capitalization, however, which result from mergers, delistings, substitutions, or rights offerings are adjusted via a proportionate change in the base value. For instance, if a corporate change adds 1 percent of the current market value (numerator), the base (denominator) is also increased by 1 percent so that the index will be the same after the capital change as it was before.

Even though it is vastly more comprehensive and representative than the Dow industrials, the S&P 500 is still a sample which tends to have more components from among the larger- and medium-sized compa-

EXHIBIT 2   Standard & Poor's Stock Price Indexes

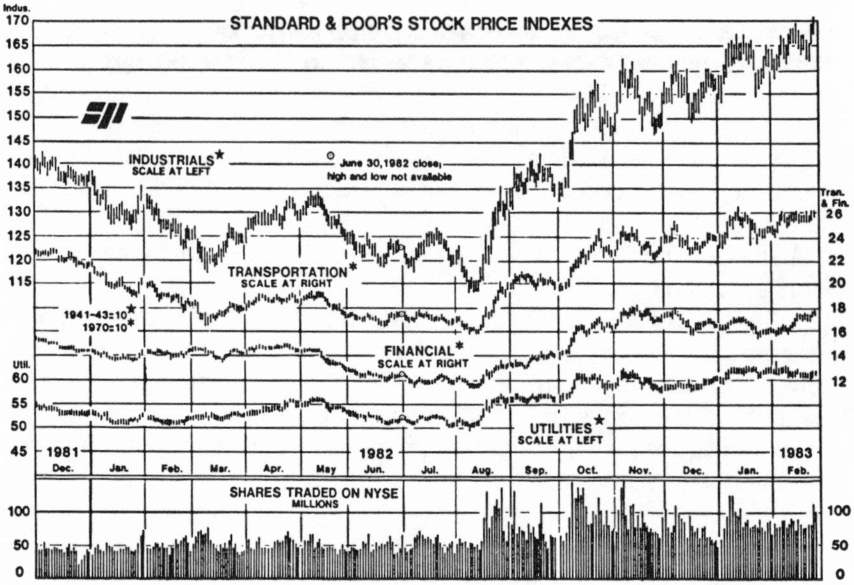

Source: Standard & Poor's Corporation, *Stock Guide*, March 1983. Reprinted with permission of Standard & Poor's Corporation.

nies. Being limited arbitrarily to 500 issues, it naturally omits roughly 1,000 other NYSE-listed companies.

Most of the news media cover the movement of the S&P 500 in their description of market developments. The S&P broad indexes are also available on the ubiquitous desk-interrogation units one finds in brokerage offices these days; they are also printed, oddly enough, on the American Stock Exchange ticker tape. The weekly figures for the dozens of industry subindexes appear in Standard & Poor's *Outlook* each week.

NYSE

The overall NYSE Common Stock Index (Exhibit 3) is the most comprehensive measure of the NYSE common stock market, consisting as it does of *every* one of the roughly 1,500 common stocks listed on the exchange. It is not based on a sample of the market, large or small (500 or 30). The composite also has four comprehensive subgroups—industrial, transportation, utility, and finance—which comprise every NYSE-listed common stock in those respective broad industrial classifications.

EXHIBIT 3 New York Stock Exchange Index

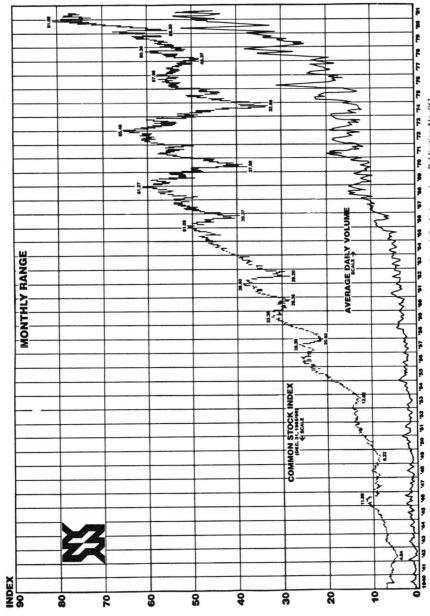

Note: January 1940 to May 1964 based on weekly closing prices; June 1964 to date based on daily closing prices. Publication No. 061

The composite has been computed on a daily-close basis from May 28, 1964. By converting a discontinued Securities and Exchange Commission index to the NYSE base (December 31, 1965 = 50) on a weekly-close basis from January 7, 1939, to May 28, 1964, the NYSE provided its index with a historical background that now goes back nearly 45 years. The component industry indexes have been calculated on a daily-close basis from December 31, 1965, while the overall index has been computed every half hour and the components hourly since July 14, 1966.

The base value was set at 50, because that figure was reasonably close to the actual average closing price of all NYSE common stocks on the base date of December 31, 1965. The index otherwise is computed in a manner similar to the method followed for the S&P 500. The adjustments, however, are more frequent because of constant additions to and deletions from the list of common stocks traded on the exchange. New stocks, for example, are included from the first day of listing. Adjustments are made to eliminate the influence of corporate changes, so that the index reflects *only* movements resulting from market activity. Thus, any change in capitalization arising from new listings, delistings, mergers, rights offerings, and the like require a proportionate change in the market value of the base figure.

The NYSE index has steadily been widening its acceptance. It now appears in most daily financial coverage—press, radio, and television. Instantaneous computations are possible via interrogation devices, while the widely disseminated consolidated ticker tape carries the readings half hourly.

Before moving on to descriptions of the indexes covering other markets, it may be helpful to compare the movements of the three major measures of price action on the NYSE. The table below shows the change from an important low at the close of the market on August 12, 1982, to the readings six months later. The Dow Jones industrials evidently understated the strength of the broader market, as measured by the NYSE Common Stock Index, by five percentage points.

Measure	8/12/82 Closing	2/11/83 Closing	Increase
Dow Jones industrials	776.92	1,046.54	39.8%
S&P 500	102.42	147.63	44.1
NYSE index	58.80	85.18	44.9

Moreover, during the 128 trading days in that six-month period, the NYSE and Dow measures moved in opposite directions 10 times—6 times the NYSE index showed a rise, while the Dow showed a decline; four times the NYSE index was down when the Dow was up.

Amex

On September 4, 1973, the American Stock Exchange (AMEX) introduced its market value index system (Exhibit 4). This comprised an overall index with a base level of 100 on August 31, 1973, historical values calculated back to January 2, 1969 and 16 subindexes. (The new index replaced a price change index which had been in effect since April 1966.)

The Amex index includes, in addition to common shares, the market value of American depository receipts of foreign companies traded on that market and warrants. Each issue is weighted according to its market value by multiplying the price per share times the number of shares outstanding. New listings must be traded for a full business day before they can be included, while suspensions and delistings result in immediate removal from the list. The customary adjustments are made for capitalization changes.

The Amex index is transmitted over the Amex's ticker network every half hour during the trading day and is carried by the major financial media. It is also available on interrogation devices.

NASDAQ

Until recent years, the only comprehensive measure of over-the-counter stock price movement was the National Quotation Bureau Industrial Average. Although this is still maintained, apparently for reasons of historical continuity, the National Association of Securities Dealers (NASD) has developed a market value weighted index to reflect the price movement of the stocks traded through the National Association of Securities Dealers Automated Quotation (NASDAQ) system. Besides a composite index, the NASD also publishes seven subindexes. The base for the NASDAQ indexes (Exhibit 5) is 100 and the base period is February 5, 1971. Daily history of the indexes begins in November 1971.

The NASDAQ index consists of all the common stocks traded in the NASDAQ system—roughly 2,400 in number. It excludes issues listed on an exchange as well as those with only one market maker. Whether an over-the-counter issue is included in the NASDAQ system depends on its size and share activity.

Prices used in the index are not based on actual transactions but are the median bid price at the time the index is computed. Continuous computations are available to market data vendors through so-called NASDAQ Level 1 terminals, with calculations at five-minute intervals through Level 2 and 3 terminals. Hourly index readings are made avail-

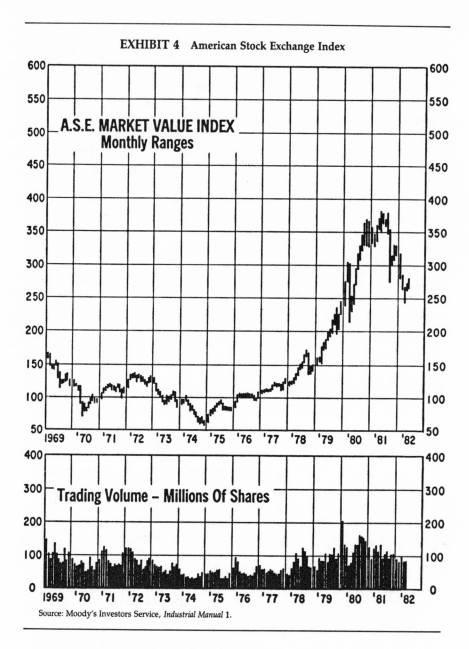

EXHIBIT 4   American Stock Exchange Index

A.S.E. MARKET VALUE INDEX
Monthly Ranges

Trading Volume – Millions Of Shares

Source: Moody's Investors Service, *Industrial Manual* 1.

able to the newswire services. Adjustments are immediate for changes in share capitalization greater than 5 percent for stocks added to or removed from the system.

In all the value-weighted indexes, a small number of extremely large companies account for a large part of the market value and thus affect

EXHIBIT 5   NASDAQ Price Index and Volume

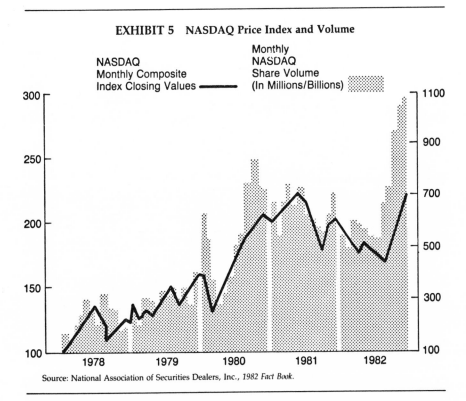

Source: National Association of Securities Dealers, Inc., *1982 Fact Book.*

the movement of the particular index. The NASDAQ index, however, is subject to a further and unique limitation. Movements of the index can be affected by dealer judgment (represented by bids) rather than the judgment of investors who have actually participated in a transaction in an auction market. In the over-the-counter market, the number of market makers may be as few as two; one dealer's change in the bid can markedly affect the median "price" which goes into calculation of the NASDAQ index.

Value Line

Although numerous other stock price indexes are compiled and published, one bears particular mention. The Value Line Composite Index (with three subindexes) consists of almost 1,500 NYSE and non-NYSE issues, distinctive in that it is an unweighted geometric index (Exhibit 6). Each component issue receives equal weight in the calculation, regardless of any measure of size of company or issue. Daily percentage changes in price are calculated, with the resulting quantities multiplied.

EXHIBIT 6   Value Line Composite Index Compared with Other Stock Market
            Indexes

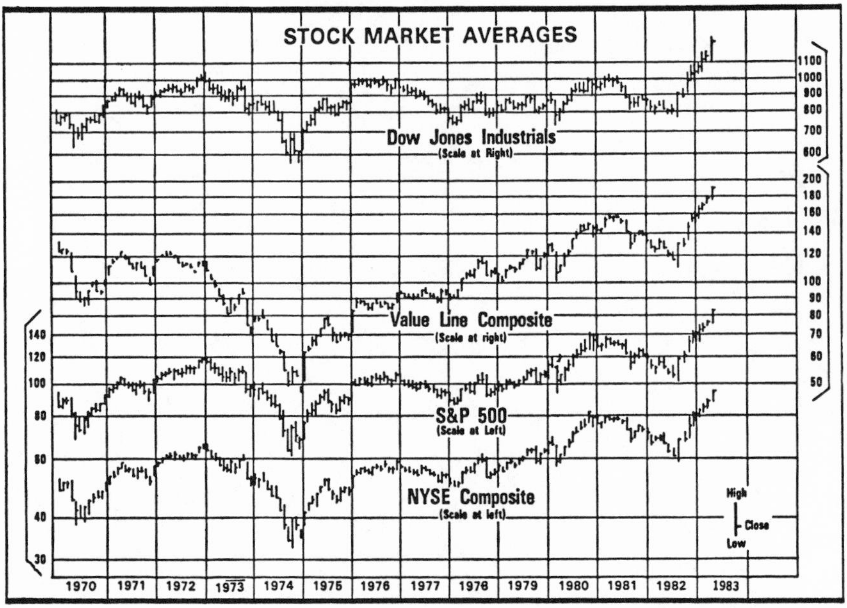

Source: "Summary of Advices and Index," *The Value Line Investment Survey*, May 13, 1983.

A geometric average is then obtained and multiplied by the previous day's average.

Attitudes toward this measure are mixed. Some consider an unweighted index superior because no issue has more importance than any other. Other observers consider it inferior for the very same reason. On balance, it does seem illogical to allow a small stock with minimal investor interest to carry the same weight as a large stock with vast numbers of individual and institutional holders.

On the other hand, the unweighted index can provide another dimension to understanding market movements. It can convey some impression of the number of issues that are acting strongly or weakly and can indicate times when other indexes are being unduly influenced by issues with heavy weightings.

Other Indexes

Various other stock price indexes and averages emanate from a variety of sources, primarily financial periodicals and investment advisory services. The most widely known examples are summarized below:

Wilshire 5000 Equity Index—total price of all stocks for which daily quotations are available, weighted by market value; prepared by Wilshire Associates, Santa Monica, Calif.

Media General Composite Stock Index—based on market value of all common stocks listed on New York and American stock exchanges and of tabulated over-the-counter stocks, using January 2, 1970, as base; published by *The Media General Financial Weekly*, Richmond, Va.

Barron's 50–Stock Average—average of prices of 50 stocks with the same dollar investment in each issue, so that equal percentage declines in varying issues have the same effect on the average (regardless of whether the price is high or low); published by *Barron's* each week.

Advisors—several investment advisory services have developed their own stock price indexes. Among the best known are the unweighted price indexes for the New York and the American stock exchanges compiled by *The Zweig Forecast*, the New York and Amex unweighted averages of *The Professional Tape Reader*, and the unweighted NYSE average compiled by *Indicator Digest* since 1965. The services use these measures as part of their analytical arsenal, and so the data are only available to subscribers.

BREADTH MEASURES

Key tools to the technical market analyst are the various measures of market breadth. They supply an insight into the market that a single measure such as a stock price index or average cannot provide. Because the underlying statistics for breadth measures are readily available on the financial pages of most daily newspapers and many weekly financial periodicals—and are frequently included in the daily market wrap-ups on financial broadcasts and telecasts—observers of the market should become familiar with them. Essentially, these measures look at the market in terms of numbers of stocks performing in various ways.

Advances/Declines

Knowing the number of issues advancing compared with the number declining and remaining unchanged provides a market dimension that may confirm or contradict what a market index shows. For example, here are four instances, drawn just from the first quarter of 1982, when the widely followed Dow Jones Industrial Average (DJIA) did not accurately reflect what was happening in the market:

Date	DJIA Net Change	NYSE Advances	NYSE Declines
Jan. 7	+ .76	512	622
Feb. 4	+2.00	473	699
Feb. 23	+1.72	498	693
Mar. 11	+ .67	527	642

These figures are published on a daily basis for the major markets: NYSE, Amex, and NASDAQ. The NYSE supplements the normal advance/decline data by providing the number of *common* issues advancing, declining, and remaining unchanged. This eliminates any distortions from preferred issues in periods of sharply changing interest rates. *Barron's* each week publishes the total number of issues advancing, declining, and remaining unchanged during the preceding week— separately for the NYSE, Amex, and NASDAQ.

High/Lows

The same sources of financial data publish each day the number of issues which traded on the preceding day at new high or low prices for the past 12-month period. *Barron's* again provides the same information on the number of issues which traded at 52-week highs or lows during the previous week–but not for NASDAQ issues. These are useful measures for assessing the underlying trend of the market, which might otherwise be masked by a single-figure price index.

VOLUME

One of the basic stock market statistics readily available from all the news media is the volume of activity. Most detail concerns the New York Stock Exchange market, but the other markets also publish their overall daily volume data. The figures are used in relation to the direction of price movements.

Reported Volume

The primary measure of volume on the NYSE is the reported share volume—i.e., the volume of shares traded and reported on the ticker system. This statistic is transmitted over the exchange's ticker network every hour, along with the index transmission. The daily total, together with the aggregate *dollar* value of trading, is also disseminated after the market's close at 4 P.M. EST. The American Stock Exchange and NAS-DAQ daily-share volume figures also appear in most newspapers covering the financial scene; dollar values are not available on a daily basis for those markets, however.

Upside/Downside Volume

In recent years, the major financial newspapers have been including, with their daily market indicators, a relatively new set of volume statistics: the volume of advancing stocks compared with the volume of declining stocks. *The Wall Street Journal* carries this information for the NYSE, Amex, and NASDAQ, but the *New York Times* supplies the figures only for the NYSE and Amex.

MARKET PARTICIPANTS

One of the most difficult tasks any observer of the stock market has is ascertaining what role the various market participants are playing at a particular time. Only for exchange members are data compiled and published regularly on their relative roles in the market and whether they are buyers or sellers on balance. Public participation (i.e., the relative distributions of individual versus institutional activity) can only be known occasionally via exhaustive sampling efforts for limited periods of time. The NYSE has conducted these so-called public transaction studies (PTS) intermittently since 1952. The last one, covering the fourth quarter of 1980, broke down the major sources of NYSE share volume as follows: members 26.9 percent, public individuals 25.7 percent, institutions/intermediaries 47.4 percent.

The net result is that it becomes extremely difficult to ascertain, in any definitive manner, which investor/trader groups are responsible for sudden surges in volume. What little information is available often becomes known only after rather substantial time lags. Nevertheless, it may be useful to apprise the reader of what can be learned about the activities of various types of stock market participants.

Institutions

As the dominant force in the markets for more than a decade, the institutions merit first attention. For over 20 years, the Securities and Exchange Commission (SEC) published quarterly purchases and sales of common stocks for four major institutional groups; budgetary restrictions, however, have forced the elimination of this data collection effort. The only institutional category for which stock market activity can be found is mutual funds. The Investment Company Institute releases monthly purchase and sale data for the funds in the month following the activity reported.

More broadly, one must examine the large block data published by the New York Stock Exchange—either the monthly releases or the daily data carried in the financial press or summarized weekly in publications such as *Barron's* (Exhibit 7). Inasmuch as the 1980 PTS showed institu-

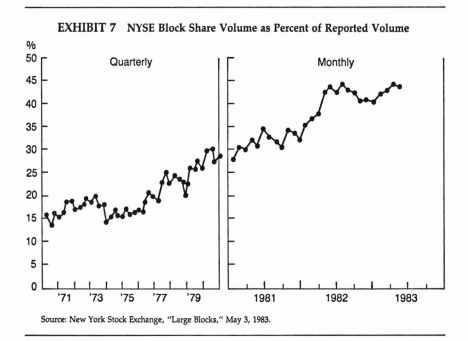

EXHIBIT 7   NYSE Block Share Volume as Percent of Reported Volume

Source: New York Stock Exchange, "Large Blocks," May 3, 1983.

tions/intermediaries accounting for nearly 90 percent of the large blocks of 10,000 shares and over traded on the NYSE, a surge in such activity permits a reasonable inference that institutional activity is on the rise. If the bulk of that activity takes place on upticks (prices higher than the last preceding price), one can further conclude that the institutions are on the buy side. If downticks predominate, the opposite conclusion, of course, is drawn. The price information is carried to a limited degree in *Barron's* and some of the investment advisory services.

Margin Traders

Each month the NYSE releases a stock market credit report (Exhibit 8) which is customarily summarized in the financial press. It carries the

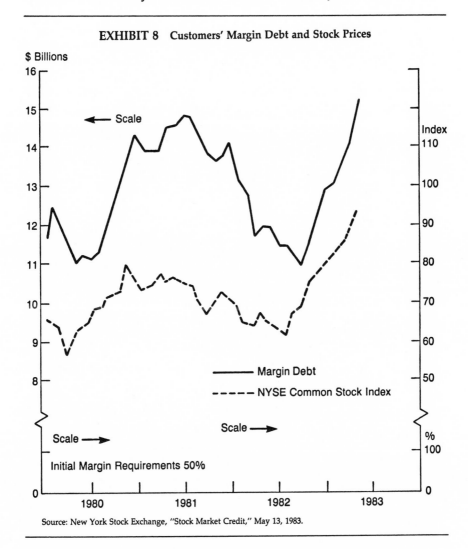

EXHIBIT 8   Customers' Margin Debt and Stock Prices

Source: New York Stock Exchange, "Stock Market Credit," May 13, 1983.

following information: customers' net debit balances, free credit balances, number of margin accounts, value of collateral in margin accounts, potential purchasing power of margin accounts, and quality of security credit. Debit balances generally rise for a combination of several reasons: margin customers have acquired more stock, margin customers have withdrawn funds from their accounts, or new margin accounts have been opened and have been used to acquire stock.

To simplify, when initial margin requirements as set by the Federal Reserve Board are 50 percent, an increase of $300 million in margin debt probably means that margin traders acquired on balance about $600 million worth of stock. At an average price of about $30 per share on the NYSE, that would mean margin accounts added about 20 million shares to their positions during the previous month. They may have accounted for a great deal more activity, buying and selling during the course of the month, but the 20 million shares would represent the net increment to their positions. Since margin customers were responsible for more than half of public individuals' activity in the 1976 and 1980 PTS, the monthly actions of this group are significant. In their present incarnation, the statistical series on credit activity go back to 1965.

Member Trading

Statistics on the purchase and sale activity of members of the New York and American stock exchanges have been published regularly since the 1930s. These weekly data appear in *The Wall Street Journal* on Mondays and in *Barron's*; monthly NYSE figures are summarized in the New York Stock Exchange's *Statistical Highlights.*

The breakdowns of member trading show purchases and sales, as well as short sales, for specialists, members on the trading floor, and members off the floor. Analysts place considerable weight on the direction of member activity in assessing the market outlook, even though much of this activity is member reaction to their customers' needs. For instance, the specialists are obliged to perform a stabilizing role in the market, so that when public investors are selling heavily, the specialists should be buying and vice versa. By the same token, "upstairs" firms doing a block-positioning business would be acquiring stock temporarily from institutional clients to accommodate their selling programs. Nevertheless, a body of analytical history has been built around ratios of member purchases to sales and around member to public activity, such as member short sales related to public short sales. No comparable data exist for the over-the-counter market.

The Short Side

Tracking what the market pessimist is doing is a relatively simple matter. First of all, the two major exchanges publish monthly data (as of the midmonth settlement date) on the so-called short interest—i.e., the amount of shares sold short and not yet covered by purchase. (Selling short, of course, merely means selling stock one does not own in the expectation of being able to make delivery at some later time at a lower price, thus profiting on the difference between the selling price and the subsequent purchase price.)

In addition, the exchanges publish weekly data on member short sales and public short sales. These statistics appear in *The Wall Street Journal* and in *Barron's*. No such data are available for the over-the-counter market. To some extent, the short interest and short sales data have lost a degree of usefulness in recent years with the advent of other forms of trading that reflect a negative view of the market or a particular stock, e.g., put options and financial futures on indexes.

In any event, the data have become somewhat distorted by short activity which has no relation to the market outlook. Short sales of stock already owned are a way of hedging a position to protect a profit or to postpone a gain into a subsequent tax year. Short sales have also come to play an important part in the activities of arbitrageurs, especially in connection with mergers or takeovers wherein the arbitrageur may purchase the stock of one of the parties and short the stock of the other.

Small Investors

Historically, the small investor was defined as the individual who bought or sold stock in odd lots, less than the 100-share standard round-lot unit of trading. Purchases and sales data (with short sales broken out separately) go back at least to 1920. They appear currently on a daily basis in most of the financial press and are often summarized weekly. Unfortunately, for the past few years, the daily data are incomplete, since a handful of brokerage firms handle the odd lots of their customers and no longer send them to the exchange. Those firms do not publish their daily odd-lot activity.

The odd-lot data were widely followed in the past on the theory that the unsophisticated small investor was likely to be making the wrong decision at important turning points in the market. As a whole, odd-lot data are less useful than they used to be. The changing level of stock prices, coupled with the greater affluence of investors, has contributed to the secular decline in the proportion of odd-lot to total trading. The small investor today is probably more likely to be dealing in 100-share and 200-share round lots.

Moreover, the odd-lot data need to be treated gingerly because of biases that have grown up on the sell side. Stock splits and stock dividends, along with employee stock purchase plans and automatic dividend reinvestment plans, create odd lots without any purchase action in the marketplace itself. Yet, when those acquisitions are liquidated, they increase the sale balance in the odd-lot area. Similarly, odd-lot short sales data have undoubtedly been affected by the availability of put options as a speculative vehicle for the pessimistic small investor.

Foreigners

Market observers are periodically intrigued by what foreigners may be doing in regard to U.S. equities. Foreign portfolio managers are purportedly extremely astute, so that their attitudes toward investment in this country are of considerable interest. Unfortunately, whether or not these managers are actually more astute than most investors, the information on what they are doing becomes available too late even to be deemed a coincident indicator.

The U.S. Treasury Department collects from banks and brokerage firms a substantial amount of detail on foreigners' purchases and sales of U.S. securities, including stocks. The data are published in the *Treasury Bulletin* and the *Federal Reserve Bulletin* on a preliminary basis about three months after the month they cover. Thus, the information may be useful to the market historian, less so to the market timer. Incidentally, the statistics are expressed in millions of dollars, not shares, and are for U.S. stocks as a whole—with no breakdown for the marketplace on which the stocks are traded or on which they were acquired or disposed of.

SPECULATIVE SENTIMENT

The final area worth examination deals with indicators of speculative sentiment. Some of the measures already described touch on this subject; a good example is the various margin statistics. While individual market analysts may have developed their own proprietary indicators, this section attempts to summarize a few that can be readily tracked through publicly available information.

Amex/NYSE Volume

One of the simplest indicators of the speculative climate merely requires a calculation of the ratio of American Stock Exchange volume to New York Stock Exchange volume. This can be done as often as daily or as infrequently as monthly; weekly seems to be about right for avoiding day-to-day aberrations without missing important shifts. The necessary underlying figures are carried on virtually every newspaper financial page, particularly in the weekend summaries.

The rationale for this measure is a logical one. Listing requirements for the Amex are not as stringent as on the NYSE; Amex companies tend to be smaller and somewhat lower in quality than NYSE companies. The average price of a stock on the Amex is about half the average NYSE stock price. Whenever the Amex "catches fire," it means that speculators are shifting their interest to the secondary and tertiary stocks that have not yet had significant price moves.

Through most of 1981 and 1982, the ratio of Amex to NYSE weekly-share volume rarely exceeded 12 percent. In many weeks it was below 8 percent. These are normal—even subnormal—parameters suggesting an absence of excessive speculative enthusiasm. If the ratio were to move over 30 percent and persist in that area for a sustained period, one could conclude that the markets were becoming more speculative. (A similar measure could be constructed to relate NASDAQ volume to NYSE volume, but with appropriately different parameters.)

Average Price

Another simple measure of speculative interest is the average price of the most active issues traded on the NYSE. Although this can be constructed on a daily basis for the list of most actives carried on most financial pages, the measure would be a bit erratic. Unexpected news affecting one or two companies could suddenly bring them to the fore and temporarily distort the list of active stocks. An average constructed from the most active issues for the entire week seems to work better; in fact, *Barron's* publishes the figure each week on its "Market Laboratory" page, with the computation already done.

Normally, because of the generally higher prices of the more widely held issues that tend to be among the most active week after week, the average price will fall somewhere in the $30–40 range. When it drops to the area of $20–25 for a sustained period, lower-priced secondary issues have captured speculative interest and are garnering abnormal attention as reflected in heavy volume.

Options Ratio

A new measure of speculative sentiment that has attracted interest in recent years is the relationship between call volume and put volume in the options market. Some data were available on over-the-counter options trading for many decades. The advent of standardized options trading on the Chicago Board Options Exchange and other markets has expanded the amount of data available on options activity.

A large amount of call volume relative to put volume suggests that investor psychology is extremely optimistic. Conversely, when traders and investors become pessimistic about the market outlook, call volume shrinks at the same time put volume expands. Inasmuch as options trading permits speculators to "play the market" without committing large sums of money, readings of the call/put ratio can be useful in assessing shifts in speculative sentiment. Thus, in a sense, this indicator supplements readings obtained from the odd-lot data. The underlying statistics for these computations appear regularly in *The Wall Street Journal*, the *New York Times*, and other leading financial dailies.

Other Measures

Numerous other indicators of sentiment abound—such as "insider trading," secondary distributions, advisory service opinions. Inasmuch as this is not intended to be a compendium of every conceivable stock market indicator or theory, the discussion has been confined to statistical measures which can generally be easily constructed or compiled from readily available sources.

As stated at the outset, the object was not to create a body of wildly successful investors; it was to help create a body of better informed observers of the stock market scene.

PART FOUR

Inflation

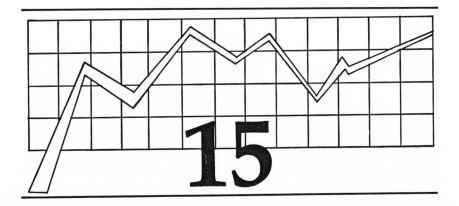

Measures of Inflation

Joel Popkin, Ph.D.
Joel Popkin and Company

The purpose of this chapter is to describe how inflation is measured. It contains an analysis and description of the concepts and definitions that underlie inflation measurement, the sources of the data the various measures require, and an evaluation of the strengths and weaknesses of the resulting measures. The chapter also contains a description of how the various measures of inflation have behaved in the period since the end of World War II.

CONCEPTS AND DEFINITIONS IN INFLATION MEASUREMENT

It is clear that in order to construct a measure of inflation, the concept of inflation requires definition. Among economists there is no single definition of inflation, and therefore no single measure. As commonly used, however, there are two connotations of the word. The first is that inflation relates to a rise in prices of a large number of goods and services. In other words, it connotes a broad-based or generalized rise in prices. The second connotation is that the rise is a fairly substantial one. A small rise in prices is not usually characterized as inflation. Thus, the period of time in the U.S. economy from 1960 to 1962, when prices rose between 1 and 2 percent per year, is not regarded as a period of inflation. There is no agreement as to a precise point at which price increases come to be characterized as inflation. It is clear from recent usage, however, that price increases at a single-digit annual rate—6, 7, 8 percent—are characterizable as inflation. If that were not so, the term *double-digit inflation*, coined to describe inflation rates of 10–20 percent that obtained in some years during the 1972–82 period, would not have been necessary. And throughout history, inflations at a rate of 50 percent or more per year have generally been characterized as hyperinflations. Thus, it would appear that there are four categories of price increases:

1. Those that are not large enough to be characterized as inflation.
2. Those that are, but are less than 10 percent.
3. Those between 10 and 50 percent, that are characterized as double-digit inflation.
4. Those in excess of 50 percent, which are characterized as hyperinflation.

As indicated, inflation is a phenomenon that describes a rise in prices of a fairly large number of goods and services. It is unusual that inflation can be produced by a rise in one (or several) items unless they are very widely purchased. And even then, much of the inflation that results will reflect the effects of the rise in that item's price on prices of other goods and services and the indirect effect on wages.

Inflation can be viewed as a decline in the purchasing power of the money used to purchase those goods and services. That raises another important issue with respect to measuring inflation. It is the issue of whose purchases and, therefore, whose dollars are being eroded. That question is typically answered in terms of two constituencies: consumers and producers. The consumer price index (CPI), compiled and published by the Bureau of Labor Statistics of the U.S. Department of Labor, measures changes in prices paid by consumers. The producer price index (PPI), also compiled and published by the Bureau of Labor Statistics, covers the prices charged by producers of manufactured, mineral, and agricultural products.

These two indexes and a few others are used to transform dollar figures on the value of U.S. output, called gross national product, into constant dollars. The resulting measure is called the gross national product in constant dollars. The overall price index reflecting the difference between gross national product in current dollars and in constant dollars is called the deflator for gross national product. It is the third major measure of inflation and is produced by the Bureau of Economic Analysis (BEA) of the U.S. Department of Commerce. Its scope includes both consumers and producers, since it measures the prices associated with the output of all goods and services in the U.S. economy.

The bulk of this chapter is devoted to describing, evaluating, and comparing the behavior of these three measures of inflation. But first, it is necessary to present and evaluate the various formulas used to compile price indexes.

PRICE INDEX FORMULAS

Measures of inflation are typically called price indexes. Their purpose is to measure inflation from one time period to the next. Since inflation is a concept that relates to a large number of goods and services, a price index is an aggregate made up of their price changes. Like any aggregate, the component parts (prices in this case) must be added up. Typically they are added up with weights; the weights are selected to reflect the importance of the various items in the purchases of whatever group to which the price index will refer. Weights are sometimes characterized as constituting the market basket for the index, particularly in the case of the CPI. Thus, the ingredients of a price index are prices and weights.

There are various ways in which the prices can be multiplied by the weights to derive the resulting index. These various approaches are called price index formulas. The most widely used formulas for constructing price indexes are the Laspeyres and Paasche index formulas, named for their originators. These formulas address the question of what weights (q's) are appropriate for use in adding up the prices (p's). The differences between the two indexes, simply put, is that in measuring the difference in prices between two periods, the Laspeyres index (L) uses weights of the first period, the Paasche index (P) weights of the second period. The formula for the Laspeyres index is:

$$L = \Sigma p_2 q_1 / \Sigma p_1 q_1.$$

The formula for the Paasche index is:

$$P = \Sigma p_2 q_2 / \Sigma p_1 q_2.$$

When economic theory is used to analyze these index formulas, the implication of their use becomes apparent. If the object of measurement is the average change in prices paid by consumers—sometimes called changes in the cost of living—then the use of the Laspeyres index results in an overestimate of that change, assuming that tastes and real incomes of the consumers remain unchanged between the two time periods. If the Paasche index is used, the result is an understatement of the cost of living. On the other hand, if one is measuring the price index associated with production, the Laspeyres index is an understatement of that price, the Paasche an overstatement.

The reason neither index is a perfect reflection of changes in the cost of living is that if changes in price from one period to the next are not the same for all of the items in the index, the consumer may substitute within some range the commodities that have become relatively cheaper for those that have become relatively more expensive. In so doing, he can offset some of the effect of inflation. If the price index formula uses weights from the initial period, those weights will not reflect the substitutions. If the formula calls for use of the weights of the second period, those weights will not reflect what happened before the price rise. When tastes and real incomes are constant, the true cost-of-living change lies somewhere between the change measured by the Laspeyres and Paasche indexes. As a result, Irving Fisher, another important contributor to price index formulas, devised his so-called ideal index, which is the square root of the product of the Paasche and Laspeyres indexes (in other words, the geometric mean of the two). This index is an exact measure of changes in the cost of living if the utility function of the consumer meets certain rather rigid assumptions. Fisher's ideal formula (F) is:

$$F = (L \cdot P)^{1/2}$$

The foregoing analysis is cast in terms of measuring price change from one time period to the next. Typically, however, price indexes measure the change among a large number of time periods. If the Laspeyres index is used, the question arises as to how long the base period weights should continue in use, because the Laspeyres index under certain conditions is an upperbound on the rate of inflation; its continued use will result in accumulated bias. However, it is costly to revise weights frequently, so revisions are not usually made in each time period. An exception is the deflator for gross national product. Every three months, the government collects a new market basket of U.S. production, although not in the detail the data for the CPI are gathered. It is used to construct several price indexes relating to the gross national product. One index is derived from the calculation of a new Laspeyres index each quarter. That is, the change in prices from T to T + 1 is measured using the weights of T, and the change in prices from T + 1 to T + 2 is measured using the weights of T + 1. The percentage changes are then linked into a chain. Such an index is called a chained Laspeyres index. A chained Laspeyres index still has the potential problem that between every two time periods it overstates inflation somewhat, though probably not nearly as much as an index with fixed weights covering a long period of time. To attempt to remedy this bias, other methods of constructing price index formulas have been devised. The best-known and most widely used basis for such indexes is that of Divisia. The weights in such an index are, in principle, changing every second. They are nonetheless approximated by discreet changes in weights. The most recent extension of the Divisia formula (D) averages the weights of two adjacent time periods and uses the result to weight up the logarithm of price relatives. That formula is:

$$D = \exp[\Sigma(s_n^2 + s_n^1) \ln (p_n^2/p_n^1)],$$

where

$$s_n^t \equiv (p_n^t q_n^t / \Sigma p_n^t q_n^t),$$

the cost share of good n in period t.

While it is important to understand the effect of using different formulas for constructing price indexes, it has been demonstrated that the practical effect of different formulas is quite small. It is greatest when there is a large change in the relative price of particular commodities which have a large weight in a market basket. An example is the change in energy prices during the 1970s. But even then, the absolute bias was very small relative to the inflation rate.

MEASURES OF INFLATION

Three measures of inflation will be discussed in this section. They are the consumer price index (CPI), the producer price index (PPI) and the GNP deflator (GNPD).

Consumer Price Index

The consumer price index is intended to measure changes in the cost of living. Conceptually, the term *cost of living* implies that the index will measure changes in the cost of acquiring market baskets that yield consumers the same level of satisfaction. The quantities in the basket can vary in response to changes in relative prices; only the satisfaction is held constant. In practice however, the quantities are held fixed, however, but the effect is small (as noted above).

The cost-of-living concept also requires that weights be based on the flows of consumption services which the consumer receives from the goods and services he purchases; satisfaction flows from using the item, even if it is not totally consumed in one use. Thus, the CPI is intended to approximate the cost-of-living index by measuring the cost, over time, of services that flow from the market basket of goods and services consumed in the base period. Because some commodities, housing in particular, are purchased at one point in time yet yield services and therefore satisfaction over a longer period of time, the price of the services rather than the price of the item itself must be used. The implementation of this service flow concept is relatively new and is limited so far only to housing.

Since 1978, when the most recent revision of the CPI was put in place, there have been two consumer price indexes; one relating to all urban consumers and the other to wage earners and clerical workers. The former is called CPI–U, the latter CPI–W.

The CPI is prepared using the Laspeyres formula. Thus, the weights are for a base period in history, and they are used throughout the time period between major revisions.

The major revisions of the index have typically been prompted by the need to revise weights, tempered by the costliness of such an undertaking. Such revisions have usually taken place about once every 10 years. The most recent revision reflects weights of 1972–73. They were collected by means of a consumer expenditure survey, perhaps the most complex survey conducted by the U.S. government. The data are collected by the Census Bureau for the Bureau of Labor Statistics. The 1972–73 survey was conducted using technology that had not been used in the past. In particular, consumer expenditures were collected quarterly throughout the time period for all but a group of frequently purchased food and personal items. Data on these items were collected through the use of a two-week diary placed in the hands of another sample of consumers. Since 1979, the consumer expenditure survey has been collected on an ongoing, quarterly basis by the Census Bureau. It will facilitate the next revision of the consumer price index.

Exhibit 1 shows the distribution of the major categories of expenditures in the present CPI market basket as determined in the 1972–73 consumer expenditure survey. These data constitute what is called the

---

EXHIBIT 1   Consumer Price Index Market Basket for All Urban Consumers

Major Group	Percent Distribution 1972–73
All Items	100.0
Food and beverages	18.8
Housing	42.9
Apparel	7.0
Transportation	17.7
Medical care	4.6
Entertainment	4.5
Personal care	1.7
Other goods and services	2.8

weight base of the current consumer price index. But there is another base mentioned more often in describing price indexes. It is called the reference base. The reference base is the year which is set equal to 100 for purposes of making international comparisons. The selection is arbitrary; any year can be chosen as the reference base, and changing the reference base from one year to another (as the government does periodically) has no effect on the rate of change of prices.

The expenditures data are broken down in the current CPI into about 265 categories. These categories are called item strata. The distribution of expenditures among these categories remains constant between expenditure surveys. This reflects the requirements of the Laspeyres index, as mentioned earlier. Within each of these expenditure classes, weights can be changed to reflect changes in product mix, a flexibility that is designed primarily to permit the introduction of new products into price indexes between revisions.

Each year, about 1.6 million price quotes are collected for the CPI in addition to about 96,000 rents. About half of the prices are for food items. The remaining ones are for nonfood commodities and services. The prices are collected in 85 areas called primary sampling units. They are collected on a bimonthly basis in many places. Price indexes are published for the United States as a whole and for 28 metropolitan areas in the United States. For most of these places where pricing is less frequent than monthly, the indexes are published only bimonthly.

Prices are collected with the use of a specification detailing rather precisely the characteristics of the item that are likely to command value in the market place. Specifications have been developed for 382 entry-level items called ELIs. An ELI specification designates the item that. price collectors try to price initially when they initiate into the sample an outlet where consumers make purchases. The sample of outlets was developed from the point of purchase survey (POPS), which was designed to provide information on the frequency with which various items are purchased in various types of outlets. The entry-level item may not be available in the outlet selected for the sample. In that case, the data collector will shift to a similar item which is available in the outlet. The substituted item is then described in a specification, and that specification is used for continuing the price collection in subsequent months. The specification provides the best assurance that the price collected each time is for the same item. When specified items cannot be found it may be a signal that an item is no longer available and a new one must be substituted.

The consumer price index for the United States was first published in 1921, at which time indexes going back to 1913 were made available. Prior to that year, there are some indexes for consumer food purchases and for some U.S. cities. The CPI is published monthly. To ensure that the index properly pertains to a month, price collection is spread throughout the month. Each index is currently released about three weeks after the close of the month to which the index pertains.

The CPI is widely used to measure the purchasing power of the consumer dollar. It is also used, perhaps even more extensively, as a means to adjust the economic terms of multiyear contracts for the effects of inflation. As an example, the CPI is used to adjust the wages of about 4.5 million workers covered by private-sector collective bargaining agreements that affect 1,000 or more workers. The CPI is used to adjust payments to social security recipients and the military and civilian retirees of the federal government. It has increasingly come to be used in contracts for rent and contracts providing for the payment of alimony.

There are a number of problems encountered in the measurement of prices used in the CPI. The most pervasive is undoubtedly the measurement of quality change. Products and services do change over time, for better and for worse. Often, it is not possible to measure prices of comparable items from one time period to another. Accordingly, an adjustment of some type may be necessary. One kind of adjustment is that necessitated because an item is not available at a particular outlet in a given month. This type of problem is usually treated by calculating the index without the price of that item from that outlet for the two months adjacent to the month for which the price is missing. A more difficult problem emerges when an item is not available in any outlet or in most outlets. That situation is illustrated by seasonal products such as winter suits, which are not available in the summertime, and strawberries, which are not widely available in the winter. Various procedures are used to handle such situations.

A third type of situation is one in which an old product is replaced by a new model. New automobiles illustrate this point. Such situations are usually handled in one of three ways. The first is that, if the differences between an old and a new model are relatively small, there may be judged to be no significant difference between the two models, and a direct comparison is made between the price of the old model and the price of the new model. A second method that is used is that of linking. Assuming prices of old models are available along with the prices of the new one in one month (e.g., September of a given year), the percentage change from August to September is calculated for the old model, and that percentage change is linked to the percentage change from September to October calculated for the new model. Another, more sophisticated method of making quality adjustments is the so-called hedonic regression approach in which prices of a family of items are regressed on their characteristics. The resulting regression coefficients reflect the market valuation of the different characteristics. In this manner, the value of a more powerful refrigerator motor (measured in terms of horsepower) can be evaluated so that, if the horsepower of refrigerator motors was increased from one year to the next, adjustments can be made for that part of the change in price that reflects just the value of the added horsepower.

While the problems associated with defining the quality of commodities are complex, those associated with the problem of defining the quality of services are even more difficult to evaluate. For example, while physicians fees have been rising, the effectiveness of treatment has perhaps increased or perhaps deteriorated. Measurement of these effects is a very difficult problem.

Producer Price Index

The second major measure of inflation is the producer price index. The index is designed to measure the prices received by producers. In principle, the producers can sell commodities or services; but so far, the index scope is limited to producer prices in the agricultural, mining, and manufacturing sector as well as those for electric power and natural gas distributed to business users.

The formula used to calculate the producer price index is the Laspeyres one mentioned earlier. The data for the weights come from information on shipments in mining and manufacturing industries collected by the Census Bureau in its quinquennial census of manufactures and mineral industries and from the agricultural statistics of the U.S. Department of Agriculture. The weights in the index since 1976 have been based on the 1972 industrial and agricultural censuses.

The use of the Laspeyres index formula poses for producers the same kind of problem its use posed in the CPI. Producers may vary their output based on changes in the relative prices of the things they produce. Thus, the Laspeyres index is an upperbound on the rate of increase in producers' prices. When the producer price index components are used, as they often are, to derive series on shipments in constant dollars, those series are biased downward because the price indexes are biased upward. Not much work has been done on calculating the effect of substitution in response to relative price change on the bias that results if one measures producers' prices using the Laspeyres index formula. However, if such research were done, it is unlikely that it would result in the finding of substantial bias. Rather, the bias would be more like that reported in connection with the CPI.

Prices for the PPI are collected largely from producers. However, some prices are based on quotations appearing in trade publications, and some are based on purchasers' prices. As of January 1982, the PPI was based on 18,000 price quotations per month on 3,450 commodities.

Eventually this data base will be expanded until all 493 mining and manufacturing industries are covered by approximately 90,000 price quotations and 6,000 published product indexes each month.

The PPI is a system of price indexes that can be aggregated in various ways, depending on the purpose to which the indexes are being put. Until 1978, the index system had been called the wholesale price index (WPI). Confusion over the use of the term *wholesale* led the bureau in 1978 to use the word *producer* to describe this price index system. The focus of the WPI was on individual commodity indexes which were then aggregated to form an index for all industrial commodities. The combination of the industrial commodities index and an index for all agricultural commodities yielded the all-items wholesale price index.

In 1978 the bureau also changed the focus of its reporting of aggregated indexes to a stage-of-process framework. The stage-of-process indexes had long been calculated but they had never received much attention. However, the industrial commodities index had the deficiency that it contained double and triple counting. If, for example, the price of iron ore went up, which made the price of steel go up, which made the price of cars go up, the index would rise in all three areas. Such multiple counting gave the index an upward bias. In order to eliminate that effect, the stage-of-process structure was made the focus of the reporting of the PPI aggregates. There are three stages of process delineated in the index system. One is for finished goods, defined as goods that will never again be touched by the manufacturing process. Another is crude materials, materials which have never been touched by the manufacturing process. The third is intermediate goods, which contains items that fall into neither category.

More recently the producer price index program has focused on the development and publication of price indexes for 4-digit standard industrial code (SIC) industries. These indexes cover both the primary and secondary products produced in the industries. The indexes are weighted using net output weights; the production of the industry that is consumed within the industry is netted out. In addition, the use of probability sampling is utilized in the development of these series; someday the entire PPI will be based on scientific sampling.

The PPI is one of the oldest continuous statistical series published by the Bureau of Labor Statistics. It was first published in 1902 and contained retrospective data beginning in 1890. It has been published monthly ever since. Most prices in the index are collected to reflect the price in effect on the Tuesday of the week containing the 13th of the month. The index is released by the Bureau of Labor Statistics about a week after the end of the month.

The PPI is used for a number of purposes. It is widely used in the escalation of commercial contracts, particularly contracts calling for the provision of commodities. A contract to build a ship, for example, might be escalated by a combination of the producer price indexes that reflect the materials used in producing the ships and wage indexes for the kinds of labor employed in shipbuilding. The PPI is also used to analyze the present and prospective course of inflation. It has been found that certain prices, components of the PPI, rise before components of the CPI. For example, the price of wheat rises before the price of bread purchased by consumers in supermarkets. Thus, the producer price index components have content bearing on the future course of consumer prices.

As is the case with the CPI, the PPI has its shortcomings. One is that it does not fully cover the manufacturing and mining sectors of the economy. In particular, it lacks prices on complicated electronic and telecommunications equipment such as computers. The BLS plans to include prices for such products ultimately. Another criticism sometimes made about the producer price indexes is that they fail to reflect actual transactions prices. The claim is that the BLS receives reports containing list prices and that, particularly in recessions, the transaction prices reflect unreported discounts from list prices. Available studies show no systematic bias, but the problem exists or has existed for some products. One solution is to collect prices from buyers. While this was done in some cases, it proved quite expensive because the same buyer does not purchase the same item month after month.

Another problem that pervades the producer price index relates to the measurement of quality change. As mentioned, quality adjustment is a very complex process, particularly in instances where there are model year changeovers in complex equipment, the costs of which are difficult to disentangle from general inflationary pressures. The best assurance that quality change is taken into account is that it be identified. To this end, tightly drawn specifications are also used to collect prices for the PPI.

The GNP Deflator

The third major measure of inflation is the deflator for gross national product. It is a Paasche index, derived implicitly by dividing GNP in current dollars by GNP in constant dollars. The latter is derived by dividing nominal dollar series on each of the GNP components by price indexes. (Most of the price indexes used are from the CPI and PPI systems.) If the implicit deflator is multiplied by GNP in constant dollars, the result is GNP in current dollars. No fixed-weighted price index will yield the correct current-dollar total when multiplied by constant-dollar GNP.

Because it is a Paasche index, the deflator for GNP changes from period to period, both because of price changes and because of changes in the composition of real output. It is not as satisfactory a measure of pure price change as a fixed-weighted index. For that reason the BEA, which produces the national income and product accounts, prepares and publishes two other price indexes related to gross national product. One is a Laspeyres-type index of the prices of the GNP components. In this index, the quantities of the various component outputs are held constant. The BEA also prepares a chain index, discussed earlier. The chain index measures the change in prices from one period to the next, using as weights the composition of output in the first period.

THE BEHAVIOR OF MEASURES OF INFLATION

Exhibit 2 depicts the behavior of the three most widely used measures of inflation in the period since the end of World War II. The chart contains percentage changes in the CPI, the PPI for finished goods, and the GNP deflator on an annual basis. The pattern of percentage changes, their acceleration and deceleration, is fairly similar among the indexes. As can be seen from Exhibit 2, percentage changes in the finished goods index of the PPI fluctuate the most. The CPI is the second most volatile of the three indexes, while the deflator for gross national product changes least. In the future, it is likely that the CPI will behave more like the GNP deflator and will fluctuate less than it has in the past. The reason is that, beginning with the index for January 1983, the BLS revised the method by which it measures housing costs in the CPI. In the past, housing costs were measured as a function of both the change in house prices and the change in mortgage interest rates. In January 1983, the BLS introduced the rental-equivalent approach to measuring the cost of housing. In this approach, the BLS attempts to measure the rents paid for dwellings with characteristics similar to those of owner-occupied houses. As a result of the fact that house prices and particularly the volatile mortgage interest rates are no longer in the CPI, the volatility of that index will diminish substantially.

Exhibit 2 shows that during the period since World War II, there have been four periods of fairly rapid inflation. The first was just prior to the Korean War. The second was during the Korean War, and the third and fourth were in the 1970s during the two episodes of large increases in the price of crude oil by OPEC. During the rest of the period, inflation was usually 5 percent or less. It rose above 10 percent only in 1974 and in 1979–81, reflecting the substantial boost in the price OPEC charged for crude oil during those time periods.

EXHIBIT 2   Annual Percentage Change in Selected Price Indexes

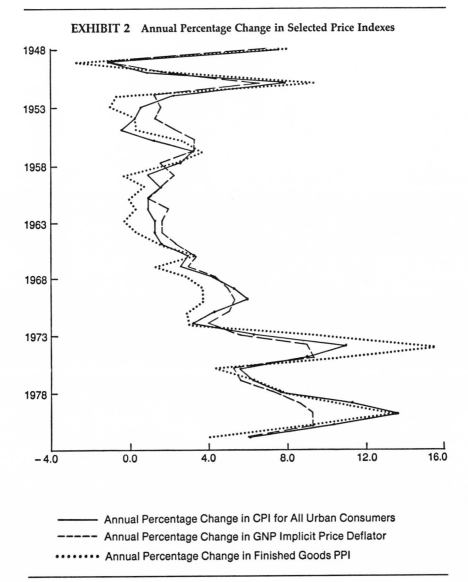

——— Annual Percentage Change in CPI for All Urban Consumers

‑‑‑‑‑ Annual Percentage Change in GNP Implicit Price Deflator

•••••• Annual Percentage Change in Finished Goods PPI

EXHIBIT 3   Annual Percentage Change in Selected Producer Price Indexes

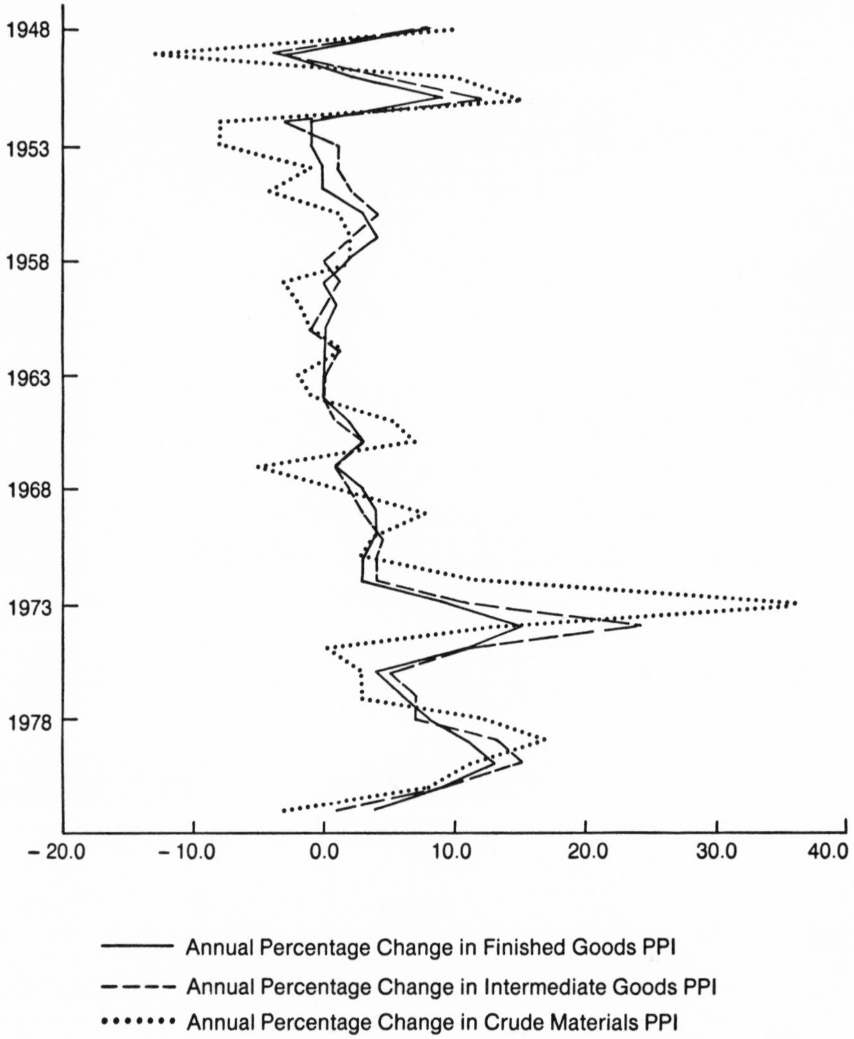

_____ Annual Percentage Change in Finished Goods PPI

– – – – Annual Percentage Change in Intermediate Goods PPI

•••••• Annual Percentage Change in Crude Materials PPI

Exhibit 3 shows the behavior of prices by stage of process. It is plotted in terms of annual rates of change from 1948 through 1982. It is clear that prices of crude materials fluctuate more than prices of intermediate goods. While less clear from the chart, prices of intermediate goods fluctuate more than prices of finished goods, particularly when fluctuations are large.

Also visible are the effects in 1951 of the Korean War and of the OPEC increases in cruce oil prices in 1973–74 and 1979–80. The crude oil increases in 1973–74 were accompanied by sizable increases in other crude materials.

One reason that prices fluctuate less as goods move from the crude to finished stage of process is that, while prices at one stage of production are materials input cost to the next stage, they are not the only input cost. If unit labor costs are rising more slowly than the prices of purchased materials, then total unit costs are rising at a weighted average of the two. So the prices firms pay for materials can rise faster than the prices they charge for their output without squeezing profit margins.

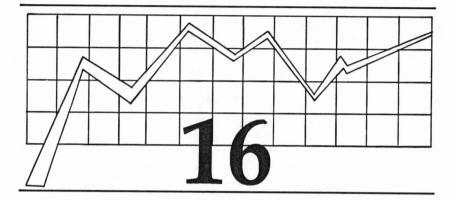

Commodity Price Indexes

John H. Ortego*
MicroEconometrics

Among the most timely, reliable, and longstanding economic indicators are commodity price indexes. The producer price indexes (PPI), for example, dating back to the beginning of the century, are usually issued by the Bureau of Labor Statistics within a month of the survey date and are subject to revision for a period of only four months thereafter. Historically, revisions have been slight. Also, several well-known commodity indexes are published on a weekly basis, and some spot and futures price indexes are available on a daily basis. By contrast, certain other inflation indicators such as the GNP deflator and its components are published only quarterly. Further, these data are subject to frequent and often significant revision for years after initial publication. The consumer price index (CPI) is published on a schedule similar to that of the PPI but has been subject to controversy, particularly with respect to the treatment of the housing component. At the same time, ongoing PPI revisions are likely creating confusion among users, and reporting has apparently become spotty.

---

* At the time of this writing, the author was Director, Industry Analysis, Chase Econometrics.

BACKGROUND

Need. It is a simple matter to track and compare the price, over time or between different geographic locations of an individual, standard specification primary commodity such as wheat or copper, since it is traded on organized exchanges. The primary data in terms of unit price serve the purpose quite well. If changes in price are to be emphasized, an index with a specific base period can be easily constructed in the form of price relatives:

$$I_{ot} = \frac{p_t}{p_0} \tag{1}$$

where p_0 is the price of a commodity in the comparison or base period, and p_t is the price at time t.

There are limitations associated with even the simple exercise above. One is that prices on organized exchanges do not necessarily reflect the many transactions negotiated elsewhere under different conditions of sale for the same commodities. Thus, although it is to be expected that other transaction prices will bear some relationship to the highly visible commodity exchange prices, an index constructed only on the basis of published prices must be regarded as merely a sample of multiple prices prevailing in the economy. For analytical purposes then, the index becomes a proxy for all these transaction prices which are unobserved and cannot be directly measured. An implicit assumption is that, while the absolute levels of all prices cannot be recorded, changes over time will be at similar rates.

Thus, as in the case of other index numbers, commodity price indexes are designed to provide an indicator of changes in magnitudes which cannot in practice be directly observed or measured. Indexes are constructed, based on a sample of transactions, to provide insight into price movements. A consequence of the process is that the accuracy and consistency of price indexes are perennially in question.

It is often desirable to capture price changes for a group of commodities as opposed to a single commodity. Composite indexes serve this purpose. If all commodities carry equal weight in an index—that is, it is unweighted—strong movements in the price of a single commodity can dominate the index. For this reason a geometric mean is sometimes employed:

$$I_{ot} = \sqrt[n]{\sum \frac{p_t}{p_0}} \tag{2}$$

where n is the number of commodities covered. In practice, logarithms are used to simplify the calculation:

$$\log I_{ot} = \frac{1}{n} \sum \log \frac{p_t}{p_0} \tag{3}$$

The problem of aggregating prices for commodities which do not share the same physical units is likewise resolved via the use of indexes. Textiles prices may be quoted in square yards, whereas those for copper are expressed in units of weight such as pounds or metric tons. Combining price relatives for nonhomogeneous commodities to arrive at some form of general price level therefore requires a value-weighting scheme. Specification of weights is another source of indexing problems.

Construction. Index weights can be fixed or variable. Indexes of the variable-weight type, which seek to measure price changes as they actually impact transactions, are generally referred to as implicit price deflators, such as the GNP deflator, the personal consumption expenditure deflator, or the producer durable equipment deflator as used in the national income and product accounts (NIPAs). Such indexes are current year–based and allow for the fact that consumers seek to conserve on high-priced commodities and tend to shift their budgets to include more lower-priced items. Deflators are not the subject of this chapter, but are discussed in the chapter on measures of inflation. For the purpose of exposition and completeness, it is sufficient to note that price deflators can be defined as:

$$I_{ot} = \sum \frac{p_t q_t}{p_o q_t} \qquad (4)$$

The prices and quantities of the numerator are of the same time period, and the index is expressed in reference to base time period prices and current time period quantities as shown in the denominator. The national income account deflators are known as Paasche-type weighted aggregative indexes.

Another method of measuring commodity price changes is to compare price changes to a given (or constant), as opposed to variable, "market basket":

$$I_{ot} = \sum \frac{p_t q_o}{p_o q_o} \qquad (5)$$

The fixed, or base-weighted, form is known as the Laspeyres index and is the most common construction methodology for commodity price indexes.

Using a simple arithmetic transformation, the Laspayres index can be expressed in terms of price relatives:

$$I_{ot} = \frac{\sum p_o q_o (p_t / p_o)}{\sum p_o q_o} \qquad (6)$$

Theory. The theoretical foundation of consumer price indexes has long been established and is grounded in economic theories related to consumption. The central argument is that the consumer seeks to maximize his satisfaction (utility in economic terms) by allocating his finite budget to items available for purchase. (Alternatively, the consumer seeks to minimize expenditures to achieve or maintain a given level of satisfaction.) When prices rise, given a fixed nominal-dollar budget, consumer satisfaction or the standard of living is presumably reduced, since the same allocation (or market basket) can no longer be purchased. The theoretical constant satisfaction (utility) index is a deflator resulting from the division of current expenditures by a base period expenditure. In fact, the consumer is continuously altering his money allocation between products and may or may not experience a change in his level of satisfaction as prices rise. Purchases of phonograph records, for example, decreased as prices skyrocketed in response to higher costs for plastic, etc. At the same time, sales of video games ballooned. Prices for video games have been rapidly declining. Since the primary buyers of both commodities are teens and preteens, and both items are directed toward filling leisure time, their substitutability does not make it at all clear that a net loss of satisfaction has been experienced.

From a practical standpoint, it is not possible to cope with continual changes in consumer market baskets, particularly where the introduction of new products, products of altered quality, or changes in consumer tastes and incomes are involved. A fixed-weight market basket is therefore employed as a proxy to measure changes in living standards, or the cost of living.

An analogous theory for producer prices, based on the theory of production, has only recently begun to emerge. Given a fixed-input market basket, the producer ideally adjusts his outputs as their relative prices change in order to maximize his profits under constant technology. (Alternatively, he would minimize input usage at constant output levels.) The ideal output price index is a constant-resources price deflator which, when divided into current-dollar revenues, yields constant-dollar (or real) output.

Since data on the change of output in response to price movements cannot be collected, the PPI is calculated as a fixed-weight Laspeyres index. It follows that the Laspeyres index is the lower bound of the ideal economic price index, since revenues could be improved if outputs were variable. As the Laspeyres index understates price rises, it tends to overstate real output.

THE INDEXES

Industrial commodity price indexes vary substantially in items covered, methods of calculation, manner of data collection, periodicity, and longevity. Each was designed to serve a specific purpose and must be used accordingly.

Spot Market Price Indexes

The timelist indexes are those published daily. Since speed in data collection is essential, prices covered in these indexes are limited to those available almost instantaneously in world markets and are, therefore, cash (or spot) prices. Futures prices, or the prices associated with delivery at a specific future date, are often available on the same basis as cash prices. No such timely data collection system generally exists for contract prices negotiated outside of exchanges.

Spot prices and futures prices on organized exchanges are available only for raw materials or partially processed materials by reason of their homogeneity. Specifications of such items are well known among traders and are commonly met by producers throughout the world. As materials are processed to serve a multitude of end users, technical specifications become almost infinite, with a corresponding decline in volumes trading for each specification. Thus, the heterogeneous nature of semifinished and finished commodities precludes the possibility of trade on organized exchanges and mitigates against the availability of spot prices.

Responding to daily nuances in the relationship between supply and demand, spot prices are necessarily more volatile than negotiated or producer prices. In fact, it is this very sensitivity to the marketplace which makes spot prices so valuable in terms of embedded information. The tone of today's spot market, if sustained any length of time, cannot help but impact negotiations which take place outside the market. Moreover, there are obvious implications for prices of goods which use the raw materials as inputs. The price of grain is a cost to beef growers, who must attempt to pass higher prices through to beef buyers if their profitability is to be preserved; alternatively, margins can be maintained at lower price levels if grain prices fall. Should the grower fail in his efforts to pass through higher prices, reduced profitability is a signal that the consumer will purchase less beef at higher prices. Under such circumstances, the grower will likely liquidate part of his breeding herd, ultimately reducing the supply of beef going to market and restoring prices to a level where profits can be made. Thus, a new regime of higher prices with reduced demand and supply is established.

Tuesday Index of Spot Market Prices.   In the United States, the publication of daily spot market price indexes was initiated by the Bureau of Labor Statistics in January 1934 at the request of the Treasury Department. Release to the general public was begun in January 1940. A new index was inaugurated in 1952, based on a sample of 22 commodities and calculated on a 1947–49 base. The old index had been based on 28 commodities and was calculated on an August 1939 base. The index was periodically rebased to correspond to the base period for other federal government indexes and is presently on a 1967 = 100 base. In 1969, computation on a daily basis was discontinued, and the index has since been published only weekly, based on Tuesday prices. In fact, the index is no longer published by the Bureau of Labor Statistics but has been carried on by the Commodity Research Bureau (CRB) since May 26, 1981. There have been some data source modifications with the transition to CRB, but it seems reasonable to assume that consistency has not been unduly impaired.

Economist. The longest-lived spot commodity price index is that generated by *The Economist* magazine and dates back to 1860. Over this long history, several revisions have necessarily been made, but the series retains its usefulness as an indicator of long-term inflation in primary materials.

Today the Economist commodity price indicators encompass 28 commodities (including multiple specifications) weighted by three-year moving averages of imports into industrial countries with a base of 1975. Since 1974, indexes have been published in both sterling and dollars, calculated back to 1970 Like the earlier indexes, the new ones contain both sterling and dollar prices, but all are now converted to dollars.

The Economist first published commodity indexes in 1864, the purpose at that time being to draw attention to the rise in prices subsequent to the gold discoveries in California and Australia. As presently constructed, the index is intended to measure changes in the raw material import bill of the noncommunist industrial world. Over the recent past, weights have changed to favor food, and metals have become more important at the expense of fibers. Where prices are administered, such as farm products in the European Economic Community or crude oil (which is deliberately excluded), the index does not reflect changes in consumer costs.

Reuters. Also weighted by the relative importance of commodities in international trade, the Reuters daily index of United Kingdom staple commodity prices is prepared by Reuters Economic Services. The index is constructed as a geometric average of 17 primary commodities and is designed to follow day-to-day changes in what is regarded as the world commodity price level relative to a base of September 18, 1931 = 100. Changes in index composition are made periodically to reflect structural changes in markets.

Dow Jones.   The Dow Jones commodity spot price indexes are essentially designed to afford a comparison between cash prices on organized exchanges and futures price 150 days subsequent. Included are 12 commodities on an equal weight basis. Unlike the other indexes cited, the Dow Jones index includes the speculative metals gold and silver.

Prior to January 1982, the Dow Jones indicators measured prices of only agricultural commodities. At the time of revision, the daily history was extended to December 31, 1974, the new base date. Both the Dow Jones and Reuters indexes are published daily in *The Wall Street Journal*.

Spot index market baskets and construction are compared in Exhibit 1.

Producer Price Indexes

Traditional.   The most widely used and most comprehensive set of commodity price indexes is the PPI, published by the Bureau of Labor

EXHIBIT 1   Commodity Spot Price Indexes: Simplified Comparison of Market Baskets

	Index Construction			
	U.S. Tuesday Spot (equal weighted geometric mean)	The Economist (moving weighted arithmetic mean)	Dow Jones (equal weighted arithmetic mean)	Reuters (Geometric weighted mean)
Food				
Beef/steers	x	4.5%	x	4%
Butter	x			
Cocoa		6.4		3
Coconut oil		1.0		
Coffee		18.3	x	11
Copra		0.3		2
Corn		6.4	x	5
Cottonseed oil	x			
Groundnuts		0.7		2
Groundnut oil		0.6		
Hogs	x			
Lamb		1.5		
Lard	x			
Rice				4
Soybeans		7.9	x	3
Soybean meal		3.6		
Soybean oil		0.7		
Sugar		6.5		7
Tea		1.4		
Wheat		3.4		14
Total food		63.2		55

EXHIBIT 1 *(concluded)*

Index Construction

	U.S. Tuesday Spot (equal weighted geometric mean)	The Economist (moving weighted arithmetic mean)	Dow Jones (equal weighted arithmetic mean)	Reuters (Geometric weighted mean)
Textiles and fibers				
Burlap	x			
Cotton	x	4.9	x	13
Jute		0.1		
Print cloth	x			
Sisal		0.1		
Wool	x	4.7		11
Total textiles and fibers		9.8		24
Metals				
Copper	x	11.4	x	9
Gold			x	
Lead	x	2.7		1
Silver			x	
Steel scrap	x			
Tin	x	3.3		2
Zinc	x	2.4		2
Total metals		19.8		14
Other				
Hides	x	2.3		
Lumber			x	
Palm oil		1.0		
Rubber	x	3.9		7
Tallow	x			
Total other		7.2		7
Total industrials		37.7		45

Note: Numbers represent percentage weights, x denotes unweighted commodities included.
Sources: Bureau of Labor Statistics, *The Economist*, *The Wall Street Journal*, Reuters.

Statistics in Table 6 of its monthly publication, *Producer Prices and Price Indexes*. Published since 1902, index coverage has grown from about 250 to approximately 3,450 commodities as of January 1982; under present plans for expansion, 6,000 indexes will eventually be listed.

PPI construction has changed significantly over its history. The first index was an unweighted (or equally weighted) average of price relatives. Presently the PPI is calculated by a modified Laspeyres formula, with weights based on the 1972 industrial census shipment values. The current base is 1967 = 100 (except for items recently introduced).

It is intended that the PPI represent the actual price for the first significant commercial transaction with respect to each commodity. Prices are ideally FOB production to avoid inclusion of transportation costs; excise taxes and subsidies to producers are also excluded. As far as possible, prices at time of shipment rather than at time of order are specified.

As originated, PPI price sampling was judgmental rather than statistical, with respect both to commodities covered and to reporters solicited. In an ongoing program begun in the late 1970s called the producer price index revision (PPIR), scientific price sampling methodology is gradually being introduced.

Stage-of-Processing. At higher levels of aggregation, the traditional (or all-commodities) type of PPI suffers from an inadequacy termed *double-counting*. For example, the prices of iron ore, steel mill products, and washing machines are all included in the all-commodities PPI by weight of their shipment values in the industrial censuses. An increase in the iron ore price is therefore implicitly reflected several times in the index, overstating its impact. To remedy such analytical difficulties, the PPIs were organized by stage-of-processing. Since 1978, when the name "producer price index" superseded the old misnomer "wholesale price index," emphasis has been placed in news releases on the stage-of-processing indexes—primarily finished goods, since this is the form in which commodities find their way to the consumer, or last buyer. Under the new scheme, iron ore forms part of the crude goods index, steel is an intermediate good, and the washing machine is a component of the finished goods index, thus avoiding much of the double-counting problem. Unfortunately, there are usually several intermediate processing stages, so double-counting remains a problem at this stage.

The weighting schemes for the traditional PPI and the stage-of-processing indexes are given in Exhibits 2 and 3. Stage-of-processing price indexes are tabulated in Tables 1–3 of the BLS publication.

Industry Price Indexes. As indicated, the traditional PPIs are commodity rather than industry oriented. There is not a direct correspondence, for example, between aggregate PPI 08, chemical and allied products, and other statistical series, such as employment or shipments, for standard industrial classification (SIC) 28 by the same name. Analysis is thus hampered, and deflators for SIC 28 must be devised on an ad hoc basis, as is done by the Bureau of Economic Analysis for use in the annual *Industrial Outlook*, published by the Commerce Department, and for aggregation to the GNP deflator in the NIPA.

Some industry and product class price indexes have been published by the BLS, based on SIC classifications. Individual products are assigned a seven-digit code by the Bureau of the Census. The product

EXHIBIT 2 Producer Price Indexes: Relative
Importance of Commodities in
Traditional Commodity-Oriented
Indexes, December 1981

All commodities	100.00%
Farm products	6.04
Processed foods and feeds	11.51
Textile products and apparel	4.89
Hides, skins, leather, and related products	0.75
Fuels and related products and power	16.73
Chemicals and allied products	6.78
Rubber and plastic products	2.56
Lumber and wood products	2.04
Pulp, paper, and allied products	7.17
Metals and metal products	12.15
Machinery and equipment	11.57
Furniture and household durables	2.86
Nonmetallic mineral products	2.95
Transportation equipment	8.70
Miscellaneous products	3.31

EXHIBIT 3 Producer Price Indexes: Relative Importance of
Commodities By Stage-of-Processing,
December 1981

Crude materials for further processing	100.00%
Foodstuffs and feedstuffs	50.63
Crude energy materials	33.61
Crude nonfood materials less energy	17.02
Intermediate materials, supplies, and components	100.00
Intermediate foods and feeds	5.35
Intermediate energy goods	17.03
Intermediate materials less foods and energy	77.63
Finished goods	100.00
Finished consumer foods	21.92
Finished energy goods	12.74
Finished goods less foods and energy	66.39

indexes are then aggregated to five-digit product classes. Industry indexes at the four-digit SIC code level are then constructed using these product class indexes and made-in-the-industry weights. Industry sector price indexes are found in Tables 9–10 of the BLS publication.

The industry price index program has depended upon price data as collected for the PPI, with attendant shortcomings. The BLS is phasing out this system by eliminating publication of those industry indexes which have been absorbed into the PPIR system, where coverage is being systematically expanded to include all 493 four-digit SIC industries.

Under the PPIR, indexes are industry rather than commodity oriented. Some seven-digit Census products included in the PPIR correspond to eight-digit commodities published in the traditional PPI commodity system. In general, however, it is usually not possible to publish meaningful average prices for individual commodities in the PPIR by reason of the broader specification range based on census definitions. Therefore, the traditional PPI will continue to serve a purpose where specific commodities are concerned.

Weighting schemes in an industry output index are based on the concept of net output, with items being selected for pricing to the extent that they are actually sold outside the industry, eliminating multiple counting. Construction of net output weights for the PPIR indexes is inherently more complex than the use of gross shipment weights in the traditional PPI commodity structure. In addition to the value of shipments data supplied by the industrial censuses, BLS uses value of materials consumed (also from the Census), data on detailed industry flows from the input-output table constructed by the Bureau of Economic Analysis, and other detailed industry data.

Historically the PPI have concentrated on the manufacturing sectors. Under the PPIR, coverage of services is planned as well. To date, railroad freight indexes by standard transportation commodity code (STCC) have been made available in Table 11 of the BLS publication, Table 12 documents selected telephone service prices, and postal services are presented in Table 13.

Import and Export Price Indexes.   Following a short-lived program after World War II, the BLS began publishing export price indexes in 1971 and import price indexes in 1973. Presently, publication is quarterly and, as of June 1982, accounted for 71 percent of the value of exports and 96 percent of the value of imports. Full coverage of nonmilitary imports and exports is planned by the end of 1983.

The level of disaggregation reported for the import/export price indexes is the four-digit standard industrial trade classification code (SITC) established by the United Nations. Prices are collected according to the specification method and are "cost, insurance, and freight" (CIF) U.S. port as far as possible for imports, and either "free on board" (FOB) factory or "free alongside ship" (FAS) for exports.

The import and export price indexes are constructed via a modified Laspeyres formula with weights in accordance with 1980 trade values. Publication is by BLS news release five weeks after the end of each quarter.

MACROECONOMIC APPLICATIONS

On first examination, the specificity of commodity price indexes might appear to rule out applications of the broad nature normally associated with macroeconomics. In fact, it is this very characteristic which permits formulation of a microcosm employed as a leading indicator of economic activity, provides the building blocks for aggregate inflation measures, traces the transmission of inflation through the economy, and provides the most consistent data for analysis of long-term price movements.

Deflator Construction.   The NIPA system, developed as an aid to measuring the economic health of the nation, requires a means of adjusting outputs and incomes to remove the illusory effects of inflation. Nominal-dollar figures are divided by price indexes or implicit price deflators to estimate constant-dollar (or real) quantities in the NIPA.

Disaggregated producer price indexes facilitate the construction, through the formation of appropriately weighted output market baskets, of deflators at the more disaggregated levels of the NIPA. Current-dollar values are then divided by corresponding deflators to form constant-dollar series. Adding together all of the constant-dollar amounts yields constant-dollar GNP. The GNP implicit price deflator results when nominal-dollar GNP is divided by constant-dollar GNP. Aside from the PPI, the CPI, import-export price indexes, and government sector indexes are used in developing the requisite deflators.

Inflation Measurement.   A comparison of the traditional all-commodities producer price index with the GNP deflator and CPI is presented in Exhibit 4. Since GNP is a value-added concept and therefore is dominated by labor costs, it is reasonable to expect that, over the long span of history, it outpaces other price indexes; that is to say, labor income has inflated more rapidly than other costs. In fact, real wage gains (the rate of gain of wages in excess of the GNP deflator or consumer price index) are regarded as an indicator of whether or not the standard of living is improving.

Growth Indicators.   A market basket termed *sensitive commodity prices* is a component of the Department of Commerce composite index of leading indicators. As shown in Exhibit 5, however, recent history does not provide a strong showing for commodity prices in the role of a leading economic indicator. On a quarterly basis, compared with real GNP, sensitive commodity prices appear to be more a coincident than a leading economic indicator. Of course, there is a time lag in the data which tends to bolster the image of prices as a leading indicator: Spot commod-

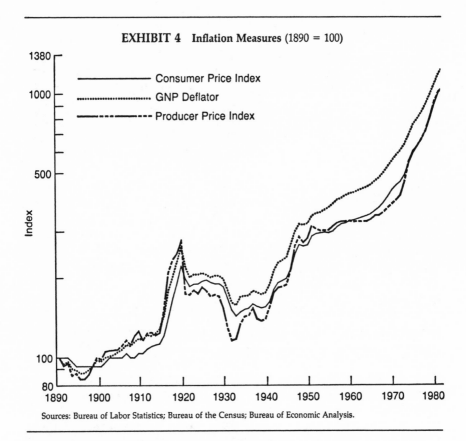

EXHIBIT 4   Inflation Measures (1890 = 100)

——— Consumer Price Index

·············· GNP Deflator

— - - — - - - Producer Price Index

Sources: Bureau of Labor Statistics; Bureau of the Census; Bureau of Economic Analysis.

ity prices are available almost instantaneously, whereas GNP data are issued quarterly and subject to significant revision. Thus, it was correct to conclude in 1982 that weakness in commodity prices was evidence of economic weakness and that the upturn begun in December presaged positive growth. Bearing in mind the international nature of many commodity prices, however, it should be noted that world economic health is reflected as well and that changes may be ambiguous with respect to the United States.

The mechanism which underlies the assumption that increases in raw commodity prices precede economic growth is that once excess inventories accumulated during recession are pared, higher prices are required to elicit added production, given that inventory liquidation implies distress pricing. On the downside, inventories accumulate involuntarily as final demand subsides and price growth abates. The latter is probably the better argument for commodity prices as a leading indicator.

EXHIBIT 5   Commodity Prices and Economic Growth, Sensitive Materials versus
GNP (quarterly data)

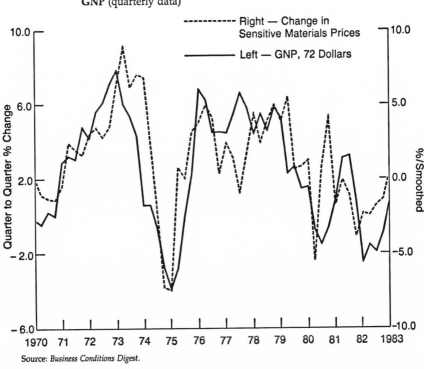

Source: *Business Conditions Digest.*

Industrial Policy.   Perhaps the greatest value of commodity-level producer price indexes is that they can be combined in customized market
baskets to suit the needs at hand. For a long period of our history, for
example, prices of farm outputs were compared to purchases to determine the farm parity ratio or the change in the relationship from a base
period, in this case usually 1910–14. In many instances, parity was an
important consideration in the formulation of government agricultural
policies such as price supports (see Exhibit 6).

Inflation Indicators.   The historical portrait which the analyst paints of
inflation is sensitive to the indexes selected and the base period or time
span of interest. The current 1967 base—if used for Exhibit 4, for example—would have clearly demonstrated the overwhelming impact of energy prices on other commodities in the 70s and the implications for
living standards (see Exhibit 7). Regardless of the research focus, the

EXHIBIT 6   Producer Price Indexes and Farm Parity: Annual Data (1910–1914 = 100)

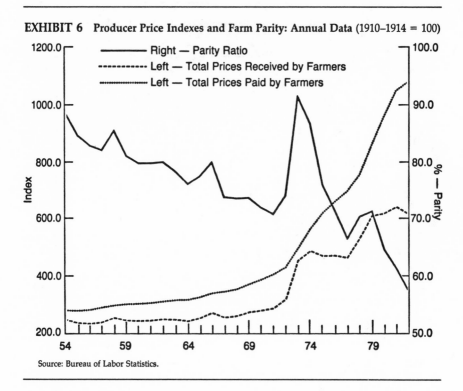

Source: Bureau of Labor Statistics.

producer price index components are ideally suited to trace the mechanism of price/cost transmission through the economy, whether by stage-of-processing or by industry.

Movements in spot prices necessarily precede the knowledge of movements in the crude materials PPI, if only because the former are reported daily and the latter monthly. New crude material price index trends usually develop in advance of the intermediate materials indexes since they serve as inputs to the manufacture of those very commodities. (Exceptions include natural gas, which is represented in both crude materials and finished goods indexes.) The premise is that higher materials costs will be at least partially passed through to buyers. If, on the other hand, input prices drop, it is assumed that knowledgeable buyers will insist on price cuts. By the same token, an increase/decrease in intermediate materials is transmitted by the manufacturer to the distributor purchasing finished goods. The distributor in turn adjusts his price to the retailer, who passes on the adjustment to the ultimate consumer; and the transaction theoretically will ultimately show up in the CPI (see Exhibit 8). As always, the reality is somewhat removed from the suppo-

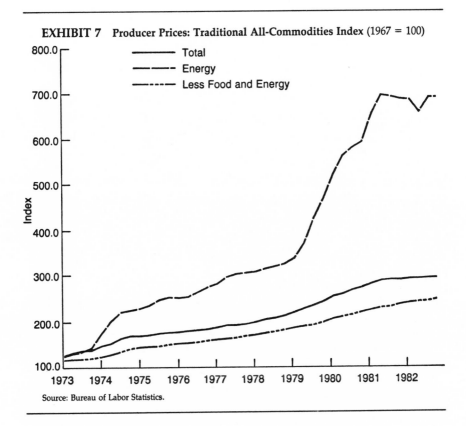

EXHIBIT 7   Producer Prices: Traditional All-Commodities Index (1967 = 100)

Source: Bureau of Labor Statistics.

sition; but the substance remains, albeit sometimes obscured. Gasoline prices, for example, are lagged one month in the PPI sample, whereas no such lag exists in the CPI.

In the analysis of inflation, it is often desirable to remove as much as possible the effects of the "uncontrollables"—food and energy. Such a presentation, by stage-of-processing, is given in Exhibit 9 and illustrates the sequential movements of the indexes as materials move through the processing chain. The finished goods PPI can be similarly related to the CPI.

The finished goods PPI, less food and energy, can be compared to unit labor costs in manufacturing (as in Exhibit 10) to estimate the underlying or core rate of inflation in the economy. Since labor makes up the bulk of embedded costs by the time a good reaches the finished stage of processing, the modest residual variation between commodity prices and unit labor costs is explained by the influence of material, energy, cost of capital, and profit margins.

EXHIBIT 8   Commodity Prices and Inflation: The Raw Materials Index and the CPI (monthly data)

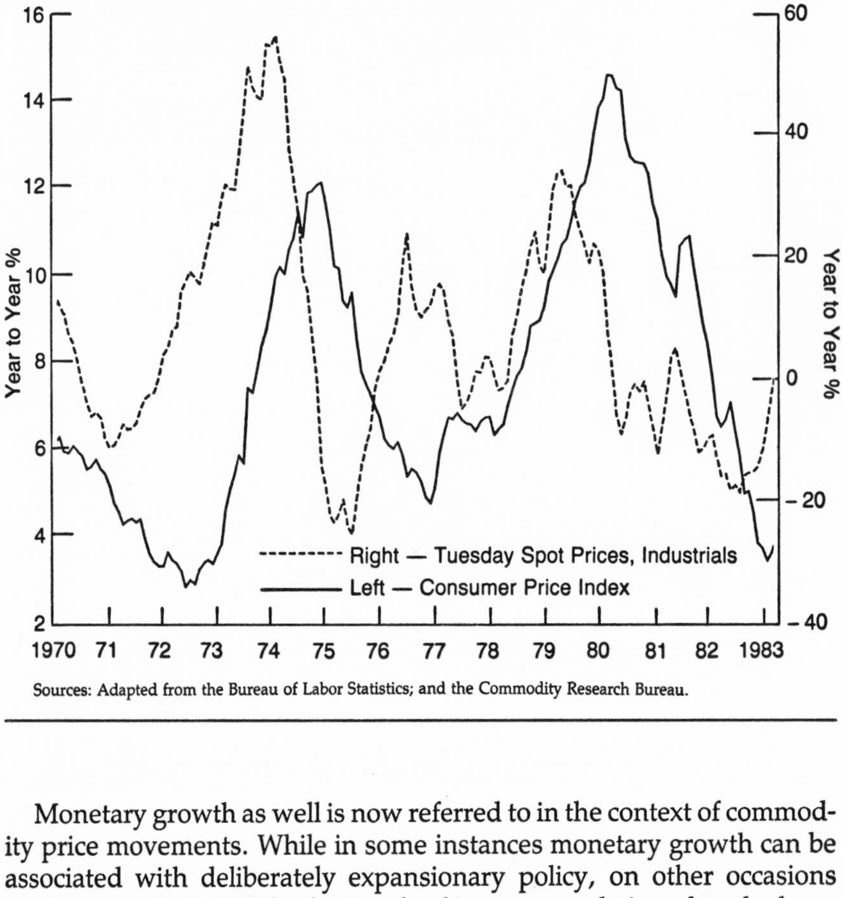

Right — Tuesday Spot Prices, Industrials
Left — Consumer Price Index

Sources: Adapted from the Bureau of Labor Statistics; and the Commodity Research Bureau.

Monetary growth as well is now referred to in the context of commodity price movements. While in some instances monetary growth can be associated with deliberately expansionary policy, on other occasions (such as the 1973 OPEC oil price shock), accommodation played a large role.

At this writing, there is widespread concern in the United States that recent high growth rates in the money supply (M1 for purposes of this discussion) inevitably foreshadow reemergence of the, by now, all too familiar inflationary spiral. The debate is frustrated by the ongoing deregulation of the financial sector and the resultant ambiguities in money supply data. In the face of these difficulties, some analysts have turned to sensitive commodity prices—that is, the Tuesday spot price index for industrials—as a barometer of inflationary pressures. It is argued that the present monetary expansion coexists with a decline in the velocity of money, an indication that the desire to hold money has increased—just the opposite of what would occur with a rise in inflationary expecta-

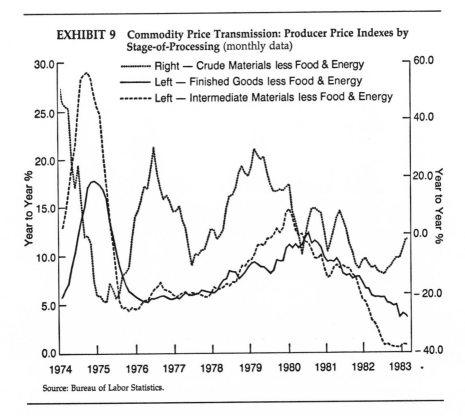

EXHIBIT 9 Commodity Price Transmission: Producer Price Indexes by Stage-of-Processing (monthly data)

.... Right — Crude Materials less Food & Energy

———— Left — Finished Goods less Food & Energy

- - - - - Left — Intermediate Materials less Food & Energy

Source: Bureau of Labor Statistics.

tions. Since velocity is not simply measured on a day-to-day basis, commodity prices are then pointed to as an appropriate indicator, with gold being identified as most closely associated with monetary conditions. Commodity prices, it is argued, are positively correlated with money velocity (see Exhibit 11).

An eight-year history of the Dow Jones cash and futures indexes are shown in Exhibit 12. Since the futures index has outrun the cash index for most of the period, it seems safe to conclude that an inflationary psychology has generally existed in the commodity markets.

Long-Term Analysis. Commodity price indexes are a standard indicator in analysis of economic cycles, long as well as short, Analysts have historically devoted considerable effort to the identification of long-term economic cycles. Almost invariably, commodity price behavior plays a central role in such investigations. Joseph Schumpeter devised a three-cycle framework which included the Kitchin cycle (a "minor cycle" of 40 months average duration, largely inventory related), the Juglar cycle

EXHIBIT 10   Commodity Prices versus Labor Costs (annual data)

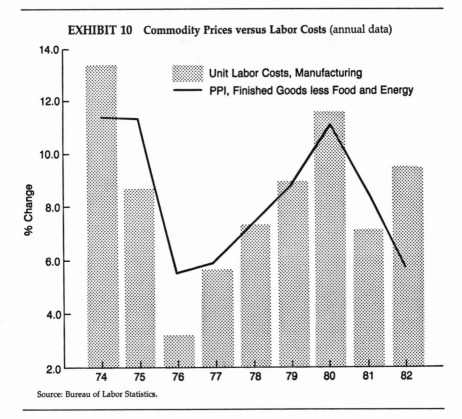

Source: Bureau of Labor Statistics.

(the standard "business cycle" of 9–10 years average duration, associated with the normal economic adjustment process and its attendant lags and accelerator mechanisms), and the 54-year average-duration Kontradieff cycle (said to be related to waves of innovation stemming from economic necessity). The more recently identified Kuznets cycle is of an intermediate, 15–20 years duration; it emphasizes construction activity, possibly responding to demographic pressures.

Wholesale or producer prices are available in greater volume than those at the retail level, particularly in early years, and thus often form the basis for analysis over the long span of history, such as the Kontradieff cycle. Based on commodity price indexes, dating back as far as the 13th century, for several countries, David Hackett Fischer, in the *Journal of the Institute for Socioeconomic Studies*, has concluded that there have been four long waves of inflation in Europe and the United States since 1000 A.D. Each wave was determined to be of approximately 100 years duration, with the most recent commencing in 1896.

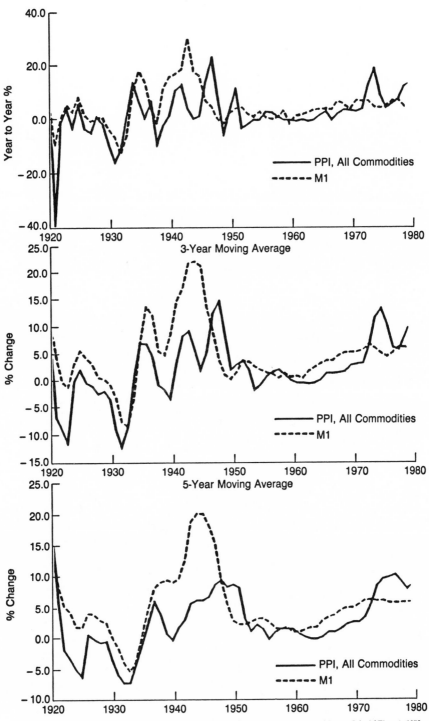

EXHIBIT 11   Commodity Prices and Money Supply Growth

Sources: Bureau of Labor Statistics; Bureau of the Census, *Historical Statistics of the United States, Colonial Times to 1970.*

EXHIBIT 12 Inflationary Expectations: Dow Jones Commodity Price Indexes (December 31, 1974 = 100)

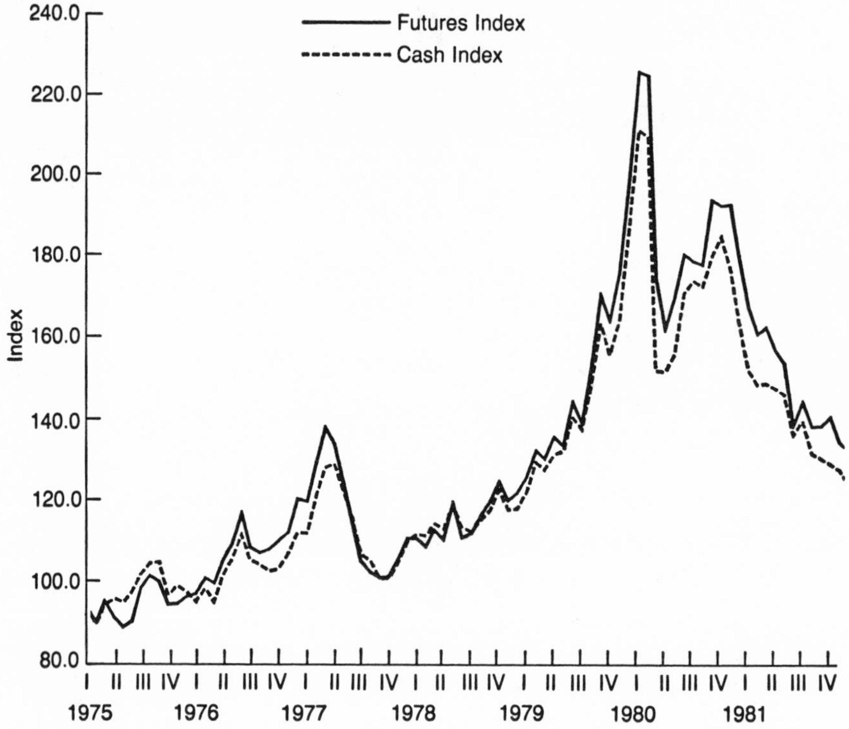

Source: Reprinted by permission of *The Wall Street Journal*, © Dow Jones & Company, Inc. All rights reserved.

Fischer argues that each wave found its origin in a large population increase which strained the supply capabilities for necessities such a food, clothing, and energy. Each episode, he contends, was ultimately reinforced by expansionary monetary and fiscal policies. Under this long-wave scheme, the major economic disruptions of the current century, such as the Great Depression, represent only deviations from trend.

The Economist and Reuters commodity indexes are plotted in Exhibit 13 as indicators of long-term inflationary cycles. The indexes are in general agreement until recently (considerable license was taken in splicing the Economist series). Historically, rapid inflation has been usually associated with the exigencies of war. Since the Second World War, however, prices no longer are inclined to revert to prewar levels once the battles are over. The economic policies which we implemented to avoid

EXHIBIT 13 Long-Term Inflation: The Economist Commodity Price Indicator versus Reuters Commodity Index (1931 = 100)

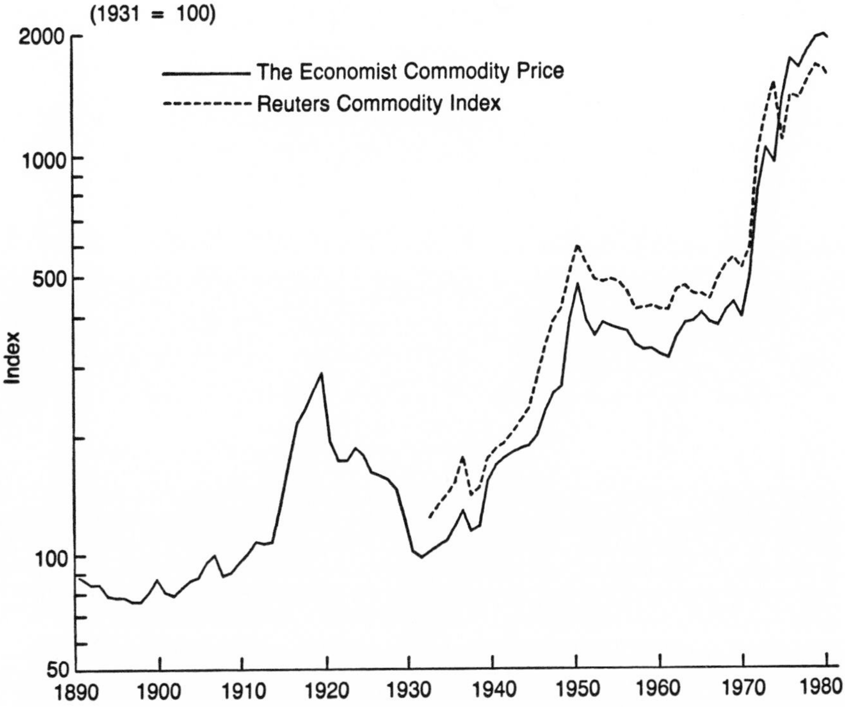

Sources: *The Economist*; Reuters.

earlier postwar depressions have imparted an inflationary bias to our economies (see Exhibit 14).

MICROECONOMIC APPLICATIONS

Although commodity price indexes are commonly used in the more abstract world of macroeconomic analysis, the greatest use by far is in concrete business or microeconomic applications. In a survey of users released in 1977, the BLS found that 45 percent of respondents were manufacturers, and the highest incidences of usage reported by all respondents were forecasting, contract escalation, inflation indication, and price trend measurements, in that order. This section is devoted to fleshing out some of these applications.

EXHIBIT 14   Long-Term Inflation: Producer Price Index, All Commodities
(annual data; 1967 = 100)

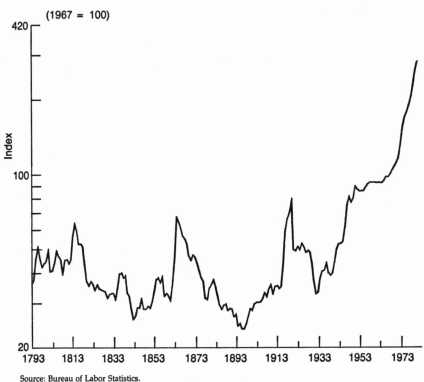

Source: Bureau of Labor Statistics.

Price Tracking and Performance Measurement.   From the standpoint of the purchasing executive, specific producer price indexes are interesting to the extent that they afford a comparison with their own experience. A buyer who, through his negotiating or shopping skills, is able to hold cost increases for purchased goods below the rate of increase in the relevant PPI (national market proxy) obtains a potential competitive advantage for his company. Conversely, price increases exceeding PPI gains affect the firm's competitive cost position adversely and may provide evidence of inferior performance.

Prices paid for commodities in the marketplace are expressed on a per-unit basis. The PPI, on the other hand, can be of rather abstract construction for price tracking and performance measurement. A one-for-one comparison may be difficult, even if changes are monitored over a period of time. In some instances, such as for many steel mill products, the BLS also lists unit costs as well as the index itself. In the case of cold-rolled carbon steel sheet, an index of 321.3 in January 1981 corresponded to a price of 23.731 cents per hundred pounds. Given one's own price history (in, say, dollars per ton) for cold-rolled carbon steel sheet and an easily calculated conversion factor, it is possible to make an explicit and direct comparison with the PPI, as depicted in Exhibit 15.

EXHIBIT 15   Price Tracking and Performance Measurement: PPI Converted to Unit Costs for Cold-Rolled Steel Sheets

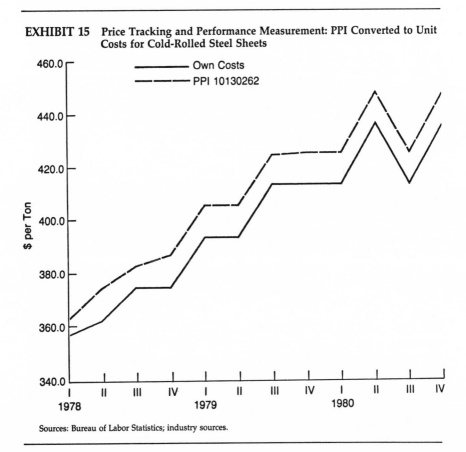

Sources: Bureau of Labor Statistics; industry sources.

The graph suggests that prices paid did approximate the PPI for the period shown, but with a lag, and that rates of change were quite similar.

Where unit prices are not provided by the BLS, the analyst can select a base period and infer his own PPI-to-unit-price conversion factor. It is often desirable to statistically formalize the relationship using regression analysis.

Escalation Clauses.   The aforementioned BLS survey of users documented that $82.7 billion of their sales were escalated by industrial price indexes, with about $93.1 billion of their purchases being so treated. These figures likely understate grossly the volume of transactions subject to escalation clauses in the economy, since 46 percent of respondents employing such practices failed to report the dollar amount.

Unforeseen inflation can place a financial burden on one or the other side of a transaction, especially when lead times are long and the potential cumulative impact comparatively large. Buyers and sellers alike often find it mutually convenient in such circumstances to specify escalator clauses in pricing contracts, thereby allowing for the effects of inflation from a base price at a base date. Ideally, the escalator clause eliminates the possibility of windfall profits or losses on either side of a transaction and is therefore fair. Misspecification, however, can introduce a new set of problems, as will be discussed later in this chapter.

Substitution.   Selection of materials in manufacturing is nothing less than a strategic decision. The relative price change between aluminum and copper is an important consideration in electrical applications; metal must be compared with wood in office furniture fabrication, and variations of composite materials currently finding use in the aerospace industry are being evaluated as substitutes for existing materials by other manufacturing sectors. Exhibit 16 dramatizes, using containers as an example, the relative price changes in materials which have shaped that industry.

Cost Analysis.   Today, purchasing executives in numerous markets monitor inflation in the inputs consumed by suppliers in order to judge the merits of requested output price adjustments. Characteristically, cost analysis requires completion of a data jigsaw puzzle, with bits and pieces gleaned from different sources being laboriously fitted together. Consistency of timing and specification frequently become luxuries, if not miracles. The exercise is nevertheless valuable and, given the relative magnitude of uncertainty to be addressed, perhaps even invaluable where information is scarcest. The more demanding the task, the lower the probability that the competition or other parties to a negotiation will duplicate it. It is in this spirit that the example which follows is offered.

In spite of the large number of PPIs published, there are many voids in the data. Not until June 1980 was a series introduced for heat exchangers (PPI 1075), a type of equipment used extensively in the process industries. The trade press and trade associations often find it necessary to fill such gaps. In this case, the construction industry standard is an index published quarterly by the *Oil and Gas Journal* and available back to 1926. Based on input-output and census data, it is possible to develop a

EXHIBIT 16   Producer Indexes and Materials Substitution, Annual Data
(1950 = 100)

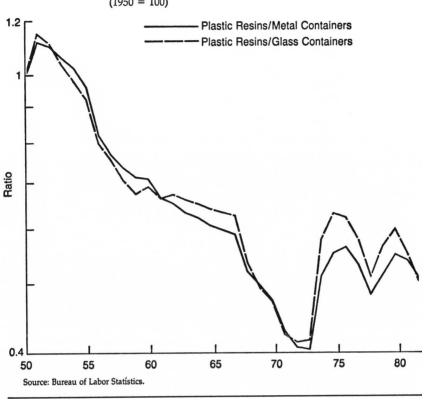

Source: Bureau of Labor Statistics.

proxy cost index for heat exchanger manufacture, assuming it is adequately represented by the data for the producing industry, boiler shops
(SIC 3443). Such a tabulation is given in Exhibit 17. Comparing the proxy
cost index against the heat exchanger index yields the results of Exhibit
18. Significant divergences are evident, indicating that other factors are
at work. Those factors include the demand side of the equation as illustrated by the rate of backlog growth also shown in the graph. Margin
implications for heat exchanger makers are obvious. A price contract
invoking an appropriately specified escalator clause would have resulted in substantial savings for buyers during much of the period,
given prudent selection of the base and the less than assured assent of
the seller.

Employing the same market basket approach, a firm's costs can be
compared to those of competitors to gauge the impact of alternative infla-

EXHIBIT 17   Industry Inputs, Boiler Shops
(SIC 3443)

	1976 Percent of Total Sales (1976 Dollars)
Intermediate purchases from:	
Iron and steel	29.5
Copper	2.4
Boiler shops	6.2
Pipes, valves, fittings	2.6
Industrial pumps, blowers, fans	1.1
Electrical industrial apparatus, nec	1.3
Wholesale trade	4.0
Business and legal services	1.6
Business travel	1.0
Other	11.8
Total purchases	61.5
Compensation of employees	24.0
Business taxes and property income	14.5
Total sales	100.0

Note: Percentages are shown only for inputs exceeding 1 percent.
Sources: Chase Econometrics Interindustry Service (input-output model), 1976 Survey of Manufactures.

EXHIBIT 18   Price versus Cost Indexes, Heat Exchangers (1970 = 100)

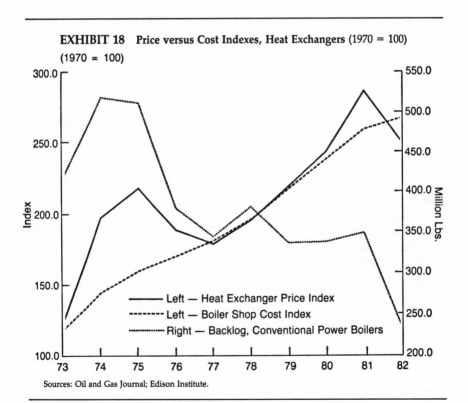

(1970 = 100)

Left — Heat Exchanger Price Index
Left — Boiler Shop Cost Index
Right — Backlog, Conventional Power Boilers

Sources: Oil and Gas Journal; Edison Institute.

EXHIBIT 19 Chemical Engineering Plant Cost Index (revised)

BLS Code No.	Weight Factor	Component	Weight Factors and Component Groups
10130246	0.254	Plates, carbon, A–36	
10130247	0.043	Plates, stainless steel	
10130276	0.043	Mechanical tubing, carbon, weld	
10130278	0.043	Mechanical tubing, stainless, weld	
1025	0.022	Nonferrous mill shapes	
Subtotal	(0.405)	Components of fabricated products	
10720102	0.183	Pressure vessels, nonaluminum	0.37 Revised fabricated equipment
10720111	0.007	Elevated water tank, field erected	
10720112	0.027	Bulk storage tank, 6,000 gal or less	
10720113	0.025	Bulk storage tank, over 6,000 gal	
10720133	0.021	Other pressure tanks	
10720138	0.082	Custom tanks, ¾ inch or less	
10720139	0.010	Custom tanks, over ¾ inch	
10720147	0.010	Petroleum storage tanks	
Subtotal	(0.365)	Typical fabricated products	
SIC 34	0.230	Fabricated products labor	
10130246	0.105	Plates, carbon, A–36	
10130264	0.030	Sheets, cold-rolled, stainless	
10130265	0.010	Sheets, electrical, alloy	
1015	0.060	Foundry and forge shop products	
1144	0.075	Industrial material handling equipment	
1147	0.025	Fans and blowers, except portable	

Excerpted by special permission from *Chemical Engineering*, 19 April 1982. Copyright © 1982 by McGraw-Hill, Inc., New York, N.Y. 10020.

EXHIBIT 19 (concluded)

Weight Factors and Component Groups

BLS Code No.	Weight Factor	Component			Revised process plant cost index
116604	0.250	Chemical industry machinery	0.14 Revised process machinery		
117301	0.035	Electric motors			
119202	0.150	Crushing, pulverizing, screening machinery			
132	0.030	Concrete ingredients			
Subtotal	(0.770)	Components of process machinery			
SIC 35	0.230	Process machinery labor		0.61 Revised equipment, machinery, and supports	
0721	0.050	Plastic construction products			
10130269	0.400	Pipe, black, carbon			
10130276	0.100	Mechanical tubing, carbon, weld			
102502	0.100	Copper and brass mill shapes	0.20 Revised pipes, valves and, fittings		
13320101	0.050	Culvert pipe, reinforced			
S1014011	0.200	Industrial valves (special index)			
S1016011	0.100	Industrial fittings (special index)			
10130261	0.057	Sheets, hot-rolled, carbon			
10130264	0.014	Sheets, cold-rolled, carbon			
1015	0.077	Foundry and forge shop products			
1025	0.060	Nonferrous mill shapes			
102502	0.053	Copper and brass mill shapes			
117301	0.036	Electric motors	0.07 Revised process instruments and controls		
1178	0.400	Electronic components and accessories			
S1014011	0.053	Industrial valves (special index)			
Subtotal	(0.750)	Components of instruments and controls			

Code	Weight	Description	Group weight	Group description	Final group weight	Final group description
SIC3622	0.063	Industrial controls labor				
SIC3823	0.187	Industrial instruments labor				
Subtotal	(0.250)	Instrument and control manufacturing labor				
114102	0.900	Industrial pumps	0.07	Revised pumps and compressors		
114103	0.050	Air compressors, stationary				
11410401	0.025	Centrifugal gas compressors, uncooled				
11410405	0.025	Reciprocating gas compressors, 1,000 hp				
102601	0.057	Copper wire and cable	0.05	Revised electrical equipment and materials		
1083	0.188	Lighting fixtures				
117301	0.306	Electric motors				
11730222	0.043	Electric generating plant, 100–125 kW				
1174	0.146	Transformers and power regulators				
1175	0.260	Switchgear, switchboard, etc., equipment				
0621	0.028	Prepared paint	0.10	Revised structural supports, insulation and paint		
10130248	0.382	Structural steel shapes				
10130255	0.077	Bars, reinforcing				
132	0.117	Concrete ingredients				
1392	0.396	Insulation materials				
S1012011	0.530	Construction materials (special index)			0.07	Buildings, materials and labor
SIC15	0.470	General building contractors				
ASACIII	0.060	Clerk, accounting, class III, annual salary			0.10	Revised engineering and supervision
ASBEV	0.330	Engineer, class V, annual salary				
ASDIV	0.470	Drafter, class IV, annual salary				
ASTII	0.140	Typist, class II, annual salary				
SIC15	0.334	General building contractors			0.22	Contract construction labor
SIC16	0.333	Heavy construction contractors				
SIC17	0.333	Special trade contractors				

EXHIBIT 20   Capital Project Cost Escalation

Quarter	Constant Dollar Expenditure (000)	Cost Index Forecast	Nominal Dollar Expenditure (000)
82.4	—	1.000	—
83.4	—	1.047	—
84.4	—	1.118	—
85.1	$ 150	1.139	$ 170.9
85.2	150	1.161	174.2
85.3	700	1.187	830.9
85.4	1,000	1.210	1,210.0
86.1	1,050	1.219	1,280.0
86.2	1,200	1.239	1,486.8
86.3	1,580	1.265	1,998.7
86.4	1,510	1.287	1,943.4
87.1	1,200	1.297	1,556.4
87.2	740	1.319	976.1
87.3	550	1.346	740.3
87.4	170	1.370	232.9
Total	$10,000		$12,600.6

---

tion scenarios, productivity gains, yield improvements, and so on. Within the firm, specific products can be modeled, and the prospects of individual divisions tracked and simulated. Using data such as presented for heat exchangers, econometric models can be developed to forecast commodity prices. Decisions can then be made about the future. Based on the market basket for chemical plant costs as published by *Chemical Engineering* magazine, Exhibits 19 and 20 depict the process for a multiyear capital expenditure.

PITFALLS

Problems associated with the use of producer price indexes as outlined in the preceding sections usually fall in the following categories:

1. Failure of the PPI to accurately reflect transactions prices.
2. Discontinuities in series publication by reason of:
   a. Program revision and resultant series deletions.
   b. Series redefinitions.
   c. Failure to report.
3. Absence of representative series by reason of noncoverage. Computers are an example.
4. Use of a series at a greater level of aggregation than appropriate.

Nonreporting. Data gaps have apparently become more numerous as the number of series reported has expanded. The probability of nonreporting by reason of inadequate sample diminishes as the level of aggregation in the PPI increases. However, the appropriateness of the index for the purpose at hand is usually improved with disaggregation. Thus, there is no clear answer for coping with nonreporting; hopefully, the BLS and/or firms will be able to improve reporting practices as economic conditions improve. In the interim, a default series can be specified for contractual or analytic purposes.

Discontinuities. In December 1980, the BLS introduced a new price subsector within the pulp, paper, and allied products aggregate: PPI 093—publications, printed matter, and printing materials. This subsector includes prices for newspaper, periodicals, and books, corresponding in essence to SIC 27. The addition of this subsector to the aggregate paper price sector was accommodated by significantly altering the distribution of weights among the components. The relative importance of PPI 091 (pulp, paper, and products excluding building papers) dropped to 45.3 percent from 96.7 percent. As a result, since that time, changes in PPI 09 have been heavily weighted toward changes in prices within the publishing sector—introducing a discontinuity in the data. The effects are shown in Exhibit 21. Using the most disaggregated PPI appropriate to the task at hand (in this case, PPI 091 or an even more disaggregated series) guards against revisions at the aggregate level.

Even eight-digit PPIs are not immune to discontinuities—the cold-rolled steel sheet PPI shown in an earlier example no longer exists. Also a casualty of the revisions, it has been replaced by PPI 1017011 for which unit cost data are no longer provided.

Misspecification. In defense contracting, there is an overwhelming bias toward specifying the producer price index for metal and metal products (PPI 10) together with a pertinent wage in escalator clauses. This tradition, aside from its obvious attraction of simplicity, undoubtedly dates back to the period when the most disaggregated forecasts available were at the two-digit PPI level (as is still generally the case in macroeconomic forecasting services).

Exhibit 22 summarizes the component-weighting scheme of the PPI for metal and metal products. Implicit in the decision to use PPI 10 as the basis for escalation is that the material inputs to the job at hand are required in approximately the proportions shown. Even out-of-hand, it seems implausible that materials consumed in building a fighter aircraft would be over 37 percent iron and steel—although the number might not be so far afield for tanks or rifles.

EXHIBIT 21   Producer Price Index Revisions with Discontinuities: Pulp, Paper, and Allied Products (annual data)

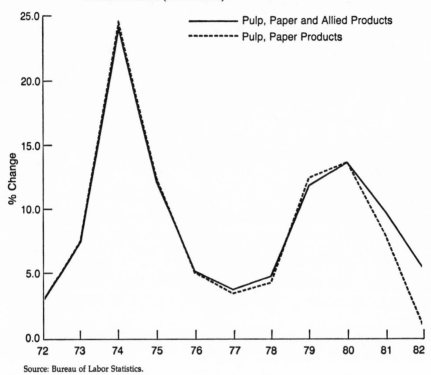

Source: Bureau of Labor Statistics.

EXHIBIT 22   Metal and Metal Products: Relative Importance*

PPI		Percent
10	Metal and metal products	100.00
101	Iron and steel	37.53
102	Nonferrous metals	22.42
103	Metal containers	4.08
104	Hardware	4.16
105	Plumbing fixtures and brass fittings	1.33
106	Heating equipment	1.53
107	Fabricated structural metal products	14.69
108	Miscellaneous metal products	14.27

* December 1981 weights normalized to 100 percent.

A further shortcoming in using a highly aggregated index in escalation clauses is the aforementioned double-counting. In aggregation, all stages of processing are counted, thus guaranteeing that an increase or decrease in the raw material price (say for iron ore) is counted several times, since it is embedded in the price of inputs to each stage of manufacturing.

The foregoing consideration would be purely academic if inflation were uniform. Such is not the case as indicated in Exhibit 23. Differential

EXHIBIT 23   Producer Price Indexes: Metal and Metal Products

		\multicolumn{5}{c}{*Percent Change*}
PPI		*1978*	*1979*	*1980*	*1981*	*1982*
10	Metal and metal products	8.7	14.2	10.4	4.9	0.5
101	Iron and steel	10.1	11.8	7.6	9.4	1.6
102	Nonferrous	6.3	26.0	16.5	−6.3	−7.7
103	Metal containers	11.6	10.6	10.9	5.7	4.0
104	Hardware	8.1	9.2	10.0	9.4	6.4
105	Plumbing fittings and brass fixtures	6.7	9.0	13.6	8.4	4.2
106	Heating equipment	5.4	7.3	10.3	8.6	5.8
107	Fabricated structural metal	9.5	9.9	8.7	9.2	3.1
108	Miscellaneous metal products	8.0	9.1	8.0	8.2	4.7
10220117	Primary aluminum ingot	6.2	11.8	18.0	7.3	−7.0
10220123	Aluminum sheet, heat treatable	19.6	21.8	4.2	8.2	0.8

inflation increases with disaggregation. Prices of heat-treatable aluminum sheet, the staple of aircraft skins, moved up very rapidly in 1979—for example, 7.6 percentage points more than PPI 10.

Accuracy.   At this writing, higher transactions costs for aluminum are not being accurately reflected in the PPI. The producer list price for aluminum ingot has been pegged at 76 cents per pound since mid-1980 but has been deeply discounted. The free market price plummeted to a low of 45 cents in the second quarter of 1982 and has surged to the 65-cent range in April. The change in the PPI for primary ingot has been strictly nominal during this period. One consequence of this stability is that PPI 102 rose a slim 3.0 percent in the first quarter of 1983; PPI 10 rose only 1.1 percent. Thus, a buyer of aluminum ingot could have seen his transactions prices go up 24 percent in the first quarter of 1983 with little recompense if he had been operating under a PPI 10 escalator or, for that matter, the PPI for aluminum ingot (see Exhibit 24).

Since the PPI often have a tendency to reflect published list prices, even in the face of pervasive discounting, it can be expected to decline more slowly than transactions prices in recession and to rise more slowly during recovery. The PPI attempt to sample spot and contract

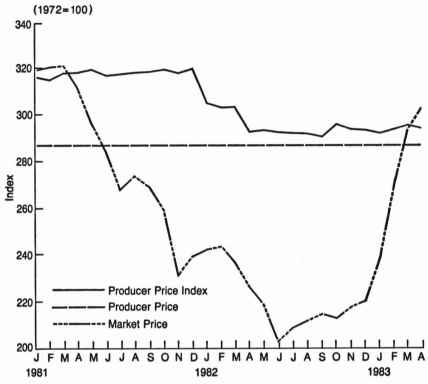

EXHIBIT 24   Producer Price Indexes, Contract and Market Prices: Aluminum Primary Ingot (monthly prices; 1972 = 100)

Sources: Bureau of Labor Statistics; *Metals Week*.

sales in the proportions of the base weight year. These proportions in reality vary with the economic cycle as buyers adjust their view of the trade-off between price and security of supply. Thus, there exists a built-in bias toward overstating inflation during downturns and understating it during upturns.

SUMMARY

Commodity prices, especially those quoted on organized exchanges, are an important statement generated by the market on how it perceives the health of the specific sectors and the overall economy. Indeed, given that almost instantaneous reaction to world events is reflected in daily and hourly exchange quotations, there is a bias toward overstatement.

With that caveat, however, there is no more timely or reliable barometer of economic sentiment than commodity prices, hence commodity price indexes.

Taken together with unequaled sensitivity to economic conditions, the ready and long-standing availability of price data places commodity indexes among the most analytically valuable of indicators. The greatest value of the PPI is as a data base which can be either recast to form specialized indexes for analysis or manipulated statistically to generate forecasts. Even greater use will result from the ongoing expansion of the PPI, the increasing sophistication of users, and the heightened cost-consciousness of business in the economic environment of the 80s.

REFERENCES

Allen, R. G. D. *Index Numbers in Theory and Practice.* Hawthorne, N.Y.: Aldine Publishing, 1975.

BLS Handbook of Methods. Washington, D.C.: U.S. Department of Labor, Bureau of Labor Statistics, 1976. Also volume I, December 1982.

"The Economist Indicators." *The Economist,* July 7, 1973; January 5, 1974; March 2, 1974; September 4, 1976; January 14, 1978; January 9, 1982; and January 15, 1983.

Fisher, F. W., and K. Shell. *The Economic Theory of Price Indices.* New York: Academic Press, 1972.

Historical Statistics of the United States, Colonial Times to 1970. Bicentennial edition, parts 1 and 2. Washington, D.C.: U.S. Bureau of the Census, 1975.

Howell, C., and W. Thomas. "Escalation and Producer Price Indexes: A Guide for Contracting Parties." Washington, D.C.: Bureau of Labor Statistics, September 1979.

"New Dow Jones Commodity, Spot Price Indexes." *The Wall Street Journal,* January 4, 1982.

PART FIVE

Firms and Consumers

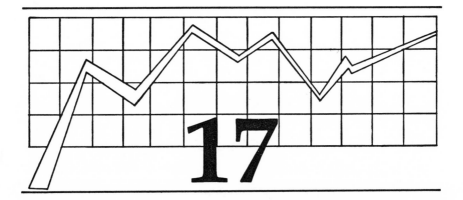

Consumer Confidence

Philip D. Nathanson, Ph.D.
Vice President and Economist
Bankers Trust Company

INTRODUCTION

Attitudes, expectations, and *sentiment* are terms that are frequently used when people refer to the psychological mood of consumers. These are distinct concepts. Attitudes reflect the feelings that consumers have about current conditions, and expectations are attitudes which have been projected to some point in the future. Both attitudes and expectations are subsumed into the larger category called consumer sentiment, or confidence.

Consumer sentiment in the United States has been measured on a regular basis since 1946 by the Survey Research Center of the University of Michigan. Its gauge, called the index of consumer sentiment, is calculated monthly and is recognized by the National Bureau of Economic Research as a leading indicator of economic activity. About 15 years ago, the Conference Board in New York City began compiling its own consumer confidence index, and it too is reported on a monthly cycle. Both indexes receive widespread attention in the media and from economic analysts in the academic world and the private sector.

With consumer sentiment as its focus, this chapter has three objectives. First, the theoretical rationale for consumer sentiment will be outlined. Second, the methodology underlying the construction of the Survey Research Center's and the Conference Board's indexes will be presented along with information about the procedures for dissemination of survey results. Third, the chapter concludes with a discussion of the strengths and weaknesses of these series.

THE ROLE OF CONSUMER SENTIMENT

Prior to World War II, consumer psychology was not generally perceived to be a determinant of variations in consumer spending. John Maynard Keynes, for example, hypothesized that consumer spending was largely a passive factor that was influenced by changes in income. Attitudes of consumers, while both positive and negative for individuals across the population, would likely cancel to zero in the aggregate. Similarly, he suggested that changes in expectations about the future would also average to zero for the whole community.

Intuitively, it is clear that confidence or sentiment is an important causal factor in any one person's spending. If, for example, an individual feels that the government is mismanaging the economy and that this will lead to a recession and possibly cause him to be laid off, he will be less likely to purchase a new car than if he is optimistic about the future. Keynes did not deny this; he merely felt that the optimists would cancel out the pessimists.

After World War II, accumulating empirical evidence indicated otherwise. Pioneering research conducted by Professor George Katona at the University of Michigan indicated that consumers do contribute to economic fluctuations far in excess of the impact of changes in their income resulting from variations in the amount disbursed by business and government sectors of the economy. More specifically, Katona found that measures of consumer sentiment provide advance indications of changes in consumers' spending and saving behavior as well as indicating major changes in expenditures for durable goods.

Keynes was probably correct that consumer sentiment was fairly steady for the general population for much of the period prior to 1936, when *The General Theory* was published. However, the tremendous advances in communications since then—radio, television and a veritable plethora of periodicals—have led to frequent and significant shifts in the population's overall psychological mood. Waves of optimism and pessimism do intervene and modify consumer responses to pure financial variables such as changes in personal income. Consumer psychology does matter. Sometimes it matters quite a bit, as we shall see later in this chapter.

Katona first measured consumer attitudes in 1945 and 1946, finding optimism that extended until 1948. This led to his forecast, subsequently borne out, that consumer spending would remain strong throughout the 1948–49 recession. What is of particular importance is that consumer sentiment is a *net* contributor to the explanation of changes in discretionary consumer spending over time. That is, it provides unique information which is not found in the other variables generally perceived to explain consumer spending, such as income and employment.

MEASURING CONSUMER SENTIMENT

The two most widely followed measures of consumer sentiment are the index of consumer sentiment (ICS), which is calculated by the Survey Research Center at the University of Michigan, and the consumer confidence index (CCI), which is constructed by the Conference Board in New York City.

Index of Consumer Sentiment

The Survey Research Center at the University of Michigan conducted and reported periodic surveys of consumer sentiment between 1946 and 1962. This was done on a quarterly basis between 1962 and December 1977, and every month since January 1978. The ICS is calculated from the response of a survey sample. The five questions which are included in the index are shown in Exhibit 1.

EXHIBIT 1   Index of Consumer Sentiment Questions

1. We are interested in how people are getting along financially these days. Would you say that you and your family are better off or worse off financially than you were a year ago?

2. Now looking ahead—do you think that a year from now you people will be financially better off or worse off or just about the same as now?

3. Now turning to business conditions in the country as a whole—do you think that during the next 12 months we'll have good times financially or bad times or what?

4. Looking ahead, which would you say is more likely—that in the country as a whole, we'll have continuous good times during the next five years or so, or that we will have periods of widespread unemployment or depression, or what?

5. About the big things people buy for their homes—such as furniture, house furnishings, refrigerator, stove, television, and things like that—for people in general, do you think now is a good or a bad time to buy major household items?

Each month, the University of Michigan conducts a representative cross-section sampling of 700 respondent households by telephone. In general, the sampling for a given month takes about four weeks. The interviewers are paid employees who ask the five questions which comprise the index along with other questions which are designed for the business clients who pay for the survey. While these other questions (which could, for example, ask about the respondent's attitude toward a tax cut) do vary, the five questions comprising the ICS never change.

Questions 1 and 5 highlight attitudes, while questions 2, 3, and 4 emphasize expectations. Although question 4 asks about the next five years, the time horizon in general is 12 months. The survey also asks whether this is a "good" or a "bad" time to make a purchase. It does *not* query about the actual intention to buy. Each question is equally weighted in the ICS. All positive replies are given a weight of 2, a neutral response receives a 1 and a negative reply, 0. Therefore, if all respondents in the survey sample gave positive responses to all questions, the ICS would have a value of 200. Alternatively, one can calculate the index level by subtracting the number of negative responses from the number of positive responses and adding the constant 100. The index base period is January 1967 = 100.

Monthly readings of the ICS are not available to the general public on as timely a basis as they are to sponsors of the survey, who purchase annual memberships for a substantial fee. These sponsors receive telephone reports soon after the Survey Research Center compiles the monthly data, and these calls are followed by detailed written analysis. Sentiment data is disseminated to the public by press conference once a quarter only. The Center publishes *Economic Outlook USA* each quarter (annual subscriptions are available at nominal cost), and this periodical contains a graph of the ICS through the most recent quarter and separate graphs for the two current components (survey questions) and the three expectational components. There is also a comparison of the ICS responses by the income levels of respondents, a breakdown which was begun in 1978. Additional survey results, such as the respondents' inflationary expectations, are presented. Generally there are several articles discussing the survey. The *Business Conditions Digest*, published monthly by the Commerce Department and available at many libraries, is a convenient source for obtaining each month's ICS level.

Consumer Confidence Index

The Conference Board has conducted, since 1967, continuous surveying of consumer sentiment and intentions to purchase homes and other durable goods, first bimonthly and then monthly since January 1978.

The consumer confidence index is calculated from the responses to the questions posed in Exhibit 2. These questions are divided into two categories: the *present situation* (questions 1 and 2) and *consumer expectations* (remaining questions). The survey questionnaire also asks about actual intentions to purchase a home, car, and other durable goods. These data are used to calculate a buying plans index. Over time, this index has not predicted or correlated with major changes in consumer spending as well as the CCI.

EXHIBIT 2 Consumer Confidence Index Questions

1. How would you rate the present general business conditions in your area:
   ☐ GOOD.   ☐ NORMAL.   ☐ BAD.
   a. SIX MONTHS from now, do you think they will be:
      ☐ BETTER?   ☐ SAME?   ☐ WORSE?

2. What would you say about available jobs in your area right now?
   ☐ PLENTY.   ☐ NOT SO MANY.   ☐ HARD TO GET.
   a. SIX MONTHS from now do you think there will be:
      ☐ MORE?   ☐ SAME?   ☐ FEWER?

3. How would you guess your total family income to be SIX MONTHS from now?
   ☐ HIGHER.   ☐ SAME.   ☐ LOWER.

For each question, the respondent is given a choice of three reply options. To compute the CCI, neutral responses are discarded, while the positive and negative replies are added together. The positive responses are then expressed as a percentage of this total for each question. Each series, or question, is then adjusted for seasonal variation. The Conference Board has two sets of monthly seasonal adjustment factors. One is for present conditions, and the other for future conditions. In general, consumer attitudes about current conditions are subject more to seasonal vagaries than are expectations about future conditions. Consumers are least optimistic about the present in February, with optimism growing over the spring and summer. On a seasonal basis, the future is perceived most optimistically in April, but this fades until bottoming in November. The total index is an arithmetic average of the seasonally adjusted responses to the five questions, with the index base period arbitrarily selected as 1969–70 = 100. The present-situation and the consumer-expectation questions are also presented as subindexes of the CCI.

Data for the Conference Board survey is collected by National Family Research, a Toledo, Ohio, marketing research firm. The survey universe is comprised of approximately 13,000 households that have consented to answer mailed questionnaires. These households are separated into "balanced panels" of 5,000 families each to be a representative demographic cross section. The panels are rebuilt every two years on the basis of census data. Each month, a survey questionnaire is sent to a different 5,000-person panel. The response rate is about 80 percent.

The monthly results of the CCI are more aggressively marketed to the press than is Michigan's ICS. They are generally reported in *The Wall Street Journal* and other newspapers about a week after each month's survey. Conference Board associates receive the findings by mail. Members of the board's Consumer Research Center receive detailed results with breakdowns geographically and by age and income.

HOW CONSUMER CONFIDENCE RELATES TO THE ECONOMY

As discussed in the previous section, the index of consumer sentiment and the consumer confidence index employ different methodologies. They are derived from different sets of questions and use different arithmetic techniques for their calculation. Furthermore, the latter index is adjusted for seasonal variation, while the former is not. However, because the methodologies are sound in concept and consistent over the life of each series, one would expect the indexes to exhibit similar patterns over time. This has been the case, as illustrated in Exhibit 3.

There are some differences in the timing of the peaks in the indexes, however. In 1972, the ICS topped out about one quarter before the CCI. The peak realized by the ICS in the second quarter of 1977 preceded the top in the CCI by nearly one year. The other major contrast is the relatively greater volatility of the CCI, which is caused by its method of calculation.

The advantages of both indexes as tools for explaining and, in some instances, forecasting consumer behavior become apparent when they are viewed in conjunction with historical data for consumer spending on durable goods and consumer indebtedness. One such relationship is presented in Exhibit 4, where the ICS is plotted against consumer spending on durable goods, a category that includes automobiles, appliances, and furniture. Periods where spending on durable goods turned downward or sluggish, as was the case in the latter three quarters of 1973 and all of 1974, were forecast by a deterioration in consumer psychology which had begun some time earlier.

EXHIBIT 3   Index of Consumer Sentiment versus Consumer Confidence Index

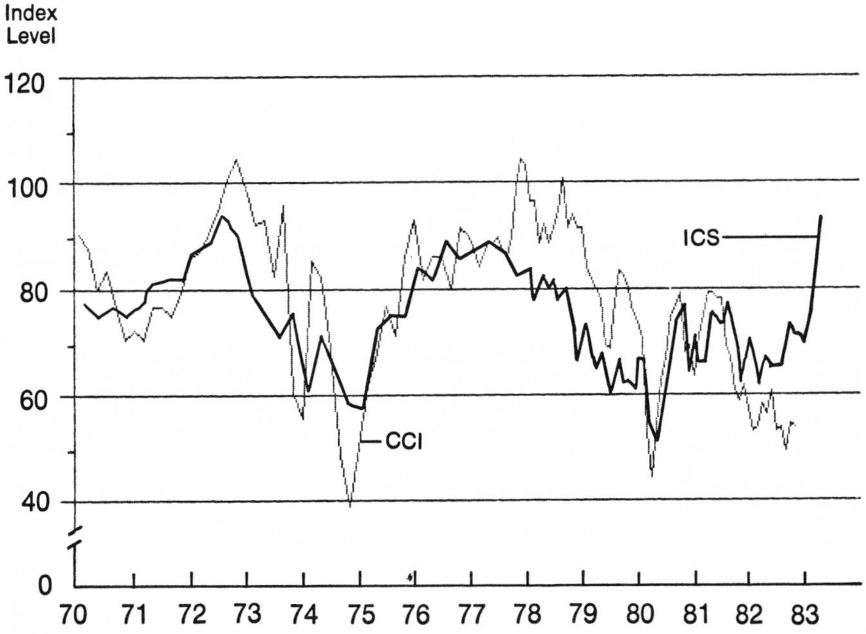

The upswings in consumer spending in 1975 and in the latter half of 1980 coincided with growing optimism. One must be cautioned against trying to correlate month-to-month variations in consumer sentiment with monthly squiggles in durable goods. In general, historical evidence suggests that consumer psychology will deteriorate before consumers rein in spending on durable goods. In contrast, there has been virtually no time lag between rising optimism and purchases.

One must be cognizant of two intervening factors which have, on occasion, distorted the traditional direct relationship between consumer sentiment and expenditures on durable goods. These factors are real interest rates and inflationary expectations. Inflationary expectations do, at some point, depress consumer psychology. The reason is that consumers know that periods of high inflation in the United States have eventually been followed by recessions or by more restrictive government growth policies. Hence, when inflation is accelerating unusually fast, consumer psychology tends to deteriorate. At the same time, one would expect spending on durable goods to increase, at least for a while. This occurs as consumers buy now to beat future price increases. Thus,

EXHIBIT 4   Index of Consumer Sentiment versus Consumer Expenditures on Durable Goods ($ billions, SA)

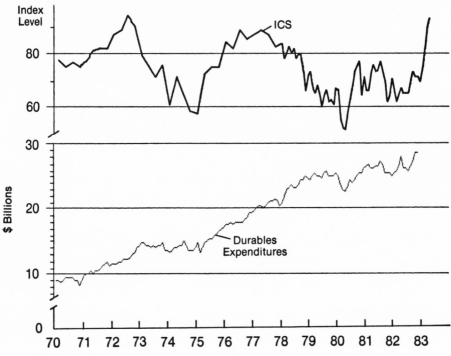

during periods of rapid inflation, the ICS could be falling as spending on durables rises. This was the case from late 1976 until the latter part of 1979. Over that period, the decline in the ICS was accompanied by a rising trend in spending on durable goods.

Real interest rates, which are defined as nominal (or market) interest rates minus the expected rate of inflation, can also distort or accentuate the traditional relationship between consumer psychology and spending. If the rate of expected inflation is rising faster than the cost of a car loan, then the consumer's real interest rate is falling. One would expect that rising inflationary expectations and rising nominal interest rates would depress the ICS readings, as was the case in 1978 and 1979. However, as inflationary expectations rose faster than nominal interest rates, the real rate of interest fell. And that tended to stimulate spending by consumers even as their psychology deteriorated over this period.

Thus, it is essential to remember that changes in inflationary psychology and real interest rates can temporarily mitigate the link between the ICS and spending, as explained above. Of course, in a period when inflationary expectations are dormant or falling and real interest rates are rising or high, then one would expect consumer spending to be somewhat more subdued than their psychology might otherwise suggest.

The Conference Board's CCI has been less distorted by sharp changes in inflationary expectations or real interest rates than has the ICS, and this can be seen in Exhibit 5. In this graph, domestic new car sales have

EXHIBIT 5 Consumer Confidence Index versus Domestic New Car Sales (millions of units, SAAR)

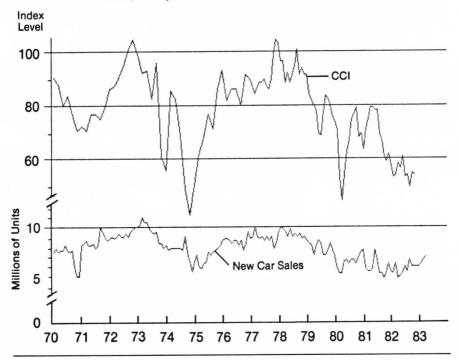

been plotted against the CCI, revealing a quite close relationship. One should also note that the CCI remained high throughout 1978, while the ICS (see Exhibit 3) was falling. It is probable that the construction of the survey questions and the way they capture inflation leads to this result.

The ICS asks survey respondents about conditions one to five years ahead, while the CCI focuses on the next six months. Consumers probably reckon that they can keep ahead of inflation for six months (hence a higher reading on the CCI), while they are not so sure about one to five years ahead (thus a lower reading on the ICS).

Another close relationship of the two indexes exists between sentiment and consumer installment debt, and this is illustrated in Exhibit 6. Consumer installment shows the net change from the preceding month, and this is defined as the change in net extensions of debt minus the

EXHIBIT 6   Index of Consumer Sentiment and Consumer Confidence Index versus Monthly Net Change in Consumer Installment Debt ($ billions, SA)

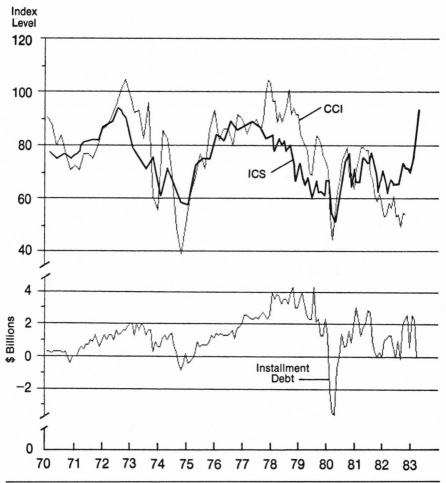

change in liquidations of existing debt. It is interesting to note that both the ICS and the CCI peaked in late 1972, well before the peak in consumer debt nearly one year later. Another top in consumer debt late in 1979 again lagged the ICS by about 12 months. The steep drop in both consumer confidence and debt in the second quarter of 1980 reflected the uncertainty associated with the imposition of credit controls. Since 1980, the variations in both sentiment indexes, particularly the ICS, have tracked fairly closely with movements in consumer debt.

Based on the evidence since 1970, it seems that in periods where secular inflation is rising, changes in consumer confidence (especially the ICS) lead similar changes in consumer debt by a significant amount of time. In contrast, where secular inflation seems to be falling (as in the decade of the 1980s), the relationship is coincidental.

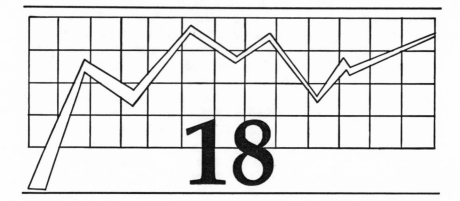

Productivity Measures

Elliot S. Grossman, Ph.D.
Associate Professor of Economics
Lubin Graduate School of Business
Pace University

Measures of productivity are measures of efficiency in the use of resources. Resources are used more efficiently when the economy is able to produce more output for the same amount of inputs (alternatively, producing the same amount of output with less inputs). Over the postwar period (1948–82), real output in the American economy rose at an annual rate of 3.2 percent. During this same period, labor input increased at a 0.8 percent rate, and capital at 3.1 percent. Thus, output increased more than the increase in the use of inputs—i.e., the U.S. economy has experienced a gain in productive efficiency.[1]

Productivity leads to increases in our material well-being, higher real wages, and downward pressures on costs and prices, and it enhances the competitive position of the U.S. economy. For these and other reasons, government and industry leaders have a strong interest in produc-

---

[1] For a review of the concept and history of productivity measures, see John W. Kendrick and Elliot S. Grossman, *Productivity in the United States: Trends and Cycles* (Baltimore, Md.: The Johns Hopkins University Press, 1980).

tivity at the economywide or sector level as well as at the industry level. However, measures of productivity are only available at the sector and broad industry levels; detailed industry and company-level productivity measures are not available and must be developed by parties interested in such measures.

Productivity is also a cyclical indicator in addition to a secular indicator as discussed above. Typically, gains in productivity slow in momentum or even decline prior to the onset of a recession. Then, before the economy bottoms out, productivity begins to rise. This leading indicator pattern is a result of the interaction between productivity, costs, profits, and prices. As the economy overheats, cost pressures rise faster than the ability of business to translate them into higher prices. Productivity falls as output growth decelerates or declines and businesses continue with the same size labor force, further increasing cost pressures. Unit profits subsequently fall, discouraging capital investment and plans for expansion.

After the recession has had a chance to play its course, businesses have had a chance to decrease the size of their labor forces, and other cost pressures have declined. With the smaller work force, productivity gains are again being experienced, and unit profits start to rise. This increase in unit profits encourages business to resume their capital and other expansion plans, thereby helping to set the stage for the coming economic recovery.

As of this writing, there are only two sources of productivity measures that are available on a continuous and consistent basis, the Bureau of Labor Statistics (BLS) of the U.S. Department of Labor, and the American Productivity Center (APC) of Houston, Texas. The BLS has been publishing, on a quarterly basis, measures of labor productivity (output per unit of labor input) for the major sectors since 1959. On an annual basis, the BLS publishes labor productivity measures for selected industries. As of 1983, the BLS has added annual measures of multifactor productivity (also known as total-factor productivity) for the major sectors.[2]

Since 1980, the APC has been publishing quarterly measures of labor and total-factor productivity for seven major sectors, and annually for 31 industry segments including the 20-two digit SIC code manufacturing industries.[3] Both the BLS and the APC measures generally extend from 1948 through the current period.

---

[2] *Productivity and Costs* (Bureau of Labor Statistics news release); Bureau of Labor Statistics, *Productivity Measures for Selected Industries, 1954–81*, Bulletin 2155, December 1982. See news release USDL83–153, April 6, 1983, on the BLS' first measures of multifactor productivity.

[3] *Multiple Input Productivity Indexes* (Houston, Tex.: American Productivity Center, published quarterly).

THE BLS MEASURE OF LABOR PRODUCTIVITY

The BLS measures labor productivity for five sectors and two subsectors: business economy, farm, nonfarm, nonfinancial corporations, manufacturing, and nondurable and durable manufacturing.[4]

Labor productivity is simply the ratio of output, measured in real (constant-dollar) terms, to labor input, measured in hours *paid*[5] for all persons:

$$\text{Labor productivity} = \text{Output/Hours paid}$$

Both output and hours are added up directly from the detailed industry estimates to the broadest sectors. That is, output and labor hours are direct aggregates and are not weighted. Thus, shifts among industry segments within sectors and among labor characteristics will affect the measured growth rate of productivity over time.[6]

Productivity and Costs Release

The quarterly report on labor productivity includes indexes on output, hours of all persons, compensation per hour, real compensation per

---

[4] According to the BLS technical notes published in their *Productivity and Costs* news release:

> Business sector output is equal to gross national product less the rest-of-the-world sector, general government, output of paid employees of private households and nonprofit institutions, rental value of owner-occupied dwellings, and the statistical discrepancy in computing the national income accounts. Corresponding exclusions are also made in labor inputs. Business output has accounted for about 77 percent of gross national product in recent years.
>
> Total manufacturing measures are computed by summing series prepared for the durable and nondurable goods sectors.
>
> The durable sector includes the following 2-digit SIC industries: primary metal; fabricated metal products; nonelectrical machinery; electrical machinery; transportation equipment; instruments; lumber and lumber products; furniture and fixtures; stone, clay, and glass products; and miscellaneous manufactures. The nondurable sector includes the following 2-digit SIC industries: textile mill products, apparel products, leather and leather products, printing and publishing, chemicals and chemical products, petroleum products, rubber and plastic products, foods, and tobacco products.
>
> Manufacturing output has accounted for about 24 percent of gross national product in recent years.
>
> Nonfinancial corporate output is equal to gross national product less the rest-of-the-world sector, general government, unincorporated business, output of paid employees of private households and nonprofit institutions, rental value of owner-occupied dwellings, the output of corporations engaged in banking, finance, stock and commodity trading, and credit and insurance agencies, and the statistical discrepancy in computing the national income accounts. Nonfinancial corporate output has accounted for about 59 percent of gross national product in recent years.

[5] For a discussion of hours paid versus worked, see Elliot S. Grossman and George E. Sadler, "Establishment Data and Productivity Measures," National Council on Employment Policy, Conference Proceedings, June 17, 1982.

[6] Ibid.

hour, unit labor cost, unit nonlabor payments, and the implicit price deflator (see Exhibit 1). In addition, for nonfinancial corporations, the BLS reports on total unit cost and unit profits (see Exhibit 2).

Measures of unit costs are particularly useful, as they highlight the impact of rising input prices and how gains in productivity can offset these cost pressures, thereby reducing inflation. Unit costs are simply the ratio of input prices to output per unit of that input. In the case of unit labor costs:

Unit labor costs = Hourly compensation/Output per unit of labor

For example, Exhibit 3 presents the growth rates between 1958 and 1982 for selected items experienced by nonfinancial corporations. The 4.3 percent increase in prices is almost equal to the increase in unit labor costs. These growth rates are almost the same, since increases in prices must by definition equal the growth in unit labor costs and unit profits (since labor costs plus profits equal total factor costs). Also, labor costs represent about 67 percent of total input costs, thereby accounting for the bulk of cost increases. Further, it is clear that the 2 percent rise in productivity has lowered the cost pressures of rising labor compensation. The information on unit nonlabor costs and unit profits allows for a more complete analysis of the components of rising prices.[7]

Labor Productivity in Selected Industries

The BLS also publishes measures of labor productivity in selected industries.[8] For most of these industries, information is provided on real output and employee hours for all employees, production workers, and nonproduction workers since 1958. The BLS Bulletin 2155 also includes charts on output per employee, output, and employee hours for each of the industries reported. Exhibit 4 reproduces the table provided in the BLS news release, indicating the level of detail of these selected industry reports.

International Comparisons of Manufacturing Productivity

The BLS has reported annually, beginning with 1950, on manufacturing labor productivity, hourly compensation, unit labor costs, and re-

---

[7] See Kendrick and Grossman, *Productivity*, especially the analysis in Chapter 4 and Tables 4–2 and 4–3.

[8] BLS Bulletin 2155, *Productivity Measures*; see also news release USDL81–358, July 21, 1981.

EXHIBIT 1 BLS Productivity and Costs Release:* Business Sector, All Persons (productivity, hourly compensation, unit labor cost, and prices, seasonally adjusted)

Year and Quarter		Output per Hour of All Persons	Output	Hours of All Persons	Compensation per Hour	Real Compensation per Hour	Unit Labor Cost	Unit Nonlabor Payments	Implicit Price Deflator
				Indexes 1977 = 100					
1982	I	100.1	106.3	106.2	151.1	96.8	150.9	136.3	145.9
	II	100.4	106.4	106.0	153.5	97.1	152.9	137.0	147.5
	III	101.3	106.7	105.3	155.9	96.7	153.8	139.9	149.1
	IV	102.0	105.9	103.9	158.0	97.6	154.9	140.7	150.1
Annual		101.0	106.4	105.4	154.5	97.0	153.1	138.5	148.1
1983	I	102.6	107.1	104.5	159.8	98.8	155.8	145.3R†	152.2R
				Percent change from previous quarter at annual rate					
1982	I	-0.8	-5.4	-4.6	7.6	4.5	8.5	-5.9	3.7
	II	1.3	0.6	-0.7	6.7	1.3	5.3	2.1	4.3
	III	3.7	1.1	-2.5	6.3	-1.4	2.4	8.9	4.4
	IV	2.6	-3.0	-5.5	5.5	3.5	2.9	2.3	2.7
Annual		0.3	-2.3	-2.6	7.2	1.0	7.0	2.4	5.5
1983	I	2.2	4.7R	2.4R	4.6R	5.0R	2.3R	13.6R	5.8R
				Percent change from corresponding quarter of previous year					
1982	I	-0.6	-2.6	-1.9	7.9	0.2	8.6	3.5	6.9
	II	-0.3	-2.4	-2.1	7.7	0.8	8.0	2.7	6.3
	III	0.3	-2.6	-2.9	7.0	1.1	6.7	1.8	5.1
	IV	1.7	-1.7	-3.3	6.5	1.9	4.7	1.7	3.8
Annual		0.3	-2.3	-2.6	7.2	1.0	7.0	2.4	5.5
1983	I	2.5	0.8	-1.6	5.8	2.1	3.2R	6.6R	4.3

* May 26, 1983.
† R = Revised.
Source: Bureau of Labor Statistics.

EXHIBIT 2 **BLS Productivity and Costs Release:* Nonfinancial Corporations** (productivity, hourly compensation, unit labor cost, unit profits, and prices, seasonally adjusted)

Year and Quarter	Output per All-Employee Hour	Output	Employee Hours	Hourly Compensation	Real Hourly Compensation	Unit Labor Cost	Unit Nonlabor Cost	Total Unit Cost	Unit Profits	Implicit Price Deflator
	Indexes 1977 = 100									
1982 I	101.8	107.9	106.0	150.9	96.7	148.3	161.8	151.8	86.1	144.3
II	102.4	107.8	105.2	153.2	96.9	149.5	166.0	153.8	82.3	145.6
III	103.6	108.0	104.2	155.4	96.4	150.0	168.3	154.8	89.6	147.3
IV	103.7	106.2	102.4	157.4	97.2	151.8	172.9	157.3	83.1	148.8
Annual	102.9	107.5	104.5	154.2	96.8	149.9	167.2	154.4	85.3	146.5
1983 I	104.9P†	107.9P	102.8P	159.5P	98.6P	152.1P	172.1P	157.3P	98.3P	150.5P
	Percent change from previous quarter at annual rate									
1982 I	0.4	-5.2	-5.6	8.6	5.4	8.1	5.7	7.4	-39.4	3.0
II	2.7	-0.4	-3.0	6.2	0.9	3.4	10.7	5.4	-16.7	3.8
III	4.6	0.6	-3.8	5.9	-1.8	1.2	5.9	2.5	40.8	4.7
IV	0.4	-6.3	-6.7	5.4	3.3	5.0	11.4	6.8	-25.9	4.2
Annual	0.8	-2.9	-3.7	7.4	1.2	6.6	10.5	7.7	-16.0	5.7
1983 I	4.6P	6.3P	1.6P	5.4P	5.8P	0.8P	-2.0P	0.0P	95.4P	4.7P
	Percent change from corresponding quarter of previous year									
1982 I	-0.5	-2.7	-2.2	8.1	0.4	8.6	12.8	9.7	-17.8	7.3
II	0.2	-3.0	-3.2	7.9	1.0	7.6	10.9	8.5	-16.7	6.4
III	1.3	-3.2	-4.4	7.2	1.4	5.8	9.9	7.0	-14.8	5.1
IV	2.0	-2.9	-4.8	6.5	1.9	4.4	8.4	5.5	-14.8	3.9
Annual	0.8	-2.9	-3.7	7.4	1.2	6.6	10.5	7.7	-16.0	5.7
1983 I	3.1P	-0.1P	-3.0P	5.7P	2.0P	2.6P	6.4P	3.6P	14.1P	4.3P

* May 26, 1983.
† P = Preliminary.
Source: Bureau of Labor Statistics.

EXHIBIT 3   Nonfinancial Corporations: 1958–1982
Growth Rates, Selected Items

Item	Rate of Growth
Hourly compensation	6.5%
Output per hours of all employees	2.0
Unit labor costs	4.4
Implicit price deflator	4.3

Source: U.S. Department of Labor, Bureau of Labor Statistics.

EXHIBIT 4   BLS Selected Industries Release: Indexes of Output per Employee Hour[1] in Selected Industries, 1976–1982, and Percent Changes 1981–1982 (1977 = 100)

SIC code	Industry	1976	1977	1978	1979	1980	1981	1982[2]	Percent change 1981–82
	Mining								
1011	Iron mining, crude ore	113.5	100.0	116.8	125.5	129.0	139.0	119.8	-13.8
1011	Iron mining, usable ore	115.9	100.0	119.2	125.6	127.5	136.8	119.3	-12.8
1021	Copper mining, crude ore	99.2	100.0	109.6	103.8	100.3	101.5	103.1	1.6
1021	Copper mining, recoverable metal	94.7	100.0	107.6	97.8	91.3	97.2	111.1	14.3
111,121	Coal mining	103.1	100.0	106.4	99.4	112.5	122.2	115.9	-5.2
121	Bituminous coal and lignite mining	103.0	100.0	106.7	99.6	112.6	122.7	116.9	-4.7
14	Nonmetallic minerals, except fuels	96.2	100.0	104.6	102.4	96.2	96.0	88.8	-7.5
142	Crushed and broken stone	93.7	100.0	109.0	108.4	103.3	100.7	96.5	-4.2
	Manufacturing								
2026	Fluid milk	99.5	100.0	108.0	116.3	124.8	129.3	131.3	1.5
203	Preserved fruits and vegetables	100.1	100.0	104.4	99.3	101.2	99.6	3/	3/
2033	Canned fruits and vegetables	102.3	100.0	103.7	101.4	100.6	99.7	3/	3/
204	Grain mill products	91.1	100.0	100.4	102.2	107.5	112.9	3/	3/
2041	Flour and other grain mill products	85.1	100.0	101.5	98.5	99.8	98.8	102.8	4.0
2043	Cereal breakfast foods	100.0	100.0	101.7	107.6	106.5	110.0	3/	3/
2044	Rice milling	88.7	100.0	92.7	96.3	111.8	117.9	3/	3/
2045	Blended and prepared flour	110.9	100.0	92.5	91.0	104.8	104.6	3/	3/
2046	Wet corn milling	83.2	100.0	102.0	110.8	129.2	143.8	3/	3/
2047,48	Prepared feeds for animals and fowls	90.1	100.0	100.8	102.0	106.2	112.6	3/	3/
205	Bakery products	93.9	100.0	97.2	94.1	92.3	94.3	91.7	-2.8
2061,62,63	Sugar	95.8	100.0	101.0	109.1	109.1	111.2	110.4	-0.7
2061,62	Raw and refined cane sugar	92.5	100.0	100.7	107.3	107.8	111.1	108.7	-2.2
2063	Beet sugar	101.7	100.0	101.2	110.9	111.7	111.4	113.1	1.5

lated measures for some 11 industrialized countries.[9] Unit labor costs are reported on both a national currency basis and a U.S. dollar basis after adjustment for changes in exchange rates. Exhibits 5, 6, and 7 present labor productivity and unit labor costs for the 11 countries as reported by the BLS.

BLS Measure of Multifactor Productivity

Labor productivity, the traditional measure of productivity as published by the BLS, is a partial productivity measure.[10] It has long been

---

[9] BLS, news release USDL83–248, May 26, 1983.

[10] See the discussion in Grossman and Sadler, "Establishment Data."

EXHIBIT 5   BLS International Comparisons Release: Output per Hour, Manufacturing (average annual rates of change 11 countries, 1960–1982)

COUNTRY	1960-82 (2)	1960-70	1970-82 (2)	1960-73	1973-82 (2)	1979-80	1980-81	1981-82
			OUTPUT PER HOUR					
UNITED STATES	2.6	2.9	2.1	3.0	1.5	0.2	2.9	-1.0
CANADA	3.5	4.3	2.2	4.5	1.4	-2.3	.8	-2.8
JAPAN	8.9	10.5	6.7	10.7	6.2	6.8	.8	1.0
BELGIUM	7.2	6.2	6.9	7.0	6.1	3.2	5.6	NA
DENMARK	5.9	6.1	5.0	6.4	4.0	1.4	5.6	3.0
FRANCE	5.4	6.1	4.7	6.0	4.6	1.6	1.6	6.9
GERMANY	5.1	5.8	4.7	5.5	4.2	1.4	2.7	1.7
ITALY	5.7	7.1	4.4	6.9	3.7	5.8	3.5	1.3
NETHERLANDS	7.1	7.1	6.0	7.6	5.1	2.1	2.6	NA
SWEDEN	4.8	6.9	2.8	6.7	2.2	1.2	.1	3.0
UNITED KINGDOM	3.5	4.3	2.8	4.3	2.5	1.2	5.7	3.4
			OUTPUT					
UNITED STATES	3.3	5.3	2.4	4.7	1.5	-4.3	2.3	-8.8
CANADA	4.5	6.7	2.6	6.3	1.3	-2.9	2.1	-12.3
JAPAN	9.7	13.4	6.2	13.0	6.0	9.4	1.0	.3
BELGIUM	5.0	6.0	2.5	6.5	1.1	-1.4	-2.5	NA
DENMARK	3.8	5.5	2.4	5.2	1.8	.0	.5	2.6
FRANCE	5.0	6.6	2.9	6.6	1.9	-.1	-2.7	-.1
GERMANY	3.6	5.4	1.8	5.2	1.5	.5	-1.4	-2.7
ITALY	5.2	7.3	3.5	6.8	3.0	6.3	-.9	-1.8
NETHERLANDS	4.7	6.6	2.3	6.4	1.8	1.7	-.9	NA
SWEDEN	3.0	5.7	.5	5.1	-.4	.0	-3.6	-.1
UNITED KINGDOM	1.3	3.3	-.8	3.0	-2.0	-9.1	-6.4	-.8

EXHIBIT 6   BLS International Comparisons Release: Unit Labor Costs, Manufacturing (average annual rates of change 11 countries, 1960–1982)

COUNTRY	1960-82 (2)	1960-70	1970-82 (2)	1960-73	1973-82 (2)	1979-80	1980-81	1981-82
		UNIT LABOR COSTS:	NATIONAL CURRENCY BASIS					
UNITED STATES	4.4	1.5	6.8	1.9	7.9	11.6	7.2	9.6
CANADA	5.1	1.3	8.7	1.8	9.5	12.6	10.3	14.2
JAPAN	5.0	2.7	5.3	3.5	2.6	-.2	6.1	2.4
BELGIUM	5.1	3.4	6.6	3.5	5.6	6.2	2.4	NA
DENMARK	6.8	4.6	8.2	5.1	7.8	9.4	3.5	7.2
FRANCE	6.3	2.4	9.7	3.1	9.9	12.6	13.2	10.8
GERMANY	4.7	2.7	5.1	3.7	4.6	7.3	4.6	3.6
ITALY	10.2	3.7	15.3	5.1	15.4	12.4	18.0	16.5
NETHERLANDS	5.4	4.6	5.7	4.8	4.3	2.8	2.1	NA
SWEDEN	6.8	2.9	10.1	3.5	10.1	9.8	12.5	3.7
UNITED KINGDOM	9.5	2.8	15.0	4.1	15.7	22.9	9.9	5.4
		UNIT LABOR COSTS:	U.S. DOLLAR BASIS					
UNITED STATES	4.4	1.5	6.8	1.9	7.9	11.6	7.2	9.6
CANADA	4.6	.7	6.7	1.9	6.5	12.8	7.5	10.9
JAPAN	7.8	2.8	9.4	4.9	6.0	-3.5	8.8	-9.5
BELGIUM	7.8	3.4	11.2	4.6	8.6	6.7	-19.3	NA
DENMARK	7.5	3.6	8.8	5.0	5.5	2.2	-18.0	-8.8
FRANCE	6.3	1.7	9.6	2.8	7.3	13.5	-11.6	-8.9
GERMANY	8.8	3.4	10.2	6.1	7.4	8.3	-15.8	-3.8
ITALY	7.4	3.6	8.5	5.4	6.8	9.2	-10.8	-2.6
NETHERLANDS	8.7	4.8	11.0	6.1	7.9	3.9	-18.5	NA
SWEDEN	7.4	2.9	9.7	4.2	7.2	11.3	-5.5	-16.9
UNITED KINGDOM	7.3	1.0	12.4	2.6	13.5	34.6	-4.4	-9.0

NA=NOT AVAILABLE
(1) RATES OF CHANGE COMPUTED FROM THE LEAST SQUARES TREND OF THE LOGARITHMS OF THE INDEX NUMBERS.
(2) FOR BELGIUM AND THE NETHERLANDS, DATA RELATE TO PERIOD ENDING 1981 ONLY.
(3) ADJUSTED TO INCLUDE CHANGES IN EMPLOYMENT TAXES THAT ARE NOT COMPENSATION TO EMPLOYEES, BUT ARE LABOR COSTS TO EMPLOYERS (FOR FRANCE, SWEDEN, AND THE UNITED KINGDOM).

NOTE: DATA RELATE TO ALL EMPLOYED PERSONS IN THE UNITED STATES AND CANADA; ALL EMPLOYEES IN THE OTHER COUNTRIES.

SOURCE: U.S. DEPARTMENT OF LABOR, BUREAU OF LABOR STATISTICS

EXHIBIT 7   BLS International Comparisons Release: Output per Hour in Manufacturing, 11 Countries, 1950–1982 (indexes: 1977 = 100)

YEAR (1)	UNITED STATES	CANADA	JAPAN	BEL-GIUM	DEN-MARK	FRANCE	GERMANY	ITALY	NETHER-LANDS	SWEDEN	UNITED KINGDOM
1950	49.4	34.7	9.8		27.5	25.3	22.0	20.9	20.0	30.7	44.8
1951	51.1	36.1	11.2		27.8	26.7	22.7	23.3	20.7	31.6	44.9
1952	52.0	37.0	11.8		27.6	27.5	24.8	24.3	21.2	31.5	43.1
1953	52.9	38.3	13.4		28.0	29.0	26.6	25.5	22.9	33.2	45.2
1954	53.7	40.0	14.3		29.2	29.8	27.7	26.8	23.7	33.2	46.7
1955	56.4	42.6	15.1		29.9	31.2	29.5	29.2	25.0	33.6	48.3
1956	56.0	44.4	16.0		30.8	33.7	30.2	30.8	26.5	35.7	48.3
1957	57.1	44.7	17.5		31.9	34.2	32.9	31.4	27.5	37.5	49.5
1958	56.9	46.2	16.4		33.0	35.4	34.5	31.9	28.1	39.2	50.5
1959	59.6	48.7	19.1		35.3	37.7	37.3	34.4	30.2	41.6	52.5
1960	60.0	50.4	22.0	32.2	36.4	39.8	40.0	36.5	31.7	43.0	55.6
1961	61.6	53.1	24.9	32.7	38.4	41.6	42.1	39.5	33.4	45.0	56.1
1962	64.3	55.9	26.0	35.0	40.4	43.5	44.8	43.7	34.5	48.3	57.5
1963	68.9	58.0	28.1	36.1	41.8	45.9	46.8	44.9	35.7	51.1	60.6
1964	72.3	60.6	31.8	38.3	45.1	48.4	50.5	47.6	38.9	55.4	64.9
1965	74.5	62.9	33.1	39.8	47.4	51.2	53.8	52.9	41.3	59.4	67.0
1966	75.3	65.1	36.5	42.6	49.8	54.8	55.7	56.4	44.0	61.8	69.5
1967	75.3	67.1	41.9	45.3	54.2	57.8	59.4	59.7	47.1	66.9	72.7
1968	78.0	71.7	47.1	49.2	59.0	64.4	63.4	64.5	52.8	73.1	78.0
1969	79.3	75.9	54.5	53.5	61.4	66.7	67.1	69.4	57.7	78.6	79.9
1970	79.1	77.0	61.4	58.8	65.3	70.1	68.2	72.7	63.0	82.0	80.5
1971	83.9	82.5	65.3	62.5	69.3	73.8	71.0	74.9	67.3	86.2	83.7
1972	88.2	86.2	72.7	69.6	75.1	78.2	75.7	81.1	72.6	90.8	90.2
1973	93.0	91.6	80.2	77.0	82.8	82.4	80.1	90.9	80.1	97.5	95.8
1974	90.8	93.6	82.1	81.5	85.5	85.3	84.5	95.3	86.7	100.9	96.5
1975	93.4	91.2	85.3	85.1	94.4	87.9	89.0	91.1	85.1	100.5	94.6
1976	97.5	96.1	93.3	93.9	98.0	95.1	95.3	98.9	96.1	101.6	98.4
1977	100.0	100.0	100.0	100.0	100.0	100.0	100.0	100.0	100.0	100.0	100.0
1978	100.8	101.7	107.9	105.0	102.4	105.7	103.3	103.0	106.6	104.3	103.3
1979	101.5	104.7	117.4	111.8	108.3	110.7	108.3	110.5	111.9	113.0	106.8
1980	101.7	102.3	125.4	115.4	109.8	112.6	109.8	116.9	114.2	114.4	108.1
1981	104.6	103.1	126.3	121.8	116.0	114.4	112.8	121.0	117.2	114.5	114.2
1982	103.6	100.3	127.6		119.5	122.3	114.7	122.6		117.9	118.2

(1) PRELIMINARY ESTIMATES FOR LATEST YEAR.

NOTE: THE DATA RELATE TO ALL EMPLOYED PERSONS (WAGE AND SALARY EARNERS, THE SELF-EMPLOYED, AND UNPAID FAMILY WORKERS) IN THE UNITED STATES AND CANADA, AND ALL EMPLOYEES (WAGE AND SALARY EARNERS) IN THE OTHER COUNTRIES.

SOURCE: U.S. DEPARTMENT OF LABOR, BUREAU OF LABOR STATISTICS

recognized by experts such as John Kendrick, Ed Denison, Dale Jorgenson, and Zvi Griliches[11] that capital as well as labor contribute to gains in productivity. In 1979, the Rees Commission, under the auspices of the National Academy of Sciences,[12] recommended to the BLS that they experiment with multifactor (i.e., total factor) productivity measures. Their reasoning is based on the fact that partial productivity measures may ignore the contribution of other factors, especially capital. To quote Rees:

> Measures of multifactor productivity show changes in the use of all measured inputs per unit of output. Measures of output per worker hour may increase only because inputs of capital or intermediate goods have been substituted for labor inputs. Thus, measures of productivity, which are more complete measures of changes in productive efficiency, generally rise less rapidly than measures of labor productivity.[13]

[11] See the bibliography in Kendrick and Grossman, *Productivity,* for references.

[12] A. Rees, "The Measurement and Interpretation of Productivity," National Academy of Sciences, 1979; and, A. Rees, "Improving the Concepts and Techniques of Productivity Measurement," *Monthly Labor Review,* U.S. Department of Labor, Bureau of Labor Statistics, September 1979, pp. 23–27.

[13] Rees, "Improving the Concepts," p. 25.

The BLS has long recognized the role of other factors, including capital. To quote their *Productivity and Costs* technical note:

> Although the productivity measures relate output to the hours of all persons engaged in each sector, they do not measure the specific contributions of labor, capital, or any single factor of production. Rather, they reflect the joint effects of many influences, including new technology, capital investment, the level of output, capacity utilization, energy use, and managerial skill, as well as the skills and efforts of the work force.

In April 1983, the BLS released their first estimates of multifactor productivity for the private business, nonfarm, and manufacturing (total, durable, and nondurable) sectors, covering the 1948–81 period (see Exhibit 8). As of this writing, they plan to update these annual series about September of each year.

EXHIBIT 8 BLS Multifactor Productivity Release: Private Business Sector, 1948–1982

Year	Productivity			Output 3/	Inputs			Capital per hour of all persons
	Output per hour of all persons	Output per unit of capital	Multifactor productivity 2/		Hours of all persons 4/	Capital services 5/	Combined units of labor and capital inputs 6/	
				Indexes 1977=100				
1948	45.3	99.0	60.0	36.8	81.3	37.2	61.3	45.7
1949	46.0	93.5	59.3	36.1	78.6	38.6	60.9	49.2
1950	49.7	98.6	63.6	39.5	79.5	40.1	62.1	50.4
1951	51.2	100.1	65.1	41.8	81.8	41.8	64.3	51.1
1952	52.9	99.3	66.3	43.2	81.8	43.5	65.2	53.2
1953	54.6	100.6	68.0	45.1	82.6	44.9	66.4	54.5
1954	55.6	96.2	67.7	44.3	79.8	46.1	65.5	57.7
1955	57.8	100.9	70.7	47.9	82.9	47.5	67.8	57.3
1956	58.5	100.0	70.9	49.2	84.2	49.2	69.4	58.5
1957	60.0	97.9	71.6	49.7	82.9	50.7	69.4	61.2
1958	61.8	94.3	72.0	48.9	79.0	51.9	67.9	65.6
1959	63.9	99.3	74.9	52.5	82.1	52.9	70.0	64.4
1960	64.8	98.5	75.4	53.3	82.2	54.1	70.7	65.8
1961	67.0	98.0	76.9	54.2	80.9	55.3	70.5	68.4
1962	69.6	101.2	79.7	57.2	82.2	56.6	71.8	66.8
1963	72.2	102.6	82.0	59.7	82.7	58.2	72.9	70.4
1964	75.3	105.2	84.9	63.3	84.0	60.2	74.5	71.6
1965	78.0	107.8	87.6	67.6	86.7	62.7	77.2	72.4
1966	80.4	108.0	89.3	71.3	88.7	66.0	79.9	74.5
1967	82.3	104.9	89.6	72.9	88.6	69.5	81.4	78.5
1968	85.1	105.5	91.7	76.7	90.1	72.7	83.7	80.7
1969	85.3	103.7	91.2	78.9	92.5	76.1	86.5	82.3
1970	86.1	98.5	90.2	78.3	90.9	79.4	86.8	87.4
1971	89.2	98.1	92.2	80.6	90.4	82.2	87.5	91.0
1972	92.3	101.0	95.2	86.0	93.2	85.2	90.4	91.5
1973	94.7	103.0	97.5	91.8	96.9	89.1	94.1	92.0
1974	92.4	96.5	93.8	89.9	97.2	93.1	95.8	95.8
1975	94.5	92.0	93.6	88.0	93.1	95.7	94.0	102.8
1976	97.6	96.1	97.1	93.7	95.9	97.5	96.5	101.6
1977	100.0	100.0	100.0	100.0	100.0	100.0	100.0	100.0
1978	100.6	101.8	101.0	105.5	104.9	103.6	104.4	98.8
1979	'99.3	100.3	99.7	107.9	108.6	107.5	108.2	99.0
1980	98.8	95.5	97.7	106.4	107.7	111.4	108.9	103.4
1981	101.2	95.8	99.3	109.8	108.4	114.6	110.5	105.7
1982	101.1	90.9	97.4	106.6	105.4	117.3	109.4	111.3

See footnotes following table 6.

EXHIBIT 9   Private Business Economy: Growth Rates of Selected Items

	Average Annual Rate of Growth		
	1948–81	1948–73	1973–81
Multifactor productivity	1.5%	2.0%	0.1%
Labor productivity	2.4	3.0	0.8
Output	3.3	3.7	2.2
Labor hours, all persons	0.9	0.7	1.4
Capital services	3.5	3.6	3.2
Combined inputs	1.8	1.7	2.0

Source: U.S. Department of Labor, Bureau of Labor Statistics.

Exhibit 9 illustrates the difference in multifactor and labor productivity growth rates. Over the 1948–81 period and the two subperiods, labor productivity recorded higher growth rates than multifactor productivity. A look at the growth rates of output and the inputs will indicate why it is so. When output went up 3.3 percent (1948–81), a labor input went up to 0.9 percent, for a measured increase in productivity of 2.4 percent. However, when the increased use of capital services is properly included in the measure, productivity now so measured increases at a lesser rate of 1.5 percent.

The method of calculating multifactor productivity differs from labor productivity in two regards. First, capital services is the total of the stock of 1972 constant-dollar equipment, structures, land, and inventories, times their respective rental prices. The measures of the stock of plant and equipment are net of depreciation, where the estimates of depreciation are based on the average lifetimes and ages, as well as deterioration rates, of various classes of plant and equipment. Thus, capital services is a weighted total, not a direct aggregate as is labor. Labor continues to be a direct aggregate of hours of different subgroups. However, the BLS continues to experiment with various methods to weight labor hours by age, sex, and educational structure. They may include weighted aggregate labor hours in the future.[14]

---

[14] To quote the multifactor release USDL83–153:

The multifactor productivity indexes are derived by dividing an output index by an input index which is a weighted average of the hours of all persons and of capital services. The output indexes are computed from measures of constant-dollar gross domestic product, derived from the national income and product accounts developed by the Bureau of Economic Analysis of the U.S. Department of Commerce.

The labor component of the input indexes is developed from measures of employment and average hours, drawn mainly from the BLS current employment statistics

The second difference from labor productivity is that multifactor productivity requires that labor and capital inputs be added together. The BLS uses each input's share of total output as weights in adding their respective indexes. These weights change each year and are the average of the current with the previous year's share. The formula for multifactor productivity is based on a discrete form of the Divisia index:

%CH(MP)
$$= \%CH(Output) - (S_L \times \%CH(Labor) + S_K \times \%CH(Capital))$$

where

$\%CH(MP)$ = Percent change in multifactor productivity
$\%CH(Labor)$ = Percent change in hours worked
$\%CH(Capital)$ = Percent change in capital services
SL = Share of labor of total output, years t and t–1
S_K = Share of capital of total output, years t and t–1

and

$$S_L + S_K = 1.$$

APC'S MULTIPLE-INPUT PRODUCTIVITY INDEX PROGRAM

The American Productivity Center has been publishing quarterly measures of total-factor productivity for seven sector groupings since 1980.

---

program (the establishment survey) and the current population survey (the household survey). The establishment survey provides information about employees on nonagricultural payrolls; the household survey about the self-employed, unpaid family workers, and those engaged in agriculture. The BLS has done considerable research on the effects on productivity growth of work force composition (changes in the age, sex, and educational structure of the work force). This work is not included in the measures published today, because more research is required.

The capital services component of the combined input indexes is developed from measures of the stock of physical assets—equipment, structures, land, and inventories—and rental prices for each type of stock. The stock measures, in turn, are derived from data in the national accounts and other sources on investment, service lives, and capital deterioration functions. The rental prices are derived from data on depreciation costs and estimates of rates of return on the capital assets.

The labor and capital components of the input indexes are combined with weights which represent each component's share of total output. The index uses changing weights where the share in each year is averaged with the preceding year's value.

Data are presented for the private business, private nonfarm business, and manufacturing sectors. The private business sector, which accounts for about 80 percent of the gross national product, includes all activities in the economy with the exception of general government, government enterprises, the rest-of-world sector, owner-occupied housing, nonprofit institutions, and private household employees. The private nonfarm business sector also excludes agriculture, but includes agricultural services.

In addition, the APC publishes annual measures for some 11 nonfarm nonmanufacturing and 20 manufacturing industry segments.[15]

The APC measure is keyed to the same definitions as the BLS measure of the business economy. Thus, the APC measure of labor productivity is the same as published by the BLS in their *Productivity and Costs* release. This consistency between the two measures allows the analysis, among sectors and industry segments, of the relationships between total factor productivity, labor productivity, output per unit of capital, and the capital-labor ratio.[16]

The APC Measure of Total-Factor Productivity

The APC measure is based on the methodology developed by Professor John W. Kendrick.[17] In this method, real output, labor hours, and capital stock are direct aggregates (unweighted totals) of industry estimates. This method parallels the BLS method for calculating labor productivity, but differs from their treatment of capital.

The APC adds together estimates of gross fixed capital stock (plant and equipment) with an imputation for the stock of land and estimates of the stock of inventory, all in constant 1972 dollars. The BLS uses respective rental prices to weight the separate components of capital. ·Further, the BLS is net of depreciation, whereas the APC measure is gross.

The APC adds together indexes of labor hours and capital stock, using shares of labor and capital of total-factor costs. Unlike the BLS method, these weights are fixed for approximately 10-year periods (1948–59, 1959–69, and 1969–78):

Total-factor productivity
$$= \text{Output}/(S_L \times \text{Labor hours} + S_K \times \text{Capital stock})$$

where

S_L = Share of labor of factor costs, a specific year
S_K = Share of capital of factor costs, specific year

and

$S_L + S_K = 1.$

Another difference between the APC and BLS methods is that the BLS

---

[15] *Multiple Input Productivity Index,* selected issues.

[16] For such an analysis, see John W. Kendrick, "Inter-Industry Differences in Productivity Growth," in *A Study in Contemporary Economic Problems* (Washington, D.C.: American Enterprise Institute, 1982).

[17] Kendrick and Grossman, *Productivity.*

measure of multifactor productivity is of the private business economy, and the APC covers the business economy.

Exhibit 10 presents growth rates for the APC and BLS measures of total-factor productivity and its components for the 1948–81 period. The

---

EXHIBIT 10 Comparison of APC and BLS
Measures: Total-Factor
Productivity and Related
Items, 1948–1981 (average
annual growth rates)

	APC	BLS
Total-factor productivity	1.8%	1.5%
Labor productivity	2.4	2.4
Output per unit of capital	0.2	−0.1
Output	3.3	3.3
Labor hours	0.9	0.9
Capital services	3.1	3.5
Total-factor input	1.5	1.8

Source: U.S. Department of Labor, Bureau of Labor Statistics; American Productivity Center.

APC measure shows total-factor productivity rising at a 1.8 percent average rate versus the BLS estimate of 1.5 percent. The major difference is the estimate of capital input. The APC estimate rises at a 3.1 percent rate, less than the 3.5 percent rate estimated by the BLS. Differences in weighting labor and capital together also account for the variance between their estimates.

APC Sector and Industry Estimates

Exhibit 11 presents estimates of the growth rates of total-factor productivity for all of the sectors and industry segments for the 1948–82 period and selected subperiods. In addition to the business economy and other major sectors reported by the BLS, and APC reports measures for the goods producing and service producing industries. The goods producing industries include manufacturing, farm, mining, and construction. Service producing includes the various nonfarm nonmanufacturing industries excluding mining and construction.

Exhibit 12 presents the trend of total-factor and labor productivity for the business economy over the 1948–82 period. The slowdown in pro-

EXHIBIT 11   Total-Factor Productivity By Major Industries of the Economy (selected periods, 1948–1982)

	Average Annual Rates of Change				
	1948–82	1948–65	1965–73	1973–79	1979–82
Business economy	1.7%	2.6%	1.7%	0.4%	−0.5%
Goods producing industries	2.3	3.5	2.3	0.4	−0.1
Service producing industries	1.3	1.8	1.3	0.6	−0.4
Farming	3.6	4.1	3.1	1.8	6.6
Manufacturing	1.9	2.6	2.3	0.7	−0.6
Food	2.9	2.9	4.1	0.1	4.8
Tobacco	1.5	2.3	2.1	0.3	−1.7
Textiles	3.4	3.9	3.0	3.7	1.9
Apparel	2.2	2.0	3.0	3.1	−0.1
Lumber	2.9	4.5	1.3	0.2	3.6
Furniture	1.8	2.1	0.8	3.3	0.4
Paper	1.8	2.2	4.0	0.0	−3.1
Printing and publishing	1.1	2.4	1.0	−1.2	−1.4
Chemicals	3.0	3.9	4.2	1.2	−1.2
Petroleum	0.5	3.4	2.0	−3.3	−10.8
Rubber	1.5	2.3	2.0	−0.5	0.1
Leather	1.5	1.0	1.7	1.2	4.4
Stone, clay and glass	1.3	2.0	0.9	0.1	0.2
Primary metals	−0.3	0.9	0.9	−2.0	−6.5
Fabricated metals	1.3	1.7	1.3	0.7	0.0
Machinery, except electrical	1.2	1.4	1.4	0.8	0.1
Electrical machinery	3.3	4.3	2.8	3.2	−0.4
Transportation equipment	1.9	3.4	2.3	0.2	−4.0
Instruments	2.6	3.6	2.5	0.9	0.7
Miscellaneous manufacturing	2.3	2.3	3.6	1.9	−0.2
Nonfarm nonmanufacturing	1.2	1.9	1.1	0.2	−0.6
Mining	0.3	2.3	1.7	−4.1	−5.8
Construction	0.3	2.4	−1.0	−3.0	−1.4
Transportation	1.6	2.0	2.4	1.2	−1.7
Railroad	2.5	4.2	1.2	0.4	2.8
Nonrail	0.9	0.5	2.7	1.2	−2.2
Communications	4.3	5.4	3.2	3.8	1.6
Public utilities	2.6	5.5	1.5	−1.0	−3.7
Trade	1.9	2.4	2.6	0.7	0.6
Finance and insurance	0.2	1.0	0.3	−1.0	−2.1
Real estate	1.4	1.9	0.0	2.6	−0.4
Services	0.3	0.3	−0.2	0.0	2.0
Nonfinancial corporate business	1.7	2.6	1.5	0.7	−0.3

ductivity gains is quite obvious after 1965 and again after 1973 and 1979. In fact, over the 1973–82 period, total-factor productivity only grew an insignificant 0.1 percent. Labor productivity exhibits similar declines in productivity growth rates over the same subperiods. Much of the decline in productivity is a major factor contributing to many of the problems the U.S. economy has been facing through the 1970s and into the

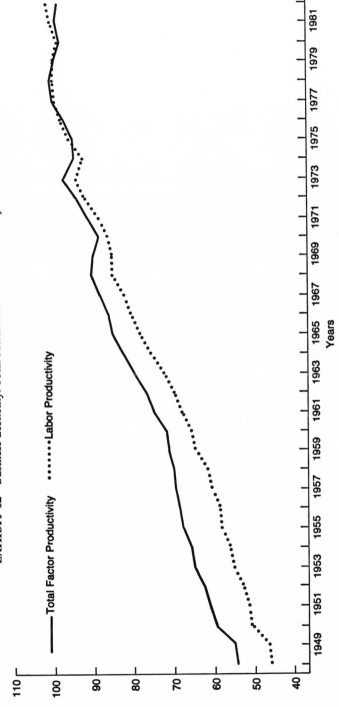

EXHIBIT 12 Business Economy: Total-Factor and Labor Productivity Trends, 1948–1982

——— Total Factor Productivity   •••••• Labor Productivity

Years

110

100

90

80

70

60

50

40

1949 1951 1953 1955 1957 1959 1961 1963 1965 1967 1969 1971 1973 1975 1977 1979 1981

EXHIBIT 13   Baking Industry: Production Productivity Report

Measure	Number of Observations	Deciles 1	Deciles 2
Pounds of product/Direct hours of labor	240	124.5	152.2
Pounds of product/Total hours of labor	229	78.6	95.7
Dollars of product/Dollars of direct payroll	210	8.48	9.59
Dollars of product/Dollars of all labor costs	210	4.07	4.62
Pounds of product/Pounds of flour	239	1.50	1.58
Pounds of product/Pounds of sugar	239	6.59	9.82
Pounds of product/Pounds of shortening	237	20.70	31.19
Dollars of product/Dollars of ingredients	240	3.79	4.07
Dollars of product/Dollars of packaging	240	19.06	22.68
Percentage of cripples	239	.10	.30
Pounds of product/Building, square feet	167	91.8	118.2
Pounds of product/Oven capacity	221	.31	.37
Dollars of product/Dollars of assets employed	227	1.58	2.05
Pounds of product/Cubic feet of natural gas	239	.57	.65
Pounds of product/Millions of BTU of energy	239	445.3	519.1
Dollars of product/Dollars of energy input	241	42.16	46.90
Dollars of product/Dollars of plant maintenance cost	234	23.24	27.88
Dollars of product/Dollars of all inputs	194	1.52	1.75

time of this writing: high inflation, low economic growth, deteriorating international competitiveness, and high unemployment.[18]

APC Benchmark Productivity Measurement Program

The APC has recently inaugurated a program to measure productivity at the detailed industry level using primary survey data. While the program has not as yet produced regularly published estimates, the APC has completed its initial work for the baking industry.[19] It is the intention of the APC to conduct the surveys and report the productivity estimates on a biannual or quarterly basis.

Unlike the other measurement programs mentioned above, the APC benchmark program requires funding and cooperation on the part of the industry being measured. However, this program is an excellent vehicle for companies to obtain detailed benchmark productivity measures geared to their particular industry. Exhibit 13 presents the results of this

[18] For further discussion on the productivity slowdown, see John W. Kendrick, "Productivity Trends and the Recent Slowdown: Historical Perspective, Causal Factors, and Policy Options," in *Contemporary Economic Problems, 1979* (Washington, D.C.: American Enterprise Institute, 1979).

[19] *Banking Industry Productivity, January–June 1982* (Houston: American Productivity Center, April 12, 1983).

		Deciles					Decile 9 over Decile 5	Decile 1 over Decile 5
3	*4*	*5*	*6*	*7*	*8*	*9*		
172.7	194.5	214.0	237.0	264.9	288.2	334.0	1.561	.582
111.5	126.4	140.2	157.8	169.1	182.8	210.7	1.503	.561
10.57	11.59	13.09	14.16	15.73	17.64	20.40	1.559	.648
5.02	5.31	5.75	6.38	6.93	7.77	9.10	1.584	.709
1.64	1.69	1.76	1.83	1.93	2.06	2.44	1.386	.852
12.29	13.76	15.00	16.35	17.77	19.74	22.82	1.521	.439
39.10	46.70	51.01	56.02	62.56	70.73	79.45	1.558	.406
4.30	4.43	4.59	4.70	4.95	5.28	5.93	1.292	.826
24.02	25.88	28.04	29.55	31.23	32.71	36.59	1.305	.680
.50	.70	.80	1.00	1.30	1.60	2.10	2.625	.125
148.0	175.9	204.4	224.8	262.2	297.8	366.1	1.791	.449
.43	.46	.53	.58	.66	.75	.89	1.675	.585
2.57	2.97	3.45	4.02	4.93	5.76	8.05	2.332	.457
.75	.81	.92	1.01	1.12	1.23	1.48	1.609	.620
571.0	649.0	703.7	771.0	842.1	921.4	1054.6	1.499	.633
51.50	56.30	61.90	67.72	74.96	80.84	94.94	1.534	.681
30.78	34.51	38.48	43.47	48.09	56.05	68.88	1.790	.604
1.85	1.91	2.00	2.10	2.22	2.33	2.48	1.240	.758

first report. Eighteen various industry-specific productivity measures are reported, including their decile variation. In this way, a company can easily determine in which decile their particular company ranks among their industry cohorts.

SUMMARY

The productivity measures provided by the Bureau of Labor Statistics and the American Productivity Center are quite useful, as far as they go. Because of the broadness of their coverage, these measures are most useful for aggregate national and industry analyses, but fall short when meeting the needs of detailed industry and company analyses.

An additional area of need is for international productivity measures. Currently, such measures only cover labor productivity and the most aggregate sectors. In an economic environment of intense international competition, industries need consistent productivity measures at the detailed industry level. Thus, the major need today is for measures which include capital and other nonlabor inputs, that are consistent, and cover greater industry detail both nationally and internationally.

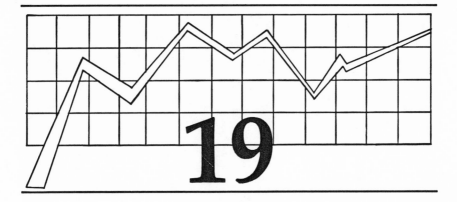

Measures of Competition

Peter Asch, Ph.D.
Professor of Economics
Rutgers University

BACKGROUND

Concepts of Competition

The notion of competition has long been one of the most fundamental and widely employed concepts in economics. Yet, if we ask on what criteria a market may be properly termed *competitive* (or *noncompetitive*), a variety of responses is likely to be forthcoming. The initial difficulty is conceptual: What precisely does the word *competition* mean?

The Structural Notion. Competition in economic analysis traditionally has been defined as a particular set of structural market conditions. Structure refers broadly to the relatively stable organizational character- istics of the market; for example, the number and size distribution of constituent firms, the ease or difficulty of entry for new firms, the nature of the product or service that is sold,[1] and the nature of product demand.

---

[1] The usual distinction is between homogeneous and differentiated goods.

426

Market structure is pertinent because it defines the competitive *environment* within which firms pursue profits and other objectives. In general, the absence of dominance by one or a few companies, easy entry for prospective rivals, and closely substitutable goods suggest a structurally competitive market. The essence of competition in this sense is the dispersion of power. No single seller or small group can exercise much control over the terms at which goods are supplied to the market.[2] Competitiveness is, in effect, powerlessness.

The attention paid to market structure by economists is at once theoretically appropriate and empirically useful. In principle, competitive market structures should lead to competitive forms of behavior (the linkages, however, are precise only in polar cases). Although significant measurement problems exist, relevant data are abundant. Some direct information on virtually every important dimension of structure is available for large numbers of American industries; and a wide variety of structure-based measures has been developed, some of which are quite useful for purposes of competitive classification.

Competition as Market Performance.   Performance refers to the observable results of the market: prices, costs, outputs, profits, innovations, etc. As Mark S. Massell has put it: "Conceptually, the ultimate judgment about the effectiveness of competition in a market should be its performance. How competitive are the prices, the production, the innovations, the consumer choices?"[3] In this view, structure or other dimensions of competition are important primarily insofar as they enable us to explain or predict performance.

Competitive market performance consists of the results that we would expect a competitive market to yield. The definition of such performance, however, encounters some significant problems, both conceptual and empirical. A fundamental difficulty is that there exists no clear competitive (or monopolistic) benchmark for many elements of performance. It may be hypothesized, for example, that a strongly competitive environment will drive firms to produce at the lowest possible cost and/or to innovate actively. But "lowest possible cost" may have no obvious dollars-and-cents translation, nor does "active" innovation suggest a well-defined rate of product or process development. In practice, then, it may prove difficult to determine whether an observed record of costs or innovations signifies a competitive result. Problems of data availability and imperfection also abound and will be discussed below.

---

[2] In the polar benchmark of perfect competition, individual firms are utterly powerless. Because each is so small in relation to the market and because all sell a homogeneous product, none can perceptibly influence market output or price.

[3] *Competition and Monopoly* (Washington, D.C.: Brookings Institution, 1962), p. 221.

Competition as a Form of Conduct.   Perhaps the most popular notion of competition—especially within the business and legal worlds—is stated in terms of market conduct. Conduct refers to the nature of strategies and decisions adopted by firms. The essence of competition is an active and independent striving for customers. Simply stated, companies "fight it out." Competition in this sense is not so much a precisely defined environment or set of results as it is a process.[4]

The antithesis of competition thus defined—i.e., monopoly—is collusive or cooperative conduct by rivals. It is the *avoidance*, however achieved, of the competitive struggle. A noteworthy aspect of competition in the conduct sense is its relative independence of market structural conditions. Active rivalry may (or may not) occur in a wide variety of structural circumstances, some of which would not appear highly competitive in traditional terms.

Although defining competition in terms of conduct is conceptually plausible, perhaps even appealing, it turns out to be the least useful approach empirically. Since conduct refers to the independence of firms' decision processes—to their stratagems and objectives—it is seldom directly observable. Some indirect measures have been suggested and will be described below, but there is no conduct-based index capable of describing competition in a precise and reliable way.

Broader Notions of Competition.   Market structure, conduct, and performance do not represent inconsistent or mutually exclusive approaches to the definition of competition. Each dimension represents a different way of posing the question: Are the firms in a market under strong pressure to act efficiently? If the answer is yes, the market is competitive. And the answers that are forthcoming on the basis of structure, conduct, and performance criteria should not as a rule prove widely divergent.

Some writers have proposed definitions of competition that are not specifically tied to these classifications. Robert Bork, for example, suggests that competition may be defined as "any state of affairs in which consumer welfare cannot be increased . . . by judicial decree."[5] And Jesse Markham has argued in somewhat the same vein that a market is "workably competitive" when "there is no clearly indicated change that

---

[4] This was Adam Smith's vision of competition. See *The Wealth of Nations* (New York: Modern Library, 1937), especially pp. 56–57. In a similar vein, Scherer refers to competition as "an independent striving for patronage by the various sellers in a market." F. M. Scherer, *Industrial Market Structure and Economic Performance*, 2d ed. (Chicago: Rand McNally, 1980), p. 10. Robert C. Brooks notes that competition "in its ordinary business sense means that rival companies attempt to divert trade from each other." "Businessmen's Concepts of INJURY to Competition," *California Management Review*, Summer 1961, pp. 89–101.

[5] Robert Bork, *The Antitrust Paradox* (New York: Basic Books, 1978), p. 61.

can be effected through public policy measures that would result in greater social gains than social losses."[6]

Such broad-gauged views of competition have real virtues, especially for policy officials. They do not, however, point us in the direction of obvious or precise measurement procedures.

Early Efforts at Systematic Measurement

The first systematic efforts to apply what might be regarded as indexes of competition and monopoly to industries did not occur in the United States until the late 1930s. Studies by Gardiner C. Means, W. L. Thorp and W. F. Crowder, Clair Wilcox, and G. Warren Nutter sought to establish the extent of competition and monopoly in broad segments of American industry.[7]

Although these studies were crude, they are highly instructive in pointing to some measurement issues that have never been resolved in fully satisfactory ways. The efforts of Means and of Thorp and Crowder were the most limited. Confined largely to the manufacturing sector of the economy, these authors examined Bureau of the Census data in order to classify industries as competitive or monopolistic. The sole criterion was a simple concentration ratio: the percentage of industry output accounted for by the largest firms, usually the top four. At least two important and persistent problems were apparent in these pioneering works:

1. Census industry and product definitions may not correspond closely to economic markets.
2. The concentration ratio taken alone is not an adequate measure of competition or monopoly in most instances.

These difficulties were quickly recognized. Nutter pointed to "overly narrow" product definitions (e.g., "men's work shoes, wood or metal fastened"), and reclassified industries whose apparent high concentration on the basis of U.S. data ignored substantial imports. He further adopted alternative cutoff points to distinguish industries of "high"

---

[6] Jesse W. Markham, "An Alternative Approach to the Concept of Workable Competition," *American Economic Review*, June 1950, pp. 349–61 (quotation at p. 361).

[7] Gardiner C. Means, *The Structure of the American Economy*, a report prepared by the Industrial Section of the National Resources Committee (Washington, D.C.: Government Printing Office, 1939); W. L. Thorp and W. F. Crowder, *The Structure of Industry*, Temporary National Economic Committee Monographs No. 27 (Washington, D.C.: Government Printing Office, 1940); Clair Wilcox, *Monopoly and Competition in American Industry*, Temporary National Economic Committee Monographs No. 21 (Washington, D.C.: Government Printing Office, 1940); G. Warren Nutter, *The Extent of Enterprise Monopoly in the United States, 1899–1939* (Chicago: University of Chicago Press, 1951).

concentration and reported upper- and lower-bound estimates of "effectively monopolized" industries.[8]

Wilcox, in a well-known statement, implied clearly that the competitive status of a market was not likely to be well described by a single concentration measure:

> Where producers are numerous, where the degree of concentration is low, where the prices charged by different firms are not identical, where these prices are not rigidly maintained over long periods of time, where the volume of production is not drastically curtailed at the onset of depression, where productive capacity is largely utilized during each of the phases of the trade cycle, where the turnover of producing units is rapid, where profits are moderate, and where the rate of business mortality is high, there is a presumption that effective competition prevails.[9]

Reasonable assessments of competition require appropriate market definitions and, in all likelihood, considerably more information than a one-dimensional index conveys. But such requirements are more easily noted than met. As we shall see, the problems they present can prove extremely stubborn.

Defining the Market

Competition is intrinsically a market phenomenon, one that occurs within some product and geographic boundaries. Most measures of competition depend, implicitly or explicitly, upon a definition of these boundaries; and the values of some competitive indexes may be highly sensitive to the way in which the scope of the market is defined.

The unavoidable task of market definition raises two distinct issues. The first is conceptual: What is a theoretically appropriate market? In principle, the answer is straightforward. A market consists of a group of "closely substitutable" goods or services. Somewhat more specifically, an appropriate market grouping (product or geographic) should be:

1. Narrow enough to exclude from the grouping all nonsubstitutes for the items within.
2. Broad enough to include in the grouping all substitutes for the constituent items.

The conceptual problem is that it may prove difficult, even impossible, to satisfy these criteria simultaneously. Market groupings that are nar-

---

[8] Nutter estimated that 17.4 percent of national income originated in effectively monopolistic industries in 1899; his estimates for 1937 ranged from 12.9 to 21.2 percent.

[9] Wilcox, *Monopoly and Competition*, p. 20.

row enough to exclude all nonsubstitutes are likely to exclude some substitutes as well; whereas broad groupings that include all substitutes are likely also to encompass some items that are not substitutes for one another.

A closely related practical problem has already been noted. Available market data, gathered mainly by the Bureau of the Census, may not correspond to theoretically appropriate markets in at least some instances. In fact it is not hard to find too-broad and too-narrow Census classifications. Prime examples of the former are pharmaceutical preparations (an industry category that embraces such nonsubstitutes as cold remedies, insulin, and chapsticks) and newspapers (an industry which the Census defines nationally, but which is in reality a collection of local and perhaps regional markets). Overly narrow product groupings include, for example, "cottage cheese," "tufted carpets and rugs," and "metal porch, lawn, and outdoor furniture."

Improper market definitions are not merely displeasing on abstract or aesthetic grounds. As noted, they may distort available indexes of market competition, almost beyond recognition in some instances. The newspaper industry, for example, shows very low concentration at the national level (the four largest firms account for only 19 percent of value of shipments); yet, this "industry" consists largely of local monopolies, a fact that is concealed in the national data. Conversely, the four-firm concentration ratio for "cottage cheese" (about 32 percent) probably overstates the importance of the leading producers, who are subject to competition from manufacturers of other cheeses and dairy products.

Summary

To this point we have noted that *competition* is a term subject to varied definition and, potentially, to a similarly varied array of measurement approaches. Early efforts at measurement highlight two issues of paramount importance: the need for appropriate market definition and the possible inadequacy of a one-dimensional competition index such as the concentration ratio. We turn now to the competition measures that have been devised and employed, largely since the 1930s.

ALTERNATIVE MEASURES: CONSTRUCTION AND DATA

In discussing alternative measures of competition, it is useful to follow the structure, conduct, and performance categories described above.

Conduct-Based Measures

As we have observed, market conduct (which refers to the actual stratagems and objectives of firms) is the least measurable aspect of competition. The basic task of a conduct index is to describe the extent to which market rivals are striving independently or acting in concert to avoid the competitive battle. Direct measurement is, as a rule, impossible. A number of indirect measures of conduct, however, may provide some useful clues to the state of competition.[10]

Stability of Firm Ranks. Collusive action creates some expectation that the relative positions of firms in the market will be stabilized. Indeed, enhancement of such market stability may be a central objective of coordination. The degree of turnover in rank of firms—e.g., of dollar sales or shipments—may thus provide a rough clue as to whether the companies are competing actively. Higher turnover rates suggest a higher likelihood of such rivalry, *ceteris paribus*. A number of rank correlation indexes are appropriate to the task.

Stability of Firm Market Shares. Where market share data are available over time, an index of share stability provides a somewhat more sensitive measure than rank turnover. The appropriate index is a correlation measure applied at two or more points in time.

Similarity of Price Movements. Where movements of price (or other supply terms) are similar among rivals over prolonged periods, clear suspicion of coordinated policies is created. There is no single numerical index that is especially convenient or appropriate to measure such similarity. The degree of similarity that is observed will additionally depend upon such factors as the degree of product or service differentiation in the market (identical or standardized items will tend to have similar prices) and perhaps upon the sophistication of business managers who do not want to arouse suspicion of illegal collusion among antitrust enforcers.

Summary. It is unlikely that such indirect measures of conduct, taken singly or as a group, will provide very clear notions about the competitiveness of a market. The difficulty is, in part, that rivalry is not a simple

---

[10] See, for example, Michael Gort, "Analysis of Stability and Change in Market Shares," *Journal of Political Economy*, February 1963, pp. 51–63; Stephen Hymer and Peter Pashigian, "Turnover of Firms as a Measure of Market Behavior," *Review of Economics and Statistics*, February 1962, pp. 82–87; and Jonathon D. Ogur, *Competition and Market Share Instability*, staff report to the Federal Trade Commission (Washington, D.C.: Government Printing Office, August 1976).

dichotomous condition. It exists in degrees ranging from completely independent to completely interdependent, or collusive. To observe and characterize these degrees is extraordinarily difficult. Conduct measures are accordingly best seen as a supplement to other types of information about the state of competition.

Structure Measures

Most competition indexes employed in economics have been structural, for reasons of theoretical appropriateness as well as data availability. Three major types of structural measures deserve attention: demand elasticity, market concentration and market shares, and entry barriers.

Demand-Elasticity Measures.   Price elasticity of demand—defined as the ratio of percentage change in quantity demanded to percentage change in price—contains considerable information about the pricing power of firms. In the extreme case of perfectly elastic demand, the seller is utterly powerless: The slightest increase in price above the prevailing (market) rate will cause sales to disappear. As we approach the opposite pole—perfectly inelastic demand—quantity demanded or sold becomes increasingly unresponsive to price changes; sellers may therefore raise prices with relative impunity.

Other things being equal, demand-elasticity values will be "high" when the market offers consumers close substitutes for the product in question, for even "small" increases in product price will then cause consumers to shift in relatively large numbers to the available alternatives. In this sense, elasticity reflects competitiveness.

In 1934, Abba P. Lerner proposed a measure of monopoly that is related to prove elasticity of demand.[11] The Lerner index is defined as:

$$L = \frac{Price - Marginal\ cost}{Price}$$

It measures the ability of the firm to set price above marginal cost, a central element of monopoly behavior which is closely related to the elasticity of demand.[12] Despite its theoretical usefulness, this measure has not been widely employed in empirical analyses. The primary reason is an absence of appropriate data, especially for marginal cost, for large numbers of firms and industries.

---

[11] Abba P. Lerner, "The Concept of Monopoly and the Measurement of Monopoly Power," *Review of Economic Studies*, June 1934, pp. 157–75.

[12] For profit-maximizing firms in equilibrium, the Lerner index is precisely the reciprocal of demand elasticity.

Concentration Measures.   Concentration measures reflect the fact that the competitive environment is shaped by both the number of firms in a market and their relative sizes (or shares). These indexes attempt to discern what has been termed the condition of "fewness"—i.e., control of the market by a small number of firms. In Tibor Scitovsky's words, they "try to express the number and size distribution of competitors in terms of a one-parameter index."[13]

The Concentration Ratio.   The most widely used concentration index is the simple concentration ratio—the joint market share held by the largest firms in the market, usually the top four or top eight. A "top four" (CR4) value of 84 percent for the cigarette industry, for example, means that the four largest cigarette manufacturers account for 84 percent of the value of industry shipments.

The concentration ratio is useful because it tells us something about the probability that a market is dominated by a few firms. The upper limit of the four-firm ratio is 100 percent, attained whenever the market consists of four or fewer firms. The lower limit varies with the number of firms in the market and is reached when all firms are of equal size. A market consisting of vast numbers of equal-sized firms will exhibit a CR4 close to zero.

The concentration ratio has three important virtues which have contributed to its widespread use:

1. It is theoretically reasonable. The index is, for example, insensitive to trivial changes in market structure, such as the entry or exit of a miniscule company.
2. It has a relatively modest data requirement. All that is needed for computation is the size of the market and of the largest firms. Additionally, concentration ratios are published periodically by the Bureau of the Census for large numbers of manufacturing industries.
3. It is easily understood.

Some shortcomings, however, are also present. The concentration ratio does not reveal much about the structure of the top firm group (a CR4 of 80 percent, for example, is consistent with the existence of a single dominant firm or four roughly equal-sized firms at the head of the market). In a sense, the index lacks detail. Where comprehensive data about the size distribution of firms in a market are available, the concentration ratio fails to exploit the information fully.

---

[13] Tibor Scitovsky, "Economic Theory and the Measurement of Concentration," in *Business Concentration and Price Policy* (Princeton, N.J.: Princeton University Press for the National Bureau of Economic Research, 1955), p. 109.

It also may be observed that in an index focusing on the largest n firms in a market, the number n is essentially arbitrary: Why look at the top four firms? Why not the top three, or five, or simply the top one? Whereas this observation is strictly correct, some arbitrariness is an inescapable attribute of virtually all concentration measures. The difficulty is not so much with the index itself, but rather with underlying theoretical ambiguity. There is no analytical framework that specifies, for example, the number of leading firms that ought to be examined.

There are, in addition, some very specific difficulties associated with the complication of Census concentration data. These have mainly to do with the diversification of many corporations, which extends even to the plant or establishment level on which the Census focuses. As a result of diversification, some portion of a company's shipments may be counted in the "wrong" industry, an error that can in turn distort measured concentration in certain cases. Caution in the utilization of published concentration ratios is therefore appropriate.

The Herfindahl Index.[14]   The Herfindahl index is a comprehensive or summary measure of concentration. It is defined as:

$$H = \sum_{i=1}^{n} \left(\frac{s_i}{S}\right)^2$$

where

> s_i = The size of any firm i in the market
> S = The size of the market
> n = The number of firms in the market

H is thus the sum of the squares of the market share of each firm in the market. In the case of single-firm monopoly, $H = 1.0$. Where the market is populated by many small firms, the value of H approaches zero.

The Herfindahl index, unlike the concentration ratio, reflects the position of every firm in the market. It has considerable theoretical appeal and is regarded by some economists as a superior concentration measure.[15] The index carries two significant limitations, however.

1. Precisely because it is comprehensive, the data requirement is demanding. Calculation of H requires the market share of every firm in

---

[14] The index was developed independently by Orris C. Herfindahl in an unpublished doctoral dissertation, "Concentration in the U.S. Steel Industry," (New York: Columbia University, 1950); and by Albert O. Hirschman, "The Paternity of an Index," *American Economic Review*, September 1964, p. 761.

[15] See George J. Stigler, "A Theory of Oligopoly," *Journal of Political Economy*, February 1964, pp. 44–61.

the market (although omission of very small companies will have little practical effect).

2. Although H values can be used to rank the concentration levels of various markets, a given absolute value of H has no simple intuitive interpretation.

Market Shares. Recent empirical research suggests that the key element in predicting the nature of market performance may be the market share of the leading one or two firms in the market—rather than more aggregate ratios.[16] Individual market shares may be interpreted as a particular type of concentration ratio, one that looks only at the largest firm. As such, this measure is subject to much the same observations as CR4.

Summary. There is a virtually limitless number of ways to measure market concentration. Indexes may generally be interpreted as weighted sums of firms' market shares. (The H index, for example, weights each share by squaring it; the concentration ratio effectively assigns a weight of 1.0 to the shares of the largest firms, and zero to all others.)

The difficulty common to all measures is analytical: There is no theory of markets that prescribes the ideal weights. Despite this difficulty, concentration remains the fundamental index of market structure; it is difficult to discuss the state of competition in a market without reference to its concentration level.

Measures of Entry Barriers.   Economists, particularly in recent years, have emphasized the critical role of barriers to entry in evaluations of competition and monopoly. As Carl Kaysen put the point some time ago, monopoly power "rests on the existence of high barriers to the entry of . . . other firms into the market."[17]

The reasoning behind this statement is straightforward. In the absence of entry barriers, any attempt by an incumbent firm to act monopolistically—e.g., to set price well above cost and earn a monopoly reward—is likely to prove self-defeating. Such behavior will attract new entrants (and/or expansion by firms already in the market). The would-be monopolist thus stands to lost substantial sales to rivals. Although it may set a high price temporarily, it has no true or lasting control.

Under these circumstances, an incumbent firm may occupy an appar-

---

[16] See especially William G. Shepherd, "The Elements of Market Structure," *Review of Economics and Statistics,* February 1972, pp. 25–37; and John E. Kwoka, "The Effect of Market Share Distribution on Industry Performance," *Review of Economics and Statistics,* February 1979, pp. 101–9.

[17] Carl Kaysen, *United States versus United Shoe Machinery Corporation,* (Cambridge, Mass.: Harvard University Press, 1956), p. 16.

ently powerful market position; it may even appear to be a monopolist. But lacking the protection of entry barriers, the company's behavior will in fact be closely constrained by actual or potential rivals—which is to say that it is subject to competitive pressure.

The implication of this argument is that factors such as market concentration and market share cannot provide the basis for a categorical evaluation of competition. At a minimum, the condition of entry also must be examined. Unfortunately, the measurement of entry barriers is usually not a simple task.

There is, in fact, some disagreement about how a barrier ought to be defined. Some writers suggest a broad approach: A barrier to entry is any condition that is expected to retard the rate at which new rivals actually enter the market in response to profit signals.[18] Others argue for a more restrictive definition: Entry barriers are, for example, costs "borne by a firm which seeks to enter an industry, but . . . not . . . by firms already in the industry."[19]

Factors that may constitute significant barriers to entry include the following:

1. *Absolute cost advantages* for established firms. If incumbents can produce more cheaply than new entrants at all (or most) output levels, the deterrent to entry is apparent. Such advantages may arise in various ways, such as control of superior productive techniques (perhaps via patent or trade secret), tying up of superior inputs or distribution outlets by means of long-term contracts, or capital market practices that impose less favorable terms on new entrants.[20]

2. *Product differentiation advantages* may originate in control over superior forms of product design (arguably not a barrier in the narrow sense) or from what Joe Bain has called the "accumulative preference of buyers" for established brands and company reputations.[21] In some in stances, customer loyalty may be tied to heavy promotional activity, especially advertising.

3. *Legal barriers*, such as the need for a government license, may effectively preclude entry into certain markets. Such barriers are highly significant in a number of areas—for example, many local markets in taxicab services and liquor sales.

---

[18] See, for example, William G. Shepherd, *The Economics of Industrial Organization*, (Englewood Cliffs, N.J.: Prentice-Hall, 1979), p. 182.

[19] George J. Stigler, *The Organization of Industry*, (Homewood, Ill.: Richard D. Irwin, 1968), p. 67.

[20] Notice, however, that high capital costs may not constitute an entry barrier narrowly defined. Such costs may confront *all* firms at the time they come into the market and, in this sense, are not confined to new entrants.

[21] Joe S. Bain, "Conditions of Entry and the Emergence of Monopoly," in *Monopoly and Competition and Their Regulation*, ed. E. H. Chamberlin (New York: Macmillan, 1954).

4. *Economies of scale* may be a deterrent to new entry, especially in conjunction with heavy initial capital requirements. Such economies imply that a prospective entrant must capture a significant share of the market in order to operate efficiently; the attempt to do so, however, will tend both to bid down product (or service) prices and to bid up the prices of factor inputs—clear discouragements to entry. Once again, however, scale economies are not barriers in the narrow sense of the term, for they apply to new and old firms alike.

As the above examples suggest, the measurement of entry barriers does not lend itself to quantitative precision. A common practice is to rank industries broadly according to ease or difficulty of entry. "High" barriers, for example, characterize such manufacturing industries as soaps, automobiles, and steel; "moderate" barriers exist in fertilizers, cigarettes, and tires and tubes; while barriers are relatively "low" in such areas as flour, textiles, and footwear. Cardinal and even finer ordinal distinctions are difficult to draw; but measurement problems do not diminish the critical conceptual role of entry barriers in evaluating market competition.

Summary.   Structural measures seek to describe the market environment within which firms operate. The alternatives above provide very basic data on this central aspect of competition. As the discussion suggests, however, no single measure is likely to prove fully adequate to the task.

Performance Measures

We have already noted one potentially significant problem in performance measures of competition: the absence of a competitive or monopolistic benchmark for some variables. Some important data problems also arise, but the importance of performance as an indicator of competition is such that extensive efforts at measurement have been attempted.

Profits.   Profits are, in a sense, the most fundamental element of firm and market performance and are also of major theoretical significance to the assessment of competition. A distinguishing characteristic of monopoly is the likelihood (although not the certainty) that profits persistently in excess of opportunity cost, or a "normal" rate of return, will be earned. For this reason, many investigators have looked to profit data as a source of information about the state of competition.

Measuring Profit Rates.   A great deal of empirical research has consisted of efforts to predict or explain variations in firm and industry profitability.[22] Among the more interesting findings are that profit rates tend to rise with such variables as market share, market concentration, entry barriers, advertising intensity (usually defined as the ratio of advertising to sales dollars), and firm and market growth rates. There is some support for the general proposition that monopolistic market structures are associated with relatively high rates of return, as traditional economic theory suggests.

As writers such as Harold Demsetz argue, however, the proper interpretation of these correlations is debatable.[23] It may be, for example, that certain firms perform in a qualitatively excellent fashion; as a consequence, they capture large shares of their markets and earn high profits. The observed result is high shares, high concentration, and high profitability; but monopoly, in Demsetz' view, is hardly the appropriate interpretation. To the contrary, these firms have outcompeted rivals, a result that he terms *competitive superiority*.

Regardless of how one may wish to interpret observed correlations, some important problems in profit rate measurement deserve attention. Empirical research commonly focuses on two accounting measures of profitability:

$$\text{Return to stockholders' equity: } \frac{Y - T}{E}$$

where:

   Y = Net income
   T = Taxes
   E = Stockholders' equity or net worth

$$\text{Return to capital: } \frac{Y - T + I}{TA}$$

where:

   Y = Net income
   T = Taxes
   I = Interest payments
   TA = Total assets

Use of these profit rates suggests a number of difficulties:

1.   The *accounting* (or *reported*) profits that these data reflect are not quite the same thing as the *economic* profits to which our analytical

---

[22] In 1974, Leonard W. Weiss cited at least 46 profit rate studies; it is likely that the number had at least doubled by the end of that decade. "The Concentration-Profits Relationship and Antitrust," in *Industrial Concentration: The New Learning*, ed. Harvey J. Goldschmid, H. Michael Mann, and J. Fred Weston (Boston: Little, Brown, 1974).

[23] Harold Demsetz, "Industry Structure, Market Rivalry, and Public Policy," *Journal of Law and Economics*, April 1973, pp. 1–9.

expectations apply. The central difference is that profit, in the economic sense, takes into account an imputed opportunity cost for owner financing—this "normal" rate of return is not counted as part of economic profits: accounting profits, in contrast, include whatever rate of return is normal to the activities of the firm. This element ought to be subtracted from observed returns, but it can be an elusive magnitude to define.

2.   Accepted accounting procedures permit companies a good deal of flexibility in the profits that they report, especially over short periods. Asset valuation is a particular problem area, and such items as depreciation, inventory valuation, and taxes are also subject to varying treatment. The result is a good deal of random "noise" in profit rate observations.

3.   The treatment of investment-like expenditures such as advertising and research and development is troublesome. These activities generate returns over relatively long periods and, for this reason, are sometimes referred to as intangible assets. Accepted accounting practice, however, typically treats these items as current expenses, a procedure that is likely to affect reported profit rates, but not in a completely consistent or obvious way.

4.   The diversification of many major corporations hinders evaluation of the profitability of particular product lines. Since profits are usually reported at the firm level, without finer breakdowns, the return earned by a firm in a given market activity may be difficult to define precisely.

. 5.   Some funds that might have found their way into net revenues (i.e., profits) will be diverted to management salaries and perquisites in certain firms. The result is an understatement of reported profits, but the understatement is not consistent across all firms.

Measuring Price-Cost Margins.   In part because of the difficulties noted above, some investigators have preferred to work with a measure known as the price-cost margin. This variable is defined as:

$$PCM = \frac{\text{Value added} - \text{Payroll}}{\text{Value of shipments}}$$

The price-cost margin roughly approximates the average margin of price over cost on an industry basis (margins are sometimes available for subsets of an industry, but not for individual firms). Based on Census data, the variable succeeds in avoiding many of the firm-specific problems associated with reported profit rates. It encounters a potentially serious difficulty, however: The PCM may not be a consistently accurate measure of profits.[24]

---

[24] See S. J. Liebowitz, "What do Census Price-Cost Margins Measure?" *Journal of Law and Economics*, October 1982, pp. 231–46.

Invention and Innovation. Technological change or innovation is a critical element of competition in many markets, especially if one takes a "dynamic," or long-term, view. Whether price is set close to average or marginal cost—traditional "static" measures of competitiveness—may be less important socially than the rate at which new products and processes are developed and introduced to the market. As Edwin Mansfield puts it: "Technological change is a key element in the competitive struggle among firms. The extent and quality of a firm's research and development program can make it an industry leader or head it for bankruptcy."[25]

Unfortunately in light of its importance, inventive and innovative activity does not lend itself to quantitative indexing. Measurement efforts that have been undertaken focus frequently on research and development spending (a reflection of technological effort or input) or on patents (an element of output). Such measures, however, are basically flawed. A dollar of R&D expenditure is unlikely to bear any close or consistent relationship to a "unit" of technological progress; indeed, what firms may choose to call research and development at times has little to do with true innovative effort.

Patents, on the other hand, do reflect inventive achievement, but in such a crude way that interpretation of the data is exceptionally difficult. A given patent may be of enormous importance or of no importance whatever; it may or may not result in the actual introduction of an innovation to the market; and the "propensity to patent" a given quantity of invention may vary widely across firms and industries.[26]

An alternative measure, the percentage of sales or revenues accounted for by new products, may be superior to patents although it suffers from definitional problems. It also tends to miss process, as opposed to product, innovations.

Innovation measurement, as noted earlier, also confronts the absence-of-benchmark problem. Clearly, technological *opportunity* varies widely from market to market. There is no way, for example, that the innovative inputs or outputs of industries such as flour milling and lumber products will match those of drugs or communications. Does an observed rate of technological progress reflect competitive pressures? This question can be answered only by comparing observations in any market with the opportunities that the market presents. Not only actual innovation but the potential for innovation must be examined, a task that is not easily accomplished.

The difficulty of the empirical problem has generated some rather melancholy assessments of attempts to measure technological progress.

---

[25] Edwin Mansfield, *Technological Change*, (New York: W. W. Norton, 1971), p. 6.

[26] The term is in F. M. Scherer, "Firm Size, Market Structure, Opportunity, and the Output of Patented Inventions," *American Economic Review*, December 1965, pp. 1097–125.

The importance of this aspect of performance, however, assures continuing empirical efforts.

Product Differentiation. Product differentiation has been mentioned above as an element of market structure—a possible barrier to entry. Alternatively, however, it can be viewed as an aspect of competitive performance. To some degree, differentiation is within the control of firms, especially in markets in which advertising is an important form of competition.

Once again, significant problems may be encountered in interpreting observed performance. Does high advertising intensity—e.g., an advertising-to-sales ratio well above the norm—signify competitive behavior, perhaps an attempt by firms to provide prospective customers with the kind of full information that will enable the market to function in "textbook" fashion? Or does it instead represent an effort to erect entry barriers via a kind of "artificial" differentiation—not so much an attempt to inform as to create impressions based on advertising messages rather than on "objective" product qualities?

Summary. Performance indexes of competition seem invariably to encounter two important measurement obstacles: the absence of a well-defined competitive (or monopolistic) benchmark with which observations can be compared and the failure of available data to match up with the magnitudes that would serve as ideal measures. Despite these difficulties, the conceptual significance of performance to any assessment of market competition remains strong. Measurement efforts continue accordingly.

AN ASSESSMENT OF COMPETITION MEASURES

The burden of the discussion above should be clear. No single index of competition can be regarded as fully adequate. The reasons are twofold: first, substantial practical difficulties in the form of data imperfections interfere with efforts to assess competitiveness, especially for large samples of industries; even categorical rankings may not always be possible. Second, competition—however we may define it—does not lend itself to precise quantitative shorthand. The concept itself is sufficiently elusive that no single statistic is likely to capture it. The indexes discussed above nevertheless serve as a basis for some very useful clues to competitiveness.

Data Problems

We have noted above the data problems that commonly arise in attempts to construct indexes of competition. These difficulties range from the unobservability of relevant variables (e.g., the conduct of firms) to "noise" or bias in the magnitudes that can be observed (profit rates, concentration, etc.).

Whether these obstacles to measurement can be held to tolerable levels depends largely on the task at hand. Broad empirical examinations frequently can be designed to avoid the worst problems, usually by confining samples to well-defined industries or to firms for which relatively good data exist. Where the task is more specific—e.g., to determine the "competitiveness of industry A"—alternative strategies may be necessary. Substantial care must be taken in examining such variables as market share, concentration, and profit rates; yet, given the proper care, these variables can serve as a basis for very useful, if not fully precise, descriptions of competition.

Conceptual Problems

Even if we had access to "perfect" firm and industry data—a delightful prospect indeed!—our problems would not be fully resolved. The underlying conceptual difficulty is that the notion of competition is not reducible to *any* one-dimensional index, however sound that index may be. Furthermore, a multidimensional measure inevitably encounters the problem of assigning weights to its various dimensions. (If, for example, we seek to devise a broad structural index that takes account of concentration, entry barriers, and demand elasticity, how are we to combine these distinctive types of information?) Our difficulty at this point has nothing to do with the goodness of data. The question is rather: What weights are correct? Economic theory simply does not provide a clear answer.

Edward H. Chamberlin compared the problem to that of measuring a person's health: "Some aspects of health can be measured and others cannot. Among the former we have body temperature, blood pressure, metabolism, weight, etc., but these do not lend themselves to the construction of a *single* quantitative index of health."[27] In a similar spirit, Morris Adelman has observed that "competition, or monopoly, is not a

---

[27] "Measuring the Degree of Competition and Monopoly," in Chamberlin, *Monopoly*, p. 267.

brute physical fact but rather a hypothesis confirmed by the available evidence. . . ."[28]

The Usefulness of Competition Measures

Plainly, anyone who seeks a simple and straightforward index of competition will be disappointed, and the disappointment will not be fully ameliorated even by the development of better data or measurement technique. The absence of an ideal index, however, does not detract from the real usefulness of many of the measures discussed above.

If we ask, for example, how competitive the widget industry is, it may be possible to come up with a reasonably cogent answer.[29] If the industry is highly concentrated, entry barriers appear substantial, reported profits are far above the norm, companies' shares of the market are stable, and prices move in close concert, we may be confident that the industry is "monopolistic." Low concentration, low entry barriers, etc., would in contrast point to competitiveness. Where the signals are mixed, the answer is less clearcut; but even this may be an accurate reflection of ambiguity in the state of that industry's competition.

Competitive judgments can seldom be rendered with complete certainty or precision, and an element of subjectivity is unavoidable in most instances. Useful judgments are nonetheless possible for large numbers of industries. Competition, meaningfully defined, is both a process and an environment. It is not fully quantifiable; but if present, it leaves some observable evidence in its wake.

---

[28] Morris A. Adelman, "The Antimerger Act," *American Economic Review*, May 1961, pp. 236–44 (quotation at p. 237).

[29] How much data digging will be necessary is a separate question. If widgets comprise a well-defined market for which the Bureau of the Census gathers data and if major widget manufacturers are not highly diversified, the task will be relatively easy. If, at the other extreme, widgets do not comprise a well-defined market—perhaps because they are subject to strong competition from other products—one may decide that the question (How competitive is the widget industry?) is not only unanswerable but is not worth answering.

PART SIX
Forecasting

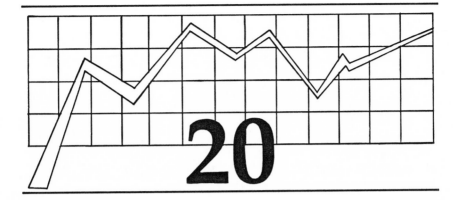

Fedwatching and the Federal Funds Market

William C. Melton, Ph.D.*
Vice President—Senior Economist
Investors Diversified Services, Inc.

Myriad factors affect the determination of interest rates, including the pace of economic activity, the mix of fiscal and monetary policies, the financing strategies of borrowers, and the preferences of investors. This chapter discusses a small subset of these factors—those directly affecting the rate on federal funds. The object is to present the basic concepts necessary to analyze the behavior of the major participants in the market as well as to describe some analytical techniques of interest to the practitioner.[1]

* Like many people, the author gets by with a little help from his friends. Critical comments and other assistance were generously provided by Irving Auerbach, Jeffrey Brummette, Louis V. B. Crandall, Kenneth D. Garbade, David S. Jones, William Jordan, Gerald Levy, Charles Lieberman, Jean M. Mahr, Christopher McCurdy, Paul Meek, Anne-Marie Meulendyke, Larry Ricciardelli, Madeleine D. Robinson, Marcia L. Stigum, Robert W. Stone, Thom B. Thurston, and Betsy B. White. Michele Farano labored mightily typing the manuscript, and Olga Vidal prepared the charts. The author alone bears responsibility for any remaining errors.

An earlier version appeared as Chapter 45 in Frank J. Fabozzi and Irving M. Pollack (eds.), *The Handbook of Fixed-Income Securities* (Homewood, Ill.: Dow Jones-Irwin, 1983).

[1] Though analysis of the federal funds market generally occupies only a portion of Fedwatchers' time, space limitations preclude discussion of techniques applied in money stock forecasting, for example.

A proper understanding of the funds market is crucial to market participants, since it is the immediate locus of Federal Reserve operations to affect the availability of reserves to the banking system—and no other single factor so influences other money market interest rates as the funds rate. Moreover, in view of the substantial rate volatility inherent in the Federal Reserve's reserves-oriented operating procedures—the potential of which was amply demonstrated during 1979–82—it is also worthwhile to consider whether—and how—the market could be made to function more efficiently.

The chapter first discusses forces affecting the funds market "in the large"—during a reserves statement week taken as a whole. Once the special character of the reserves market has been roughed out, the focus of the analysis shifts to the market "in the small"—the day-to-day behavior of market participants and the relation of that behavior to the potentially highly volatile daily movements of the funds rate. Throughout, the emphasis is on the (in)ability of market participants to understand and quantify factors affecting the market and, thus, to estimate the equilibrium funds rate. In that activity (among others), "Fedwatchers"—an apt vernacular description of the (sometimes) highly expert analysts of Fed policy—have a key role. In order to understand clearly the forecasting activities of Fedwatchers as they relate to the funds market, the next two sections discuss the major factors affecting bank reserves positions as well as the strategy of Federal Reserve open market operations. The chapter concludes with some thoughts on the inefficiencies created by the paucity of information available to market participants (relative to that in the hands of the Fed) together with suggestions as to how they might best be ameliorated.

Before proceeding to the analysis, a few definitional comments are in order. In referring to the federal funds market, most of the discussion actually has in mind the market for loans of immediately available funds typically settled via the Fed Wire. That market comprises not only federal funds proper (i.e., typically unsecured loans of immediately available funds through which member banks may secure reserve-free balances from certain categories of financial institutions) but also the market for repurchase agreements (RPs).[2] Since the security involved in loans of immediately available funds is largely unimportant in the analysis, this distinction is ignored.

---

[2] For discussions of the regulatory and other distinctions between federal funds and repurchase agreements, see Charles M. Lucas, Marcos T. Jones, and Thom B. Thurston, "Federal Funds and Repurchase Agreements," Federal Reserve Bank of New York *Quarterly Review,* Summer 1977, pp. 33–48; and Marcia L. Stigum, *The Money Market* (Homewood, Ill.: Dow Jones-Irwin, 1983).

THE RESERVES MARKET: IN THE LARGE

One of the most powerful techniques in the economist's analytical toolbox is the concept of a market equilibrium defined by demand and supply functions. The simple model typically ignores all dynamic aspects of price formation as well as risk aversion and the imperfect quality of available information—the very factors that account for some of the most interesting (and bizarre) behavior in the funds market. Nevertheless, precisely because the model is so austere, it can, if properly applied, focus the analysis on a set of fundamental determinants of the equilibrium interest rate that might otherwise be difficult to identify. In that spirit, this section uses a simple graphic model of the reserves market to illustrate some of the peculiarities of the supply and demand for reserves and to trace their consequences for the nature of equilibrium in the funds market as well as the Federal Reserve's implementation of monetary policy.

Supply of Reserves

The Federal Reserve controls the supply of reserves available to the banking system, though its control is imprecise in the very short run, principally due to the unpredictability of certain so-called operating factors (about which more later). For analytical purposes, the supply of reserves may be decomposed into two components: nonborrowed reserves and borrowed reserves. Nonborrowed reserves are those supplied by the Fed through acquisition of assets for its own account, other than through extension of accommodation credit through the discount window. Borrowed reserves are those supplied through accommodation lending.

Prior to October 6, 1979, the Fed attempted to alter the supply of nonborrowed reserves in whatever amount was required to maintain the federal funds rate at a target level. Afterward, the Fed adopted a reserves-oriented operating procedure—often described simply as "nonborrowed reserves targeting"—which, to a first approximation, required that the supply of nonborrowed reserves be kept on a target growth path.[3] For present purposes, the nature of the growth path is of secondary importance; the key point is that, unlike the period prior to

---

[3] The Fed continues to specify upper and lower bounds for the funds rate, but these differ from the pre-October 1979 bounds in that they are much wider and serve only to prompt consultations when they are breached. They do not constitute an operational constraint on the System account manager.

October 6, 1979, the supply of nonborrowed reserves is now essentially unresponsive to the funds rate.

In contrast, the supply of borrowed reserves continues to respond to the funds rate, though in a complex fashion that is the result of the peculiar historical evolution of the Fed discount window.[4] In essence, the Fed views borrowing as a privilege and not a right. Operationally, that principle generally means that one individual bank should not borrow too frequently; and when it does borrow, it should demonstrate an inability to secure funds in the market. The obvious way to do that is to bid aggressively for funds without successfully covering the reserves deficiency before applying to the discount window. Otherwise expressed, the willingness of a discount officer to accept a bank's request for accommodation is likely to be an increasing function of the spread of the funds rate over the discount rate.[5] However, the precise nature of that relationship depends on banks' *attitudes* toward borrowing from the Fed. For that reason, discount window borrowing has sometimes been viewed as demand determined, although it clearly is a channel for the supply of reserves.

It is now possible to assemble these two components of the Fed's supply of reserves in a diagram. As Exhibit 1 indicates, the supply schedule is vertical at lower levels of the funds rate and becomes positively sloped at higher rates.

Since borrowing is, for all practical purposes, the only channel for additions to the aggregate reserves of the banking system, the funds rate should not be above the discount rate when borrowing is at essentially "frictional" levels. Otherwise expressed, the reserves supply

---

[4] A key purpose of the Federal Reserve Act of 1913 was to establish a "lender of last resort," a central bank function first clearly defined by Walter Bagehot, the prominent 19th-century English economist, historian, and literary critic, who is also credited with the invention of the Treasury bill and the founding of the *Economist* magazine. Bagehot viewed the central bank as the ultimate source of liquidity in a financial crisis and framed the principle that credit extended under such circumstances should be charged an above-market interest rate to ensure that the central bank would be the last resort of banks in trouble and the first of their borrowing sources to be paid off as the crisis waned. In contrast, the Federal Reserve generally has sought to maintain its discount rate below the funds rate and to empty the (implied) threat of nonaccommodation in order to maintain discipline over banks seeking assistance. The logic to this approach is that banks experiencing temporary difficulties ought not to be penalized by the Fed for their misfortune. Were Bagehot alive today, he surely would point out that such an approach also reduces the incentive of banks to take measures to forestall the occurrence of such events.

[5] Discount window borrowings fall into two categories—short-term adjustment credit and extended credit. Extended credit includes long-term assistance provided by the Federal Reserve to certain troubled financial institutions. Since its volume is essentially unresponsive to the funds rate, it is best regarded as functionally a component of nonborrowed reserves, or the so-called operating factors. Short-term adjustment credit corresponds directly to the concept of borrowing employed in the text.

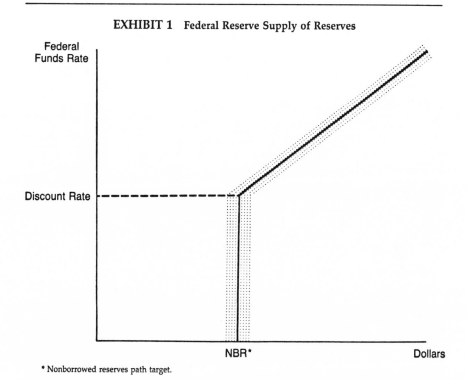

EXHIBIT 1 Federal Reserve Supply of Reserves

Federal Funds Rate

Discount Rate

NBR*   Dollars

* Nonborrowed reserves path target.

function begins to take on a positive slope at that approximate funds-rate level.

However, though this point is conceptually clear, a practical problem of interpretation arose from time to time when a surcharge on frequent borrowings by large institutions (those with deposits of $500 million or more) was applied.[6] Since the rules have provided that an institution must borrow in more than a specified number of statement weeks in the recent past in order to be subjected to the surcharge, the "effective" discount rate (i.e., the rate that banks perceive as the opportunity cost of reserves) was made a complex function of the volume of borrowing in past weeks as well as banks' inherently subjective appraisal of the likeli-

---

[6] Effective March 17, 1980, through May 7, 1980, the surcharge was set at 3 percent. Thereafter, it was eliminated, only to be reinstituted at a 2 percent level effective November 17, 1980, subsequently raised to 3 percent on December 5, 1980, and to 4 percent on May 5, 1981. Effective October 1, 1981, the surcharge was reduced to 3 percent, reduced again to 2 percent on October 13, 1981, and then eliminated entirely effective November 17, 1981.

hood that they might have to borrow in the future.[7] About all that could be said in practice was that the effective discount rate lay somewhere between the basic discount rate and that rate plus the surcharge.[8]

Finally, it is important to note that—for reasons that will be explored in more detail later on—the supply of nonborrowed reserves is not perfectly controlled by the Fed, at least over a period as short as a few weeks. As a result, the supply of nonborrowed reserves may actually fluctuate in a *range* around its estimated amount. In addition, though the relation of discount window borrowing to the funds rate is theoretically precise, in practice it is at times highly variable. The uncertainty thus introduced into the supply of nonborrowed and borrowed reserves is represented in Exhibit 1 by the shaded area around the supply schedule.

Demand for Reserves

Banks' demand for reserves is usefully decomposed into two components: required reserves and excess reserves. (Excess reserves are defined residually as the difference between total reserves and required reserves.)[9]

The computation of required reserves is fairly complex. Effective February 2, 1984, the reserves maintenance period was changed from seven days starting on Thursday and ending on Wednesday to fourteen days starting on Thursday and ending on the second Wednesday following.

---

[7] Specifically, until October 1, 1981, the rules stipulated that the surcharge would apply to an institution borrowing during (*a*) two successive statement weeks or (*b*) more than four weeks during a *calendar* quarter. Such an arrangement had the effect that, in a quarter in which borrowing had been modest, banks found themselves possessed of excess "tickets" as the quarter end approached, with the result that their attitude toward borrowing became more aggressive, making the effective discount rate plunge toward the basic rate. That process was especially evident during the first and third quarters of 1981. The Fed responded by altering the rules effective October 1, 1981, to replace the calendar quarter with a "moving quarter" consisting of the current statement week plus the 12 prior weeks. That change meant that there could never be a glut of "tickets" unless borrowing were at essentially frictional levels for a protracted period of time.

[8] Two considerations apparently caused the Fed to view the surcharge as a useful supplement to the basic discount rate. First, since the stringency of discount window administration varies considerably from one Federal Reserve district to another, subjecting frequent users of accommodation credit to the surcharge guarantees at least a minimum of uniformity of treatment of similar banks in different districts. In addition, with the surcharge structure in place, the "effective" discount rate tends to rise toward the full (i.e., basic plus surcharge) rate as borrowing pressure increases. Other things equal, that feature made the funds rate more responsive to borrowing pressure and was at least superficially consistent with the spirit of the operating procedures.

[9] Reserves can be maintained in two forms: collected deposits at a Federal Reserve Bank and holdings of vault cash. Deposits are measured during the current reserves maintenance period, but vault cash held approximately four weeks earlier counts as reserves during the current period.

Simultaneously, reserve requirements on *transactions* deposits—demand deposits and so-called "other checkable deposits" (mainly NOW accounts)—were made almost contemporaneous with the new two-week reserves maintenance period. Specifically, a bank's average level of transactions deposits in the two-week period starting on Tuesday two days prior to the beginning of the maintenance period and ending on Monday two days prior to the end of the maintenance period is multiplied by the applicable reserve requirement percentage to calculate reserves required to support the bank's transactions deposits. Since the *deposit computation period* for transactions deposits thus overlaps with the *reserves maintenance period* on twelve out of fourteen days, this system of reserve requirements is loosely described as "contemporaneous," in contrast to the previous "lagged" system in which weekly average deposits were used to compute required reserves in the one-week maintenance period two weeks later.

Under the current system, reserve requirements on nontransactions deposits are calculated on the basis of their two-week average four weeks prior to the maintenance period.

In the current maintenance period, reserves required to support nontransactions deposits are completely predetermined by events of four weeks earlier. In principle, the almost-contemporaneous reserve requirement applied to transactions deposits allows banks in the aggregate to alter their transactions deposits—and thus their required reserves—by varying their extension of credit. The system is too new to permit a verdict as to the practical importance of this effect. However, most would probably agree that the responsiveness of deposits to changes in interest rates during a maintenance period is quite small. Consequently, banks' demand for reserves with which to cover their reserve requirements is probably quite unresponsive to interest rates during the reserves maintenance period.

The second component of reserves demand, excess reserves, is generally kept at the most minimal levels consistent with the state of the art of funds transfers and management of banks' reserves positions.[10] In general, the large money-center banks, which devote substantial resources to managing their reserves positions, maintain their average excess reserves in the neighborhood of zero. The bulk of excess reserves—which do not earn interest—is held by smaller banks, for whom the cost savings from more precise management of reserves positions is less than the expense of staffing themselves adequately to monitor their positions.

---

[10] For a useful overview of the impact of increasing technological sophistication and reserves accounting changes on the behavior of excess reserves, see David C. Beek, "Excess Reserves and Reserves Targeting," Federal Reserve Bank of New York *Quarterly Review*, Autumn 1981, pp. 15–22.

Although the cost incentive induces banks generally to maintain their excess reserves at "frictional" levels, a modest degree of interest sensitivity remains in their demand for excess reserves. The reason is that Federal Reserve regulations permit banks to carry into the next reserves maintenance period a deficiency or excess in the bank's reserves position—provided that it is within a specified percentage of the bank's required reserves and provided further that the bank does not post deficiencies for two weeks in succession.[11] Although banks may have excesses in successive periods, the carry-over from the prior period to the current one may not be counted toward the current period's reserve position in such a case. Thus, if the funds rate is abnormally high at the end of a period, a bank with a small deficiency can reduce its funding cost by covering it in the following period, when (it is hoped) the rate is lower. Similarly, a soft funds rate at the end of the period may prompt potential sellers of funds to carry over small excesses rather than to sell the funds at an abnormally low rate.[12] The result is that federal funds are not a completely perishable commodity; to a very limited extent they can be "stored" in the current reserves maintenance period and "consumed" in the following period (alternatively, "consumed" this period and "replenished" in the next). That imparts a modest degree of interest sensitivity to banks' demand for excess reserves.

The amount of reserves required to support nontransactions deposits is known with great precision due to its computation from deposit levels in prior weeks. But that is not true of reserves required to support transactions deposits. Accordingly, the demand for total required reserves is uncertain during the maintenance period, and that fact is indicated in Exhibit 3 by the shaded area around the demand schedule for required reserves.

In addition, the demand for excess reserves can be highly erratic at times, reflecting (among other things) banks' imperfect knowledge of

---

[11] The regulations introduced in February 1984 provided that the "carry-over" percentage be three percent for six months, two and one-half percent for six months after that, and two percent from February 1985 onward.

[12] Assuming a bank's reserves position in the current period is even and that it was even or deficient in the prior week, the expected profit from buying funds to carry into the next week is simply the spread of the rate expected to prevail next week over the current rate. However, if the bank carried in an excess from last week, that amount will be lost, thus reducing the expected profit. Consequently, for a bank contemplating "doubling up" in this way, the break-even funds rate (i.e., the current funds that makes the expected profit zero) can be found by using the following formula:

$$\text{Break-even funds rate} = \frac{\text{Carry-over from this period}}{\text{Carry-over from last period} + \text{Carry-over from this period}} \times \text{Funds rate expected next period}$$

their true reserves positions as well as interest rate expectations. This uncertainty is indicated in Exhibit 2 by the shaded area around the demand schedule for excess reserves.

Summing banks' demand for required reserves and excess reserves, the demand for total reserves has the shape shown in Exhibit 3. Reflect-

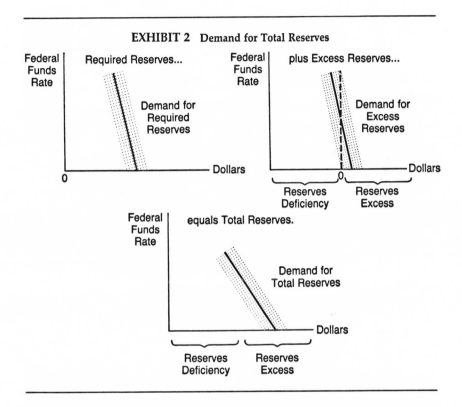

EXHIBIT 2   Demand for Total Reserves

ing the limited ability of banks to store excess reserves, the function has a steeply negative slope, indicating a modest responsiveness of reserves demand to interest rates.

Market Equilibrium

Having defined the properties of the supply and demand for reserves during a statement week, it remains to put them together to analyze the nature of the market equilibrium and, in particular, the source of the potential volatility of the funds rate.

EXHIBIT 3   Equilibrium in the Federal Funds Market

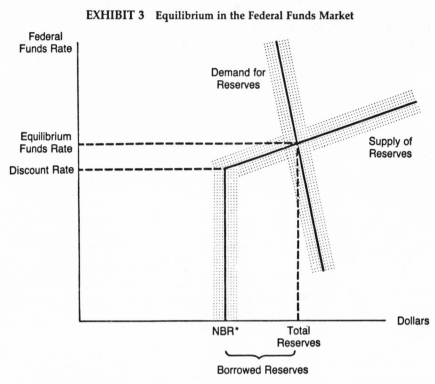

* Path target for nonborrowed reserves (actually path target plus a small, frictional amount of borrowed reserves).

Exhibit 3 shows the equilibrium funds rate determined by the inter-section of the supply and demand functions discussed earlier. The equi-librium is reasonably stable so long as the amount of borrowing from the discount window remains above frictional levels. In that case, the spread of the funds rate over the discount rate is determined by banks' reluctance to borrow (alternatively, the firmness of discount window administration).[13] Unanticipated shocks to the demand for excess re-

---

[13] This underscores the radically different role of the discount rate in the post-October 6, 1979, period compared with its earlier function. Prior to that time, the funds-rate target set the trading range for the funds rate, and the discount rate was merely adjusted from time to time to keep it in line with the funds rate (i.e., to keep the spread from becoming enlarged). That helped enforce discipline at the discount window. In contrast, the dis-count rate now serves as the base for the funds-rate structure, with the spread determined by the degree of borrowing pressure. Consequently, although a discount-rate increase in the earlier period need have no impact on the funds rate, an increase now would be expected to lift the funds rate by an almost identical amount.

serves are offset by equal movements of borrowed reserves, with relatively modest impacts on the funds rate. Of course, if something should cause the slope of the borrowing function to increase (e.g., an increase of "discipline" exerted on banks by the Fed's discount officers) then the impact on the funds rate will be greater.

Moreover, if borrowing becomes depressed—perhaps as a result of slow growth of the money supply and, thus, of required reserves relative to the target for nonborrowed reserves—then the equilibrium funds rate is determined by the intersection of the vertical supply schedule for nonborrowed reserves with the *almost* vertical reserves demand schedule. In that situation, small errors in the Fed's supply of nonborrowed reserves and small shocks to banks' demand for excess reserves can produce large movements of the funds rate. Moreover, an attempt by the Fed to keep nonborrowed reserves greater than required reserves will enlarge excess reserves while forcing borrowing to frictional levels, so that a pell-mell drop of the funds rate may well ensue, reflecting the "perishability" of the excess funds.

In other words, though the funds market is always volatile due to shocks of various sorts, it is especially so when borrowing is so low that the discount rate may cease to serve as a prop under the funds rate. The Fed, of course, is well aware of that fact and is not likely to allow a "free-fall" to develop. It has several options available to forestall such a situation. Perhaps the most obvious is to revert to some kind of funds-rate targeting. That is essentially what was done in the May–June 1980 period, when borrowing was at frictional levels and the funds rate repeatedly challenged or breached the lower limit of the funds-rate band then in force. As noted earlier, targeting the funds rate causes the Fed to lose control of nonborrowed reserves through supplying or draining whatever amount is necessary to keep the funds rate at the desired level. Another way to brake the decline of the funds rate without explicitly targeting its level is to depress the supply of nonborrowed reserves sufficiently to maintain borrowings—at least for a time—at an above-frictional level. This approach was employed during March–April 1981 and again in autumn of that year. In terms of Exhibit 4, the policy shifts the whole supply function to the left, thereby keeping some distance between the demand function and nonborrowed reserves. Such an approach is obviously akin to funds-rate targeting, but the key difference is that the Fed does not "endogenize" its provision of nonborrowed reserves. Moreover, since the objective presumably is to allow the funds rate to decline in a reasonably restrained fashion, a simultaneous reduction of the discount rate would be appropriate. That way, the funds rate (in principle) will decline without entering the free-fall zone.

Even more akin to funds-rate targeting was the approach followed from late 1982 through the present (Spring 1984). The Fed for all practi-

cal purposes adopted discount-window borrowings as its operating target. Except for some minor policy-related adjustments and occasional
errors in reserves provision, the volume of borrowed reserves was maintained about unchanged during the period. The discount rate was held
constant at 8½ percent. Naturally, under these circumstances the funds
rate was relatively stable as well, at least in comparison to prior years. In
this approach, the Fed's supply of nonborrowed reserves *was* endo-
genized.

Excursus: Total Reserves Targeting

In general, monetarist economists advocate tight control of the supply of reserves. That implies a role for the discount rate that is radically
different from its role in nonborrowed reserves targeting. Instead of
serving as a prop *under* the funds rate as in Exhibit 3, a "penalty"
discount rate is advocated that would be kept well above the normal
trading range of the funds rate. That way, as depicted in Exhibit 4, the

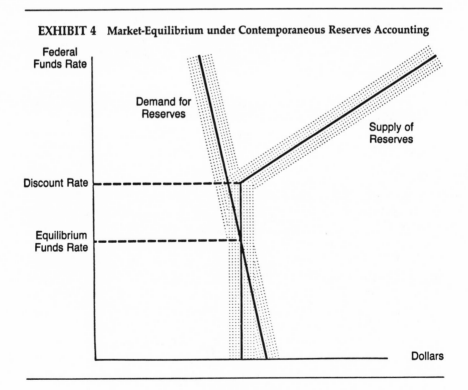

EXHIBIT 4   Market-Equilibrium under Contemporaneous Reserves Accounting

relevant range of the reserves supply function is vertical, while the demand for reserves is sharply negatively sloped. As a result, the funds rate under total reserves targeting would be more volatile than currently, not because of the contemporaneous calculation of required reserves on transactions deposits—in fact, *despite* that feature—but because of the lack of interest sensitivity in the relevant portion of the reserves supply function. Control over the supply of reserves obviously would become more precise. However, there could well be substantial slippage between reserves and the money supply. In particular, if the enlarged reserves carry-over provisions introduced in February 1984 were retained, the increased interest sensitivity of demand for excess reserves will allow banks to temporarily defer adjustments in deposits, thus impairing somewhat the precision of monetary control.

Most econometric evidence suggests that total reserves targeting would at best improve monetary control marginally over the span of a month or so without affecting its precision over longer time horizons. Thus one's attitude toward the choice between total reserves targeting and nonborrowed reserves targeting is importantly conditioned on the importance one attaches to short-run monetary control as well as the greater interest rate volatility likely to be associated with total reserves targeting.

Fed Tracking Paths

Up to this point, the analysis has focused on the funds market at a point in time in which the supply of nonborrowed reserves is held constant. In general, the Fed defines a short-run growth path for nonborrowed reserves thought to be consistent with the short-term monetary growth target adopted by the Federal Open Market Committee (FOMC).

It is useful to visualize graphically the tracking paths for nonborrowed and total reserves and to relate them to the funds market model developed earlier. Exhibit 5 depicts, in two panels, a stylized tracking path for nonborrowed reserves. The difference between that path and the path of total reserves is obviously equal to borrowed reserves. In the top panel, total reserves increases rapidly, propelled by the rising levels of required reserves produced by deposit growth exceeding the short-term target rate. As a result, borrowing increases. In terms of Exhibit 3, the demand for reserves is shifting to the right, increasing borrowed reserves and with it the funds rate. Parenthetically, it should be noted that on occasion the Fed has acted to accelerate the adjustment of interest rates by depressing the nonborrowed reserves path to increase the amount of borrowing pressure quickly. In terms of Exhibit 3, such a

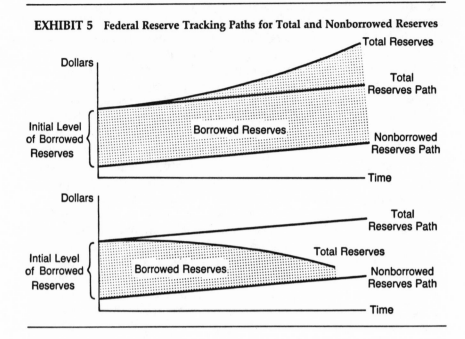

EXHIBIT 5   Federal Reserve Tracking Paths for Total and Nonborrowed Reserves

policy shifts the supply of reserves to the left. The trajectory of total reserves shown in the bottom panel of Exhibit 5 is produced by stagnating deposit growth. As total reserves approaches the nonborrowed reserves path (i.e., as borrowing declines toward zero), the nonborrowed reserves path must be adjusted downward if the funds rate is not to enter into the free-fall zone.

Rationale for Reserves Targets

The rationale for the Fed's adoption of the reserves-oriented operating procedures was to speed the adjustment of the funds rate to a deviation of monetary growth from target. Although the earlier operating procedures (which embodied narrow tolerance ranges for the funds rate) in principle could have been used to react equally as fast, in practice the funds rate was quite slow to respond.[14] The most likely explana-

---

[14] Studies of the Fed's speed of reaction to deviations of money growth from target in the pre-1979 period uniformly found a slow response. See, for example, Gary Stern and Paul De Rosa, "Monetary Control and the Federal Funds Rate," *Journal of Monetary Economics*, February 1976.

tion is that the Fed at the time was operating in a political environment in which sensitivity to short-run volatility was much greater than at present, while concern with the longer-run problems of monetary growth and inflation was less pronounced. In addition, the FOMC is like almost any other committee in that it is cautious in reacting to new and typically tentative data; consequently, whatever its target may be, that target will probably be adjusted slowly. In a sense, the new procedure represented a middle ground between funds-rate targeting and a full-fledged total reserves targeting procedure incorporating contemporaneous reserves accounting and a penalty discount rate. As noted earlier, the latter procedure would provide almost instantaneous adjustment of the funds rate, at the cost of a large degree of rate volatility.

The reserves-oriented procedures retain an active role for the FOMC and the staff and do not work mechanically as some monetarists have occasionally envisioned. First, the FOMC must decide the relative emphasis to be given the various monetary aggregates. As the Fed has pointed out repeatedly, in a period of rapid change in the payments mechanism, a determination as to the appropriate transactions measure is no trivial task. Second, given the desired emphasis, the Committee must set short-run paths to correct for deviations from the annual targets; moreover, adjustments must be made by the staff for the frequent short-run shifts in the reserve multiplier resulting from changes in the relative proportions of reservable components of the monetary aggregates. Third, some degree of judgment must be employed in responding to changes in an aggregate that are suspected of being transitory in nature. Finally, when establishing the intermeeting reserves tracking paths, the FOMC must exercise discretion in setting the initial amount of borrowing (though as a rule it is kept close to levels prevailing before the meeting). Although the FOMC thus has a large judgmental input under the reserves-oriented operating procedure and although in all likelihood the committee's response is slow as before, there is a key difference between the new procedures and the old: Under the reserves-oriented procedures, slow adjustment of the reserves path by the FOMC does not inhibit the funds rate from reacting promptly, wheres the old procedures often delayed precisely that response. On the other hand, to the extent that the volume of borrowed reserves is itself the effective operating target, reactions of the funds rate *will* be inhibited, much as they were under the old procedures.

Studies by the staff of the Federal Reserve Board suggest that faster adjustment of the funds rate increases the likelihood of monetary targets being hit, though it is unclear whether still faster adjustment speeds (as probably would be produced through total reserves targeting) might be desirable or whether the present adjustment speed produced by nonborrowed reserves targeting itself is too fast.[15] An attempted resolution of these issues would carry the discussion far beyond the confines of this chapter. The crucial point here is that a faster adjustment speed increases funds market participants' need for information concerning factors affecting the market equilibrium far beyond what was adequate in the past. The next section explains how funds traders attempt to solve that problem.

THE RESERVES MARKET: IN THE SMALL

This section changes the focus of the analysis from the supply and demand for reserves in the reserves maintenance period as a whole to the adjustment of banks' reserves positions and the Fed's provision of reserves *during* the period.

Supplying Reserves: The Fed's Problem

In supplying nonborrowed reserves during the reserves maintenance period, the Fed typically tries to hit its target.[16] That target may be derived from short-run growth objectives for primarily M1 as was the case during 1979–82, or it may be inferred from a desired level of "reserves pressure"—i.e., discount-window borrowings. In either case, the task is complicated by the at times highly erratic movements of the so-called operating factors. Easily the most variable such factor is Federal Reserve float, the weekly average of which can swing by $2 billion or more in response to seasonal interruptions in the payments system or to acute operational problems. (Float and other operating factors are discussed in more detail below.) In contrast, the average weekly reserves provision called for by the growth path for nonborrowed reserves is only on the order of about $50 million. The upshot is that, for the most part, the Fed's open market operations are "defensive" in nature; that is, they are intended to offset a swing in reserves availability produced by float or some other operating factor rather than to provide the small increment of reserves called for by the target.

Moreover, given the overall need to add to or drain from the weekly average level of reserves, the Fed still must decide the *timing* of open market operations during the reserves maintenance period. Several factors influence the timing decision. First, the information available to the Fed's Open Market Desk (hereafter, Desk) concerning reserves supplies

---

[15] For evidence on this question, see *New Monetary Control Procedures*, Board of Governors of the Federal Reserve System, February 1981.

[16] For an excellent description of the daily routine of the Desk, see Paul Meek, *U.S. Monetary Policy and Financial Markets* (New York: Federal Reserve Bank of New York, 1982).

generally becomes more complete and reliable as the period progresses. All other things equal, then, the Desk would probably prefer to delay arranging any open market operations.

Also, the Desk on occasion may attempt to smooth out swings in the availability of reserves during the period so as to avoid unnecessary volatility in the funds market. Since banks must meet reserve requirements on an average basis for the period as a whole, *intra*period swings in reserves availability in principle need have no impact on the funds rate. Indeed, if banks were able to anticipate the movement in availability with confidence, they could passively allow their reserves positions to mirror the swing, and there would be no impact on the funds rate. In practice, banks are highly uncertain about their reserves positions—as is discussed further below—and the funds rate is likely to respond to major daily imbalances between banks' "normal" reserves positions and actual availability. Though such funds-rate movements may mislead some market participants, the Fed in recent years has been much less inclined than in the past to smooth out swings in availability. Nevertheless, if projections suggest a very large excess of reserves emerging prior to a weekend, the Desk probably would want to offset the glut on Thursday or Friday rather than see the funds rate temporarily depressed. Similarly, if the reserves market appears generally in balance prior to the weekend, with a major excess supply expected to emerge later, then the Desk's natural inclination would be to delay the reserves-draining operation until after the weekend. On the other hand, moderate intraperiod swings in reserves availability probably would be ignored.

Smoothing adjustments may also be necessitated by variations in the distribution of discount window borrowing during the period. The problem is rooted in the institutional phenomenon that virtually all discount window borrowing by large banks (abstracting from long-term credit extensions) is done on only two days: Friday and Wednesday.[17] If, as is usually the case, the discount rate is below the Fed funds rate, Friday is the preferred day to borrow. This is because borrowing on that day counts for three days, thus magnifying the favorable impact of the below-market discount rate on a bank's average funds cost for the week. (Primarily regional banks can succeed with such a tactic; discount window administration at the New York Federal Reserve Bank is generally acknowledged to be more stringent than in other Federal Reserve districts.) Indeed, as Exhibit 6 illustrates, the Wednesday percentage of

---

[17] When small banks borrow from the discount window, they frequently do so for every day of the statement week. The reason is that such banks almost always are sellers of federal funds, so that if they have sustained a reserve drain so large that it cannot be covered by reducing funds sales, there may be no practical alternative to seeking accommodation for a number of days.

EXHIBIT 6   Behavior of Federal Reserve Adjustment Borrowing

	Average Federal Funds Rate Less Discount Rate	Average Borrowed Reserves	Avg. Net Borrowed Reserves	Wednesday Borrowing as a Percentage of Week Total			
				Mean	Std. Dev.	Min.	Max.
1976	%−0.44	$ 85	$−134	40.6%	24.4%	7.8%	82.1%
1977	0.06	464	250	29.4	22.4	7.6	92.8
1978	0.40	868	671	20.5	9.9	7.5	56.3
1979	0.88	1338	1116	19.6	9.0	7.0	47.7
1980	0.79	1232	934	28.1	24.0	4.1	97.2
1981	0.11	1266	964	27.2	15.6	7.5	89.2
1982	1.21	876	516	32.0	20.0	6.2	88.3
1983	0.59	664	167	33.5	21.7	3.7	86.3

Note: Borrowing data have been adjusted to remove extended credit advanced to certain institutions. The discount rate includes the discount-rate surcharges applied at various times during 1980–81. Since the surcharge was not binding for several months in 1981, the difference between the funds rate and the fully surcharged discount rate is deceptively small for that year.

total borrowing is negatively related to the overall level of borrowing. In 1976, when banks actually averaged net free reserves and the funds rate was low relative to the discount rate, Wednesday borrowing averaged about 40 percent of the total. During 1978–79, when borrowing traffic was much greater and the funds rate was correspondingly higher than the discount rate, the Wednesday percentage was about half as large, reflecting the greater attractiveness of Friday borrowing. However, during 1980–83 the Wednesday percentage on average was substantially higher than in 1978–79 and more erratic, despite the fact that average borrowing was about the same in both periods. Though the reasons for that phenomenon are not clear, it is probably related to the advent of the reserves-oriented operating procedures in late 1979 and perhaps to the effect of the discount rate surcharge on banks' borrowing behavior.

The substantial variability of the distribution of borrowing traffic during the reserves maintenance period can create problems for the Desk. For example, if for some reason borrowing is unexpectedly high early in the period, the period's borrowing target may have been fulfilled—or even overfulfilled—leaving nothing to be done on the final Wednesday. The result would be downward pressure on the funds rate unless the Desk entered the market to drain out some of the excess.[18] Such an

---

[18] In a sense, Friday borrowing is "demand-determined," largely reflecting banks' efforts to take advantage of a (possibly) below-market discount rate. By the final Wednesday afternoon, however, the total amount of borrowing remaining to be done is almost completely determined by reserves availability earlier in the period. That means that on the final Wednesday (and perhaps somewhat earlier) the funds rate responds to the scale of borrowing and not the other way around as on a Friday.

operation would involve a deliberate, though probably temporary, departure from the nonborrowed reserves path rather than merely a decision with regard to the timing of reserves availability during the maintenance period.[19]

Once the Desk has formed a view with regard to the desirable timing of any operations affecting reserves availability, it must choose an instrument to accomplish the objective. Basically, the decision involves a choice between (1) permanent reserves operations versus temporary ones and (2) various alternative kinds of temporary operations. In order to avoid interfering with the market's determination of interest rates, the Desk tries to minimize its presence in the market. Thus, if there is a need to add reserves over a substantial period of time (e.g., during the late-year holiday season), the natural course is to make one or more outright purchases of securities. One way this can be done is to buy them from the foreign central banks for whom the New York Fed acts as agent and securities custodian. Such a transaction would be arranged internally and would involve no operations in the market; it thus serves as a convenient device to reduce the Fed's presence in the market. The major limitation of that kind of transaction is that the decision to buy or sell securities is made by the foreign customers, so that the Fed can take advantage of a timely opportunity to carry out its reserves-adding task this way, but it cannot create that opportunity itself. In the event that no such opportunity appears, the Fed must instead purchase the securities in the market by asking dealers for their offers.[20] Regardless of how the outright purchase (sale) of securities is arranged, its purpose is to relieve the Fed of the necessity of repeatedly carrying out temporary additions (drains) of reserves for a protracted period of time.

In the event of a need to drain reserves over a substantial time period, a sale of securities to foreign accounts, if possible, would be convenient. But in this case, there is another nonmarket option as well: The Fed can bid to redeem some of its maturing bills at the regular weekly auction of

---

[19] On not a few occasions, the desk has made precisely such a departure in nonborrowed reserves provision in order to offset swings of borrowing. For details, see Paul Meek and Fred J. Levin, "Implementing the New Operating Procedures: The View from the Trading Desk," in *New Monetary Control Procedures.*

[20] By law, the Federal Reserve may not bid to increase its holdings of maturing Treasury bills or coupons in an auction. The original purpose of this restriction apparently was to prevent the Treasury from selling unlimited amounts of securities directly to the Fed; instead, the Treasury was to be subject to the discipline of the market. At present, the main practical justification for the restriction is that any attempt by the Fed to enlarge its holdings in an auction would, in effect, reduce the size of the offering to the public below the size announced, thus tending to produce an unexpectedly high price (low yield) on the issue. That could be disadvantageous to securities dealers and others submitting competitive bids for the issue.

Treasury bills. To do so, the Fed submits a noncompetitive tender for an amount smaller than its holding of the maturing issues. The major limitation of this approach is that the Fed obviously can redeem only as much as it holds of the maturing issues and in practice would not want to disrupt the auction process by concentrating a large redemption in a single auction. Consequently, only reserves drains in amounts of $500 million or so are likely to be implemented in this fashion. Larger operations will involve outright sales of securities in the market.[21]

When a reserves need is perceived to be temporary, affecting only one or a few statement weeks, The Fed's preferred action is to arrange repurchase agreements (RPs) with the dealers.[22] That injects reserves for the duration of the RPs and is operationally simpler and less obtrusive than would be an outright purchase of securities followed by an outright sale.

RPs can be arranged by the Fed for its own account—so-called System RPs—or by the Fed as agent for its customers.

The Federal Reserve Bank of New York performs a number of banking services for foreign central banks and several international organizations. Typically the Fed handles their very short-term investments by in effect doing RPs with them, using securities in the Fed's portfolio as collateral.[23] The total of such short-term investment balances is sometimes informally referred to as the "internal RP pool," reflecting the fact that the investments are processed internally at the Fed for the most part, with no private market participants involved. When the Desk wishes to inject reserves by reducing the portion of the pool invested with the Fed, it does so by executing some of the investment orders with the dealers as so-called "customer RPs." What remains of the pool is invested with the Fed and is described on the Fed's balance sheet as "matched sale-purchase transactions executed internally with customer accounts" (more on these below).

Since the Fed treats the pool as one of several operating factors affecting reserves availability, there is no difference between the reserves

---

[21] In practice, outright sales of securities are rather rare. They sometimes occur early in the year to implement a seasonal drain of reserves. In addition, outright sales tend to be associated with reductions of reserve requirements, which otherwise might produce a substantial reserve excess.

[22] See *Monetary Control Procedures*.

[23] In effect, an RP is a collateralized loan. When a dealer arranges an RP, (s)he transfers title to a security to the lender in exchange for cash. At maturity, the transaction reverses. The security is returned to the dealer, and the lender receives the original principal plus interest due. A so-called "reverse RP" operates in exactly the same way, except the dealer temporarily lends out cash in exchange for a security.
For more details, see Stigum, *op. cit.*

impact of System and customer RPs—though that fact is not always recognized by market participants. If they are functionally identical, then what explains the Fed's choice between them? As a rule, the Fed employs customer RPs when it estimates a reserves need to be small.[24] The largest customer RP ever arranged totaled only $3 billion, and the average size is $1–2 billion. In contrast, System RPs have been executed fairly often for amounts as great as $6–7 billion. The feasible size of customer RPs is fundamentally limited by the available volume of foreign investment orders, which generally average $2–3 billion. Moreover, since the foreign orders primarily constitute working cash balances of central banks, it is rather unusual for the Desk to arrange multiday customer RPs, though some have occurred. Thus, if a multiday RP is needed, a System transaction is the most likely alternative. Finally, for institutional reasons, only Treasury and agency securities are eligible collateral for customer RPs, although those securities as well as certain bankers' acceptances are eligible for System RPs.[25] When there is an ample "floating supply" of collateral, arranging customer RPs presents no problem; but if collateral is rather scarce, a premium (i.e., a lower-than-market rate) would be expected to be charged on the customer RPs.[26] Rather than have its customers disadvantaged in such a fashion, the Fed would probably prefer to execute the foreign orders internally and arrange System RPs in the market.[27] In fact, if the collateral shortage were severe, the Desk might experience difficulty in executing the desired amount of System RPs.[28] When faced with such a situation in the past, the Desk frequently has preannounced its RPs (e.g., notified dealers on Wednesday afternoon of its intention to do RPs on the following Thursday) in order to encourage dealers and their customers to keep collateral available for use with the System RPs.

---

[24] When the Fed was targeting the funds rate, customer RPs frequently were employed to signal that the Fed had no objection to the current funds rate but wanted to add reserves to meet a modest estimated reserve need. The new operating procedures have obviated that practice.

[25] Moreover, until relatively recently, collateral for customer RPs was priced at market value, and that for system RPs was priced at par value. That meant that the dealer required more collateral per dollar of customer RPs than of system RPs. Currently, collateral for both forms of RPs is priced at market value, including any accrued interest.

[26] Before 1972, only securities owned by dealer firms recognized by the Federal Reserve Bank of New York—so-called primary dealers—were eligible collateral for RPs. Since then, securities obtained by the firms through separate transactions with their customers are also eligible.

[27] When foreign orders are executed internally (i.e., not passed through to the market as customer RPs), the Fed pays an average rate obtained when it surveys dealers.

[28] A collateral shortage may exist when the floating supply of eligible securities in the hands of dealers and their customers is relatively small, as when widespread expectations of rising interest rates cause dealers and banks to trim their holdings of securities.

A temporary reserves-draining operation is simpler because matched sale-purchase transactions (MSPs), which are functionally equivalent to reverse repurchase agreements, can be used to remove the temporary reserves glut.[29] Here again, however, there may be a delicate problem of choice of technique. Frequently, market participants show relatively poor proposals to the Fed for multiday MSPs for an abundantly clear reason: They are being asked to extend the Fed a fixed-rate loan when they have at least some grounds for suspecting that the rationale for the MSPs might be to reduce the availability of reserves. All other things equal, such an operation would raise short-term interest rates and thus would increase their costs of funding that loan.[30] Proposals are more competitive for overnight MSPs or for multiday MSPs when market participants generally recognize the need to drain reserves. As a result, the Fed may well encounter a situation in which it is simply unable to drain a sufficient amount of reserves via multiday MSPs arranged, for example, on Thursday (without, that is, accepting rates well above the going market rate) and thus must return for more on Friday. This problem can be alleviated somewhat by offering simultaneously overnight and multiday MSPs.

Finally, if inadequate proposals prevent the Desk from achieving the desired reserves add (drain), the Treasury may be asked to alter the balances in its account at the Fed. Such an operation would take care of the problem if an additional drain is called for, but there can be difficulties when Treasury balances are used to inject reserves. The reason is that Treasury deposits must be collateralized; and if banks have insufficient collateral available, they will remit the balances back to the Treasury's Fed account, thus frustrating the reserves injection. In any event, manipulation of Treasury balances to adjust reserves positions is done relatively infrequently; in general, balances in the Treasury's Fed account are maintained close to a weekly average of $3 billion.[31]

---

[29] Since the Federal Reserve Act prohibits the Federal Reserve banks from borrowing from the public, reverse RPs were and are viewed as an illegal transaction for the Fed. However, in 1966, a sudden temporary increase in float resulting from a disruption of airline service prompted the innovation of the matched (cash) sale- (forward) purchase agreement. The agreement is structured as two separate transactions and is therefore legal under the act's authorization to buy and sell securities. Moral: There's more than one way to skin a cat! Operationally, MSPs are less time-consuming for the Desk than are RPs, since the Fed controls the collateral. That is, the Fed can specify the one or two bill issues in its portfolio that are to be used in the MSPs and set the prices easily. For RPs, however, the Fed must accept whatever eligible collateral the dealers wish to offer, and the pricing task is commensurately greater.

[30] On the other hand, if the MSPs are widely perceived to be required to offset a reserve excess due to movements of the operating factors, then proposals likely will be more competitive.

[31] This procedure was reintroduced in November 1978, when new regulations were adopted governing Treasury tax and loan accounts. For details, see Joan E. Lovett, "Treasury Tax and Loan Accounts and Federal Reserve Open Market Operations," Federal Reserve Bank of New York *Quarterly Review*, Summer 1978, pp. 41–46.

Banks' Problem: Managing Reserves Positions

The key objective of a bank in managing its reserves position during a reserves maintenance period is to maintain its weekly average level of excess reserves as close as possible to zero. The reason is that excess reserves earn no interest and may be applied to a bank's reserve requirement in the subsequent period only to a limited extent. The two principal areas of uncertainty affecting a bank as it begins the period are the scale of its needs for funds and the level of the federal funds rate during the course of the period. The latter was especially volatile during 1979–82. The former is the result of the net flow of collected funds to the bank during the period. For the most part, it reflects transfers in and out of deposit accounts; but it is also affected by maturing securities and other sources of funds. For a small bank serving primarily retail customers, uncertainty concerning its funds need may be minor. In contrast, large money-center banks sometimes sustain net increases or decreases of 20 percent or more in their demand deposits in a single day. If such movements are so erratic as to be essentially unpredictable, then the bank faces a difficult task in controlling its reserves position.

In addition, a bank's funds trader works under several major constraints as he or she attempts to home in on the zero excess reserves target. First, as noted earlier, a modest deficiency of required reserves may be carried in from one maintenance period to the next, but significant penalties will be incurred if the bank is deficient in the second period. Thus, following a deficiency, a funds trader must exercise special care to end up even or in an excess position subsequently. If an excess is carried over in two consecutive periods, the first carry-over is lost, so that also involves a cost. Second, the Federal Reserve does not allow banks to have an overnight overdraft in their reserves accounts (that would constitute a loan by the Fed). Recently the Fed has gone even further and has discouraged banks from allowing overdrafts to occur in their accounts *during* the business day. That limits the ability of a funds trader to maintain a "short" position in a reserve account. Third, it is generally rather late in the day before the funds trader can know what the closing position in his or her Fed account will be; that operational constraint limits somewhat the trader's willingness to take a view in the funds market earlier in the day.

Most funds traders cope with these constraints by covering their reserves need incrementally during the two-week maintenance period, as available information concerning their average reserves need becomes more refined with each passing day.[32] Moreover, even if the trader feels

---

[32] The major exception is that a funds trader consciously preparing to borrow from the Fed discount window will purposely try to stay in a deficit position before going to the window. In doing so, the trader will generally not sell funds—the Fed would frown on that—but rather will avoid buying funds by refusing to bid at the market rate.

confident about his or her reserves need and the direction of the funds rate, the inability to run a deficit in the reserves account limits the trader's ability to "take a view." For example, a trader who expects the funds rate to decline will want to have a "short" position in the reserves account (i.e., to have less reserves in the account than necessary to cover that day's normal portion of the total weekly reserve need), which the trader will cover later (it is hoped) at a lower rate. But the constraint on daylight and overnight overdrafts limits the trader's ability to do that. Similarly, a trader who expects the funds rate to increase will want to have a "long" position now, followed by a sufficiently short position later as to make the excess reserves average about zero over the period as a whole. Here again, the overdraft constraint limits the amount of funds that can be sold later and thus the size of the long position that can be taken now. In fact, even if they have a well-defined rate outlook, large money-center banks typically run deficit positions during most of the maintenance period, which they cover starting on the final Monday. That minimizes the risk that they may be caught with surpluses early in the period that would prevent making excess reserves average zero (or close to it) without running an overdraft later in the period. (The mirror image of this process is that small banks and other sellers of funds that have much less uncertainty concerning their positions run surpluses during most of the period.)

To a very minor extent, the overdraft constraint may be offset by arranging transactions in the forward market for Federal funds. In the forward market, traders buy or sell funds today for settlement on future days when the transaction can be covered in the cash market. This device thus allows traders the possibility of realizing a potentially substantial spread between the rate at which they sell funds and the rate at which they buy them (if they guess right) without having to arrange all the transactions on the same day and without running an overdraft on any day.

However, volume in the forward funds market is very small relative to total transactions and is even smaller now than in the recent past. The primary reason for the decline in activity is the demise of so-called Eurodollar arbitrage, a technique by which large banks were able to reduce their effective required reserves.[33] Arbitrage created an incentive for forward funds transactions to be arranged for Friday and Monday in order to lock in the profit from the transaction. Before September 1980, such forward trades frequently accounted for 10 percent or more of total funds trades on those days.[34] However, by late 1981 forward trades—

---

[33] The best description of Eurodollar arbitrage is Warren L. Coats, Jr., "The Weekend Eurodollar Game," *Journal of Finance*, June 1981, pp. 649–60.

[34] The basis for these statements is the author's inspection of the records of trades kept by one of the largest federal funds brokers.

though more dispersed throughout the week—generally accounted for only about 1 percent of total volume; and on a fair number of days, there was no forward trading at all. Moreover, such trading as there was tended to be limited to a handful of banks.

Intraperiod Pattern of the Funds Rate

The preceding discussion has outlined the essential relationships a funds trader should consider when forming a view as to the likely course of the funds rate during the two-week reserves maintenance period. First, one needs to know the Fed's implied target for borrowing during the period. Assume also that actual borrowing closely approximates the target. Then, by solving the relationship between borrowing and the spread of the funds rate over the discount rate—a relationship that appears to have changed substantially since the introduction of contemporaneous reserve requirements in February 1984—a notion of the funds rate can be formed consistent with the borrowing target (given the discount rate). And *that* is the level at which a funds trader should expect to trade. Forming a view, in essence, is the process of gauging the extent to which the current funds rate differs from that equilibrium rate.

Alas, it's not that simple in practice. To start with, as the period begins on Thursday, the funds trader knows neither the Fed's target for borrowed reserves nor the actual level of borrowing during the preceding period. Add to that the fact that the relation between borrowing and the funds rate is uncertain, particularly when the "effective" discount rate is unknown (as in the case of a surcharge applied to the basic rate), and it is apparent that several layers of uncertainty obscure the funds trader's perception of the equilibrium rate.

In this setting, many funds traders rely on a second-best approach. In effect, they filter recent movements of the funds rate in order to define the current equilibrium (or notionally "fair") rate.[35] This procedure makes a great deal of sense during the period, as an emerging reserve imbalance tends to persist for a while, causing serially correlated movements in the funds rate. From the informational point of view, the technique has much less merit in analyzing trading in two separate maintenance periods, since (as noted earlier) reserves provision is largely separated between them. Nevertheless, the initial Thursday opening rate is very strongly correlated with the rates at which funds traded on previous days. (Trading during the final Wednesday after-

---

[35] Conceptually, this process is similar to the way dealers in a thin market try to use transactions data to determine the equilibrium price of a security. For an excellent description and analysis of such behavior, see Kenneth D. Garbade, *Securities Markets* (New York: McGraw-Hill, 1982), Chapter 26.

noon, when the market is generally thin and often erratic, seems to be ignored in setting the opening rate.)

As a result of traders' notional equilibrium—as well as the enlarged "carry-over" provisions in effect since February 1984—the funds rate is sometimes slow to adjust to a change in the degree of borrowing pressure in the banking system. One reason is that such a change may only begin to be evident in the reserves market in late Wednesday trading, and events at that time are erratic anyway and consequently are given little weight by funds traders. Moreover, in some cases, a reserves stringency (if widespread) may be manifested initially not as an increase of borrowing but as a negative excess reserves position. As banks seek to avoid reserves deficiencies in the subsequent period, the funds rate should belatedly increase. Finally, if borrowing has been at very low levels for some time, banks may feel little initial concern about seeking accommodation at the Fed window; and as long as that attitude persists, the full effect of increased borrowing pressure will be delayed.[36]

The notional equilibrium funds rate is obviously compatible with the incremental approach to covering reserves positions discussed earlier, in that both depend on an assumption that it is impossible to determine precisely where the funds rate ought to trade. In the absence of such well-defined knowledge, both techniques represent second-best methods with which funds traders can cope.

Nevertheless, it would be a mistake to assume that any sluggishness of the funds rate is solely attributable to funds traders. The Fed's Open Market Desk also from time to time uses movements in the funds rate as a check on its reserves projections. The logic of the approach is to use the information contained in funds-rate movements to verify the existence of an imbalance in the reserves market. Thus, if the borrowing target has not changed appreciably, but the funds rate is moving sharply higher (lower), that suggests that some disturbance to nonborrowed reserves has created a reserves shortage (excess). The Desk probably would use this kind of information only in relation to large movements of the funds rate, ignoring smaller changes. However, such a tactic should in principle induce a tendency toward serial correlation in the funds rate, since movements of the rate away from its previous level will be more likely to prompt offsetting open market operations. Ironically then, the existence of such second guessing on the part of the Fed lends some credence to funds traders' notional equilibrium funds rate. The Desk, for its part, has pointed to market expectations of open market

---

[36] Exactly that is what appears to have happened during the August–October period of 1980. Though borrowing pressure on banks was mounting steadily, the funds rate was relatively slow to respond. As a result, the Fed undertook special measures, including increases in the discount rate, to achieve the desired effect. See Meek and Levin, "Implementing the New Operating Procedures."

operations as reducing the usefulness of the funds rate as an indication of reserve need.[37]

During the reserves maintenance period, the funds rate responds to a *perceived imbalance* in the reserves market. Such an imbalance will be only temporary because as the funds rate adjusts to a level consistent with inducing the implied amount of borrowing from the discount window, the imbalance is relieved. As noted earlier, borrowed reserves to a large extent are provided at three points in the two-week period—two Fridays and the final Wednesday. Hence, in order to increase borrowing, the Fed generally will need to create a palpable reserve shortage early in the period in order to put upward pressure on the funds rate in time to induce the called-for traffic at the discount window on Friday night. If the funds rate does not respond immediately, for whatever reason, then pressure should intensify later in the period, as enlarged borrowing needs finally begin to become apparent to funds traders. If the funds rate is rising during the period's final days, the increased tightness will generally produce a higher rate at the following Thursday opening, which in principle could induce the desired average weekly volume of borrowing. The same basic procedure operates in reverse when the Fed is in process of easing pressure on bank reserves positions.

The principal problem this convoluted procedure presents to a funds trader is that of distinguishing the daily rate gyrations due only to unevenness of borrowing (given the period's total) from adjustments designed to create a change in the total. It is not an easy task, but it is greatly facilitated if one has a clear conception of the pattern of open market operations that would be most likely to produce an even distribution of borrowing at the pace of the previous period. A deviation from such a pattern may signal to a funds trader a possible shift in the funds rate before the end of the period.

ANALYTICS OF RESERVES: A CHILD'S GUIDE TO FLOAT AND OTHER MYSTERIES

The starting point for anticipating and interpreting open market operations is the ability to estimate the extent to which forces outside the direct control of the Fed are increasing or decreasing banks' needs for reserves. Exhibit 7 summarizes the most important such influences. The first category is those factors that create a reserves need for banks (i.e., those for which an increase implies an added need for the banking system to hold reserves in the form of deposits at the Federal Reserve

---

[37] For a description of the frequency and relative success with which the Fed has used this technique, see Meek and Levin, ibid.

EXHIBIT 7   **Factors Affecting Reserves** (statement week ended
January 20, 1982; $ millions)

Factors creating reserves need:

1.	Required reserves*	+2,268	
2.	Excess reserves	+140	
3.	Currency in circulation	−1,385	
4.	Treasury deposits at Federal Reserve banks	+643	
5.	Miscellaneous liabilities	−191	
6.	Total		+1,475

Factors reducing reserves need:

7.	Vault cash†	+111	
8.	Float	+2,651	
9.	Advances	−50	
10.	Miscellaneous assets	+165	
11.	Total		+2,877
12.	Total reserve need (6 less 11)		−1,402

Note: Data are changes in weekly average levels. Beginning February 2, 1984, the reserves maintenance period was lengthened from one week to two weeks.
* Adjusted for required reserves covered through holdings of vault cash.
† Held by institutions maintaining reserves balances at a Federal Reserve bank; data reflect holdings two weeks prior to the statement week.

banks). They include required reserves as well as excess reserves. In addition, certain factors drain funds from these reserve accounts, such as Treasury deposits at the Federal Reserve banks, currency in circulation, and a variety of other minor items. The mechanism involved is simple: An increase of Treasury deposits, for example, involves a transfer of funds from bank reserves accounts to the Treasury's account at the Fed, thus reducing reserve availability. Similarly, when the nonbank public increases its holdings of currency, banks must replenish their stocks by obtaining currency from the Fed (either directly or via a correspondent bank) in exchange for debits to their reserve accounts.

The second basic category of reserves factors includes those for which an increase reduces banks' reserves needs. Because vault cash (held four weeks ago) counts as reserves, an increase (other things equal) reduces the need for reserves from other sources. Easily the most variable factor in this category is Federal Reserve float (essentially the discrepancy between the *scheduled* availability of checks and other cash items presented to the Fed for collection versus the *actual* volume of collections posted). Since float for the most part reflects the degree to which the check-processing system is functioning smoothly, it swings erratically in response to seasonal pressures on the collection process as well as to acute disruptions of normal procedures (e.g., airport closures due to bad weather or computer malfunctions).[38] Last but not least,

---

[38] The classic description of techniques used by the Fed and Fedwatchers to predict float is Irving Auerbach, "Forecasting Float," in *Essays in Money and Credit* (New York: Federal Reserve Bank of New York, 1964), pp. 7–13. A more recent, though less analytical, discus-

borrowings from the Fed obviously reduce the reserves needed by banks from other sources.

In order to compute the amount of reserves to be supplied (drained) during the maintenance period, the total change of the factors reducing reserves needs is subtracted from the total change of factors increasing reserves needs. If the result is positive (negative), the Fed needs to add (drain) reserves.

Of course, as a practical matter, both the Fed and Fedwatchers rely on estimates of factors that may diverge considerably from their actual values, especially in the case of such a volatile factor as float. For example, as Exhibit 8 shows, projections of the total weekly average reserves need made by the System Open Market Desk staff on Thursday morning of the statement week diverged from the actual by an average absolute amount of about $673 million. Exceptionally, the Thursday projections were wide of the mark by a couple of billion dollars or more. In part, however, it is misleading to judge the precision of the Fed's forecasts by the Thursday projections, since daily data streams into the Fed, allowing forecasts to be revised. In any event, the estimates are still more refined later in the period.[39]

The information available to Fedwatchers compares very poorly with that available to the Fed itself. Fedwatchers, for example, receive data on discount-window borrowing and most operating factors on Thursday evening each week. Data for required reserves, excess reserves, and vault cash are computed as two-week averages and are released every other Thursday. The only daily data received by Fedwatchers is for Treasury balances, and that is available from the Treasury only with a two-day lag. Despite these handicaps, some of the more astute Fedwatchers maintain a forecast accuracy closely approximating the Fed staff's Thursday/Wednesday accuracy. But even they are often in error concerning open market operations, since they may lack vital information on the course of developments in the current maintenance period.

Once one knows the value of the reserves need as given on line 12 of Exhibit 7, there remain two additional steps to be taken before computing the amount of open market operations. First, if RPs (MSPs) were

sion is Arline Hoel, "A Primer on Federal Reserve Float," Federal Reserve Bank of New York *Monthly Review*, October 1975, pp. 245–53. FInally, readers wondering what the current Federal Reserve Board chairman had to say about float some years back may find interesting Hobart C. Carr, Madeline McWhinney, and Paul A. Volcker, "Federal Reserve Float," in *Bank Reserves: Some Major Factors Affecting Them*, 2d ed. (New York: Federal Reserve Bank of New York, 1953).

[39] As Exhibit 8 shows, during 1979–80 the average absolute error of Fed projections of current-week reserve need available on Wednesday morning was $144 million—substantially lower than the error in the Thursday projections, but definitely still of an order of magnitude capable of producing erratic behavior in the funds market on Wednesday afternoons. Similar errors in the current system of two-week maintenance periods would have a smaller impact due to the enlarged carry-over provision.

EXHIBIT 8 Federal Reserve of New York Projection Errors by Major Component for Selected Years* (weekly average, $ millions)

	Nonborrowed Reserves (market factors)		Float		Treasury Deposits		Currency in Circulation		Other Factors		Addendum: Required Reserves	
	$|\bar{e}|$	$|\bar{\Delta}|$	$|\bar{e}|$	$|\bar{\Delta}|$	$|\bar{e}|$	$|\bar{\Delta}|$	$|\bar{e}|$	$|\bar{\Delta}|$	$|\bar{e}|$	$|\bar{\Delta}|$	$|\bar{e}|$	$|\bar{\Delta}|$
One Week Ahead (Thursday) Forecasts												
1977–78	711	1,867	592	873	409	1,681	152	453	158	628	31	597
1978–79	887	1,435	861	1,189	334	692	140	519	221	776	65	707
1979–80	673	1,057	619	918	350	535	170	551	176	646	155	724
One Day Ahead (Wednesday) Forecasts												
1977–78	118	1,867	110	873	41	1,681	52	453	55	628	17	597
1978–79	176	1,435	182	1,189	49	692	54	519	73	776	35	707
1979–80	144	1,057	140	918	37	535	30	551	73	646	48	724

* From third statement week in October to second statement week in October of following year.

$|\bar{e}|$ = mean absolute forecast error.

$|\bar{\Delta}|$ = mean absolute change.

Source: Reprinted from Paul Meek and Fred J. Levin "Implementing the New Operating Procedures: The View from the Trading Desk," in *New Monetary Control Procedures*, Board of Governors of the Federal Reserve System, February 1981.

executed in the prior week, the runoff from their average level in that week to zero in the current week will create a reserves drain (add), in addition to that indicated on line 12. Second, as noted earlier, the Fed may execute internally the temporary investment orders of its foreign central bank customers, or it may pass them through to the market as customer RPs. If the volume of orders executed increases, the result is an increased reserves need. In that respect, the foreign orders resemble other factors creating a need. As a matter of simplicity, the Desk personnel add the change in foreign orders (i.e., the average level of orders available for execution in the current week minus the average level of orders *actually* executed in the previous week) to the reserves need given on line 12. If the Deity is disposed to ease the Desk's job, the result will be zero, and no operations in the market will be necessary. That does not happen often, however.

STRATEGY OF OPEN MARKET OPERATIONS

During the year, both the reserves need (line 12) and the reserves need adjusted for runoffs of RPs and MSPs and for changes in foreign investment orders, have a pronounced seasonal pattern. Currency and demand deposits follow distinct multiweek swings and also fluctuate around certain dates—for example, holidays and tax payment dates. Float behavior is also strongly influenced by holidays. In principle, even the large swings of reserves need could be met through arranging large amounts of RPs, but a number of considerations argue against such a tactic. First, the amount of collateral required easily approaches $10 billion or so and could well exceed the floating supply of "free" collateral in the hands of dealers and other financial institutions (mainly commercial banks). The result would be that the Desk would be unable to adhere to its nonborrowed reserves target. Moreover, even if the amount of collateral were adequate, the fact that banks would repeatedly begin the reserves maintenance period with a severe reserves deficiency (until the need was met through RPs) would probably create considerable upward pressure on the funds rate. For these reasons, provision of at least some portion of the reserves need through outright purchases of securities is desirable, and outright transactions are closely related to swings in seasonal reserve needs as well as changes in reserve requirements.

There are, of course, various ways to do outright transactions. First, as noted earlier, a suitable foreign customer order may present an opportunity for the Fed to effect the permanent addition (drain) of reserves without recourse to transactions with dealers. Such an approach is consistent with the Fed's desire to minimize its presence in the market; but it presents problems to Fedwatchers, who do not learn of the existence of the transaction until the Fed's release of reserves data following the maintenance period in which it was executed. Another means by which the Fed can achieve a permanent reserve drain is to bid to reduce its holdings of maturing bills in a Treasury auction—for example, the regular Monday auction of three- and six-month bills. In such a case, Fedwatchers will learn of the redemption when the results are announced in the evening of the day of the auction. Since settlement for the auctioned bills is the following Thursday, Fedwatchers in this case will know the size of the reserves impact a couple of days before it actually occurs. In many cases, the Fed will have no choice but to execute an outright transaction in the market. Such transactions usually are arranged on Wednesday for settlement the following day, though they do occur on other days as well, sometimes for skip-day settlement. Fedwatchers can only guess at the size of the transaction, since the Fed does not announce it; typically, more than a week elapses before the size of the outright transaction becomes known to the market through the Fed's release of reserves data.

Given the decision to effect a permanent addition (drain) of reserves, the Fed must decide how many securities of what type to purchase (sell). The alternatives are Treasury bills, Treasury coupon securities, and federal agency securities. In general, bills are the preferred instrument. The bill market is more liquid than the market for any other money market instrument, so that the large transactions arranged by the Fed (frequently on the order of $1–2 billion) will not have much impact on rates in the market. Since the Fed prefers not to exercise undue influence on market rates, that is an important consideration. On the other hand, there is some incentive for the Fed to allocate at least some of its holdings to coupon securities so as to provide a core of permanent reserves without the need repeatedly to roll over large amounts of maturing issues. Operationally, the problem with coupon purchases is that the amounts in dealer hands are frequently rather modest relative to the size the Fed requires, so that the Fed generally must solicit offers for a wide variety of issues in order to have flexibility to obtain competitive rates and to maintain the desired maturity balance.[40] That means a sizable task of computing yields for a large number of issues and extends the time required for the transaction to be processed. Otherwise expressed, a coupon "pass" is an ordeal for the Desk. Even worse is an agency pass. Since supplies of agency issues in dealer hands are typically light, even for short-term issues, offers must be solicited for many

---

[40] This problem is obviously less severe in the period immediately following the settlement of an auction of Treasury coupon securities when dealer holdings typically are rather ample. Not coincidentally, most of the Fed's purchases of coupon securities are made at such times.

maturities of each agency's issues necessitating an arduous computation of yields, followed by comparison of spreads between the rates on issues of different agencies. Thus, it comes as no surprise that agency passes are infrequent.

In the final analysis, the desired mix of permanent and temporary reserve injections must inevitably depend on subjective judgments by the System account manager. Nevertheless, there are certain situations for which temporary reserves injections or drains are particularly appropriate. A good example would be a four-week period in which the first maintenance period requires, say, a $1 billion weekly average addition to reserves, followed by a $1 billion drain in the following period. This could be accomplished easily be executing $2.3 billion three-day RPs on each Friday ($2.3 billion × 3 days ÷ 7 days = $1 billion) and doing no RPs in the subsequent period, producing a $1 billion weekly average reserves drain. That approach obviously has the merit that it minimizes the need for the Fed to enter the market.

In practice, of course, matters are rarely that straightforward. In the first place, estimates of reserves need are only that—estimates. Second, repeated execution of temporary reserves injection (drain) operations may at times serve an ancillary purpose by affecting the psychological attitude of funds traders. For example, in an environment in which the funds rate has declined substantially in past weeks, funds traders may be apt to anticipate still further declines in the current maintenance period. One way in which the Fed may temper such expectations without departing from the nonborrowed reserves path (i.e., without temporarily forcing higher borrowing) would be to arrange open market operations so that, for several weeks, RPs are necessary. Then banks would start each period short of reserves and would therefore probably bid more aggressively for funds.[41]

Needless to say, to monetary policy purists, such behavior smacks of the old procedure of funds-rate targeting, and some critics have suggested that the Fed should reduce the frequency with which it arranged RPs.[42] Of course, the vast majority of temporary reserves injections (drains) are not related to the kind of expectations alteration described above but are required by very short-term movements in the operating

---

[41] A simpler way to achieve the same objective would be to undersupply nonborrowed reserves, but that approach obviously would involve a departure from the nonborrowed reserves path.

[42] For example, Milton Friedman has criticized the Fed for an excessive amount of RP activity. See Milton Friedman, "Monetary Policy: Theory and Practice," *Journal of Money, Credit and Banking*, February 1982, pp. 98–118. For a critique and correction of Friedman's charges by two officers of the Open Market Desk, see Fred J. Levin and Anne-Marie Meulendyke, "A Comment," *Journal of Money, Credit and Banking*, August 1982, pp. 399–403, as well as Friedman's reply in the same issue, pp. 404–6.

factors. Even so, since late 1982 the Desk has executed some form of RP in the last three days of practically every reserves maintenance period, contributing to a level of RP activity substantially greater than that which drew the critics' ire. The object apparently is to guard against the possibility of the funds rate plunging due to an unintended, temporary excess of reserves. Whether one thinks the tactic justified or not thus has a great deal to do with whether or not one believes the Fed should do anything at all to damp interest-rate volatility.[43] Professional economists have sharply divided opinions on that issue.

Nevertheless, there is one respect in which the frequency of execution of RPs could be reduced with only a trivial change in techniques. It is not widely appreciated among market participants that multiday system RPs typically are "withdrawable"—that is, the dealer participating in the transaction may give notice to the Fed by 1:30 P.M. on the day the dealer wishes to terminate the agreement. As a result, if the Fed arranges, say, a 7-day RP on Thursday with a "stop" rate (the lowest accepted rate) of 10 percent, but the market RP rate declines to 9½ percent by Friday, then a substantial and essentially unpredictable portion of the dealers who entered into the RPs with the Fed on Thursday now have a palpable economic incentive to withdraw, leaving the Fed with the job of coming back into the market to arrange more RPs so as to prevent a reserves scarcity from emerging. Not only that, but if rates rise after Thursday and dealers respond by lightening their positions, then their reduced financing needs may also cause them to withdraw from the RPs, putting still further pressure on the funds market.

At this point, the reader may well be wondering why the Fed would allow its RPs to be withdrawable in the first place, especially since non-withdrawable RPs are standard among other market participants. The best explanation appears to be that the withdrawable RP is an institution that has survived the circumstances that originally made it useful. Before 1966, when the first MSPs were executed, any reserves draining was accomplished through outright sales of securities. Thus, if the Fed had done RPs early in the week in response to a perceived reserve need but later found itself faced with a need to drain reserves, then to the extent that the soft funds rate caused RPs to be withdrawn, the reserve drain would be accomplished automatically and, in particular, without requiring an outright sale of securities.[44] Obviously, however, MSPs make this particular feature of RPs redundant.

---

[43] In terms of Exhibit 3, the object is to maintain banks' reserves demand schedule on the sloped portion of the reserves supply schedule *at all times* during the reserves maintenance period so that an unintended increase in nonborrowed reserves does not prompt a plunge in the funds rate.

[44] Sometimes, however, the withdrawal of RPs in those days was not altogether automatic. The story is told of a System open market account manager who was confronted

Presumably because of the interest rate risk involved, dealers generally have participated in a smaller portion of the Fed's multiday MSPs and (very rare) multiday nonwithdrawable RPs than have their so-called customers (primarily banks). Consequently, if multiday RPs were made uniformly nonwithdrawable, a smaller volume of less attractively priced proposals generally would be submitted, and that might impair the Fed's ability to execute as many transactions as desired.[45] One way to cope with that problem would be to offer one-day and multiday RPs simultaneously, as is frequently done with MSPs. Another would be to execute outright transactions more often.

With the exception of customer RPs, the Fed does not disclose the size of a temporary addition (drain) of reserves, and that presents problems for Fedwatchers and other market participants. Some participants attempt to cope by monitoring the stop rate on the transaction. The conventional wisdom is that a low (high) stop on an RP (MSP) relative to the market rate indicates an "aggressive" operation. But in fact, monitoring the stop is a very poor substitute for knowing the size of the transaction relative to the size of the reserve need. The reason is that the stop rate in general depends on the size of the transaction *and* the distribution of proposals submitted to the Fed. As Exhibit 9 illustrates, the flatter the "tail" of the proposals (i.e., the narrower the range from the highest to the lowest rates shown to the Fed), the less responsive is the stop rate to variations in the size of the transaction. Consequently, there is no unique relation between the stop relative to the market and the aggressiveness of the operation. Moreover (as noted earlier), in some circumstances, dealers and perhaps also their customers are likely to be loath to submit very competitive proposals to the Fed—for example, multiday MSPs in general and RPs when dealers are holding negligible or short positions.

---

with a need to drain reserves after multiday RPs had been executed earlier in the week. Though the funds rate was softening, no withdrawals were forthcoming. Upon investigation, it turned out that a large block of the RPs was held at a major dealer firm. Accordingly, the account manager telephoned the firm's head trader and asked whether he would like to withdraw his RPs. The head trader replied that he was not interested. Then the account manager said that he would appreciate it if the RPs were withdrawn. Again the offer was declined. Before hanging up, the account manager observed that he was certain to remember this event the next time the head trader was in a jam and needed a favor. About 10 minutes later, a phone call to the Desk announced the withdrawal of the RPs.

[45] Recall that dealers desire to do RPs primarily to finance their inventory of securities, though many do run a so-called matched book quite independently of their securities position. Consequently, if the inventory being financed by a multiday nonwithdrawable RP were liquidated, the dealer would suddenly be in a long funds position that could not be eliminated by the simple device of withdrawing from the RP. For the same reason, customers account for a larger than normal portion of multiday MSPs as well as RPs when dealers have very light or net short positions.

EXHIBIT 9 Hypothetical Distributions of Proposals for Repurchase Agreements and Matched Sale-Purchase Agreements

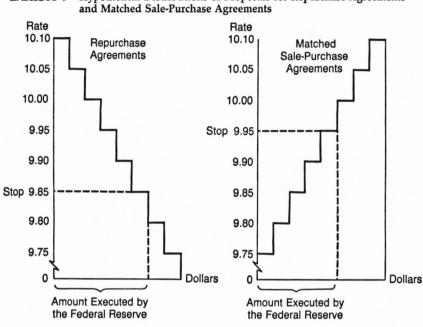

DOES FEDWATCHING MATTER?

Essentially, Fedwatching comprises three analytical techniques. First, like many other economists, a Fedwatcher makes projections, whether formally or subjectively, of the level of economic activity, especially as it bears on variables in which the Fed is thought to be particularly interested (e.g., one or more measures of the money stock). In this same general area, the federal budget may be analyzed both for its overall macroeconomic impact as well as for the more direct impact on financial markets of the scale and timing of Treasury financing needs. The second focus is the forecasting and interpretation of bank reserves positions and the Fed's open market operations. Most of this chapter has been devoted to explaining the objectives and techniques of such analysis. Flowing naturally from the first two is the third area of interest: the projection of interest rates in money and capital markets. As far as the operation of a financial institution in general and a securities dealer firm in particular is concerned, the latter is the most important of all.

The first and the last of these activities will always be necessary, but there is no intrinsic reason for projection of reserves positions and open market operations to be part of the job. In performing such an analysis, Fedwatchers merely duplicate and improve upon, if possible, the projections routinely generated by the Fed staff to guide the desk. Moreover, as the preceding discussion has illustrated, the best efforts of Fedwatchers often fall far short of the quality of the Fed staff's projections, primarily because of major delays in the receipt of information by market participants.

As noted earlier, the consequence of this lack of information is greater uncertainty among funds traders as to the degree of borrowing pressure being placed on banks and thus the equilibrium funds rate, so that funds traders are impelled to be more or less aggressive in bidding for funds than they otherwise would be. Indeed, in a sense, the quantity of information provided to the market has been sharply *reduced* since the advent of the nonborrowed reserves targeting procedures in 1979. Prior to that time, by targeting the funds rate, the Fed effectively communicated all information necessary to determine the equilibrium funds rate with precision. Market participants concentrated their analytical energies on divining the next change in the funds-rate target and had to do little more than watch the Fed's "intervention points" (the funds rate at which reserves were added or drained) to determine the equilibrium rate. Since late 1979, however, Fedwatchers and funds traders have had to process information on reserves to estimate the equilibrium rate. In principle, there is nothing wrong with that, and of course the procedures have advantages for monetary policy. The main disadvantage—potential volatility of the funds rate—is due in substantial part to the unavailability of current information concerning factors affecting reserves.

Suppose that market participants were perfectly informed concerning reserves factors and the Fed's intended supplies of nonborrowed reserves. Then they would have a fairly precise idea of the equilibrium funds rate, and any change of the Fed's policy with respect to reserves supplies would be followed immediately by a change in the perceived equilibrium funds rate—and thus of the actual funds rate. The prompt implementation of such a change, when called for by the Fed's monetary aggregates targets, is of course the rationale for its operating procedures. The only question is how rapidly the change is to occur. In that context, the Fed seems to be of two minds: On the one hand, its operating procedures are designed to speed the adjustment of the funds rate to deviations from monetary targets; but on the other hand, the information supplied to the market is far from adequate to allow participants to estimate confidently an equilibrium rate to which they can respond. As a result, when the equilibrium is changing, the actual funds rate probably will lag behind, but may even rush ahead. That kind of response is inconsistent with a fully efficient market. Moreover, even if the equilibrium rate is not changing, uncertainty caused by swings in intraperiod borrowing traffic contributes to a dispersion of trades around the equilibrium rate.

Needless to say, the flow of information to the market can never be perfect. But the Fed could supply to the market at almost negligible cost all daily information on factors affecting reserves, thus enhancing the ability of market participants to interpret their environment. Even better, the Fed could announce to the market its own projections of operating factors as well as the size of all open market operations carried out. Doing so would scarcely interfere with the Fed's ability to conduct its operations. On the contrary, it could facilitate them in certain cases (such as multiday MSPs).

Several considerations in addition to the usual bureaucratic inertia may account for the Fed's reluctance to provide such data. First, the Fed may suspect (no doubt correctly in some cases) that the wealth of data to be released would prove confusing to some market participants. Moreover, since the float data, for example, are subject to a variety of "as of" adjustments, the Fed could argue that on some occasions data released might be misleading if not supplemented with background information on the continuing flow of such adjustments. Another consideration that probably influences the Fed's attitude is that the occasional large size of revisions to factor estimates could be embarrassing. Finally, the Fed may believe that release of the full set of reserves data and projections might "tie the hands" of the Desk, conveying to the market an impression of a need for open market operations when the Desk had grounds to suspect that some other factor (such as a prospective swing in the volume of foreign investment orders) might invalidate a superficial interpretation of the data and projections. In such a case, the market might be misled by the Fed's abstaining from open market operations.

These are not trivial considerations, but their significance is unduly magnified when they are advanced with an implicit assumption that the market functions efficiently now. For example, coping with the complexity of reserves data and the revisions constantly being made would indeed tax the patience of almost anyone, but it could hardly be argued to be more trying than the patently inadequate techniques *currently* employed for the same purpose. Similarly, revisions to projections are a source of embarrassment to all forecasters, and all Fedwatchers regularly eat their humble pie in large portions; but that is merely evidence of the job's difficulty. In any event, the Fed regularly releases data on its major weekly forecast errors anyway. Finally, the "tie our hands" argument only applies when the market is deprived of the knowledge that the Fed questions the accuracy or interpretation of the projections; otherwise, it has no force. In sum, the objections typically advanced against timely release of reserves data have little merit. Ironically, they had more substance when the Fed was targeting the funds rate.

In view of the pivotal role of the funds market in implementing monetary policy, the market's striking inefficiencies are of major concern. Though the reserves-projecting activities of Fedwatchers constitute a logical and—under the circumstances—crucial response to the problems, this response is not the most effective way to improve the operation of the funds market.

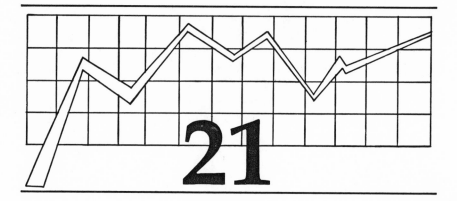

Measures for Evaluating Forecasts*

H. O. Stekler, Ph.D.

Professor of Economics
Industrial College of the Armed Forces
National Defense University

After economic or financial forecasts have been prepared and issued, their accuracy should be evaluated so that procedures for correcting the errors can be developed. This chapter deals with the measures used to evaluate quantitative forecasts of such economic variables as GNP, consumption, and investment.

GNP forecasts usually are composed of predictions for a number of subaggregates; and for every forecaster or model, these predictions are generally available for a number of years. In one evaluation study, Stephen McNees had thousands of forecasts which he could have examined.[1] Obviously, each of these forecasts cannot be compared in any meaningful way with each of the outcomes. Therefore, criteria have been developed for making these comparisons.

The procedures used in forecast evaluations consist of two dimensions. The first involves the adoption of a summary measure for compar-

---

* The views expressed in this chapter are those of the author and do not necessarily reflect the views of the National Defense University or the Department of Defense.

[1] Stephen K. McNees, "An Evaluation of Economic Forecasts," *New England Economic Review*, November–December 1975, pp. 3–39.

ing errors across techniques or forecasters. The second stage is to select standards against which the forecasters will be judged.

EVALUATION MEASURES

Summary Measures

After the time period has occurred to which the prediction refers, it is possible to calculate the forecast error. Define P_t as the prediction of the level of an economic variable (such as GNP) for a particular period and A_t as the observed level of that variable for the same period. Then the forecast error is:

$$e_t = P_t - A_t$$

The time series of these observed errors can then be combined into a number of summary measures.

Two summary measures of forecast errors which are frequently used are the mean square error:

$$MSE = \frac{\sum_{t=1}^{n} e_t^2}{n} \tag{1}$$

and the mean absolute error:

$$MAE = \frac{\sum_{t=1}^{n} |e_t|}{n}. \tag{2}$$

The error could be measured either as the discrepancies between predicted and actual levels or between the predicted and actual changes of the variables which were forecast. The recent evaluations have tended to focus on the errors which are derived from the actual and predicted changes, frequently expressed as percentage changes. This increased emphasis on changes is appropriate, for we are concerned about the ability of the forecaster to predict the economy's movements.

The same measures could be derived when the forecasts are issued and evaluated as changes—i.e., GNP will increase by $30 billion in the next quarter, or GNP will grow at a 4.0% rate during the next quarter. The forecast error based on changes[2] is:

$$e_t = (P_t - A_{t-1}) - (A_t - A_{t-1})$$

but the associated MSE and MAE measures are derived as before.

---

[2] For one-step-ahead forecasts, the level and change errors would be identical; i.e., $A_t - P_t = (A_t - A_{t-1}) - (P_t - A_{t-1})$. They would differ for predictions made for more than one period in advance.

Use of the Measures: Standards of Comparison

For any forecaster's predictions of any particular variable, neither the MSE nor the MAE provides meaningful information by itself. These descriptive statistics may be compared with similar statistics obtained from the output of other forecasters. This comparison would enable the observer to determine which forecaster best predicted the variables in question. Also, these summary measures may be compared with similar statistics obtained from alternative models. The comparison in this case would indicate whether a forecaster were superior to a particular type of model. Frequently, the accuracy of forecasts obtained from naive models or time series regressions are used for this comparison. The rationale for this comparison is that forecasters should perform at least as well as the simplest models from which predictions could have been derived.

Time series regressions or autoregressions are generally even more stringent standards, since all of the past values of the variables being predicted are used to obtain estimates for future periods. These regressions are of the form:

$$X_{t+1} = a_o + a_1X_t + a_2X_{t-1} + a_3X_{t-2} + \cdots \tag{3}$$

In recent years, there have been major developments in time series analysis and methodology. Analyses of these new techniques, known as ARIMA or Box-Jenkins methods, are clearly beyond the scope of this chapter, which deals with the measures involved in forecast evaluation.[3]

In comparing any particular set of forecasts with the predictions obtained from the naive models, it should be noted that the first naive model, which predicts no change ($P_t = A_{t-1}$), represents a more stringent test when the variables to be predicted display irregular period-to-period fluctuations. On the other hand, the second naive model, which extrapolates last period's change ($P_t - A_{t-1} = A_{t-1} - A_{t-2}$), is more relevant when the variable has a strong underlying trend. Associated with the first naive model, a statistic U developed by Henri Theil[4] is now widely used in forecast evaluations. It compares the root mean square error for the forecasts which are being evaluated, with the same measure obtained from the standard of comparison, the first naive model.[5] This U statistic is:

$$U = \frac{\sqrt{\Sigma(\Delta P_t - \Delta A_t)^2}}{\sqrt{\Sigma\Delta A_t^2}}. \tag{4}$$

---

[3] Basic references for these new time series techniques are George E. P. Box and Gwilym M. Jenkins, *Time Series Analysis* (San Francisco: Holden Day, 1970); and C. W. J. Granger and Paul Newbold, *Forecasting Economic Time Series* (New York: Academic Press, 1977).

[4] Henri Theil, *Applied Economic Forecasting* (Amsterdam: North-Holland Publishing, 1966).

[5] It should be noted that the U coefficient is similar in concept to a comparison of the MAE relative to the average absolute change.

If U is equal to zero, the forecasts are perfect. If U is greater than one, the forecasts being evaluated displayed errors which were larger than those which would have been generated by the first naive model.

Although the second naive model and time series regressions have been used as standards of comparison, no statistic comparable to Theil's U coefficient has been developed for these analyses. In these cases, analysts usually just list the mean square errors of the various forecasts, including those of the naive or time series model.

Extensions of the Measures: Sources of Errors

In addition to providing a basis for comparing forecaster performance, these measures may also be used to determine some of the possible *sources* of errors. For example, the MSE, $\Sigma (\bar{P}_t - \bar{A}_t)^2/n$ may be decomposed:

$$\frac{1}{n} \Sigma (\bar{P}_t - \bar{A}_t)^2 = (\bar{P} - \bar{A})^2 + (S_p - S_A)^2 + 2(1 - r)S_p S_A \qquad (5)$$

where $\bar{P}$ and $\bar{A}$ are the means:

$$\bar{P} = \frac{1}{n} \Sigma P_t$$

$$\bar{A} = \frac{1}{n} \Sigma A_t$$

S_p and S_A are the standard deviations:

$$S_p^2 = \frac{1}{n} \Sigma (P_t - \bar{P})^2$$

$$S_A^2 = \frac{1}{n} \Sigma (A_t - \bar{A})^2$$

and r is the correlation coefficient between the predicted and actual values.

If the first term in (5) is nonzero, the forecasts are said to be biased— i.e., on average there is a difference between the actual and predicted values of the variable. This bias may be attributable either to over- or underestimates, but the bias which has been most commonly observed is the underestimate of the change in the variable.

The second term in (5) measures the difference between the standard deviations of the predicted and actual variables. It has been argued that under certain circumstances the standard deviations of the predictions should be less than that of the observed values.[6] This type of error is due to unequal variations.

Finally, the third source of error is due to incomplete covariation between the actuals and predictions. In optimal predictions, this should be the largest source of the forecast errors, and in empirical studies, this has indeed been the case.

Since the second (i.e., unequal variation) component of (5) may not vanish even when optimal forecasts are issued, a second decomposition of MSE was suggested by Theil.[7] In this case:

$$\frac{1}{n} \Sigma(\bar{P}_t - A_t)^2 = (\bar{P} - \bar{A})^2 + (S_p - rS_A)^2 + (1 - r^2)S_A^2 \qquad (6)$$

where the variables are defined as previously. The first component of (6) still measures the bias and may be interpreted as before. However, the interpretation assigned to the second and third components of (6) would differ from that attributed to the errors of (5). In this new decomposition of the MSE, the second component measures the regression error and the third the disturbance.

The regression error is related to the slope of the relationship between the predicted and the actual values in the regression:

$$A_t = a_o + a_1 P_t$$

If the prediction is optimal, the value of a_1 should be 1 and the second term of (6) should be zero.[8] This measure has been extensively used to test whether published forecasts are optimal and to devise correction factors to make the forecast optimal.[9]

Finally, the disturbance portion of the error is the nonsystematic component of the forecast error. There is no correction factor which can be applied to eliminate it.

USES OF THE EVALUATION MEASURES

How Good Were the Forecasts? Magnitude of the Errors

In using these measures to judge past GNP forecasts, it is thus important to consider both their absolute accuracy and their performance rela-

---

[6] Michio Hatanaka, "The Underestimation of Variations in the Forecast Series: A Note," *International Economic Review*, February 1975, pp. 151–160; and Paul A. Samuelson, "Optimality of Sluggish Predictors under Ergodic Probabilities," *International Economic Review*, February 1976, pp. 1–7.

[7] See Theil, *Applied Economic Forecasting*.

[8]
$$a_1 = \frac{\Sigma(P_t - \bar{P})(A_t - \bar{A})}{\Sigma(P_t - \bar{P})^2} = \frac{rS_A}{S_p}$$

If the coefficient is 1, $(S_p - rS_A)^2 = 0$, and there is no regression error.

[9] See Dennis A. Ahlburg, "Forecast Evaluation and Improvement," *Journal of Forecasting*, forthcoming; and David J. Smyth, "Short-Run Macroeconomic Forecasting," *Journal of Forecasting*, January–March 1983, pp. 37–49.

tive to alternative standards.[10] Using either root mean square or mean absolute percentage errors, recent studies have found that the predictions of real GNP one year ahead were within 1–3 percent of the observed levels.[11] In addition to applying the measure to the predictions of the *levels* of GNP and its components, these studies have also examined the errors of the predictions of the *changes* in GNP and components.

For various subperiods between 1959 and 1976, the errors averaged about 30 percent of the observed change. Moreover, the U coefficients for the various real GNP forecasts for 1970–75 ranged between .4 and .8, but were lower (i.e., more accurate) for the price deflator forecasts.[12] Comparable findings about the magnitude of these errors were derived from another set of forecasts issued for the entire decade of the 1970s.[13]

Finally, the GNP and price deflator predictions of 12 forecasting groups were compared with the predictions of an autoregressive mechanism. Most of the forecasters outperformed this autoregressive benchmark. Moreover, the superiority of these forecasts increased the longer the forecasting span.[14] These recent findings about the relative superiority of the econometric forecasts over those generated by autoregressions are similar to other studies involving econometric forecasts.[15]

Given these results, what can one say about the quality of the forecasts? If the U coefficients are less than one, this means that the forecasts were superior to those generated by a naive model which predicted no change, period after period. This is not a particularly stringent standard when applied to variables which display trends. Beating a benchmark autoregression which makes even larger errors does not enhance the quality of these predictions. Moreover, when the predictions of the components of GNP are examined, the forecasts for many of these variables have U's which exceed one.

Nevertheless, these observed results led McNees to conclude that the forecasts were good but did not show the minimum feasible errors that economists could have made. However, using a different breakdown of

---

[10] Stephen K. McNees, "The Forecasting Record for the 1970s," *New England Economic Review*, September–October 1979, pp. 1–21.

[11] Carl F. Christ, "Judging the Performance of Econometric Models of the U.S. Economy," *International Economic Review*, February 1975, pp. 54–74; McNees, "The Forecasting Record"; and Victor Zarnowitz, "An Analysis of Annual and Multiperiod Quarterly Forecasts of Aggregate Income, Output, and Price Level," *Journal of Business*, January 1979, pp. 1–33.

[12] Zarnowitz, "An Analysis."

[13] McNees, "The Forecasting Record."

[14] Ray C. Fair, "An Evaluation of a Short-Run Forecasting Model," *International Economic Review*, June 1974, pp. 285–303; and Stephen K. McNees, "The Recent Record of Thirteen Economists," *New England Economic Review*, September–October 1981, pp. 5–21.

[15] Albert A. Hirsch, Bruce T. Grimm, and Gorti V. L. Narasimham, "Some Multiplier and Error Characteristics of the BEA Quarterly Model," in *Econometric Model Performance*, ed. Lawrence R. Klein and Edwin Burmeister (Philadelphia: University of Pennsylvania Press, 1976), pp. 108–125; McNees, "The Forecasting Record."

the errors as reported, it is possible to formulate a different basis for evaluating these forecasts.[16]

Were the Forecasts Really That Good?

McNees noted that the large errors were not randomly distributed over the period of the 1970s but rather were clustered sequentially.[17] For instance, all of the largest real GNP errors occurred between 1974I and 1976I, "when the forecasts indicated little about the future course of the economy."[18] The inflation rate forecasts showed similar tendencies with serious errors from the third quarter of 1973 to the third quarter of 1975 and from the fourth quarter of 1978 on.

Sometimes the real GNP and the price deflator forecasts offset each other, thus providing more accurate nominal GNP forecasts. However, these offsetting errors would certainly have obscured the major trends, and the greater accuracy of nominal GNP should not be considered a virtue.

Therefore, the question still remains: Can economists make accurate predictions for periods during which there are either cyclical fluctuations or changes in fundamental relationships? Or is accuracy only attainable during "normal" periods? Victor Zarnowitz's results, showing smaller errors in 1961–68 relative to earlier and later periods, suggests the latter hypothesis.[19]

A recent unpublished study by A. Yermilov addresses this question directly.[20] For the period 1977–82, he examines the accuracy of the forecasts which are collected and tabulated monthly by Eggert Economic Enterprises. These forecasts are obtained from leading business and economic organizations. As an example, the root mean squared error (RMSE) of the forecasts of real GNP for this period are presented in Exhibit 1. They quite clearly show that the forecasts are more accurate in the first half of the period then in the second half, when two recessions (1980 and 1981–82) occurred. In fact, the RMSE of the forecasts exceeded the absolute value of the observed change in both 1980 and 1982 and was 57 percent of the change in 1981.

Similar results (Exhibit 2) were obtained from the predictions of the GNP price deflator. The acceleration of inflation in 1978 and 1979 and the deceleration of price increases in 1982 were not well predicted.

---

[16] McNees, "The Forecasting Record."

[17] Ibid.

[18] Ibid., p. 19.

[19] Zarnowitz, "An Analysis," p. 13.

[20] A Yermilov, "An Analysis of the Accuracy of the Blue Chip Short-Term Macroeconomic Forecasts," mimeo.

EXHIBIT 1 RMSE of Forecasts of Percent Changes of Real GNP, 1977–1982

Forecasters	1977	1978	1979	1980	1981	1982	Average
American Express	0.39	0.43	1.10	1.44	1.30	2.41	1.35
Bank of America	0.33	0.40	0.79	1.26	1.32	2.49	1.33
Bankers Trust	0.22	0.39	0.26	1.04	0.99	3.35	1.52
P. Berstein	0.20	0.34	0.71	1.13	0.98	2.98	1.54
Brown Brothers Hariman	*	0.26	0.46	1.54	1.13	2.96	1.64
Business Economics	0.59	0.40	0.60	1.10	2.24	2.02	1.41
Cahners Publishing	*	1.30	0.28	1.84	1.02	4.02	2.17
Chamber of Commerce	*	0.44	0.75	0.97	0.90	3.88	1.97
Chase Manhattan Bank	0.26	0.20	0.67	0.58	1.11	2.19	1.10
Chase Econometric	0.22	*	0.29	0.91	1.13	2.93	1.67
Citibank	0.20	0.46	0.52	0.75	0.48	2.28	1.10
National Bank of Cleveland	0.22	0.28	0.58	0.75	0.63	2.97	1.34
Conference Board	0.37	0.39	0.31	1.13	1.32	2.22	1.19
Harris Trust	0.25	0.25	0.88	.45	1.99	1.77	1.26
E. I. du Pont	0.54	0.37	0.86	0.71	0.55	3.63	1.57
Eggert Econ. Ent.	0.68	0.13	0.90	1.20	0.33	3.75	1.66
Equitable Life	0.44	0.25	0.56	0.80	1.29	3.07	1.43
Evans Economics	*	*	*	1.27	0.52	3.65	2.30
General Electric	0.17	0.37	0.58	1.25	*	*	0.61
Irving Trust	*	*	1.63	0.58	0.93	3.64	2.11
Arthur D. Little	0.34	0.27	0.49	0.52	1.74	3.66	1.75
Manufacturers Hanover Trust	0.68	0.25	0.54	0.87	1.77	2.40	1.30
Michigan Econometric	0.53	0.61	0.41	1.01	0.61	2.45	1.34
Morgan Guaranty	0.50	0.36	0.93	0.65	0.70	2.77	1.27
Pennzoil	0.78	0.32	0.71	1.03	0.90	2.98	1.41
Philadelphia National Bank	0.19	0.31	0.82	0.74	1.32	3.04	1.43
Prudential Life	0.41	0.35	0.31	0.76	1.59	1.92	1.09
Security Pacific National Bank	0.22	0.38	0.67	0.96	1.53	2.81	1.39
UCLA Business Forecast	0.23	0.60	0.67	0.91	0.69	2.77	1.38
U.S. Trust	0.18	0.47	0.32	1.04	0.82	3.19	1.45
Wharton Econometric	0.56	0.44	1.11	0.88	0.87	2.83	1.42
Average Eggert's	0.25	0.16	0.48	0.63	0.95	2.97	1.30
Average excluding 32	0.37	0.39	0.66	0.97	1.09	2.90	1.47

* Figures not available.
Source: A. Yermilov, "An Analysis of the Accuracy of the Blue Chip Short-Term Macroeconomic Forecasts," mimeo, p. 5.

These results suggest that forecasters tend to make their most serious mistakes during periods when the economy is experiencing significant changes. While these periods are inherently more difficult to predict, it is just during such periods that more accurate forecasts are required.

Which Method or Forecaster Is Best?

A main intent of forecast evaluations was to determine whether there was a method, model, or forecaster which performed the best. In the

EXHIBIT 2 RMSE of Forecasts of Percent Changes of the GNP Deflator, 1977–1982

Forecasters	1977	1978	1979	1980	1981	1982	Average
American Express	0.53	1.02	1.21	0.63	0.51	2.10	1.13
Bank of America	0.39	1.22	1.52	0.60	0.49	1.85	1.15
Bankers Trust	0.36	1.29	0.82	0.89	0.33	1.85	1.08
P. Berstein	0.20	1.64	1.15	0.83	1.10	1.08	1.15
Brown Brothers Hariman	*	1.29	1.64	0.71	0.55	1.79	1.29
Business Economics	0.44	1.39	1.63	0.81	0.68	1.81	1.26
Cahners Publishing	*	0.80	1.35	1.15	0.46	1.69	1.20
Chamber of Commerce	*	0.78	1.30	0.44	0.55	1.22	0.94
Chase Manhattan Bank	0.21	1.18	1.40	0.98	0.58	1.28	1.07
Chase Econometric	0.57	*	0.89	1.07	0.51	1.86	1.18
Citibank	1.09	1.65	1.06	0.49	0.68	1.35	1.15
National Bank of Cleveland	0.38	1.34	1.38	0.71	0.66	1.39	1.11
Conference Board	0.53	1.18	1.57	0.94	0.99	0.98	1.08
Harris Trust	0.95	0.96	0.87	0.72	0.85	1.17	0.96
E. I. du Pont	0.75	1.59	1.78	0.73	0.35	1.39	1.23
Eggert Econ. Ent.	0.33	0.83	1.93	0.98	0.63	1.42	1.16
Equitable Life	0.41	1.08	1.59	0.49	0.35	2.14	1.22
Evans Economics	*	*	*	0.35	0.30	1.45	0.90
General Electric	0.28	0.54	0.62	0.85	*	*	0.59
Irving Trust	*	*	0.93	0.30	1.18	0.94	0.88
Arthur D. Little	0.38	0.98	2.48	0.62	0.71	1.20	1.25
Manufacturers Hanover Trust	0.83	1.24	1.49	1.61	1.14	1.18	1.29
Michigan Econometric	0.37	1.15	1.21	0.26	0.34	1.47	1.02
Morgan Guaranty	0.70	1.51	1.41	0.51	0.55	0.78	1.01
Pennzoil	0.09	1.09	1.53	0.59	0.58	1.99	1.18
Philadelphia National Bank	0.31	0.99	1.22	0.75	0.48	1.52	0.98
Prudential Life	0.30	1.15	0.76	0.39	0.25	1.75	0.95
Security Pacific National Bank	0.51	1.26	1.18	0.37	0.60	1.63	1.04
UCLA Business Forecast	0.48	1.04	1.33	0.65	0.55	1.29	1.00
U.S. Trust	0.65	1.46	1.32	0.78	0.58	1.75	1.18
Wharton Econometric	0.73	1.12	1.42	0.58	0.44	2.08	1.25
Average Eggert's	0.36	1.19	1.34	0.52	0.39	1.52	1.01
Average excluding 32	0.49	1.17	1.33	0.70	0.60	1.51	1.09

* Figures not available.
Source: A. Yermilov, "An Analysis of the Accuracy of the Blue Chip Short-Term Macroeconomic Forecasts," mimeo, p. 16.

early evaluations, the issue was whether judgmental[21] or econometric procedures yielded superior results. Currently, there is an interest in possible differences between the forecasts of econometric models and those obtained from time series equations. It is possible that the distinction between methods may not matter, for the techniques often blend together.[22]

[21] For a discussion of the procedures used in judgmental forecasting, see William F. Butler, Robert A. Kavesh, and Robert B. Platt, eds., *Methods and Techniques of Business Forecasting* (Englewood Cliffs, N.J.: Prentice-Hall, 1974).

[22] The models are not used as is, but are judgmentally adjusted to take account of information (such as strikes) which had not been incorporated into the model. For a

Moreover, it is now accepted that no single forecaster or model is consistently superior over time to any other individual or model[23] in forecasting GNP or its components.[24]

If this finding continues to remain valid, future forecast evaluations will need to be refocused. Instead of searching for the "best" forecasts, these evaluations should be used to determine why particular types of errors occur or how either the inputs used in forming the predictions or the characteristics of the forecasting process itself affect the accuracy of the forecasts. The next few sections deal with some typical topics relating to this subject—that is, the role of judgment and the length of the forecasting horizon.

The Role of Judgment

The role of judgment can best be observed by comparing the record of an econometric model which has been subjectively adjusted with its accuracy when it is not adjusted.[25] The use of judgment in constructing the forecast has improved the predictive accuracy of the econometric models. This can best be observed by comparing the errors of the actual, or ex ante, forecasts which were released by the model builders with the similar errors of the ex post (i.e., after the fact) estimates that the model would have generated for the same period. The existing evidence indicates that the ex ante model forecasts are considerably more accurate than the ex post estimates obtained by using the actual known values and solving the models.[26] Thus, it can be concluded that judgment plays a crucial role in increasing the predictive accuracy of the econometric model and that the predictive accuracy of a model run by a fine-tuning

---

discussion of adjustment procedures, see George R. Green, Maurice Liebenberg, and Albert A. Hirsch, "Short- and Long-Term Simulations with the OBE Econometric Model," in *Economic Models of Cyclical Behavior*, Studies in Income and Wealth No. 36, ed. Bert G. Hickman (New York: National Bureau of Economic Research, 1972) pp. 25–131; and Yoel Haitovsky, George Treyz, and V. Su, Forecasts with *Quarterly Macroeconomic Models* (New York: National Bureau of Economic Research, 1974). Recent analyses have also shown that econometric and time series methods may not be that distinct. See Arnold Zellner, "Statistical Analysis of Econometric Models," *Journal of the American Statistical Association*, September 1979, pp. 628–43.

[23] The forecasts of time series models have not been as extensively analyzed as have the predictions of other methods. It may be appropriate to undertake such an analysis to verify this result.

[24] See Christ, "Judging the Performance"; McNees, "The Forecasting Record"; and Zarnowitz, "An Analysis."

[25] One model is not subjectively adjusted (see Fair, "An Evaluation"). Rather, it is reestimated each time before it is used for predictions.

[26] See Christ, "Judging the Performance"; and H. O. Stekler, "Forecasting with an Econometric Model: Comment," *American Economic Review*, December 1966, pp. 1241–48.

forecaster is superior to the performance of the model alone.[27] This may also explain why the subjectively adjusted forecasts using ex ante exogenous data are better than the forecasts using the actual observed exogenous data.[28]

Forecast Accuracy and Forecast Horizon

Both public and private decisions are frequently based on forecasts made for some period(s) distant in the future. Thus, forecast evaluations often consider how the accuracy of these distinct forecasts diminishes when the length of the forecast horizon is increased.

Most studies which evaluate multiperiod forecasts covering a span of quarters have examined this relationship between accuracy and the length of the forecast horizon. All the results quite clearly show that the mean absolute errors increase in proportion to the span of the forecast.[29] However, there is no consensus about the meaning of these results.

Zarnowitz suggests that "the predictive value . . . of forecasts . . . further than a few quarters ahead must be heavily discounted."[30] On the other hand, McNees argues that the accuracy of the forecasts does not deteriorate with the length of the span. U coefficients do not increase with the forecast horizon.[31] While the observed errors increase with the span, so do the actual changes, thus accounting for the relative stability of the U coefficients.

---

[27] We shall not consider the problems, procedures, and controversies involved in comparing the models themselves. For these issues, see Christ, "Judging the Performance"; Ronald L. Cooper, "The Predictive Performance of Quarterly Econometric Models of the U.S.," in *Econometric Models*, ed. Hickman, pp. 813–947; Phoebus Dhrymes, E. Philip Howrey, Saul H. Hymans, Jan Kmenta, Edward E. Leamer, Richard E. Quandt, James B. Ramsey, Harold T. Shapiro, and Victor Zarnowitz, "Criteria for Evaluation of Econometric Models," *Annals of Economic and Social Measurement*, July 1972, pp. 291–324; Gary Fromm and Lawrence R. Klein, "The NBER/NSF Model Comparison Seminar: An Analysis of Results," *Annals of Economic and Social Measurement* 5, no. 1 (1976), pp. 1–27; Granger and Newbold, *Forecasting Economic Time Series*; and E. Philip Howrey, Lawrence R. Klein, and Michael D. McCarthy, "Notes on Testing the Predictive Performance of Econometric Models" in *Econometric Model Performance*, eds. Klein and Burmeister, pp. 108–25. For an interesting discussion about the value of econometric models, see the "Symposium on Forecasting with Econometric Methods," *Journal of Business*, October 1978.

[28] If the forecaster considers his preliminary estimates unreasonable, he will adjust both the model and his estimates of the exogenous variables (see Christ, "Judging the Performance," p. 59).

[29] Stephen K. McNees, "An Evaluation of Economic Forecasts: Extension and Update," *New England Economic Review*, September–October 1976, pp. 30–44; McNees, "The Forecasting Record"; and Zarnowitz, "An Analysis."

[30] Zarnowitz, "An Analysis," p. 31.

[31] Stephen K. McNees, "The Forecasting Record."

Further work is obviously needed in this area both to interpret the results and to determine which procedure is most appropriate for analyzing this question.

Have the Forecasts Improved over Time?

Finally, over time, has there been an improvement in the profession's ability to predict GNP? The record suggests that despite all the advances in theory and modeling that have occurred, the accuracy of the forecasts has not improved monotonically over the past 20 years. The errors in the 1960s were less than those of the 1970s,[32] and the large errors in the 1970s occurred at the end of the period.[33]

However, it has already been noted above that the forecasters tend to do best in periods of normality and make large errors when there are cyclical fluctuations or structural changes. Both of these phenomena occurred during the 1970s, making that period more difficult to predict. Thus, a relevant question that still remains unanswered is: Has there been an improvement in forecasters' abilities to predict GNP during periods when cyclical fluctuations or structural changes occur? This question might be answered by examining the forecasts for any time sequence of nonnormal, however defined, periods.

CRITIQUE OF THE FORECASTING MEASURES

The first section of this chapter explained the existing measures which are used to evaluate economic forecasts and was followed by a discussion of the applications found for these measures and the issues which have been addressed in the analyses of forecasting errors. This last section deals with a critical evaluation of the measures.

The summary measures which have been described above do not explicitly consider turning-point errors. In that sense, the measures are deficient because failures to predict the direction of movement of the economy are among the most serious of forecast errors. However, in defense of these measures, it should be noted that all of these are quantitative in nature and are designed to measure the accuracy of quantitative predictions. Other measures have been developed to identify turning-point errors in qualitative indicators such as the leading series. In any

---

[32] Zarnowitz, "An Analysis."

[33] See McNees, "The Forecasting Record." Smyth, "Short Run Macroeconomic Forecasting," obtained similar results when he examined the forecasting record of the OECD.

event, analyses of the individual quantitative forecasts would reveal whether or not turning-point errors occurred.[34]

One of the criticisms leveled against the most frequently used measure, MSE, is that the process of squaring individual errors makes it extremely sensitive to one or a small number of extremely bad forecasts. However, it has been argued that the MSE corresponds closely to the economist's quadratic loss function, where a single large loss is penalized much more heavily than a number of smaller losses. In a similar fashion, large forecast errors are penalized much more heavily.

Over the past 25 years, there have been significant advances in the methodology and measures used for evaluating forecasts. However, much still remains to be done. The lack of consensus about an appropriate measure for evaluating multiperiod forecasts have already been mentioned. Other areas where opportunities for further research exist include: (1) the development of statistical tests for determining whether the errors of a particular forecaster are *significantly* different than those of another individual; (2) the application of measures to determine whether the accuracy of an aggregate forecast such as GNP is due to accurate predictions of each component or to offsetting errors among the components;[35] and (3) the possible development of a measure which adjusts the error penalties for the ease or difficulty in predicting the event.

These methodological developments should not be undertaken for their own sake nor merely for the purpose of generating a new set of evaluation measures. These statistics and procedures must be developed primarily to improve our knowledge about the sources of forecast errors, so that we may better understand and improve the forecasting process.

---

[34] These turning-point errors could be identified through a prediction-realization diagram (Theil, *Applied Economic Forecasting*).

[35] A measure for analyzing the (non)existence of offsetting errors was developed in the early 1970s and has been applied in the works of Haitovsky et al., *Forecasts with Quarterly Macroeconometric Models*; and H. O. Stekler and R. William Thomas, "Forecasts of a Regional Construction Model: An Evaluation." *Economics Letters* 6 (1980), pp. 387–92.

Author Index

Subject Index